# ROCK AND POP TIMELINE

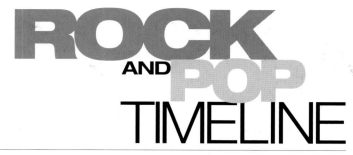

# ROCK AND POP TIMELINE

## How music changed the world through four decades

Johnny Black

**WITH CONTRIBUTIONS FROM**

Hugh Gregory

Andy Basire

THUNDER BAY
P·R·E·S·S

San Diego, California

**Thunder Bay Press**

An imprint of the Advantage Publishers Group

5880 Oberlin Drive, San Diego, CA 92121-4794

**www.thunderbaybooks.com**

All notations of errors or omissions should be addressed to
Thunder Bay Press, Editorial Department, at the above address. All
other correspondence (author inquiries, permissions) concerning the content
of this book should be addressed to

Outline Press Ltd
Unit 2A Union Court
20-22 Union Road
London, SW4 6JP
England

**ISBN 1-59223-052-0**

Library of Congress Cataloging in Publication Data available upon request.

Printed in Hong Kong

1 2 3 4 5 07 06 05 04 03

ART DIRECTOR Nigel Osborne
EDITOR Paul Quinn
DESIGN Denise Wright

Origination by Hong Kong Scanner Arts International Ltd
Printed by Colorprint Offset

# Contents

## The **1960s**

# The **1990s**

# 21st **Century**

# Introduction

# The

## The Roots Of The Rock Revolution

**T**HE ORIGINS OF THE SOUNDS enjoyed in the 1960s, 1970s, and beyond, can almost all be traced back to the 1950s – so it's here we have to start when looking for the musical influences of our 40 years of rock & pop.

The first question that occurs to anyone foolhardy enough to consider creating a history of rock music is also the hardest one to answer – when exactly did rock'n'roll start? It's a question with no definitive answer. Put a bunch of experts together in a room to debate it and you'll get several answers. One will point out that the terms 'rock' and 'roll' were in common use among America's black population back in the 1920s, as fairly interchangeable synonyms for having a real good time – usually involving a man and a woman, and often, but by no means always, horizontally.

Another will insist that rock'n'roll was not really born until the two terms came together in a song. But as far back as the 1934 movie *Transatlantic Merry-Go-Round*, jazz vocal trio The Boswell Sisters can been seen singing a ditty entitled 'Rock And Roll.' And in 1939, when country vocalist Buddy Jones recorded 'Rockin, Rollin, Mama' for Decca Records, he could be heard yelling, "I love the way you rock and roll." But this was hardly rock'n'roll music as we know it now.

The genre's start should perhaps be pushed forward to March 5th 1951, when an up-tempo, stomping song called 'Rocket 88' was recorded by Jackie Brenston, backed by Ike Turner's Kings Of Rhythm, in Memphis, Tennessee. Brenston's finest moment is often claimed as the first rock'n'roll record. One further point in its favor is that the profits from 'Rocket 88' enabled its producer, Sam Phillips, to start his Sun Records studio and label which, in due course, would

**BILL HALEY KICK-STARTED** the rock'n'roll revolution when his 1954 track 'Rock Around The Clock' was used on the soundtrack of the following year's teen-rebellion flick *Blackboard Jungle*. The effect on audiences was instant and extreme. It literally caused riots in some city cinemas. But when fans eventually got to see Haley (left) in the flesh, the polite, balding 30-year-old rockabilly bandleader didn't quite meet expectations. Enter Elvis...

# Fifties

launch Elvis Presley on an unsuspecting world. Yet, in terms of its sound, style and beat, this hymn to the Oldsmobile 88, the fastest car on American roads at the time, is actually no more a rock'n'roll record than 'Rock The Joint' by Jimmy Preston, or 'The Fat Man' by Fats Domino, both recorded two years earlier.

All we can say for sure is that, by the start of the 1950s, the term was already in circulation, and various streams of American music were unwittingly poised to fuse together into something that everyone would, by the middle of the decade, be calling rock'n'roll.

But it can't be stressed too often, or too loudly, that music doesn't exist in isolation. It is, to a large extent, a reflection of an evolving culture – social and political – which gives birth to the music, nurtures it, and ultimately dictates whether it will live or die.

## Rebels With A Cause

It could be argued that US Senator Joseph McCarthy ranks high on the list of those who set the agenda that made rock'n'roll inevitable. As the 1950s opened, democratic America was in the grip of McCarthy's Communist witch hunts. The senator was convinced that the US State Department was riddled with, and possibly even controlled by, "Reds under the beds," and his obsession with digging out this evil extended into the arts. His lists of potential Communists for

**BROADWAY AND HOLLYWOOD** musicals played a significant role in the musical culture of the 1950s – this was, perhaps, the peak of their influence. Before and during the rock'n'roll boom, 1950s teenagers – who included Elvis, Buddy Holly, even The Beatles – were familiar with show tunes from movies they'd seen, such as *Guys And Dolls*, starring two 1950s icons, Frank Sinatra and Marlon Brando (left). Other classic musicals of the era included *Singin' In The Rain*, *Oklahoma*, *Carousel* (featuring the anthemic 'You'll Never Walk Alone'), and the daddy of them all, *South Pacific*, the soundtrack to which remains one of the biggest-selling non-rock records ever.

**COLD WAR PARANOIA** was rife in the 1950s, and the unseen threat from an 'alien' culture – when it wasn't manifested in McCarthyist persecutions – was often allegorised by movie makers as a humanity-threatening invasion by genuine aliens from outer space, or from mutants created by exposure to nuclear radiation. The heyday of the sci-fi b-movie can also be pinpointed as the root of electronic music. For instance, in an attempt to create an other-worldly atmosphere in *The Day The Earth Stood Still*, composer Bernard Herrmann used an ethereal musical device called a theremin – which in turn inspired Brian Wilson to use one on The Beach Boys' 'Good Vibrations.'

**FRANK SINATRA WAS IN** his musical prime in the 1950s, with a long list of 'swinging' hit albums and movie credits to his name. But he wasn't at all keen on rock'n'roll, as personified by Elvis Presley, describing it as "the most brutal, ugly, vicious form of expression." Perhaps this reflected both his genuine distaste for this relatively unsophisticated musical style and a fear for his own career. Indeed, old-style popular music was under serious threat: the crooners and swing balladeers were becoming an endangered species – with the odd exception, such as Sinatra. His legendary status was secure, and in fact grew as he got older, living in a sometimes uneasy co-existence with rock. Frank would even invited Elvis on to his TV show... eventually.

investigation included actors, painters, poets, and naturally musicians. Like most artists, musicians dislike being categorised, and particularly despise anything that smacks of repression or censorship. McCarthy's heavy-handed investigations and public inquisitions created a climate in which musicians felt obliged to respond by challenging his hypothetical status quo. Anything that upset the applecart would be seen as good – so the time was ripe for something new and radical to emerge.

Happily, there was also an audience waiting. The term teenager started being used in the 1940s, to describe those increasingly outspoken young people who, unlike the youth of previous generations, now often had the benefit of a college education. Whether well-schooled or not, they certainly had a new set of expectations about what they wanted out of life – largely fueled, it must be said, by a new breed of aspirational advertising campaign, beamed into most homes via television. Teenagers now either controlled a significant amount of their parents' disposable income, or earned their own, and the increased spending power of this newly identified group would become a vital spur to the growth of rock'n'roll.

Another burning political issue of the era was segregation. In theory, America was an integrated nation, a land of equal opportunity. In practice, the black and white communities lived dramatically different lives. In the southern states, especially, 'coloreds' were routinely barred from theaters, bars, and restaurants. Their job prospects were severely limited, they could only

**ROMANTIC COMEDY** movies, pairing the likes of Rock Hudson and Doris Day (left), were considered 'adult' in their day. But they conformed to post-war stereotypes, pairing a strong, clean-cut, middle-class, obviously white, and usually wealthy hero, with a slightly dizzy, vulnerable, and decidedly virginal heroine. It's an image that the jive-dancing rock'n'rollers, in their scruffy leathers and jeans, pointedly failed to identify with. They preferred the rebellious image embodied by Brando or James Dean.

sit in the back seats of buses, and their children were obliged to go to all-black schools. This was a situation which the new generation of teenagers would soon begin to find unacceptable.

At the start of the decade, few kids from the black 'underclass' in society had access to television, but most of them were glued to their radios for long periods. A sign of changing times had come in October 1948 when the Memphis, Tennessee, radio station WDIA changed to an all-black music format, making it a pioneer in this type of programming. Steve Cropper, later to become the guitarist for Booker T & The MGs, and producer at the core of the Stax studio sound, has recalled how, as a white teenager in Memphis during 1951, he "started listening to the black spiritual stations on the radio. That music has such rhythm and feeling – it was great, and I loved it." Cropper's experience was not untypical. Hundreds of thousands of white teenagers were listening to black music, and loving it. By the same token, black kids could now tune in to hear the white stations – just to make sure they weren't missing anything.

But even those teens who were listening to stations that reflected their own ethnic origins found themselves exposed to, and caught up by, the newly emerging rock'n'roll. White 1960s pop idol Bobby Vee, for example, later recalled: "The upper Mid-West, where I grew up, was agricultural, and I came to rock'n'roll through country music. I was listening to the country station and they started playing Elvis Presley and Carl Perkins." One of the first nicknames given to Elvis was The Hillbilly Cat, reflecting his country music origins, but Elvis was equally inspired by the black musicians who befriended him in Memphis. B.B. King, for example, has said, "I knew Elvis before he was popular. He used to come and be around us a lot. There was a pawn shop where we used to hang out on Beale St [Memphis], and that was where I met him."

It was this collision of white country music with the black roots of gospel and blues that would take rock'n'roll to a mass audience. On May 14th 1955, 'Rock Around The Clock' by Bill Haley & His Comets entered the US Top 40 singles chart (a year after it was recorded), on its way to becoming the first rock'n'roll record ever to reach Number One. Yet a cursory glance at Haley's origins reveal he had been previously been burdened with such patently hillbilly slogans as, "Yodelling Bill Haley – Singing Cowboy." It's also interesting to note, in retrospect, that Haley's label, Decca, had no idea how to promote 'Rock Around The Clock' when it was released. They initially tucked it away on the b-side of a single called 'Thirteen Women' and listed it on the label as a "fox-trot."

By the time Elvis Presley hit Number One with 'Heartbreak Hotel,' almost a year later, in April 1956, rock'n'roll had clearly become not just the most significant new musical form of the decade, but a rallying point for youth of every colour and creed.

## Noisy New World

**H**eated discussions about whether rock'n'roll was fathered by Jackie Brenston, Bill Haley, or even the Boswell Sisters, will run and run. There's general agreement, though, that rock'n'roll would never have taken off if the electric guitar hadn't been invented. The acoustic guitar was widely employed in jazz in the 1920s, but only as a rhythm instrument, because its low volume would not allow soloing – or at least not in a big-band situation. The first amplification system for a guitar was in fact designed for Hawaiian guitars (which were briefly fashionable at the time) by Adolph Rickenbacker and his colleagues. But once it had been invented, jazz and swing big-bands cottoned on fast to the benefits, and guitarists like Charlie Christian

**WHEN NOT LISTENING** to rock'n'roll records, 1950s teenagers were offered other, more wholesome distractions. In 1958, for instance, the Wham-O company (already renowned for its Wham-O slingshot) made some large plastic hoops and invited people to put them round their waists and shimmy, so that the hoops would spin. And people did – in fact Wham-O sold 25 million 'hula-hoops' in just two months – making it the biggest US toy fad ever. The Soviet Union, meanwhile, insisted the hula hoop demostrated the "emptiness of American culture." Wham-O, undeterred, went on to develop the Frisbee and the Hacky Sack...

**TELEVISION SETS GRADUALLY** started appearing in most homes in America, and a few of the more affluent ones elsewhere in the world, during the 1950s. Now you barely needed to leave the house, especially after Swanson's invented the frozen TV dinner in 1954, and the craze for pre-cooked pizzas began... Stars like Lucille Ball and Bob Hope (together below) became national treasures, more through their TV shows than their earlier movie work.

BUDDY HOLLY impressed 1950s teenagers, not only with his tuneful rock'n'roll songs and distinctive country-style vocal twang, but also with his guitar – a brand new Fender Stratocaster, affectionately known as a Strat. Launched in 1954, the Strat was by no means the first electric guitar, but it was new, and looked radically different from previous designs – far removed from 'electrified-acoustic' guitars used by the jazz band players. The electric bass, on the other hand, took a bit longer to catch on.

became musical icons for a new breed of 'electric' guitarists of the 1940s and 1950s. The amplified guitar proved ideal for early R&B and rock'n'roll players who needed to create a big sound from a small number of musicians.

And another timely new development helped this big new sound reach a mass audience. In January 1949, RCA introduced a revolutionary new music-carrying format, the 45rpm seven-inch record. This new disc had several advantages over the old 78s, not least that it was less breakable, lighter, and more compact. Just one month later, RCA completed the double whammy by marketing a 45rpm auto-changing record player, which stacked records for playing one after the other. You couldn't do that with fragile, easily scratched 78s. The 45s were pressed with a ring of raised plastic around the label, which kept the surfaces apart. Better yet, the ring was serrated, so the discs interlocked and wouldn't slip while playing. Simple, but very clever. Teenagers loved the new format – they could take a lightweight box of rock'n'roll hits to each other's houses, and play half a dozen tracks without needing to stop dancing. By 1958, over 98 per cent of record sales were in the 45rpm format.

Such was their popularity that in 1956 the Chrysler automobile company decided to install a 45rpm auto-change record player in every new Chrysler Imperial car. Hard to believe now, maybe, but true. It was fitted under the dashboard. And, amazingly, the device seems to have worked – although figures don't exist for any sudden increase in road accidents while records were being changed.

Just as the 45rpm single was synonymous with the rise of 1950s rock'n'roll, so of course was the juke box. This wasn't a new development – the concept dated back 50 years, and the first Wurlitzer juke box was made in 1937 – but the idea of having your favorite rock'n'roll stars 'playing' in your local coffee bar or drug store proved irresistible to 1950s teenagers. Any young buck could demonstrate his cool to his peers by choosing the right tracks, and could use

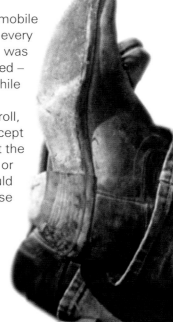

the discs to relay messages of undying love to the object of his affection, without the embarrassment of actually having to say anything.

Radio, though, remained the major way for music to reach the masses. Teenagers were glued to their sets every night, waiting for the latest rock'n'roll record. But coming up fast behind radio, especially towards the end of the decade, was television. Live music – relatively cheap to stage and instantly gratifying – was a staple of TV programming from the earliest days: popular crooner Perry Como had his own TV series from the late 1940s, and the New York-based *Ed Sullivan Show* was a variety entertainment featuring regular music acts alongside dancing seals and contortionists.

The *Steve Allen Show* also featured occasional rock'n'roll performers. Its host once commented: "It was television that made Elvis's success possible. What his millions of young fans responded to was obviously not his voice, but Elvis himself. His face, his body, his gyrations, his cute, country-boy persona." Allen reckoned 90 per cent of Elvis's initial following was female, and responded to him on a mostly visual level: "Elvis had no mature adult fans at all. Most Americans over 50, in fact, were critical of him." There's an undoubted element of truth here, but it overlooks the power of the music itself. Viewers, as well as listeners, knew what kind of music they liked.

Country music got its first regular dedicated TV outlet when long-running Nashville-based radio show *The Grand Ole Opry* hit the screens in October 1955, and then when controversial DJ Alan Freed's *Rock'N'Roll Dance Party* aired for the first time in April 1956, rock'n'roll had its own window on the world.

Freed crashed and burned in the payola scandals, as we'll see, and was quickly overtaken as a youth spokesman by clean-cut Dick Clark, whose daily pop slot, *American Bandstand*, brought the biggest stars of the era flocking to Philadelphia to be on the show, such was its drawing power.

# Hail Rock'N'Roll

Looking back to the start of the decade, a glance at the *Billboard* pop singles chart for January 1950 reveals singing cowboy Gene Autrey reigning supreme with his rendition of 'Rudolph The Red-Nosed Reindeer.' It might be tempting to dismiss this as a Christmas novelty hit, except that in the context of other 1950 chart toppers – 'If I Knew You Were Coming (I'd Have Baked A Cake)' by Eileen Barton, or 'Chattanooga Shoeshine Boy' by Red Foley – Autrey's success was pretty much par for the course. The standard fodder for Americans of all ages was swing-jazz, crooners, and country music. But in January 1950, a new studio business, The Memphis Recording Service, had opened down in Memphis, Tennessee, at 706 Union Avenue. Founded by radio engineer Sam Phillips, it would become the home of Sun Records, whose artists would include Elvis Presley, Jerry Lee Lewis, and Carl Perkins.

But Phillips (who lives until 2003, just as our story concludes) didn't start Sun Records with the intention of making rock'n'roll history. It was his way of addressing an entirely different problem. "Negro artists in the South who wanted to make a record

**JAZZ MUSIC WAS STILL** enormously popular in the 1950s – the US either favoring the 'hard bop' of Art Blakey's Jazz Messengers, or the smoother 'cool' jazz of Miles Davis (right), while the UK seemed to prefer more 'trad' forms like Dixieland. Swing-jazz was enjoying huge mainstream support, with singers like Ella Fitzgerald (inset) at the peak of her popularity. Just as the new 45rpm disc was perfect for pop singles, so the 33rpm long-player was a major advance for jazz, allowing much more room for extemporised solos and musical development than the three-minute limit of the old 78 format. Jazz was also invaluable for introducing some hip new buzz words to the musical community, and soon to the wider world – among those most used at the time were: crazy, cool, cat, bug, dig, drag, funky, hip...

**AS WELL AS THE FENDER** Strat, the other 1950s musical instrument design to stand the test of time is the Gibson Les Paul – named after the man whose idea it was, guitarist Les Paul. (Paul's other claim to fame, perhaps wider in its impact, was his development of multi-track tape recording.) Although developed before the Strat – and possessing what the company's own literature describes as an "unusual tone" – the Les Paul guitar only comes into its own in the late 1960s, when its thick, full sound proves a hit with blues-rock stars like Eric Clapton and Jimmy Page. That starts a fanatical revival of interest in the Les Paul, and turns some of the 1950s models into lusted-after collectors' items.

just had no place to go," he'd explain. "I set up a studio just to make records with some of those great Negro artists."

From the 1920s up until the 1950s, music made by black musicians was distributed and sold almost exclusively to a black audience, usually under the banner of 'race records.' The mainstream music industry knew there was a potentially vast black market out there, but for 30 years they chose not to engage with it, for a variety of reasons, ranging from simple racism to sheer ignorance. Primarily black musical forms – including blues, jazz, and gospel – could reach a white market, but usually only when performed by white artists. Chess Records of Chicago began to change all that. The label was launched by Polish immigrant Leonard Chess, who saw that Chicago had become a center for musicians from the deep South, who had often traveled there from the plantations of Mississippi. And he knew there would be a market for their music. Chess went on to become home to Chuck Berry, Bo Diddley, Willie Dixon, and a host of other R&B talents, who would in turn find white imitators, from Elvis Presley to The Rolling Stones and beyond. Chess's recordings still inspire over 50 years later.

The other main plank on which rock'n'roll would build its foundation was country music. Although often berated for its redneck attitudes, there's no denying that the melodic purity, sweet vocal harmonies, and lyrical directness of country were enjoyed by many black listeners. And it's worth remembering that Ray Charles, Solomon Burke, and other black artists either first found crossover success with country songs, or frequently included them in their recorded output.

Once the new hybrid music had gone public, with the crossover success of Haley, Presley, Buddy Holly, Eddie Cochran, Gene Vincent, and others, it quickly gathered popularity – but not without resistance. Just as McCarthy had picked on the Communists at the start of the decade, so the North Alabama Citizens Council was able to imagine a complex conspiracy centred around Elvis, decrying rock'n'roll as, "a means of pulling the white man down to the level of the Negro. It is part of a plot to undermine the morals of the youth of our nation."

Even popular and talented artists who should have known better, from Rosemary Clooney to Frank Sinatra, felt the need to belittle the emerging form for what they perceived as its lack of musicality and low moral standards. By then, though, rock'n'roll had gathered considerable commercial momentum. In stark contrast to the singles chart back in 1950, the Number One hits for the final

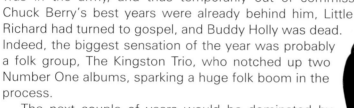

**THE MOVIE THAT STARTED** it all, 1955's *Blackboard Jungle*, starred Glenn Ford as a harassed teacher facing insubordination and the odd knife-wielding thug in a wild inner-city New York school. Sidney Poitier had an early role as one of the hoodlum ringleaders. Oddly, although the movie has passed into legend for its role in the birth of rock'n'roll, the track 'Rock Around The Clock' was untypical of the soundtrack, which was mostly jazz.

**AT THE END OF THE FIFTIES,** Jerry Lee 'Killer' Lewis was, like the other two great pioneers of rock'n'roll, Chuck Berry (above) and Little Richard, all but finished in terms of his influence on the pop charts and the development of popular music, for reasons which we'll explore later. For many, this was proof that rock'n'roll was dead. Fortunately for us, a whole new era had just begun.

year of the decade included not just Elvis Presley, but black artists such as Lloyd Price and Wilbert Harrison.

To demonstrate just how much popular music had broadened and diversified during the 1950s, we could look at a typical day in the life of the US music industry as the end of the decade neared. On July 1st, 1959, for example, jazz giants The Dave Brubeck Quartet were recording 'Take Five' in New York; at the same time country star Johnny Horton was committing 'Johnny Reb' to tape in Nashville; and at Capitol Records' studio, work was finishing on the Broadway cast recording of Cole Porter's *Kiss Me Kate*.

Out on the live circuit, a similar picture emerges. That same evening, The Everly Brothers were headlining the International Frontier Fair in Detroit, Michigan, while B.B. King was picking up $500 for a club gig in Shreveport, Louisiana. New York, meanwhile, saw the curtain rise on two strikingly different packages. At the Apollo theater in Harlem, Brook Benton, Wilbert Harrison, and The Shirelles were pulling in a devoted black clientele. Meanwhile, at The Albany Theater, Frankie Avalon, Connie Francis, and Annette Funicello were wowing the white teens. Integration was coming, but it was not exactly in a hurry.

By the end of the 1950s, rock and pop music had reached a crucial point. Elvis was in the army, and thus temporarily out of commission. Chuck Berry's best years were already behind him, Little Richard had turned to gospel, and Buddy Holly was dead. Indeed, the biggest sensation of the year was probably a folk group, The Kingston Trio, who notched up two Number One albums, sparking a huge folk boom in the process.

The next couple of years would be dominated by teen idols who were, to all intents and purposes, old-style crooners with rock'n'roll haircuts, carefully manufactured by the music industry to replace the rebelliousness of rock with something much safer and more easily manipulated. To the casual observer, it looked as if rock'n'roll was almost on its last legs.

But of course, the casual observer couldn't possibly have known that Johnny & The Moondogs, an obscure British group playing clubs around Liverpool, included three young men called John Lennon, Paul McCartney, and George Harrison. Or that on January 12th, 1959, Detroit factory worker Berry Gordy had borrowed $800 from his family's loan fund to start his own record label, which he would call Tamla. Or that a young Memphis record store owner called Jim Stewart was making the first recordings for what would soon become Stax Records... Rock'n'roll's darkest hour had come, as always, just before the golden dawn.

# The Sixties

# 1960

## January–April

### Paid In Full

**F**EBRUARY 8TH: A GOVERNMENT subcommittee in the US starts a public hearing on the subject of DJs accepting money and gifts in return for broadcasting particular records – a corrupt but common music business practice known as 'payola', which in fact dates back to the dawn of radio, if not before. The highest-profile targets are Alan Freed and Dick Clark. Clark, described at the time as "the single most influential person" in the pop industry, admits in testimony that he has a financial interest in many records he's played on his TV show, *American Bandstand*, and offers to surrender these. He's let off lightly, told by chairman Oren Harris, "You're not the inventor of the system, or even its architect. You're a product of it. Obviously, you're a fine young man." Clark goes on to establish himself as a pillar of the US music industry, and was still broadcasting and running his own production

---

### JANUARY

- **4TH: THE FIRST NEW US NUMBER ONE** single of the Sixties is 'El Paso' by Marty Robbins – it's also the longest record to reach the top spot in the charts to date, at around five minutes. The same day, existentialist writer Albert Camus dies when the car in which he's a passenger veers into a tree at 80mph: Camus once remarked there would be no more meaningless way to die than in an automobile accident.
- **12TH: RELEASE OF THE** first (and last) feature film in Smell-O-Vision: while audiences watch *The Scent Of Mystery*, smells including garlic, paint, coffee and seawater are released through small pipes under the cinema seats at appropriate moments. The experiment is not popular, and soon scrapped.
- **19TH: *THE SURFER*,** the first magazine dedicated to surfing, is launched in California by John Severson to cover the new craze sweeping the US (though in fact surfing itself dates back centuries, and was documented by Captain Cook and his crew on their travels around the Pacific islands way back in the 1770s).

### FEBRUARY

- **1ST: FOUR BLACK STUDENTS** refuse to leave a whites-only cafeteria in a Woolworth's store in Greensboro, North Carolina. They repeat the action, joined by friends and supporters, over the next few days. News of the sit-ins spreads and leads to similar direct actions elsewhere, aimed at repealing the notorious 'Jim Crow' laws on racial segregation and discrimination, and precipitating major advances in the US civil rights movement. One of the protesters' rallying cries is 'We Shall Overcome' – chosen in 2002 by Secretary Of State Colin Powell as his favourite political song, and described by him as "the negro national anthem."
- **9TH: THE FIRST GOLD STAR** is laid on the Hollywood Walk Of Fame, by actress Joanne Woodward. Since then over 2100 have been added – including Alan Freed (see top of the page).

- **12TH: AT CHESS STUDIO,** Chicago, Illinois, Chuck Berry records 'Bye Bye Johnny,' 'Jaguar And Thunderbird,' 'Drifting Blues,' and other tracks. It's a difficult period for Berry (as we'll see next month in particular), with his career in the doldrums.
- **17TH: THE EVERLY BROTHERS** sign a $1m ten-year contract with fledgling Warner Brothers Records (originally just a movie-making company, long before the AOL-Time-Warner multimedia mega-conglomeration).
- **20TH: THE ROCKING KINGS,** featuring 17-year-old guitarist James Marshall Hendrix (later known as Jimi), appear at Washington Hall in his hometown, Seattle, Washington. He's playing his first guitar, a Supro Ozark.
- **29TH: FIRST PLAYBOY CLUB** opens, in Chicago; Newsweek calls it "Disneyland for adults."

- **JANUARY 1ST: JOHNNY CASH PERFORMS** a New Year concert for the prisoners at San Quentin penitentiary, California – one of several gigs he is invited to perform there from 1958 onwards (he's pictured here in the mid 1960s). One particularly impressed inmate is a young Merle Haggard, serving time for attempted robbery: after years of petty crime, this event inspires Haggard to concentrate on music and, after gaining early parole, he will have his own first country hit by 1963.

and communications company into 2003. On the other hand, Alan Freed (pictured here), who is widely acknowledged to have been first to bring rock'n'roll to the masses via his *Moondog* radio shows and concerts in the early 1950s – is less co-operative, claiming he has been payed merely as a consultant. Though he is a former musician himself – playing trombone in a band called The Sultans Of Swing (no doubt where Dire Straits got the song title from) –

Freed's name does appear on some dubious writing credits, famously on Chuck Berry's 'Maybellene', alongside Russ Fratto, a printer who just happened to be another creditor of Berry's label, Chess. Freed is charged with receiving illegal gratuities and fined around $2000. His career falters, he falls out with one employer after another, and slides into alcoholism and premature death at the age of 43 – though he is posthumously inducted into the Rock & Roll Hall Of Fame at its inauguration in 1986, and given a star on the Hollywood Walk Of Fame in 1991. After this 1960 test case, and in an attempt to safeguard the "captive audience" of American youth from what's seen as the demoralising effects of rock'n'roll and its corrupt business practices, Massachussetts State Representative Tip O'Neill demands investigations into yet more radio station employees, and before long payola is officially pronounced illegal across the US. Not that this stops it, of course: it still carries on, every day, even now – if often in rather more subtle and inventive ways.

# 1960
## January–April

## MARCH

- **3RD: ELVIS PRESLEY**, on the way home after his two-year stint in the army, most of which was spent in Germany, stops off for a couple of hours at Prestwick Airport in Scotland. It's his first and last visit to the UK. He signs autographs for the few lucky fans who received a tip-off, and warms himself in the officers' mess while the military plane is refueled. Back in the US, he begins to concentrate on a career in movies, starting with *GI Blues.* The same day, Lucille Ball files for divorce from her husband and famous TV comedy partner, Desi Arnaz.
- **8TH: ALFRED HITCHCOCK'S PSYCHO** is released, with eerie score by composer Bernard Herrmann. As it happens, this unforgettable soundtrack was an afterthought – Hitch originally wanted no music at all in the movie.
- **11TH: CHUCK BERRY**, having been convicted by a jury in Missouri of transporting a 14-year-old girl from El Paso, Texas, to St Louis for "immoral purposes," is sentenced to five years in prison and fined $5000. On appeal, the trial is deemed unfair due to racial comments made by the judge, and a retrial is ordered.
- **14TH: THE SILVER BEATS**, later to find success as The Beatles, audition to play at The Latham venue, Seaforth, Liverpool, UK.
- **20TH: START OF A BUSY WEEK** for Elvis Presley – at his first post-army recording session in Nashville, Tennessee, he cuts six songs, including his next single, 'Stuck On You.' The day afterwards, he receives a black belt in karate – his first of many. A week later he'll guest in a recording of Frank Sinatra's TV show (to be broadcast in May), for which he receives $125,000 – a record-breaking fee at the time. This will be Elvis's last television appearance until his triumphant and leather-clad *Comeback Special* (see 1968).
- **21ST: IN SHARPEVILLE**, South Africa, police fire into a crowd of demonstrators, killing 69 – most of whom are shot in the back – and injuring 180. They've been protesting against the apartheid 'pass law,' which compels all black South Africans to carry ID books, or face imprisonment. The massacre hastens international sanctions against the country's apartheid regime.

## APRIL

- **1ST: THE APRIL ISSUE** of *Motor Trend* magazine announces that the Car Of The Year is the Chevrolet Corvair from General Motors. It's the first and most radical of a new breed of 'compact' cars launched for 1960 by the big three manufacturers – the Ford Falcon and Chrysler's Plymouth Valiant are the rival compacts – as an alternative to the outsize excesses of 1950s motoring (those gas-guzzling giants with huge tailfins and acres of chrome). And of course a chance to stem European imports. The Corvair also marks a revolution in US car design because it has the engine at the back and trunk up front. But it proves just too unusual for most American drivers at the time – its awkward handling and general safety issues further hinder its popularity – and it's finally doomed by Ralph Nader's critical, campaigning mid-Sixties book *Unsafe At Any Speed*.
- **4TH: RCA VICTOR** becomes the first company to issue all their pop singles simultaneously in stereo and mono, starting with Elvis's 'Stuck On You.' That evening, at the 32nd Academy Awards ceremony, *Ben-Hur* wins 11 Oscars – more than any other movie until *Titanic* in 1997.
- **13TH: IN THE SAHARA** desert of southern Algeria, France tests its first atomic bomb, becoming the world's fourth nuclear power after the US, USSR and UK.
- **18TH: THE ALBUMS** The

## Something Else

- **APRIL 17TH: AT THE END OF** a British tour, 21-year-old Eddie Cochran is killed when his hired taxi cab slams into a concrete lamp-post in Chippenham, Wiltshire, en-route from Bristol to London's Heathrow Airport, where he is due to catch a flight home next day. Cochran's fiancee, songwriter Sharon Sheeley, and his friend Gene Vincent are both hurt in the crash (Vincent already had a limp from an earlier accident), but Eddie himself suffers critical brain damage and will die after some hours in a coma. According to Sheeley, he was singing 'California Here I Come' during the journey. Musical Director Ray McVay, initially intending to travel with them in the cab, had to stay behind to make room for Cochran's amplifier and guitars. Police arriving at the scene don't realise who is involved in the accident at first, but suspect it must be musicians because of the equipment debris on the road. One young police cadet in attendance is Dave Dee (ne Harman) who goes on to form successful Sixties UK pop band Dave Dee, Dozy, Beeky, Mick & Tich.

*Kingston Trio,* and *The Kingston Trio At Large* both earn gold discs from the Recording Industry Association of America (RIAA) for these pioneers of the US folk revival. The Kingston Trio's banjo-and-12-string-guitar-wielding folksy style and close harmonies, with a dash of calypso and casual humor, is extraordinarily popular at the time: at one stage they have four albums in the Top Ten

simultaneously, a feat only matched by megastars like The Beatles and Elton John in later years.
- **23RD: USING A BORROWED** 16mm movie camera, 35-year-old engineer Tim Dinsdale famously films the Loch Ness Monster in the Scottish highlands – or is it just a distant motor boat? (Dinsdale spends the rest of his life trying to prove Nessie's existence.)... On the same date, John Lennon and Paul McCartney can be spotted performing as The Nerk Twins at the first of two gigs in a pub owned by a cousin of Paul's in Caversham, Berkshire, in the south of England.
- **30TH: FATS DOMINO RECORDS** 'Walking To New Orleans' at Cosimo Recording Studio, New Orleans, Louisiana. It will become his 23rd US Top 40 hit (and his 14th in the UK).

## Detroit Spinner

**M**AY 16TH: **HAVING** received a paltry royalty cheque from Chess Records, who are distributing a record he co-wrote with Smokey Robinson of The Miracles, young songwriter/producer, former boxer, car-worker and budding entrepreneur Berry Gordy Jr, from Detroit, Michigan (pictured here in glamorous movie-star pose), is persuaded to start independently distributing his own records, featuring an array of local talent, on the Tamla and later Motown labels. The original idea is apparently that solo artists will record for Tamla and groups for Motown, but this proves unworkable – indeed UK releases are later issued under the unified Tamla Motown banner, and there will be several subsidiary labels, such as Miracle, Gordy, Latino, Soul, Workshop Jazz, and Morocco.

## MAY

- **1ST: IN AN INTERVIEW** published in the *New York Daily News*, jazz/ballad singer Peggy Lee claims, "Rock'n'roll is fading."... Meanwhile, above the Soviet Union, a new US spy plane, the U2, is shot down and its pilot held captive for 17 months. Dramatically increasing East-West tensions, this event becomes known as 'The U2 Incident'... Next week, Paul 'Bono' Hewson is born in Dublin.
- **15TH: THE FIRST OPTICAL LASER** is demonstrated by Theodore Maiman. Initially without much practical use, lasers have since become essential for CDs, eye surgery, and extravagant light shows.

- **22ND: THE LARGEST EARTHQUAKE** ever recorded occurs in southern Chile, measuring 9.5 on the Richter scale. Over 2000 people are killed – relatively few considering the quake's magnitude. The resulting tidal wave, or tsunami, spreads thousands of miles across the Pacific, as far as Japan, drowning hundreds of people in the process.
- **23RD: THE EVERLY BROTHERS'** debut single on Warner Brothers, 'Cathy's Clown', hits the US Number One spot for the first of five weeks. It will actually be their last ever US Top Five hit, though they have five more in the UK.

### Don't Cry For Me

- **MAY 11TH: ADOLF EICHMANN**, the former German SS officer who led the Jewish genocide in World War II, is captured in Argentina, where he's lived under a false name since the war. He is smuggled out of the country to stand trial in Israel, is later found guilty of mass-murder, and is hanged in May 1962... Meanwhile back in the music world, Gene Vincent records 'Pistol Packin' Mama' (originally planned as a duet with Eddie Cochran) at EMI's Abbey Road Studios in London. His backing group, The Beat Boys, includes 16-year-old keyboard player Clive Powell, who changes his name to Georgie Fame when he joins Billy Fury's band The Blue Flames.

## JUNE

- **6TH: ROY ORBISON** releases what will be his first major hit, 'Only The Lonely', having had no luck persuading Elvis or the Everlys to record the song. It reaches Number Two in the US, and Number One in the UK (in October this year).
- **7TH: PRINCE ROGERS NELSON** – eventually to find fame as plain old Prince – is born in Minneapolis, Minnesota. He's named after his father's jazz band, the Prince Rogers Trio... On the same day, free hearing aids are distributed for the first time on the UK National Health Service.
- **10TH: BRITISH GROUP** Johnny Kidd & The Pirates release their new single, the self-written spikey-guitar-riff-driven classic 'Shakin' All Over', which will peak at Number One on the UK charts.
- **13TH: 'ALLEY OOP'** by the Hollywood Argyles (one-hit wonders created by Gary Paxton, who goes on to produce Bobby Pickett's 'Monster Mash' in 1962) enters the US singles chart, on its way to Number One. The song is about a comic-strip caveman character, and the recording features top session drummer Sandy Nelson playing on garbage cans. An almost simultaneous cover version is released by Dante & The Evergreens, produced by Herb Alpert and Lou Adler, which makes it to 15 on the US charts.
- **23RD: TWO MONTHS** after his death, Eddie Cochran has his first and only Number One single when 'Three Steps To Heaven' tops the British charts... The same day, Dr Martin Luther King Jr has a private meeting with presidential candidate John F. Kennedy in New York to discuss civil rights.
- **25TH: JOHN LEE HOOKER** plays at the second *Newport Folk Festival*, Newport, Rhode Island – a historic appearance which, along with Muddy Waters' set at the following week's *Newport Jazz Festival*, introduces a new generation to authentic blues performers, and helps launch the 1960s folk-blues revival.
- **30TH: THE REPUBLIC OF CONGO** gains independence from Belgium, and the young, charismatic Patrice Lumumba becomes its first ever elected Prime Minister. His progressive, anti-colonial views win him powerful international enemies, and he is soon ousted, then assassinated in January 1961, to be replaced by Joseph Mobutu.

## JULY

- **4TH: THE USA INTRODUCES** its new official flag, with a 50th star added for the latest state in the union, Hawaii.
- **6TH: US PRESIDENT EISENHOWER** starts trade sanctions against Cuba, firstly by cancelling sugar imports, in the hope that economic hardships will lead the Cuban people to overthrow their communist-style government, which has deposed the US-friendly dictator Batista and begun acquiring and nationalising US interests on the island.
- **12TH: CHILDREN'S DRAWING** toy Etch-A-Sketch is created by Ohio Arts – originally with the hope of being a one-off Christmas novelty – and has remained in production virtually unchanged ever since. Around the same time, Danish-made Lego is first seen in the UK, before being distributed in the US by Samsonite the following year; and Mattel, makers of Barbie, produce the first talking doll, Chatty Cathy... Meanwhile Floyd Cramer, "Nashville's top session pianist," records his first of three hits, 'Last Date', for RCA Records in Nashville, Tennessee.
- **21ST: 'APACHE' BECOMES** the first of over 20 Top 20 UK hits in the 1960s for The Shadows. Added to their 30-odd hits backing Cliff Richard, this means in total they'll have more UK hits than The Beatles. They're also the first group to popularise the two-electric guitars/electric bass/drums line-up, back in 1958 (when they were known as The Drifters). Strangely, despite their Buddy Holly looks and Fender Strat-derived, foot-stomping instrumentals, The Shadows make no impact whatsoever on the US charts, where Danish guitarist Jorgen Ingmann has a one-off hit with his cover version of 'Apache' in 1961. But Shadows leader and twang guru Hank Marvin becomes the inspiration for a whole new generation of guitarists, including Jimmy Page, Neil Young, Peter Frampton, Eric Clapton, Brian May, Mark Knopfler, and Ritchie Blackmore.

Using borrowed money, plus earnings from hits he's co-written for Jackie Wilson – including 'Reet Petite' – Gordy sets up his home studio as a base, grandly calling it Hitsville USA, and proceeds to create "The Sound Of Young America" for the next couple of decades. No other record company will have as much Top Ten success in the Sixties: in 1964 alone Gordy sells three million albums and 12 million singles, a remarkable ten per cent of America's top 100 hits for that year. He goes on to release classic tracks – written by prolific in-house teams like Holland/Dozier/Holland and Whitfield & Strong – for Stevie Wonder, The Four Tops, Martha Reeves, Diana Ross, Smokey Robinson, The Jackson Five, and Lionel Richie. Some of the artists nurtured by Gordy will subsequently complain of poor contracts and domineering work practices, and lawsuits become a regular occurrence – a trend that might well eventually contribute to Gordy's decision to sell out to MCA in June 1988 (though he cannily retains the ownership of Jobete, Motown's publishing arm). "I earned 367 million dollars in 16 years," he's quoted as saying in 1976. "I must be doing something right."

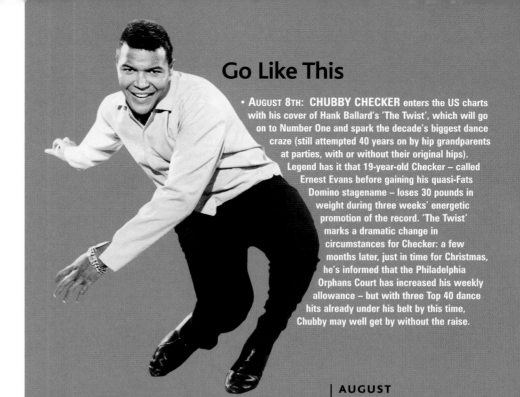

## Go Like This

- **AUGUST 8TH: CHUBBY CHECKER** enters the US charts with his cover of Hank Ballard's 'The Twist', which will go on to Number One and spark the decade's biggest dance craze (still attempted 40 years on by hip grandparents at parties, with or without their original hips). Legend has it that 19-year-old Checker – called Ernest Evans before gaining his quasi-Fats Domino stagename – loses 30 pounds in weight during three weeks' energetic promotion of the record. 'The Twist' marks a dramatic change in circumstances for Checker: a few months later, just in time for Christmas, he's informed that the Philadelphia Orphans Court has increased his weekly allowance – but with three Top 40 dance hits already under his belt by this time, Chubby may well get by without the raise.

### AUGUST

- **JULY 18TH: FILMING BEGINS** (in Nevada, US) on *The Misfits*, the last completed movie of both Clark Gable and Marilyn Monroe... Around the same time, Elvis Presley finishes making *GI Blues*. Despite the impression you might get looking at this still from the movie, with co-star Juliet Prowse, Elvis is soon to be voted 'Least Cooperative Actor Of 1960' by the Hollywood Women's Press Club. Undeterred, he goes on to act in over 25 more features during the decade. Given the quality of some of these movies, it's hardly surprising he's uncooperative.

- **1ST: EIGHTEEN-YEAR-OLD** gospel singer Aretha Franklin records her first pop tracks for Columbia Records, where she's been signed by John Hammond. She will record eight albums for the label in the next six years, with only limited success, especially outside the R&B chart.
- **2ND: TINA TURNER** makes her recording debut, with partner Ike (there's some dispute over whether they're officially married at the time) on 'A Fool In Love.'
- **18TH: CONTRACEPTIVE PILL** Enovid is made available in the US (though not in the UK for another year), ushering in a new era of sexual freedom... The same day, the American Corona satellite takes the first photos of Earth from space. Perhaps mostly photos of people having sex.
- **19TH: BELKA AND STRELKA**, aboard the Soviet Union's Sputnik 5, become the first dogs to survive a trip into space. One of Strelka's puppies is later given to President Kennedy as a gift.
- **23RD: DEATH OF LYRICIST** and musical theatre giant Oscar Hammerstein II. Writer of many of the 20th century's best loved songs – in collaboration with composers such as Jerome Kern and Richard Rodgers – Hammerstein's last completed work was *The Sound Of Music*.
- **29TH: 'WALK, DON'T RUN'** by The Ventures peaks at Number Two in the US. An old track, written by revered jazz guitarist Johnny Smith, and recorded in 1957 by Chet Atkins, The Ventures make it their own with this proto-surf version, and it remains their biggest hit.

## Oh Carole

NOVEMBER 21ST: 'Will You Love Me Tomorrow?' by The Shirelles enters the US Hot 100 at Number 88, on its way to Number One. Not only is this track memorable for being the first US Number One by an all-female group, it's also the first for young husband-and-wife songwriting team Gerry Goffin and Carole King, who will go on to supply hits for The Drifters, The Monkees, Billy Fury, Helen Shapiro and Rod Stewart, among many others. The couple met in 1958 when Goffin was working in a pharmacy and King was attending Queen's College in New York City. After rubbing shoulders with other aspiring writers like Paul Simon and Neil Sedaka (who wrote his mis-spelt 1959 hit 'Oh Carol' about King – before she was married, naturally), the pair team up and start writing songs for Don Kirshner and Al Nevins' music publishing company, Aldon, based in the Brill Building on Broadway. Some of Goffin & King's biggest Sixties hits include 'Take Good Care Of My Baby' (a Number One for Bobby Vee in August 1961), 'The Loco-Motion' (a 1962 Number One for Little Eva – who is the couple's babysitter at the time), 'Chains' (The Cookies, 1962 – later covered by The Beatles), 'Up On The Roof' (The Drifters, 1962), 'Go Away Little Girl' (Steve Lawrence, 1962), 'One Fine Day' (The Chiffons, 1963), 'I'm Into Something Good' (UK Number One for Herman's Hermits in 1964), 'Some Of Your Lovin'' and 'Goin' Back' (Dusty Springfield, 1965-66), 'Don't Bring Me Down' (The Animals, 1966), 'Pleasant Valley Sunday' (The Monkees, 1967), and '(You Make Me Feel Like) A Natural Woman' (Aretha Franklin, 1967). King also starts to carve out a career separate from Goffin, not only co-writing The Everlys' 'Crying In The Rain' with Howard Greenfield, but also as a performer, recording 'It Might As Well Rain Until September,' which reaches Number Three in the UK in 1963, Number 22 in the US. Although this is not her solo debut – that was

## SEPTEMBER

• 2ND: **HAVING FLED** from the Chinese occupation of Tibet last year, the 14th Dalai Lama, Tenzin Gyatso, and his fellow asylum seekers set up the Tibetan parliament-in-exile is its new home of Dharamsala, in the mountains of northern India, with the blessing of Indian prime minister Jawaharlal Nehru.

• 11TH: **THE CLOSING CEREMONY** of the *17th Olympic Games* is held today. Highlights of the competition have included legendary Ethiopian marathon runner Abebe Bikila, who smashed the world record running in his bare feet, becoming the first African to win an Olympic medal; and Cassius Clay winning the light heavyweight boxing gold medal for the USA – this is before he gains a few pounds and changes his name to Muhammad Ali.

• 14TH: **THE ORGANISATION** Of Petroleum Exporting Countries (OPEC) is formed by Iraq, Iran, Kuwait, Saudi Arabia, and Venezuela.

• 24TH: **LAUNCH OF THE USS ENTERPRISE** – no, not the *Star Trek* one (that's not till 1966… or should that be the 22nd century?), but in fact the world's first nuclear-powered aircraft carrier.

• 25TH: **IN LOS ANGELES, CALIFORNIA**, 16-year-old Barry White (not yet embarked on his singing career as the Walrus Of Love) is released from jail after serving three months for stealing 300 car tyres. Don't ask...

### Grand Ole Patsy

• SEPTEMBER 3RD: **SINGING 'THERE HE GOES,'** Patsy Cline makes one of many appearances at the *Grand Ole Opry* in the Ryman Auditorium, Nashville. It's broadcast as part of NBC's radio series *The Prince Albert Show*, named after its tobacco-brand sponsors.

## OCTOBER

• 2ND: **CANDID CAMERA**, the first fly-on-the-wall ordinary-people-as-stars TV show, originally launched in the late 1940s, starts a new regular slot on CBS, to great popular acclaim.

• 3RD: **'STAY' BY MAURICE WILLIAMS** & The Zodiacs (complete with unfeasibly high falsetto chorus) enters the US singles chart, where it will peak at Number One – becoming the shortest record ever to top the charts, at just over one-and-a-half minutes long.

• 10TH: **RAY CHARLES** enters the US Top 40 with 'Georgia On My Mind,' which will give him his first of three Number Ones.

• 15TH: **RINGO STARR**, drummer with Rory Storm & The Hurricanes, deputises for Pete Best when The Beatles back Lou Walters of The Hurricanes during a recording session in Akustik Studio, Hamburg, Germany.

• 17TH: **US MUSIC BIZ NEWSPAPER** *Billboard* reports that Dion & The Belmonts have "ankled one another's scene". In plain English, they've split up.

• 24TH: **THE ALBUM LOVE IS THE THING** by Nat King Cole (recorded in 1957 with some lush orchestration by Gordon Jenkins) is awarded a US gold disc by the RIAA. After initially being at Number One for eight weeks, it has by now been lodged in the album chart for nearly two years.

• 27TH: **THE TRIAL OPENS IN LONDON**, UK, to decide whether the new, uncensored version of *Lady Chatterly's Lover* from Penguin Books is an "obscene" publication. After five days the jury decides it's not, and the paperback goes on to sell two million copies in the next 12 months – albeit 30 years too late for author DH Lawrence to benefit... Meanwhile, after failing to sell his song 'Stand By Me' to his former band The Drifters, singer Ben E. King records it himself in New York City, with Jerry Leiber and Mike Stoller producing – assisted by a newcomer to the studio world, Phil Spector. The song takes six months to chart, and almost another 26 years to reach Number One (and even then only in the UK) when it's re-issued on the back its appearance in the Rob Reiner movie of the same name.

• OCTOBER 7TH: **CINEMA RELEASE** of Roman epic *Spartacus*, directed (mostly) by Stanley Kubrick. Kubrick was not first-choice director, and had numerous on-set clashes with star and executive producer Kirk Douglas (seen here on high horse). The film still manages to win four Oscars. It also helps end the Hollywood 'blacklist' era by using and openly crediting screenwriter Dalton Trumbo, one of ten artists jailed in 1950 for refusing to co-operate with Senator McCarthy's Un-American Activities anti-communist trials.

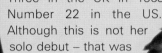

back in 1959 when she made 'Oh! Neil' as a response to Sedaka's 'Oh! Carol' – it marks the direction in which her career will develop. In the late 1960s Goffin and King divorce, and King sets up the Tomorrow label with journalist Al Aronowitz – her first release is a version of 'Some Of Your Lovin''. She then forms the group The Myddle Class, which includes bass player Charles Larkey, but the resulting album disappears without trace. King moves to the West Coast and forms another group with Larkey (whom she subsequently marries), plus session guitarist Danny 'Kootch' Kortchmar and drummer Jim Gordon. Called The City, the group's debut, *Now That Everything's Been Said,* is released on Lou Adler's Ode label. Even though the group soon disbands – because King is apprehensive about playing live – the album has its fair share of fine songs, such as 'Wasn't Born To Follow', which The Byrds covered for the soundtrack of the cult movie *Easy Rider.* King also does session work, notably playing piano on James Taylor's album *Sweet Baby James* (she writes his hit 'You've Got A Friend'),

before cutting the album *Carole King: Writer.* Featuring Larkey, Kortchmar, Taylor and drummer Russ Kunkel, this proves to be a template for the classic *Tapestry* album which, from its release in 1971, goes on to sell over 20 million copies worldwide. On it she famously re-interprets the old Shirelles door-opener, transforming 'Will You Love Me Tomorrow?' from a singalong pop ditty into a heart-wrenching, world-weary ballad. By now established as a solo artist, she releases ten more albums in the 1970s, though none quite attain the status of *Tapestry.* Rod Stewart has a UK hit with 'Oh No Not My Baby' in 1973, but in more recent years King has been less prolific. She's worked with Goffin now and again since their divorce, while he's collaborated successfully with Michael Masser on chart-toppers like 'Do You Know Where You're Going To?' (Diana Ross, 1973) and 'Saving All My Love For You' (Whitney Houston, 1985). On January 17th 1990, Carole King and Gerry Goffin will be inducted together as a songwriting team into The Rock & Roll Hall of Fame.

## NOVEMBER

- **3RD: JOHNNIE RAY** – pre-Elvis teen heart-throb, tagged The Sultan Of Sob for his tear-shedding stage act – begins a residency at the Basin Street East club, New York City, with the George Shearing Quintet and the Quincy Jones Orchestra.
- **5TH: MACK SENNETT**, movie producer from the silent era, dies at the age of 80. Known in his day as The King Of Comedy, Sennett first introduced audiences to Charlie Chaplin and the Keystone Cops, and founded Hollywood's Studio City.
- **9TH: TODAY'S GENERAL ELECTION** result reveals that John Fitzgerald Kennedy will become 35th president of the United States – having been helped by televised debates opposite his less photogenic rival Richard Nixon. At 43, JFK will be the youngest ever US leader, as well as the first Catholic to hold the office... On the same date (presumably having voted earlier in the day) Lightnin' Hopkins – one of the "rediscovered" middle-aged bluesmen benefitting from the Sixties folk-blues revival – records the album *Lightnin'* at Fantasy Studios, Berkeley, California.
- **10TH: BOBBYSOX TEEN IDOL** Fabian hosts an *After-School Coke Party* for his young fans in the lobby of the Paramount Theater, New York City. Ah, these innocent times...
- **16TH: HOLLYWOOD ICON CLARK GABLE** dies, aged 59, having suffered a heart attack a few weeks after filming ended on *The Misfits.*
- **17TH: LOUIS ARMSTRONG** arrives in Salisbury, Rhodesia (later known as Zimbabwe) on his second tour of Africa.
- **19TH: IN SAN FRANCISCO**, Elvis Presley threatens passengers in his car with a gun, believing they have insulted him. The singer is known to be suffering mood swings, presumed to be caused by work-related stress. He's also a big fan of guns, and always carries at least one – even, in later years, when he's on-stage.

## DECEMBER

- **1ST: IN THE SHOWBIZ** pairing of the year, wholesome teenage pin-up actress Sandra Dee (who played surfing heroine Gidget in the first-ever beach movie in 1959 – which was made before Dee actually learned to swim) marries singer and actor Bobby Darin in a secret ceremony in New Jersey. The marriage lasts seven years.
- **3RD: THE ARTHURIAN MUSICAL** *Camelot,* written by Alan Jay Lerner and Frederick Loewe, opens at the Majestic Theatre, New York. Co-starring with Richard Burton is Julie Andrews, who's already spent three years on-stage in Lerner & Loewe's *My Fair Lady* playing Eliza Doolittle.
- **5TH: THE NEW NUMBER ONE** album in the US is Elvis's *GI Blues.* Meanwhile Elvis's last hit single, 'Are You Lonesome Tonight?' has provoked something of a literal response: at least three 'answer' records are released (by Thelma Carpenter, Dodie Stevens and Ricky Page), all entitled, rather earnestly, 'Yes, I'm Lonesome Tonight'... On the same day, The Crickets release 'Peggy Sue Got Married.' One of the last songs Buddy Holly wrote before he died in that plane crash in February 1959, it was intended as a follow-up to his hit 'Peggy Sue'. Vocals are supplied this time by 17-year-old David Cox – who will die four years later, in a plane crash.
- **9TH: DOMINICK DEVARTI** sells his pizzeria in Ypsilanti, Michigan, to Thomas Monaghan, who decides to keep the trading name, Dominick's. Devarti objects to this, so Monaghan changes it slightly, to Domino's – a company which by 2003 will be claiming to sell around 400 million pizzas a year in over 50 countries... Meanwhile in the UK tonight, TV viewers will sit down (without any pizza, almost certainly) to watch the first episode of *Coronation Street*, which – having sensibly changed its name from *Florizel Street* at the last minute – will become Britain's longest running soap opera. It still hasn't quite caught up with CBS's *Guiding Light,* a show that premiered on American TV in 1952, and on radio way back in 1937.
- **16TH: THE WORST AIR DISASTER** of the decade occurs when two passenger planes collide in mid-air and spray debris over New York, killing 134 people, including six on the ground.
- **19TH: BRENDA LEE'S** seasonal chestnut 'Rockin Around The Christmas Tree' makes its first appearance in the US Top 40 (though she recorded it back in 1958). The UK would have to wait until 1962 to enjoy hearing it... Meanwhile, Bing Crosby's 'White Christmas' enters the US Top 40 for the third time in five years... On the same day, Frank Sinatra makes his first recordings for his own newly launched label, Reprise – even though his deal with Capitol Records is yet to end.
- **26TH: YOUNG BARRY, ROBIN AND MAURICE GIBB**, later to become known as The Bee Gees, begin two weeks of appearances in a pantomime, *Jack & The Beanstalk,* at the Rialto Theatre, Sydney, Australia.
- **27TH: RAY CHARLES RECORDS** 'One Mint Julep' at Van Gelder Recording Studio, Hackensack, New Jersey. The track is arranged and conducted by Quincy Jones.
- **31ST: THE FARTHING** (quarter-penny) is withdrawn from circulation in the UK... And on the same day, 'Shop Around' by The Miracles enters the US Top 40, giving Berry Gordy's Tamla label its first million-seller. It won't be the last.

## Reet Petite And Gone

**F**EBRUARY 15TH: **SINGER** Jackie Wilson is shot twice in the chest by Juanita Jones – described at the time as a "deranged female fan," but most likely an aggrieved lover – in his New York apartment. Wilson survives, but his injuries mean he loses a kidney, and one of the bullets has to be left in place because it's too close to his spine to be removed. When he is discharged from hospital after a few weeks he discovers that, despite being at the peak of success, he is flat broke, and his house has been repossessed by the Internal Revenue Service. Sadly there's worse to come. Always a heavy drinker, and brawler, with a few dubious business connections, his wife divorces him in 1965 because of his serial adultery, and in 1970 his 16-year-old son is shot dead. In 1975, with his career more or less confined to the cabaret circuit, 41-year-old Wilson

**JANUARY**

**FEBRUARY**

- **1ST: NEIL SEDAKA**, Dion, Bo Diddley, The Drifters, Chubby Checker, Little Anthony, The Skyliners, Johnny Burnette, Bobby Vee, and Dante & The Evergreens play the last of ten days in the *Christmas Rock'N'Roll Show* at the Paramount Theater, Brooklyn, New York.
- **9TH: BOBBY VEE** is on his way to his first million-seller when his version of the Gene Pitney composition 'Rubber Ball' peaks at Number Six on the US singles chart (Number Four in the UK). Eighteen months earlier Vee was fronting a band called The Shadows, up in Fargo, North Dakota, and briefly hired a keyboard player by the name of Elston Gunn – whose real name was Bob Zimmerman, soon to become Dylan.
- **10TH: THRILLER WRITER** Dashiell Hammett, author of *The Maltese Falcon* and *The Thin Man*, dies at the age of 66... On the same day, one of the world's largest hydro-electric power plants, at Niagara Falls on the US-Canadian border, begins generating electricity.
- **12TH: AFTER SIX YEARS**, Big Joe Williams makes his last appearance as vocalist for the Count Basie Band, at the Harlem Apollo, New York City, and embarks on a solo career.
- **13TH: IN AN EPISODE** from the first season of Hanna-Barbera series *The Flintstones*, Fred cuts a record, adopting the stage-name Hi-Fye.
- **15TH: THE PRIMETTES** are signed to Berry Gordy Enterprises and Tamla Records – having been rejected initially and told to go away and finish

school. Gordy doesn't like the group's name, though, so the female vocal four-piece change it to The Supremes. It will take them seven flop singles, and slimming down from a quartet to a trio, before they have any kind of impact on the charts.

## You Looking At My Island?

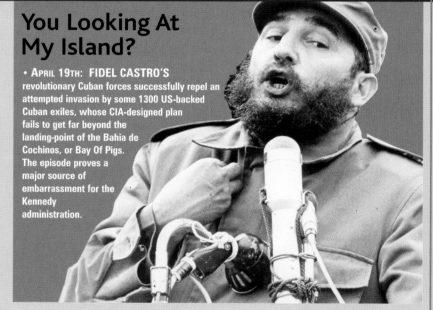

- **APRIL 19TH: FIDEL CASTRO'S** revolutionary Cuban forces successfully repel an attempted invasion by some 1300 US-backed Cuban exiles, whose CIA-designed plan fails to get far beyond the landing-point of the Bahia de Cochinos, or Bay Of Pigs. The episode proves a major source of embarrassment for the Kennedy administration.

- **20TH: JOHN F. KENNEDY** is sworn in as the new American president. During his inaugural address in Washington DC, he famously proclaims: "Ask not what your country can do for you, but what you can do for your country."
- **21ST: DEL SHANNON** arrives at Bell Sound Studios, 237 West 54th St, New York City, to record his latest composition, 'Runaway.'
- **24TH: ASPIRING FOLK SINGER** Bob Dylan arrives in a wintry New York City, having driven from Madison, Wisconsin, in a four-door Pontiac. That evening he performs a few songs (mostly Woody Guthrie numbers) at an 'open-mike' hootenanny night at the Café Wha? in Greenwich Village. The Café Wha? is a famous 'beat/rock' club of the 1960s, a popular hangout for poets, writers, comedians and musicians. Dylan isn't the only performer to start his career here – others include Bill Cosby, Jimi Hendrix, Richard Pryor, Bruce Springsteen, and Kool & The Gang, who all learn their trade at this New York institution (which still exists in 2003). Dylan plays several

early gigs here – at which time one of the club's waitresses is Mary Travers, who later finds fame herself in folk trio Peter, Paul & Mary.

- **9TH: THE BEATLES DEBUT** at The Cavern, Liverpool, UK, with a lunchtime session. Their first evening gig there is not until March 21st.
- **24TH: FOSSIL HUNTERS** find skull and bone fragments that suggest mankind has been around a million years longer than previously thought... And the *Festival Du Rock* has been taking place in Paris, bringing unprecedented scenes of mayhem to the French capital. National hero Johnny Hallyday is one of the headliners, but at the Vince Taylor & The Playboys' show, squads of gendarmes are called to quell a riot. British-born Taylor, occasionally known as the 'Black Leather Rebel,' also happens to be brother-in-law to Joe Barbera, of *Flintstone* creators Hanna-Barbera.

collapses on-stage, and never fully recovers: he spends most of the next eight years in a coma, and dies in January 1984, without ever speaking again, let alone singing. The man that some call 'The Black Elvis,' and whose dynamic stage act enthralled the likes of Elvis himself, James Brown, Michael Jackson and Prince, will end up buried in an unmarked pauper's grave – though he is later given a headstone and posthumously inducted into The Rock & Roll Hall Of Fame. In 1986 his re-released 'Reet Petite' reaches Number One in the UK.

## What'd I Do?

**A**PRIL 24TH: Legendary rock'n'roll pioneer Jerry Lee Lewis reaches the US Top 40 for the first time in almost three years, with a cover of Ray Charles' 'What'd I Say.' Incredibly this "Rompin', stompin', piano-playing son-of-a-bitch" (as he once describes himself in *Time* magazine) only has three Top Ten hits to his name, all before 1958. In the late 1950s/early 1960s he goes through a disastrous period when the scandal breaks that he's married his cousin's 13-year-old daughter, Myra Gale Brown (right) – even though it's all perfectly legal in their part of the deep South. Lewis later has some success as a country artist, though many regret the forced curtailment of his rock'n'roll career. It's said that when John Lennon gets to meet Lewis, one if his icons, in 1973, the ex-Beatle kneels down and kisses Jerry Lee's feet.

---

### MARCH

- **10TH: THE NINTH ANNUAL** *New Musical Express (NME) Poll Winners Concert*, held at the Empire Pool, Wembley, London, is televised to an audience estimated at 15 million. Connie Francis presents awards to Adam Faith, The Shadows and skiffle king Lonnie Donegan. Performing live are guitarist Bert Weedon (whose *Play In A Day* book earns him the nickname "The man who taught the world to play guitar"), Billy Fury, Emile Ford & The Checkmates, Adam Faith, The John Barry Seven, and Cliff Richard & The Shadows.
- **25TH: ELVIS PRESLEY STAGES** his last live show for eight years, at Block Arena, Pearl Harbour, Hawaii.

### APRIL

- **8TH: WHOLESOME BRITISH** balladeer Craig Douglas gets into trouble when his cover version of Gene McDaniels' US hit '100 Pounds Of Clay' is banned by the BBC for its religious fundamentalist lyrics – suggesting that God created woman out of mud. Douglas re-records it with new words, and has his hit.

- **12TH: RAY CHARLES** scoops four US Grammy Awards, for Best Male Vocal Performance, Best Single, Best Album, and Best Song... The same day, Yuri Gagarin becomes the first human to orbit the earth – or at least the first to come back alive (Soviet space-race secrecy being what it is). A hero on his return, ironically Gagarin dies when his

plane crashes during a refresher lesson in 1968.
- **17TH: FORMER BARBER** Paul Revere and his band The Raiders – who dress like colonial soldiers on-stage – enter the US Top 40 with the Jerry Lee Lewis-style piano-led instrumental 'Like, Long Hair,' their first of 15 hits over the next ten years. Unfortunately, just as his debut hit makes the charts, Revere is drafted (into the real armed forces), so his place has to be taken on a promotional tour by keyboard player Leon Russell.
- **17TH: 27-YEAR-OLD ROCKABILLY** guitarist Clarence 'Charlie' Shivers (of whom Scotty Moore once said, "If Charlie had decided to give up building bridges and turn professional, we'd all have had to look for new jobs"), dies in a freak methane gas explosion on a farm.
- **24TH:** Bob Dylan earns himself $50 playing harmonica on the album *Midnight Special* by Jamaican-American star Harry Belafonte's. It's young Bob's recording debut.

- **MARCH 15TH: THE E-TYPE JAGUAR** is introduced at the *Geneva Auto Show*. Costing around $6,000 (more than a Corvair but less than a Ferrari), it's an instant and enduring classic sports car, not to mention style icon.

MAY | JUNE

## A Cavern In The Town

**A**UGUST 2ND: **ALREADY** Liverpool's favourite band, The Beatles begin a residency at its most happening club, The Cavern. Named after Paris jazz haunt Le Caveau, the Cavern first opened its doors at 10 Mathew Street in Liverpool on Wednesday 16th January 1957 to the sounds of the Merseysippi Jazz Band. Initially a jazz-only venue, they gradually relax this policy: local jazz fans might have complained, but as the beat boom takes off, so do the Cavern's financial fortunes. John Lennon first played there as far back as August 1957 when, coinciding with the UK's skiffle craze, the venue welcomed his early group The Quarrymen. A week earlier, Ringo Starr is said to have debuted there with the Eddie Clayton Group; Paul McCartney first climbed on the stage in January 1958, though George Harrison didn't play there till the first Beatles lunchtime gig at the venue on 9th February 1961. The Cavern's lunchtime Beatle shows have

---

• **2ND: JIMMY (NOT YET JIMI)** Hendrix is arrested in Seattle, Washington, for being in a car that has been taken without the owner's consent.
• **5TH: ASTRONAUT ALAN SHEPARD** is the first American to leave the planet, when his tiny Freedom 7 space capsule is blasted into space for just 15 minutes. During an unexpected and uncomfortable four-hour delay on the Florida launchpad, he famously discovers the inadequate toilet facilities in early space suits. Shepard will eventually get to walk on the moon, in 1971, at the age of 47 – being of such advanced years, he naturally needs to hit a few golf balls while he's there.
• **9TH: AT COLUMBIA UNIVERSITY**, New York City, the first composition for synth is presented – using RCA's half-million dollar, room-sized Mark II Electronic Music Synthesizer – by American composer, mathematician and musical theorist, Milton Babbitt.
• **12TH: TONY SHERIDAN** and The Beatles sign a one-year recording contract with Bert Kaempfert of Polydor Records in Hamburg, Germany... Meanwhile, in the hills above Los Angeles, a brush fire destroys dozens of houses, but spares the famous Hollywood sign.
• **25TH: PRESIDENT** Kennedy, during a joint session of Congress, states: "I believe that this nation should commit itself to achieving the goal, before this decade is out, of landing a man on the moon and returning him safely to the Earth."

• **2ND: THE FIRST SUCCESSFUL** prosecution of record counterfeiters takes place in Hackensack, New Jersey.
• **5TH: AS IT HITS** Number One on the US singles charts, Roy Orbison earns a gold disc for one million sales of 'Running Scared'.
• **8TH: MARVIN GAYE** releases his debut album, *The Soulful Moods Of Marvin Gaye*, in the US.

• **16TH: RUDOLF NUREYEV**, Russian ballet star, skips off a proposed plane journey at Le Bourget airport in Paris and asks local police for asylum.
• **21ST: BOBBY VEE** records the Goffin & King song 'Take Good Care Of My Baby' at United Recording Studios, Hollywood, California.
• **25TH: ONE OF ALAN FREED'S** rare West-Coast concerts, at the Hollywood Bowl, Los Angeles, California, features Brenda Lee, Jerry Lee Lewis, Bobby Vee, B.B. King, The Shirelles, The Ventures, Clarence 'Frogman' Henry, and The Fleetwoods.
• **26TH: GLADYS KNIGHT** hits Number One on US R&B chart with 'Every Beat Of My Heart'.

• **MAY 13TH: GARY COOPER** dies, from cancer of the spine, at the age of 60. Of his 93 movies the most famous is 1952's *High Noon*, for which he won an Oscar.

gone down in musical history – in fact it's during one of these sessions, on November 9th 1961, that Brian Epstein makes his way down those 18 well-worn steps into the heaving, sweaty vault to witness for himself the exhilarating cacophony he's heard so much about. The Beatles success means they soon outgrow the club (their last lunchtime show here is 4th February 1963, and their last ever date on 3rd August 1963), but they leave behind a thriving scene, with bands such as the (pictured) Gerry & The Pacemakers, The Swinging Blue Genes, Rory Storm & The Hurricanes, and King Size Taylor all building sizeable fan bases – and pre-fame Cilla Black checking coats. By 1973 the venue is forced to close when bad financial management and the need for renovation stretch the purse strings too far. It's moved across the road (to a venue that would later become famous in the punk era as Erics) – but in late 1981 the original site is excavated, the brickwork saved and used to re-build The Cavern to the original dimensions (if a little deeper). In 1984 The Cavern will again opens its doors at 10 Mathew Street, Liverpool.

## Free Thinking

**M**AY 28TH: THE BARBED-WIRE wrapped Amnesty International candle is first lit by British lawyer Peter Benenson, incensed by Antonio Salazar's Portuguese regime handing seven-year jail sentences to two students who had the temerity to drink a toast to freedom. As Benenson states: "Thousands of men and women are imprisoned and tortured because they express political or religious views that differ from their governments," despite the UN Declaration Of Human Rights ("Everyone is entitled to freedom of speech, belief, thought, and opinion.") With the stated aim of alerting the public to breaches of the declaration, by 1962 there are AI groups in nine countries around the world, including the US, 'adopting' around 200 'prisoners of conscience' – which by the end of the decade will have risen to 4000. Their first high-profile fund-raising concert takes place in 1976.

**JULY**

**AUGUST**

- **3RD: 'QUARTER TO THREE'** by Gary 'US' Bonds reaches Number One on the US Top 40 – it'll be his only chart topper, although he has nine hits in all, the last of which, in 1982, will be produced by one of his young fans, Bruce Springsteen.
- **5TH: RAY CHARLES** records 'Unchain My Heart' and 'Hit The Road Jack' in New York City. The call-and-response number 'Hit The Road Jack' becomes his second US Number One single, after 1960's 'Georgia On My Mind'.
- **13TH: HAVING COMPLETED** a long season in Germany, The Beatles return home to the UK, and start off a series of local dates with a show at St John's Hall, Tuebrook, Liverpool.
- **21ST: IT'S ANNOUNCED** that Capitol Records is threatening to sue its biggest star, Frank Sinatra, because his latest album for his own new Reprise label, called *Swing Along With Me*, is felt to be confusingly similar to one he's just made for Capitol titled *Come Swing With Me*. The latter is the

singer's last contractually obliged release for his old label, and generally felt to be one of his weakest albums, probably for that very reason (perhaps also because Sinatra has been distracted by his recent involvement in the presidential campaign for his friend John Kennedy). The Reprise album's title is changed to *Sinatra Swings*, but still outsells Capitol's effort.
- **26TH: *VARIETY* MAGAZINE** reviews a recent show at the Village Gate, New York City, by the Aretha Franklin Trio, declaring her to be "a stylish singer who can play lively piano." Despite this, her only Top 40 hit around this time is a cover of the old Al Jolson warbler 'Rock-A-Bye Your Baby With A Dixie Melody,' which struggles to rise to Number 37 on the US charts. The earth-shaking Atlantic years are still a long way off.
- **29TH: THE FIRST DICK CLARK** *Caravan Of Stars* tour opens in Atlantic City, New Jersey, featuring Chubby Checker, Bobby Rydell, Gary US Bonds, Freddy Cannon, The Shirelles, Duane Eddy, and Johnny & The Hurricanes.

## First Bricks In The Wall

- **AUGUST 13TH: CONSTRUCTION BEGINS** on the Berlin wall, conceived by the East German government to prevent its citizens defecting. Within seven days it's 45km long, and 1.5 meters high, dividing the city into East and West-controlled sectors. It stays up for 28 years.

- **12TH: BRITISH SCHOOLGIRL** star Helen Shapiro – not yet 15 years old – enjoys the first of two UK Number Ones in a row with 'You Don't Know,' written by John Schroeder and Mike Hawker, who also write the follow-up, the Ivor Novello-award-winning 'Walking Back To Happiness'.

- **15TH: PIONEERING BLUES** vocalist 'Stick' McGhee dies of cancer. His best-remembered song is 'Drinking Wine Spo-Dee-O-Dee', in 1949.
- **21ST: 'WHO PUT THE BOMP'** (In The Bomp Bomp Bomp)' by Barry Mann enters the US chart, where it will peak at Number Seven. Thankfully,

Mann goes on to write some better songs, usually in partnership with his wife Cynthia Weill – penning such classics as 'You've Lost That Lovin' Feeling' (with Phil Spector), 'I Just Can't Help Believing,' 'Saturday Night At The Movies,' and 'We've Gotta Get Out Of This Place.'

# 1961

## Espresso Bongo

**B**Y 1961, beatniks have largely become figures of fun, stereotyped in the press and in movies as black-clothed, drug-taking weird-beards mouthing poor poetry and patting bongo drums. They gained their name and notoriety in the late 1950s when, in the era of Sputnik and cold war Soviet obsessions, such 'alternative,' free-thinking, and vaguely-threatening youths – followers of the 'beat' poets and writers (Jack Kerouac, Allen Ginsberg, Neal Cassady, and William Burroughs) – are disparagingly called 'beatniks,' much to the annoyance, it must be said, of the artists themselves. It was Kerouac, author of *On The Road* (published in 1957, and the ultimate in good old stream-of-consciousness travel writing) who initially coined the word 'beat' – conceived as a play on the terms beat-up (as in 'put-upon') and beauty, with some rhythmic

---

### SEPTEMBER

• **SEPTEMBER 29TH:** *NEW YORK TIMES* music critic Robert Shelton raves about a Bob Dylan gig at Gerdes Folk City, describing him as "a cross between a choirboy and a beatnik" who is "bursting at the seams with talent." The rest of the music industry agrees, and on 26th October Dylan signs on the dotted line to become a Columbia Records artist. He starts recording his debut album, *Bob Dylan*, at Columbia's Studio A in New York on 20th November – it costs $400 to make.

• **4TH: FOLK MUSIC** makes one of its so-far rare ascents to the Number One slot in the form of 'Michael' (as in 'Row The Boat Ashore,' a 19th century slave song), as performed by a banjo-led acoustic five-piece called The Highwaymen, all fresh out of university. There's clearly a movement stirring here...

• **11TH: MOTOWN** girl-group The Marvelettes make their US chart debut with 'Please, Mr Postman,' which will go on to reach Number One in both the R&B and pop music charts

• **12TH: VOCALIST** and songwriter Chris Kenner, from New Orleans, Louisiana, records his original version of the much-covered 'Something You Got,' co-written with Fats Domino.

• **15TH: CALIFORNIAN GROUP** The Pendletones, later to become The Beach Boys, meet with publisher Hite Morgan, who invites them to record their song 'Surfin'' at his home studio. The band name is changed without their knowledge before the record is released, and they play their first gig as The Beach Boys on New Year's Eve 1961 in Long Beach California, at a memorial concert for Ritchie Valens (who died with Buddy Holly in 1959).

---

### OCTOBER

• **1ST: ROGER MARIS,** playing with the New York Yankees, hits his 61st home run of the season – breaking Babe Ruth's record... Meanwhile John Lennon and Paul McCartney of The Beatles begin a two-week holiday in Paris, during which they are persuaded to re-style their hair in a fashion similar to their friend, the photographer Jurgen Vollmer. The Beatle cut is born.

• **17TH: WITH THE LPS** *Rockin' At The Hops* by Chuck Berry and *The Best Of Muddy Waters* under his arm, Mick Jagger meets Keith Richards in Dartford Railway Station, south London, UK. They form a strong friendship and, soon after, start The Rolling Stones.

• **22ND: JOSEPH HELLER'S** novel *Catch-22* is published, and a new phrase for an impossible dilemma enters the language. Heller's original title for the book was *Catch-18*, but it is changed just before publication to avoid confusion with another book being released at the same time with the word 18 in the title.

• **23RD: THE USSR DETONATE** the largest ever thermonuclear device – the 50 megaton 'Tsar' bomb – in the Arctic Ocean off northern Russia. It was meant to be even bigger, but there were no planes that could carry it. This leads to the development of the intercontinental ballistic missile (ICBM), and a further escalation of the arms race.

overtones added to the mix: Kerouac's belief was that there's a nobleness and sanctity in the downtrodden. In 1959, Allen Ginsberg – the closest thing to a father figure that the beat movement had – dismissed the term 'beatnik,' saying: "It seems a word of insult usually applied to people interested in the arts." Beatniks start to gravitate to coffee houses (beatniks are largely to blame for the espresso & cappuccino craze), or folk or jazz clubs, where they can share thoughts, verses, and music – this concept persists into the 21st century in some more bohemian urban areas. Black clothing is preferred (much like the later goths), the typical look for a beatnik being roll-neck sweater (often long or baggy), skinny slacks or jeans, and chunky-framed glasses, preferably dark, for the intellectual or just plain mysterious look. Male beatniks classically sport a beret and a goatee beard too. And they often speak their own hip language – taken to its logical limit in the stage act of Richard 'Lord' Buckley, and the early work of 'beat'

comedian (from the more radical wing), Lenny Bruce. If you ain't a beatnik, you must be a square, daddy-o. Dig? The Beatles' famous mop-top image owes something to beatnik fashion as well: on their early travels in Germany and France the band break from their rock'n'roll teddy boy look in favor of black clothes and long-fringed dishevelled hairdos – at least until Brian Epstein tidies them up. British comedian Tony Hancock's 1961 movie *The Rebel* (titled *Call Me Genius* in the US) sees him lampooning the avant garde artistic beatnik set (one of whom is incongruously played by a very young Oliver Reed). Then in January 1962 comes what must be the final nail in the beatnik coffin, when an article in the *New Musical Express* is headed, 'They Plan To Make Pat Boone A Beatnik.' It's clear the game must be up. By the mid 1960s beatniks will have been replaced in the mainstream public's disaffection by hippies – who carry the torch by adopting Allen Ginsberg as counter-cultural guru for their own generation.

## NOVEMBER

• 9TH: **A LIFE-CHANGING** lunchtime for record store owner Brian Epstein. This is the day he visits The Cavern Club in Mathew Street, Liverpool, UK, to see The Beatles for the first time. He's been inundated with requests for copies of the record they made in Germany with Tony Sheridan – in fact Epstein believes at first they must be a German band. When he finds out they are local, and what's more they're playing at The Cavern, not far from his shop, he and his assistant, Alistair Taylor, go to check them out for themselves. Epstein recalls being impressed by their humour and charm as well as their music. Within a month he is their manager.

• 13TH: **'JUST OUT OF REACH'** becomes the first single by soul pioneer Solomon Burke (see small photo of this big man) to enter the US Top 40, where it will peak at Number 24. Though he never gets higher than Number 22 in the mainstream pop charts (with 'Got To Get You Off My Mind' in 1965), Burke will quickly gain a reputation among the genre's cognoscente – which includes Atlantic label producer Jerry Wexler – as the greatest soul singer of them all. He is also one of the most charismatic and unusual (even by the often outlandish standards of soul artists): for

instance, as well as being a former 'wonder boy preacher', and a bishop, and having a church named after him, he's also a qualified undertaker, and has a habit of wearing a crown and regal robes on-stage. Burke will enjoy a revival and belated acclaim some 40 years later.

• 25TH: **REQUIRED TO** enroll for military service, the Everly Brothers join the US Marines at San Diego, California – but only for six months.

• 27TH: **BASS PLAYER BILLY COX** hears the guitar playing of US army private James Marshall Hendrix from outside a service club at Fort Campbell, Kentucky. (Hendrix enlisted voluntarily before being drafted into the military.) Cox and Hendrix form a group, The King Kasuals, and are soon playing locally.

## DECEMBER

• 4TH: **VEE JAY RECORDS** of Chicago, Illinois, release Gene Chandler's classic 'Duke Of Earl,' which will become his only Number One hit. Originally recorded with his group The Du-Kays, its memorable 'Doo-doo-doo' refrain is based on the group's vocal warm-up routine. Strangely, in the UK the song won't become a hit until it is covered by Fifties-style rock'n'roll revivalist band Darts in 1979.

• 8TH: **'SURFIN'', THE DEBUT SINGLE** by The Beach Boys, is released on Candix Records in the US – but it'll be another nine months before they make any impression on the US charts, and some two-and-a-half years till they hit the UK Top Ten.

• 14TH: **THE HIT SINGLE** 'Big Bad John' by Jimmy Dean – the moving tale of a giant-sized miner who heroically perishes while saving his colleagues – is awarded a US gold disc by the RIAA.

• 18TH: **'THE LION SLEEPS TONIGHT'** by The Tokens, based on traditional South African song 'Wimoweh' (previously recorded in Zulu by Miriam Makeba, and performed in concert by folk group The Weavers), becomes the first African song to reach Number One in the USA – albeit sung by an all-white group from New York.

• 22ND: **ON HIS WAY HOME** to Hibbing, Minnesota, for Christmas, Bob Dylan stops off to record some some songs in Minneapolis. The resulting tape will become the basis of what's considered the first bootleg, *Great White Wonder*...

• OCTOBER 2ND: **'RUNAROUND SUE'** by Dion enters the US singles chart, where it will climb all the way to Number One. Dion DiMucci (left) has had a couple of previous Top Five hits, when he was backed by The Belmonts, with 'Teenager In Love' and 'Where Or When'; now he's gone solo he will have another half a dozen hits in the Sixties, including 'The Wanderer' in December 1961 – about an itinerant, womanising tattoo collector (he's the man with 'Rosie' on his chest) – and the more political 'Abraham, Martin & John' in 1968. But 'Runaround Sue' will remain his only US chart-topper.

# 1962

## January–April

### American Folkies

**I T'S NOT OVERSTATING** the case to say that most popular music of the 20th century can be traced back to two strands of American folk music: black ex-slave songs, such as spirituals and blues, and white country – which itself can be traced further back to the UK and Ireland. It's equally true that the US folk music boom of the late 1950s/early 1960s largely shapes the later music scene. Taking their influences from Woody Guthrie, Pete Seeger (& his group The Weavers), Burl Ives and Josh White, this new collection of folkniks are eloquent, intelligent and in the main, fiercely political (many vocal in

## JANUARY

- **1ST: THE BEATLES** are turned down by Decca Records, whose A&R man Dick Rowe enters the history books when he advises them that, "Groups with guitars are out." Rowe did later try to make amends by signing The Bachelors... oh yes, and The Rolling Stones.
- **13TH: IN A UNIQUE** achievement, nearly 18 months after it's been US Number One, Chubby Checker's 'The Twist' returns to the top of the charts. After two weeks it's replaced – but only by Joey Dee & The Starliters' 'Peppermint Twist,' yet another of the dozens of records cashing-in on the insatiable twisting craze, currently reaching its frenetic peak. Other examples include The Marvelettes' 'Twistin' Postman,' Sam Cooke's 'Twistin The Night Away,' plus Checker's own 'Let's Twist Again' and 'Slow Twistin.' Even Frank Sinatra gets in on the act, with 'Everybody's Twisting.' In the meantime a teenager from Essex, UK, claims to have set a world record by dancing the Twist non-stop for 33 hours.
- **14TH: SIX PEOPLE DIE** following an outbreak of smallpox in Britain – one of the victims is a pathologist who contracted the virus after conducting a post mortem. Parliament considers vaccinations for everyone.
- **15TH: CHRISTIAN DIOR** protégé Yves Saint Laurent opens his own fashion house in Paris. The Algerian-born designer, initially criticised for his flamboyantly excessive use of colour, was just 21 when he worked his way to the top job at Dior.

## FEBRUARY

- **4TH: JOHN STEEL** of the Kansas City Five, a band from Newcastle, UK, receives enough 21st birthday cash to be able to buy himself a black pearl Premier drum kit with Zildjian cymbals. The group will eventually evolve into The Animals.
- **7TH: TROYAL BROOKS** is born in Tulsa, Oklahoma. Using his middle name, Garth, he will go on to dominate the US country music scene in the 1990s.
- **13TH: PRODUCTION BEGINS** on the movie version of Harper Lee's 1961 Pulitzer Prize-winning novel *To Kill A Mockingbird*. It will win three Academy Awards, including one for star Gregory

Peck, who plays lawyer Atticus Finch, taking on the task of defending a black man in a prejudiced Southern town. It also marks the movie debut of actor Robert Duvall in the role of child-like and misunderstood Boo Radley (a name borrowed by a UK band in the 1990s).
- **16TH: BILLY VAUGHN**, the most successful orchestra leader of the rock and pop era, is awarded three gold discs by the RIAA for his albums *Blue Hawaii, Sail Along Silvery Moon* and *Theme From A Summer Place*.
- **19TH: HAVING HAD HIS RETRIAL**, and been convicted of those "immoral purposes," Chuck Berry starts his prison sentence. He's

### Cliff Hanger

- **JANUARY 11TH: BRITISH PIN-UP** Cliff Richard becomes the first homegrown artist to go straight onto the UK singles chart at Number One, with the theme from his new movie *The Young Ones*.

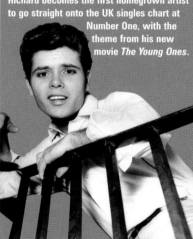

released in October 1963 – by which time some of his new disciples, like The Beach Boys, The Beatles, and The Rolling Stones, will have been spreading the Chuck Berry gospel, leaving the door open for an (albeit short-lived) 1960s revival...
- **20TH: ASTRONAUT JOHN GLENN** – following on from the brief but significant debut trip into space by Alan Shepard the previous year – becomes the first American to orbit the Earth. Glenn later becomes a US senator.
- **21ST: THE DIRECTOR OF THE CIA** compiles and submits an "estimate of the Communist objectives, capabilities, and intentions in South-East Asia" for the Kennedy government in the US.

- **JANUARY 4TH: ANDY WILLIAMS** records the song 'Moon River' for Columbia Records in New York. Written by Henry Mancini & lyricist Johnny Mercer, and sung by Audrey Hepburn (left) in the 1961 Blake Edwards' movie *Breakfast At Tiffany's*, it helps Mancini to win an amazing four Grammys for his work on the film soundtrack. The song is adopted as a virtual signature tune for easy-listening crooner Williams, and he uses it as a theme song in his long-running Sixties TV shows – though strangely it never becomes a hit single for him. In fact it is taken to Number One (in the UK) by a namesake, though no relation, Danny Williams.

their opposition to racial segregation, the military draft, McCarthyism, blacklists, censorship, the Cold War and of course later Vietnam) – although clean-cut acts like The Kingston Trio, Limeliters and New Christy Minstrels take up a less confrontational stance. A fine example of this new radical folk is a trio put together by Albert Grossman – before he discovers Bob Dylan – comprising Mary Travers, Paul Stookey and Peter Yarrow. Peter, Paul & Mary help define the era with albums like *Moving* and *In The Wind* (1963), and hit singles like Seeger's 'If I Had A Hammer' and Dylan's own 'Blowin' In The Wind'. The trio also follow the folk tradition of recording songs for children with 'Puff The Magic Dragon' (any drug associations resolutely denied). The Warners label have one of their most successful years ever in 1962/63 due largely to the success of P, P & M. The flood gates are opened, and a deluge of folk performers follow – including Joan Baez, Phil Ochs, Judy Collins, Loudon Wainwright, John Prine, Woody's son Arlo Guthrie, and Tim Hardin...

## Alexis's Corner

**MARCH 17TH:** **ALEXIS KORNER'S** new and already influential white blues band Blues Incorporated plays at the opening night of the soon-to-be legendary Ealing Club in west London. The nucleus of the group is Korner, harmonica virtuoso Cyril Davies, Ken Scott (piano) and Dick Heckstall-Smith (saxophones), but the rest of the line-up is drawn from a loose-knit bunch of young players who join in when they can – for instance tonight it includes two future Rolling Stones (Mick Jagger and Charlie Watts), and future Cream bassist Jack Bruce. Since joining the Chris Barber Band in 1949, Alexis Korner has been in the vanguard of the British blues and R&B boom. A fine guitarist and singer in his own right, Korner can be seen as a catalyst and father figure for a whole generation of young musicians – not just the future Stones but also Bruce, Clapton and Baker of Cream, Peter Frampton, Steve Marriot, Graham Bond, Long John Baldry, and Paul Jones of Manfred Mann. Korner never gives up searching for and nurturing fresh talent: he will be involved in discovering and naming Paul Kossoff's group, Free, and will record an album with Robert Plant, pre-Led Zeppelin. Still inspiring as a performer and DJ till the end, Korner dies from cancer on New Year's Day 1984, at 55.

## MARCH

---

## APRIL

• **7TH:** **THE BEATLES** perform for the first time wearing matching suits (made by Liverpool tailor Beno Dorn), shedding their previous "greasy" leather look, as John Lennon describes it. Tonight's gig, at the Manchester Playhouse, is recorded and will become their first BBC radio broadcast, on a show called *Teenager's Turn - Here We Go*.

• **10TH:** **'HEY BABY'** by Bruce Channel reaches Number One in the US. While on a UK tour, Channel's harmonica player, Delbert McClinton, gives an impressed John Lennon a few harmonica lessons.

• **23RD:** **THE CREAM** of Britain's rock'n'rollers – Billy Fury, John Leyton, Marty Wilde, Joe Brown, Shane Fenton, Jackie Lynton, The Tornados, and Peter Jay & The Jaywalkers, play in a pop package tour at the Granada venue, Sutton, UK.

• **30TH:** **FILMING ENDS** on the first James Bond movie, *Dr No*, with Sean Connery and Ursula Andress. When it's screened to Bond author Ian Fleming he's not over keen, but it's a hit with the public, starting a 40-year love affair – while Monty Norman's '007' theme becomes the most famous Sixties guitar riff.

• **24TH:** **THE SHADOWS'** guitar instrumental 'Wonderful Land' reaches Number One in the UK where it will sit for eight weeks... The same weekend, President Kennedy is due to stay with Frank Sinatra at his house in Palm Springs, California (according to Sinatra's Eighties biographer Kitty Kelley) – but JFK is persuaded by his brother Bobby, the Attorney General, to change his plans because of the singer's perceived links with organised crime. It's decided instead the president will stay at the nearby house of Bing Crosby – an avowed Republican, but at least politically clean. The job of telling Frank is given to his Rat Pack buddy Peter Lawford – Frank is not amused, and blames Lawford, who claims he is then excommunicated from the 'clan' and dropped from various up-coming Sinatra movies.

HARRY SALTZMAN and ALBERT R. BROCCOLI PRESENT **THE FIRST JAMES BOND FILM!** IAN FLEMING'S **DR NO** TECHNICOLOR **SEAN CONNERY** ANDRESS · WISEMAN · LORD KITZMILLER · GAYSON DAWSON · MARSHALL BERNARD LEE

• **7TH:** **'NIGHT TRAIN'** by James Brown is released in the US on King Records. It's still representative of his 'soul' side, as he's yet to introduce the world to the funk.

• **10TH:** **STUART SUTCLIFFE**, Scottish-born art school buddy of John Lennon's, and original bass player with The Beatles, dies in Germany, from a brain haemorrhage, at the age of just 21. He's been living there with his girlfriend Astrid Kirchherr, having opted to quit the group and concentrate on being an artist rather than a musician. The Beatles learn of his death when they arrive a couple of days later to start a seven-week residency at The Star Club in Hamburg. Despite their grief, the show must, and indeed does, go on. During this stint they support the likes of Little Richard, Ray Charles and Gene Vincent.

• **14TH:** **IT'S REPORTED** that the Johnny Jenkins Combo has signed to Confederate Records in the US. The singer in the band is called Otis Redding.

• **16TH:** **WALTER CRONKITE** makes his *Evening News* debut on CBS Television. During his 19 years as anchor man on the program, 'Uncle Walter' will become an American institution, and popularly regarded as the "most trusted man in the US."

• **21ST:** **STILL ONLY 27**, Elvis Presley notches up his 16th American Number One with 'Good Luck Charm' (it's also his 11th Number One in the UK).

## Ring-A-Ding Rhythm

• **APRIL 27TH:** **MR ACKER BILK** appears on *This Is Your Life* on UK TV, and around the same time receives a gold disc for over a million sales of his single, 'Stranger On The Shore,' which has now been in the UK charts for over five months. Bowler-hatted clarinettist Bilk has also taken the US by storm, climbing into the Top Five – and by May he'll become the first

UK artist to have a US Number One, nearly two years before The Beatles get there. (Strangely, in a marked parallel with the four young Liverpudlians who would follow him to the US, Bilk and his Paramount Jazz Band also honed their art by playing long sets in German bars.) Although 'Stranger On The Shore' is a smoochy instrumental ballad, Bilk is best known as part of the British 'trad jazz' boom of the late 1950s/early 1960s, alongside Ken Colyer, Chris Barber, and Kenny Ball (who just had a US Number Two hit in February 1962 with 'Midnight In Moscow'). Trad is essentially a revival of American Dixieland and 'traditional' jazz – celebrating the music's roots, as opposed to the current modern or alternative strains. Mr Bilk also crops up in a new movie which blends trad jazz and rock'n'roll, titled *It's Trad, Dad* in the UK (in the US it's *Ring-A-Ding Rhythm*). Directed by Richard Lester – who'll go on to make the two major Beatle movies – it stars Helen Shapiro (pop trivia notes: Shapiro was once apparently in a teenage band with Marc Bolan, and was the first British artist to have a Number One hit in Japan), and Craig Douglas, with guest appearances by Chubby Checker, Gary US Bonds, Gene Vincent, Del Shannon, Gene McDaniels – plus, as the movie's UK title suggests, the leading lights of the trad jazz scene. Sadly, like all fashions, trad proves short-lived, and once the sound of beat groups and modern dances like The Twist begin to dominate people's consciousness, trad music falls into decline around the mid 1960s, relegated to boozy Sunday lunchtimes in British pubs.

## Original And Best?

**A**UGUST 16TH: BRIAN EPSTEIN informs The Beatles' drummer Pete Best that he is fired, and is to be replaced by Ringo Starr (as soon as Ringo shaves off his beard). Misunderestimating Best's devastation – not to mention that of the fans, for whom Pete is a good-looking favourite – and expecting gentlemanly behaviour in all business dealings, Epstein is shocked when Pete fails to turn up for tonight's gig... Drummers in bands seem to be particularly vulnerable to getting dropped – in later years both Pearl Jam and The Clash shed sticksmen that many of their fans wish they hadn't, and 1970s UK rockers Uriah Heep get through four in only three albums (and doubtless inspire *Spinal Tap* writers along the way). And most pertinently, 23 years after Pete

Best gets the boot, avowed Beatles fans Oasis do exactly the same thing to their original drummer Tony McCarroll – who, obviously aware of the parallels, promptly hires Jens Hill, the lawyer who represented Pete Best, to take up his claim for unpaid royalties. Of course it's not only the drum stool that gets whipped away – the music world is littered with casualties where the axe has fallen on an unwanted member: bands like Black Sabbath and the ever-changing Rainbow seem to operate a revolving-door policy, while King Crimson and Guns N' Roses retain little except the bandname. Prince and David Bowie have between them probably sacked enough musicians to form a reasonable orchestra. John, Paul, George & Pete sounds faintly ludicrous now, yet if history had taken a slightly different course we might equally have had Bunny Livingstone & The Wailers, or Bob Montgomery & The Crickets...

- **12TH: THE TEMPTATIONS** make their US R&B singles chart debut with 'Dream Come True.' Their first success in the mainstream pop charts is two years away yet.
- **13TH: THE BEACH BOYS** have their first recording session for their new label, Capitol Records, in Los Angeles. They record 'Surfin Safari,' 'Lonely Sea,' and '409.' Even at this early stage their three main themes are clear: surf, girls and automobiles. 'Surfin Safari' is no-nonsense beach music, with talk of "loading up the Woody" (classic Forties-style wood-paneled station-wagon, ideal for putting surfboards on top) and impressing the "honeys." 'Lonely Sea' is a love song with the surf as a metaphor; and '409' indulges Brian Wilson's own passion for cars – in this case a souped-up Chevrolet 409.
- **19TH: GENE PITNEY** (seen here in mid-song) enters the US singles chart with the Burt Bacharach/Hal David song 'The Man Who Shot Liberty Valance,' based on the 1962 John Ford western of the same name, starring John Wayne, James Stewart and Lee Marvin (though the song doesn't actually appear in the movie). It will become Pitney's first Top Five hit.
- **24TH: ROY ORBISON** is among the guests attending Bob Dylan's 21st birthday party in Greenwich Village, New York City.
- **26TH: THE ISLEY BROTHERS** release their classic version of 'Twist And Shout.' It becomes their first Top 20 hit, and will be covered by The Beatles on their debut album (and issued as a single in the US only in 1964.) The Isleys have been performing since the early 1950s, when they were a gospel trio, but will enjoy their most successful period in the late 1960s/early 1970s.

- **2ND: 'TWIST BABY'** by Owen Gray is the first single to be released by Island Records, owned by Chris Blackwell, a wealthy white Jamaican who just launched the label last year and has now set up a London office to import West Indian music to the UK. Island will go on to become one of the UK's most important independent labels... Meanwhile, Stanley Kubrick's movie version of Vladimir Nabokov's highly controversial 1955 novel *Lolita* opens in New York. James Mason, Shelley Winters, Peter Sellers, and Sue Lyon star.
- **6TH: AT EMI'S ABBEY ROAD** studios, The Beatles audition for producer George Martin, who will shortly sign them to the company's Parlophone label.

### A Little Bit Country

- **JUNE 1ST: RAY CHARLES** releases a ground-breaking new album, *Modern Sounds In Country & Western Music*. Already at home with sophisticated jazz, stomping R&B and soulful blues, Charles stuns many fans by venturing into the previously white preserve of country music. As it happens, both parties will gain: country is suddenly seen as slightly more 'cool,' and Ray becomes hugely popular with a whole new audience. *Modern Sounds* tops the US album charts for 14 weeks, and spawns the million-selling single 'I Can't Stop Loving You,' a US and UK Number One.

- **16TH: BOBBY VINTON** has his first US Top 40 single as 'Roses Are Red (My Love)' enters the chart, where it will peak at Number One.
- **23RD: THE SOUNDTRACK** album of the movie *West Side Story* – which won ten Oscars in April – hits the top of the charts in the US, and will stay there for seven weeks.

- **4TH: THE EVERLY BROTHERS** begin a 50-city US tour which will run until 20th August.
- **7TH: 'BREAKING UP IS HARD TO DO'** by Neil Sedaka enters the US Top 40 chart. It's the songwriter's first Number One in his own right – and it will also be his last for some 12 years.
- **9TH: ANDY WARHOL HAS** his "first show of real art in a real gallery" at Irving Blum's Ferus Gallery on La Cienega Boulevard in West Hollywood, LA (till August 4th). It features Warhol's soon-to-be-famous series of 32 different canvases of Campbell's soup cans. His explanation is simply that he likes the soup. Originally selling for $100 per painting, gallery owner Blum decides to pay Warhol $1000 for the set – 40 years later they are worth over $10m. During the exhibition a nearby grocery store advertises Campbell's soup in their window, saying: "The real thing for only 29 cents a can."
- **11TH: THE ERA OF GLOBAL** broadcasting begins with the launch of the Telstar communications satellite by the American Telephone & Telegraph company. The satellite will shortly beam black & white pictures from Maine in the US to Cornwall in the UK and Brittany in France.
- **22ND: JACKIE ROBINSON,** former Brooklyn Dodgers player who broke the 'color barrier' when he joined the Major League in 1945, becomes the first black man to enter the Baseball Hall Of Fame.
- **23RD: MARVIN GAYE** releases 'Stubborn Kind Of Fellow,' his first hit single in the US.
- **30TH: PAUL ANKA** turns 21, and is now able to take control of the vast wealth he has amassed as a teen pop star, singing self-written hits like 'Diana,' 'Lonely Boy,' and 'Puppy Love.'

# 1962
## May–August

- **AUGUST 5TH: THE BODY OF MARILYN MONROE** is discovered at her Hollywood apartment – the press are intrigued to note that she is found lying naked on her bed, next to a bottle of sleeping pills and a telephone. Conspiracy theories have surrounded her death ever since: is it suicide, or a murder staged to look that way? Romantically linked with both President John Kennedy and his brother Bobby, Monroe is known to have powerful, and potentially dangerous friends. Star of *The Seven-Year Itch*, *Gentlemen Prefer Blondes,* and *Some Like It Hot,* her 31st movie, *Something's Got To Give*, remains unfinished when she dies, at the age of 36.

## AUGUST

- **2ND: ARETHA FRANKLIN** makes her small screen debut on US TV's *American Bandstand*... Also today, 44-year-old shopkeeper Sam Walton celebrates his first month in discount retailing – probably by cutting his prices even more. By 1966 he will have opened 15 so-called Wal-Mart stores... and by 1985 *Forbes* magazine calculates he is the richest man in America. Walton himself dies in 1992, but his multinational empire continues to grow and spread. On a good day, it's said, global sales can top one billion dollars.
- **9TH: ROBERT ZIMMERMAN** legally changes his name to Bob Dylan.
- **11TH: BOOKER T** & The MGs' instrumental classic 'Green Onions' is released on Stax Records in the US.

- **13TH: QUINCY JONES** & His Orchestra record 'Soul Bossa Nova' – used 35 years later as the theme to *Austin Powers: International Man Of Mystery*. Known to friends as Q, Jones' musical track record is second to none: since his early teens he's been playing trumpet or writing arrangements for artists such as Ray Charles, Lionel Hampton, Tommy Dorsey, Count Basie, Duke Ellington, Dinah Washington, and Dizzy Gillespie... And we haven't even got to his movie scores, or his production work in the 1970s and 1980s with Michael Jackson... or his remarkable 26 Grammy Award wins (and nominations for a record-breaking total of 76)...

- **JUNE 19TH: *THE MUSIC MAN*,** the movie version of the hit stage musical, opens in Mason City, Iowa (the real 'River City' of the story). Seven-year-old co-star Ronnie Howard, who lisps his way through 'Gary Indiana,' will go on to star in *Andy Griffith* and *Happy Days* on TV, as well as becoming an Oscar-winning Hollywood director.

# He's A Rebel

**N**OVEMBER 3RD: THE CRYSTALS' 'He's A Rebel' is at Number One in the US, signalling the start of Phil Spector's career as the 1960s greatest producer – as well as one of its most disturbed (though there's plenty of competition for that particular title – see Joe Meek on the opposite page for a start). Born in the Bronx, New York on Boxing Day 1940 to parents who were first cousins (and his father committed suicide when he was only nine years old), Spector once even immortalised his psychiatrist in a track called 'Dr Kaplan's Office,' and took the title for 'To Know Him Is To Love Him' (a Number One hit for his early band The Teddy Bears) from his father's gravestone... Spector continually walks a tightrope between genius and lunacy – from turning up at the Brill building in 1960 and sleeping on Leiber & Stoller's office couch, starting his own Philles record label and becoming a millionaire at 21, to retiring to the seclusion of his Beverly Hills mansion at 26, apparently because of American radio's failure to embrace what he feels is his greatest work, 1966's 'River Deep Mountain High' by Ike & Tina Turner. (It's said his relationship with radio stations is poor because he won't play the payola game.) Dubbed the Tycoon Of Teen by Tom Wolfe, Spector's attention to detail is obsessive, and he's known to spend hours going over the same few bars of music. His 'Wall Of Sound' production style has been endlessly emulated (he is a major influence on The Beach Boys' Brian Wilson) but seldom recaptured. Co-writing the songs with Ellie Greenwich and Jeff Barry, Spector elevated the art of production to a new level, with his arranger Jack Nitzsche, concocting "little symphonies for the kids" by multi-layering of instruments, and always with a fanatical dedication to mono recording (instead of the new-fangled and, as he saw it, less powerful stereophonic sound).

## SEPTEMBER

- **1ST: 'SHERRY'** by The Four Seasons enters the US Top 40, destined for Number One – their first of four in the 1960s (plus there's a belated one in 1976, as we'll see later).
- **8TH: BOBBY 'BORIS' PICKETT** & The Crypt Kickers' mock-horror single 'Monster Mash' enters *Billboard*'s Hot 100 at Number 85, beginning a six-week climb to the top, where it arrives just in time for Halloween. It's reportedly banned in the UK at the time by the BBC (too scary), and isn't a hit there until it's re-released in 1973. In-between times it'll be covered by The Bonzo Dog Doo-Dah Band... Also on the 8th, Peter Paul & Mary debut in the US charts with the Pete Seeger and Lee Hays song 'If I Had A Hammer.'
- **11TH: THE BEATLES**, with session drummer Andy White instead of Ringo, record their debut single, 'Love Me Do,' at Abbey Road, London. It's released in the UK on October 5th – though not in the US until May 1964... And Marvin Gaye records 'Wherever I Lay My Hat (That's My Home)' for Tamla Records, in Detroit, Michigan.
- **30TH: RACE RIOTS** are sparked when James Meredith becomes the first black student to enrol at the University of Mississippi, in accordance with the new desegregation laws. President Kennedy orders federal marshalls to escort Meredith after his entrance is initially blocked by troopers sent by Gov Ross Barnett. Three people die in the ensuing riots.
- **SEPTEMBER 26TH:** *THE BEVERLY HILLBILLIES* **is first broadcast on US TV: it will attract the biggest viewing figures of any TV show in 1962/63. Its theme tune, 'The Ballad Of Jed Clampett' by veteran bluegrass duo Lester Flatt & Earl Scruggs (& their Foggy Mountain Boys), even dents the charts at Number 44. Flatt and Scruggs also make a few guest appearances on the show, as old family friends. Forty years later, CBS plan to create a 'reality' TV version of the series, putting a genuine poor rural family in a Beverly Hills mansion and filming the outcome.**

## OCTOBER

- **1ST: THE BEACH BOYS** release their debut album, titled *Surfin' Safari*, in the US.
- **2ND: JOHNNY CARSON** takes over as host of NBC's late-night talk-show *The Tonight Show*, which he will present for the next 30 years: over 4,500 shows.
- **4TH: TEN YEARS** before he finally gets to become James Bond, Roger Moore stars as suave thief-cum-sleuth Simon Templar when a UK TV version of Leslie

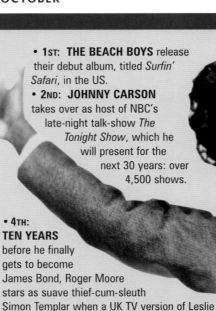

Charteris' *The Saint* is launched. Though he plays the part for seven years, and it will make him famous, Moore is not Charteris' fist choice – he would have preferred Cary Grant. Moore is, however, headhunted for the Bond role at an early stage, but is fully committed to *The Saint* at the time.
- **13TH: DON EVERLY** of The Everly Brothers collapses on the stage of the Prince Of Wales Theatre, London, during rehearsals. After two suicide attempts in The Savoy hotel he is too drugged on amphetamines to perform. Phil goes on and does the tour alone.
- **28TH: TODAY SEES** the eventually peaceful resolution of the Cuban Missile Crisis, a confrontation that's come perilously close to a nuclear exchange. US President Kennedy and Soviet Premier Khrushchev initially argue over US aggression towards communist Cuba, prompting the Russian leader to offer to install long-range missiles on the island. These are apparently spotted by US U2 spy planes, and Kennedy is persuaded to order a naval blockade. After tense diplomatic exchanges, both parties agree to leave Cuba alone and the crisis ends. But the cold war goes on...

- **OCTOBER 8TH: FIVE YEARS AFTER** abandoning rock'n'roll for religion, Little Richard makes his comeback at the Gaumont Theatre, Doncaster, UK, on a bill shared with Sam Cooke. To the dismay of the crowd, Richard sings only gospel for the first half of the show – but after the interval, he rocks again.

For a masterclass in heroically overblown recording sessions, listen to 'You've Lost That Lovin' Feelin'' by The Righteous Brothers or 'Walking In The Rain' by The Ronettes, or the same group's 'Baby I Love You' (covered by The Ramones in 1979, when they mange to tempt Spector out of retirement). Shakespeare once noted, "Ambition should be made of sterner stuff," but while Spector's ego is vast it will also prove very fragile, and in the later Sixties his erratic behaviour will become far more apparent than his studio wizardry: numerous drunken episodes, stories of guns being fired into studio ceilings, and elevators being used as toilets, are all evidence that things are slipping out of his grasp. He goes on to produce intermittently for John Lennon, George Harrison, and his wife Ronnie (of The Ronettes). In 1977 Leonard Cohen will disown Spector's work on *Death Of A Ladies Man* as soon as it is released. In 2003 Spector gives an interview to the UK's *Daily Telegraph* in which he admits to taking drugs for personality disorders, and speaks at length about his unhappiness: "I have not been well," he says. "I wasn't well enough to function as a regular part of society, so I didn't. I have devils inside that fight me." Just days later he will be arrested on suspicion of murder... For a few years in the early 1960s, though, Phil Spector proves to be one of the most astonishing producers of his, or any other, generation.

## A Star Is Born

• DECEMBER 22ND: THE FIRST BRITISH rock band to top the US singles chart is The Tornados, with the TV-satellite-inspired instrumental 'Telstar,' written and produced by Joe Meek. Once described once as part Thomas Edison, part Phil Spector, with a dash of B-movie director Ed Wood, Meek's early production work is revolutionary: overloading compressors, ladling on echo, multiple overdubs and creating lo-fi sound effects with kitchenware, combs, bottles and flushing toilets. Despite hits with John Leyton, Heinz, and The Honeycombs, Meek grows increasingly paranoid – personally and professionally (he's sure his ideas are being stolen). Things finally come to a head in 1967, when he shoots his landlady, then himself, and dies at the age of 37.

# 1962
## September–December

**NOVEMBER**

**DECEMBER**

• 2ND: US TRADE MAGAZINE *Billboard* reveals that songwriting/production team Jerry Leiber and Mike Stoller have started their own record labels, called Daisy and Tiger. One of the most successful hit-creating duos of the 1950s, originally turning out R&B numbers for the likes of Ray Charles, Jimmy Witherspoon and Big Mama Mae Thornton (who first recorded their song 'Hound Dog'), they wrote numerous hits for Elvis Presley including 'Jailhouse Rock,' 'Loving You,' and 'King Creole,' plus comedy numbers like 'Yakety Yak' and 'Charlie Brown' for The Coasters. In the early 1960s they penned Ben E King's 'Spanish Harlem' and 'Stand By Me,' but the launch of their own labels is not their most fruitful venture, and they sell up in the mid 1960s. Their later, more mature style is best reflected in Peggy Lee's genre-defying 1969 hit, 'Is That All There Is?'.
• 5TH: THE VAN DU PUT FAMILY from Belgium and their doctor are found not guilty today of the mercy killing of their daughter Corinne, who was born without arms due to the drug Thalidomide. An ingredient found in sedative

medicines, and used by expectant mothers in the early stages of pregnancy to prevent morning sickness, Thalidomide is soon proven to be responsible for hundreds of such deformities, mainly in the UK, Germany and Canada, since it was introduced in 1959 (it was never approved in the US). The drug is quickly withdrawn. Forty years later it is back in use as a treatment for, among other things, leprosy.
• 9TH: THE MIRACLES release a new single, 'You've Really Got A Hold On Me,' in the US.
• 13TH: AN IBANEZ GUITAR bought on

September 1st by James (*still not Jimi*) Hendrix in Clarkesville, Tennessee, is returned to the store because he can't afford to keep up the payments.
• 17TH: THE KON-RADS play a gig at Cudham Village Hall in Kent, UK. Their saxophone player, named David Jones, will, in a few years, become David Bowie.
• 27TH: THE FIRST *MOTOR TOWN REVUE* – a two-month long all-Motown package tour featuring The Miracles, Supremes, Mary Wells, Marvin Gaye, The Contours, Marvelettes, Martha & The Vandellas (pictured) and Little Stevie Wonder – plays a date in Tallahassee, Florida.

• 5TH: WILLIAM PERKS (soon to be known as bass player Bill Wyman) is introduced to the Rolling Stones at the Red Lion pub, Sutton, south London, UK.
• 9TH: THE MANNE-HUG QUARTET, later to become Manfred Mann, headlines the Marquee Club in central London for the first time.
• 14TH: MARINER 2, the first successful interplanetary spacecraft, sends back close-up pictures of the red-hot surface of Venus.
• 15TH: *THE FIRST FAMILY* by Vaughan Meader, is the first record to dare to poke fun at the US president – and it tops the US album charts for 12 weeks.
• 20TH: THE OSMOND BROTHERS make their debut on NBC-TV's *Andy Williams Show*.

• SEPTEMBER 10TH: THE LONDON PREMIERE of David Lean's lavish widescreen epic *Lawrence Of Arabia*, starring Peter O'Toole and Omar Sharif.

## The Hardest Working Man In Show Business – In Person!

• OCTOBER 24TH: JAMES BROWN records a live set at the Apollo Theater, Harlem, New York City, which will become his classic album *Live At The Apollo*. He may not be the easiest man to work with – his musicians are fined for bum notes, or even having scuffed shoes on-stage – but his results are inspired. His label, King, is at first unconvinced a live album will sell, so Brown has to dip into his own savings to make this recording. The result is still a classic of its type, and ensures Brown's live audiences will mushroom.

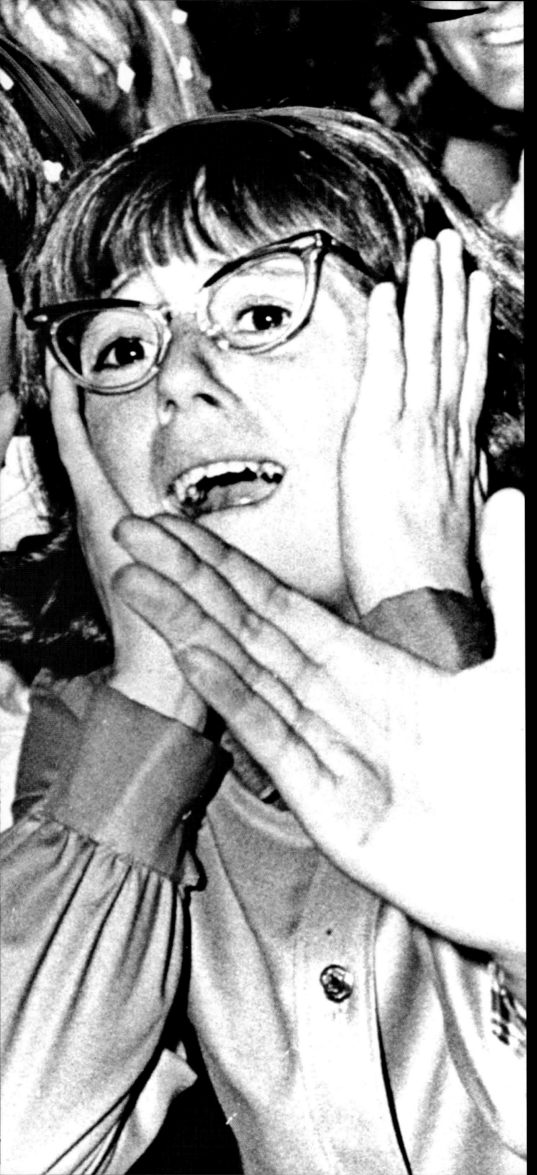

# 1963

## THE SCREAMING BEGINS

Having just had their first UK Top 20 hit with 'Love Me Do' at the end of 1962, The Beatles cram the next six months with national tours, showcases, promotional interviews, and TV & radio performances. It pays off. By the summer of 1963 they'll have had two Number One singles and a Number One album, plus their own radio series on the BBC, and even a dedicated fan magazine in the UK. Throngs of teenage girls turn up everywhere they appear, risking life and limb for a glimpse of the boys. In October, when the band appears at the London Palladium, the unprecedented scenes, inside and out, lead the press to coin a new phrase to describe this unbridled hysteria: Beatlemania.

And they've not even reached America yet...

# 1963

## January–April

### JANUARY

- **1ST: SAM COOKE** appears at a New Year's Day gospel concert in New York City.
- **3RD: THE ROLLING STONES** play at The Marquee, London, as support group to Cyril Davies' R&B All Stars.
- **5TH: DIONNE WARWICK** has her first US singles chart entry with 'Don't Make Me Over,' which will peak at Number 21.
- **7TH: GARY 'US' BONDS** files a law suit against Chubby Checker: Bonds thinks Checker has plagiarised his single 'Quarter To Three' in his hit 'Dancin' Party.'
- **25TH: HAVING JUST** arrived from Texas, Janis Joplin plays her first San Francisco gig in a North Beach coffee house, where she passes a hat to raise cash.
- **26TH: THE ROOFTOP SINGERS** hit Number One in the US with a version of an obscure 1930s song, 'Walk Right In.'

### FEBRUARY

- **8TH: WHEN BOB DYLAN** and Happy Traum play together in the basement of Gerde's Folk City, New York City, their performance is recorded and will eventually be released as a bootleg, known as *The Banjo Tape*.
- **9TH: PAUL AND PAULA** top the US singles charts with the call-and-response number 'Hey Paula.'
- **11TH: THE BEACH BOYS** are in the studio in Los Angeles, working on the tracks 'Let's Go Trippin',' 'Miserlou' (both songs previously recorded by Dick Dale & his Del-Tones), 'Honky Tonk,' and Brian Wilson's 'Noble Surfer.'
- **14TH: HAROLD WILSON** becomes the new leader of the British Labour Party, succeeding the late Hugh Gaitskell.
- **22ND: 'PLEASE PLEASE ME'** by The Beatles reaches Number One in the *NME* singles chart (though not, controversially, in the official BBC charts), sharing the slot with 'The Wayward Wind' by Australian yodeller Frank Ifield.
- **23RD: 'HE'S SO FINE'** by female group The Chiffons, which has already been rejected by 14 record labels, enters the US chart on its way to Number One.

### MARCH

- **2ND: MARVIN GAYE**, Lou Christie, The Four Seasons, Paul & Paula, Dick & Dee Dee, The Crystals and Herb Alpert's Tijuana Brass and host Chubby Checker appear in the *Limbo Party* at the Cow Palace, San Francisco.
- **5TH: PATSY CLINE** (aged 30) and two other country music stars, Cowboy Copas and Hawkshaw Hawkins, are killed in a plane crash in Tennessee, on the way back from a charity benefit. Cline, who's had hits with 'Walking After Midnight,' 'I Fall To Pieces,' and 'Crazy' – all delivered with the trademark crack in her voice – will become an iconic figure, blazing a trail for other strong female country acts to follow. In 1985 her life is made into a bio-pic with Jessica Lange.
- **19TH: FIFTY FOLK SINGERS** convene at The Village Gate, Greenwich Village, New York City, to protest against the ATV show *Hootenanny*, which has refused to allow Pete Seeger & The Weavers to appear because of their left-wing politics.
- **22ND: IN AUSTRALIA**, the Bee Gees release their debut single, 'The Battle Of The Blue And The Grey.'

### APRIL

- **6TH: 'PIPELINE' BY THE CHANTAYS** becomes the first official surfing hit when it enters the US Top 40, eventually peaking at Number Four. But Dick Dale & The Deltones are still the cult heroes of the genre – their 'Let's Go Trippin',' released back in October 1961, is regarded as the birth of surf music, although it only reached 60 on the chart at the time... The Drifters are also new on today's Top 40 with 'On Broadway,' co-written by Barry Mann, Cynthia Weill, Jerry Leiber and Mike Stoller... Meanwhile Britain and the US sign the Polaris Missile Sales Agreement, allowing joint production of the first submarine-launched nuclear ballistic missile, to replace the UK's own unsuccessful Blue Streak and Skybolt missile projects. The following week, on the 15th, 70,000 people march through central London on a CND protest against nuclear weapons – a number of the protesters having walked from the British nuclear military base at Aldermaston in Berkshire, 50 miles west of London.
- **7TH: YUGOSLAVIA** declares itself a socialist republic, and Marshall Joseph Tito, who's been prime minister/president since 1945, names himself "President For Life."
- **14TH: THE BEATLES** nip down to the Crawdaddy Club in the Station Hotel, Richmond, south London to check out up-and-coming band The Rolling Stones.
- **22ND: GENE VINCENT'S** recording contract with Capitol Records expires, and is not renewed.
- **23RD: BOB DYLAN** has his final recording session for the album *Freewheelin'* at Studio A, Columbia Recording Studios, New York City, during which he records 'Girl Of The North Country,' 'Masters Of War,' 'Walls Of Red Wing,' 'Talking World War III Blues,' and 'Bob Dylan's Dream.'

## Smokey On Top

- **FEBRUARY 16TH: 'YOU'VE REALLY GOT A HOLD ON ME'** by The Miracles – written and sung by their frontman William 'Smokey' Robinson – reaches Number One in the US R&B chart. A cover version is recorded by The Beatles in July, and appears on their second album.

- **MARCH 21ST: THE LAST 27 INMATES** leave Alcatraz Island prison in San Francisco Bay, which has fallen into disrepair and become too expensive to run. Apart from Al Capone, its most famous inmate was killer Robert Stroud, known as The Birdman of Alcatraz (portrayed on film by Burt Lancaster, left) – although, despite the nickname and his genuine knowledge and love of aviculture, Stroud was never actually allowed to keep birds while at Alcatraz.

## Three Cool Rats

**J**ANUARY 23RD: FRANK SINATRA, Dean Martin and Sammy Davis Jr (seen here on-stage together, up to some shenanigans), kick off a three-week stint at the Sands Hotel, Las Vegas, Nevada. Popularly known as The Clan or The Rat Pack – a term originally applied to a drinking clique led by Humphrey Bogart, though after Bogie's death Sinatra became the "chairman of the board" with a coterie that included Martin, Davis, actor Peter Lawford, and comedian Joey Bishop – their best-known early outing is the heist romp *Ocean's Eleven*, followed by a string of lesser movies and always-popular stage shows. Their typical live act is an anarchic, often booze-fuelled cocktail of song, dance, impersonations and comedy, with a high level of hit-and-miss improvisation and in-jokes. By 1964 the Rat Pack hey-day is all but over, though they re-unite from time to time for the odd shindig and benefit concert.

## New Groove

• MARCH 18TH: 'THE GIRL FROM IPANEMA' is recorded in New York City. Written by Brazilian piano player Antonio Carlos Jobim, it's performed by Jobim, João Gilberto (revered Brazilian singer and guitarist), and Stan Getz, renowned jazz saxophone player. Getz's interest in Brazilian music dates back to 1962 when he worked with guitarist Charlie Byrd on the Number One album *Jazz Samba*, at the time an innovative blend of jazz and South American grooves, which spawned the instrumental hit 'Desafinado.' But one difference on 'The Girl From Ipanema' is the untutored but charming vocal of João's wife, Astrud Gilberto (seen here on the right, with Stan and João), on what is her first recording. Although it's João's voice that opens the track (with an extraordinary, buzzing, guitar-like hum), and sings the original Brazilian lyric, Astrud picks it up in English, and a legendary musical moment is created. At first the song is simply an album track, but when it's finally released as a single in the summer of 1964, in a shorter English-only version, it causes a sensational reaction, and ignites an international passion for samba, bossa nova, the glamorous beaches of Rio de Janeiro, and all things Brazilian...

• MARCH 4TH: THE BEACH BOYS release 'Surfin' USA,' their first US Top Ten hit, as well as their UK Top 40 breakthrough. This posed photo shows (right to left) Brian Wilson, Mike Love, Carl Wilson, David Marks (a 16-year-old friend who's joined the group for 18 months while Al Jardine is at college), and Dennis Wilson, the only surfer among them.

## Surf, Sand... & Songs

**JUNE 15TH:** Jan & Dean (pictured left, in off-beach apparel) release 'Surf City,' co-written by Brian Wilson of The Beach Boys. The song will reinvent Jan Berry and Dean Torrence as the new musical pin-ups of the surf craze. Though they've been having pop hits since 1959 (including 'Linda,' the sleeve of which features a photo of Linda McCartney as a child, though the song isn't actually about her – it's a long story), the duo will soon come to embody the ethos of surf music, complete with candy-striped shirts and ringing harmonies. Other tracks will include 'Honolulu Lulu,' 'Ride The Wild Surf,' and even 'Sidewalk Surfing,' celebrating the Sixties precursor to skateboarding. Like The Beach Boys, they also cater to that other California teenage boy obsession, fast cars, with tracks like 'Drag City,' 'Dead Man's Curve,' and 'Little Old Lady From Pasadena' (about a speed-freak granny with a hot-rod Dodge in her garage).

This summer also sees the explosion of the beach movie – low-budget, no-brainer, good-time scripts with lots of dancing and 'making out' on the California sand to a soundtrack of Dick Dale & His Del-Tones, and of course Jan & Dean. It's a trend that lasts only a few years, but makes teen movie idols of cherubic former Disney Mouseketeer Annette Funicello, clean-cut pop singer Frankie 'Venus' Avalon, and shimmying go-go dancer Candy Johnson (above).

---

- **10TH: THE ROLLING STONES** record their debut single, 'Come On,' at Olympic Studios, London, UK.
- **12TH: THE PRODUCERS OF** CBS's *Ed Sullivan Show* refuse to let Bob Dylan perform his song 'Talking John Birch Society Paranoid Blues' – they've heard it at rehearsal, and are worried by its scathing attack on American anti-communist neurosis. Dylan won't back down, and his slot on the show is dropped... Later this month his second album, *The Freewheelin' Bob Dylan,* will be released in the US – on CBS. No doubt irritated by the *Ed Sullivan* incident, and unimpressed by poor sales of Dylan's debut, CBS drop 'John Birch' and a few other songs from the album. This still leaves classics like 'A

Hard Rain's A-Gonna Fall' and 'Blowin' In The Wind,' and the LP becomes an international landmark in Dylan's career.
- **15TH: PETER, PAUL & MARY** collect awards for Best Folk Recording and Best Performance By A Vocal Group for their hit 'If I Had A Hammer' at the fifth annual Grammy Awards. Other winners include Best Rock'N'Roll Recording – 'Alley Cat' by the splendidly named Danish performer Bent Fabric; and Best R&B Recording – 'I Can't Stop Loving You' by Ray Charles. If there were an award for Worst Band Name it would undoubtedly have to go to The Rocky Fellers, a father-and-sons act who've had a recent US hit with 'Killer Joe' – their family name really is Feller, but that's no excuse.
- **18TH: THE INFECTIOUS** Jimmy Soul calypso song 'If You Wanna Be Happy' ("make an ugly woman your wife") hits US Number One.

- **21ST: FINAL EPISODE** of the TV crime series *The Untouchables* – starring Robert Stack as crime-busting FBI agent Eliot Ness – is aired on ABC in the US. Though

hugely popular, the show is criticised for its "gratuitous and senseless violence." It originally only runs for four years, but becomes a worldwide hit – including in France, where it's called *Les Incorruptibles*.
- **24TH: THE INFLUENTIAL BLUES** slide guitarist Elmore James dies of a heart attack in Chicago, Illinois, at the age of 45.
- **28TH: VALIUM** is introduced. Roche's brandname for the sedative diazepam soon becomes America's most prescribed drug, only overtaken by Prozac in the late 1980s.

---

## Let Freedom Ring...

- **AUGUST 28TH: BOB DYLAN, MAHALIA JACKSON**, Joan Baez, Odetta, Peter, Paul & Mary and other musical celebrities turn out to support Martin Luther King when he delivers his "I have a dream" speech on the steps of the Lincoln Memorial in Washington DC. Referring to Lincoln's emancipation of the slaves 100 years earlier, and the promise which that entailed, Dr King states: "America has given the Negro people a bad check which has come back marked 'insufficient funds' ... We can never be satisfied as long as a Negro in Mississippi cannot vote and a Negro in New York believes he has nothing for which to vote ... I have a dream that my children will one day live in a nation where they will not be judged by the color of their skin but by the content of their character ... when all of God's children, black men and white men, Jews and Gentiles, Protestants and Catholics, will be able to join hands and sing in the words of the old Negro spiritual: Free at last! Free at last! Thank God Almighty, free at last!"

Daddy. Follow-ups include Bikini Beach, Muscle Beach Party, How To Stuff A Wild Bikini, and Beach Blanket Bingo, considered to be one of the best, with a cameo by Buster Keaton and a score by lounge music guru Les Baxter.

Surf music becomes popular in its own right, whether or not you have access to a surfboard or indeed a beach, and guitarist Dick Dale becomes a cult hero – initially around Southern California, but his influence spreads thanks to tracks like 'Let's Go Tripping' on the beach party movies – and he is the main inspiration for other classics of the instrumental genre such as 'Wipe Out' (The Surfaris), 'Let's Go' (The Routers), and 'Pipeline' (The Chantays).

As for Jan & Dean, their career is halted by Jan's near fatal car accident in 1966, and his subsequent paralysis, but the duo will eventually make a heroic return to the musical stage, and they continue touring into 2003.

The first of the series, *Beach Party* – in which a stuffy, bearded anthropologist arrives to research youth culture, without getting emotionally involved, of course – even has brief appearances from Brian Wilson and, strangely, Vincent Price, who steals the movie with the one-line part of Big

## JUNE

• **JUNE 12TH: CLEOPATRA**, the epic of doomed love on the Nile, premieres in New York – all four hours of it. Not only over-long, it's also way over-budget, and at $50 million dollars (at 1963 prices) is probably still the most expensive movie ever made – no computer-generated sets and crowd scenes here. It's also famed for the on and off-screen romance between co-stars Elizabeth Taylor and Richard Burton – married to other people at the time, though not for long.

• **3RD: POPE JOHN XXIII** dies, to be replaced by Pope Paul VI.
• **6TH: 'DA DOO RON RON'** by The Crystals, produced by Phil Spector, peaks at Number Three on the US singles chart.
• **25TH: GEORGIOS PANAYIOTOU** is born in Finchley, London. He will become George Michael.

• **MAY 21ST: THIRTEEN-YEAR-OLD** Little Stevie Wonder releases his second album, The 12-Year-Old Genius ('13-year-old' would have been impressive, but wouldn't have scanned so well). Recorded live at a ballroom in Detroit, Michigan, the single 'Fingertips Parts One & Two' soon becomes the first live recording to top the US charts. Little Stevie has a dozen more hits before turning 20.

## JULY

• **1ST: THE ZIP CODE** is introduced by the US Postmaster General.
• **6TH: SURF CLASSIC** 'Wipe Out' by The Surfaris enters the US Top 40, where it will ride to Number Two. Almost entirely instrumental (apart from the manic laughing and the words "Wipe out!," the track is also a big hit in the UK, despite their minimal interest in surfing... Meanwhile, in Iran, where surfing is not high up the agenda either, Ayatollah Khomeini is among more than 30 Muslim religious leaders arrested for trying to topple the regime of Shah Mohammed Reza Pahlevi. Shiite mobs are recruited by these religious leaders, who are opposed to the Shah's land reforms and new rights for women. Three unveiled women are massacred by one of the mobs.
• **9TH: THE JOURNEYMEN**, including John Phillips, later to lead The Mamas & The Papas, play at The Shadows, Washington DC, with comedian Bill Cosby as their supporting act.
• **11TH: I LEFT MY HEART** In San Francisco, the recent album by Tony Bennett (pictured here looking in fine voice for a man with no heart) is awarded a US gold disc by the RIAA.

• **15TH: THE US, USSR AND UK** open talks towards a nuclear test ban treaty. They eventually agree that no more bomb tests should be carried out – unless they're underground. Out of sight...
• **20TH: INDONESIA** announces it will rename the Indian Ocean the 'Indonesian Ocean.' No one else seems to agree.
• **21ST: COMMUNIST CHINA** and Soviet Russia fail to resolve their ideological differences after two weeks of secret meetings in Moscow. The Soviet Union advocates "peaceful coexistence" with the West, while China views this as surrendering to capitalism.
• **23RD: NEIL YOUNG** has his first recording session in Winnipeg, Canada, as part of his group The Squires.
• **26TH: AFTER A FOUR-YEAR BREAK**, the *Newport Folk Festival* returns at Newport, Rhode Island. The three-day event features Bob Dylan, Joan Baez, Phil Ochs, Tom Paxton, Ramblin' Jack Elliott, and Peter Paul & Mary, while bluesman John Lee Hooker – who's recently had his biggest international hit with 'Boom Boom' – plays on the first and third days.

## AUGUST

• **3RD: MARTHA & THE VANDELLAS** release a new single, 'Heatwave,' in the US.
• **8TH: THE KINGSMEN** release 'Louie, Louie' on Jerden Records in the US... Meanwhile, the biggest robbery in British history takes place when a mail train is halted by a sabotaged rail signal. The 15 Great Train Robbers, including Ronald Biggs and Buster Edwards, steal £2.6 million, mainly old bank notes on their way to be incinerated. No guns are fired, but one of the train staff is severely injured after being repeatedly hit about the head. Biggs will later achieve further notoriety by singing (if that's the word) with

the Sex Pistols, while Edwards will be immortalised (ahem) on screen by Phil Collins in *Buster*.
• **9TH: A NEW UK POP SHOW**, *Ready Steady Go*, has its debut TV broadcast, featuring Bob Dylan, The Rolling Stones and The Who.

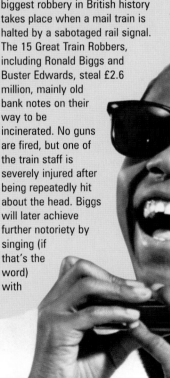

# 1963

## Dusty

**O**CTOBER 11TH 1963: SUCCESSFUL UK folk trio The Springfields announce they are to split, and their singer Dusty (real name Mary O'Brien) is going to pursue a solo career. Although the group was only formed three years ago, their brand of folk and country has won many admirers, especially in the US where their version of 'Silver Threads And Golden Needles' managed to climb to Number 20. 'Island Of Dreams' and 'Say I Won't Be There' both hit Number Five in the UK before the group disbands. Dusty's brother Tom will concentrate on songwriting, penning the theme for the movie *Georgy Girl* (starring Lynn Redgrave), and several other hits for The Seekers. Mike Hurst, the third member of the trio, becomes a staff producer at Philips, before producing the 1970s British rock'n'roll revival group Showaddywaddy. Dusty meanwhile reinvents herself as both a grand balladeer and pop diva (as well as TV star), able to reinterpret the greatest contemporary writers. Recording songs by Bacharach & David, Goffin & King, Pomus & Shuman, and the like, she invites comparison with vocalists such as Dionne Warwick or even jazz-pop stylist Nancy

Wilson. Dusty's debut solo hit, 'I Only Want To Be With You' (released on November 8th), is the first song to be featured on BBC TV's new flagship chart show *Top Of The Pops*, on January 1st 1964. This is followed up with a string of successes, such as 'I Don't Know What To Do With Myself' (two years before Warwick's version), 'Wishin And Hopin',' and 'You Don't Have To Say You Love Me.' By 1968 Dusty will be ready to try something new and, encouraged by her new US label Atlantic and its top production team of Jerry Wexler, Tom Dowd, and Arif Mardin, she moves into the more soulful territory of Aretha Franklin. But the resulting album, *Dusty In Memphis*, fails to appeal to her fans – despite the critics' plaudits and hit singles like 'Son Of A Preacher Man' (a Top Ten in both the US and UK). Very gradually her career begins to tail off, and one of the UK's best vocal talents spends most of the next two decades languishing in a musical limbo, recording only occasionally and with very limited success, most often to be found providing backing vocals on studio sessions. At least until 1987...

## Songs About Cars

• SEPTEMBER 9TH: 'LITTLE DEUCE COUPE' is released by The Beach Boys, and will become their fifth US hit – and also the latest in a long history of popular songs about automobiles. The fashion dates from the start of the 20th century, when the car was becoming a common sight, and brandnames were cited right from the off, in songs like 1905's 'In My Merry Oldsmobile,' or 'Jolly Old Ride In A Glide.' The view was not always positive in the early days – there's a 1912 song by Irving Berlin called 'Keep Away From The Fellow Who Owns An Automobile,' largely because of their dangers and unreliability, and the idea that a couple could easily become stranded miles from home (deliberately or otherwise). And the young Cole Porter wrote perhaps the first auto injury song with 1910's 'The Motor Car.' By the 1940s/50s, speed and sex-appeal become the big attractions – the curvy chassis (with running boards) and large engines of 1930s cars like the '32 Ford 'Deuce' Coupe appeal to hod-rod racers (the Deuce features in the 1973 movie American Graffiti). Other famous car songs: 'Rocket 88,' about a 1949 Oldsmobile with a V-8 engine, a bunch from Chuck Berry, Janis Joplin's 'Mercedes Benz,' Prince's 'Little Red Corvette,' Springsteen's 'Pink Cadillac'...

# 1963
## September–December

• NOVEMBER 25TH: PRESIDENT JOHN F. KENNEDY is buried at Arlington National Cemetery, Virginia. The man who is accused of assassinating him three days earlier, Lee Harvey Oswald, is by now dead too, shot by small-time crook Jack Ruby while in police custody in Dallas... Meanwhile at home in Los Angeles, shocked by news of JFK's death, Brian Wilson of The Beach Boys writes 'The Warmth Of The Sun.' Out of respect, Phil Spector delays the launch of his cheery Xmas album *A Christmas Gift To You*; and Stanley Kubrick postpones the cinema release of his new political black comedy, *Dr Strangelove*.

### SEPTEMBER

• 8TH: *MURRAY THE K'S HOLIDAY REVUE* plays the last of ten days at the Brooklyn Fox Theater, New York City, featuring Ben E. King, Little Stevie Wonder, Jan & Dean, The Drifters, The Shirelles, Gene Pitney, The Miracles (including Smokey Robinson), Paul & Paula, The Angels, The Dovells, Jay & The Americans, The Tymes, The Chiffons, and Randy & The Rainbows.
• 11TH: THE ALAN PRICE RHYTHM AND BLUES COMBO plays a midnight set at The Downbeat Club, Newcastle, UK. This is the first appearance together of the quintet that will later name itself The Animals.
• 14TH: THE RONETTES make their US Top 40 singles chart debut with the Phil Spector production 'Be My Baby,' which will peak at Number Two.
• 20TH: ERIC CLAPTON plays one of his first gigs as guitarist for The Yardbirds, at Studio 51, Leicester Square, London, UK.
• 21ST: BOBBY VINTON takes the US Number One slot with 'Blue Velvet.'
• 23RD: WHEN BO DIDDLEY records a live BBC Radio session for the show *Saturday Club* in London, his backing group is The Rolling Stones.
• 29TH: JUDY GARLAND'S first and only TV series starts on CBS. Despite guests like Sinatra, Dean Martin, Mickey Rooney, Count Basie, and Donald O'Connor, the show is pulled after six months. Strained at times, it's still felt to contain some of her best work.

### OCTOBER

• 4TH: A ROCK PACKAGE tour arrives at the Vets Memorial Auditorium, Columbus, Ohio. For $1.75 fans can see Sam Cooke, Dion, Bobby 'Blue' Bland, Baby Washington, The Tymes, The Kingpins, Little Willie John, and Freddie Scott.
• 5TH: LITTLE RICHARD gives a welcome boost to poor ticket sales when he joins an Everly Brothers UK tour at The Gaumont, Watford, UK. Other acts on the bill include Bo Diddley, Mickie Most, The Rolling Stones, Julie Grant, and The Flintstones.
• 7TH: THE FIRST LEARJET has its maiden test flight. International travel for wealthy pop stars will never be the same again, as for the next 20 years the name Lear will become synonymous with the luxury private jet. Inventor William Lear does rather tarnish his reputation

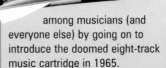

among musicians (and everyone else) by going on to introduce the doomed eight-track music cartridge in 1965.
• 12TH: JIMMY GILMER & The Fireballs reach Number One in the US with 'Sugar Shack.' It goes on to become the year's best-selling song in America.
• 13TH: FIFTEEN MILLION British viewers tune in to see The Beatles' debut on the UK TV show *Sunday Night At The London Palladium*, as hordes of screaming fans wait outside the venue. Beatlemania has arrived.

### NOVEMBER

• 2ND: RUFUS THOMAS enters the US Top 40 singles chart with 'Walkin' The Dog.'
• 13TH: THE ALBUM *In The Wind* by Peter, Paul & Mary is awarded a US gold disc by the RIAA.
• 21ST: THE DAVE CLARK FIVE enter the UK singles chart with 'Glad All Over,' bound for Number One.

### DECEMBER

• 7TH: 'DOMINIQUE' BY THE SINGING NUN is the new Number One single in the US, keeping the Kingsmen's 'Louie Louie' off the top. It's written and sung by Belgian-born nun Jeanine Deckers, also known by the French stagename Soeur Sourire (Sister Smile) – she becomes a reluctant star with this unexpected hit, though her only financial goal was to raise money for the convent. She wins a Grammy award, and is even the subject of a fictionalised 1965 biopic starring Debbie Reynolds. Eventually, after leaving the convent and dabbling in drugs and modern living, she sets up a school for autistic children with her friend Annie Pescher. Tragically, in 1985, hounded by Belgian authorities for payment of tax on her Sixties earnings, even though she'd given everything away, she and Annie kill themselves in a suicide pact.
• 11TH: FBI AGENTS PAY a $240,000 ransom for the return of kidnap victim Frank Sinatra Jr, and he is soon found wandering around Bel Air. Later two men receive life sentences for the kidnap, despite insisting it was just a publicity stunt.
• 12TH: THE BEATLES become the first act ever to knock themselves off the top of the UK singles chart when 'I Want To Hold Your Hand' replaces 'She Loves You.'
• 22ND: IN AUSTRALIA, twins Robin and Maurice Gibb leave school. They are already playing in the family group, The Bee Gees.
• 31ST: FORMERLY KNOWN as The Ravens, The Kinks make their live debut at The Lotus House Restaurant in London, UK.

## None Finer

• DECEMBER 14TH: DINAH WASHINGTON is found dead at home in Detroit, Illinois, from an overdose of alcohol and diet pills, at the age of just 39. Known as the Queen Of The Blues, though equally at home with jazz, R&B, and pop, her best-known records include 'What A Diff'rence A Day Makes,' 'Mad About The Boy,' and a couple of hit duets with Brook Benton.

# 1964

## January–April

### Got The T-Shirt?

**P**RIOR TO 1964, only Elvis Presley has generated any significant merchandising revenue, but with The Beatles comes a flood of associated artifacts – to such an extent that by late 1963 Beatles' manager Brian Epstein is concerned that their merchandising is out of control. He's particularly worried that The Beatles are not receiving their fair share of the profits, but Epstein is also concerned that the shoddy nature of many items – from plastic guitars to cheap lockets and jigsaws – will reflect badly on his boys. Lacking time to oversee this headache himself, Epstein dumps the

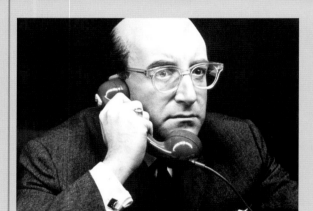

• JANUARY 29TH: DR STRANGELOVE (Or How I Learned To Stop Worrying And Love The Bomb) is finally released, having been held over from December 1963 in the wake of the Kennedy assassination. Stanley Kubrick's satirical black comedy about cold war relations stars Peter Sellers in several roles, including a fictional US president (seen here).

• **1ST: FIRST EVER** edition of the long-running UK TV show *Top Of The Pops* is transmitted on the BBC, starring The Rolling Stones, Dusty Springfield and The Dave Clark Five.
• **4TH: 'LOUIE LOUIE'** by The Kingsmen peaks at Number Two on the US singles chart.
• **9TH: ROD STEWART** makes his stage debut with Long John Baldry's Hoochie Coochie Men at The Marquee, London.
• **11TH: THE SUPREMES** have their first US Top 30 singles entry when the Holland/Dozier/Holland composition 'When The Lovelight Starts Shining Through His Eyes' reaches Number 23.
• **13TH: BOB DYLAN** releases a new album, *The Times They Are A-Changin'*, in the US.
• **15TH: THE WHISKEY A GO GO** night club and music venue opens on Sunset Boulevard in West Hollywood, Los Angeles, famously featuring go-go dancers in cages.
• **18TH: PLANS ARE UNVEILED** for building the enormous twin-towered World Trade Center in New York City.

## Ladies & Gentlemen, Here Are The Beatles

• **FEBRUARY 9TH: SEVENTY-THREE MILLION** Americans tune in to view The Beatles' first US TV performance on the *Ed Sullivan Show*. Police around the country report an abnormally low crime rate tonight...

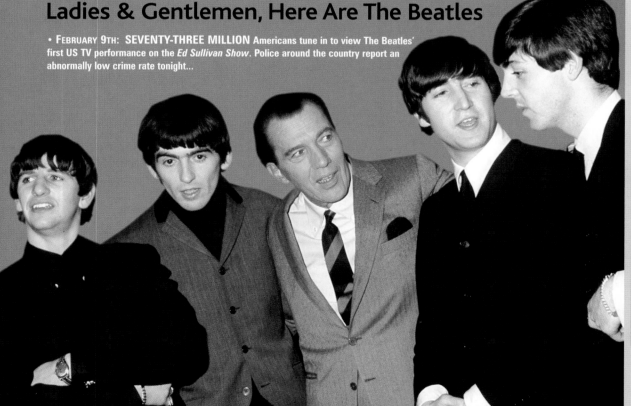

• **FEBRUARY 25TH: FORMER OLYMPIC** boxing champion Cassius Clay defeats Sonny Liston to claim the World Heavyweight title. He announces his conversion to Islam and a change of name to Muhammad Ali.

• **1ST: IN THEIR HOTEL SUITE** in Paris, France, Beatles manager Brian Epstein informs them they have secured their first US Number One with 'I Want To Hold Your Hand.' They'll have six more before the end of the year (not counting the Lennon/McCartney song 'World Without Love,' taken to the top of the charts by Peter & Gordon). The British Invasion has begun.
• **6TH: LONDON AND PARIS** agree to build a rail tunnel under the English Channel, after prolonged consultation by the Channel Tunnel Study Group set up in 1957. The tunnel won't actually open for another 30 years.
• **8TH: INDIANA GOVERNOR** Matthew

job onto his lawyer, who, in turn, invites Nicky Byrne, a London music business dabbler, to start a new Beatles merchandising company. It's a measure of just how radical this concept is that Byrne doesn't leap at the chance. Astonishingly, when the contract is drawn up, Byrne is asked to choose whatever share of the profits he wants to receive, so he puts down the first figure that comes into his head – 90 per cent. The deal is done and Epstein, without even seeing the contract, is assured that matters are now under control... When The Beatles hit Number One in America with 'I Want To Hold Your Hand' in February 1964, the Reliant Shirt Corporation pays Byrne's company an instant $25,000 for the right to make Beatle T-shirts. A million are sold in three days and, shortly after, Capitol Records offers Byrne a cool $500,000 to buy his company. The buoyant US economy means that the purchasing power of

American teenagers is considerably higher than that of their counterparts in the UK, whom they outnumber five to one. According to the *Wall Street Journal*, Beatle goods would account for $5m of US spending before year's end. Byrne remembers handing a cheque for $9,700 to Brian Epstein when he flew into New York on February 7th. Delighted at first, Epstein asks Byrne, "How much of this do I owe you?", to which Byrne replies, "Nothing, Brian – that's your ten per cent." Byrne has just banked $97,000. Lennon and McCartney are unhappy that Epstein has missed out on this commercial bonanza, but they may be appeased slightly in April when they reportedly receive a cheque for $140,000 – their share of the previous four months profit just from sales of Beatles chewing gum. The merchandise list quickly expands to include egg cups, dolls, plastic windmills, crayon sets, airbeds, ice cream, bow ties, edible licorice discs, masks, balloons, pillowcases, panties, garters, coat hangers, talcum powder, bread rolls, biscuits, cutlery, wallpaper, ottomans, and berets... The first steps have been taken along the road that will lead, inexorably, to Kiss face masks, Britney bra-tops and even the official Jimi Hendrix Golf Cart.

## MARCH

Welsh is one of many politicians who asks local radio stations to ban 'Louie Louie' by The Kingsmen because of speculation that the (mostly unintelligible) lyrics are obscene. The song's publisher offers $1000 to anyone who can prove it... The same day, George Harrison buys his first Rickenbacker 12-string electric guitar (pictured here). Its huge, chiming sound – soon heard to great effect on 'A Hard Day's Night' – earns it the name "The Beatles' secret weapon."

- **12TH: NEW YORK CITY SONGWRITERS** Wes Farrell and Bert Berns register the song 'My Girl Sloopy.' It will become a huge hit for The McCoys under the name 'Hang On Sloopy,' and will also be recorded by The Yardbirds.
- **14TH: PRESIDENT MAKARIOS** of Cyprus rejects an Anglo-UN offer of help to keep peace between the island's Greek and Turkish communities.
- **18TH: SONNY & CHER** make their first recording together, a re-working of Don & Dewey's hit 'The Letter.' It's released under the name of Caesar & Cleo on Vault Records in the US.
- **20TH: THE BAND FORMERLY** known as The Detours play their first gig using their new name, The Who, at the Oldfield Hotel, Greenford, west London. They will shortly change their name to The High Numbers, before becoming The Who once again.

## Millie Makes It Big

- **APRIL 23RD: SKA MAKES** its first appearance on the US charts when 'My Boy Lollipop' by Jamaican-born Millie Small enters the Hot 100. It reaches Number Two in June, three months after it's done the same in the UK (where she's billed simply as Millie). The authentic arrangement is by legendary guitarist Ernest Ranglin, while session harmonica player is a then almost unknown Rod Stewart.

- **2ND: AN INSTITUTE FOR** Scientific Atheism is set up in Moscow with the aim of eliminating religious prejudice in the Soviet Union.
- **5TH: GENE PITNEY** enters the UK singles chart with 'That Girl Belongs To Yesterday,' an operatic ballad written by Mick Jagger and Keith Richards of The Rolling Stones and wrapped up in dramatic brass and piano. It will peak at Number Seven.
- **8TH: MALCOLM X** announces he is splitting from the Black Muslim movement led by Elijah Muhammad to form the Black Nationalist Party, stating: "There can be no revolution without bloodshed, and it is nonsense to describe the civil rights movement as a revolution."
- **9TH: THE TRIDENTS**, a UK rock band featuring guitarist Jeff Beck, apply for an

audition with the BBC, hoping to gain work on radio.
- **10TH: ASPIRING FOLK DUO** Simon & Garfunkel record Paul Simon's song 'The Sound Of Silence' for Columbia Records in New York City. It will eventually become their first US Number One – almost three years later.
- **23RD: JOHN LENNON'S** first book of poetry, *In His Own Write*, is published in the UK.
- **26TH: CHUCK BERRY**, recently released from prison, records 'No Particular Place To Go,' which will give him his first US Top Ten hit since 'Johnny B Goode' in 1958. At the same recording session, at Chess Studios, Chicago, Illinois, Berry cuts 'Promised Land,' 'Brenda Lee,' 'Big Ben Blues,' and, with Bo Diddley, 'Chuck's Beat' and 'Bo's Beat.' Berry's chart renaissance is short-lived, and after this year he won't have another hit till 1972 – but he's still a musical role model for 1960s rockers: John Lennon once said, "If you tried to give rock'n'roll another name, you might call it Chuck Berry."
- **28TH: UK WAXWORKS MADAME TUSSAUDS** announces that The Beatles are to become the first pop act to be cast in wax for the museum. This may explain George and Paul's poses in that *Ed Sullivan Show* photograph opposite...
- **30TH: MODS AND ROCKERS,** whose cultural and musical tastes (soul, suits and scooters versus leathers, grease and rock 'n'roll) seem worth fighting over, clash in the UK seaside resort of Clacton, followed a few weeks later by battles in Brighton, Margate, and Southend.

## APRIL

- **6TH: SOVIET PREMIER** Khrushchev denounces the Chinese view on how the world could survive atomic war saying, "Only a child or an idiot would not fear war."
- **3RD: BILLBOARD** magazine reports that The Beatles now hold all of the Top Five positions in the American singles chart, with 'Can't Buy Me Love' at Number One. They also occupy the top six places in the Australian singles charts.
- **16TH: WHEN THE ROLLING STONES** release their eponymous debut album in the UK, there are already 100,000 advance orders.

- **20TH: PREMIERE OF ELVIS'S** latest film, *Viva Las Vegas* (not his worst, by a long way), co-starring Ann-Margaret, with whom Elvis is being romantically linked. The pair eventually get married in May 1967 – although not to each other.
- **24TH: JOAN BAEZ,** the folk singer, refuses to pay 60 per cent of her income tax as a protest against US expenditure on the military.
- **27TH: THE NEW AFRICAN** nation of Tanzania is created by the union of Tanganyika and Zanzibar.

- **APRIL 17TH: FORD LAUNCH THE MUSTANG** 'pony' car, aimed squarely at the the hip young consumer. After a short but intensive TV advertising campaign, Ford sells 22,000 Mustangs on the first day. Over 400,000 are on the road within a year.

# 1964

May–August

## Suck And Blow

AUGUST 1ST: *BILLBOARD MAGAZINE* reports that sales of harmonicas have rocketed because of their use by such contemporary stars as Bob Dylan, Stevie Wonder, The Rolling Stones, The Yardbirds, and The Beatles. Introduced to America by the German Hohner company just over a century ago, and beloved of blues bands everywhere, the harmonica will, believe it or not, remain the world's best-selling musical instrument, for the next 40 years.

## The Hits Keep Coming

DURING THE 1960S, the songwriting team of Burt Bacharach and Hal David bestrides the international music scene like a colossus. Based in the Brill Building on Broadway, along with all the other songwriters of the day, they knock out a seemingly endless sequence of hits for Dionne Warwick, Jackie De Shannon, Herb Alpert, Dusty Springfield, Gene Pitney, The Drifters, and The Walker Brothers, among others. Despite their prolific pop output they manage to find the time to score movies such as What's New Pussycat?, Alfie, Casino Royale and Butch Cassidy & The Sundance Kid. However by the early 1970s, Bacharach's partnership with David is effectively over — Burt's marriage to actress Angie Dickinson ends around the same time as well —

## MAY

- **4TH: THE PULITZER PRIZE** committee decides that there is no fiction, music or drama that's worthy of its prizes this year.
- **10TH: LOCAL GROUP THE ZOMBIES** win first prize in the Herts Beat Music Contest at Watford Town Hall, Hertfordshire, UK. A few weeks later they record 'She's Not There' in West Hampstead, London. By the end of the year it will have reached Number Two in the US singles charts.
- **14TH: THE WATERS** of the river Nile are diverted from their normal course to begin the next stage of construction of the Aswan dam. The dam will raise the level of the Nile nearly 200 feet and create a huge lake.
- **16TH: 'MY GUY'** by Mary Wells, written for her by Smokey Robinson, tops the charts in the US.
- **19TH: FORTY MICROPHONES** are discovered hidden in the walls of the US Embassy in Moscow.
- **21ST: SESSION GUITARIST** James Marshall Hendrix records 'Testify' with The Isley Brothers.
- **24TH: A BAD DECISION** by a referee starts a riot at a soccer

game between Argentina and Peru that leaves 300 people dead and 500 injured. Most of those killed are trampled to death.
- **27TH: ECCENTRIC BRITISH** rocker Screaming Lord Sutch starts his own radio station, Radio Sutch, in a fort on the River Thames, near London. He will later repeatedly stand for parliament as leader of the Monster Raving Loony Party, and invariably lose his deposit by getting too few votes.

- **27TH: JAWAHARLAL NEHRU**, the first prime minister of independent India, dies of a heart attack in New Delhi at age 74. Acclaimed for his neutralist foreign policies, Nehru attracts a million-and-a-half mourners along the route of his funeral cortege. He is survived by his only daughter, Indira Ghandi.
- **28TH: THE PLO** (Palestine Liberation Organisation) is formed.

## JUNE

- **3RD: DEAN MARTIN** makes life as difficult as possible for the Rolling Stones on their first US TV appearance (on a show called *The Hollywood Palace*) by constantly making fun of their appearance. "Their hair's not long," he quips, "It's just smaller foreheads and higher eyebrows." The following week, taking a break during their first US tour, the Stones drop in at Chess Studios in Chicago, Illinois, where they jam with Chuck Berry, Muddy Waters and Willie Dixon.
- **4TH: THE BEATLES'** first world tour starts at KB Hallen, Copenhagen, Denmark, with Jimmy Nicol standing in for drummer Ringo Starr who has collapsed from exhaustion.
- **6TH: THE DIXIE CUPS** hit Number One on the US Top 40 with 'Chapel Of Love,' originally written for The Ronettes.
- **14TH: NELSON MANDELA** is flown from Pretoria to Cape Town, South Africa, and taken out to Robben Island in Table Bay after being sentenced to life imprisonment on terrorism charges. Mandela, who was born in 1918 into the royal family of

the Tembu tribe in the Transkei, gained a law degree and opened the first African legal practice in the country, before taking up the black nationalist cause in 1944... Also, Francois Duvalier names himself president for life in Haiti – mass executions follow.
- **16TH: COMEDIAN LENNIE BRUCE** once again finds himself on trial on charges of obscenity. Hounded by the authorities and the media, his life, and his act, becomes more and more obsessed with legal matters.
- **17TH: THE SUPREMES** release their new single – another Holland/Dozier/Holland classic, 'Where Did Our Love Go' – which begins a run of five consecutive Number One hits.
- **22ND: LAST EPISODE** of the original *Twighlight Zone* TV series is screened tonight, after six years of scary stories, hosted by Rod Serling, and that famous atonal theme tune.
- **30TH: CONNIE FRANCIS**, the US's biggest female pop star between 1958-64, enters the Top 40 for the last time.

- **MAY 1ST: The original** line-up of The Yardbirds, including Eric Clapton on guitar, release their first single 'I Wish You Would' in the UK... On the same day, anarchic US composer and bandleader Spike Jones dies – he was a pioneer of musical sound effects and the 'novelty' song in the 1940s and 1950s.

and he enters a lean patch. In 1981, in partnership with Carole Bayer Sager, Peter Allen and Christopher Cross, he returns with 'Arthur's Theme', from the soundtrack of the Dudley Moore movie, which becomes a massive hit and picks up the Academy Award for Best Song. Thereafter hits like 'That's What Friends Are For' (Dionne Warwick) and 'On My Own' (Patti LaBelle and Michael McDonald) begin to roll through once again. During the 1990s, as Bacharach's reputation begins to grow, yet again, with a younger generation of musicians, he collaborates with Elvis Costello on Painted From Memory. On top of that, Bacharach's career is celebrated at Radio City Music Hall with Luther Vandross, Barenaked Ladies, Chrissie Hynde, Wynonna Judd, Elvis Costello and All Saints; an album rather grandly titled One Amazing Night is issued. But, perhaps, the 'piece de résistance' is Bacharach's cameo in the movie Austin Powers (1997).

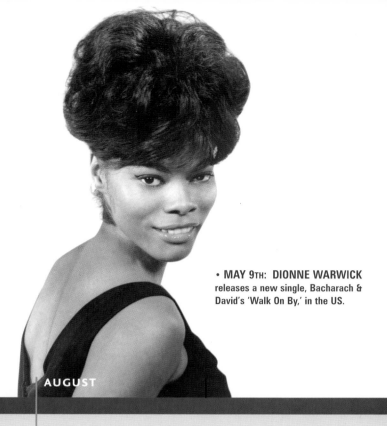

• **MAY 9TH: DIONNE WARWICK** releases a new single, Bacharach & David's 'Walk On By,' in the US.

## JULY

## AUGUST

• **AUGUST 26TH: DISNEY MUSICAL** *Mary Poppins* is released, starring Julie Andrews and Dick Van Dyke. It will be nominated for 13 Oscars, and win five, including Best Original Song for 'Chim Chim Cher-ee.'

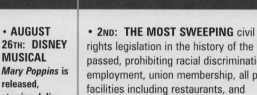

• **2ND: THE MOST SWEEPING** civil rights legislation in the history of the US is passed, prohibiting racial discrimination in employment, union membership, all public facilities including restaurants, and federally-funded programs.

• **4TH: ON US** Independence Day, appropriately enough, 'I Get Around' becomes the first Number One for the all-American Beach Boys. But over half the singles in this week's US Top Ten are by British acts.

• **5TH: BELFAST R&B BAND** Them, fronted by Van Morrison, record 'Gloria.'

• **6TH: PREMIERE OF THE FIRST** Beatles movie *A Hard Day's Night*, directed by Richard Lester, with a screenplay by Liverpool writer Alun Owen, and co-starring Wilfrid Brambell as Ringo's grandfather. When it's first screened in America, on August 12th, *Time* magazine calls it "rubbish," and recommends it should be avoided at all costs. This doesn't make any difference to the fans (the soundtrack also becomes the quickest-selling LP in history), or the band's rapid ascent to superstardom... Around this time, Paul McCartney gives his dad a racehorse as a present.

• **12TH: LEVON HELM & THE HAWKS** (later to become The Band) record 'Do The Honky Tonk' at Pop Ivey's Summer Gardens, Port Dover, Ontario, Canada.

• **14TH: US SENDS 600** more troops into Vietnam, following major setbacks for South Vietnamese forces... Two weeks later, Washington promises to send 5,000 more 'advisers'.

• **24TH: MARVIN GAYE** records 'How Sweet It Is (To be Loved By You)' for Tamla Records, in Detroit, Michigan.

• **26TH: THREE DAYS** of racial riots in Rochester, New York, cause one death and 350 injuries. The catalyst is the crash of a police helicopter on a building, killing two.

• **31ST: THE RANGER 7 PROBE** sends back the first close-up photos of the moon, and then crashes... The same day, country star Jim Reeves is killed in a plane wreck near Nashville, Tennessee.

• **JULY 18TH: THE FOUR SEASONS** (pictured on the right) head the US Top 40 with 'Rag Doll.' Fronted by Frankie Valli, the group has already had four US Number Ones, dating back to 'Sherry' in 1962 – but this will be their last until 1976.

• **7TH: THE** *FOURTH NATIONAL* *Jazz & Blues Festival* is held in Richmond, Surrey, with the Rolling Stones topping the bill. The Yardbirds and the Graham Bond Organisation also appear. One of the supporting bands, Nightshift, features up-and-coming guitarist Jeff Beck... Also today, the US government gives President Johnson greater authority to strike back against the communists in North Vietnam, whom the president claims have made unprovoked attacks on US ships in the Gulf Of Tonkin – though many Americans express misgivings about the deepening US military involvement in Vietnam.

• **12TH: IAN FLEMING**, creator of James Bond, dies. He will not live to see the release of *Goldfinger*, the third Bond movie and the first to establish the winning formula... On the same day, South Africa is barred from the Tokyo Olympics because of its apartheid policy.

• **19TH: THE BEATLES** start a US tour at The Cow Palace, San Francisco, supported by The Righteous Brothers, Jackie De Shannon and The Exciters.

• **28TH: BOB DYLAN** reportedly turns The Beatles on to marijuana in the Delmonico Hotel, New York City.

• **29TH: THE FOUR TOPS** enter the US Top 40 for the first time, with 'Baby I Need Your Lovin'.'

# 1964

September–December

## TV Triumphant

**S**EPTEMBER 17TH: OVER THE NEXT week, five new TV shows debut in the US: *Bewitched*, *The Addams Family*, *The Fugitive*, *The Munsters*, and *The Man From UNCLE*. Not a bad week. All of human life is there – so long as you include witches, the undead, and the disembodied. *Bewitched* makes a household name of Elizabeth Montgomery, who stars as suburban witch Samantha. The show will become infamous when Samantha's husband Darren undergoes an unexplained transformation, as original actor Dick York leaves through illness and is replaced by Dick Sargent... The men from UNCLE – suave secret agents Robert Vaughn (as Napoleon Solo) and David McCallum (as Illya Kuryakin, seen here), battling the global crime organization THRUSH – are almost like pop stars themselves, beseiged by teenage girls in the street, and featuring on bubble gum cards and the like. McCallum later even presents a pop music TV show (*Hulabaloo*) in character as Kuryakin.

### SEPTEMBER

- **4TH: THE ANIMALS** make their live US debut at the Paramount Theater, Brooklyn, New York, along with Jan & Dean, Chuck Berry and Del Shannon. The following day, their organ-driven version of 'House Of The Rising Sun,' an old blues standard made famous by Josh White, hits Number One in the US (having already done the same in the UK).
- **5TH: 'DANCING IN THE STREET'** by Martha & The Vandellas – with one of the most powerful backbeats heard on record to date – peaks at Number Two on the US charts.
- **10TH: THE KINKS** reach Number One on the UK singles chart with 'You Really Got Me' – often cited as the first heavy metal track, due to its raw, distorted guitar chord-riff.
- **11TH: THE BEATLES** refuse to take the stage at the Gator Bowl, Jacksonville, Florida, until they are assured that they will be playing in front of a non-segregated audience.
- **16TH: SAM COOKE**, The Everly Brothers and the Righteous Brothers are the stars when a new all-pop music television show, *Shindig*, premieres on ABC in the USA. Cooke will be dead before the end of the year (see story top right).
- **25TH: BRIAN EPSTEIN** turns down a $7 million offer from a group of US businessmen to buy out the Beatles contract.
- **27TH: THE WARREN COMMISSION** investigating the assassination of President Kennedy issues a report concluding that Lee Harvey Oswald was the sole assassin, though it also calls for a reform of the Secret Service. Their 'lone assassin' conclusion is later contradicted by a House committee investigation in 1978.

- **28TH: ADOLPH 'ARTHUR' MARX**, best known as Harpo – the silent, be-wigged, harp-playing Marx brother – dies at age 70.

### OCTOBER

- **5TH: ART ARFONS** sets a new land speed record: 434mph. Ten days later, Craig Breedlove becomes the first person to exceed 500mph.
- **6TH: HAVING RECENTLY** moved on from The King Bees, singer Davy Jones, later known as David Bowie, fronts The Mannish Boys as they have their first recording session at Decca studios in London.
- **9TH: DR GEORGE JAMES** cites poverty as the third highest cause of death in the US... Meanwhile, in line with a Musicians Union ruling not to comply with South Africa's apartheid regime, The Rolling Stones cancel a proposed tour there. Other groups refusing to go include The Swinging Blue Jeans and Freddie & The Dreamers.
- **10TH: THE SHANGRI-LAS** release the teen angst and death single 'Leader Of The Pack' in the US. It's their only Number One – but the UK obviously can't get enough of it, as it's a hit there on three separate occasions: in 1965, 1972, and 1976.

- **14TH: DR MARTIN LUTHER KING** JR is awarded the Nobel Peace Prize as a "peaceful warrior for civil rights." At 35 he is one of the youngest ever recipients of this award. Not everyone is impressed, though: J. Edgar Hoover, director of the FBI, calls King, "the most notorious liar in the country."
- **15TH: COLE PORTER**, legendary US composer and lyricist, whose songs include 'Night And Day,' 'I Get A Kick Out Of You,' and 'Let's Do It,' dies at the age of 73.
- **16TH: THE BRITISH LABOUR PARTY** regains power after 13 years of Conservative rule. "Nice place we've got here," jokes Harold Wilson, stepping inside 10 Downing Street in London, after scraping to victory by 14 seats. His new government will be the first to set up a Ministry Of Technology, and also grant licenses for oil and gas companies to start drilling in the North Sea... Meanwhile Communist China announces it has exploded its first atomic bomb, but insists it will never be the first to use nuclear arms.
- **17TH: NIKITA KHRUSHCHEV** is ousted by Leonid Brezhnev, who will take Khrushchev's job as First Secretary of the Communist Party. Aleksei Kosygin will take over as Soviet prime minister.
- **19TH: SIMON & GARFUNKEL** release their debut album, which has the unwieldy but intriguing title *Wednesday Morning, 3am – Exciting New Sounds In The Folk Tradition*.
- **22ND: EMI** reject an audition tape by the High Numbers, who will subsequently achieve world fame as The Who.
- **28TH: THE TAMI SHOW** (Television Audience Measurement Index) is recorded in Santa Monica, California, with an amazing line-up of The Rolling Stones, James Brown, Chuck Berry, The Beach Boys, The Supremes, Jan & Dean, Marvin Gaye, Smokey Robinson, Gerry & The Pacemakers, Billy J. Kramer, The Barbarians and more.

- **OCTOBER 17TH: UK GROUP MANFRED MANN** – another force in the British invasion of the States – ascend to the US Number One slot with 'Do Wah Diddy Diddy.'

## The Story Of Big O

**SEPTEMBER 26TH: ROY ORBISON** hits Number One in the US with 'Oh Pretty Woman,' which will quickly become his biggest and best-remembered hit (credited to Roy Orbison & The Candy Men). In October the song will also top the charts in the UK, where The Big O, as he's called, is the most popular US singer of the early 1960s. Orbison's dramatic, quasi-operatic tales of heartbreak and unrequited love take full advantage of one of the finest and most original voices of his generation. He cuts 15 hits between 1960 and 1965, including 'Only The Lonely,' 'Running Scared,' 'Crying,' 'In Dreams,' and 'It's Over.' 'Oh Pretty Woman' – reputedly dedicated to his wife, Claudette, sells seven million copies. He divorces her shortly afterwards on the grounds of cruelty, when she has an affair with a builder.

Orbison and Claudette later reconcile and re-marry, but within months, in 1966, she is killed on her motorbike. Two years later, Roy's two eldest sons die when the family home burns to the ground. After this Orbison's career goes into a decline until 1988, when he teams up with Bob Dylan, George Harrison, Jeff Lynne and Tom Petty to form The Traveling Wilburys. Just as he's enjoying a revival, he dies of a heart attack, on December 6th 1988.

## Death Of A Soul Man

• **DECEMBER 11TH: AFTER AN EVENING** at PJ's club in Los Angeles, soul singer Sam Cooke is shot dead by the manageress of the Hacienda Motel in Watts. It's claimed he's been trying to rape Elisa Boyer, a girl he had picked up that evening. The coroner declares it justifiable homicide. A tragic and tawdry end for a great soul inspiration. Cooke's biggest hits include 'You Send Me', 'Chain Gang' and 'Wonderful World', and his influence was wide, from Otis Redding and Marvin Gaye to Rod Stewart and Mick Jagger. He died at the age of 33.

---

## NOVEMBER

• **NOVEMBER 1ST: WHEN THE DAVE CLARK FIVE** sing 'Glad All Over' on the *Ed Sullivan Show* in New York, their host points out that, unlike The Rolling Stones, they are "nice, neat boys."

• **3RD: US PRESIDENT JOHNSON** wins his first election, and remains in the White House.

• **10TH: AUSTRALIA** introduces the draft to fulfil its commitment in Vietnam.

• **11TH: TOM JONES RECORDS** 'It's Not Unusual', his second single and first international hit, in Decca Studios, West Hampstead, London.

• **13TH: POPE PAUL VI** gives his jewelled tiara to the world's poor. The Vatican also announces the official exoneration of the Jewish race of any guilt in the crucifixion of Jesus.

• **16TH: JUDY GARLAND**, appearing at the London Palladium, is joined onstage by her 18-year-old daughter Liza Minnelli. It is the first time they have sung together publicly.

• **19TH: GARY LEWIS** & The Playboys record the Al Kooper composition 'This Diamond Ring' at Western Studios, Los Angeles, California. Lewis is the son of comedian Jerry Lewis, and he will have nine Top 20 US hits in the next two years, though this will be his only Number One.

• **21ST: B.B. KING** plays at the Regal Theater, Chicago, Illinois. The performance is recorded and will be released as an album, *Live At The Regal*, in 1965.

... Also in November, Jan & Dean release 'Sidewalk Surfing', a tribute to the new craze that will eventually become internationally popular as skateboarding. The sound effect at the beginning of the record is Dean Torrence falling off.

## DECEMBER

• **4TH: THE JOURNAL** of the American Medical Association reports that heavy cigarette smokers are three times more likely to die prematurely than non-smokers.

• **10TH: TWENTY-ONE MEN**, including a sheriff and deputy, have been arrested by federal agents in connection with the deaths of three civil rights workers near Jackson, Mississippi. All are members of the Ku Klux Klan or White Knights.

• **12TH: THE RIGHTEOUS BROTHERS** release a new single, 'You've Lost That Lovin' Feeling', which becomes their first hit – not only an international Number One, but also one of the most played records ever on American radio.

• **14TH: MICHAEL BROWN**, of The Left Banke, meets dancer Rene Fladen at a New York recording studio. He falls in love and is inspired to write two songs about her – 'Walk Away Rene' (later covered by The Four Tops) and 'Pretty Ballerina'.

• **15TH: CANADA ADOPTS** the Maple Leaf as the national emblem and flag (replacing the old British colonial flag).

• **21ST: ROLLING STONES** drummer Charlie Watts releases his first book, a biography of Charlie Parker entitled *Ode To A High Flying Bird*... The same day, the British House Of Commons votes to end the death penalty.

• **24TH: BEACH BOYS** leader Brian Wilson suffers a nervous breakdown aboard a plane headed for a concert in Houston, Texas. It's not his last...

• **28TH: OTIS REDDING** records 'That's How Strong My Love Is' and 'Mr Pitiful' for Volt Records.

• **31ST: DONALD CAMPBELL** (son of Sir Malcolm Campbell, the British speed ace of the 1930s,) now sets a new world water speed record of 276.3mph at Lake Dumbleyung in Western Australia. In July he set a new land speed record in his car Bluebird, achieving 403mph at Lake Eyre. The feat of breaking both land and water records in a single year is unique.

• **DECEMBER 19TH: THE SUPREMES** have their third US Number One in just four months, thanks to 'Come See About Me,' hot on the heels of November's 'Baby Love.' By May 1967 the trio will have had no fewer than ten Number One singles, making them the most successful US female group ever.

# 1965

## SUPREMES IN THEIR PRIME

The Supremes have just made an album called *A Little Bit Of Liverpool*, although it's clear that with Motown writers like Holland/Dozier/Holland in their corner, and a perfect line-up of Florence Ballard, Mary Wilson, and Diana Ross, they have little need for such bandwagon-jumping gimmicks. In fact their latest single, 'Come See About Me,' will shortly become The Supremes' third consecutive million-seller, knocking The Beatles off the top spot – something they'll do again to both The Beatles and The Rolling Stones in the course of 1965, as the trio notch up another three US Number Ones. The quintessential Motown girl group, The Supremes soon become the biggest-selling female outfit of all time.

# 1965
## January–April

## Violence Claims Malcolm X

**M**ALCOLM X is shot dead at a rally of the Organisation of Afro-American Unity (OAAU) in Manhattan, New York, on , the 21st of February, a Sunday. Born Malcolm Little, in Omaha, Nebraska, the radical black separatist leader has rejected his original name as a legacy of slavery since becoming a Black Muslim in 1952. He is killed as he begins addressing an audience of 400. Three men shoot him 15 times at close range. In their murder trial it will emerge that all three are members of the Black Muslim organisation, headed by Elijah Muhammad, with whom X has had a bitter split.

## Unforgettable Nat

• **FEBRUARY 15TH: NAT 'KING' COLE** dies of lung cancer in Santa Monica, California. Born Nathaniel Coles, in Montgomery, Alabama, he was the son of a preacher who moved his family north to Chicago when the boy was four. By that time, Nat had already started the piano. He became an important and influential jazz pianist, following in the tradition of Earl Hines. Occasionally his King Cole Trio would do vocal numbers, and in 1944 he scored a pop hit with 'Straighten Up And Fly Right', supposedly based on one of his father's sermons. Soon he was much better known as a singer of mellow ballads, achieving 27 US top 40 hits between 1954 and his death.

### JANUARY

• **1ST: IRISH R&B BAND** Them, fronted by vocalist Van Morrison, enter the UK singles chart with 'Baby, Please Don't Go'. Playing guitar on the record is Jimmy Page, who goes on to form Led Zeppelin three years later.

• **3RD: THE FENDER GUITAR** company, maker of the Stratocaster and Telecaster, is bought by CBS for $13 million.

• **4TH: US PRESIDENT JOHNSON** announces new social reform programmes, including Medicare and Medicaid... The same day, poet T.S. Eliot dies at 76. He once wrote, "Things have a terrible permanence when people die." So true.

• **15TH: THE WHO'S** first single, 'I Can't Explain,' is released in the UK.

• **20TH: THE BYRDS** record Dylan's 'Mr Tambourine Man' at Columbia Studios, Hollywood, California.

• **24TH: WINSTON CHURCHILL DIES**, age 90, having suffered a stroke nine days beforehand. The funeral for Britain's wartime Prime Minister – held a week later – is attended by 3,000 mourners from 110 different countries (up to 350 million watch the service on television). Queen Elizabeth also attends, the first time a monarch has ever attended the funeral of a subject.

### FEBRUARY

• **1ST: AMERICAN-BORN SINGER PJ PROBY** is banned by the ABC Theatre Chain in the UK for purposely splitting his tight trousers on-stage in an attempt to drive his audiences into a wild frenzy... On the same day, James Brown records 'Papa's Got A Brand New Bag'. It finally reaches the mainstream charts in August, giving Brown his first Top Ten hit, and and signalling the birth of funk.

• **2ND: INDONESIA** becomes the first country to withdraw from the United Nations.

• **3RD: MORE THAN 1,000** black schoolchildren are arrested for truancy and unlawful assembly in Alabama. This follows the arrest of Dr Martin Luther King Jr and 770 others for picketing a county courthouse, during furious protests about segregation and voting rights violations .

• **6TH: THE RIGHTEOUS BROTHERS** hit Number One in the US singles chart with the Phil Spector-produced 'You've Lost That Lovin' Feeling'. They will stay there for two weeks.

• **7TH: NICKNAMED "THE BRITISH BOB DYLAN,"** Donovan (full name Donovan Leitch) is signed to Pye Records... And Britain bans cigarette advertising on television.

• **11TH: THE JOHNNY CASH** album *Ring Of Fire* is certified gold by the RIAA in the US.

• **12TH: ARAB PRESSURE** forces West Germany to halt military shipments to Israel.

• **13TH: BRIAN WILSON** performs live with the Beach Boys for the last time until the mid 1970s. He's decided to concentrate his energies on studio work, and will go on to produce much of his most creative and complex work in the next two years, at least until the wheels come off after 'Good Vibrations.' Brian's first touring replacement on bass and vocals is session man Glen Campbell, long before he becomes a solo star – though by April, Bruce Johnston has been brought in on a more permanent basis, becoming only the second Beach Boy (after Dennis Wilson) who actually surfs.

• **16TH: FOUR PEOPLE** are held over a plot to blow up the Statue Of Liberty, the Liberty Bell, and the Washington Monument.

• **22ND: ON A PRIVATELY** chartered BOAC Boeing 707, The Beatles fly to the Bahamas and book into the Balmoral Club, Cable Beach, to begin filming their second movie, *Help!*

# Vietnam: Into The Abyss

• **FEBRUARY 1965 SEES A DRAMATIC ESCALATION** of the Vietnam conflict, with the beginning of 'Rolling Thunder,' an almost unbroken campaign of US air raids lasting three years, and the first battles involving American troops. The war had its origins in the 1930s, when the country was a French colony. A Vietnamese nationalist rebellion, under the leadership of a young communist called Ho Chi Minh, was brutally crushed. During the Second World War, the French agreed a truce with the invading Japanese. Ho Chi Minh's Viet Minh forces attacked both, and at the end of the war he was in effective control of the northern part of Vietnam after the Japanese surrender. The French, meanwhile, attempted to reassume power in the South. This split was recognised in 1954, when a peace conference divided the country, leaving North Vietnam under the communists and South Vietnam under a new democratic (if corrupt) government. The conflict continued, however, and soon began to involve the US, which committed itself to the survival of South Vietnam, sending first economic and military aid and then military advisers. On August. 4, 1964, things took a turn for the worse when North Vietnamese torpedo boats allegedly attacked US destroyers in the international waters of the Gulf of Tonkin. (It was later revealed that President Johnson expressed doubts the attack ever actually occurred.) A resolution in congress permitted President Johnson to wage all-out war on the North without a formal declaration. It did not end until 1975, when North Vietnam took Saigon. Vietnam was formally reunified in July, 1976, and Saigon renamed Ho Chi Minh City. US casualties numbered more than 50,000 dead. South Vietnamese were estimated at more than 400,000, and Viet Cong and North Vietnamese at more than 900,000. Opposition to the war had grown as television beamed the suffering of both civilians and conscripts around the world. Demonstrations in New York City in 1969 only attracted 25,000 marchers but several hundred thousand would gather a few years later. Most demonstrations were peaceful, but acts of civil disobedience intended to provoke arrest were common. Although much of the protest came from students, there was also opposition from the clergy, politicians, and people such as Dr. Benjamin Spock. The election of Richard Nixon in 1968 and his reduction in US ground forces did little to placate the protestors, and his decision to invade Cambodia in 1970 led to massive demonstrations on college campuses. At Kent State University, on May 4th, 1970, four students were shot and killed by the Ohio National Guard.

**MARCH**

**APRIL**

• **1ST: BIRMINGHAM'S SPENCER DAVIS GROUP**, featuring 16-year-old Steve Winwood, play their first headline gig at The Marquee Club, Soho, London.

• **2ND: THE MOVIE VERSION** of Rodgers & Hammerstein's *The Sound Of Music* premieres at the Rivoli Theater, New York. It went on to win five Oscars, including a best director award for Robert Wise, but nothing for star Julie Andrews.

• **5TH: REG DWIGHT**, later known as Elton John, quits school to work as a messenger for Mills Music, a music publisher, in London.

• **13TH: IT'S ANNOUNCED** that Eric 'Slowhand' Clapton is leaving The Yardbirds. Session guitarist Jimmy Page is approached as his replacement, but declines. He recommends Jeff Beck, currently with the up-

and-coming Tridents. Beck says later he is persuaded to take the job because it means he gets a free suit, as you can see.

• **18TH: SOVIET COSMONAUT** Aleksei A. Leonov is the first man to leave an orbiting spacecraft and float in space. Television viewers in the Soviet Union and Europe watch him emerge from the capsule and do a somersault... The same day, 'King Of The Road' by Roger Miller enters the UK singles chart, where it will peak at Number One.

• **20TH: WAYNE FONTANA** & The Mindbenders enter the US Hot 100 singles with 'Game Of Love' which will go all the way to Number One.

• **21ST: 3,200 PEOPLE** begin a freedom march from Selma to Montgomery. Federal Judge Frank Johnson orders Governor George Wallace to refrain from 'harassing or threatening' the protesters... Three days later, 25,000 freedom marchers reach Montgomery, where Dr King tells the crowd "We are on the move and no wave of racism will stop us." -Then, on the 25th, Viola Liuzzo, a white civil rights supporter, is shot dead for transporting freedom marchers. Four Klan members are later arrested but Klan leader Robert Shelton insists it's all a communist plot to destroy U.S. right wing.

• **30TH: A SHIPMENT** of raw LSD arrives at Owsley Stanley's Bear Research Group in Laffler Road, Los Angeles. Owsley is now ready to become the main supplier of hallucinogenics to the West Coast musical community. The drug, originally created for medicinal purposes, would not become illegal for another year.

• **3RD: 'SUBTERRANEAN HOMESICK BLUES'** by Bob Dylan enters the US Hot 100, where it will peak at Number 39. The single, an angry protest number driven by electric guitar, marks Dylan's definitive shift from folk to rock.

• **10TH: FREDDIE & THE DREAMERS** – representing the novelty end of the British Invasion – take the Number One spot on the US charts for two weeks with 'I'm Telling You Now'. They went on to have several more hits, but their comedy

antics would fall out of favour as rock turned more serious in the later part of the 1960s.

• **11TH: WEMBLEY'S EMPIRE POOL**, London, hosts the 1965 NME Poll Winners Concert, featuring The Beatles, Rolling Stones, Moody Blues, Kinks, Searchers, Dusty Springfield, Herman's Hermits, Georgie Fame, The Animals, Them, Wayne Fontana, Donovan, Freddie & The Dreamers, Cilla Black and Tom Jones.

• **19TH: ON THE FIRST DAY** of studio work on the album *Otis Blue*, Otis Redding records a stereo version of 'I've Been Loving You Too Long' at Stax Studios in Memphis, Tennessee. The whole album will be completed in two days.

• **24TH: PRESIDENT SUKARNO** of Indonesia decrees that all foreign-owned enterprises in the country are to be seized.

• **25TH: A BAND OF 2,000** segregationists marching through the centre of Atlanta, Georgia, is forced to detour when someone tosses a smoke bomb in their path. Lester Maddox, their leader, tells the assembled motley crew of Klansmen and other anti-integrationist groups, that "deadly, bloody and ungodly communism threatens our very existence." Meanwhile, speaking at a music industry function in London that evening, CBS Records President Goddard Leiberson predicts, "There will be a growth in album sales such as you've never seen before."

• **29TH: AUSTRALIA** agrees to send 800 troops to Vietnam, despite mounting opposition at home.

• **23RD: STAN LAUREL** (left), British-born half of comedy pioneers Laurel & Hardy, dies at the age of 74. The world scratches its head in a bewildered fashion and mourns.

# The Summer Of Legs

**M**ARY QUANT introduces the mini-skirt at her Bazaar boutique in King's Road, Chelsea, London. It becomes a world sensation, and for the first time young working people are leading fashion rather than trying to emulate the wealthy. Some claim Quant adapted the mini-skirt from a French designer, but she had a good response: "It wasn't me or Courrèges who invented the miniskirt anyway – it was the girls in the street who did it." Mary's best-known girl in the street was Twiggy (right), discovered as a teenager working in a hair salon. Starting as a Quant model, Twiggy became an international star through records and movies. Quant, meanwhile, went on to create one more fashion sensation – hot pants – in line with her view that "A woman is as young as her knees."

**MAY**

**JUNE**

- **1ST: WITH ADVANCE** orders of 600,000, British band Herman's Hermits soar to the US Number One slot for the first of three weeks of the year with 'Mrs Brown You've Got A Lovely Daughter.' Meanwhile, their previous single, 'Silhouettes' is still at Number Five.
- **2ND: EARLY BIRD**, a new communications satellite, sends television pictures from the US to the UK for the first time... Meanwhile, after a coup in the Dominican Republic against national leader Donald Reid Cabral, US President Johnson sends troops, ostensibly to protect American lives and interests. In fact, he intends to shore up the regime against what he believes to be a takeover by Cuban-backed communists. The Americans are later replaced by an international peace keeping force.
- **3RD: THE WARLOCKS**, an early incarnation of the Grateful Dead, record instrumental demos at a studio in Los Angeles.
- **7TH: IAN SMITH'S** Rhodesian Front Party wins a decisive victory by taking all 50 parliamentary seats contested in the general election, strengthening his resolve to win independence from Britain and to consolidate his racially exclusive political policies. Few of Rhodesia's four million blacks have the legal right to vote.
- **9TH: BRITISH ROCK** royalty, including The Beatles, Donovan, Paul Jones of Manfred Mann and Eric Burdon of The Animals, turn out to see Bob Dylan play at London's Royal Albert Hall.

- **11TH: A CYCLONE** in Pakistan kills up to 5,000 and leaves five million homeless.
- **12TH: ATLANTIC RECORDS** signs Wilson Pickett to a recording contract.
- **14TH: FRANCES PERKINS**, the first woman Cabinet member in US history, dies, age 83. Asked whether it was ever a handicap being a woman, she responded: "Only when climbing trees."
- **22ND: AN EARLY LINE-UP** of Pink Floyd plays at the Summer Dance, Homerton College, Cambridge, UK.
- **24TH: BRITAIN ADOPTS** the metric system. Theoretically, at least.
- **25TH: SONNY BOY WILLIAMSON** (aka Rice Miller – not to be confused with the other Sonny Boy Williamson who died in 1948) dies today at the age of 65.
- **29TH: THE BEACH BOYS** take the US Number One slot for the first of two weeks with 'Help Me, Rhonda.' On the same day, their eighth album, *Today!*, peaks at Number Four in the US.

- **JUNE 15TH: USING ROCK MUSICIANS** currently working on Bob Dylan's new album, Columbia Records producer Tom Wilson overdubs electric guitar and drums onto 'Sounds Of Silence' by acoustic folk duo Simon & Garfunkel, hoping it might be a hit during the current folk-rock boom. The due first got together in the mid-1950s, calling themselves Tom & Jerry.

- **1ST: BOB DYLAN** and Joan Baez are among those in a Vietnam peace march in London. Most of the UK musical aristocracy are notable by their absence.
- **3RD: THE AMERICAN** Folk Music Tour with Rambling Jack Elliot, the Reverend Gary Davis, Buffy Saint-Marie, Josh White, Julie Felix, and Derroll Adams opens at the Town Hall, Birmingham, UK.
- **5TH: THE US STATE DEPARTMENT** finally admits that troops in Vietnam "have a combat role." Two weeks later, a further 21,000 are on their way, and by the end of July another 50,000.
- **11TH: RICK & THE RAVENS**, a group including Ray Manzarek, later to play for The

Doors, plays at Ports O'Call, San Pedro Marina, California. Because the contract calls for a six-piece group, Manzarek's friend Jim Morrison stands in with the band, pretending to play guitar.
- **14TH: PAUL MCCARTNEY** of The Beatles records 'Yesterday' in Abbey Road Studios, London.
- **18TH: A LEGAL BLOOD** alcohol limit for drivers will be introduced, the UK Government says. The US resists making alcohol in the blood an automatic offence until the 1980s.
- **21ST: AT THE RED DOG SALOON**, Virginia City, Nevada, San Francisco 'underground' rock pioneers The Charlatans play their first gig, dressed as wild-west oulaws.
- **24TH: JOHN LENNON'S** second book, *A Spaniard In The Works*, is published.
- **26TH: THE BYRDS' FIRST SINGLE**, a jangling cover of Bob Dylan's Mr Tambourine Man, hits the US Number One spot for the first of two weeks.

## Sonny & Cher

# 1965
May-August

- **AUGUST 21ST: SONNY & CHER** top the US singles chart with 'I Got You Babe'. Two weeks later, they will achieve a British number one as well. Sonny and Cher met in 1963 when he was working for Phil Spector in Hollywood. A year later they married, and then signed to the Atlantic subsidiary Atco as a duo. Sonny scribbled the words of their hit on a piece of cardboard after working on it late into the night. Cher complained she couldn't read his writing. They would have a series of hits in the 1960s before resurfacing in the 1970s in The Sonny and Cher Comedy Hour, a family tv show. The couple would separate in 1974 and then divorce, with Cher thriving as a solo artist.

### JULY

- **11TH: SOVIET PREMIER** Kosygin announces an increase in defense spending, due to the "deterioration of the world situation." That's how it looks in America, too. The US is struggling with Soviet-backed Vietnam, and China has the Bomb.

- **1ST: THE EDITOR** of the *Rand Daily Mail* and two of his journalists are arrested after printing allegations of barbaric conditions in South Africa's prisons... On the same day, regulations in America change so that AM radio stations may duplicate no more than half their programmes on their FM affiliates. The way is now open for the rise of FM rock radio.
- **3RD: 'RIDE YOUR PONY'** by former boxer Lee Dorsey brings the sound of New Orleans R&B to the US singles chart.
- **12TH: THE MOODY BLUES** throw a party at their house in Roehampton, UK. Guests include The Beatles' Paul McCartney and George Harrison, Rod Stewart, Marianne Faithfull, Sandie Shaw, the US soul singer Doris Troy, Viv Prince of The Pretty Things, and Hilton Valentine of The Animals.
- **15TH: US PROBE MARINER 4** sends the first close-up photos of Mars back to Earth.

- **16TH: THE MONT BLANC** tunnel, linking Italy and France, is opened by French President De Gaulle and Italy's President Saragat.
- **20TH: THE LOVIN' SPOONFUL** release their debut single, 'Do You Believe In Magic?', in the US. It will peak at Number Nine.
- **22ND: FIGURES SHOW** that 1964 was the worst year this century for crime in London, the UK capital.
- **25TH: BOB DYLAN** is booed by some of the more traditional members of the audience at the *Newport Folk Festival* because he has introduced a "new sound" to his music, incorporating electrical instruments. Initially this involves The Butterfield Blues Band, but Dylan enjoys the experience so much he decides to put together a touring band of his own, and drafts in The Hawks, who will soon change their name to The Band.

### AUGUST

- **2ND: AUTHORITIES** in Texas, New Mexico, Oklahoma, and Kansas are inundated with reports of unidentified flying objects. The air force later insists it was probably only Jupiter or a star, like Rigel or Betelgeuse, both of which were in the part of the sky where the sightings were reported.
- **5TH: OTIS REDDING** releases 'Respect' on Volt Records in the US.
- **8TH: THE STAX REVUE**, featuring Wilson Pickett, Booker T & The MGs, and The Astors, plays the first of two nights at the 5/4 Ballroom, Los Angeles.
- **15TH: THE LARGEST CROWD** so far for a rock show – 56,000 fans – sees The Beatles play live at Shea Stadium, New York City. The audience includes Mick Jagger and Keith Richards of the Rolling Stones, who also hang out with the group at their hotel… The same day, racial tensions in the US explode in the Watts area of Los Angeles, as the streets are overrun by people rioting, looting, and setting fires. Five days of violence leave 30 dead, hundreds injured, 2000 arrested,

and property damage estimated at $40 milion. The riots were triggered by the arrest of a suspected drunk driver.
- **19TH: AUSCHWITZ SURVIVORS** and relatives protest at what they see as very light prison terms for 16 ex-warders found guilty of murder – only six of the warders get life sentences.
- **27TH: PRESIDENT JOHNSON** lifts the draft exemption for married men... On this day, The Beatles meet Elvis, at his house in Bel Air, Los Angeles, where he lives when he's filming in Hollywood. Sadly there seem to be no pictures of this informal get-together by the world's biggest musical phenomenons. The Beatles are star-struck, by all accounts, and particularly impressed that Elvis has a pool table, and also the first remote controlled TV they've seen. When they arrive, Elvis is playing bass, while watching his huge-screen TV with the sound down. After a chat, the Beatles plug in some instruments that are lying around and proceed to have an impromptu jam with The King.

- **AUGUST 13TH: JEFFERSON AIRPLANE** play their debut gig at the opening night of The Matrix, a San Francisco club run by Marty Balin, the band's vocalist and leader. Originally intended to be a folk-rock band, Jefferson Airplane quickly came to epitomise the West Coast genre known as acid-rock. They were rapidly signed up by RCA Records for a remarkable $20,000. After the release of their first album, in 1966, vocalist Signe Anderson would be replaced by Grace Slick from local rivals the Great Society. In this incarnation, the Airplane would go on to have top ten hits with 'White Rabbit' and 'Somebody To Love' and to become a huge and long-running touring act.

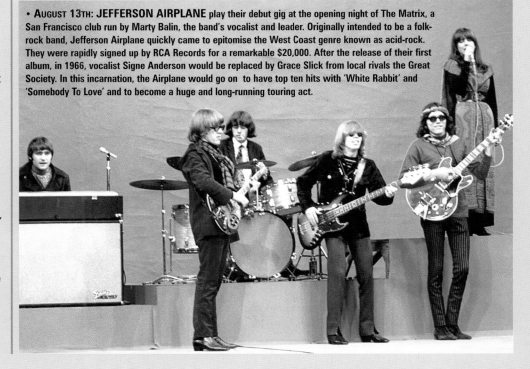

## Too Much Monkee Business

**H**ITCHING A RIDE on the coat-tails of the Beatles' *Hard Days Night*, The Monkees are a manufactured band, conjured up through adverts in *The Hollywood Reporter* and *Daily Variety*: "Madness!! Folk and roll musician singers for acting roles in new TV series." No fewer than 437 people reply, including Steven Stills and Danny Hutton (soon to be in Three Dog Night). Some even claim that Charles Manson auditions. In the end, the gig goes to (left to right) Davy Jones, Peter Tork, Mike Nesmith and Mickey Dolenz. The first show airs on NBC in September 1966, resulting in an immediate Number One hit with *Last Train To Clarkesville*. With songs from the likes of Carole King, Neil Diamond and Neil Sedaka, and expert session playing from Glen Campbell, Leon Russell and David Gates, the band will front a string of quality pop hits. But the puppets want to be real boys and write their own material. Peter Tork fights to buy himself out – for $160,000 – and it is all over by 1970.

• **1ST: INDIA AND PAKISTAN** continue to battle in air and on ground in Kashmir. Three weeks later a cease-fire is agreed at the UN, but it lasts less than a week as fighting breaks out again between Hindus and Muslims in Kashmir. Meanwhile, Indian troops exchange fire with Chinese forces on the border with Tibet.

• **4TH: THE WHO** visit Battersea Dogs' Home in south London to choose a guard dog, parking their van outside. The van is broken into and most of their equipment stolen... Meanwhile, Nobel Peace Prize winner, theologist, musician and philanthropist Dr Albert Schweitzer dies at his hospital in Gabon, west Africa.

• **5TH: SAN FRANCISCO** writer Michael Fallon applies the term 'hippie' to the city's counterculture in an article about the Blue Unicorn coffeehouse where LEMAR (Legalize Marijuana) & the Sexual Freedom League meet.

• **11TH: UK POP PAPER** *Melody Maker* runs a feature about The Preachers, a band from Bromley in Kent, whose 15-year-old guitarist is Peter Frampton.

• **SEPTEMBER 15TH:** *I SPY* begins in US – it's the first TV series to have a black star: Bill Cosby. At the same time, *Lost In Space* is launched, featuring Robot (above, with Jonathan Harris as Professor Zachary Smith). Also today, Ford introduces a range of cars equipped with eight-track cartridge players.

• **23RD: THE WALKER BROTHERS**, an American trio resident in Britain, reach Number One in the UK with the Bacharach/David song 'Make It Easy On Yourself.'

• **25TH: GRAVEL-THROATED** ex-New Christy Minstrel turned protest singer, Barry McGuire, takes the apocalyptic 'Eve Of Destruction' to the US Number One position for one week.

• **29TH: THE USSR ADMITS** it has been supplying weapons to North Vietnam.

• **NOVEMBER 29TH: MIDDLE-AGED UK** schoolteacher Mary Whitehouse forms the National Viewers and Listeners Association to campaign against "indecency" in the media.

• **2ND: STARTING A TEN-SHOW** headlining tour in Czechoslovakia, Manfred Mann become the first rock band to perform behind the Iron Curtain.

• **4TH: POPE PAUL VI**, the first pontiff ever to visit the US, arrives in New York to make an urgent appeal for peace, insisting, "The real threat to peace does not come from progress or science but from man himself."

• **5TH: BOB DYLAN** begins recording sessions for the album *Blonde On Blonde* in Columbia Recording Studios, New York City.

• **6TH: PATRICIA HARRIS**, the first black US ambassador, takes up her office, in Luxembourg.

• **7TH: OPENING OF** the Post Office Tower (later Telecom Tower) in London. At 580 feet, it is the UK's tallest building. The Empire State Building in New York, at 1,250 feet, is the world's tallest.

• **8TH: JOHN LEE HOOKER** plays in the American Folk Blues Festival in Hamburg, Germany... Meanwhile negotiations between British Prime Minister Harold Wilson and Rhodesian Prime Minister Ian Smith break down when Wilson insists upon black majority rule in Rhodesia.

• **15TH: COUNTRY JOE & THE FISH** play at the San Francisco State College Vietnam Day Committee Teach-In.

• **16TH: AT AN ANTI-VIETNAM** war rally in Berkeley, California, Allen Ginsberg is first to use the term 'Flower Power' as a hippie-friendly way of encouraging a non-violent uprising.

• **18TH: A COLLEGE STUDENT** named David Miller is the first person to be arrested under a new federal law, after burning his draft card during an anti-war demonstration. If convicted, he could be sentenced to five years in jail and fined $10,000.

## Moptops Of The British Empire

• **26TH: THE BEATLES** are awarded MBE (Member Of The British Empire) decorations by Queen Elizabeth, at Prime Minister Harold Wilson's behest. They are the first pop band to be given such an honour (known familiarly as a 'gong'), and it prompts some war verteran to return their awards in protest. George Harrison later claims that when they first received the official government papers through the post they thought they were being called up for the army. It's also said the band sneak into the Buckinghan Palace toilets and smoke a joint before receiving their medals.

# Stones In The Studio

- **SEPTEMBER 6TH:** **THE ROLLING STONES** begin two days of recording 'Get Off Of My Cloud' at RCA Studios, Los Angeles. It will become their second US Number One in a row, after '(I Can't Get No) Satisfaction.' Consciously marketed by their manager Andrew Loog Oldham as the antithesis of the clean-cut, bright and bouncy Merseybeat pop of the Beatles, the Rolling Stones set out their stall as mad, bad and dangerous to know. Pitching hard edged blues against the Beatles melodic power pop, the Rolling Stones will be the inspiration for every camp, preening, but determinedly heterosexual front man, every louche, aloof, artful cigarette sporting guitarist, in fact every hard-edged rock band to follow. The band's line-up had been fixed in 1963 with the addition of Bill Wyman and Charlie Watts. Their debut single, in June of that year was Chuck Berry's 'Come On,' followed by 'I Wanna Be Your Man,' a gift from John Lennon and Paul McCartney. By the summer of 1965, and the release of '(I Can't Get No) Satisfaction,' they are already superstars and are starting a string of Top Ten singles that will run for the next eight years.

## NOVEMBER

- **19TH:** **THE SCOURGE** of America's communists, the House Unamerican Activities Committee, turns its attention to the Ku Klux Klan.
- **20TH:** **SAX PLAYER** Earl Bostic, who succeeded in both jazz and R&B worlds, dies age 52.
- **21ST:** **ELVIS PRESLEY'S** original bass player, Bill Black, who played on the King's early Sun recordings, dies from a brain tumour.
- **28TH:** **THE PENTAGON** lowers the standard for military volunteers.
- **31ST:** **THE MOTHERS OF INVENTION**, led by guitarist Frank Zappa, play at The Action, Hollywood, California.

- **2ND:** **QUAKER NORMAN MORRISON** burns himself to death outside the Pentagon in an anti-Vietnam war protest. A week later, the trend for immolation as a viable protest continues as Roger LaPorte sets himself alight outside the UN.
- **5TH:** **THE DOORS** play one of their first professional gigs, at the Pioneer Club Boat Ride, in Los Angeles.
- **6TH:** **THE SAN FRANCISCO** music scene takes a step towards the 'Summer Of Love' when the Grateful Dead, Jefferson Airplane and The Charlatans perform at the Fillmore (the first show ever put on by promoter Bill Graham)... And Edgar Varese, the French-born American composer and pioneer of electronic music, dies at the age of 81.
- **11TH:** **THE CHINESE GOVERNMENT** accuses the US and USSR of collaborating in a plot for world domination.
- **16TH:** **SAN FRANCISCO-BASED** innovator Bill Ham demonstrates a complex system of lights and slides which he calls a 'light show'. This will become a vital ingredient of rock shows in the psychedelic era.
- **17TH:** **BRIAN WILSON** of the Beach Boys goes into the studio to start work on the album *Pet Sounds* in Los Angeles.
- **24TH:** **A FOUR-DAY EVENT**, The Blues Bag, begins at the Café Au Go Go in New York City's Greenwich Village, featuring John Lee Hooker, Muddy Waters, Otis Spann, Fred Neil and the Blues Project.

- **24TH:** **NUMBER OF WEEKLY** US troop deaths in Vietnam reaches a peak of 240 (reliable figures on the Viet-Cong side are not available). Three days later, 50,000 marchers descend on Washington in the latest peace demonstration.
- **25TH:** **ARMY CHIEF** Joseph Mobutu deposes President Joseph Kasavubu in the Congo and installs himself as head of the government.
- **27TH:** **KEN KESEY** – author of *One Flew Over The Cuckoo's Nest* – and his followers The Merry Pranksters make their first public 'acid tests' spiking US soft drink Kool-Aid with LSD. The exploits of this jolly outfit are later recounted by Tom Wolfe in his *Electric Kool-Aid Acid Test*. Later, Kool-Aid will be used by the cult leader Jim Jones to poison his followers in Guyana.

## DECEMBER

- **2ND:** **THE USS ENTERPRISE** becomes the first nuclear-powered aircraft carrier to take part in a hostile engagement when it launches air strikes against Viet Cong guerilla bases near Bien Hoa in Vietnam.
- **3RD:** **THE BEATLES'** new album Rubber Soul is released as they set off on what will turn out to be their final UK tour... The same day, three members of the Ku Klux Klan are convicted in Montgomery, Alabama, for the murder of a civil rights worker.
- **4TH:** **IT TRANSPIRES** that US Number One 'Turn Turn Turn' by the Byrds (written by Pete Seeger) takes its lyrics from The Book Of Ecclesiastes in the Bible... Meanwhile, Keith Richards is knocked unconscious after receiving an electric shock from a microphone.
- **10TH:** **THE NOBEL PEACE PRIZE** is awarded to UNICEF (the United Nations Childrens Fund), in Oslo. Set up in 1946 – and initially called the United Nations International Children's Emergency Fund – UNICEF's stated purpose is to help children whose lives have been devastated by war.
- **11TH:** **DUNHILL RECORDS** announces the signing of The Mamas And The Papas to a $10,000 recording contract. On the same day, The Isley Brothers sign to Motown... Later that night, when The Myddle Class (featuring David Palmer, later to sing on Steely Dan's first album) play at Summit High School Auditorium in New Jersey, they are supported by a band which has just changed its name to The Velvet Underground.
- **22ND:** **A TEMPORARY 70MPH** speed limit is introduced in Britain, covering all previously unrestricted roads, including motorways. The 'temporary' limit will not become permanent until 1978.
- **24TH:** **BOTH SIDES** agree a Christmas truce in Vietnam.
- **30TH:** **FERDINAND E. MARCOS** becomes the Philippine republic's sixth president.

## Big In Japan – The Sixties

- **BY THE MID 1960S, JAPAN** has become the world's third biggest record sales market, after the US and the UK. It's not long before Western bands start to realise this: US surf group The Ventures are one of the first to pick up on the Japanese market, touring there in early 1965, and enjoying even greater (and longer-lasting) acclaim than in the States. Their instrumental style is reflected in home-grown Japanese 'eleki' – as in 'electric guitar' music – which develops further when The Beatles arrive for their first tour in June 1966, inspiring a whole new breed of vocal-led groups: garage bands taking British and American influences and blending them with Japanese vocals to create a very distinctive hybrid. They call this 'GS' – which stands for 'group sounds' – simply because it's easier to pronounce in Japan than 'rock'n'roll'. GS heroes include The Spiders (who make the first GS record in May 1965), The Bluejeans, The Bunnys, The Tigers, The Jaguars, The Wild Ones, The Golden Cups, The Carnabeats, The Taxman, and later psychedelic acts like The Mops.

# 1966

## January–April

### JANUARY

- **1ST: IN HIS NEW YEAR** message, Pope Paul VI makes an appeal for peace in Vietnam... Meanwhile Simon & Garfunkel's revamped single 'The Sounds Of Silence' hits the US Number One spot – which comes as a surprise to the duo, who have actually split. They hastily reform.
- **6TH: SINGER-SONGWRITER** Neil Diamond signs a contract with Bang Records to supply four singles in 12 months.
- **10TH: PAKISTAN AND INDIA** sign another peace accord... Next day, Indian prime minister Lal Bahadur Shastri dies. He will be replaced by Indira Gandhi, 48-year-old daughter of Pandit Nehru, independent India's first prime minister. She becomes the second female head of government in modern history (after Mrs Bandaranaike of Ceylon).
- **11TH: MILITARISTIC** right-wing anthem, 'The Ballad Of The Green Berets' by Staff Sgt Barry Sadler, is released in the US.
- **17TH: THE US LOSE** an H-bomb when a B52 collides with a fuel supply plane over the coast of Spain. Fortunately, especially red-faced Pentagon staff, they find it a few months later.
- **20TH: 'KEEP ON RUNNING'** knocks The Beatles' 'Day Tripper' off the top of the UK charts. It's the fourth single by Birmingham's Spencer Davis Group.
- **21ST: FIRST NIGHT** of the three-day *Trips Festival* at the Longshoremen's Hall in San Francisco, featuring The Grateful Dead, Big Brother & The Holding Company, The Loading Zone, Chinese New Years' Lion Dancers & Drum & Bugle Corps, Stroboscopic Trampoline, and Ken Kesey & His Merry Pranksters... George Harrison isn't there, because he got married today to Patty Boyd, whom he met when filming *A Hard Day's Night* (she played a schoolgirl). Later his friend Eric Clapton, infatuated with her, will write 'Layla' for her and set about stealing her.
- **24TH: LOVE, LED** by guitarists Arthur Lee and former Byrds roadie Bryan MacLean, begin recording their eponymous debut album at Sunset Sound Recorders, Hollywood.
- **31ST: AFTER A MONTH OFF**, the US re-starts bombing in North Vietnam.

### FEBRUARY

- **1ST: BUSTER KEATON,** the great silent movie comedian, dies at the age of 70... As does gossip queen Hedda Hopper, at 75.
- **3RD: PAUL McCARTNEY** of The Beatles goes to see Little Stevie Wonder play at The Scotch of St James, London. In 16 years time, they will have a Number One hit together...
- **4TH: A JAPANESE BOEING 727** crashes in Tokyo Bay leaving 133 dead.
- **7TH: US ROCK MAGAZINE** *Crawdaddy* hits the streets.
- **15TH: BOB DYLAN** is recording 'Sad Eyed Lady Of The Lowlands' at Columbia Music Row Studios, Nashville, Tennessee.
- **18TH: AT GOLD STAR STUDIOS** in Hollywood, Brian Wilson of The Beach Boys starts work on 'Good Vibrations'.
- **24TH: THE DOORS** begin a three-month engagement as the house band at The London Fog, Sunset Strip, West Hollywood, California, where they earn $10 each per day for playing five sets every night from Thursday to Sunday.
- **25TH: CHER RELEASES** a new single, 'Bang Bang (My Baby Shot Me Down)', in the US.

- **JANUARY 12TH:** *BATMAN*, starring Adam West (left) as the caped crusader, is screened for the first time on US television. Guest stars over the next two years include Cesar Romero as The Joker, Frank Gorshin as The Riddler, Burgess Meredith as The Penguin, and singer Eartha Kitt as Catwoman.

## One From His Baby

**FEBRUARY 26TH:** **NANCY SINATRA** takes the US Number One position with 'These Boots Are Made For Walkin'', a week after doing so in the UK. Frank's little girl has already had numerous failed singles by this time, but this will be the first of a series of hits written and produced for her by Lee Hazlewood, who'd launched Duane Eddy's career in the 1950s. Nancy's only other Number One, though, is 'Something Stupid,' her 1967 duet with her dad, Hazlewood, meanwhile, goes on to cult fame and eventual semi-retirement in Sweden, releasing occasional and idiosyncratic albums, including his 1999 'comeback,' the snappily-titled *Farmisht, Flatulence, Origami, ARF!!! and me.*

## Repugnant Or Obscene?

• **MARCH 21ST:** **JUSTICE WILLIAM BRENNAN,** at the Massachusetts State Supreme Court, reverses the earlier verdict of Judge Eugene A. Hudson, which declared that William Burrough's book The Naked Lunch is obscene due to its graphic scenes of cannibalism and overt sexual references. Justice Brennan agrees with the assertion that the book may be "repugnant, but not obscene." The Naked Lunch is the last literary work to have a major censorship trial in the United States. Burroughs was born into a wealthy Missouri family in 1914 – his grandfather invented the first adding machine – and began writing at the age of 10. But he did not publish his first novel, Junky, until 1953. His next book, Queer, dealt with the homosexual relationship between two skid-row drug addicts, and was ignored by the public. Burroughs subsequently found it hard to get published. The Naked Lunch was eventually published in the US in 1962, whereupon Theodore Mavrikos, a bookseller in Boston, Massachusetts, was arrested for selling obscene literature. All parties agree to prosecute the book, rather than Mr Mavrikos, and Judge Brennan clears it.

**william s. burroughs NAKED LUNCH**

---

**MARCH**

• **2ND:** **LEAVING LOS ANGELES** in his beloved Pontiac hearse, Neil Young is spotted by Stephen Stills, going the other way. Stills had met Young when he was still in Canada, and recognised his distinctive vehicle. They agree to meet up the following day to play together, which leads to the formation of Buffalo Springfield.
• **3RD:** **'DEDICATED FOLLOWER OF FASHION'** by The Kinks enters the UK singles chart. It's a satirical look at the fashion victims on the streets of 'Swinging London', and marks a shift in Ray Davies's songwriting towards more 'English' subject matter and delivery.
• **4TH:** **THE LONDON EVENING STANDARD** publishes an interview in which John Lennon of The Beatles declares, "We're more popular than Jesus Christ

right now." This leads to record-burning in some particularly religious communities. Three weeks later, they court yet more controversy when the infamous 'Butcher cover' is shot by photographer Robert Whitaker in his studio in Chelsea, London. It shows the band dressed as butchers, surrounded by headless dolls and

strips of meat.
• **13TH:** **ROD STEWART** leaves Steampacket, the blues band created by Long John Baldry and featuring Brian Auger and Julie Driscoll.... Meanwhile, in his first official act since taking control of Indonesia, General Suharto tells the military to eradicate the Communist party.
• **19TH:** **PAUL REVERE & THE RAIDERS** (pictured above) release a new single, 'Kicks,' in the US – one of the first ever anti-drug rock songs.
• **20TH:** **THE SOCCER** World Cup trophy is stolen in London, but is unearthed a week later by Pickles the dog... This evening, James Brown heads the bill at a Madison Square Garden show also featuring The Young Rascals, Len Barry, and the Shangri-Las.

**APRIL**

• **1ST:** **HAVING RECENTLY** changed his name from David Jones to avoid confusion with the Monkees singer, David Bowie releases 'Do Anything You Say' on Pye Records. It fails to chart... That night, The Move, featuring Roy Wood, Carl Wayne and Bev Bevan, play at The Marquee in London for the first time, as a support act. They will soon begin a residency, but their wild stage antics (smoke bombs, pyrotechnics, and destroying televisions with axes) get them sacked and replaced by The Who...
• **6TH:** **AT STUDIO 3**, Abbey Road, London, The Beatles begin working on tracks which will become the album *Revolver*. The first song recorded is their most adventurous to date: 'Tomorrow Never Knows'.
• **8TH:** **THE VELVET UNDERGROUND** And Nico perform for the first time as part of Andy Warhol's Exploding Plastic Inevitable at the Dom on St Marks Place, New York City.

Tickets are $6 and the show makes $18,000 in its first week.
• **9TH:** **PERCY SLEDGE** releases a new single, 'When A Man Loves A Woman', in the US... That night, Jeff Beck collapses on-stage while playing a Yardbirds gig in France.
• **10TH:** **WRITER EVELYN WAUGH** dies, aged 62.
• **12TH:** **A CORVETTE** driven by Jan Berry, of surf duo Jan & Dean, collides with a gardener's truck in Beverly Hills, Los Angeles. The singer, who has just received his call-up papers, is in a coma for a month and remains partially paralyzed.
• **14TH:** **THE SANDOZ CORPORATION** In Switzerland suspends distribution of LSD.
• **17TH:** **FORMER HARVARD** psychology professor Timothy Leary is arrested on charges of narcotics possession.
• **22ND:** **THE TROGGS** release a new UK single, 'Wild Thing.'
**30TH:** **THE YOUNG RASCALS** achieve a US Number One with 'Good Lovin''.

## New York Says No War

• **MARCH 31ST:** **PEACE MARCHES** and protests against the Vietnam War continue to get bigger as more than 20,000 people take part in the latest demonstration in New York.

# 1966

May-August

**MAY**

**JUNE**

## It's A Family Affair

• MAY 7TH: **THE MAMAS & THE PAPAS** achieve their first US Number One with 'Monday Monday.' More even than the psychedelic sounds of the Summer of Love, the precise harmonies of The Mamas & The Papas come to epitomize the carefree, idyllic lifestyle of California. The Mamas & The Papas were formed in August 1965 when folk singer and songwriter John Phillips and his wife Michelle (right of picture) joined forces with Dennie Doherty and Cass Elliott (left of picture). Success comes with 'California Dreamin', the first of several million sellers, includng 'Words Of Love,' 'Dedicated To The One I Love,' and 'Creeque Alley'. John and Michelle separate – Michelle is fired on June 28th, 1968 – and the group disbands. Cass Elliott successfully goes solo, but dies on July 29th, 1974, in London, following a heart attack brought on by obesity. Michelle Phillips acts in movies like *The Long Goodbye* and in the *Dallas* spin-off *Knot's Landing*. John produces several solo albums and co-writes 'Kokomo', the Beach Boys' Number One. He too will die of heart failure, on March 18th, 2001, after years of erratic living and a liver transplant.

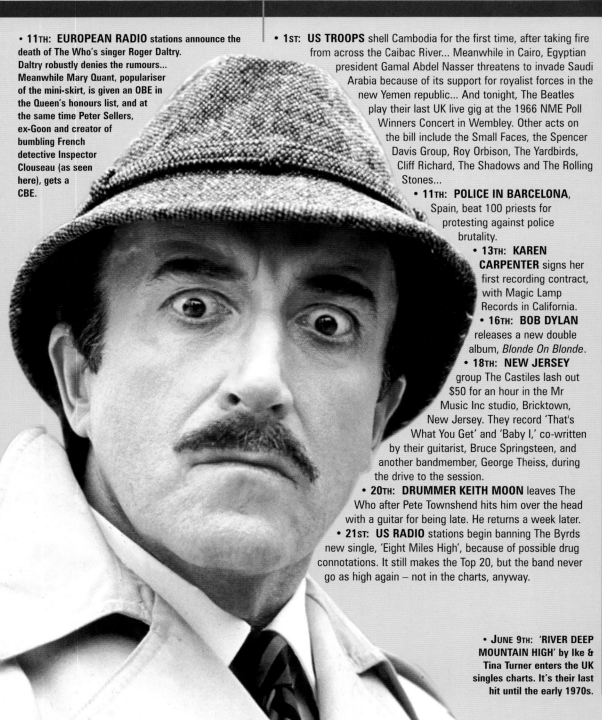

• **11TH:** **EUROPEAN RADIO** stations announce the death of The Who's singer Roger Daltry. Daltry robustly denies the rumours... Meanwhile Mary Quant, populariser of the mini-skirt, is given an OBE in the Queen's honours list, and at the same time Peter Sellers, ex-Goon and creator of bumbling French detective Inspector Clouseau (as seen here), gets a CBE.

• **1ST:** **US TROOPS** shell Cambodia for the first time, after taking fire from across the Caibac River... Meanwhile in Cairo, Egyptian president Gamal Abdel Nasser threatens to invade Saudi Arabia because of its support for royalist forces in the new Yemen republic... And tonight, The Beatles play their last UK live gig at the 1966 NME Poll Winners Concert in Wembley. Other acts on the bill include the Small Faces, the Spencer Davis Group, Roy Orbison, The Yardbirds, Cliff Richard, The Shadows and The Rolling Stones...

• **11TH:** **POLICE IN BARCELONA**, Spain, beat 100 priests for protesting against police brutality.

• **13TH:** **KAREN CARPENTER** signs her first recording contract, with Magic Lamp Records in California.

• **16TH:** **BOB DYLAN** releases a new double album, *Blonde On Blonde*.

• **18TH:** **NEW JERSEY** group The Castiles lash out $50 for an hour in the Mr Music Inc studio, Bricktown, New Jersey. They record 'That's What You Get' and 'Baby I,' co-written by their guitarist, Bruce Springsteen, and another bandmember, George Theiss, during the drive to the session.

• **20TH:** **DRUMMER KEITH MOON** leaves The Who after Pete Townshend hits him over the head with a guitar for being late. He returns a week later.

• **21ST:** **US RADIO** stations begin banning The Byrds new single, 'Eight Miles High', because of possible drug connotations. It still makes the Top 20, but the band never go as high again – not in the charts, anyway.

• JUNE 9TH: 'RIVER DEEP MOUNTAIN HIGH' by Ike & Tina Turner enters the UK singles charts. It's their last hit until the early 1970s.

• MAY 7TH: **THE BEACH BOYS** release *Pet Sounds*, created by leader Brian Wilson, lyricist Tony Asher and the pick of Los Angeles's studio players. Richly textured, innovatively arranged, and a long-term critical favorite.

• **1ST:** **FOR THE LAST OF FIVE** consecutive nights, Love headline the Whisky-A-Go-Go, West Hollywood, California, supported by the Doors. It's during these gigs that Elektra Records boss Jac Holzman sees The Doors and resolves to sign them.

• **3RD:** **THE PAUL BUTTERFIELD BLUES BAND**, Albert King. B.B. King and Fred Neil begin two weeks of shows at the Café Au Go Go, Greenwich Village, New York City. Neil's band includes Harvey Brooks, Al Kooper, John Sebastian, Felix Pappalardi, Dino Valenti and Karen Dalton.

• **4TH:** **'HOLD ON I'M COMIN''** by Sam & Dave enters the US Hot 100.

• **6TH:** **JAMES MEREDITH**, the first black student to enrol at the University of Mississippi, is shot in the back on a civil rights march. He survives... Meanwhile, Bill Graham is granted a license to run concerts at the Fillmore Auditorium in San Francisco, a former ballroom and roller-skating rink

## Bring Out The Dead

**JULY 1ST:** The Grateful Dead, formerly the Warlocks, release their debut single, 'Don't Ease Me In/Stealin'', on Scorpio Records. But singles will never be very important to the Dead. They become the house band for Ken Kesey's celebrated 'Acid Tests,' a series of LSD parties and events taking place in San Francisco in 1966 before possession of the drug is criminalized. Although the group's albums lack finesse, the Grateful Dead are superb live. Nominally led by guitarist Jerry Garcia, they win their spurs playing a lo-fi mix of blues, folk and country, but it is the long improvised guitar solos that dominate *Live/Dead* (1970) where they extend themselves. At length the studio albums *Workingman's Dead* (1970) and *American Beauty* (1971) demonstrate a grasp of country rock that is beyond the reach of their contemporaries. Furthermore, as the 1970s become the 1980s, Grateful Dead generate more income at the box office than any other group.

### JULY

that will become a crucial venue for psychedelic music.
• **7TH: DRUMMER GINGER BAKER** rings Melody Maker journalist Chris Welch to announce that he is forming a band with Eric Clapton of John Mayall's Bluesbreakers and Jack Bruce of Manfred Mann. (The group will be known as Cream)... The same day, Ronald Reagan wins the Republican nomination for governor of California.
• **15TH: THE END OF THREE DAYS** of youth riots in Amsterdam, Netherlands.
• **25TH: A SUMMER SPECTACULAR CONCERT** is held at Hollywood Bowl, Los Angeles, featuring the Beach Boys, The Byrds, Lovin' Spoonful, Love, Sir Douglas Quintet, Captain Beefheart, The Outsiders and The Leaves.

• **AUGUST 3RD: COMEDIAN LENNY BRUCE** dies of a drug overdose. Phil Spector says it was more likely a "police overdose." Virtually unable to work after being banned from most venues on obscenity grounds, Bruce was declared bankrupt last year.

• **JULY 23RD: ACTOR MONTGOMERY CLIFT** (pictured with Elizabeth Taylor), dies of a heart attack at 45.

• **1ST: AS PRESIDENT DE GAULLE** disagrees with the structure, leadership and nuclear policy of NATO, France pulls its armed forces out of the North Atlantic Treaty Organisation (for the next 27 years) and requests that all other Allied troops be withdrawn from French soil. NATO headquarters is moved to Brussels, in Belgium.
• **4TH: THE BEATLES** are attacked in Manila after accidentally snubbing President Marcos's wife – they are lucky to escape serious injury.
• **5TH: FORMER ANIMALS'** bassist Chas Chandler sees Jimmy (soon to be Jimi) Hendrix at The Café Wha? in New York City, and decides there and then to become his manager.
• **16TH: TOMMY JAMES & THE SHONDELLS** reach Number One in the US with 'Hanky Panky.'
• **29TH: BOB DYLAN** crashes his motorbike and suffers serious injuries, including concussion and several broken vertebrae in his neck. He chooses to retire from public view while he recuperates. Rumours began to circulate that he has severe brain damage or is actually dead... This is also the night Cream play their first ever gig, at the Twisted Wheel, Manchester, UK.
• **30TH: ENGLAND,** who are hosting the soccer World Cup, win the competition, beating West Germany 4-2 during extra time in the final.
• **31ST: MORE RACIAL UNREST** in the US, this time on the streets of Chicago, New York, and Cleveland. Many are killed or injured.

### AUGUST

• **9TH: THE ROLLING STONES** are awarded a gold disc by the RIAA for US sales of their album *Aftermath*.
• **11TH: ON THE FIRST DAY** of their fourth US tour, a Beatles press conference is hastily convened in Chicago, Illinois, to counter the damage – including bans and record burnings – being done to the group's reputation by John Lennon's notorious "more popular than Jesus" comment. The group have already been banned from South Africa because of the remark, and they are pelted with garbage on stage when they reach Memphis.
• **15TH: IN CHINA,** in an effort to 'purify' their communism, senior party officials, artists and intellectuals suspected of having pro-Western or pre-revolutionary ideas are being denounced and rounded up by the Red Guard and sent to work in the fields.
• **16TH: A $100,000 CAMPAIGN** is mounted to launch the first single by The Monkees, 'Last Train To Clarksville'.
• **18TH: THE DOORS** sign a provisional recording contract with Elektra Records... On the same day, the first pictures of the Earth taken from the Moon are sent back to the US by Surveyor 1. It's not the first space craft to land successfully on the moon, though – the Soviet Union did that in February, with the un-manned Luna 9.
• **20TH: THE SUPREMES,** The Temptations and Stevie Wonder play at Forest Hills Tennis Stadium, New York.•
• **29TH: FRUSTRATED** by endless touring, with thousands of screaming fans drowning out their primitive amplification, The Beatles play their last live gig at Candlestick Park, San Francisco.

## Spoonful Of Lovin'

• **AUGUST 13TH: THE LOVIN' SPOONFUL'S** first US Number One is 'Summer In The City.' These ex-folkies from Greenwich Village, New York, take their name from the average male ejaculation.

# 1966

## TV, Jim, But Not As We Know It

**B**OLDLY GOING where no television show has gone before – ask any Trekkie about the Mark Of Gideon, Elaan of Troyius or indeed Tribbles if you want to find out exactly where – *Star Trek* begins on September 8th, 1966, as a slightly camp sci-fi show, only emerging in later years as a ratings, licensing, and merchandising monster. The show's creator Gene Roddenberry (born in El Paso, Texas on August 21st, 1921) grew up on such radio, comic-book and movie serials as *The Lone Ranger*, *The Shadow* and *The Green Hornet*. He would go on to fly nearly 100 missions during World War II, winning the Distinguished Flying Cross, before joining the Los Angeles Police Department. While working in their press office, he became involved with television police series and set about becoming a screenwriter. By 1960 he had a contract with Screen Gems. Shortly afterwards, Roddenberry saw *Master of*

**SEPTEMBER**

**OCTOBER**

## Donovan Makes The Most Of It

- **SEPTEMBER 3RD:** **DONOVAN HAS** his only US Number One with 'Sunshine Superman'. The record was a move away from folk towards pop, with the help of producer Mickie Most.

- **6TH: MARGARET SANGER**, an early advocate of birth control dies at 82.
- **10TH: THE SUPREMES** replace Donovan at Number One with 'You Can't Hurry Love'... The Beatles' *Revolver* tops the US album charts, and will do so for six weeks.
- **11TH: PRESIDENT CHARLES DE GAULLE** oversees French nuclear testing at Mururoa Atoll... Meanwhile, two months into its first season, *The Newlywed Game* is being described by critics as an all-time low in television. But is already one of the most popular shows on TV. Created by Chuck Barris (who also devised *The Dating Game*), it's presented by former DJ Bob Eubanks, who promoted the Beatles at the Hollywood Bowl.
- **18TH: THREE MORE**

new TV series have just begun in the US: *Mission Impossible*, *I Dream Of Jeannie*, and *The Green Hornet*, which features a young Bruce Lee as the hero's martial arts-practising sidekick, Kato.
- **20TH: IN BOMBAY**, India, where he is taking sitar lessons from Ravi Shankar, George Harrison becomes the first of The Beatles to meet with the Maharishi Mahesh Yogi.
- **21ST: VARIETY MAGAZINE** publishes a review of young folk singer Joni Mitchell at the Seven Of Clubs, Toronto: "Miss Mitchell, with her high cheekbones, flaxen-color hair and a crystal clear voice, is bound for bigger things."
- **28TH: HAVING MOVED** to London, Jimi Hendrix begins auditions to find the musicians who will form the band he will call The Experience.

- **6TH: THE DRUG LSD** is outlawed in the US.
- **7TH: JOHNNY KIDD**, frontman of The Pirates, is killed in a car crash... And four East Germans dig under the Berlin wall to flee to the West.
- **9TH: JOHN LENNON** and Yoko Ono meet for the first time at the Indica Gallery in London... Meanwhile the US reports that the Vietnam War is now costing $2 billion a month. Nonetheless, the military request yet more troops to be sent.
- **10TH: SIMON & GARFUNKEL** release the album *Parsley, Sage, Rosemary And Thyme* in the US.
- **11TH: GINGER BAKER** collapses after playing a 20-minute drum solo at Sussex University, UK.
- **12TH: BLUESOLOGY**, whose pianist Reg Dwight will later change his name to Elton John, play at the Disco Blue discotheque in Ryde, Isle Of Wight, UK.
- **14TH: GRACE SLICK** performs as vocalist for Jefferson Airplane for the first time.
- **15TH: POLICE ARREST** Hurricane Carter, a former top-ranked middleweight boxer, and charge him with the murder of a bartender and two customers in Paterson, New Jersey. Amid suspicions of a miscarriage of justice, the case will attract high-profile interest, including the Bob Dylan song 'Hurricane'...

- **OCTOBER 15TH: THE FOUR TOPS** (left) have their second US Number One (and their first in the UK) with the Holland/Dozier/Holland number 'Reach Out I'll Be There.'

The World – a kind of *20,000 Leagues Under The Sea* but in an 1870s airship, manned by an idealistic 'band of brothers' – which led to the idea of *Star Trek*. He took it to Desilu, the production company owned by comedienne Lucille Ball and her husband Desi Arnaz. They produced a pilot called 'The Cage,' starring Jeffery Hunter as Captain Christopher Pike. But NBC turned it down, taking the unusual step of ordering a second pilot. Hunter quit, so 'Where No Man Has Gone,' featured William Shatner as Captain James T Kirk. The first real episode, 'Man Trap,' will follow. It does not have an easy run and the series is cancelled in 1969. But it makes a successful transition onto the big screen in the late 1970s, and returns to television as *The Next Generation* in 1987, finally becoming a lucrative and long-term franchise. In later years, Roddenberry will describe Star Trek as "*Wagon Train* to the stars." On October, 1992, a year after his death, a canister of his ashes is put on board the shuttle Columbia, and Gene Roddenberry finally makes his own journey into space.

## Say It Loud...

- **OCTOBER 30TH:  THE BLACK PANTHER PARTY** for Self-Defense is founded by black activists Huey Newton and Bobby Seale. Their aggressive stance, and list of revolutionary demands, attracts opposition from older civil rights campaigners, but reflects a new attitude among some black Americans.

NOVEMBER                    DECEMBER

- **16TH:  FOLK SINGER** Joan Baez is arrested at an anti-Vietnam war demonstration in Oakland, California, and jailed for ten days.
- **22ND:  THE BEACH BOYS** release their new single, the ground-breaking 'Good Vibrations'... The same day, in the UK, double agent George Blake (serving 42 years for spying) scales the outer wall of Wormwood Scrubs jail in London, using a homemade rope ladder strengthened with knitting needles... And tragedy strikes in Aberfan in Wales as 144 people, 116 of them children, are killed when a slag heap made of mining waste collapses onto the village after being soaked by constant heavy rain, engulfing the local school and several nearby houses.
- **27TH:  CHINA EXPLODES** an A-bomb in a guided missile.

## Sing A Song Of Disney

- **DECEMBER 15TH:  WALT DISNEY DIES,** having been ill with cancer for some time. Though the Disney empire was obviously built on animation, the movies' musical soundtracks were always crucial. As movie critic Leonard Maltin put it: "Music was the foundation of Walt Disney's success." This was clear from his early *Silly Symphony* and *Mickey Mouse* shorts to *Snow White*, *Pinocchio* (which prompted the first ever "original soundtrack" album, released in 1940), *Fantasia*, *Mary Poppins*, up to *The Lion King* and beyond.

- **5TH:  AS INTENDED,** The Monkees reach Number One in the US Top 40 singles chart with 'Last Train To Clarksville'.
- **8TH:  RONALD WILSON REAGAN** is elected governor of California... And Edward W. Brooke, attorney general of the state of Massachusetts, wins a seat in the US Senate, the first black person to do so in 85 years.
- **10TH:  PRIME MINISTER HAROLD WILSON** announces that Britain will join the European Economic Community. It doesn't happen until 1973.
- **11TH:  A PARTY** is held in London to welcome Motown act The Four Tops to the UK. Guests include John Lennon and George Harrison of The Beatles, Mick Jagger, Keith Richard and Charlie Watts of the Rolling Stones, Donovan and Eric Burdon.

- **12TH:  RIOTS ON** Sunset Strip, Los Angeles, in which teenagers protest against a police curfew in the area, inspire Stephen Stills of Buffalo Springfield to write his song 'For What It's Worth.'
- **18TH:  PINK FLOYD** play at the *Philadelic Music For Simian Hominids* event at Hornsey College of Art, London.
- **19TH:  THE SUPREMES** have their eighth US Number One with 'You Keep Me Hanging On.'
- **22ND:  BLUES LEGEND** Mississippi John Hurt dies, at 73.
- **25TH:  THE JIMI HENDRIX EXPERIENCE** make their London debut at a The Bag O' Nails.
- **27TH:  THE YARDBIRDS** US tour ends badly. Jimmy Page and Jeff Beck threaten to quit the band.

- **1ST:  TOM JONES**, having sung the theme song to the latest James Bond movie, *Thunderball*, starts a seven-week run at Number One in the UK with a tear-jerker, 'The Green Green Grass Of Home'.
- **3RD:  RAY CHARLES** is convicted on charges of possession of heroin and marijuana and given a five-year suspended sentence and $10,000 fine.
- **10TH:  THE ELECTRIC PRUNES** release their classic psychedelic single, 'I Had Too Much To Dream Last Night.'
- **14TH:  BIG BROTHER & THE HOLDING COMPANY**, featuring Janis Joplin, record a single, 'The Last Time,' for Mainstream Records.
- **16TH:  THE JIMI HENDRIX EXPERIENCE** release their debut single, 'Hey Joe,' in the UK.
- **17TH:  THE CHINESE** government claims that US planes have attacked its embassy in Hanoi, Vietnam.
- **24TH:  TOMMY JAMES** & The Shondells record 'I Think We're Alone Now,' their fourth US hit, which will reach Number One in 1967.
- **31ST:  THE MONKEES'** 'I'm A Believer,' written by struggling songwriter and performer Neil Diamond, is the new US Number One single.
- **23RD:  INFLUENTIAL PSYCHEDELIC** club UFO opens in London... And the last edition of UK pop show *Ready Steady Go* is screened. The rights to the archive material are subsequently bought by Dave Clark (of The Dave Clark Five), who suspiciously appear in almost every show when edited selections are televised in the mid 1980s.
- **27TH:  REPORTS BEGIN** to emerge of heavy civilian casualties in bombed-out Hanoi.
- **29TH:  BRITAIN LAUNCHES** a new peace initiative in an attempt to end the long-running war in Vietnam. It clearly fails.

- **DECEMBER 12TH:  LONDON PREMIERE** of the movie *Thunderbirds Are Go*, based on the successful Gerry Anderson TV series, spinning sci-fi adventure stories around string-operated puppets to surprisingly popular effect. The movie features 'guest' puppets such as The Shadows...

# 1967

## DOORS BREAK ON THROUGH

This is the year The Doors make a name for themselves beyond the Los Angeles area, releasing their groundbreaking debut album, and the Number One single 'Light My Fire.' Taking their name from Aldous Huxley's work *The Doors Of Perception*, a study of his own experiments with hallucinogenic drugs, the band is controversial from the start. Singer and lyricist Jim Morrison – seen here in a quieter on-stage moment – enthusiastically models himself after the greek god of wine and orgiastic excess, Dionysos (although he thankfully draws the line at the human sacrifice part). Morrison's uncompromising stand, coupled with a rampant drink and drug consumption, inevitably bring conflict with police forces and local authorities, who make various attempts to curb his apparently outrageous and lewd conduct, on and off the stage, but only succeed in intensifying the singer's legendary status and obsessive following.

# 1967

## January–April

### Gee Men

- **APRIL 14TH:** "THE MOST SIGNIFICANT TALENT since The Beatles," claim Polydor Records, releasing 'New York Mining Disaster 1941,' the major label debut single by the Bee Gees. After starting out in Australia, they move back to Britain before achieving a string of hits around the world in 1967 and 1968, including 'Words,' 'Massachusetts,' and 'I've Gotta Get A Message To You.'

## Young Rebels

- **FEBRUARY 4TH: BUFFALO SPRINGFIELD**, the influential Los Angeles band co-founded by 22-year-old Canadian Neil Young (seen here) and Texan Stephen Stills, release the single 'For What It's Worth' in the US. The song is widely adopted as an anthem for the disillusioned, anti-war youth of America. Three decades later, its sparse riff will become a popular choice for the sampling generation, creating new tracks for various artists in the 1990s. Stephen Stills, who originally wrote the number, was earlier turned down at an audition to form The Monkees – they say because his teeth weren't good enough – and the role was given instead to his friend and blond lookalike Peter Tork.

## JANUARY

- **1ST: A GIANT FREAKOUT** takes place at London's Roundhouse. Bands on the bill include Pink Floyd, The Who, and The Move.
- **2ND: AN AGREEMENT** comes into force between Elvis Presley and his manager, Colonel Tom Parker, which awards the colonel an astonishing 50 per cent of Presley's recording royalties and movie earnings.
- **3RD: CARL WILSON** of the Beach Boys refuses to join the US Army after being drafted, claiming his right to be a conscientious objector.
- **5TH: RAUL DE THUIN**, a 76-year-old Belgian, is paid by the American Philatelic Society to stop forging stamps. Over the years Thuin has sold his work to unsuspecting collectors for millions of dollars, but as the APS can't seem to stop him it decides to pay him off instead.
- **13TH: THE BEATLES'** manager Brian Epstein publicly announces a merger between his company, NEMS, and RSO, owned by entrepreneur Robert Stigwood... The same day, in an interview with UK magazine NME, Cliff Richard says he intends to retire from music and teach religious instruction in schools. He doesn't say when, and 36 years later he still hasn't.
- **14TH: 20,000 HIPPIES** turn out for The Human Be-In at Golden Gate Park, San Francisco, with music from Jefferson Airplane, Big Brother and the Holding Company, and Quicksilver Messenger Service. Similar events are held on the same day in Los Angeles and New York City.
- **15TH: THE FIRST SUPER BOWL** is played, bringing together the champions of the American Football League and the National Football League, at the memorial Coliseum, Los Angeles, California. The Green Bay Packers beat the Kansas City Chiefs 35-10... And tonight, after much argument, The Rolling Stones sing a censored version of their new single, 'Let's Spend The Night Together' (changing the chorus to 'Let's Spend Some Time Together'), on the *Ed Sullivan Show*. For all the host's complaints about their attitude and appearance, he knows the band are a popular draw – this is the Stones' fifth appearance on his show since 1964.
- **21ST: THE FIRST BLACK GOVERNMENT** takes power in the Bahamas, which has been a British colony for nearly 200 years.

## FEBRUARY

- **1ST: THE BEATLES START WORK** on what will become the title track to the album *Sgt Pepper's Lonely Hearts Club Band* in EMI Studio 2, Abbey Road, London... Meanwhile, plans are scrapped to build massive dams in the Grand Canyon, Arizona, US.
- **10TH: THE BEACH BOYS**, ? And The Mysterians (of '96 Tears' fame), The Left Banke, The Electric Prunes, and Keith (who's just had a hit with '98.6') play at the Convention Hall, Miami Beach, Florida.
- **13TH: THERE'S PANDEMONIUM** at London's Heathrow Airport as fans try to get a glimpse of The Monkees arriving for their first promotional tour of Britain.
- **14TH: THE HOLLIES PLAY** at The Whiskey-A-Go-Go in Los Angeles. In the audience are David Crosby of The Byrds and Steve Stills of Buffalo Springfield, who decide to steal Graham Nash and form a band with him.
- **18TH: ROBERT OPPENHEIMER**, scientific director of the project to build the atom bomb, dies age 62. After seeing the effects of the bomb on Japan, he opposed the development of the hydrogen bomb and had his security clearance taken away. He went on to campaign for arms control.
- **20TH: KURT COBAIN**, future leader of Nirvana, is born in Gray's Harbour Community Hospital, Aberdeen, Washington.
- **25TH: SELF-CONFESSED BOSTON** strangler Albert DeSalvo escapes from the mental ward of a correctional institution, but is immediately apprehended.

## Do Right Woman

• **WHEN ARETHA FRANKLIN** arrives at FAME Studios in Muscle Shoals, Alabama, on 24th January, 1967, she is on the brink of a breakthrough. Discovered by John Hammond, who has been instrumental in the careers of everyone from Billie Holiday to Bob Dylan, the gospel-raised Franklin has not responded well to the jazz idiom he favors for her. But then Atlantic Records producer Jerry Wexler books her into FAME – it stands for Florence Alabama Music Emporium – a remote studio he has previously used in concocting a string of soul hits. On the first day of a projected one week album session, Aretha and the house band manage one track, the magnificent 'I Never Loved A Man (The Way I Love You),' and part of the b-side, 'Do Right Woman, Do Right Man.' Then a drunken, racially-charged dispute breaks out between Franklin's then-husband Ted White and one of the musicians. Studio owner Rick Hall attempts to calm White, and makes things worse. Wexler ends the session. Recording only restarts, in New York, after tempers have cooled. Wexler never uses FAME again, but it has done the trick. Aretha tops the R&B charts for nine weeks and rides high in the pop charts. Moreover, she has found her sound. Atlantic releases an album bearing the same title as the single, and carefully steers the Queen of Soul towards the album-buying rock audience.

**MARCH**

**APRIL**

---

Though he has admitted the crimes, he is not formally convicted, but sentenced on other serious charges for which there is more evidence. A controversial movie starring Tony Curtis as *The Boston Strangler* will be released in 1968. DeSalvo himself is murdered in prison in 1973.

• **FEBRUARY 3RD:** **MARVIN GAYE** begins recording 'I Heard It Through The Grapevine' for Tamla Records in Detroit, Michigan. Written by Motown songsmiths Norman Whitfield and Barrett Strong, this much-covered track is not released by Gaye for more than 18 months, which leaves time for Gladys Knight to jump in and take her version to Number Two in the US charts in December 1967. In the meantime, Gaye records and releases two albums and a dozen singles – including 'Ain't No Mountain High Enough' and 'Your Precious Love' – with Tammi Terrell (seen here with Marvin). This inspired partnership is only ended by Terrell's tragically premature death from a brain tumour, in 1970, at just 23 years old.

• **2ND:** **AT THE NINTH GRAMMY AWARDS,** Best Contemporary Group Performance goes to the Mamas & The Papas for 'Monday Monday.'

• **3RD:** **AS PART OF A PACKAGE TOUR** headed by Roy Orbison and The Small Faces, Jeff Beck unveils the Jeff Beck Group, featuring vocalist Rod Stewart, bassist Ron Wood and drummer Ray Cook, at The Astoria, Finsbury Park, London.

• **4TH:** **A PROMOTIONAL** film for Cream's 'I Feel Free' is banned from US TV because authorities believe people may be offended by the band appearing dressed as monks.

• **9TH:** **THE WIFE** and daughter of Soviet dictator Joseph Stalin walk into the US embassy in New Delhi, India, and announce to astonished ambassador Chester Bowles that they wish to defect to the West.

• **10TH:** **THE WORLD'S FIRST** confirmed set of octuplets is born, in Mexico City... And the Grateful Dead release their eponymous debut album.

• **12TH:** **INDIRA GANDHI** is re-elected as Indian prime minister.

• **15TH:** **THE VELVET UNDERGROUND** release their debut album, *The Velvet Underground And Nico*, in the US. Protegees of Andy Warhol, they get him to design the cover, which features a 'peelable' banana painting with the instruction "Peel slowly and see."

• **26TH:** **NEW YORKERS** have their own version of the Be-In, first seen in San Francisco, as 10,000 turn Central Park into a

• **APRIL 8TH:** **SANDIE SHAW** (above) becomes the first British act to win the *Eurovision Song Contest*. Performing barefoot at the annual event (this year in Vienna, Austria), she wins with 'Puppet On A String'.

kite, balloon and bubble-strewn Day-Glo theme park.

• **31ST:** **DIVERS ARE INSPECTING** the wreck of the giant Torrey Canyon oil tanker which went aground some two weeks ago spilling 30,000 tonnes of oil onto the coast of Cornwall in the UK. Bombs and Napalm were dropped to try and sink the tanker and burn off the oil, but more than 100 miles of scenic coastline have been polluted... The Jimi Hendrix Experience grab the headlines tonight, as Jimi sets fire to his guitar on the first night of a Walker Brothers package tour at the Astoria, Finsbury Park, London.

*Andy Warhol*

• **1ST:** **UN SECRETARY GENERAL** U Thant renews his call for an end to the war in Vietnam. He's ignored as well. Three days later the US loses its 500th warplane in the conflict.

• **2ND:** **STEVE WINWOOD** leaves the Spencer Davis Group to form Traffic.

• **3RD:** **CREAM START** two days recording sessions at Atlantic Studios, New York City, during which they record 'Strange Brew' and 'Lawdy Mama' with producer Felix Pappalardi and engineer Tom Dowd.

• **7TH:** **THE TURTLES**, The Buckinghams, Tommy James & The Shondells, The Electric Prunes, Lou Christie, Bryan Hyland, The Royal Guardsmen, The Blues Magoos, and others play at the Memorial Coliseum, Jacksonville, Florida.

• **13TH:** **POLICE USE TEAR GAS** and batons to dispel a riot when The Rolling Stones play their first gig behind the Iron Curtain in Warsaw, Poland. 100 fans are injured.

• **12TH:** **THE US GREYHOUND** Bus Company starts to run tourist trips through San Francisco's 'Hippyland.'

• **15TH:** **FRANK AND NANCY SINATRA** reach Number One in the UK and US simultaneously with 'Somethin' Stupid.'

• **16TH:** **THE NATIONAL CATHOLIC REPORTER** newspaper publishes leaks from a commission on birth control, appointed by the Pope, which show that most of its members would allow contraception for married couples in some circumstances.

• **24TH:** **SOVIET COSMONAUT** Vladimir Komarov dies as his craft crashes due to a tangled parachute... The same day, the new military regime in Greece bans miniskirts (on women) and long hair (on men), and shortly afterwards, beards (on tourists, male or female). The ban will stay in place for several years.

• **25TH:** **KONRAD ADENAUER**, West Germany's first post-war chancellor – widely credited with leading his country back to economic prosperity – dies aged 91, having only retired in 1963.

• **29TH:** **THE 14-HOUR** Technicolor Dream is held at Alexandra Palace in north London, featuring Pink Floyd, John's Children (with Marc Bolan, pre-Tyrannosaurus Rex), Tomorrow (with Steve Howe, later of Yes), and The Flies.

# Happening In Monterey

**J**UNE 16TH: *THE MONTEREY POP FESTIVAL* begins at the county fairgrounds in Monterey, northern California, marking the start of what becomes known as The Summer Of Love. Organised largely by John Phillips of The Mamas & The Papas (though he didn't initiate the project), the three-day event features Buffalo Springfield, The Grateful Dead, The Association, Simon & Garfunkel, The Byrds, Big Brother & The Holding Company, The Animals, Ravi Shankar, Otis Redding, The Who, and Jimi Hendrix. The Beach Boys have withdrawn from their Saturday evening headline spot, citing pressure of recording work, and also Carl Wilson's imminent court case for draft evasion. It's estimated that more than 50,000 people turn up, though only 20,000 buy tickets and are allowed in. Not as famous as the later *Woodstock* festival, Monterey will come to be seen as a better and more enjoyable gig for all concerned. It's also a landmark event for several of the performers. Janis Joplin's manager doesn't want her performance filmed, but fortunately for posterity she persuades him otherwise. Otis Redding wins over a whole new audience of rock fans. And The Who, not widely known in the States beforehand, crash through 'My Generation,' trashing their gear and sending a wake-up call to the more laidback concert-goers. Most memorable, however, is the triumphant US homecoming of Jimi Hendrix, mesmerising his audience and iconically setting fire to his Stratocaster guitar at the climax of 'Wild Thing'.

## MAY

## JUNE

- **1ST: ELVIS PRESLEY** marries Priscilla Beaulieu at the Aladdin Hotel, Las Vegas, Nevada.
- **3rd: DESPITE** a request from General Westmoreland, the US commander, President Johnson refuses to increase the number of US troops in Vietnam. He will change his mind in August and send another 45,000.
- **5TH: SCOTT MCKENZIE** releases the flower power anthem 'San Francisco (Be Sure To Wear Flowers In Your Hair),' written by John Phillips of The Mamas & The Papas.
- **8TH: MUHAMMAD ALI** is indicted for draft evasion. As he puts it, "I ain't got no quarrel with those Vietcong." He's found guilty, fined $10,000 and given a five-year jail sentence. He avoids prison on appeal, but loses his WBA title and boxing license, and is out of the ring for three years.

The conviction is quashed in 1971.
- **11TH: ROLLING STONES** Mick Jagger, Brian Jones and Keith Richards are all now facing drugs charges.
- **20TH: THE YOUNG RASCALS** top the US singles chart with 'Groovin.'
- **28TH: 65-YEAR-OLD** yachtsman Francis Chichester completes his epic solo voyage around the world, arriving back at Plymouth, UK, in his yacht Gypsy Moth IV.
- **29TH: THE JIMI HENDRIX EXPERIENCE**, Pink Floyd, The Move and The Cream play at the Barbecue 67, in the Tulip Bulb Auction Hall, Spalding, UK.
- **30TH: IBO LEADER** Lieutenant-Colonel Odumegwu Ojukwu, declares the independence of Biafra, Nigeria's eastern region and homeland of the Ibo people. The move follows 18 months of tribal violence in which Ibos living in other regions have been the principal victims.

- **MAY 16TH: PRESIDENT DE GAULLE** of France vetoes Britain's entry into the European Economic Community (EEC), delivering his much-quoted 'Non!'

- **1ST: THE BEATLES** release their new album, 'Sgt Pepper's Lonely Hearts Club Band,' in the UK. It goes straight to Number One, where it stays for 23 weeks (in the US it stays at the top for 15 weeks)... Meanwhile John Lennon's newly painted Rolls-Royce (with psychedelic fairground artwork by Dutch design team The Fool) has been set upon by an old lady as it drives through London. Offended by the sacrilegious vandalism of such a British institution, she swings her umbrella at the car and shouts, "You swine!"
- **2ND: DAVID BOWIE'S** debut album is released on Deram Records, featuring typically quirky early tracks such as 'My Little Bombadier,' 'There Is A Happy Land,' and 'Come And Buy Me Toys'. Still no joy in the charts... 'Space Oddity' is two years away yet.
- **7TH: THREE MEMBERS** of San Francisco band Moby Grape are found with schoolgirls in the back of their car and are arrested for "contributing to the delinquency of minors."

## King Of The Court

- **JULY 5TH: BILLIE JEAN KING** wins the ladies' title at the Wimbledon Lawn Tennis Championship in the UK – as well as most other tournaments in the world this year. She will go on to acquire a total of 20 Wimbledon titles, a record held until Martina Navratilova equals it in 2003.

- **8TH: PROCOL HARUM'S** 'A Whiter Shade Of Pale', with suitably obscure psychedelic lyrics and a melody borrowed from Bach, takes up residence at the top of the UK singles chart for six weeks. It reaches Number Five in the US.
- **10TH: AFTER JUST SIX DAYS** the war between Israel and its Arab neighbours ends when Israel agrees to a hurriedly arranged UN ceasefire. Israel has captured extensive territory from Egypt, Jordan and Syria, including Jerusalem, the West Bank, the Gaza Strip and the Golan Heights. There is little hope the peace will last.
- **19TH: IN AN INTERVIEW** carried by the *Daily Mirror*, a UK tabloid newspaper, Paul McCartney of The Beatles admits to having taken LSD.
- **25TH: OUR WORLD** becomes the first television programme to be broadcast worldwide via satellite. The highlight of the show is The Beatles live performance of 'All You Need Is Love,' which John Lennon wrote especially for the show. His brief from the BBC was "Keep it simple."
- **27TH: MICK JAGGER** and Keith Richard are found guilty of drug offences and sentenced to three months in jail, prompting The Times to run the famous editorial, 'Who breaks a butterfly on a wheel?'. In support, The Who record and release two Jagger-Richards songs, 'Under My Thumb' and 'The Last Time', billing themselves as 'The Who In Support Of Mick & Keith'. A month later both successfully appeal.
- **29TH: BLONDE BOMBSHELL** Jayne Mansfield dies in a car crash.

# Which One's Pink?

• **MAY 23RD: THE PINK FLOYD** record their breakthrough single 'See Emily Play' at Sound Techniques, Chelsea, London. It's written by singer/ guitarist Syd Barrett (on the right in this photo), who joined Roger Waters, Nick Mason and Rick Wright – originally performing as the Architectural Abdabs – in 1965. Barrett renamed the band after Georgia bluesmen Pink Anderson and Floyd Council, and Pink Floyd (originally The Pink Floyd Sound) soon became the hippest band on London's psychedelic scene. Their debut album, *The Piper At The Gates Of Dawn,* is released in August to great critical and cult acclaim – but within a year, Syd's grip on reality becomes a worry...

**JULY**

**AUGUST**

• **2ND: AFTER SEEING** Cream play at London's Saville Theatre, George Harrison's wife Pattie Boyd is introduced to Eric Clapton at a party in 24 Chapel Street, the home of Beatles' manager Brian Epstein.

• **6TH: FIGHTING BREAKS** out between Nigerian troops and the breakaway Biafran Army.

• **7TH: THE BEATLES** release their new single, 'All You Need Is Love/Baby, You're A Rich Man.'

• **8TH: ACTRESS VIVIEN LEIGH**, best known as Scarlett O'Hara in Gone With The Wind, and former wife of Laurence Olivier, dies of tuberculosis, age 53. The couple had married in 1940 and divorced in 1960.

• **9TH: LOVE**

• **AUGUST 27TH: BRIAN EPSTEIN**, the Beatles manager since 1961, dies from an "accidental" overdose of Carbitral sleeping tablets. He is just 32.

**BEGIN** recording their third album, *Forever Changes*, in Sunset Sound Recorders, Los Angeles.

• **14TH: THE NATIONAL GUARD** is called in to quell racial disturbances in Newark, New Jersey. The death toll over the following four days hits 26, with more than 1,500 hurt and 1,000 arrested... Ten days later, race riots erupt in Detroit, where in three days 38 are killed and hundreds arrested as federal troops intervene.

• **15TH: 'SOCIETY'S CHILD,'** a controversial inter-racial love song by teenage singer-songwriter Janis Ian, peaks at Number 14 on the US Top 40.

• **16TH: THE JIMI HENDRIX EXPERIENCE** pull out of a totally unsuitable supporting slot on The Monkees' US tour. He's recently been criticised by the Daughters Of The American Revolution, who claim his act is "too erotic."

• **17TH: JOHN COLTRANE**, the leading exponent of 'modal' improvisation, dies at the age of 40. Hugely influential, Coltrane constantly changed musical languages, yet his playing was always rooted in gospel, blues and an attempt to emulate the human voice. In 1971 the African Orthodox Church Of John Coltrane is established in San Francisco.

• **21ST: ALBERT JOHN MVUMBI LUTHULI** dies when he is struck by a train. A South African civil rights leader, member of the ANC and advocate of non violent rejection of racism, he received the Nobel peace prize in 1961.

• **26TH: FRANCE'S PRESIDENT DE GAULLE** causes consternation by calling for the liberation of French Canadians, declaring "Long live free Quebec" (in French, naturally) on a visit to the Montreal World Fair – Expo 67.

• **29TH: THE DOORS' SINGLE** 'Light My Fire' hits the top of the US charts.

• **1ST: STOKELY CARMICHAEL**, former chairman of the Student Nonviolent Co-ordinating Committee, has called for a black revolution in the US, insisting: "They taught us to kill [in Vietnam], now the struggle is in the streets of the United States."

• **5TH: VAN MORRISON** releases his first solo single, 'Brown Eyed Girl.'

• **9TH: "I HAVE HIGH HOPES** of dying in my prime," Joe Orton confided to his diary in July, 1967. Less than one month later, Britain's most promising comic playwright is murdered by his lover Kenneth Halliwell in their London flat. Halliwell then kills himself with an overdose of 22 Nembutal sleeping pills, washed down with the juice from a tin of grapefruit.

• **13TH: FLEETWOOD MAC** make their live debut at the National Jazz & Blues Festival, Windsor, UK.

• **15TH: THE MARINE OFFENCES ACT** comes into force in the UK, outlawing 'pirate' radio stations, which have been broadcasting from ships and redundant military installations off-shore. Radio London packs up after playing its last record, The Beatles' 'A Day In The Life,' but Radio Caroline continues to defy the law. Not at all coincidentally, the BBC's new pop music station, Radio One, is launched the following month, having hired some of the same pirate DJs.

• **19TH: KNOW RADIO** in Denver, Colorado, bans all Beatles' records because they apparently advocate 'trip-taking.'

• **26TH: 'ODE TO BILLY JOE'** by Bobbie Gentry (above) reaches Number One in the US.

• **27TH: DIANA ROSS** &The Supremes headline the First Annual Motown Sales Convention at the Roostertail nightclub, Detroit, Michigan. Other acts appearing include Stevie Wonder, The Spinners and Gladys Knight & The Pips.

# Old Toons Are The Best

**SEPTEMBER 1967: MGM** ceases production of the *Tom & Jerry* cartoon series, which has been made almost continuously since 1940. It was originally made by the Hanna/Barbera/Quimby team, until 1957 when Hanna & Barbera were let go and set up on their own. After several years in the wilderness, Tom & Jerry get a new lease of life thanks to the great Chuck Jones (of Bugs Bunny and Roadrunner fame), who becomes available for work after Warner Brothers close their cartoon division in the mid 1960s. In its last year, the show explores such modern themes as robots, space stations, satellites, missiles and hi-tech spying, but MGM still sees no future for short films. The pair largely survive in rerun form, until *The Tom & Jerry Kids* in the 1990s... Music is vital in animation, and three composers stand out: Hoyt Curtin, whose credits include *The Flintstones* and *Top Cat*; his pioneering predecessor at Warners, Carl Stalling; and of course Scott Bradley at MGM, best known for his inventive orchestrations behind Tom & Jerry's adventures – from manic chases to getting hit in the face by a garden rake.

**SEPTEMBER**

**OCTOBER**

- **1ST:** THE ALBUM *Are You Experienced* by The Jimi Hendrix Experience, is released in the US.
- **2ND:** MITCH RYDER & The Detroit Wheels play at the Village Theatre, New York City, supported by Vanilla Fudge.
- **9TH:** SAM AND DAVE release a new single, 'Soul Man,' in the US.
- **12TH:** CALIFORNIAN GOVERNOR Ronald Reagan suggests leaking news to the Viet Cong that America is ready to use nuclear weapons, in an effort to bring a quick end to the long-running and unpopular war. His suggestions are not widely held to be helpful... And Canned Heat begin a 13-day season at the Café Au Go Go, New York City.
- **14TH:** THE US announces plans to give India $1.3 million to buy contraceptives.
- **17TH:** FORTY-TWO SPECTATORS are killed and more than 600 injured in riots at a soccer match in Turkey... And Jim Morrison of The Doors is asked to amend the line "Girl we couldn't get much higher" in their song 'Light My Fire' for transmission of the *Ed Sullivan Show* in New York. He refuses, and the song is broadcast intact, much to Ed's annoyance.

- **23RD:** THE BOX TOPS reach Number One in the US singles chart with 'The Letter'... And Ray Charles releases 'In The Heat Of The Night,' theme song from the movie starring Rod Steiger and Sidney Poitier (below).

- **OCTOBER 17TH:** THE ROCK MUSICAL *Hair* ('The American Tribal Love Rock Musical') opens in New York for a limited run of six weeks at the new Shakespeare Public Theater. It's the first time so much naked flesh (and hair) has been seen on a 'legimate' theatre stage, and causes immediate outcry. Yet by the time it transfers to the Biltmore Theater on Broadway in April 1968 it's so popular it runs non-stop until July 1972 – a total of 1,742 performances. Created by two unemployed actors, James Rado and Gerome Ragni, with a score by Galt McDermot, *Hair* also introduces us to some epoch-reflecting songs like 'Aquarius' (as in "This is the dawning of the age of...").

- **1ST:** TRAFFIC'S FIRST LIVE GIG in the UK takes place at the Saville Theatre, London, on the same bill as Pink Floyd.
- **6TH:** *THE DEATH OF HIPPY* event is held in San Francisco, to mark the crass commercialisation which has overtaken the ideals of the Love & Peace generation.
- **7TH:** 'HIGHER AND HIGHER' by Jackie Wilson reaches Number One on the *Billboard* R&B chart.
- **8TH:** CLEMENT ATTLEE, ex-British Prime Minister dies, aged 84. His landslide-winning post-WWII Labour government put through through the most radical and ambitious set of social reforms and anti-poverty measures the country has ever seen, including the National Health Service, great expansion of public housing, secondary education, and a new National Insurance scheme.
- **9TH:** LATIN AMERICAN revolutionary hero Ernesto Guevara is

reported to have been killed by Bolivian troops. An Argentinian by birth (and a doctor by training) Guevara was Fidel Castro's right-hand man in the Cuban revolution. His image will adorn the bedroom walls of many a student for years to come.
- **16TH:** THE HEAD of the US Food & Drug Administration (FDA), Dr James L. Goddard, equates the dangers of marijuana with those of alcohol, and calls for the removal of criminal penalties for possession of the drug. His advice is ignored.
- **20TH:** THE FIRST COUNTRY MUSIC Association Awards show, hosted by Bobbie Gentry, chooses Eddy Arnold as Entertainer Of The Year.
- **21ST:** AS AN ANTI-VIETNAM WAR protest, Allen Ginsberg, The Fugs, Norman Mailer and others attempt to levitate The Pentagon in Washington, DC. They fail, but they do get some valuable publicity.
- **25TH:** A BILL LEGALISING

abortion for the first time is passed by the British parliament in London. The US follows suit in 1973.

- **THE FOOL** are a busy bunch these days, not only painting cars and property (like the Beatles Apple boutique, and the Aquarius Theater in LA when the musical *Hair* arrives there), but also several star guitars, for the likes of The Beatles and Cream – including Eric Clapton's famous 1961 Gibson SG (right).

## Folk Hero

- **OCTOBER 3RD: WOODY GUTHRIE** dies at the age of 55, having suffered from the inherited degenerative diease Huntington's chorea for over ten years. A major influence on Bob Dylan and countless other singer-songwriters (you can see from this photo he was a proto-punk too – his guitar carried the legend, 'This Machine Kills Fascists'), he was also a great and tireless campaigner for social justice and reform. He also had an unusually liberal attitude to the business aspects of music, particularly song publishing – witness the following excerpt from one of the small mimeographed songbooks he would send to people who wanted the lyrics to his songs: "This song is copyrighted in the US, under seal of copyright #154085, for a period of 28 years, and anybody caught singin' it without our permission will be mighty good friends of ourn, cause we don't give a dern. Publish it. Write it. Sing it. Swing to it. Yodel it. We wrote it, that's all we wanted to do. – W.G."

# 1967
### September–December

## NOVEMBER

- **4TH: DIONNE WARWICK** enters the US singles chart with the Burt Bacharach-Hal David song, 'I Say A Little Prayer,' which will be her biggest hit to date, peaking at Number Four. In the UK, the track isn't a hit until Aretha Franklin covers it in August 1968.
- **5TH: MONKEE DAVY JONES** opens a clothing store in New York, called Zilch.
- **8TH: HARRY NILSSON** (below) records the Fred Neil

song 'Everybody's Talkin'' at RCA Studio B, Los Angeles. It will be used on the soundtrack of the movie *Midnight Cowboy* in 1969, when it will become the first hit for Nilsson, who has by then dropped the Harry.
- **9TH: *ROLLING STONE*,** America's first national rock magazine, is launched in San Francisco, giving away a free roach clip with every issue. The first cover carries a picture of John Lennon making the movie *How I Won The War*, and an editorial piece about who made money from the *Monterey Festival*. Publisher Jann Wenner gathers together some of the most literate and informed writers around – including Ralph J. Gleason, Hunter S. Thompson, Lester Bangs, and later Cameron Crowe, future Hollywood director – and they fearlessly opine on all issues of concern to the youth of America, with rock'n'roll as a barometer of social change.
- **11TH: THREE US STAFF** sergeants are released by the Viet Cong to display solidarity with the struggle of black Americans.
- **17TH: A TWO-DAY LOVE-IN** is held at the Palais De Sports in Paris. Soft Machine play, as do Dantalion's Chariot, featuring one Andy Somers (who will later resurface as Andy Summers in the Police).
- **21ST: JOAN BAEZ** sings for reporters and is then arrested and charged with disturbing the peace at the latest in a long line of anti-draft demonstrations in Oakland, California.
- **25TH: THE NEW US NUMBER ONE** single is 'Incense And Peppermints' by the Strawberry Alarm Clock. (Psychedelia is alive and well.)
- **29TH: JOE RONCORONI** of Jonjo Music in London writes to Peter Gabriel, a pupil of the exclusive Charterhouse private boarding school, about his unsigned band Genesis, inviting him to a meeting in London. The band will eventually sign to the label, which is owned by pop 'personality' Jonathan King.

## DECEMBER

- **2ND: *PISCES AQUARIUS CAPRICORN & JONES*** becomes the fourth US Number One album in a year for The Monkees. On the same day, their 'Daydream Believer' tops the singles chart.
- **3RD: 53-YEAR-OLD SHOPKEEPER** Loius Washkansky has his life prolonged by some 18 days by becoming the first heart transplant patient. The operation, which takes six hours, is performed by Dr Christiaan Barnard in Cape Town, South Africa. Fortunately the life expectancy of patients undergoing this operation improves with practice – the record is now over 20 years.
- **4TH: THE APPLE BOUTIQUE,** owned by The Beatles, opens on Baker Street in central London, complete with psychedelic mural by, yes, The Fool.
- **9TH: NICOLAE CEAUCESCU** becomes chairman of the Romanian Communist State Council – essentially dictator of Romania. He wins popular support for his independent political course, which openly challenges the dominance of the Soviet Union over Romania. Twenty years later, things will be very different... Meanwhile, tonight, Pink Floyd appear at the recently opened Middle Earth club in London. They've played over 300 gigs this year.

## Shipping News

- **DECEMBER 8TH: AFTER 31 YEARS** at sea, The Queen Mary arrives at the end of her last cruise. Sailing into Long Beach, California, she becomes a permanent fixture as the Queen Mary Seaport, a floating hotel/restaurant/ shopping complex. Her sister ship, the Queen Elizabeth, has a more dramatic fate, when she is destroyed by fire while undergoing a refit in Hong Kong harbour in 1972. Her replacement, the QE2, launched in 1967, will remain the flagship of shipping giants Cunard for the next 37 years.

- **DECEMBER 10TH: FOUR DAYS AFTER RECORDING** his vocals on '(Sittin' On) The Dock Of The Bay,' Otis Redding is killed (along with four of his touring band The Bar-Kays) when his plane crashes into Lake Monoma, Wisconsin, in the US. Shocked and distressed, his good friends in the Stax studio team, guitarist/producer Steve Cropper and the rest of Booker T & The MGs, nevertheless soon face the agonising task of completing the backing track and mixing the song for release. It'll become an international hit – Otis's first, and last, Number One.

- **10TH: THE WORLD'S FIRST 'COMMERCIAL'** nuclear blast is detonated by El Paso Natural Gas in New Mexico.
- **13TH: GREECE'S KING CONSTANTINE II** flees to Rome after an abortive attempt to regain control comes to nothing.
- **16TH: THE BAND BLOOD SWEAT & TEARS** is launched before 450 invited guests at The Scene, New York City....
- **19TH: THE COWSILLS** earn a US gold disc for the hit single 'The Rain, The Park And Other Things'.
- **21ST: THE TEMPTATIONS** release a new single, 'I Wish It Would Rain,' in the US.
- **24TH: CREEDENCE CLEARWATER REVIVAL** form in San Francisco.

# 1968

## January–April

• MARCH 19TH: WELSH SINGER TOM 'THE VOICE' JONES starts the first of several cabaret stints in Las Vegas, Nevada. It's said that one of these shows, at the Flamingo club, influences Elvis Presley to resurrect his live performing skills and head in the same direction, abandoning his floundering movie career. Jones – a long-time Elvis fan – first met his hero in 1965, and was amazed to find Elvis was a fan of his too. The pair remained friends till Elvis's death.

### JANUARY

• 1ST: **GUITARIST DAVE GILMOUR** is invited to join Pink Floyd, in an effort to prop up the band because Syd Barrett is now pretty much dysfunctional as a result of LSD abuse. Syd will finally leave the band in April.

• 3RD: **THE BYRDS** release the album *Notorious Byrd Brothers* in the US.

• 4TH: **JIMI HENDRIX** is arrested in Gothenburg, Sweden, after a hotel room smashing incident.

• 5TH: **ALEXANDER DUBCEK**, considered by many to be a liberal reformer, takes over as the First Secretary of the Czechoslovakian communist party... Meanwhile in the US, noted child-rearing expert Benjamin Spock is indicted for counselling youngsters to resist the draft.

• 6TH: **ROCKING IRISH CROONER** Val Doonican (that's 'rocking' as in 'chair') gently nudges the Beatles' *Sergeant Pepper* off top of the UK album charts.

• 10TH: **LOVE AFFAIR** debut in the UK singles chart with their cover of Robert Knight's US hit 'Everlasting Love', the song which blows open the practice of using session men instead of group members.

• 12TH: **THE BAND** record 'The Weight' at A&R Recording, New York City.

• 18TH: **SINGER EARTHA KITT** speaks out against the Vietnam War while she's a guest at the White House in Washington DC. Although First Lady Mrs Johnson is visibly upset by Miss Kitt's outburst, they part cordially.

• 20TH: **JOHN FRED & HIS PLAYBOY BAND** hit the US Number One slot with 'Judy In Disguise (With Glasses)'.

• 28TH: **A US AIR FORCE B-52** bomber carrying four hydrogen bombs crashes into ice off Greenland. Defence Department officials say the bombs were "unarmed so there is no danger of a nuclear explosion"... Elsewhere, The Small Faces and The Who are asked to leave a plane in Australia (presumably while it's on the ground) for making an air hostess cry.

### In The Year 2001...

• APRIL 2ND: **STANLEY KUBRICK'S** *2001: A Space Odyssey*, based on the book by Arthur C. Clarke, is released to mixed reviews – some find it unbearably slow and obtuse, thanks to its minimal dialogue and disjointed images. But it gradually gains a reputation as the most influential sci-fi movie ever, noted for its special effects, its audacious score of classical music (notably Richard Strauss' *Also Sprach Zarathustra*), and its talking computer, HAL.

### FEBRUARY

• 1ST: **THE JIMI HENDRIX EXPERIENCE** begins a US tour at The Fillmore, San Francisco, with Albert King, John Mayall's Bluesbreakers and Soft Machine.

• 3RD: **THE NEW US NUMBER ONE** single is 'Green Tambourine' by the Lemon Pipers – the almost acceptable face of 'bubblegum music.' This sickly-sweet confection includes such toe-tappers as The 1910 Fruitgum Co singing 'Simon Says,' The Ohio Express's 'Yummy Yummy Yummy (I Got Love In My Tummy)' (surely a thinly veiled innuendo), and Crazy Elephant's 'Gimme Gimme Good Lovin' – not to mention Kasenetz-Katz Singing Orchestral Circus and 'Quick Joey Small (Run Joey Run).' So we won't mention that.

• 5TH: **NEAL CASSADY**, beatnik and counter-culture icon, dies after a drinking binge, at 41.

• 10TH: **THE BEATLES** move all their business affairs from NEMS to their own newly formed Apple company, soon to open premises at 95 Wigmore Street, London.

• 12TH: **JIMI HENDRIX** plays a show for students at his old school, Garfield High in Seattle. He is then awarded an honorary diploma – not bad for someone who dropped out of school at 14.

• 14TH: **FLEETWOOD MAC** record their second single, 'Black Magic Woman,' in CBS Studios, New Bond Street, London.

• 15TH: **LITTLE WALTER JACOBS**, blues harmonica player and sideman for Muddy Waters, dies age 38 after being stabbed in a street fight in Chicago.

• 22TH: **GENESIS** release their debut single, 'The Silent Sun.'

# I May Not Get There With You...

**A**PRIL 4TH: **THE 39-YEAR-OLD** civil rights leader Rev Dr Martin Luther King Jr is assassinated as he leans over a second-floor balcony outside his room at the Lorraine Motel in Memphis, Tennessee. His death sends shock waves through America, and riots erupt in many towns and cities, leading to thousands of arrests. James Brown goes on national TV to try to calm things down. Despite his advocacy of non-violence, King knew his own violent death was always a possibility as he stood up to those who opposed civil rights. He once stated, "A riot is the language of the unheard." The night before his death he told his audience, "I may not get there with you, but I want you to know tonight that we as a people will get to the promised land." Conspiracy theories and loose ends abound. James Earl Ray is identified and convicted as the lone killer. But while there's no doubt Ray is a racist thug who may well have wanted King dead, there's also a fair chance he's been set up to take the rap for disposing of such a potentially divisive individual. Even Dr King's family later come to believe that Ray was not to blame.

## MARCH

- **1ST: ELTON JOHN'S** first solo single, 'I've Been Loving You Too Long,' is released by Philips records in the UK. Several members of his former band, Bluesology, go on to form Soft Machine.
- **3RD: A TANKER** with 5.7 million gallons of oil on board splits in half in San Juan harbour in Puerto Rico.
- **7TH: ELVIS PRESLEY** records 'A Little Less Conversation' at Western Recorders, Los Angeles. The song will be largely overlooked for more than 30 years until a re-mix propels it to Number One in the US and UK during 2002... Also today, Bill Graham opens the Fillmore East in New York, as an East-Coast mirror to

his legendary San Francisco Fillmore venue, which he's run since 1966.
- **16TH: A UNIT OF THE US ARMY**, led by Lt William L. Calley, invades the South Vietnamese hamlet of My Lai, an alleged Viet Cong stronghold, killing unarmed civilians, including women and children (the final army estimate for the number killed will be 347). The incident remains unknown to the American public until the autumn of 1969, after which it becomes a byword for the depravity of war. It probably isn't a unique incident, but Calley is the one who gets caught. He is court-martialled and sentenced to life imprisonment, though his sentence is later reduced by President Nixon and

he is released on appeal in 1974.
- **18TH: THE STEVE MILLER BAND** releases its debut single, 'Sittin' In Circles,' in the US.
- **20TH: ERIC CLAPTON** of Cream is busted for possession of narcotics at the home of Buffalo Springfield member Stephen Stills in the Topanga Canyon, LA.
- **21ST: FIGURES SHOW** that road deaths in the UK have fallen by 23 per cent in the three months since the introduction of breath tests for drink-driving.
- **27TH: WILLIE JOHN**, the originator of the classic 'Fever' dies of pneumonia while serving a sentence for manslaughter in Washington State Penitentiary.

- **MARCH 4TH: THE MOTHERS OF INVENTION, led by Frank Zappa**, release the album 'We're Only In It For The Money,' in a spoof Sgt Pepper-like sleeve. Zappa always courts notoriety, with an ironic disdain that enchants some, alienates others, and passes many by completely. But over the coming years he proves to be not only a razor-sharp wit, but a remarkable guitarist and composer.

## APRIL

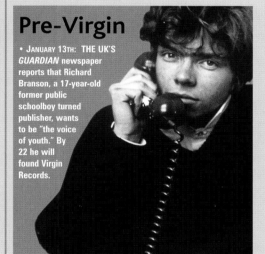

### Pre-Virgin

- **JANUARY 13TH: THE UK'S** *GUARDIAN* newspaper reports that Richard Branson, a 17-year-old former public schoolboy turned publisher, wants to be "the voice of youth." By 22 he will found Virgin Records.

- **3rd: DONOVAN RECORDS** 'Hurdy Gurdy Man' and other tracks in London with producer Mickie Most.
- **6TH: TOMMY JAMES & THE SHONDELLS** release a new single, 'Mony Mony', in the US... And Hugo Montenegro (plus His Orchestra & Chorus) enters the US Top 40 with a version of the title song from the recent Sergio Leone movie 'spaghetti western' *The Good, The Bad, And The Ugly* (starring Clint Eastwood, Lee Van Cleef, and Eli Wallach – you're left to work out which is which). At the same time, the theme's composer, Ennio Morricone, reaches Number Four on the US album charts with the original soundtrack album from the movie. It's his biggest ever hit.
- **7TH: JIM CLARK,** Scottish-born Grand Prix champion, and one of the world's greatest racing drivers, dies during an unimportant Formula Two race at Hockenheim, Germany, when his car inexplicably leaves the track and hits some trees at 150mph. Clark is just 32.
- **11TH: PRESIDENT JOHNSON** signs the US Civil Rights Act of 1968 while pleading for an end to the rioting which has erupted since the slaying of Martin Luther King.
- **14TH: PINK FLOYD** introduce an electronic sound projector called the 'azimuth coordinator' at their Albert Hall show in London. Always at the cutting edge of music technology, especially at live shows,

they will also be the first band to experiment with quadraphonic sound (using four sound channels instead of the usual two).
- **19TH: THE FBI** says it is seeking an escaped convict, James Earl Ray (who now apparently goes by the alias of Eric Starvo Galt), for the murder of Martin Luther King.
- **20TH: PIERRE TRUDEAU** is sworn in as Canada's 15th Prime Minister today, succeeding the retired Lester Pearson... And Deep Purple make their live debut at Tastrup, near Copenhagen, Denmark.
- **21ST: AFTER 32 AFRICAN NATIONS** say they will boycott the Olympic Games if South Africa is admitted, the Olympic Committe votes to bar South Africa from the competition.
- **22ND: STUDENT RIOTING** breaks out at Columbia University and students occupy five buildings. The sit-in ends when New York City police swarm onto the campus early on the 30th to evict them.
- **27TH: DIONNE WARWICK** enters the US singles charts with the Burt Bacharach/Hal David song 'Do You Know The Way To San Jose?'

- **APRIL 18TH: AMERICAN BUSINESS** tycoon Robert McCulloch purchases London Bridge (which is due to be replaced) for more than $2 million, and moves it brick-by-brick from the British capital to Arizona to become the centre-piece of a new town, Lake Havasu City. Legend has it that McCulloch thinks he is actually buying the far more spectacular Tower Bridge, with its famous raising and lowering bascules, but this is just a good story. In fact, his purchase proves very astute, and this incongruous 19th century English landmark spanning a desert lake becomes the second most popular tourist attraction in Arizona, after the Grand Canyon.

# Herb High

**J**UNE 22ND: HERB ALPERT tops the US singles chart with 'This Guy's In Love With You.' Dedicated to his wife, singer Lani Hall, this is the trumpet player's first Number One, and the first US Number One for writers Bacharach & David. It's also the first time Herb's sung on a record, and the biggest hit to date for his own label, A&M. After writing hits for Sam Cooke and Jan & Dean, Alpert, with partner Jerry Moss, makes A&M into a very successful record company.

- **1ST: MILITANT LEFT-WING** students occupy the University of Paris at Nanterre, and two days later 500 more are arrested at the Sorbonne. Within three weeks, France is nearing paralysis as millions of workers occupy factories, mines and offices. A furious President de Gaulle vows to use force if necessary to prevent what he calls a Communist dictatorship. His speech is sharply criticised by Francois Mitterrand, head of the Federation of the Left.
- **2ND: MORE THAN 2000** people set off on the Poor People's March from Memphis to Washington, originally inspired by Martin Luther King and encouraged by Senator Robert Kennedy – neither of whom would live to see its resolution. When the marchers arrive, in May, they encamp in a makeshift shanty town they call Resurrection City, in the heart of Washington DC, often in torrential rain and squalid conditions, until they are forcibly removed by police after six weeks. Though it unites all races and colours, the campaign is too anti-capitalist to get broad support, and it peters out.
- **3RD: THE BEACH BOYS** begin a US tour with pop guru the Maharishi Mahesh Yogi at Singer Bowl, New York City. The Maharishi chants on-stage and delivers words of wisdom to the audience – but the experiment is not successful, and poor ticket sales cause the tour to be abandoned. The Beach Boys' popularity has slumped ever since their non-appearance at the

very hip *Monterey Festival*, and is now at an all-time low – only 18 months after they were voted Top Band In The World in an *NME* readers' poll.

- **4TH: ASPIRING UK** pop group The Freehold play their first-ever gig, at the Marine Theatre in the sleepy seaside resort of Lyme Regis, Dorset. Their drummer is a young hopeful called Phil Collins.... Most of the town's residents, meanwhile, are probably at home watching Welsh songstress Mary Hopkin on UK TV talent show *Opportunity Knocks*. Hopkin is spotted by Twiggy, who

recommends her to Paul McCartney (seen here with Hopkin), who then signs her to Apple and produces her world-wide hit 'Those Were The Days'. She also goes on to represent the UK in the *Eurovision Song Contest* in 1970, which does little for her career.
- **6TH: JONI MITCHELL'S** debut album, Songs To A Seagull, is released in the US.
- **7TH: RIOT POLICE** storm the stage at a festival in Rome while controversial band The Move are playing. History doesn't record whether the police are assuming the chorus to 'Fire Brigade' is an actual cry for help.
- **9TH: RUSSIAN TROOPS** are reported to be massing near the Czech border in both Poland and East Germany.
- **10TH: AT A MONKEES** recording session, Neil Young plays lead guitar on the track 'You And I', which will appear on

the album Instant Replay.
- **13TH: US AND NORTH VIETNAMESE** diplomats open formal talks in Paris today aimed at ending the war in Vietnam.
- **18TH: *THE MIAMI POP FESTIVAL*** (also known as the *Underground Pop Festival*), begins at the Gulf Stream Race Track, Hallandale, Miami, Florida, with the Jimi Hendrix Experience, John Lee Hooker, Frank Zappa, Blue Cheer, Arthur Brown and Eire Apparent.
- **22ND: THE NUMBER ONE** hit single and 1960s dance classic 'Tighten Up' by Archie Bell & The Drells is awarded a US gold disc by the RIAA. This comes as good news to Bell himself, who is currently abroad on military service. When he gets home he finds that several imposter acts have been cashing in on his unavoidable absence. They even include an all-white version of Archie Bell & The Drells.

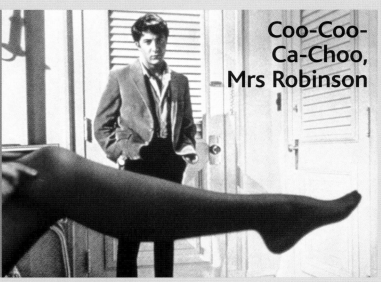

## Coo-Coo-Ca-Choo, Mrs Robinson

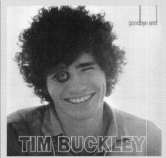

- **2ND: TIM BUCKLEY** plays the last of 13 nights at the Troubadour, Los Angeles. His most recent album (his second) is *Goodbye And Hello*, which features the track 'I Didn't Ask To Be Your Mountain,' written for his estranged wife and baby son, Jeff – who, 23 years later, will perform the song in a tribute to his father at St Ann's Church in Brooklyn, New York *(see 1991)*.
- **3RD: ANDY WARHOL** is shot by Valerie Solanis, a slightly disturbed actress who had occasionally worked on Warhol's movies. The incident will later inspire a song by Lou Reed and The Velvet Underground ('Andy's Chest'), and a 1996 movie (*I Shot Andy Warhol*). Warhol survives, after hours of heart surgery, but he never completely recovers – either physically or artistically.
- **5TH: RECORDING OF** *It Must Be Dusty* TV show, at Studio D, Elstree Studios, Borehamwood, Hertfordshire, UK, during which Jimi Hendrix and Dusty Springfield duet on Mockingbird.
- **7TH: SIRHAN BISHARA SIRHAN** is indicted by a Los Angeles grand jury on a first-degree murder charge for the assassination of Senator Robert

## Open Doors

**A**UGUST 2ND: 'HELLO, I LOVE YOU' by The Doors reaches Number One in the US. They will go on to make just six studio albums in a short but eventful career, curtailed in July 1971 when singer Jim Morrison is found dead in a Paris bathtub. The band were formed in Los Angeles in 1965 by film students Morrison and Ray Manzarek, whose keyboards will define their sound as much as Morrison's doomy vocals. Taking their name from William Blake, via Aldous Huxley, the group go on to create both endless controversy – Morrison faced jail for exposing himself on stage – and some great music, from live favourites like 'Light My Fire' to the sublime 'Riders On The Storm.'

### JULY

### AUGUST

Kennedy at the Embassy Room of the Ambassador Hotel two days ago. The New York senator was shot three times and died in hospital despite a 20-hour operation. Sirhan is a Palestinian Arab, and it is claimed he was motivated by Kennedy's Israeli sympathies. Conspiracy theory ahoy! Sirhan was clearly seen shooting the senator, yet it is later claimed that some of the wounds show the bullets came from another direction... As with his brother JFK's shooting in 1963, crucial evidence is clearly suppressed in the haste to convict a 'crazed lone assassin.' Sirhan is sentenced to life in prison. In March 2003, still incarcerated in a California jail, he will be refused parole for the 12th time.

- **12TH: THE ROLLING STONES**, Dusty Springfield, Scott Walker, Cliff Richard, Status Quo, The Association, Love Affair, Don Partridge, Amen Corner, The Herd, The Move, The Tremeloes, and Dave Dee, Dozy, Beaky, Mick & Tich play at the *NME Poll Winner's Concert*, Empire Pool, Wembley, London.
- **13TH: DURING A CALIFORNIAN VISIT**, George Harrison and Ringo Starr of The Beatles jam with David Crosby (The Byrds, CSN&Y) and Peter

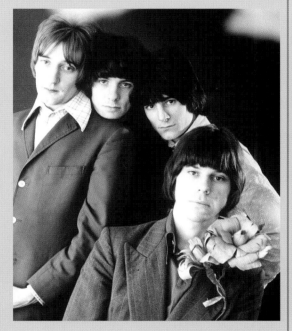

Asher (Peter & Gordon) at the Willow Glen, Los Angeles, home of The Monkees' Peter Tork... Around this time The Beatles also decide the Maharishi was "a mistake." John Lennon targets him in 'Sexy Sadie' ("You made a fool of everyone") which will appear on the band's next album later in the year.

- **22ND: THE JEFF BECK GROUP** (above) makes its US debut at the Fillmore East, New York. The singer is Rod Stewart, and the bass player Ron Wood.
- **29TH: PINK FLOYD** perform at the first free festival in Hyde Park, London – support comes from Jethro Tull, Roy Harper, and a new duo called Tyrannosaurus Rex.

- **JULY 17TH: THE BEATLES'** animated movie *Yellow Submarine* premieres at the London Pavilion. In fact The Beatles only make a brief guest appearance at the end of the movie – elsewhere their voices are imitated, rather loosely, by actors.

- **1ST: THE BAND** release their mold-breaking debut album, *Music From The Big Pink*. The back-to-basics blend of down-home traditional US music with rock instrumentation and tight harmonies presents a refreshing alternative to the current trends for psychedelia, acid-rock, or bubblegum pop.
- **10TH: ERIC CLAPTON** announces the break-up of Cream, because of "loss of direction"... And tonight, The Nice are banned from appearing at the Albert Hall, London, after burning an American flag on stage.... Meanwhile, in the US, child psychologist Dr Spock and three others get two years in jail for giving advice on draft evasion.
- **23RD: HENRY 'HANK' AARON** of the Atlanta Braves hits his 500th home run. He's already sick of people wondering whether he'll break Babe Ruth's 30-year old record of 714. Just give him a few more years (six years, to be exact).
- **23RD: FIVE YOUNG HOPEFULS** from Gary, Indiana, calling themselves The Jackson Five, arrive in Detroit, Michigan, to audition for Berry Gordy at Motown Records.
- **29TH: THE BYRDS** start a tour of South Africa, with the exception of recent recruit Gram Parsons, who refuses to go, due to the country's apartheid policies. Parsons (below) ends up leaving the band and launching The Flying Burrito Brothers with ex-Byrds colleague Chris Hillman. It's Parson's genuine love of country music that makes him a catalyst for what later becomes known as 'country-rock' – though he might have preferred "Cosmic American Music." Although he never has a hit single or even album to his name, he acquires almost mythical status as a cult figure – if anything enhanced by his tragically early death in 1973.

- **3RD: YES PLAY** their first gig together – at East Mersea Youth Camp, Essex, UK. Unlikely as it sounds, in just over three months they'll be playing at London's Royal Albert Hall, as support act at the farewell gig of superstars Cream.
- **5TH: RONALD REAGAN,** ex-actor and governor of California, joins the US presidential race for the first time.
- **6TH: CITIZENS OF CZECHOSLOVAKIA** donate money and goods to the state in an attempt to save the country from bankruptcy. Two weeks later, after Alexander Dubcek refuses to abandon his liberal experiment in the country, Soviet tanks roll into Prague. Angry Czechs fight back with whatever they can lay their hands on.
- **7TH: THE BEE GEES** enter the UK singles chart with 'I've Gotta Get A Message To You,' which goes all the way to Number One, and will also become their first US Top Ten success.
- **17TH: THE RASCALS'** 'People Got To Be Free' tops the US singles chart for the first of five weeks.
- **24TH: ANTI-WAR CAMPAIGNER** Country Joe McDonald and two of his band, The Fish, are attacked by Vietnam War veterans in a lift at the Democratic Party National Convention in Chicago, Illinois... Meanwhile, France explodes its first H-bomb in the Pacific.
- **26TH: APPLE RECORDS** releases its first four singles, including 'Hey Jude' by The Beatles and 'Those Were The Days' by Mary Hopkin.

# 1968

September–December

**SEPTEMBER**

**OCTOBER**

- **2ND: AT LEAST** 11,000 people are reported to have been killed in earthquakes in Iran over the past two days.
- **3RD: STREET FIGHTING MAN** by The Rolling Stones is banned in Chicago, Illinois, following recent riots at the Democratic Convention in that city.
- **7TH: A GROUP CALLING ITSELF** The New Yardbirds is on tour in Scandanavia. Guitarist Jimmy Page has hired a new singer, bass player and drummer since the original Yardbirds line-up has just dissolved. The new members are named Plant, Jones and Bonham. To all intents and purposes, the new group is Led Zeppelin – they just haven't changed their name yet.
- **8TH: HUEY NEWTON,** leader of the Black Panther party, is convicted on charges of voluntary manslaughter in the death of John Frey, a policeman from Oakland, California.
- **14TH: FIRST US TV** appearance of cartoon pop group The Archies, whose single 'Sugar Sugar' will sell over six million copies... Meanwhile James Brown enters the US charts with 'Say It Loud, I'm Black And I'm Proud (Part 1).'

- **27TH: STEVIE WONDER,** Gladys Knight & The Pips, Shorty Long, Bobby Taylor & The Vancouvers, appear at Gilroy Stadium, Gary, Indiana. Opening the show, on their home turf, is the Jackson Five.

- **1ST: FRENCH ARTIST** Marcel Duchamp dies, aged 81. A pioneer of the dada movement in the early 20th century, he gained notoriety for exhibiting a copy of the Mona Lisa sporting a moustache, and a series of bizarre 'ready-mades' or 'found objects,' including a bicycle wheel and a urinal.

At one show he invited visitors to destroy the exhibits. Duchamp was a fanatical chess player. One of his last public activities was a musical chess match earlier this year against avant garde composer John Cage (held in Toronto, Canada) where moving each piece triggered an electric cell in the chessboard and played a musical note, as well as activating coloured lights.
- **2ND: MOTOWN RECORDS** files a $4m suit against songwriters /producers Holland-Dozier-Holland for breach of contract, on the basis that the trio has not delivered any new songs since 1967. The three writers decide to set up on their own, but neither they nor Motown ever regain the non-stop hit production schedule they attained in the early 1960s. Though their talents are sorely missed, Motown carries on successfully with a new writing and production team known as The Corporation, which mainly consists of boss Berry Gordy, Deke Richards, Fonze Mizell, and Freddie Perren. And of course they still have an impressive roster of artists, like The Jackson Five, Stevie Wonder, Marvin Gaye, Smokey Robinson, Diana Ross and The Supremes.
- **12TH: BIG BROTHER & THE HOLDING COMPANY,** still fronted by Janis Joplin, hit Number One on the US album charts with Cheap Thrills, which has also spawned their one and only hit single, the classic 'Piece Of My Heart.' Janis's last performance fronting the band will be on December 1st, after which the band will split – though it will later reform without Joplin.
- **13TH: IT'S REPORTED** that singer and songwriter John Sebastian has quit the Lovin' Spoonful to start a solo career.
- **15TH: STEVIE WONDER** puts out a new single, 'For Once In My Life,' in the US. When it's released in the UK in December it

- **SEPTEMBER 21ST: ARTHUR BROWN** (as in The Crazy World Of) enters the *Billboard* Top 40 for the first and only time with his pyromaniacal party-piece 'Fire,' a former UK Number One, which will climb to Number Two in the US.

becomes his biggest hit yet.
- **18TH: TOMMIE SMITH** and John Carlos, gold and bronze medalists in the Olympic 200-meter sprint, are suspended from the Games and expelled from the village for raising their fists in black power salutes at the medal ceremony.
- **19TH: JIMMY PAGE'S** New Yardbirds play their last date under that name at Liverpool University, after Keith Moon suggests they will go down like 'the proverbial lead zeppelin.'
- **20TH: FORMER FIRST LADY** and JFK widow Jackie Kennedy weds Greek millionaire shipping tycoon Aristotle Onassis... And Dick Fosbury wins gold in the Olympic high jump with the revolutionary new Fosbury Flop – a backwards flip over the bar, rather than the conventional straddle.
- **25TH: JIMI HENDRIX'S** *Electric Ladyland* is released in the UK, a month after its launch in the US, where it's already battling with *Cheap Thrills* for the Number One spot.
- **26TH: WHEN PINK FLOYD** appear at Imperial College, London, their support band is Smile, featuring Brian May and Roger Taylor, both future members of Queen.
- **31ST: REVOLUTIONARY** rock act the MC5 record their debut album, *Kick Out The Jams* at the Grande Ballroom in Detroit.

## Who's Baba

**S**EPTEMBER 22ND: IT'S THE FIRST DAY of recording sessions for The Who's rock opera *Tommy* at IBC Studios, London. It will not, strictly speaking, be the first rock opera to be released – that dubious honor will go to The Pretty Things and their *SF Sorrow* album, released in December, while *Tommy* is still being made – although Who leader Pete Townshend later claims he has been working on the *Tommy* concept for years. It is while working on *Tommy*, the story of a deaf, blind and mute boy whose only outlet is his mastery of pinball, that Townshend first draws inspiration from Meher Baba, an Indian man-god, or 'avatar,' who hasn't spoken since 1925. He did write, however, that "When I break my silence, the impact of my love will be universal." Unfortunately for the world, he will die, still silent, in 1969.

**• DECEMBER 10TH: THE ROLLING STONES BEGIN** filming their TV special Rock'n'Roll Circus at Intertel Studios, Wembley, London. Guests include John Lennon and Yoko Ono, Eric Clapton, Taj Mahal, Jethro Tull, Marianne Faithfull, and an exotic collection of circus performers.

## NOVEMBER

**• DECEMBER 3RD: IT'S MORE THAN seven years** since Elvis Presley has stood in front of a live audience, and in that time he's become more or less musically redundant. Tonight's televised 'Comeback Special' (just called *Elvis* at the time) changes all that. The show's highlight is undoubtedly the section in which Presley, decked out in leather, performs an off-the-cuff greatest hits set to a rapt audience, joking and jamming with two of his original Fifties band-members, Scotty Moore and D.J. Fontana. It proves Elvis still has plenty to offer as a performer, and reignites his career – at least until years of Las Vegas eventually blunts the edges.

**• 1ST: THE FIRST OFFICIAL** Beatle solo album – the movie soundtrack *Wonderwall* – is released by George Harrison on Apple Record ... Meanwhile President Johnson tells the nation in a televised speech that he has ordered a stop to all US air, naval, and artillery bombardments in North Vietnam.

**• 5TH: RICHARD MILHOUS NIXON** is elected President of the United States, succeeding in what he failed to do eight years previously... Also, for the first time in US history, a black woman is elected to the House of Representatives.

**• 7TH: THE DOORS** are banned from Veterans Memorial Coliseum in Phoenix, Arizona, after Jim Morrison excites the crowd to a near-riot. Meanwhile Beate Klarsfeld, 29, hits Chancellor Kurt Georg Kiesinger in the eye at the closing of his Christian Democratic Union's national congress in West Berlin. Mrs Klarsfeld was dismissed two years ago as secretary of the French-West German youth service after she had published an article describing Kiesinger as a "Nazi" and "murderer" due to his dubious war record. Her life story is later made into a movie starring Farrah Fawcett.

**• 8TH: CYNTHIA LENNON** is divorced from John. Three days later, the album *Two Virgins*, by John and Yoko, is released – its cover, which shows the pair naked, is rejected by many shops, so the record is distributed in a paper bag.

**• 11TH: ON THE STAGE** of the London Palladium, Diana Ross of The Supremes makes a plea for racial harmony and is given a two-minute standing ovation.

**• 12th: NEIL YOUNG'S** solo debut album, *Neil Young*, is released in America... On the same day, the US Supreme Court voids an Arkansas law banning the teaching of evolution in public schools.

**• 16TH: GLEN CAMPBELL** enters the US singles chart with the Jimmy Webb composition 'Wichita Lineman,' which will peak at Number Three.

**• 22ND: THE BEATLES** release their double-album *The Beatles* in a plain white sleeve – from here on popularly known as *The White Album*... And Arlo Guthrie's album *Alice's Restaurant* is released in the US. It includes a 22-minute song about a real restaurant, later turned into a movie.

**• 26TH: CREAM PLAY** their farewell show at the Albert Hall, London, UK The show is filmed for posterity.

**• 5TH: GRAHAM NASH** announces his intention to leave The Hollies to form Crosby Stills & Nash.

**• 14TH: EVEN WITHOUT** the help of Holland-Dozier-Holland, Tamla Motown holds the first three positions on the US singles chart: Marvin Gaye is Number One with his definitive cover of 'I Heard It Through The Grapevine'; Diana Ross & The Supremes are Number Two with 'Love Child'; and Number Three is Stevie Wonder with 'For Once In My Life.'

**• 16TH: ALMOST 500 AGO,** King Ferdinand and Queen Isabella of Spain banished Jews from their country. Today, that order is officially rescinded. A gathering of 700 Spanish, Jewish, and other officials hear the proclamation at the opening of a Madrid synagogue – the first built in Spain for 600 years... And Creedence Clearwater Revival's eponymous debut album – which peaked at Number 52 but spent 17 steady-selling months on the chart – is certified gold in the US.

**• 17TH: DESPITE COMPLETE LACK OF ADVERTISING,** queues of young people throng to see Lyndsey Anderson's controversial, anti-establishment film If... at the Paramount Plaza in London. Originally shelved as too risky by the distributors, it's only being shown at all because Roger Vadim's Barbarella is doing so badly... Both movies go on to gain a cult following over the years.

**• 18TH: JOHN AND YOKO** host 'an alchemical wedding' at the Royal Albert Hall. London, and sit in a bag. They call it bagism – the rest of the world isn't sure what it is, but kind of sniggers behind its hand.

**• 20TH: JOHN STEINBECK,** author of *East Of Eden, Of Mice And Men*, and *The Grapes Of Wrath*, dies at the age of 66.

**• 21ST: PETER TORK** buys himself out of The Monkees for $160,000.

**• 27TH: THE THREE APOLLO 8 ASTRONAUTS** return safely to earth after becoming the first people to orbit the moon. During the trip, on Xmas Eve, they take the first ever photos of the Earth from the moon.

# 1969

## GIANT LEAP FOR MANKIND (SMALL STEP FOR BOWIE)

On July 20th 1969, just eight years after President John F. Kennedy first proclaimed the USA's intention to put a man on the moon – and only five months before the end-of-decade deadline he imposed – Neil A. Armstrong and Edwin E. 'Buzz' Aldrin Jr pilot their Apollo 11 lunar module, named Eagle, to a landing on the Sea Of Tranquillity at 4:17pm Eastern daylight time. Some six hours later, as Armstrong steps down from the landing craft to become the first person to set foot on the moon, he tells the hundreds of millions watching the scene on television, "That's one small step for man, one giant leap for mankind." The following night, to celebrate the event, Motown artists Stevie Wonder, David Ruffin, Chuck Jackson, and Gladys Knight & The Pips perform a concert in Mount Morris Park, Harlem, New York. The moon landing also helps propel a young David Bowie to stardom – though that may not have been part of JFK's original plan – as his breakthrough hit 'Space Oddity' is released almost simultaneously with the events in space. That's assuming it really is in space, of course. To the disgust and indignation of NASA and the astronauts involved, sceptics will later claim that the TV coverage and photographs, and perhaps the whole trip, have been faked – mocked up in the Nevada desert for Cold War propaganda purposes. Hoax-theorists point to inexplicable inconsistencies in the images: for instance, in this picture, close examination of the reflection on Buzz Aldrin's helmet clearly shows Elvis Presley in his white, sequinned Las Vegas suit...

# 1969

## January–April

- **3RD: POLICE AT NEWARK AIRPORT**, New Jersey, confiscate 30,000 copies of Lennon & Ono's *Two Virgins* because the cover is considered obscene.
- **4TH: BUBBLEGUM MUSIC** production company Kasenetz-Katz Associates reports an 85 per cent sales increase in the last year, adding up to $25m worth of records sold by the likes of Ohio Express and 1910 Fruitgum Company... Meanwhile, in Northern Ireland, Unionist militants ambush a civil rights demonstration by the left-wing People's Democracy group, protesting against 'gerrymandering' in local councils, as their four-day march from Belfast reaches Derry. The opposition to the civil rights marchers is

led by the Reverend Ian Paisley, founder and leader of the Free Presbyterian Church.
- **6TH: THE US** presidential salary is raised from $100,000 to $200,000 a year. It will stay the same for 30 years, at which point it is doubled again.
- **7TH: GOVERNOR OF CALIFORNIA** Ronald Reagan asks the state legislature to "drive criminal anarchists and latter-day fascists" off university campuses... Three weeks later, California is declared a disaster area, though not because of Mr Reagan — not only have two days of flooding and mud slides caused at least 11 deaths, but some of California's finest coastline is being threatened with major pollution as an offshore oil well near

Santa Barbara blows out, spewing thousands of gallons of oil into the ocean.
- **11TH: CARTONS AND SHOPPING BAGS** of beans, rice, and canned meat pile up on the steps of St Patrick's Cathedral as thousands of New Yorkers donate food for starving Biafrans, stricken by famine in the midst of the Nigerian civil war. A ship has also been sent from the people of Ireland, who feel a special connection thanks to the strong historical presence of Catholic missionaries in this part of Africa.
- **15TH: CROSBY, STILLS & NASH** sign a recording contract with Atlantic Records in the US.
- **16TH: TWO SOVIET SOYUZ** spacecraft dock in orbit, and remain joined for four hours while cosmonauts 'spacewalk' from one to the other... Meanwhile back on Earth, ten paintings, including a Rembrandt, are defaced at the Met (Metropolitan Museum of Art) in New York.
- **17TH: LED ZEPPELIN** release their eponymous debut album in the US.
- **18TH: BOXER LIONEL ROSE** is named Australian Of The Year, the first time the honour has been given to an Aboriginal Australian. Rose has won 32 of his 34 professional bouts, and was also voted Fighter Of The Year by the World Boxing Council in 1968.
- **25TH: CREEDENCE CLEARWATER** Revival release the single 'Proud Mary' in the US, where it will peak at Number Two... And NASA unveils its moon landing craft for the first time.
- **30TH: THE BEATLES** make their final public appearance together — a free concert at lunchtime on the roof of Apple Records HQ in London, which is eventually halted by the police. The event is filmed and incorporated into the *Let It Be* movie, released next year.

- **4TH: YASSER ARAFAT** is elected leader of the Palestinian Liberation Organisation (PLO).
- **8TH: ON HER BBC TV** show, Lulu — a Scots singer who had a US Number One in 1967 with the theme from the Sidney Poitier movie *To Sir With Love* — performs one of the songs competing to be chosen as this year's UK entry for the *Eurovision Song Contest*. It's called 'I Can't Go On Living Without You' and is written by the unknown team of Elton John and Bernie Taupin. Their song isn't selected to go forward. It is beaten by 'Boom Bang-A-Bang,' which incredibly goes on to tie for first place in the final event. Which just about sums up the *Eurovision Song Contest*. In ten days time, Lulu will marry Maurice Gibb of the Bee Gees.
- **10TH: FOURTEEN DIE**, and 68 are hurt as New York digs its way out of the biggest snowstorm in seven years.
- **14TH: US MAFIA BOSS** Vito Genovese dies from a heart attack while serving a 15-year prison sentence for drug smuggling.
- **17TH: JOHNNY CASH** and Bob Dylan begin recording together in Nashville, Tennessee. Only one song from the sessions is ever released, 'Girl From The North Country,' which appears on Dylan's *Nashville Skyline* album.
- **19TH: LINDA RONSTADT**,

## Everyday Funk

- **FEBRUARY 15TH:** 'EVERYDAY PEOPLE' by Sly & The Family Stone is the new Number One single in the US. Formed in 1966 as The Stoners by singer, songwriter, producer, and funk guru Sylvester Stewart (aka Sly Stone), the band has already had a Top Ten hit in 1968 with 'Dance To The Music.'

## Men Of The World

**J**ANUARY 10TH 1969: Fleetwood Mac, in their original incarnation (Mick Fleetwood, Peter Green, John McVie, Danny Kirwan, and Jeremy Spencer), begin three days of recording at Tempo Sound, New York City, working on the single 'Man Of The World,' a future UK Number Two hit. Meantime their current release, 'Albatross,' a dreamy guitar-based instrumental, is just about to become the first UK Number One.

## Smothers Smothered

• **APRIL 4TH:** *THE SMOTHERS BROTHERS COMEDY HOUR* is cancelled by CBS after a two-year run, largely due to the show's anti-establishment humour. According to rumour, President Nixon has been putting pressure on the broadcasters because he doesn't want his authority and Vietnam policy ridiculed. He is aware of the extent to which the Smothers and their scriptwriters satirised the previous president, Lyndon Johnson, during his administration. Although mild by later standards, the show's satire is ahead of its time on US TV. Talented writers like Steve Martin and Rob Reiner get their start working for the brothers. The Smothers themselves are gifted musicians, veterans of late 1950s beat clubs, and contemporary musical guests invited on to the shows include The Who, The Doors, and George Harrison. One of the final straws is a controversial episode back in December 1968, when Grace Slick, the new singer with guests Jefferson Airplane, 'blacks up' for their performance and gives a Black Power salute in the studio.

**MARCH**

**APRIL**

---

formerly of The Stone Ponies, makes her debut as a solo artist at The Whisky A Go Go, Los Angeles.

• **23RD: KING SAUD OF SAUDIA ARABIA** dies. He hasn't been the reigning monarch since 1964 when he was deposed and replaced by his brother Faisal.

• **27TH: THE GRATEFUL DEAD** begin recording their live double album *Live Dead* at the Fillmore, San Francisco.

• **FEBRUARY 3RD: BORIS KARLOFF**, English-born Hollywood movie actor, best known for playing Frankenstein's monster in the 1930s, dies at the of age 81. His real name was William Pratt.

• **1ST: THE DOORS' SINGER** Jim Morrison is arrested at Dinner Key Auditorium in Miami, Florida, for exposing himself on stage.

• **2ND: THE FIRST FLIGHT** of Anglo-French supersonic passenger aircraft Concorde: "Finally the big bird flies," as the pilot says.

• **4TH: THE LONGEST TRIAL** ever seen at London's Old Bailey court ends with notorious East End gangsters the Kray twins, and four others, found guilty of murder. The Judge, Mr Justice Melford Stevenson, says the twins should not be released for 30 years. As it happens, neither will live long enough to be free again.

• **5TH:** *CREEM* MAGAZINE is launched in the US.

• **6TH: THE FOUR TOPS** come to the end of a week of Dutch dates, with a show in Amsterdam at the Grand Gala du Disque.

• **10TH: JAMES EARL RAY** is jailed for 99 years for the murder of Martin Luther King.

• **12TH: PAUL McCARTNEY** marries Linda Eastman, daughter of American show business lawyer Lee Eastman... Meanwhile, at the *11th Annual Grammy Awards*, Album Of the Year is *By The Time I Get To Phoenix* by Glen Campbell (right). The same artist's 'Wichita Lineman' is Best Engineered Recording (pretty good tune too, by Jimmy Webb).

• **15TH: 'DIZZY' BY TOMMY ROE** reaches Number One on the US singles chart – it's his second chart topper, and the song goes on to reach Number One twice in the UK, once for Roe in April this year, and then for comedian Vic Reeves and The Wonder Stuff in 1991.

• **17TH: GOLDA MEIR**, who once taught public school in Milwaukee, Wisconsin, is sworn in as Israel's fourth premier. Mrs Meir was opposed by Agudat Israel, a religious party whose adherents insist Jewish men should not look at "strange women."

• **20TH: JOHN LENNON** marries Yoko Ono in Gibraltar, and two days later they start their 'bed in for peace' at the Amsterdam Hilton – as commemorated in this summer's hit Beatle single 'The Ballad Of John And Yoko'.

• **22ND: NEW ORLEANS** R&B combo The Meters make their first dent in the US national charts by spending one week at Number 34 with the amusingly titled 'Sophisticated Sissy'. Eight years later the group will have evolved into The Neville Brothers.

• **28TH: DWIGHT D. EISENHOWER**, former Commander of US Forces in WWII and 34th president, dies at the age of 78.

• **30TH: A COURT** in Boston, US, decides not to ban lesbian movie *The Killing Of Sister George* after respected film critic Julie Crist testified that it is among the year's top ten movies and is definitely not pornographic.

• **31ST: GEORGE HARRISON** and his wife are fined $1,500 for possession of marijuana.

• **1ST: IT'S REPORTED** that The Beach Boys are suing Capitol Records for $2m worth of unpaid royalties and producer's fees.

• **2ND: MARVIN GAYE** releases a new single, 'Too Busy Thinking About My Baby' on Tamla Records in the US. The b-side is 'Wherever I Lay My Hat (That's My Home),' which will be a UK Number One some 14 years later for Paul Young.

• **3RD: US DEATHS** in Vietnam now stand at 33,641 – passing the Korean War total.

• **8TH: THE WORLD'S** first recipient of a totally artificial heart dies only four days after the ground-breaking life-saving operation... Meanwhile, popular crooner Andy Williams releases his rather inappropriately-timed (but memorably jolly) single 'Happy Heart.'

• **9TH: KING CRIMSON** play their first gig at the Speakeasy in London. Meanwhile, Sikh bus workers in Wolverhampton in the UK win a two-year battle to wear their turbans at work.

• **13TH: A SPANISH** historian declares that Columbus, discoverer of America, was a Basque pirate.

• **16TH: ELEKTRA RECORDS** boots polemical rockers the MC5 off the label after continual protest from parents and some retailers upset by the band's liberal use of the "f-word"... Meanwhile 'The Israelites' by Desmond Dekker (right) becomes the first reggae song to top the UK charts. It will make the US Top Ten in the summer.

• **20TH: THE BRITISH GOVERNMENT** sends 1,000 troops to Belfast as the bus station and nine post offices are fire-bombed. Two days later, Bernadette Devlin, a diminutive, 21-year-old Irish woman just elected to Parliament, holds the House of Commons spellbound with her maiden speech deploring the oppression of both Roman Catholics and Protestants in Northern Ireland. A few days later, 500 more British troops are to be sent into the province.

• **21ST: CANNED HEAT** are signed up to play at the *Woodstock Festival* for a fee of $13,000.

• **22ND: THE FIRST HUMAN** eye transplant is carried out, in Houston... Meanwhile, Aretha Franklin's new single is 'I Can't See Myself Leaving You'... And The Carpenters are signed to A&M Records by company founder Herb Alpert.

• **26TH:** *HAIR*, the soundtrack LP from the hippy musical, reaches Number One on the US albums chart for the first of 13 weeks.

• **28TH: AT 11 MINUTES PAST MIDNIGHT**, at his country home, Charles de Gaulle formally announces that he will step down as president of France.

# 1969

May-August

## Astral Traveler

• **MAY 19TH:** **THE US SUPREME COURT** overturns the conviction – and 30 year jail sentence – of drug guru Dr Timothy Leary, arrested in 1965 for carrying a tiny amount of marijuana into Mexico. He stays free, pending the appeal, which he wins and voids two federal anti-marijuana laws. The court says these laws – which require someone to notify authorities and pay a tax when purchasing or importing the drug – violate the fifth Amendment. Leary subsequently announces his intention to run for election as governor of California (against Ronald Reagan). But the odds are somewhat stacked against him – especially since President Nixon labels him "the most dangerous man in America" because of his counter-cultural proclamations. A psychologist by profession and a hedonist and experimenter by inclination, Leary is a marked man. After another marijuana bust, a court in Nixon's California homeland duly sentences him to 10 years. This time he goes to an open prison, escapes and is recaptured in Afghanistan in 1972, only being released in 1976. His personal life is not the happiest: his first wife committed suicide in 1955, and 35 years later his daughter follows suit. A guru on the lecture circuit, Leary now discovers he has cancer. He approaches death, like life, as an adventure to be embraced, as often as not in the public eye. Having discovered the Internet, he plans to die online – but goes in his sleep. His ashes go into space.

• **5TH:** **ELVIS PRESLEY** releases a new single, 'In The Ghetto,' in the US.
• **6TH:** **BECAUSE OF HIS** 1968 drug conviction, John Lennon's 'standing visa' is withdrawn by the US Embassy in London.
• **9TH:** **THE VATICAN** announces the demotion of St Christopher, patron saint of travelers, and 200 other saints.
• **10TH:** **THE TURTLES** and The Temptations perform at the White House, Washington, DC. Rumour has it that two Turtles snort cocaine off Lincoln's desk.
• **13TH:** **PRESIDENT NIXON** calls for a draft lottery to be introduced for the first time since World War II. The idea is that men between the age of 18 and 26 are called up for military service based on randomly drawn birth dates. In the first lottery draw, on December 1st, the 'lucky' winning birthday is September 14th.
• **15TH:** **THE VAN** carrying Fairport Convention home from a gig crashes, killing drummer Martin Lamble and Richard Thompson's girlfriend Jeanne Franklin, a clothes designer. Jack Bruce dedicates his first solo album, *Songs For A Tailor*, to her.
• **16TH:** **PETE TOWNSHEND** is arrested after he kicks a stage invader in the groin at a Who gig – it transpires the man is an undercover cop trying to warn the Fillmore audience of a fire.
• **24TH:** **WHEN TOM JONES** opens at the Copacabana, New York City, a woman in the audience throws him her panties – initiating one of popular music's most enduring rituals.

• **6TH:** **ROD STEWART** signs a solo recording contract with Mercury Records.
• **7TH:** **BLIND FAITH** make their debut with a free concert in Hyde Park, London, supported by Richie Havens, Donovan, Edgar Broughton Band, and the Third Ear Band.
• **13TH:** **ARETHA FRANKLIN**, Ray Charles, Sam & Dave, and the Staples Singers are the featured acts at The Soul Bowl 69 in the Houston Astrodome, Texas.
• **17TH:** **THE US CONCLUDES** that the Soviets are not in fact trying to gain first-strike nuclear capability.
• **18TH:** **PRESIDENT NIXON**, following a meeting with South Vietnamese President Nguyen Van Thieu at Midway Island, announces that the US will withdraw 25,000 soldiers, the equivalent of a combat division, from Vietnam by the end of August. Aside from placating domestic critics, the troop withdrawal seems designed to put pressure on North Vietnam in the Paris peace talks.
• **20TH:** **GEORGES POMPIDOU** succeeds Charles de Gaulle as president of France.
• **27TH:** **'JE T'AIME MOI NON PLUS'** by Jane Birkin and Serge Gainsbourg is banned by British radio stations, for its suggestive 'noises,' but it will still reach the UK Number One position.
• **28TH:** **THE ALBUM** Crosby, Stills & Nash enters the US album chart.
• **29TH:** **ELVIS PRESLEY PLAYS** his official comeback concert at NBC Color City, Burbank, in California.

• **JUNE 22ND:** **JUDY GARLAND DIES**, shortly after her 47th birthday. An all-round entertainer since childhood, considered by her peers and fans alike to be the greatest talent to come out of Hollywood, she first came to fame playing Dorothy in the 1939 movie *The Wizard Of Oz*.

• **AUGUST 15TH:** *THE WOODSTOCK FESTIVAL* begins at Bethel, New York state. It's 70 miles from Woodstock, but the organisers use the more marketable name of Bob Dylan's birthplace. They promise locals 50,000 guests for the three days. At least ten times that many turn up. There are two deaths and two births, atrocious weather and worse trips. In between all that, festival-goers see Canned Heat, Creedence Clearwater Revival, Grateful Dead, Janis Joplin, Jefferson Airplane, Santana, The Who, and Crosby Stills & Nash. But mostly people will remember Jimi Hendrix 's searing 'Star Spangled Banner.'

# Peace, Love And Room Service

JUNE 1ST: ANTI-WAR SONG 'Give Peace A Chance' is recorded in a suite at the Queen Elizabeth Hotel in Montreal during another 'bed-in' by John Lennon and Yoko Ono. The song was put together by Lennon the previous day after a bedside chat with radical local rabbi Abraham Feinberg. The world's press and television crews record the singalong (which will quickly become a favourite with protest groups around the world), which also features Dr Timothy Leary, comedian Tommy Smothers – who joins Lennon on acoustic guitar – and British singing star Petula Clark, whom Lennon once described as his favourite female singer. The resulting single, credited to The Plastic Ono Band, will give Lennon his first hit without The Beatles, and is followed up later in the year by the more brutal 'Cold Turkey.' Incidentally, over 30 years later, you can spend a nostalgically romantic night or honeymoon in the same Montreal hotel bedroom, for $400.

# Losing A Stone

• JUNE 9TH: BRIAN JONES LEAVES The Rolling Stones, the band he founded in 1962. "I want to play my kind of music," he says, "which is no longer The Stones music." In fact his departure comes by mutual agreement with the other Stones, as everyone realises his contributions are becoming limited. Initially the creative leader and most musically talented member of the group (a multi-instrumentalist and blues aficionado), he has gradually become hampered by a drink and drug-induced haze. On July 3rd, a few weeks after leaving the group, Jones will be found dead in the swimming pool at his recently acquired mansion in Sussex, England (the former home of A.A. Milne, creator of Winnie-The -Pooh), in circumstances that have never been entirely explained. Jones' last recorded work is featured on the Stones album Let It Bleed, to be released in December 1969. On July 5th, the remaining Stones (plus new guitarist Mick Taylor) turn a free concert in London's Hyde Park into a tribute to Jones – ironically entering their most commercially successful period without their former leader.

## JULY

• JULY 11TH: DAVID BOWIE RELEASES a new single, 'Space Oddity,' in the UK. It's his breakthrough record – perfectly timed to take full advantage of the space-mania caused by this month's moon landing (the BBC even uses it during its TV coverage) – although it takes a couple of attempts to make its full impact, eventually peaking at UK Number Five in September. The song then takes another three-and-a-half years to break the US Top 40 (in a re-worked version), by which time Bowie will have adopted his Ziggy Stardust personna. The original recording is famous for its use of the hand-held battery-operated Stylohone keyboard, played with a pen-like stylus (and popularised by Australian entertainer Rolf Harris), and for pre-Yes session man Rick Wakeman playing mellotron throughout.

• 1ST: SESSIONS BEGIN in EMI's Abbey Road Studios, London, which will result in the album Abbey Road, the final studio work by The Beatles. Paul McCartney is the only Beatle present on this first day, working on the track 'You Never Give Me Your Money'.... Meanwhile, Sam Phillips, the man who first recorded Elvis Presley, sells Sun Records to Shelby Singleton for an undisclosed sum.

• 8TH: BONNY THE SPACE MONKEY – the 11th primate to be involved in NASA rocket missions – dies after emergency splashdown. He's the last US monkey sent into space for 14 years, until test runs in the space shuttle era.

• 9TH: US DEPARTMENT OF AGRICULTURE suspends use of the widely used pesticide DDT pending the results of a study. Though miraculously effective against malaria-carrying mosquitoes, health concerns (it's discovered that DDT is absorbed and stored in human bodies for many years) and increasing insect immunity will bring about a complete ban in 1972.

• 12TH: ZAGER & EVANS reach Number One in the US singles chart with 'In The Year 2525 (Exordium & Terminus)'. Six weeks later it reaches the top of the UK charts as well. The song was written by Evans in half an hour for the Nebraska duo's motel lounge set. The got so many requests for it, they decided to record it.

• 18TH: THE UNDECLARED WAR between Honduras and El Salvador that erupted four days ago over a disputed soccer match and took the lives of 1,000 people may be drawing to a close after both governments accept a four-point peace plan drafted by the Organization of American States.

• 19TH: TED KENNEDY, younger brother of the assassinated John and Robert, drives off a bridge in Chappaquiddick, Massachusetts, and leaves Mary Jo Kopechne, his 28-year-old passenger, dead inside the sunken car. He does not report the incident until the next morning. It will come to haunt him and to end the Kennedy political dynasty.

## AUGUST

• AUGUST 9TH: FIVE PEOPLE, including actress Sharon Tate, wife of movie director Roman Polanski, are found slaughtered in the LA home of record producer Terry Melcher (son of actress Doris Day). The words 'Pigs' and 'Helter Skelter' are daubed around the house in the victims' blood. The crimes are eventually traced to psychopathic white supremacist Charles Manson and his 'Family' of followers. Manson, a Beatles-obsessed amateur guitarist and songwriter who has spent most of his life in prison for theft and assault, has started a cult based on the idea that the black race would rise up in a racial Armageddon he calls 'Helter Skelter' (after the meaningless Beatles song on the White Album). Manson himself, who believes he is Christ reincarnated, would hide out until the killings are finished, then he (with The Beatles, of course) would assume control of the world. The killings – orchestrated, though not carried out, by Manson – are an ettempt to kick-start the genocide, as he tries to implicate local black communities. The plan backfires, Manson is arrested, and in April 1971, after the longest murder trial in US history, he and three female accomplices are found guilty and sentenced to death – later commuted to life in prison.

• 5TH: THE BEATLES make their first use of a synthesizer, when George Harrison overdubs Moog sounds onto 'Because.'

• 11TH: DIANA ROSS INTRODUCES a new group she admires, The Jackson Five, to an audience of 350 invited guests in the Daisy Club, Beverley Hills, California.

• 16TH: 'SUGAR SUGAR' by The Archies enters the US Top 40, destined for Number One in both the US and the UK.

• 18TH: MICK JAGGER is accidentally shot in the hand while filming the outlaw movie Ned Kelly in Australia.

• 31ST: US BOXER ROCKY MARCIANO, the only heavyweight champion to retire undefeated, dies in a plane crash at the age of 46... And in the UK, Bob Dylan headlines the Isle Of Wight Festival, with three of The Beatles in the audience.

# 1969
## September–December

**Wonderful Jimmy**

- **DECEMBER 27TH: JIMMY CLIFF**, Jamaican-born singer and composer, releases 'Wonderful World, Beautiful People', his first worldwide hit, reaching Number Six in the UK and 25 in the US. It's taken from his excellent second album, *Jimmy Cliff/Wonderful World*. The next single, the moving protest song 'Vietnam,' is put out only as a b-side in the States...

## SEPTEMBER

- **1ST: COLONEL KHADAFY** (otherwise known as Gadhafi, or Qadaffi, or any one of about a dozen different ways his Arabic name can be written) takes power in Libya while 79-year-old Crown Prince Idris I is undergoing medical treatment abroad.
- **13TH: JOHN LENNON'S** Plastic Ono Band, Chuck Berry, Little Richard, Gene Vincent, Jerry Lee Lewis, Bo Diddley, The Doors, Chicago and Alice Cooper play at the Toronto Rock'N'Roll Revival Concert at the city's Varsity Stadium...

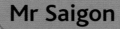

And Santana's eponymous debut album makes its first appearance on the US charts, where it will peak at Number Four, and remain for 108 weeks.
- **15TH: BRITISH HEAVY ROCK** pioneers Deep Purple, who've already had US hits with 'Hush' and 'Kentucky Woman' (apparently on a label run by Bill Cosby), come over all progressive when they perform keyboard player Jon Lord's symphonic rock composition *Concerto For Group And Orchestra* with the Royal Philharmonic Orchestra at London's Royal Albert Hall.
- **20TH: THE BRITISH BOARD** of Trade releases figures showing that, for the first time in the history of the UK recording industry, album production has outstripped singles.

### Mr Saigon

- **SEPTEMBER 4TH: HO CHI MINH**, the revolutionary communist leader of North Vietnam, dies aged 79. A life-long fighter against colonial rule – initially France, but later the intervention of the US – he is posthumously honoured in 1976, after the re-unification of Vietnam, when former South Vietnamese capital Saigon is renamed Ho Chi Minh city in his honour.

- **SEPTEMBER 26TH: THE BEATLES** release their new album, *Abbey Road*, in the UK. It's their final work together, recorded after the *Let It Be/Get Back* sessions but released first. The famous cover shot, on the zebra crossing outside the historic EMI studio in north London, adds fuel to the bizarre rumour that Paul McCartney has died. To some warped minds this is demonstrated by his bare feet in the photograph. The rationale is that Lennon, in white, represents God, Ringo in black is the undertaker, and George in denim is the gravedigger, and there are enough supposed backward messages scattered around their recordings to keep obsessives occupied for years to come.

## OCTOBER

- **1ST: CONCORDE BREAKS** the sound barrier for the first time, causing its soon-to-be-familiar sonic boom.
- **5TH: MARVIN GAYE**, The Four Tops, The Originals and Martha & The Vandellas all perform at the Black Business And Cultural Exposition in the International Amphitheater, Chicago, Illinois.
- **10TH: FRANK ZAPPA** releases his first solo album, *Hot Rats,* in the US.
- **11TH: MUDDY WATERS** is injured in a car wreck outside Chicago – three others are killed.
- **16TH: LEONARD CHESS**, co-founder of Chess Records, dies of a heart attack at the age of 52. Emerging from the Aristocrat label he ran with his brother Philip (whose star was Muddy Waters), Chess built a roster including names like Howlin Wolf, Jimmy Rogers, Little Walter, Sonny Boy 'Rice Miller' Williamson, Elmore James, Chuck Berry and Bo Diddley, Otis Rush, Etta James, and Buddy Guy.

**FRANK ZAPPA**

**HOT RATS**

- **18TH: AMERICA'S NEW NUMBER ONE** single is 'I Can't Get Next To You' by The Temptations... Meanwhile in Honolulu, Paul Kantner of Jefferson Airplane is arrested for possession of marijuana. He later claims he has been set up, although police say they found him crawling around the bushes outside his house with a joint hanging out of his mouth... And also today, in a major blow to the diet food industry, the US government bans the use of cyclamates as artificial sweeteners. Cyclamates are at this time used in more than 250 foods and soft drinks. In 1996 sodium cyclamate will be cleared for use in the UK, despite research evidence that suggests it can cause atrophy of the testicles in monkeys. Not to worry...
- **19TH: LED ZEPPELIN** release their second album, *Led Zeppelin II*.

- **23RD: AMERICAN CHILDREN'S BOOK** author Art Linkletter tells a White House conference on drugs that, "Every rock'n'roll station is sending out, 18 hours a day, messages to kids that are right over the heads of our generation ... every time one of the Top 40 hit records is played, it is an advertisement for trips." Linkletter blamed his daughter's recent suicide on LSD... And further scientific research is released today, claiming that large doses of monosodium glutamate are found to produce brain damage in mice. Mice immediately start cutting down on their Chinese food intake.
- **27TH: ELTON JOHN** and Bernie Taupin write their first hit, 'Your Song,' on the roof of Mills Music, 20 Denmark Street, in London's Tin Pan Alley.
- **31ST: KING CRIMSON** – a musically adventurous 'progressive-rock' outfit (below), whose line-up at this point includes Robert Fripp and Greg Lake – release the LP *In The Court Of The Crimson King*, comprising long, classically-inclined odysseys with suitably long titles. It reaches Number Five in the UK.

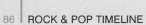

**N**OVEMBER 29TH: THE NEW ALBUM from Canadian blues-rockers Steppenwolf (called *Monster*) is released on the back of their songs 'Born To Be Wild' and 'The Pusher,' which feature in the recent genre-creating road movie *Easy Rider*. It stars Dennis Hopper, Peter Fonda, and Jack Nicholson, seen here heading out on the highway, looking for adventure, or indeed whatever comes their way – like perhaps a pile of drugs and some terminal road-rage. 'Born To Be Wild' will be a hit again in the UK in 30 years' time, thanks to its use in a TV commercial for a wholewheat breakfast cereal.

## Get Your Motor Running...

## NOVEMBER

## DECEMBER

- **1ST: 'SUSPICIOUS MINDS'** by Elvis Presley is the new Number One single in the US. It's the reinvigorated Elvis's first US chart topper since 1962... Meanwhile The Faces sign to Warner Brothers – the band consist of ex-Small Faces Ian McLagen, Ronnie Lane and Kenny Jones, plus Ron Wood and Rod Stewart, formerly of The Jeff Beck Group. Stewart's simultaneous solo career causes some friction within the band, especially when it results in them being billed as Rod Stewart & The Faces.
- **5TH: BLACK PANTHER** leader Bobby Seale is given four years for contempt of court in Chicago.
- **9TH: SIMON & GARFUNKEL** record the songs 'Bridge Over Troubled Water' and 'So Long, Frank Lloyd Wright' for Columbia Records.
- **11TH: DOORS' SINGER** Jim Morrison is forcibly removed from a Continental Airlines flight at Phoenix, Arizona, and arrested for causing a disturbance while intoxicated.
- **15TH: JANIS JOPLIN** is arrested in Tampa, Florida, for using "vulgar and indecent language" on-stage.
- **19TH: APOLLO 12** astronauts walk on the moon, and set up a research station.
- **25TH: JOHN LENNON** returns his MBE in protest at UK involvement in the Nigerian-Biafran war, Vietnam, and his latest single, 'Cold Turkey,' slipping down the charts.

- **2ND: CINDY BIRDSONG** of The Supremes is kidnapped from her Hollywood home by maintenance man Charles Meaker, but the singer manages to escape by leaping from his moving car on Long Beach Freeway, where she is rescued by passing police officers.

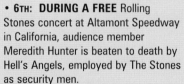

- **6TH: DURING A FREE** Rolling Stones concert at Altamont Speedway in California, audience member Meredith Hunter is beaten to death by Hell's Angels, employed by The Stones as security men.
- **8TH: JIMI HENDRIX** goes on trial for drug possession.
- **18TH: BRITISH PARLIAMENT** votes to outlaw capital punishment.
- **20TH: TWO EARLY BOOTLEG ALBUMS** appear in record racks in Chicago, Illinois. They are the appropriately titled *Stealin'* by Bob Dylan and *Liver Than You'll Ever Be* by The Rolling Stones.
- **24TH: WILLIE SUTTON** is released from Attica prison, New York. Now a white-haired man of 68, Sutton was once a debonair thief known as The

Actor who, when asked why he robbed banks, memorably explained, "That's where the money is."

- **27TH: *LED ZEPPELIN II*** becomes the final US Number One album of the 1960s. The final Number One single is 'Someday We'll Be Together' by Diana Ross & The Supremes, which is the last time Ross is together with The Supremes. In the UK, *Abbey Road* holds off *Led Zeppelin II* until February 1970, while the last Number One single of the Sixties is the sickly sentimental 'Two Little Boys' by multi-faceted (and three-legged) Australian artist Rolf Harris (above), who had a US Number three hit in 1963 with 'Tie Me Kangaroo Down, Sport.'

- **31ST: HAVING SPLIT** with Mitch Mitchell and Noel Redding in the summer, Jimi Hendrix plays his first show with his Band Of Gypsys – drummer Buddy Miles and old army pal bassist Billy Cox – at the Fillmore East, New York. They will disband after just three gigs: the final appearance is at a peace rally in Madison Square Garden, New York, where, in front of 20,000 people, Hendrix stops the show saying, "Sorry, we just can't get it together."

- **NOVEMBER 15TH: THE FIRST JACKSON FIVE** record to enter the US Top 100 singles is 'I Want You Back.' The family outfit will have four consecutive US Number Ones over the next year, and more than 20 hits (in both the US and UK) during the 1970s and early 1980s. Their huge success is arrested somewhat when youngest brother Michael goes solo...

# The Seventies

# 1970

## January–April

## Whole Lotta Led

**A**PRIL 13TH: 'WHOLE LOTTA LOVE' by Led Zeppelin is awarded a US gold disc. It's the band's biggest single, peaking at Number Four in the US. Guitarist Jimmy Page formed the band in 1968 as the New Yardbirds, recruiting John Paul Jones, a session player and arranger, singer Robert Plant – once with the ludicrously monikered Hobbstweedle, and The Band Of Joy – and, on Plant's recommendation, drummer John 'Bonzo' Bonham, who had been working with Joe Cocker and Chris Farlowe. Their debut album was recorded in a two week rush and then, renamed Led Zeppelin, they headed off to support Vanilla Fudge in the US. By January 1969, their reputation was such that Iron Butterfly refused to follow them on stage. Their debut album *Led Zeppelin*, released on Atlantic after Jerry Wexler signed them on Dusty Springfield's

### JANUARY

• **3RD: WITH JOHN LENNON** away on holiday, the other three Beatles get together in Abbey Road Studios, London, for the first time in four months, to record Harrison's 'I, Me, Mine,' a final addition to the *Let It Be* album and soundtrack. It will be the last real 'Beatles' recording session ever – or at least for 24 years, until the same trio, George, Paul and Ringo, reconvene to cobble together Lennon's 'Free As A Bird' in 1994.

• **4TH: NEIL BOLAND,** chauffeur for Who drummer Keith Moon, dies in a bizarre incident outside a disco in Hatfield, UK – Moon's car is attacked by skinheads and Boland is run over when a panicked Moon, a non-driver, attempts to drive off.

• **5TH: THE SON OF RUDOLF HESS,** Hitler's former deputy, meets British officials to plead for his father's release from Spandau prison in West Berlin, where he's been held since the Nuremberg trials at the end of World War II. Hess is now the only prisoner left in

Spandau, and in failing health. The request is denied. Hess stays there until his death in 1987.

• **7TH: MAX YASGUR,** the farmer on whose property Woodstock was held last year, is sued for $35,000 for damage to neighbouring property caused by festival-goers.

• **11TH: BRITISH HARD-ROCK QUARTET** Free record 'All Right Now' at Trident Studios, London.

• **14TH: AN EXHIBITION** of John Lennon's erotic lithographs is opened in London, but will be shut two days later by the police, who remove eight prints under the Obscene Publications Act.

• **15TH: DIANA ROSS** leaves The Supremes.

• **17TH: THE DOORS** show at the Felt Forum, New York City, is recorded for their in-concert double album *Absolutely Live*.

• **18TH: IN HIGHGATE CEMETERY,** London, Karl Marx's grave is daubed with swastikas and partially blown up.

• **20TH: IN WHAT'S BILLED** as the "Fight Of

The Century," 46-year-old former champion Rocky Marciano knocks out Muhammad Ali in the 13th round. In fact, the fight is faked. Ali is banned from competitive matches and so the two boxers collaborated in the filming of 70 one-minute fight sequences, involving (mostly) pulled punches. These were then edited together to make it look like a real fight. Different endings were shot, and the final result decided by computer just before broadcast. Marciano lost 50 pounds in weight during training for the fight (and wore a wig to hide his baldness), but sadly will never see the finished product, as he dies before it is screened.

• **21ST: THE FIRST COMMERCIAL** flight of a 'Jumbo Jet' sees 330 passengers fly from New York to London aboard a Pan Am 747-100.

• **24TH: ROBERT MOOG** begins marketing the Mini-Moog synthesizer (left).

• **28TH: ARTHUR ASHE,** the black tennis player ranked third the United States, is denied a visa to play in South Africa because of his view of apartheid.

• **29TH: THE STEVE MILLER BAND** plays the first of four nights at the Fillmore West, San Francisco.

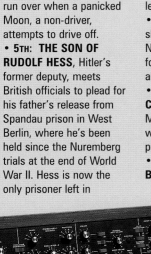

### FEBRUARY

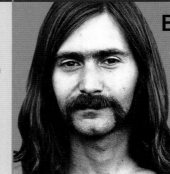

## Eternal Spirit

• **FEBRUARY 28TH: ONE-HIT WONDER** Norman Greenbaum releases 'Spirit In The Sky,' which soars to US Number Three. He will later, less successfully, release 'The Egg Plant That Ate Chicago' under the pseudonym Dr West's Medicine Show & Jug Band. The song 'Spirit In The Sky,' though, will achieve the rare feat of topping the UK charts three times, with three different acts, in 1970, 1986 and 2003.

• **3RD: RENOWNED PHILOSOPHER,** mathematician, and political activist Bertrand Russell dies at the age of 97. He was the founding president of the Campaign For Nuclear Disarmament (CND) in the 1950s, and spent a week in prison in 1961, at 88 years old, for his part in a sit-down protest.

• **5TH: IN THE PARIS THEATRE,** London, David Bowie and his new guitarist Mick Ronson tape a session for underground DJ John Peel's *Sunday Show*.

• **9TH: THE VATICAN IN ROME** calls on Catholic priests to affirm their celibacy on a yearly basis.

• **10TH: A HUGE AVALANCHE** in Val d'Isere, a ski resort in the French Alps, kills 39 people and injures 60.

• **14TH: SIMON & GARFUNKEL'S** most successful album, *Bridge Over Troubled Water*, enters the Billboard album chart in the US, where it will peak at Number One, and stays there for ten weeks. In the UK it holds the Number One position for a record 41 weeks, and remains in the charts for 300.

• **15TH: AFTER 18 PEOPLE** are arrested in a riot during a Sly & The Family Stone concert at Constitution Hall, Washington DC, the right-wing pressure group Daughters Of The American Revolution successfully demand a ban on rock shows at the venue.

• **17TH: FRANK SINATRA** is cleared of having any mafia connections by the New Jersey Commission of Inquiry into Organised Crime.

• **22ND: POWERFUL PROMOTER** Bill Graham offers Bruce Springsteen's group Steel Mill a recording contract, after they make a three-song demo at his studio in San Francisco. They turn it down.

• **28TH: THE GROUP PLAYING** as The Nobs tonight in Copenhagen is actually Led Zeppelin. Airship heiress Frau Eva Von Zeppelin has taken legal action in a doomed attempt to prevent "four shrieking monkeys" from using the family name.

• **20TH: THE TRIAL OF THE CHICAGO SEVEN** turns farcical. They are accused of plotting to incite a riot at the 1968 Democratic convention – their Yippie party had put forward a pig for the presidential nomination. Defendant David Dellinger remonstrates with Judge Julius Hoffman, to shouts of "right on" from supporters. His attorney, meanwhile, calls the judge a "racist, a fascist and a pig." All are acquitted of the plot, but five – Dellinger, Rennie Davis, Thomas Hayden, Abbie Hoffman, and Jerry Rubin – are found guilty of crossing state lines with intent to incite a riot.

• **25TH: RUSSIAN-BORN** abstract painter Mark Rothko, best known for his 'colour-field' canvases, commits suicide in his New York studio, aged 67.

recommendation, was an immediate smash. Their fearsome manager Peter Grant instigated a no-single policy at home (they put out half-a-dozen in the States), which succeeds in increasing their mystique. And their blazing blues/rock music got a helping hand from the good looks of all four band members, in particular Robert 'Percy' Plant. His vocals will be directly responsible for legions of heavy metal yodelers in the years to come. 1969's *Led Zeppelin II* maintains the momentum, but this time the band, and Page in particular, are rather lax about acknowledging their influences. 'Whole Lotta Love' and 'Lemon Song,' in particular, owe a lot to Willie Dixon's 'You Need Love' and Howlin' Wolf's 'Killing Floor' – with a dash of Robert Johnson for good measure. This will later come back to haunt them in the form of lawsuits, but by the start of 1970, according to the UK's *Financial Times,* the group has made $5 million in US sales alone. It's hard to overstate the huge effect Led Zeppelin have on a music scene still in the throes of psychedelia – and bigger and better is to come in the decade ahead.

## MARCH

- **2ND: LONDON RECORDS** begins a legal action in the UK against four Californian record outlets for selling the Rolling Stones' bootleg album *Liver Than You'll Ever Be.*
- **8TH: DIANA ROSS BEGINS** her solo career with eight nights of shows at Framingham, Massachussetts.
- **11TH: AT THE TWELFTH ANNUAL GRAMMY AWARDS**, Blood Sweat & Tears win Best Album, Best Musical Arrangements and Best Contemporary Instrumental Performance; Joni Mitchell wins Best Folk Performance for 'Clouds'; Crosby, Stills, Nash & Young win Best New Artist.
- **16TH: SINGER TAMMI TERRELL** dies of a brain tumour, still only 24 years old. She had undergone six operations in the last 18 months, after first collapsing into Marvin Gaye's arms on-stage.
- **18TH: FORMER ROLLING STONES** manager Andrew Loog Oldham's Immediate label goes into liquidation... Also, Country Joe McDonald is convicted of obscenity and fined $500 for leading a Worcester, Massachussetts, concert crowd in his celebrated "F-U-C-K" cheer.
- **20TH: DAVID BOWIE MARRIES** Angie Barnett in Bromley, Kent, UK. The pair met at a King Crimson launch party.
- **23RD: THE WDAS SOUL SPECTACULAR** is staged in the Convention Hall, Philadelphia, Pennsylvania, featuring Smokey Robinson & The Miracles, Wilson Pickett, Kool & The Gang, Chairmen Of The Board, The Moments, Judy Clay, and The Five Stairsteps. After fighting breaks out in the audience, two girls are hospitalised with gunshot wounds, and three boys with stab wounds.
- **24TH: A STAMP COLLECTOR** from Pennsylvania pays $280,000 for a tiny red one-cent 1856 Guiana (present-day Guyana) stamp, which is expected to double in price over the next ten years.
- **27TH: MARIAH CAREY** is born in New York City.

**• MARCH 11TH: PABLO PICASSO** donates more than 800 of his works to a museum in Barcelona – mostly his early, pre-Cubist paintings from his 'blue' and 'rose' periods. The 88-year-old artist has not lived in Spain since General Franco seized power in 1939 (he backed the communist side against Franco's fascists in the Spanish civil war), but he obviously still has a deep love for Spain. Still producing up to 200 works a year, he dies in France in 1973 – two years before Franco's demise.

- **1ST: JOHN LENNON** issues an April Fool press release saying he and Yoko have both checked into a sex-change clinic – in fact he's at Arthur Janov's London clinic to undergo treatment for heroin addiction. The creative result of Janov's harrowing primal scream therapy includes memorable tracks like 'Mother' on the forthcoming *Plastic Ono Band* album later this year. Lennon later said that he went to Janov because he had a father complex, previously manifested in his enthusiasm for the Maharishi – and Elvis.
- **3RD: BRITISH COUNTRY-ROCK** band Brinsley Schwartz hire a Boeing 707 to take 133 British journalists to see them play their US debut at the Fillmore East in New York. It seems like a good promotional coup... except that the chartered plane is delayed, and most of the scribes, having indulged heavily in the free in-flight alcohol, arrive tired and emotional – pissed in both the US and UK senses – and many don't even make it to the show. Those that do, give it a terrible review anyway... The band are so deflated they almost break up, but go on to become one of the most significant groups on the UK 'pub rock' circuit. Their bass player is Nick Lowe (seen

here) who, as well as becoming son-in-law to Johnny Cash (by marrying his step-daughter Carlene Carter), will produce artists like The Pretenders, Elvis Costello, John Hiatt, and The Fabulous Thuderbirds, as well having a US hit of his own with 'Cruel To Be Kind' in 1979, and writing 'What's So Funny 'Bout Peace Love And Understanding,' later covered by Curtis Stigers on the soundtrack of the movie *The Bodyguard.*
- **4TH: UK POP NEWSPAPER** *New Musical Express* runs the headline: "Keith Emerson and Greg Lake to form new group." The group is Emerson, Lake & Palmer.
- **7TH: *THE LORDS AND THE NEW CREATURES***, a book of poetry by Jim Morrison of The Doors, is published in the US.
- **11TH: APOLLO 13** is launched as the US's third trip to the moon, but an oxygen leak two days later forces the astronauts to abandon ship and return to

Earth in the lunar module, a job for which it was clearly not designed. The crew finally splashes down safely in the Pacific after a further four tense days.
- **22ND: MILLIONS OF** US citizens march to mark the nation's first celebration of Earth Day.
- **25TH: 'ABC' BY THE JACKSON FIVE**, written and produced by the Motown 'Corporation,' knocks The Beatles' 'Let It Be' off the top of the US charts, and becomes the second of their four Number Ones in a row.
- **25TH: MULTI-RACIAL BAND** Pacific Gas And Electric are booed off stage in North Carolina by racists and later shot at as they drive away.
- **26TH: MASTERS & JOHNSON** publish *Human Sexual Inadequacy,* their follow-up to 1966's best-selling *Human Sexual Response.* It doesn't sell quite as well, presumably because people are less keen to ask for the book by name.
- **30TH: ALLMAN BROTHERS BAND** road manager Twiggs Lyndon is arrested for murder following the stabbing of a New York City night club proprietor... And President Nixon announces he has sent US troops into Cambodia to destroy sanctuaries in that country for Communist guerilas.

MARCH

APRIL

## None More Black

• **AUGUST 29TH:** **BLACK SABBATH'S** *PARANOID* enters the UK chart. The band is fronted by 21-year-old John 'Ozzy' Osbourne, with bass player Terry 'Geezer' Butler, drummer Bill Ward, and guitarist (Frank) Anthony Iommi – who actually lost several fingertips early in his career and had to learn to play with home-made prosthetics. Sabbath will have most success as an album and live act, becoming a huge influence on later hard rock. If anyone puts the heavy into metal, it's Sabbath – yet they started as a blues-jazz fusion band in Birmingham, UK in 1967, using names like Polka Tulk, and The Earth Blues Company. They finally named Black Sabbath after a Boris Karloff movie, and quickly became seen as exponents of the darker side of rock. In fact, the band's flirtation with horror and so-called 'satanic' obsessions are nothing but boys' fantasy games ("We just liked the name," as Iommi says), and their place in music history is better served by recalling their heavyweight riffing and raw aggression, inspiring the likes of Metallica and Nirvana.

• **1ST:** **WHILE BOB DYLAN** is recording the album *New Morning* at Columbia Studios, New York City, George Harrison drops by and participates in the session – Dylan also covers Harrison's 'If Not For You' on the record.

• **4TH:** **FOUR STUDENTS** are killed on Kent State University campus in Ohio by US National Guard soldiers during an anti-Vietnam war protest. (Of the four killed only one was even taking part in the demonstration). The incident horrifies Neil Young into writing the song 'Ohio' the following day, which will become a hit for Crosby, Stills, Nash & Young. California Governor Ronald Reagan has previously been quoted on the subject of student unrest as saying, "If it takes a bloodbath, then let's get it over with…" And Seymour Hersh, the freelance reporter who broke the story of the My Lai massacre in Vietnam – and consequently received death threats from anonymous soldiers – is awarded the Pulitzer prize for international reporting. Hersh continues to be one of the US's few cutting-edge, if controversial, political investigative journalists over the next 30 years.

• **7TH:** **HOWLIN' WOLF RECORDS** 'The Red Rooster' in London, with a band including Eric Clapton, Hubert Sumlin, Steve Winwood, and Rolling Stones Bill Wyman and Charlie Watts.

• **8TH:** **THE BEATLES** release their final album, *Let It Be*. Their final single is the US release of 'The Long And Winding Road.'

• **16TH:** **TWO DAYS** after personal clashes have split the group, *Déjà Vu* by Crosby, Stills, Nash & Young reaches Number One on the US album chart.

• **25TH:** **PETER GREEN LEAVES** Fleetwood Mac, the band he formed in 1967, to join a religious order, having given all his money to the poor… Meanwhile the stock market in New York falls 20 points to a seven-year low. The two events are probably unrelated.

• **1ST:** **MARVIN GAYE** starts work on a new single, 'What's Going On', for Tamla Records in Detroit, Michigan – it represents a move in a more serious, spiritual and environmentally conscious direction… And Syd Barrett makes a shambolic appearance at *Extravaganza '70* at London's Olympian Stadium – he plays 'Effervescing Elephant,' 'Terrapin,' 'Gigolo Aunt,' and 'Octopus,' and is backed by Dave Gilmour and Humble Pie drummer Jerry Shirley.

• **3RD:** **TO ENSURE** that The Kinks' new single 'Lola' (left) can be played on the non-commercial BBC, singer Ray Davies has to substitute the words "cherry cola" instead of the brand name "Coca Cola" – unfortunately this entails flying 6,000 miles back to the UK from his tour in the US to record the replacement word, and then flying straight back.

• **7TH:** **BRITISH WRITER E.M. FORSTER** – author of *A Room With A View*, *Howards End*, and *A Passage To India* – dies at the age of 91.

• **12TH:** **SIR LAURENCE OLIVIER** has been made Lord Olivier of Brighton, and a member of the British House Of Lords – he is the first actor to get a peerage.

• **21ST:** **BRAZIL BEAT ITALY 4-1** to win the soccer World Cup in Mexico. Widely considered one of the most talented teams ever to play the game (with a line-up that includes the legendary Pele), Brazil are allowed to keep the trophy because they have now won it three times.

• **22ND:** **PRESIDENT NIXON** signs into law a measure reducing the voting age from 21 to 18 – and immediately calls for a court challenge to the new legislation to determine its constitutionality.

• **23RD:** **CHUBBY CHECKER IS ARRESTED** in Niagara Falls and charged with possession of marijuana and hashish.

• **26TH:** **TEN YEARS AFTER**, featuring guitarist Alvin Lee, play at the Aragon Ballroom, Chicago, Illinois, supported by B.B. King, Brownsville Station, and Mott The Hoople.

• **27TH:** **THOUSANDS OF YOUNG GAY MEN** and women march from New York's Greenwich Village to Central Park in what one organizer calls "a new militancy among homosexuals." … Also today, The Band, Janis Joplin, Grateful Dead, Delaney & Bonnie, Traffic, Buddy Guy, Mountain, Tom Rush, Sea Train, Melanie, and Ten Years After play at the Canadian National Expo Grandstand, Toronto, Canada, as part of the Festival Express – a tour that travels around the country by train

• **JUNE 22ND:** **ELTON JOHN RELEASES** his first album in the US (his second in the UK), called simply *Elton John*. It includes the hit single 'Your Song.' Critics and public alike quickly take to Elton – in August *LA Times* reviewer Robert Hilburn writes: "Rejoice. Rock music, which has been going through a rather uneventful period recently, has a new star. He's Elton John, a 23-year-old Englishman, whose debut Tuesday night at the Troubadour was, in almost every way, magnificent … His music is so staggeringly original … He's going to be one of rock's biggest and most important stars."

## Killing Joke

- **MAY 16TH:** **ROBERT ALTMAN'S MOVIE** *M\*A\*S\*H* wins first prize at the *Cannes Film Festival.* A brutal black comedy about a mobile army surgical hospital on the front lines in the 1950s Korean War, its parallels with the wretched Vietnam conflict were all too clear. Starring Donald Sutherland, Elliot Gould, Sally Kellerman, Robert Duval, and Gary Burghof as Radar (the only actor to transfer to the even more successful TV series a few years later), the movie is also notable for its bleakly ironic theme song, 'Suicide Is Painless,' a Number One hit in the UK in 1980, and a Top Ten when covered by The Manic Street Preachers in 1992.

**AUGUST**

- **3RD:** **THE THREE-DAY** *Second Atlanta Pop Festival* begins in Gainsville, Georgia, featuring The Allman Brothers, Captain Beefheart, John Sebastian, Mountain, Procol Harum, and Johnny Winter. The event, and in particular its drug-related problems (local medics declare the area "an official health disaster zone"), will prompt Georgia governor Lester Maddox to seek legislation banning rock festivals in the state... Meanwhile, in Northern Ireland, a gun battle between British troops and IRA snipers continues in Belfast, after a night of violence in which three civilians are killed and ten soldiers wounded. Bombs have also been exploding throughout the city.
- **8TH:** **BECK HANSON** is born in Los Angeles. He will find fame as innovative 1990s slacker-rock icon Beck.
- **11TH:** **THREE DOG NIGHT** climb to Number One in the US with 'Mama Told Me Not To Come'.
- **12TH:** **THE MOVE** start work on a new track, '10538 Overture,' which will eventually be released as the debut single for Roy Wood's new band, Electric Light Orchestra.
- **18TH:** **AN OPEN-AIR CONCERT** in London's Hyde Park features Pink Floyd, Roy Harper, Kevin Ayers, Edgar Broughton Band, Formerly Fat Harry, and Lol Coxhill. Jim Morrison of The Doors is a member of the audience.
- **21ST:** **THE NEW ASWAN 'HIGH' DAM** is finished across the Nile in southern Egypt, creating the huge Lake Nasser, and allowing widescale crop irrigation – though it has also displaced the ancient Nubian people, the world's oldest-known black culture. Thanks to an international campaign, the temple of Abu Simbel and four huge statues of Ramses have been raised 200 feet so they won't be submerged, but many other Nubian archeological sites are flooded and lost for ever.
- **30TH:** **ROLLING STONES** publicist Les Perrin announces that the band has ended its relationship with manager Allen Klein... And 28 British children damaged in the womb by the drug Thalidomide, prescribed for their mothers' morning sickness, are awarded damages totalling £485,000.

- **JULY 25TH:** **THE CARPENTERS** reach Number One in the US with the Bacharach/David song '(They Long To Be) Close To You.' Easy-listening siblings Richard and Karen will go on to sell around 50 million records in the 1970s alone, and win two Grammys and an Oscar before Karen's early death in 1983.

- **1ST:** **DEREK & THE DOMINOES**, featuring Eric Clapton, begin their first UK tour at the Roundhouse, Dagenham, Essex, UK... Also, the biggest hit of the summer in the UK, 'In The Summertime' by skiffle/jug band Mungo Jerry (below), breaks into the US Top 20, where it will peak at Number Three.

- **2ND:** **THE FIRST KNOWN** interracial marriage in Mississippi history is conducted.
- **4TH:** **THE MEDICINE BALL CARAVAN**, a traveling rock festival headed by the Grateful Dead with The Youngbloods, B.B. King, Alice Cooper, Stoneground, Doug Kershaw, Delaney & Bonnie, and Sal Valentino, leaves San Francisco, planning to travel across the US and on to the UK... And Jim Morrison is arrested after crashing drunkenly into somebody's front porch in Los Angeles. (He was in a car.)
- **6TH:** **ON THE 25TH** anniversary of the dropping of the atomic bomb on Hiroshima, Japan, a peace festival is held at Shea Stadium, including sets from Janis Joplin, Paul Simon, and Steppenwolf.
- **8TH:** *BLOOD SWEAT & TEARS 3* tops the US album chart for the first of two weeks... And Janis Joplin buys a headstone for blues singer Bessie Smith, who died in 1937,

bleeding to death after being turned away from a whites-only hospital after a car wreck.
- **11TH:** **THE REV DANIEL BERRIGAN** is arrested at Block Island, Rhode Island. The 49-year-old Jesuit priest was convicted in 1968, along with his brother (also a priest), of destroying draft records to protest against the Vietnam War. He has been the first priest to appear on the FBI's Most Wanted list.
- **12TH:** **EX-CHICKEN SHACK** singer Christine McVie joins her husband John in Fleetwood Mac.
- **13TH:** **PHIL COLLINS**, drummer for Flaming Youth, sees an advert in UK music mag *Melody Maker*: Genesis are looking for a new drummer – their fourth. Their original drummer, Chris Stewart, left in 1968 to go traveling, and later writes a best-selling book, *Driving Over Lemons*, about his experiences.
- **22ND:** **NEIL YOUNG** releases his third solo album, *After The Goldrush*, in the US.
- **29TH:** **THE SECOND DAY** of the *Third Isle Of Wight Festival* features The Doors, Joni Mitchell, Sly & The Family Stone, Free, John Sebastian, Emerson, Lake & Palmer, Mungo Jerry, Spirit, and an under-par Jimi Hendrix. This is the biggest and most disorganised of the island events. Afterwards promoters the Foulk brothers, who lose $180,000 on the event, announce there will be no more Isle Of Wight festivals: "It started as a beautiful dream, but it's become a monster."

## President Meets King

**D**ECEMBER 21ST: US PRESIDENT Richard Nixon meets Elvis Presley at the White House, Washington DC, to discuss the singer's offer to act as a "federal agent at large" in the fight against drug use. Nixon has recently made an appeal for the lyrics of rock songs to be screened and, if found to contain drug references, banned – and also, in an attempt to discover the causes of the generation gap, he and Vice President Agnew watched films of simulated acid trips and subjected themselves to hours of protest music. Elvis, who is nothing if not patriotic, has sent Nixon a hand-written letter saying, "I am glad to help just so long as it is kept very private," adding, rather curiously, "I have done an in-depth study of drug abuse and Communist brain-washing techniques." Clearly in awe of the president, Elvis feels the need to include a biography of himself, and a note about his recent nomination as one of "America's Most Outstanding Young Men." He also offers a personal gift (a Colt 45 pistol), and finishes off by saying, rather touchingly, "I would love to meet you just to say hello, if you're not too busy..."

• OCTOBER 24TH: **HAVING SHORTENED** their name from the unwieldy Tyrannosaurus Rex, released the album *Electric Warrior*, and embarked on a 17-date tour, T. Rex enter the UK charts with 'Ride A White Swan,' the first of ten UK Top Five singles over the next three years. (Only one, 'Get It On (Bang A Gong)' is a US hit.) Fronted by guitarist, singer and songwriter Marc Bolan, T.Rex will be at the forefront of so-called glam-rock, or glitter-rock – a particularly British phenomenon, with UK acts like Wizzard, Slade, Roxy Music, and Gary Glitter barely registering in the US charts, although The Sweet do marginally better, and of course David Bowie practically makes glam-rock his own with Ziggy Stardust. Its high-camp spirit is soon reflected in US artists such as Alice Cooper and The New York Dolls.

### SEPTEMBER

• 1ST: **THE WORLD'S** first computer chess tournament opens in New York.

• 3RD: **AL 'BLIND OWL' WILSON,** guitarist for Canned Heat, dies of a barbiturate overdose at the age of 27, in the LA home of bandmate Bob Hite.

• 8TH: **ALL THE MAJOR FILM STUDIOS,** except Fox, start proceedings against ABC and CBS TV companies for making their own movies – an alleged contravention of the 'antitrust' monopolies law.

• 12TH: **DURING HIS FIRST US** tour since 1957, Elvis Presley plays at the Miami Beach Convention Center, Miami, Florida. Jim Morrison of the Doors attends the show.

• 14TH: **US VICE PRESIDENT** Spiro T. Agnew, speaking in Las Vegas, Nevada, speaks out against The Beatles for making drug references in such songs as 'With A Little Help From My Friends.'

• 20TH: **IN MIAMI, FLORIDA,** Jim Morrison is acquitted of charges of "lewd and lascivious behaviour," but guilty of indecent exposure and profanity.

• 25TH: **ERICH MARIA REMARQUE** dies at 82. He was the author of German World War I novel *Im Westen Nichts Neues* (translated as *All Quiet On The Western Front*), a soldier's view of the horrors of war.

• 26TH: **IT'S ANNOUNCED THAT** The Jackson Five have sold ten million singles in the last nine months.

• 28TH: **STUDENTS BURN** draft cards in a memorial at Kent State University, Ohio.

### OCTOBER

• OCTOBER 1ST: **CURTIS MAYFIELD** leaves The Impressions to pursue a solo career. His biggest hits will stem from the 1972 movie *Superfly*.

• 3RD: **THE EUROPEAN PRIESTS ASSEMBLY** votes to end celibacy after a week-long conference in Amsterdam. (Right place at the right time.)

• 8TH: **THE NOBEL PRIZE** for literature goes to dissident Russian Alexander Solzhenitsyn, who decides not to go to Sweden to pick up his prize as he doesn't want to risk being permanently separated from his family in Russia.

• 10TH: **NEIL DIAMOND** has the US Number One single with 'Cracklin' Rosie.'

• 11TH: **THE MINISTER** at the parish of St John The Divine in the UK urges the legalization of marijuana.

• 12TH: **A ROCK MEMORABILIA AUCTION** is held in the Fillmore East, New York City. Up for sale are a Cadillac once owned by The Beatles, one of Paul McCartney's Shetland jumpers, and a flute

# Janis & Jimi, RIP

• **OCTOBER 4TH: JANIS JOPLIN DIES** at the age of 27, having overdosed on heroin in the Landmark Hotel, Los Angeles, little more than two weeks after Jimi Hendrix is found dead, at the same age, in the Samarkand Hotel, London. As well as being personal tragedies, these deaths deprive the music world of the leading male and female rock talents of the day. Janis has been working on the classic Pearl album with her new backing group, The Full-Tilt Boogie Band, and just has one too many drug-and-alcohol binges. Jimi's death, on September 18th, has never been entirely demystified: his death certificate records an "open verdict," simply stating "Inhalation of vomit [due to] barbiturate intoxication." Did he mean to kill himself when he took seven sleeping tablets? Or did he just want to sleep and shut out his troubles: he's known to have been unhappy with the way his music is going. Was Janis doing the same with heroin and booze? Her career has been on the up, but real happiness has always seemed to elude her.

belonging to Ian Anderson of Jethro Tull.

• **15TH: AUSTRALIA'S BIGGEST BRIDGE**, the West Gate Bridge in Melbourne, collapses, killing 33 people... Meanwhile in the US, After four years' work by more than 10,000 construction workers, the first tenants move into the lower floors of the World Trade Center (Number One, the north tower), in Manhattan, New York. It will take two more years for the upper floors to be ready in the 110-storey, 415-meter-high edifice, and for the second tower to open.

• **21ST: BLACK SABBATH** appear as guests on a children's TV show in the UK.

• **2ND: TIM BUCKLEY** releases the album *Starsailor* in the US – 30 years later, the name will be borrowed by a UK band who manage to lure Phil Spector out of retirement to produce them.

• **4TH: SESAME STREET**, the new series from the Children's Television Workshop, featuring Jim Henson's Muppets, is approved as good viewing for children by the Educational Testing Service. Henson goes on to develop the Muppets into stars in their own right, with their own long-running TV show. (As you can see, Miss Piggy was also influenced by glam-rock.)

• **5TH: THE ROLLING STONES** turn down the chance of signing Matthew Southern Comfort to their new label, insisting "They're not funky enough."

• **7TH: THE PRESIDENT OF MGM RECORDS**, Mike Curb, wishing to filter out artists who are promoting drug use and other forms of degeneracy, drops 18 acts, including such seemingly homely names as 1950s teen queen Connie Francis and family group The Cowsills.

• **11TH: BOB DYLAN'S LARGELY** impenetrable, stream-of-consciousness novel *Tarantula* is published.

• **12TH: FASHION DESIGNER MARY QUANT** launches a new collection, including the all-in-one "dish cloth" jump-suit... Meanwhile in the US, scientists report the first artificial synthesis of a living cell.

• **15TH: PAUL McCARTNEY** instigates legal proceedings to bring The Beatles to an end.

• **19TH: THE DEATH TOLL** from the cyclone and tidal wave that struck the Ganges Delta in Pakistan a week ago has been put at 150,000 by officials.

• **25TH: SPIRIT RELEASE** their acclaimed album, *Twelve Dreams Of Dr Sardonicus*... The same day, R&B and free-form jazz saxophonist Albert Ayler is found drowned in the Hudson river. The death remains unexplained.

• **28TH: SANTANA REACH** Number One in the US albumswith the Latin-rock crossover *Abraxas*.

• **NOVEMBER 21ST: 'I THINK I LOVE YOU'** by The Partridge Family reaches Number One on the US Top 40. It's taken from the new hit ABC TV series about a musical family who start a band – based, it's said, on the real-life Cowsills (who were originally asked to star, but refused when told their mother was to be replaced by actress Shirley Jones). The series makes a teen idol out of singer/actor David Cassidy, who goes on to have a successful solo career.

• **1ST: DIVORCE** is legalized in Italy for the first time.

• **2ND: THE US SENATE** votes to give 48,000 acres of New Mexico back to Taos Native Americans.

• **4TH: THE ALBUM *SUPERSESSION***, a set of musical jams featuring Mike Bloomfield, Al Kooper and Stephen Stills, is awarded a gold disc in the US.

• **6TH: THE ROLLING STONES** documentary *Gimme Shelter* has its US premier on the one-year anniversary of the concert at Altamont.

• **7TH: DEEP PURPLE** are the latest band to find themselves receiving a hard time at the hands of German fans who believe all concerts should be free. Upwards of 1000 "troublemakers" have been turning up outside shows, encouraging people to damage the venue and then following the band back to their hotels where they throw stones up at the windows.

• **10TH: NORMAN BORLAUG**, the crop expert whose research on new strains of high-yielding rice and wheat has led to a Green Revolution in developing countries, is awarded the Nobel peace prize... And Myra Lewis files for divorce from her husband, Jerry Lee, on grounds of physical abuse and mental cruelty.

• **12TH: 'TEARS OF A CLOWN'** by Smokey Robinson & The Miracles reaches Number One on the US Top 40 singles chart... And The Doors play their last show with Jim Morrison as vocalist, at The Warehouse, New Orleans, Louisiana. In a state near collapse, Morrison pushes himself to continue performing, but finally snaps, smashing the microphone onto the stage and storming off.

• **15TH: THE US FOOD & DRUG ADMINISTRATION** orders the recall of more than one million cans of tuna fish because of a risk of mercury contamination.

• **18TH: AN ATOMIC LEAK** forces hundreds to flee a nuclear test site in the Nevada desert, US.

• **26TH: BRITISH OLYMPIC RUNNER** Lillian Board, a silver medalist in Mexico in 1968, dies of cancer in a Bavarian clinic at the age of 22.

• **30TH: SPAIN'S GENERAL FRANCO**, under pressure in Europe, cancels the death sentences of six Basques.

• **DECEMBER 16TH: ALL FIVE CREEDENCE CLEARWATER REVIVAL** albums and five of their singles (including 'Up Around The Bend,' 'Down On The Corner,' and 'Bad Moon Rising'), are certified gold in the US. The most recent album from the California four-piece, *Cosmo's Factory*, reaches Number One in both the US and UK, and marks the peak of their career. Their gutsy, riff-laden rock, flavoured with country blues and swampy R&B, strikes a resonant chord, but sadly personal differences (basically the Fogerty brothers falling out) bring about the band's premature demise.

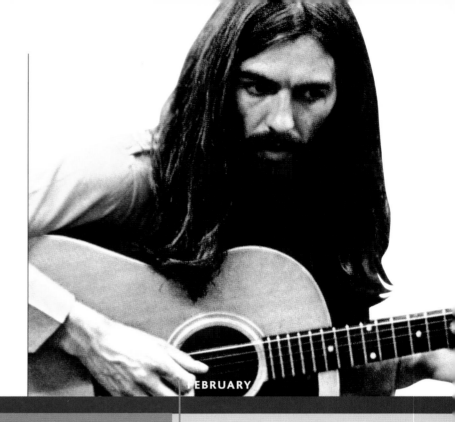

# 1971
## January–April

- **2ND: CIGARETTE ADVERTISING** is banned on US TV – the ban should have started yesterday, but was postponed to allow some extra ads before the up-coming NFL Super Bowl.
- **6TH: REPORTS OF 'STONED'** American soldiers prompts General Creighton Abrams, commander of US forces in Vietnam, to order officers to conduct searches to weed out marijuana growers and smokers in South East Asia... Meanwhile, back home, chemists at the University Of California, Berkeley, announce the first synthetic production of growth hormones.
- **13TH: EMERSON, LAKE & PALMER** release their eponymous debut album.
- **19TH: FRANK ZAPPA** – never one to hide his low opinion of journalists – gets bored with a UK press conference for his upcoming film *200 Motels* (featuring Ringo Starr, and Keith Moon as a nun) and leaves the stage, after insisting, "There's one sequence in the movie where a girl journalist comes onstage and sits in a chair and begins to ask me a series of really banal questions."
- **23RD: DAWN** begin a three-week run at Number One in the US

- **JANUARY 8TH: LAYLA (& OTHER ASSORTED LOVE SONGS)**, the double album debut by Eric Clapton's latest band, Derek & The Dominoes, is released today.

## She Wore It Well

- **JANUARY 10TH: FRENCH FASHION DESIGNER** Gabrielle 'Coco' Chanel dies at the age of 87. The 20th century's most influential name in haute couture, she first found fame in the 1920s, then enjoyed a revival in the 1950s (despite her dubious political leanings in the war years). As Mary Quant once put it, she "invented modern clothes." She revolutionised women's fashion by borrowing from men's wardrobes and fabrics, as well as introducing Chanel No5 perfume, bobbed hair, and the ubiquitous 'little black dress.'

with 'Knock Three Times.'

- **25TH: MAJOR GENERAL IDI AMIN DADA** seizes power in Uganda, killing all troops and officials who remain loyal to deposed leader Milton Obote. Amin later solidifies his position by dissolving Parliament and outlawing political parties... And Grace Slick gives birth to a baby girl (the father is Jefferson Airplane's Paul Kantner). Initial plans to name the child god (with a small g) are abandoned and they settle on China. Years later China will go on to become an MTV 'VJ' presenter, alongside Frank Zappa's equally exotically named offspring, Dweezil and Moon-Unit...
- **27TH: DAVID BOWIE** arrives in America to play his first dates there... Meanwhile over in Britain, in a letter to *The Times* newspaper in London, the self-styled Angry Brigade claim responsibility for a string of bomb attacks on right-wing political and corporate targets, in which property is damaged by small explosions but no one killed or injured (sometimes fortuitously). Disparaged in the press as "drop-outs with brains," the group claim to be directing their anger against the inequalities caused by the unfettered expansion of international capitalism, or as one of their members, John Barker, later puts it, "The twin evils of exploitation and elitism." Barker is one of four 'angries' who is caught and sentenced to ten years in prison. Another, Jake Prescott, later apologises to government minister Robert Carr and his family, whose house he bombed – he even sends them a Christmas card, which Carr's wife describes as "the best Christmas present I ever had." Perhaps because it didn't explode.

- **1ST: A US FEDERAL SURVEY** of marijuana use on college campuses reveals 31 per cent of students have tried it and 14 per cent are regular smokers. Of course. there is a large margin of error here – assuming that some people won't admit to taking illegal substances, and some take so much they can't give a serious answer – or maybe even remember the question.
- **4TH: NEW YORK'S MAYOR LINDSAY VISITS** Detective Frank Serpico in hospital. Serpico, who is part of an investigation into police corruption, has received a bullet wound in the head. It might be small consolation at the time, but in 1973 his story will be made into a hit movie starring Al Pacino.
- **6TH: THE ROLLING STONES** announce that their next UK tour will be the last before they go into exile in France for a year to avoid tax.
- **7TH: GUITARIST TOM FOGERTY** quits Creedence Clearwater Revival... Women finally get the right to vote in Switzerland, though three weeks later the all-male electorate in Lichtenstein votes to refuse women the vote. They recant in 1984.
- **10TH: AN EARTHQUAKE** measuring 6.7 on the

- **APRIL 3RD: THE TEMPTATIONS** top the US singles chart with the Whitfield/Strong song 'Just My Imagination (Running Away With Me).'

Richter scale strikes the San Fernando valley, 50 miles north of LA, resulting in 51 deaths – it could have been a lot more, had it not happened at 6am.
- **13TH: VICE PRESIDENT SPIRO AGNEW** hits three spectators with his first two shots at the *Bob Hope Classic* golf tournament. Disgusted, he jumps into a golf cart and leaves the course.
- **14TH: A QUARTET** called The Engaged Couples

# George Gets The Sue Me, Sue You Blues

JANUARY 2ND: FORMER BEATLES GUITARIST George Harrison dominates the US charts with his triple album *All Things Must Pass* and his single 'My Sweet Lord,' both of which take the Number One positions. But there's an unhappy twist to the story: on February 10th, Harrison will be sued by lawyers representing the publishers (Bright Tunes) and writer (Ronald Mack) of The Chiffons' 1963 hit 'He's So Fine,' who claim that 'My Sweet Lord' sounds suspiciously similar to their record. When the case finally comes to court, some five years later, the judge will decide that parts of the songs are so alike, Harrison must have copied the

earlier track, albeit subconsciously – which, in the judge's opinion, is no defense. Harrison will be found guilty of copyright infringement because the law does not require "intent to infringe". He is ordered to pay damages to Bright Tunes, amounting to $587,000 plus interest. Legal wranglings mean the case rolls on in court for another 20 years. It did not help when, after his contract is termnated, Harrison's lawyer Allen Klein decides to buy Bright Tunes. Mack, meanwhile, gains nothing from the case – he died in the mid-1960s. Harrison will subsequently launch his own record label, Dark Horse, but his public profile remains low (by choice) until 1981...

GEORGE HARRISON
ALL THINGS MUST PASS

**MARCH**

**APRIL**

plays its first gig at the Festfolk Quartet nightclub in Gothenburg, Sweden. Unhappy with their performance, they disband immediately. By the middle of 1972, they will be back together again under a new name – Abba.
• **15TH: THE WHO** launch Pete Townshend's new rock concept piece *Lifehouse* – but the project is a failure, the planned album scrapped, and the best of the songs will be reworked to appear on *Who's Next*... Meanwhile, the UK changes to decimal money from the old pounds, shillings and pence.
• **17TH: JAMES TAYLOR** (below) makes his first major television appearance, singing 'Fire And Rain' on the *Johnny Cash Show*.

• **18TH: AUSTRALIAN MEDIA MOGUL** Rupert Murdoch takes control of London Weekend Television in the UK.
• **20TH: YOUTHS PROTEST IN ATHENS**, Greece, about the enforced shearing of long hair.

• **1ST: A BOMB EXPLODES** in the Senate wing of the Capitol, causing damage but no injuries.
• **5TH: FM RADIO STATIONS** are instructed by the Federal Communications Commission (FCC) that they must not broadcast songs perceived as encouraging drug use, including the likes of 'Puff The Magic Dragon' by Peter, Paul & Mary, 'Lucy In the Sky With Diamonds' by The Beatles, or 'White Rabbit' by Jefferson Airplane.
• **8TH: SILENT MOVIE COMEDIAN HAROLD LLOYD** dies at the age of 77.
• **9TH: LONDON WEEKEND TELEVISION** appoints a new chief executive, after the Independent Broadcasting Authority tells Rupert Murdoch he cannot run both LWT and a national newspaper.
• **13TH: THE ALLMAN BROTHERS** play and record a gig at the Fillmore East, New York City, regarded by many as their breakthrough show.
• **14TH: THREE DOG NIGHT** release a new single, 'Joy To The World,' in the US. It will go all the way to Number One.
• **16TH: AT THE GRAMMY AWARDS**, Simon & Garfunkel collect six awards for *Bridge Over Troubled Water*. Both the album and single of the same name have been US and UK Number Ones – but by the time they collect these Grammys the duo have split and gone their separate ways.
• **20TH: JANIS JOPLIN** reaches Number One on the US singles chart with the posthumous release of 'Me & Bobby McGee.'

• **APRIL 21ST: THE ROLLING STONES** release their new album *Sticky Fingers* – the original cover of which, designed by Andy Warhol features an actual working zipper.

• **2ND: DAVID BOWIE RELEASES** the album *The Man Who Sold The World*. The original cover features a reclining Bowie in drag, but this is considered too much for some markets, so a number of alternatives are supplied.

• **6TH: IGOR STRAVINSKY DIES** at 88. The ever-controversial Russian composer (his 1913 *Rite Of Spring* caused audiences to riot in anger) came to the US in 1939... And Cat Stevens opens at The Troubadour, Los Angeles, for six nights. His support act is a young Carly Simon.
• **10TH: A BOOTLEGGING OPERATION** at the National Manufacturing Company in Phoenix, Arizona, is raided by US Federal Marshals who impound thirty tons of equipment.
• **22ND: PRESIDENT-FOR-LIFE** of Haiti, Francois 'Papa Doc' Duvalier, dies at 61. Within hours, Jean-Claude 'Baby Doc' Duvalier is sworn in as the new dictator of the impoverished republic.
• **24TH: 700 VIETNAM** veterans toss away their war medals in Washington, as more than 200,000 anti-war demonstrators rally on Capitol Hill.

## Nice Suits, Boys

• **FEBRUARY 13TH: THE OSMONDS** reach Number One on the US Top 40 singles chart with the Jackson Five-like 'One Bad Apple.' It'll be the family's only US Number One, though 13-year-old Donny has one of his own in September with 'Go Away Little Girl.' In the UK, though, The Osmonds become the biggest thing in teenage fan hysteria since The Beatles – Donny alone has six Top Ten hits, including three Number Ones, before his 16th birthday. Even nine-year-old baby brother Jimmy has a UK chart-topper with the intensely irritating 'Long-Haired Love From Liverpool,' while sister Marie comes close with 'Paper Roses.' Eventually the others sideline their own stagework to produce Donny & Marie's mindless TV shows – with inevitably unhappy results. But 30 years laters, a comeback looms...

## Now Be Thankful

JULY 24TH: *A CONCERT OF Contemporary Folk and Traditional Folk Music* is held at Tupholme Manor Park, Lincoln, UK, celebrating the new wave of folk-rock acts from Britain and the States. They include James Taylor, The Byrds, Tom Paxton, Buffy St Marie, Incredible String Band, Pentangle, Sandy Denny, Tim Hardin, Steeleye Span, Ralph McTell, Dave Swarbrick & Martin Carthy, and Sonny Terry & Brownie McGhee. Folk-rock is a kind of traditional music with added electric guitars and drum kits. In the US, it can be heard in the music of The Band and Gram Parsons, while in Britain there's a full-blown movement, led by groups like Fairport Convention. Here they are (left) in a classic early line-up, although by 1971 both Sandy Denny (seated) and Richard Thompson (far left) will have left to go solo. Denny, unsurpassed as a singer in this genre, will return briefly, but dies tragically young after a fall in 1978. Thompson, a perennially underrated guitarist, will create his singular version of folk-rock for the next 30 years, initially with his wife Linda, and latterly alone. Fairport Convention, in varying line-ups, plough on into the 21st century.

**MAY**

**JUNE**

**JULY**

- **1ST: THE ROLLING STONES** release their latest single, 'Brown Sugar,' in the US – it'll give them their sixth US Number One.
- **5TH: INDIA APPEALS** for urgent aid for 1.8 million Bangladeshi refugees, while at the same time denying allegations that it has meddled in Pakistan's civil war.
- **6TH: IKE & TINA TURNER** are awarded a US gold disc by the RIAA for their cover of the Creedence Clearwater Revival song 'Proud Mary.'
- **7TH: DUKE ELLINGTON**, at the age of 72, announces his intention to tour Russia.
- **12TH: MICK JAGGER** marries Bianca Perez Morena de Macias in St Tropez, France. Paul McCartney, Ringo Starr, and Eric Clapton are among the guests.
- **13TH: GRACE SLICK** is badly injured in a car accident.
- **14TH: ASPIRING ROCKER** Bruce Springsteen unveils his new group, Dr Zoom & The Sonic Boom, at The Sunshine Inn, Asbury Park, NJ. The band size fluctuates between five and 30 members.
- **15TH: AFTER PINK FLOYD** have performed at the Crystal Palace Bowl Garden Party in south London, it emerges that many of the fish in the lake in front of the stage have died. The general consensus is that they've died from exposure to high noise levels, rather than from fear after catching sight of the 50-foot inflatable octopus the band have brought with them... And Donald Duncan, the inventor of the yo-yo and the parking meter, dies at 78.
- **18TH: CAROLE KING** debuts the songs from her new album, *Tapestry*, live at The Troubadour, Los Angeles.
- **21ST: SIXTY WESTERN WRITERS** and intellectuals, including Jean Paul Sartre and Simone de Beauvoir, denounce Fidel Castro for his treatment of Cuban poet Herberto Padilla, imprisoned without charge after daring to criticise elements of the revolution.
- **25TH: MURDER CHARGES** against Black Panthers Bobby Seale and Ericka Huggins are dropped in Connecticut due to the trial being prejudiced by undue publicity.
- **31ST: THIRTY-ONE FANS** require treatment after their drinks are spiked with LSD at a Grateful Dead gig in Winterland, San Francisco... And Queen Elizabeth II asks Parliament to increase her annual grant.

- **JUNE 26TH: JONI MITCHELL** releases her fourth album, the austere and intensely personal *Blue*, having just had a UK hit with the upbeat (but pointed) 'Big Yellow Taxi' last year. Combining withering wit and fragility, Mitchell becomes, rightly or wrongly, the yardstick for every emancipated female singer-songwriter who follows her in the next 30 years.

- **1ST: THE TWO-ROOMED HOUSE** in Tupelo, Mississippi, where Elvis Presley was born is opened to the public.
- **5TH: TICKETS** for an upcoming appearance by Grand Funk Railroad at Shea Stadium, NY, sell out in 72 hours.
- **6TH: THE LAST EVER** *Ed Sullivan Show* is broadcast on US TV, featuring Gladys Knight & The Pips.
- **9TH: J.J.CALE** finishes recording his solo debut album, *Naturally*, at Bradley's Barn, Mount Juliet, Tennessee.
- **12TH: THE SOUTH AFRICA** broadcasting company lifts its ban on Beatles records... And the four founding members of The Eagles play together for the first time, as the support band for Linda Ronstadt on the Tomorrowland stage at Disneyland, California.
- **14TH: FRANK SINATRA** retires – not for the last time.

- **26TH: IN LOS ANGELES**, Bill Withers makes his first live appearance – on the same day he releases his debut LP.
- **27TH: FIVE THOUSAND MARCH** in a gay rights rally in Central Park, New York.
- **30TH: THREE COSMONAUTS** who've set a world endurance record orbiting the earth are found dead when their Soyuz spacecraft returns to earth.

- **5TH: AN ITALIAN GOVERNMENT-SPONSORED** day-long festival, which includes an assortment of Italian acts, plus Led Zeppelin headlining, brings 15,000 fans into the outdoor Vigorelli Velodromo stadium. But the day ends in violence. Clashes first occur outside the stadium between ticketless fans and police. Then, during Led Zeppelin's set, small fires begin erupting in the audience, stones are thrown, police fire tear gas, and the band finally quit as the police baton-charge rioters.

## Lost In France

- **JULY 3RD: AT 27, JIM MORRISON** of The Doors dies of a heart-attack in his bath in Paris, France. His grave, at the Père Lachaise cemetry in Paris, quickly becomes a shrine for the disaffected youth of the world to visit (on back-packing trips), carve lovelorn graffiti, or just stop and have a think and a smoke – at least until security is tightened in the 1990s after the movie-led Doors revival.

- **10TH: FOR TONIGHT'S GIG** at Brookdale Community College, Lincroft, New Jersey, Dr Zoom & The Sonic Boom have changed their name, wisely, to The Bruce Springsteen Band.
- **21ST: CAROLE KING'S SINGLE** 'It's Too Late' is certified gold in the US by the RIAA.
- **25TH: THE BEACH BOYS** release *Surf's Up*, the album that signals something of a comeback. Its title track is a left-over Brian Wilson track from 1967's abandoned *Smile* project, and stands out as the album's strongest and most poignant song.
- **31ST: JAMES TAYLOR** reaches Number One on the US Top 40 singles chart with his cover of the Carole King song 'You've Got A Friend,' which features backing vocals by Joni Mitchell... And Apollo 15 astronauts David R. Scott and James B. Irwin take the first ever buggy-ride on the moon.

# So Long, Louis

- **JULY 6TH:** **LOUIS 'SATCHMO' ARMSTRONG** dies at 70 (though his exact date of birth is unclear). One of the great pioneers of jazz cornet and trumpet playing since his work with King Oliver and Fletcher Henderson in the 1920s, he was also an important bandleader and a remarkable vocal stylist – not to mention one of the great handkerchief users of the age.

## AUGUST

- **3RD:** **PAUL McCARTNEY** announces the formation of a new band that includes himself, wife Linda, drummer Denny Seiwell, and former Moody Blues guitarist/singer Denny Laine. The band will not choose a name until September, but apparently Turpentine is being seriously considered.
- **4TH:** **EMERSON LAKE & PALMER'S** eponymous debut album is awarded a US gold disc by the RIAA.
- **6TH:** **THE NITTY GRITTY DIRT BAND** start work on their classic triple-album set, *Will The Circle Be Unbroken,* at Woodland Sound Studios, Nashville, Tennessee. The album brings together several generations of country-inspired musicians by featuring The Dirt Band alongside such country legends as Mother Maybelle Carter, Earl Scruggs (and his banjo too), Doc Watson, Roy Acuff, Merle Travis, and Jimmy Martin.
- **9TH:** **EMERGENCY POWERS** are introduced in Northern Ireland as 12 die in riots.
- **13TH:** **KING CURTIS** is stabbed to death outside his New York apartment. The 37-year-old sax player is best known for his work with the Coasters. Aretha Franklin and Stevie Wonder will attend his funeral four days later.
- **21ST:** **P.J. PROBY** finds the audience at the Piper, a club in Preston, Lancashire, UK, confused by his loss of weight and new beard. Some even have their doubts about the performer's true identity. The police are called to check Proby's signature, and in the end the show only goes ahead when the club owners offer £1,000 to anyone who can prove that the main act isn't him.
- **22ND:** **CAMPBELL'S** recalls cans of chicken soup in Texas after finding deadly botulism in some of them.
- **26TH:** **THE BEE GEES** are awarded a US gold disc by the RIAA for their Number One hit single, 'How Can You Mend A Broken Heart?'
- **31ST:** **THE ROLLING STONES** begin a $29m legal suit against former manager Allen Klein, claiming that he has failed to represent the band's interests properly.

- **AUGUST 1ST:** **THE FIRST OF TWO** Concerts For Bangladesh begins at Madison Square Garden, New York City. The brain-child of ex-Beatle George Harrison, it brings together many of his buddies to raise funds for UNICEF's efforts in war-torn Bangladesh. They include Eric Clapton (a rare outing at this drug-dazed period), Bob Dylan, Ringo Starr, Billy Preston, Leon Russell, and sitar guru Ravi Shankar.

## He Wears It Well

**• OCTOBER 2ND:** ROD STEWART'S album *Every Picture Tells a Story* dethrones Carole King's *Tapestry* after 15 weeks at Number One on *Billboard*'s best-selling LP chart. Stewart will remain a member of the Faces until 1975, alongside guitarist Ron Wood, ex-Small Faces drummer Kenney Jones, bass player Ronnie Lane, and keyboard player Ian McLagan. But he has always run a solo career parallel to his day jobs, since his early outings with Long John Baldry's Steampacket and the Jeff Beck Group. He makes his first small inroads in the US with *The Rod Stewart Album* (1969). By 1970, and the release of *Gasoline Alley*, he is better known as a solo act than as part of the Faces. This year's solo follow-up (pictured right) even finds itself in direct chart competition with the Faces' 1972 release, *A Nod's As Good As A Wink To A Blind Horse.* It is no surprise that after that things will gradually deteriorate, culminating in 1973 with Lane's departure from the band, to be replaced by Tetsu Yamauchi. From then on the focus will be firmly on Rod Stewart, and his commercial success and personal fame will skyrocket.

**SEPTEMBER**

**OCTOBER**

**• 4TH:** PAUL AND LINDA McCartney reach Number One in the US with 'Uncle Albert/Admiral Halsey' from their album *Ram*, which *Rolling Stone* has even-handedly described as "the nadir in the decomposition of Sixties' rock so far."

**• 18TH:** PINK FLOYD perform at the Classical Music Festival in Montreux, Switzerland, the first rock band to do so. They play *Atom Heart Mother*, the 23-minute title track of which features a choir and brass section. And The Bay City Rollers enter the UK singles chart for the first time with 'Keep On Dancing,' which will peak at Number Four. After this things go a bit quiet for the band – at least until 1974...

**• 19TH:** THE US ARMY stops using the words "Kill! Kill!" during bayonet drill. Instead, recruits are told to shout the less specific "Yah! Yah!"

**• 20TH:** US CONGRESSMAN Evan Bayh begins a speech in Congress with the words. "Mr President, I desire to pay tribute to a family of five young black musicians and singers from Gary, Indiana..." His speech goes on to praise the Jackson Five's contribution not only to music but to the status of black Americans generally, and ends with, "Indiana and the nation are proud of the Jackson Five."

**• 21ST:** THE HIT SINGLE 'Ain't No Sunshine' by Bill Withers is certified as a US gold disc by the RIAA. It's the first hit for the 33-year-old Virginian, and is produced by Booker T. Jones.

**• 21ST:** THE US REVEALS the existence of eight unanswered letters from Ho Chi Minh seeking aid against French colonial rule in Vietnam in 1945.

**• 24ST:** BOB DYLAN is in Studio B, Columbia Recording Studios, New York City, working on various tracks including 'You Ain't Going Nowhere' and 'I Shall Be Released.'

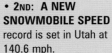

**• OCTOBER 30TH:** THE ALBUM *IMAGINE* by John Lennon & The Plastic Ono Band reaches Number One on the US album chart, and does the same in the UK. It's his first chart-topping LP since leaving The Beatles and his biggest hit until 1980. The title track will virtually become his epitaph.

**• 2ND:** A NEW SNOWMOBILE SPEED record is set in Utah at 140.6 mph.

**• 14TH:** SLY & THE FAMILY STONE release their most celebrated album, *There's A Riot Going On*.

**• 15TH:** FORMER TEEN IDOL Rick Nelson is booed while playing an oldies show at Madison Square Garden, New York City, for daring to perform new material. Incensed by the crowd's response, he later pens the song 'Garden Party,' which goes to Number Six on the US charts and heralds a new period of success.

**• 23RD:** THE INDIAN GOVERNMENT is offering each man $13 and a sari for his wife if he is willing to have a vasectomy. India faces a population of one billion by the year 2000.

**• 28TH:** BRITAIN ENTERS the European Common Market, although opinion is divided in the country as to the merits of this move.

**• 29TH:** DUANE ALLMAN of the Allman Brothers Band, who played slide guitar on 'Layla,' dies in a motorcycle accident in Macon, Georgia.

**• 29TH:** KEN RUSSELL'S FILM *The Devils* is released, inspired by the affair of the possessed nuns of Loudun in 1634... Also around this time, Clackers, or Klick-Klacks, the craze of the summer, are gradually banned from school playgrounds everywhere and start disappearing from stores. It has emerged that the hard acrylic balls which make that satisfyingly irritating clack when struck together have a tendency to shatter into tiny sharp fragments.

## Horrorshow

**• NOVEMBER 1ST:** *A CLOCKWORK ORANGE*, based on the book by Anthony Burgess, is premiered in the US. Delinquent Alex, played by Malcolm McDowell (left), and his teenage 'droogs' murder and rape at will (while talking their own Nadsat language). The movie's shocking portrayal of senseless violence leads to its being widely banned, and director Stanley Kubrick receives death threats. At his insistence, it's withdrawn, and not shown until after his death in 1999.

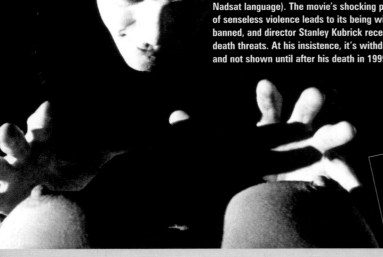

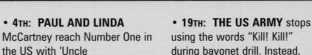

**• SEPTEMBER 27TH:** BLACK SABBATH are awarded a US gold disc by the RIAA for their album *Masters Of Reality*.

## Can Ya Dig It?

**N**OVEMBER 22ND: ISAAC HAYES' 'Theme From *Shaft*' ascends to Number One on the *Billboard* Hot 100. This is 29-year-old Hayes' first solo hit single, though he's had three big-selling albums in the past three years, typical of which was his debut *Hot Buttered Soul*. Throughout the 1960s Hayes was a leading light at Stax, the far-sighted multi-racial soul label set up in Memphis, Tennessee, by Jim Stewart and his sister Estelle Axton. Stax was home to such greats as Booker T & The MGs, Otis Redding, Rufus & Carla Thomas, and Sam & Dave. Hayes was producer, session musician, and writer (with David Porter) on many Stax releases, but becomes a star in his own right thanks to *Shaft* and subsequent movie and live work. His career will get an unexpected late boost, thanks to some badly-drawn kids from South Park.

**NOVEMBER**

**DECEMBER**

• 2ND: **A HURRICANE** and ensuing tidal wave takes 6,000 lives in India.

• 4TH: **THE RAINBOW THEATRE** in London (formerly home to the Beatles Christmas shows when it was the Astoria) opens its doors with a three-date stint by The Who. Also lined up in the near future are Alice Cooper, The Doors, Mountain, The Faces, The Grateful Dead, and Family.

• 6TH: **CHER REACHES** Number One in the US with 'Gypsies, Tramps, And Thieves.'

• 9TH: **CHICAGO IS AWARDED** a US gold disc by the RIAA for the four-disc set *Chicago Live At Carnegie Hall*... And the BBC is inundated with complaints after a boy swears on *Woman's Hour*.

• 10TH: **TWO WOMEN** are tarred and feathered in Belfast, Northern Ireland, for dating British soldiers.

• 13TH: **DAVID CASSIDY**, teen heartthrob of the *Partridge Family,* has his first solo US Top 40 hit single with the 'Cherish.'

• 15TH: **THE PEOPLE'S REPUBLIC OF CHINA** joins the United Nations, and representative Chiao

Kuan-hua promptly rebukes its members for allowing the superpowers "to manipulate and monopolize" them.

• 16TH: **ROGER DE LOUETTE**, a former French intelligence agent, pleads guilty to charges of smuggling $12 million worth of heroin into the United States.

• 19TH: **B.B. KING** marks his 25th year in showbusiness by starting a European tour in London, UK.

• 20TH: **FIRST DAY** of the eight-day Fiesta del Sol, Puerto Rico, which features the Allman Brothers (minus Duane), Beach Boys, Chambers Brothers, Ike & Tina Turner, John Mayall, Jose Feliciano, Lamb, Mountain, Poco, Procol Harum, Richie Havens, Stevie Wonder, and Ten Years After.

• 24TH: **BRITAIN AND RHODESIA** agree greater political rights for black Rhodesians , which could lead eventually to a black government.

• 25TH: **HALF OF CARNABY STREET** in London is sold for $8.5 million.

• 26TH: **CANING OF STUDENTS** as punishment in schools is outlawed in the UK.

• 1ST: **THE MODERN LOVERS**, led by Jonathan Richman, play at Uncle Sam's Dance Palace in the Hotel Continental, Cambridge Common, Boston, Massachussetts. In a few years they will go on to become pioneers of the mid-1970s punk rock explosion.

• 3RD: **DURING A FRANK ZAPPA** concert at Montreux Casino in Switzerland, the venue burns down (taking $50,000 worth of Zappa's gear with it), inspiring Deep Purple to write their song 'Smoke On The Water'... It's not a good month for Zappa: a week later he is attacked onstage at The Rainbow Theatre in London by audience member Trevor Howell, who is jealous because his girlfriend says she loves the avant-garde rock star. Pushed into the orchestra pit, Zappa sustains a broken leg, fractured skull, and concussion. He is taken to a nearby hospital but refuses treatment describing it as 'absolutely filthy.'

• 4TH: **'AMERICAN PIE** (Parts I & II)' by singer-songwriter Don McLean enters the US Top 40 singles chart, en route to Number One, where it'll stay for four weeks. Its theme is "the day the music died" – the 1959 death of Buddy Holly.

• 11TH: **JOHN AND YOKO** perform a benefit concert for John Sinclair, former manager of political rockers MC5, who has been sentenced to ten years in prison for possessing marijuana... Meanwhile

in the UK, comedian Benny Hill hits the top of the charts with 'Ernie (The Fastest Milkman In The West)'

• 14TH: **DETECTIVE FRANK SERPICO** has his day in court, telling the Knapp Commission how he tried to inform high-ranking New York City officials of police corruption – who then failed to act on the allegations.

• 16TH: **THE UN GENERAL ASSEMBLY** approves a treaty banning the use of biological weapons.

• 17TH: **DAVID BOWIE** has his first US album release with *Hunky Dory*. It reaches Number 93 on the album chart.

• 19TH: **BOTH THE CATHOLIC AND PROTESTANT** churches criticize the MPAA system for rating movies.

• 26TH: **A BAND OF VIETNAM** veterans takes control of the Statue Of Liberty in a dramatic anti-war statement.

• 28TH: **LOU REED** arrives in London to start recording his first solo album with guitarist Steve Howe and player Rick Wakeman – both of whom have recently joined Yes.

## Sweet Gene

• OCTOBER 12TH: **AFTER SUFFERING FROM** a bleeding ulcer for months, 1950s rock idol Gene Vincent dies of a seizure in Newhall, California. Vincent had a huge hit with 'Be Bop A Lula' in 1956, though his real tastes ran more to the blues. He was a great musical – and sartorial – influence, particularly on the young John Lennon and teenage guitarist Jeff Beck.

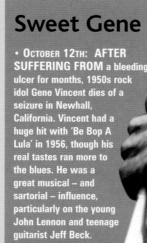

# 1972
## January–April

• APRIL 19TH: **ROBERTA FLACK** is awarded a US gold disc by the RIAA for her hit single 'The First Time Ever I Saw Your Face.' Written in 1963 by folk singer Ewan MacColl for his wife Peggy Seeger to perform, it is Flack's first Number One. She follows up with 'Killing Me Softly With His Song,' inspired by seeing Don McLean live, and 'Feel Like Makin' Love.'

## JANUARY

• **JANUARY 1ST: CAT STEVENS** releases the single 'Morning Has Broken,' a version of a popular English hymn, which will give him one of his biggest hits. A talented songwriter as well as a singer, with credits including 'The First Cut Is The Deepest,' 'Wild World,' 'Matthew & Son,' 'Moon Shadow,' and 'Father & Son,' Stevens will turn his back on the pop world in 1979, having become a devout Muslim and changed his name to Yusuf Islam.

• **JANUARY 1ST: THE NEW CAROLE KING** album, *Music*, goes to Number One on the *Billboard* chart, where it remains for three weeks... And French entertainer Maurice Chevalier dies at 83.

• **15TH: THE J. GEILS BAND** scores its first US hit single when 'Looking For A Love' enters the Top 40.

• **16TH: ROSS BAGDASSARIAN**, the man behind The Chipmunks, dies at 52. Calling himself David Seville, he used sped-up tape machines to create the Chipmunk voices, and his numerous recordings included two US Number Ones in the late 1950s.

• **22ND: TOP SONGWRITING-PRODUCTION** team Holland-Dozier-Holland settle out of court with Motown Records, which had sued them when they left the label.

• **JANUARY 27TH: MAHALIA JACKSON** possibly America's greatest gospel singer, dies at the age of 71. Born in New Orleans, she started her singing career in Chicago's Greater Salem Baptist Church. She once insisted, "I don't work for money – I sing because I love to sing,"

## FEBRUARY

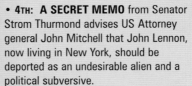

• **FEBRUARY 19TH: HARRY NILSSON** tops the US singles chart with the song 'Without You,' written by Pete Ham & Tom Evans of Badfinger (central pair in inset photo). It's ironic that Nilsson's best-known tracks are cover versions (1969's 'Everybody's Talkin'' was written by Fred Neil), since he started as a songwriter in his own right, having two of his early songs recorded by Phil Spector's Ronettes. The story of UK band Badfinger is one of the most tragic in rock: after early success, including being feted by the Beatles and signed to Apple, financial and personal crises will lead both Ham & Evans to hang themselves – Ham in 1975 and Evans in 1983.

• **4TH: A SECRET MEMO** from Senator Strom Thurmond advises US Attorney general John Mitchell that John Lennon, now living in New York, should be deported as an undesirable alien and a political subversive.

• **5TH: T.REX** reach Number One on the UK singles chart with 'Telegram Sam.'

• **10TH: DAVID BOWIE** reveals his new incarnation as Ziggy Stardust at the Toby Jug pub, Tolworth, London.

• **12TH: AL GREEN** hits US Number One with 'Let's Stay Together' – Green achieved his first US Top 40 singles chart entry six months earlier with 'Tired Of Being Alone.'

• **15TH: LEGISLATION** intended to curb the rise of bootleg recordings by giving copyright protection to sound recordings comes into effect in the US.

• **18TH: NEIL YOUNG** is awarded a US gold disc for the album *Harvest*.

• **19TH: GEORGIO MORODER** (who will go on to have hits with Donna Summer, Sparks, and Blondie) helps Chicory Tip top the UK charts with the first ever synthesizer-driven Number One, 'Son Of My Father.' Many people take an instant dislike to the instrument... Meanwhile Wings release 'Give Ireland Back To The Irish' (another song inspired by Bloody Sunday), and the BBC immediately bans it.

• **22ND: THE IRA** attack British army Parachute Brigade headquarters in Aldershot, Hampshire, as a reprisal for Bloody Sunday but succeed only in killing six civilians (kitchen staff and a priest).

• **JANUARY 20TH: PINK FLOYD** give their first live performance of *Eclipse*, at The Dome, Brighton, UK. A month later they present its London premiere under its new name, *Dark Side Of the Moon*, with four shows at the Rainbow Theatre. The later studio version will go on to become one the most successful albums of all time.

# Sunday Bloody Sunday

**J**ANUARY 30TH: BRITISH PARATROOPERS fire on unarmed demonstrators in the Bogside area of Londonderry, Northern Ireland, killing 13 people and wounding several more. They have been protesting against the UK government's decision to introduce internment in Northern Ireland: it can now hold without trial those it suspect of being terrorists. The government tribunal into the incident clears the soldiers, who say they were under fire. This exacerbates problems in the region, but 26 years later, after constant protests, a full scale inquiry is begun. The incident will become the inspiration behind many songs in years to come, perhaps most notably Irish band U2's 'Sunday Bloody Sunday.'

## MARCH

## Soft Bread

• **JANUARY 7TH: BREAD,** fronted by david gates, earn a US gold disc for their melt-in-the-mouth folk-rock ballad 'Baby I'm A Want You.'

• **1ST: THE EAGLES** begin recording their debut album in London... And a 14-year-old British schoolboy, Timothy Davey, is sentenced to six years in prison for drug offences in Turkey. Despite appeals, including approaches from Prime Minister Edward Heath, he won't be released until he is 17, in May 1974.
• **2ND: THE PIONEER** spacecraft begins its 21-month journey to Jupiter.
• **3RD: HERALDING A PERIOD** of intense creativity, Stevie Wonder releases a new album, *Music Of My Mind*, in the US.
• **6TH: JOHN LENNON'S** temporary US visa is revoked (due to drug convictions), leaving him with a long drawn-out battle ahead to gain a green card
• **10TH: WALTER DEJACO,** the man responsible for designing the gas chambers at Auschwitz, is freed by an Austrian court becaue of "insufficient evidence" to convict him of a crime.
• **13TH: CLIFFORD IRVING** admits to a New York court that he fabricated Howard Hughes'

autobiography after receiving a $750,000 advance from his publishers. Irving was banking on the publicity-shy millionaire's notorious reclusiveness to get away with the plan.
• **14TH: AT THE 14TH** Annual Grammy Awards, Carole King wins Record Of The Year for 'It's Too Late,' Song Of The Year for 'You've Got A Friend,' Album of The Year for *Tapestry*, plus Best Female Vocal Performance. 'Ain't No Sunshine' by Bill Withers is Best R&B Song.
• **15TH: ECCENTRIC DJ ROBERT W MORGAN** takes his life in his hands by playing Donny Osmond's 'Puppy Love' non-stop for 90 minutes on Los Angeles radio station KHJ.
• **18TH: JACKSON BROWNE** releases a new single, 'Doctor My Eyes,' in the US.
• **20TH: MARLON BRANDO'S** son Christian is found after being kidnapped. The perpetrators say they were paid by Christian's mother.
• **25TH: AMERICA** reach Number One on the US singles chart with 'A Horse With No Name.'

## APRIL

• **1ST: BURT REYNOLDS** appears naked in *Cosmopolitan* magazine... Meanwhile four people die during the *Mar Y Sol Festival*, Vega Baja, Puerto Rico, which stars The Allman Brothers, Emerson Lake & Palmer, Fleetwood Mac, Black Sabbath, B.B. King, and the J. Geils Band. For barely-known singer-songwriter Billy Joel, there's another reason to remember the day, because he is spotted by talent scouts from CBS Records.
• **8TH: TODD RUNDGREN** releases a new single, 'I Saw The Light,' in the US.
• **11TH: PAUL McCARTNEY** is fined for taking cannabis into Sweden.
• **15TH: THE ROYAL SCOTS DRAGOON GUARDS** find themselves surprise visitors to the UK's *Top Of The Pops* studios as their version of 'Amazing Grace' tops the UK Charts.
• **16TH: ELECTRIC LIGHT ORCHESTRA,** Roy Wood's new band, make their live debut at The Fox And Greyhound, Park Lane, Croydon, England.
• **20TH: APOLLO 16,** the penultimate lunar mission, piloted by astronauts John Young and Charles Duke Jr, lands on the moon and stays for more than 71 hours. They will splash-down safely seven days later in the Pacific, bringing 200 pounds of moon rock back for study.
• **22ND: JOHN FAIRFAX** and Sylvia Cook become the first people ever to row across the Pacific Ocean.
• **24TH: JOHN LENNON** and Yoko Ono's 'Woman Is The Nigger Of The World' is released and promptly banned almost everywhere.
• **27TH: PHIL KING,** manager of the Blue Oyster Cult, dies after being shot in the head 13 times with a .38 Magnum handgun by a gambling associate.

• **FEBRUARY 28TH: PRESIDENT NIXON'S** historic meeting with Mao Tse-Tung in China ends positively after "serious and frank talks" and the exchanging of gifts – Giant Pandas from China and Musk Oxen from the US.

# 1972

May–August

## Fame Is The Drug For Me

**AUGUST 19TH: ROXY MUSIC RELEASE** their debut single, 'Virginia Plain,' inspired by a painting by frontman Bryan Ferry. This is art-rock: Andy Mackay (sax), Phil Manzanera (guitar) Paul Thompson (drums) and Brian Eno (synthesizer) have dabbled, too. So it is appropriate that it will take the risqué cover art of 1974's Country Life (above), rather than music, to bring them to America's attention.

Elsewhere, however, they are the new sensation – a fabulous creation boasting glamour, wit, and a modicum of artistic chaos. Record-buyers bored with denim, bombast, and the 15-minute guitar solo place the Roxy Music album and the first two singles straight into the UK charts. But after For Your Pleasure, the follow-up, self-proclaimed 'non-musician' Eno leaves, taking the band's radicalism with him. Ferry sets a course for mainstream success with albums like Stranded, Country Life and Siren, but everyone involved has solo projects, and the band are never single-minded enough to conquer the world. Eno, meanwhile, quietly becomes a great producer and musical inspiration.

## MAY

- **2ND: BRUCE SPRINGSTEEN'S** 15-minute audition with CBS's legendary A&R man John Hammond extends to two hours. Later tonight Springsteen plays at The Gaslight Club in New York City.
- **3RD: LES HARVEY** of UK band Stone The Crows is electrocuted on stage in Swansea, Wales. The band's vocalist Maggie Bell, who is also Harvey's girlfriend, collapses (from grief) and is rushed to hospital.
- **5TH: PAUL SIMON**, Carole King, James Taylor, Chicago, Quincy Jones and Judy Collins perform in a benefit concert to raise funds for the US presidential campaign of George McGovern.
- **6TH: DR HOOK & THE MEDICINE SHOW** enter the US singles chart for the first time with a Shel Silverstein song, 'Sylvia's Mother.'
- **7TH: BICKERSHAW FESTIVAL** is held near Wigan, Lancashire, UK, with the Grateful Dead, Hawkwind, Third Ear Band, Donovan, Incredible String Band, Wishbone Ash, Captain Beefheart, and Family.
- **15TH: IN THE US**, Arthur Bremer, an attention-seeking white misfit, fires five close-range shots at George Wallace, the segregationist governor of Alabama, at a rally in Laurel, Maryland. Wallace survives, but a bullet damages his spinal cord, paralyzing him.
- **22ND: CEYLON BECOMES** Sri Lanka after gaining independence from the UK... Meanwhile in Denver, Colorado, Creedence Clearwater Revival play their last show.
- **23RD: RICHARD NIXON** becomes the first US President to visit Russia and signs a pact with Leonid Brezhnev aimed at reducing the risk of war.
- **28TH: THE MAN WHO** gave up the UK throne to marry Wallis Simpson in 1936 dies in Paris at 77. The Duke Of Windsor was King Edward VIII for just 325 days.
- **MAY 29TH: WHEN THE** New York Dolls perform at the Diplomat Hotel, New York City, Gene Simmons and Paul Stanley are inspired to start their band, Kiss.

- **JULY 1ST: SLADE REACH** Number One on the UK singles chart with 'Take Me Bak 'Ome.' In the US, they must wait until the 1980s to achieve even modest success as a hard rock band. But in the UK this will be the second of six chart-toppers, all propelled by poor haircuts, bad spelling, and glam-rock glad rags.

**JUNE**    **JULY**    **AUGUST**

- **3RD:** **SALLY PRIESAND**, ordained at the Isaac M Wise Temple in Cincinnati, Ohio, becomes the first woman rabbi.
- **5TH:** **MICHAEL JACKSON** of the Jackson Five appears on *The Dating Game*, and chooses 'bachelorette' Latanya Simmons.
- **9TH:** **JOHN LENNON**, Bob Dylan and George Harrison are in the audience when Elvis Presley belatedly makes his New York concert debut, at Madison Square Garden.
- **9TH:** **FOLLOWING TREATMENT** for suicidal depression brought on by heroin addiction, Johnny Winter is discharged from River Oaks Hospital, New Orleans, Louisiana.
- **9TH:** **ONE OF THE PICTURES** that has come to epitomise the horror of the war in Vietnam – the image of a young girl, Pahn Thi Kim Phuc, running naked towards the camera after tearing off her clothes to escape burning napalm – is published after American planes accidentally bomb a Vietnamese village.
- **15TH:** **75,000 PEOPLE** attend a rally in Texas that evangelist Billy Graham refers to as a 'religious Woodstock.'
- **16TH:** **GERMAN POLICE** capture the last remaining member of the notorious Baader-Meinhof 'Red Army Faction' when they arrest Ulrike Meinhof in Hanover (Andreas Baader was arrested two weeks previously in Frankfurt).
- **17TH:** **FIVE MEN** are arrested at the Watergate complex in Washington, DC, attempting to bug the offices of the Democratic National Committee, opponents of the sitting president. Meanwhile, in the UK, *Twenty Dynamic Hits* on K-Tel is the UK's Number One album, a landmark for a television-advertised compilation.
- **20TH:** **THE TALLAHATCHIE BRIDGE**, featured in Bobbie Gentry's song Ode To Billy Joe, collapses into the muddy water that also swallowed up Billy Joe McAllister.
- **24TH:** **'TAKE IT EASY,'** the debut single by promising country-rock outfit The Eagles, enters the US singles charts.

- **JUNE 3RD:** **JETHRO TULL** top the US album charts with *Thick As A Brick*.

- **2ND:** **WHEN CULT** Californian band Spirit cancel a gig at The Greyhound, Croydon, UK, they are replaced by Genesis.
- **12TH:** **BOB MARLEY** plays at Paul's Mall, Boston, Massachussetts, US.
- **15TH:** **ELTON JOHN'S** album *Honky Chateau* begins a five-week run at Number One in the US. It contains future hit singles 'Rocket Man' and 'Honky Cat.'

- **16TH:** **SMOKEY ROBINSON** plays his farewell gig with The Miracles in Washington DC. He will be replaced by Billy Griffin.
- **17TH:** **A PERSON** or persons unknown blows up the Rolling Stones' PA truck in Montreal. It remains unclear if the act was a political or musical statement.
- **20TH:** **THE POLICE FORCIBLY** remove an aboriginal camp, set up to draw attention to land rights, outside the Australian parliament building in Canberra, which aboriginals claim is built on land of special significance.
- **22ND:** *THE EAGLES* enters the US album charts.
- **29TH:** **SCREAMING LORD SUTCH** is arrested in London with four naked women as part of a publicity stunt to promote his upcoming tour.

## Watts Going On

- **AUGUST 20TH:** **A SPECTACULAR END** to this year's Watts Summer Festival, with today declared 'Wattstax Day' at the LA Coliseum. The festival has been held every year since 1968, to commemorate the 1965 south Los Angeles riots, remember the 34 who died, and raise money for local community projects. This year's special concert is subsidised by the Stax Records label, so the ticket price is kept to $1 for the day. Over five hours, it features a huge line-up of Stax favorites, including The Staples (above), Isaac Hayes, Rufus & Carla Thomas, Eddie Floyd, The Bar-Kays, Albert King, Billy Eckstein, The Stylistics, and comedian Richard Pryor. Also performing are the controversial Watts Prophets, a trio of performance poets who first got together at a writing project established after the riots by Hollywood screenwriter Budd Schulberg. Their radical political stance and strong live act propel them towards making perhaps the first rap album, 1971's *Rappin' Black In A White World*. A film of the *Wattstax* concert comes out in 1973 and is re-issued in a 30th anniversary special edition in 2003.

- **1ST:** **LOU REED** starts recording sessions for his album *Transformer* in Trident Studios, London, UK.
- **4TH:** **HOTLEGS** change their name to 10cc and release the doo-wop-style pop hit 'Donna.'
- **12TH:** **THE O'JAYS** secure their first US Top 40 hit single with 'Back Stabbers.'
- **22ND:** **RHODESIA IS BANNED** from the Munich Olympics.
- **27TH:** **RUSTY**, a local folk duo featuring Declan McManus (the future Elvis Costello), play at the Temple Bar, Liverpool, UK.
- **31ST:** **IN ONE DAY AT THE MUNICH OLYMPICS**, US swimmer Mark Spitz wins five gold medals, among them the 100 and 200-metre freestyle, and the 100 and 200-metre butterfly. By the end of the Games, he will win two more gold medals, making seven in all.

# 1972
## September–December

## SEPTEMBER

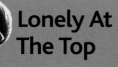

- **1ST: BOBBY FISCHER** becomes the first US citizen to win the world chess championship. (Boris Spassky finally resigns the match by telephone.) Fischer's victory, in Reykjavik, Iceland, ends 24 years of Soviet domination of the title.
- **2ND: HEADLINERS** at the Bull Island Festival, Indiana, are Canned Heat, Brownsville Station, Black Oak Arkansas and Pure Prairie League.
- **5TH: EMERSON, LAKE & PALMER** (ELP) are awarded a US gold disc for their album *Trilogy*... Next week The Hollies will get one for sales of the hit single 'Long Cool Woman In A Black Dress.'
- **12TH: WHEN**

**THE FACES** headline Madison Square Garden, New York City, support acts include a Charleston dancing troupe, a Scottish piper, and a Dixieland jazz band.
- **14TH: TWO BRITISH** trawlers are sunk by Icelandic gunboats during the 'Cod War.'
- **22ND: THE ORIGINAL LINE-UP** of Jefferson Airplane plays its last date together at Winterland, San Francisco... And Idi Amin gives Uganda's 8,000 Asian citizens 48 hours notice to leave the country.
- **26TH: THE PHILIPS N1500**, the first commercially available home video cassette recorder becomes available to schools and colleges in the UK - although the general public must wait until the end of 1973 before they can get their hands on one.

### Lonely At The Top

- **SEPTEMBER 9th: HAVING SPENT** four weeks at the top during July and August, Gilbert O'Sullivan's 'Alone Again Naturally' now returns to the US Number One spot for another week. His bizarre original image seems to represent a nostalgic snapshot of a Depression-era orphan, with flat-cap, pudding-basin haircut, and short trousers. His nerve is much admired, although most are relieved – not least for him – when he switches to stripey sweaters and a curly perm.

## OCTOBER

- **OCTOBER 18TH: FORMER SUPREME DIANA ROSS** makes her movie debut when *Lady Sings The Blues* opens in US cinemas, with Ross in the leading role as the great jazz singer Billie Holiday, who died in 1959.

- **2ND: LED ZEPPELIN** begin a Japanese tour with the first of two nights at The Budokan, Tokyo.
- **6TH: 147 PEOPLE** are killed and 700 more injured in a train wreck in Mexico
- **10TH: GODFATHER OF SOUL** James Brown, visits the White House, Washington DC, to discuss America's race and drugs problems with President Richard Nixon.
- **13TH: A PLANE CRASH** in the Andes leaves a Uruguayan rugby football team to survive a ten-week ordeal in freezing conditions without food. The 16 survivors will eventually need to eat their dead fellow passengers to survive. The event later inspires a TV special called *When Football Players Eat Their Friends*. No, that's a lie. In fact it's the subject of a thoughtful 1993 movie, entitled *Alive!*
- **14TH: AN EDITED VERSION** of The Temptations' 11-minute album track 'Papa Was A Rolling Stone' is released as a single in the US. It'll become the group's fourth (and final) Number One hit.

- **21ST: THE SOUNDTRACK** album to the 'blaxploitation' movie *Superfly*, by Curtis Mayfield, reaches Number One in the US album chart.
- **24TH: STEVIE WONDER** releases his new single, the enormously funky 'Superstition.'

- **OCTOBER 10TH: DAVID BOWIE** is in the US to promote his album *The Rise And Fall Of Ziggy Stardust & The Spiders From Mars* and with it his new persona. It has been acclaimed in the UK, and the first few dates of his tour, including New York's VIP-filled Carnegie Hall, have been a resounding triumph. But tonight he's playing an 11,000-capacity hall in St Louis, Missouri, and fewer than 200 people have turned up. Bowie charms them by inviting them all into the orchestra pit, and performing a special, intimate show. The LP still doesn't sell well, but the legend grows...

## Deadly Games

**S**EPTEMBER 5TH: a group of eight Palestinian gunmen from a group called Black September infiltrate the Israeli team's rooms at the Olympic games in Munich, Germany. They kill two immediately, hold the other nine and demand that Israel releases 200 prisoners. Within 24 hours, seven terrorists will be dead – but so will all the hostages, killed at the airport when their captors realise a rescue attempt is under way.

LOU REED - TRANSFORMER

• DECEMBER 8TH: **LOU REED** releases *Transformer*, the classic album that marks his escape from the shadow of the Velvet Underground, his 1960s band. Reed, born Louis Firbank in Freeport, Long Island, in 1942, had abruptly left the Velvets, one of the most celebrated bands of their era, in 1970. But within two years he was ready to make a leap forward. Produced by David Bowie and Mick Ronson, *Transformer* boasts some of the most important and admired songs of Reed's career, notably 'Walk On The Wild Side,' 'Perfect Day,' and 'Satellite of Love'. After that, things would be less smooth, with Reed veering wildly from the overblown pop of *Sally Can't Dance* (1974) to walls of feedback and white noise on *Metal Machine Music* (1975). The 1980s would bring five strong albums, including *New York,* a triumphant onslaught on racists, extreme right wing politicians, consumerism and more. Reed then turns once again to John Cale on *Songs For Drella* (1990) and the death obsessed *Magic And Loss* (1992). There continue to be reunions for the Velvets, and some less inspired Reed on record. But only a fool would write him off at this stage.

### NOVEMBER

• 4TH: **THE NEWCASTLE BIG BAND** play at the Guildhall, Newcastle, UK. Among its members is Gordon Sumner, later to find fame as Sting.... In the US, Johnny Nash begins four weeks at No1 in the Top 40 singles chart with 'I Can See Clearly Now,' and the Communist Party headquarters in New York is firebombed.
• 6TH: **21-YEAR-OLD NEW YORK DOLLS** drummer Billy Murcia dies while on tour in the UK after a girl pours coffee down his throat while he is asleep, suffocating him
• 7TH: **RICHARD NIXON** is re-elected US president by a huge majority.
• 9TH: **PALEOANTHROPOLOGIST RICHARD LEAKEY** finds 1.8 million-year-old skull at Koobi Fora in Africa
• 11TH: **BERRY OAKLEY**, bass player with the Allman Brother Band, crashes his motorbike, barely a mile from where fellow bandmember Duane Allman also crashed and died just one year previously.
• 12TH: **FOR A GIG IN YORK**, Pennsylvania, Bruce Springsteen's backing musicians are referred to for the first time as The E Street Band.
• 13TH: **THE BBC** celebrates 50 years since it was awarded its monopoly of the UK airwaves.
• 17TH: **THOUSANDS LINE THE STREETS** to celebrate the return of Juan Peron to Argentina after a 17-year long exile.
• 18TH: **STEELY DAN** release a new single, 'Do It Again,' in the US... And Crazy Horse guitarist and songwriter Danny Whitten, author of the much-covered 'I Don't Want To Talk About It,' dies of a heroin overdose before he reaches 30.
• 23RD: **BOB DYLAN** and his wife Sara arrive in Durango, Mexico, to work on the movie *Pat Garrett & Billy The Kid*.

### DECEMBER

• 2ND: Mott The Hoople fail to climb above Number 37 on the US charts with 'All The Young Dudes,' despite having David Bowie, who wrote the song, on backup vocals, guitar and production. It has just reached Number Three in Britain... Meanwhile, the Moody Blues – the second line-up, with the more ethereal Justin Hayward and John Lodge replacing R&B-rocker Denny Laine – finally have a big hit in the US. Oddly it's with a five year old track, 'Nights In White Satin,' whose unforgettable melody will torment the UK charts no fewer than five times in just 12 years.
• 6TH: **THE PUBLIC PROSECUTOR'S OFFICE** in Nice, France, confirms that arrest warrants have been issued for Rolling Stones guitarist Keith Richards and girlfriend Anita Pallenberg for violating French drug laws.
• 9TH: **HELEN REDDY** reaches Number One on the US Top 40 with 'I Am Woman'... And Louella Parsons, veteran US gossip columnist, who, with Hedda Hopper, was once the most influential and feared critic in Hollywood, dies at 91.
• 11TH: **MORE AMERICAN** astronauts land on the moon, via Apollo 17. This is to be the last such mission and the astronauts (Cernan and Schmitt) leave a plaque which reads, "Here man completed his first exploration of the moon."
• 13TH: **£11.25 MILLION** ($18m) in compensation is offered to Thalidomide victims in the UK.
• 14TH: **SEALS & CROFT** are awarded a US Gold Disc by the RIAA for the single 'Summer Breeze.'
• 23RD: **CHUCK BERRY IS DISPLACED** from the top of the UK charts after four weeks. Sadly, the track that's given the godfather of rock guitar his first Number One is the cringeworthy 'My Ding-A-Ling.' It's a mercy for all concerned when it's gone, except it's replaced by Jimmy Osmond singing 'Long Haired Lover From Liverpool.'
• 24TH: **THE MANFRED MANN EARTH BAND** have a concert in Miami stopped due to "excessive noise levels," which results in a riot.
• 25TH: **ROBERT SMITH**, future leader of The Cure, gets his first guitar as a Christmas present... Meanwhile the Nicaraguan capital of Managua is devastated by an earthquake that kills 10,000.
• 26TH: **HARRY S. TRUMAN**, former US president (1945-53) dies at 88.

### This Song Is About You

• NOVEMBER 3RD: **CARLY SIMON MARRIES** James Taylor at her apartment in New York City. The marriage will end stormily after 11 years. Next month Simon will release her biggest hit, 'You're So Vain,' inviting endless speculation as to the song's target. Suspects include Mick Jagger (though he sings on the track, so that's a twist), Warren Beatty, Cat Stevens, and Kris Kristofferson. She might even have been using her imagination. As she says: "Who cares? Like all riddles, it's best unsolved".

# 1973

## DON'T SHOOT ME, I'M ELTON JOHN

In the 1970s, Reginald K. Dwight – short, bespectacled, and prematurely balding – transforms himself into the greatest rock'n'roll showman and song-seller of the age. As well as epitomizing all the flamboyant pop excesses, and inventing a few new ones, he works hard at his craft – creating pop gems with lyricist Bernie Taupin and promoting them around the world, as Frank Sinatra might say, not in a shy way. After 48 manic gigs across America in two months at the end of 1972, Elton does the same thing all over again less than a year later, breaking stadium attendance records set by Elvis Presley along the way. And he does it with some style – big clothes, big glasses, big shoes (apparently his eight-inch platform boots are even checked for drugs at Los Angeles airport). At his Hollywood Bowl gig on September 7th 1973, he brings on a live crocodile to waddle across the stage during 'Crocodile Rock,' (his first Number One from the new album, *Don't Shoot Me I'm Only The Piano Player*), and has lookalikes of people like Marilyn Monroe, The Beatles, the Pope, Frankenstein's monster, the Queen, and Groucho Marx appearing on-stage, with pornstar Linda Lovelace as MC. Plus palm trees, doves, multi-coloured grand pianos, the whole bit... He likes to enjoy himself, does Elton. And then on a BBC show for DJ John Peel at Christmas 1973, he'll be hamming it up on a barrel-house piano, playing cheesy carols and singalong medleys of everything from Victorian music-hall favourites like 'Knees Up Mother Brown' and the 'Hokey Cokey' to Bob Dylan numbers. The serious result of all this tomfoolery, and considerable musicianship, is that Elton is officially the most successful artist of the 1970s, just ahead of Paul McCartney, and the third biggest act of the rock era, behind only Elvis and The Beatles. Over the first 30 years of his career, he will average a US Top 40 hit every six months.

# 1973
## January–April

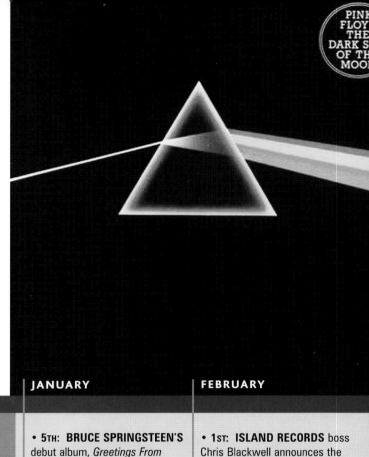

PINK FLOYD THE DARK SIDE OF THE MOON

## No Noel

• **MARCH 26TH:** NOEL COWARD dies at the age of 74. A quintessentially British actor and playwright, his best known musical compositions include 'Mad About The Boy,' and 'Mad Dogs And Englishmen.'

### JANUARY

• **5TH: BRUCE SPRINGSTEEN'S** debut album, *Greetings From Asbury Park, NJ,* is released in America. It fails to chart.
• **7TH: IN THE US** Earl Clarke pays $153,000 for Hitler's bulletproof Mercedes 770-K.
• **13TH: ERIC CLAPTON STAGES** his comeback with a live all-star concert at The Rainbow, London.
• **14TH: ELVIS PRESLEY** makes his historic *Aloha From Hawaii* satellite concert to an audience estimated at over one billion.
• **16TH: SINGER CLARA WARD**, a major inspiration for Aretha Franklin, dies.
• **23RD: THE AUDIENCE GOES WILD** when Neil Young interrupts his show at Madison Square Garden, New York City, to announce that a cease-fire has been declared in the Vietnam War. Four days later a truce is signed in Paris which marks the end of US action in the country. Overall US casualties in the war are said to be approaching 50,000 (the Vietcong closer to one million), and the war has cost almost $110 billion. US bombing does however continue for some time due to what are called "cease fire violations."
• **27TH: 'SUPERSTITION'** becomes Stevie Wonder's first US Number One since 1963.
• **27TH: *AMERICAN GRAFFITI*** is premiered in San Francisco.
• **30TH: GORDON LIDDY** and James McCord are convicted of spying on the Democratic headquarters in the Watergate building. McCord later reveals to Judge Sirica that many top White House officials are involved.

### FEBRUARY

• **1ST: ISLAND RECORDS** boss Chris Blackwell announces the formation of Mango Records, a label intended to groom reggae artists for international success.
• **3RD: ELTON JOHN** tops the US Hot 100 with 'Crocodile Rock.'
• **6TH: WORK BEGINS** on what will become the world's tallest building, the CN Tower in Canada (553.33 meters or 1,815'5"). The building will be topped off in June of 1976.
• **8TH: MAX YASGUR**, the owner of Woodstock farm, dies of a heart attack at the age of 53.
• **14TH: DAVID BOWIE** collapses from exhaustion on stage during a midnight Valentine's Day concert at Radio City Music Hall, New York City.
• **16TH: JOHN MARTYN** releases his second solo album, *Solid Air*.
• **22ND: ISRAEL SHOOTS DOWN** a Libyan airliner for failing to land after flying over an Israeli military airfield in the Sinai – 74 people die... And Roberta Flack is awarded a US gold disc for her hit single 'Killing Me Softly With His Song.'
• **23RD: 'BLINDED BY THE LIGHT,'** the debut single from Bruce Springsteen, is released in the USA. It fails to chart.
• **24TH: AFTER PLAYING** a final gig at the Capitol Theater, Passaic, New Jersey, The Byrds call it a day.

# Dark Side Of The Floyd

**J**ANUARY 18TH: **PINK FLOYD** start work on their album *Dark Side Of The Moon*, with its immaculately-produced tales of everyday madness and paranoia, at Abbey Road studios, London... It'll be released in March, proceed swiftly to US Number One (with a nice US-only Top 20 single in 'Money'), will have generated a gold disc for the band by April, and over the next 30 years will sell more than 34 million copies – not to mention spending more time on the charts than any other record, notching up 741 weeks on the *Billboard* Top 200 (591 of them – that's 11 years, consecutively). But despite spending well over 300 weeks on the UK charts, it never actuallly makes it to Number One there, even though 1970's far less commercial *Atom Heart Mother* did. Funny old world. Floyd will put that right with the follow-up in 1975.

• **APRIL:** **THE WAILERS** have moved on since their mid-1960s ska period (see inset photo). Left to right, Bunny Livingston, Bob Marley, and Peter Tosh have been developing their mature reggae sound – as well as their dreadlocks – having spent some time in the early 1970s working with Jamaican dub guru Lee 'Scratch' Perry. Perry installed a new rhythm section, the Barrett brothers – Aston on bass and Carlton on drums – which rounded out and tightened the musical unit. After three Perry-produced albums, including *Soul Rebels* and *African Herbsman*, The Wailers strike a deal with long-time reggae supporter Chris Blackwell and his UK-based Island label. The first album from this partnership, *Catch A Fire*, is released this April, to rave reviews but not enormous sales, especially in the US. November's follow-up, *Burnin'*, will contain the song 'I Shot The Sheriff,' which Eric Clapton will make famous, drawing attention to its source as he does so. Sadly by the end of the year, the old trio is no more – but a new set of Wailers will help Marley to fame.

---

## MARCH

• **MARCH 28TH:** **MARLON BRANDO REFUSES** his Oscar for his role in *The Godfather* as a protest at Hollywood's portrayal of native Americans.

• **3RD:** **SLADE REACH NO1** in the UK singles chart with 'Cum On Feel the Noize.'

• **4TH:** **SCIENTISTS IN CALIFORNIA** discover that the rings of Saturn are made up of large chunks of solid matter.

• **5TH:** **OCCASIONAL JIMI HENDRIX MANAGER** Michael Jeffries dies in a plane crash in France (there have however been claims he was never on the flight and is still alive today, possibly camping out with Jim Morrison and Elvis).

• **6TH:** **ELTON JOHN** has his first US No1 album with *Don't Shoot Me I'm Only The Piano Player*.

• **8TH:** **PAUL McCARTNEY** is charged with growing pot on his farm in Scotland... and Ron 'Pigpen' McKernan, keyboard

player with the Grateful Dead, dies from liver failure at just 27.

• **20TH:** **A&R MAN PAUL NELSON** signs The New York Dolls to Mercury Records.

• **24TH:** **THE O'JAYS** reach Number One on the US Top 40 singles with 'Love Train'... Meanwhile at the other end of the love spectrum, Alice Cooper's *Billion Dollar Babies* enters the album charts on its way to becoming his first Number One LP in the US and the UK.

• **26TH:** **PRODUCER AL KOOPER** takes Lynyrd Skynyrd into Studio One, Atlanta, Georgia, to begin recording their breakthrough album: *Pronounced Leh-nerd Skin-nerd*.

• **26TH:** **THE FIRST WOMAN STOCKBROKER** in 171 years sets foot on the floor of the London Stock Exchange

• **29TH:** **DR HOOK** & The Medicine Show realise an ambition expressed in the song 'Cover Of The Rolling Stone'.

• **MARCH 12TH:** **LAST EPISODE OF** *Rowan & Martin's Laugh-In* is aired in the US. Actress Goldie Hawn got her break as one of their regular cast.

---

## APRIL

# Four Long Weeks

• **APRIL 21ST:** **DAWN (FRONTED BY TONY ORLANDO)** reach Number One simultaneously on the UK and US singles charts, and stays there for a month, with 'Tie A Yellow Ribbon Round The Old Oak Tree' – a classic example of a record aimed straight down the middle of the road through Middle America. An old-fashioned feel-good sing-along: the kind of thing you find yourself humming before you even realise it. The song, and the actual tying of yellow ribbons around trees, is later adopted by families of homecoming US troops after various conflicts abroad.

• **1ST:** **MOVES ARE MADE** in India to save the tiger from extinction.

• **4TH:** **PAPERS ARE UNCOVERED** at the Vatican which prove aides to Pope Pius XII and probably even the Pope himself, knew of the Nazi extermination camps but failed to speak out against them.

• **7TH:** **THE STEELY DAN** single Reeling In the Years enters the US Top 40.

• **13TH:** **WHEN THE J.GEILS BAND** perform Give It To Me on US tv show In Concert, network censors remove the phrase 'get it up' from the lyric.

• **14TH:** **GIVING IT ALL AWAY**, a single from Roger Daltry's solo album Daltry, enters the UK charts. The album, produced by Adam Faith, contains songs by Leo Sayer and David Courtney.

• **21ST:** **THE DOOBIE BROTHERS** release a new single, Long Train Runnin', in the US.

• **28TH:** **BRUCE SPRINGSTEEN** and his band perform as Chuck Berry's backing group at the University Of Maryland.

• **30TH:** **THE EDGAR WINTER BAND** earns a US gold disc for the album They Only Come Out At Night.

## Gone West

- **August 31st:** **JOHN FORD,** US movie director, dies at 78. Best known for his classic western adventures, he also made *The Quiet Man* and *The Grapes Of Wrath* (and is seen here between James Stewart and John Wayne).

# All The Presidents' Henchmen

**MAY 7TH 1973:** **REPORTERS** Carl Bernstein and Bob Woodward, who've been investigating the Watergate bugging and conspiracy scandal (and are later portrayed on screen by Dustin Hoffman and Robert Redford, right), help the *Washington Post* get a Pulitzer Prize. Although two of the president's top staff have already resigned, Nixon himself still denies any knowledge of the affair or any cover-up. In June, sacked advisor John Dean implicates the president, saying he discussed the details with him many times; then in July it's revealed that Nixon routinely records all converstations and phone calls in his office, so he could easily prove his innocence – but he refuses to hand over these tapes to the Senate Watergate committee. Calls for his impeachment increase...

**MAY**

**JUNE**

- **1st:** *MARVIN GAYE DAY* is proclaimed in Washington DC. During the day Marvin performs twice in the city – first at Cardova High School, then at the Kennedy Center.
- **2nd:** **THE LEBANESE** Civil War begins when 29 people die as the army clash with Palestinian refugees.
- **5th:** **LED ZEPPELIN** attract 56,000 punters to their gig in Tampa, Florida, and break the long-standing concert attendance record which had been set by The Beatles at Shea Stadium in the mid 1960s.
- **8th:** **NATIVE AMERICAN INDIANS** are finally persuaded to leave Wounded Knee in South Dakota, the site of the 1890 massacre of 200 Sioux by Federal Troops. They had occupied the area for 69 days in an attempt to draw attention to civil rights violations and broken US Government treaties... And at the Music Hall, Boston, Mass., Paul Simon starts his first solo tour since the breakup of Simon & Garfunkel.
- **12th:** **TOM WAITS** releases his debut album, *Closing Time*, in the US. It fails to chart – as indeed, shamefully, do his next 16 LPs. Tom's delivery and wit are too rough for polite tastes.
- **14th:** **THE FIRST US** space station Skylab is launched.
- **23rd:** **CLIVE DAVIS,** president of Columbia Records in the US, is sacked for misuse of company cash. He is alleged, for example, to have spent $20,000 of Columbia's money on his son's bar mitzvah.
- **28th:** **RONNIE LANE** leaves the Faces and forms Slim Chance. His old band replaces him with Japanese bass player Tetsu Yamauchi.

- **May 25th:** **THE VIRGIN RECORDS** label is launched in the UK by slick 'hippy' entrepreneur Richard Branson. Its first release is *Tubular Bells* by Mike Oldfield, a one-man orchestra who never really re-creates the same level of originality or success again – although he does reproduce *Tubular Bells* several times.

- **1st:** **ROBERT WYATT,** drummer with Soft Machine and Matching Mole, falls from a third-storey window while drunk at a party, and causes permanent damage to his spine. After six months convalescence he continues his music career from a wheelchair.
- **3rd:** **ALICE COOPER** plays at Madison Square Garden, New York City.
- **6th:** **BARRY WHITE** is awarded a US gold record by the RIAA for his hit single 'I'm Gonna Love You Just a Little More Baby.'
- **20th:** **THE 20TH** Anniversary Edition of US rock TV show *American Bandstand* features Three Dog Night, Paul Revere &The Raiders, and Little Richard.
- **21st:** **BREAD** play their last ever concert, at the Salt Palace, Salt Lake City, Utah, US.
- **23rd:** **10CC REACH NUMBER ONE** in the UK with 'Rubber Bullets.'
- **24th:** **EAMON DE VALERA** finally steps down as Ireland's President, at the age of 90. He was the world's oldest statesman.
- **28th:** **THE *BRITISH RE-INVASION TOUR*** arrives in the US. The package includes Hermans Hermits, Gerry & The Pacemakers, Wayne Fontana, and The Searchers.
- **29th:** **IN OSAKA,** Japan, Deep Purple play their last show with singer Ian Gillan and bass player Roger Glover (although they will rejoin the band as part of later reunion packages). They are replaced by unknown vocalist David Coverdale, and Glenn Hughes on bass.

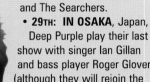

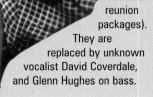

- **July 3rd:** **AT THE END OF** his gig at the Hammersmith Odeon, London, UK, David Bowie announces his "retirement" from showbusiness – which comes as a shock not only to the audience but to the band as well. A press release next day confirms Bowie has quit live performing – but in fact it soon turns out it's only Ziggy Stardust who's retiring. This photo is from Ziggy's last photo shoot, taken later this year, and the enigmatic eye-patch is actually for medical reasons, as Bowie has conjunctivitis at the time.

**Enter The Dragon**

• JULY 20TH: **BRUCE LEE** dies at the age of 32. American-born, he lived in Hong Kong for most of his early life, and trained in martial arts there before displaying his astonishing talents on-screen. At 21 he studied philosophy at Washington University, Seattle, while teaching Kung-Fu to his fellow students – amazing everyone with his strength, speed, and stamina (with his famous two-finger push-ups and the one-inch punch, flooring an opponent with minimal arm movement). Lee first came to wider attention when he landed the part of Kato, sidekick to the Green Hornet in the TV show of that name in the late 1960s. He recovered fully from a severe back injury in 1970 to star in a series of soon-to-be-cult martial arts movies, moving between Hong Kong and Hollywood, delivering titles like *The Big Boss* (*Fists Of Fury*), and *Enter The Dragon* to an unsuepecting US public. Acknowledged as the best in his field, Lee was also in great demand as a martial arts teacher, with some high-profile students such as James Coburn and Steve McQueen. His death has come as a complete shock: apart from recent headaches he seems in supreme health. The official cause is a cerebral edema – swelling of the brain caused by fluid congestion. But, of course, all kind of intrigue and rumour abounds – compounded in 1993 when his actor son Brandon is killed...

## JULY

## AUGUST

• 1ST: **SLADE** set a new UK gig attendance record when they draw 18,000 people to their show at Earl's Court, London... Three days later their drummer Don Powell is hurt in a car accident that kills his girlfriend. He will suffer memory problems for some time afterwards but remains part of the band.
• 5TH: **SOULFUL SINGER** Dobie Gray earns a US gold disc for his hit single 'Drift Away.'
• 6TH: **QUEEN** release their first single 'Keep Yourself Alive.' Their debut album is released a week later.
• 12TH: **RESEARCHERS IN SWEDEN** develop a test to detect marijuana in human blood. Hippies the world over giggle uncontrollably and head for the fridge.
• 13TH: **US ACTOR** Lon Chaney Jr dies at 67 years of age.
• 15TH: **DURING A SHOW** supporting Edgar Winter's White Trash and Sly & The Family Stone, Ray Davies announces, from the stage of the *White City Festival* in London, UK, that he is leaving The Kinks.
• 18TH: **BRITISH ACTOR** Jack Hawkins dies, after compliactions arising from an operation to have an artificial voice-box fitted. He had his own larynx removed after cancer in 1966, but still continued acting – for the last seven years of his career his voice was dubbed by other sound-alike actors.
• 28TH: **THE LARGEST ATTENDANCE** recorded at a rock festival, 600,000, is achieved by the Watkins Glen Summer Jam, outside New York, featuring the Allman Brothers, The Band and the Grateful Dead.
• 30TH: **THALIDOMIDE VICTIMS** win compensation of £20 million ($35m) as the 11-year case, fought by the *Sunday Times* finally ends.

• JULY 14TH: **WHEN THE EVERLY BROTHERS** appear at Knotts Berry Farm in California, US, Phil smashes his guitar and storms off stage. The duo breaks up immediately afterwards.

• 1ST: **THE ALLMAN BROTHERS BAND** releases the album Brothers And Sisters in the US. It'll be their first and only Number One record, and features the Southern band's biggest hit single, 'Ramblin' Man.'
• 2ND: **IN LOS ANGELES** Superior Court, John Phillips, leader of the Mamas & The Papas, lodges a $9m legal suit against Dunhill Records, which he claims has defrauded him and his group.
• 6TH: **STEVIE WONDER** is seriously injured in a car crash in North Carolina, and remains in a coma for four days.
• 11TH: **KISS** are seen by record producer Bill Aucoin while playing in New York City. He is so impressed that he immediately offers them a deal,

• AUGUST 25TH: **THE NEW NUMBER ONE** on the US singles chart is 'Brother Louie' by The Stories. It's a cover version of a track by UK band Hot Chocolate, written by their founding members Errol Brown (left) and Tony Wilson, and taken into the UK Top Ten earlier in the year.

to be made final within the next two weeks.
• 12TH: **JONI MITCHELL**, Neil Young and The Eagles play the second of two nights live at the Topanga Canyon Corral, Los Angeles, California.
• 17TH: **PAUL WILLIAMS** of The Temptations commits suicide in his car in Detroit, Michigan, aged 34.

### Pin-Up Girl
• JULY 2ND: **BETTY GRABLE**, Hollywood musical actress and top WWII pin-up (whose film studio, 20th Century Fox, famously insured her legs for $1 million), dies from cancer at the age of 56.

# 1973

September–December

## End Of Thick Vinyl

**O**CTOBER 17TH: OPEC OIL-PRODUCING states based in the Middle East react to the current Arab-Israeli war by announcing they will be putting oil prices up by 70 per cent, and slashing supplies to countries supporting Israel. Just before Christmas, the Shah of Iran opts for a 100 per cent increase. The subsequent oil shortages cause panic and drastic measures around the world. In the US, drivers accustomed to cheap gasoline have to wait in long lines and pay three times the previous price, as well as sticking to a new fuel-conserving speed limit of 55mph. Everyone has to get used to energy saving (reminded by the SOS slogan: Switch Off Something). Many UK workers are put on a three-day week. Even the record industry is affected – oil-derived vinyl becomes precious, and LP records start becoming physically thinner than they were in the 1960s.

---

## SEPTEMBER

### Ring Master

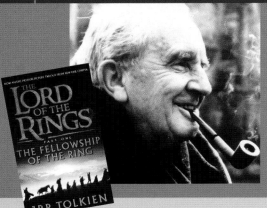

• **SEPTEMBER 2ND:** **J.R.R. TOLKIEN,** author of *The Lord Of The Rings* and *The Hobbit,* dies at 81. The books he began writing for his children will, in 20 years time, become an epic movie event.

• **1ST: PAUL MCCARTNEY** and Wings begin recording the album *Band On The Run* at EMI Studios, Lagos, Nigeria.

• **7TH: SCOT JACKIE STEWART** becomes world champion racing driver for the third time... Meanwhile Ray Charles and Otis Rush feature in the *Second Ann Arbor Blues & Jazz Festival*... And a Royal Navy frigate is accused of attacking an Icelandic gunboat in the North Sea with carrots.

• **8TH: MARVIN GAYE** reaches Number One on the US Top 40 with 'Let's Get It On.'

• **10TH: THE BBC BANS** 'Star Star' by The Rolling Stones, a song about groupies, originally entitled 'Starfucker.'

• **11TH: PRESIDENT SALVADOR ALLENDE** is overthrown by a US-supported military junta. Allende supposedly shoots himself, but many believe he is actually assassinated.

• **12TH: THE JIM CROCE** song 'Time In A Bottle' is featured heavily in the ABC TV drama *She Lives*. The next day, orders for the song begin pouring in at record stores across America. Croce has already had a US chart-topper earlier this year, with the single 'Bad Bad Leroy Brown.' But 'Time In A Bottle' will become his best-known song – and tragically, his own memorial, because he doesn't live to see it become his second Number One. On September 20th, eight days after the TV movie creates such fresh interest in his music, Croce is flying to a gig in Louisiana when his chartered plane crashes into a tree, and he dies at the age of 30.

• **14TH: ELTON JOHN,** dressed as a gorilla, invades the stage during an Iggy Pop performance at Richards Nightclub, Atlanta, Georgia.

• **16TH: B.B. KING,** Muddy Waters, Dr John, The James Gang, John Mayall, and Lynyrd Skynyrd begin a 20-date tour of the US.

• **19TH: GRAM PARSONS,** former guitarist from the Byrds and Flying Burrito Brothers, dies at 26. An inquest fails to find a conclusive cause of death, though traces of alcohol and drugs are found in his bloodstream. His body is later stolen by his manager and, following Parsons' desire to be buried in the desert, burned at Joshua Tree.

---

## OCTOBER

• **4TH: CROSBY STILLS NASH AND YOUNG** are re-united for the first time in two years when the other three join Stephen Stills onstage during a solo performance.

• **8TH: THE FIRST COMMERCIAL** radio station in Britain opens its doors when LBC (London Broadcasting) takes to the air.

• **9TH: PAUL SIMON** is awarded a US gold disc for the single 'Loves Me Like A Rock.'

• **10TH: US VICE-PRESIDENT** Spiro Agnew resigns over charges of tax evasion.

• **11TH: ELVIS PRESLEY** divorces Priscilla, who receives $1.5 million and $4,200 a month as settlement, as well as half the sale of the house ($750,000) plus a five per cent interest in two of Elvis's publishing companies.

• **12TH: ABBA RELEASE** their UK debut single, 'Ring Ring.' It fails to make much impact.

• **13TH: THE POINTER SISTERS** have their first US hit single, when 'Yes We Can Can' peaks at Number 11.

• **15TH: A BLOW AGAINST** radio censorship is struck when the US Supreme Court rules that, "The government cannot, consistent with the First Amendment, require a

• **OCTOBER 20TH: THE SYDNEY OPERA HOUSE** is formally opened by Queen Elizabeth II (although the first public performance, a version of Prokofiev's opera *War And Peace,* happened a month ago on September 28). Started in 1959, the building was intended to take four years, but its design proved enormously complex, costly and controversial. It will come to symbolize Australia.

broadcaster to censor its music."

• **20TH: THE STEVE MILLER BAND** releases a new single, 'The Joker,'. which gives the band its first US Top 40 singles entry. They also earn a gold disc for the album of the same name. The single will be a belated UK Number One for Miller when it's re-released in 1990 (yes, because it's used in a TV commercial).

---

### Knight To Remember

• **OCTOBER 27TH: GLADYS KNIGHT & THE PIPS** reach Number One on the US Top 40 singles chart with 'Midnight Train To Georgia.'

- NOVEMBER 12TH 1973: **THE OFFICIAL BIRTH-DATE OF HIP-HOP.** The Universal Zulu Nation is founded today in New York by Afrika Bambaataa, a former gang member who's borrowed his new name from a 19th century Zulu chief in South Africa (changing it from the less colourful Kevin Donovan). Taking inspiration from the Zulu tribe's code of honour and bravery, the idea is to encourage local street gangs to do something positive and creative with their time and energies – which leads to an explosion of DJs, rappers, break-dancers and graffiti artists, and the start of what becomes known as 'hip-hop' culture. Bambaataa's vision is for a peaceful, multi-ethnic co-existence, with music as a unifying factor – although he's a musically astute DJ in his own right, he's best known as an instigator of community events and performances, and doesn't put anything on vinyl until the acclaimed 'Planet Rock' in 1982. The person credited with being the main innovator on the musical side of hip-hop is Jamaican-born Clive Campbell, better known as Kool Herc, whose trademarks include extending his eclectic set of soul, funk, jazz and old R&B tracks by repeating 'breakbeat' sections (long before the days of samplers), using two turntables, and 'rapping' over the top.

## NOVEMBER

- 4TH: **PINK FLOYD** and Soft Machine play a benefit for Robert Wyatt at the Rainbow in London.
- 5TH: **A PERFORMANCE** of The Who's *Quadrophenia* shambles to a premature end when Pete Townshend storms off stage. But the band does return to play some older songs.
- 9TH: **BILLY JOEL RELEASES** *Piano Man,* his breakthrough album in the US, taking him into the Top 40 albums (and singles) chart for the first time.

- 10TH: **ELTON JOHN** reaches Number One on the US (and UK) album chart with *Goodbye Yellow Brick Road,* which includes the future hit 'Candle In The Wind.'
- 11TH: **A LIVE MOTT THE HOOPLE** concert, broadcast today on 30 US radio stations, is later revealed to have consisted entirely of studio tracks with applause dubbed on at the beginning and end of each song.
- 13TH: **JERRY LEE LEWIS'** son is killed in a car accident at 19.
- 17TH: **'PHOTOGRAPH'** by Ringo Starr goes to Number One on the US singles chart. John Lennon is now the only former Beatle not to have had a solo Number One in the US – he has to wait another year.

- 19TH: *BRAIN SALAD SURGERY* is the new album from classically-oriented prog-rock trio Emerson, Lake & Palmer. It's their fourth album, but the first on their own Manticore label (named after a mythical beast on their LP *Tarkus* – this is the early 1970s, after all). *Brain Salad* is also notable for its striking cover art (below). It's the first time many people have seen the work of H.R. Giger, who will later design the creature in *Alien*.

- 20TH: **COMEDIAN ALLAN SHERMAN,** the man behind hit record 'Hello Muddah, Hello Fadduh,' dies at 48... And Tangerine Dream begin recording their groundbreaking electronic album *Phaedra* at The Manor, Shipton-on-Cherwell, Oxfordshire, UK.
- 24TH: **AUSTRALIAN ABORIGINES** get the vote.
- 26TH: **FORMER SHADOW** John Rostill is electrocuted by his guitar, at 31.
- 29TH: **CHARLIE RICH** has a US Top 40 entry with the country hit 'The Most Beautiful Girl In The World.' By the middle of December it'll be the US Number One, and reaches UK Number Two next spring.

## DECEMBER

- 1ST: **FOUNDING FATHER** of modern Israel, and the country's first prime minister, David Ben Gurion, dies aged 87... And The Carpenters reach Number One on the US Top 40 singles with 'Top Of The World.'
- 2ND: **THE WHO** are imprisoned after trashing a hotel room in Montreal, Canada.
- 7TH: **A FORMER** manager of Fleetwood Mac, Clifford Davis, claims ownership of the band's name, and sends a fake band on tour.
- 10TH: **THE LEGENDARY** CBGB's club is opened by Hilly Kristal on The Bowery in East Greenwich Village, New York City.
- 14TH: **JOHN PAUL GETTY II,** the teenage grandson of the oil tycoon, is finally set free by his Italian kidnappers after part of his ear had been cut off and sent, together with a ransom note, demanding $750,000 to his grandfather who paid the ransom.
- 20TH: **SPANISH PRIME MINISTER** Luis Carrero Blanco is killed when a bomb explodes as his car passes.
- 31ST: **AC/DC** play their first ever gig at The Chequers Club, Sydney.

- **DECEMBER 26TH:** *THE EXORCIST* (below) is released, and quickly acknowledged as the scariest film yet made. The use of extracts from *Tubular Bells* on the soundtrack gives Mike Oldfield's opus an edgy new dimension too.

- **DECEMBER 20TH: BOBBY DARIN DIES** after surgery to replace a faulty heart valve – he's just 37, but he's had heart problems since childhood, when he caught rheumatic fever while growing up in poverty in the New York Bronx. A singer and multi-instrumentalist, as well as an actor and all-round showman, Darin had over 20 mostly easy-listening pop hits between 1958 and 1967, including 'Dream Lover,' 'Mack The Knife,' 'Things,' and 'If I Were A Carpenter.' His high-profile celebrity marriage to teen starlet Sandra Dee ended in 1967. Darin held stongly left-wing political views (he was once booed on-stage for singing a protest song), and was traumatised by the death of Robert Kennedy. In 2003 his life will be the subject of a new film from actor and fan Kevin Spacey.

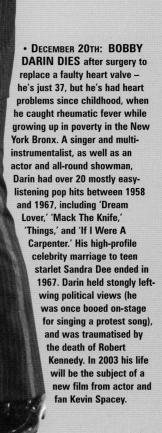

# 1974
## January–April

## Abba Arrive

**A**PRIL 6TH: **ABBA WIN** the *Eurovision Song Contest,* singing the self-written 'Waterloo' (having failed in their attempt to qualify last year with 'Ring Ring.') In the only known instance of *Eurovision* throwing up anything other than totally cheesy pop or obscure one-hit wonders, 1974's Swedish winners (whose bandname comes from their four first-names: Anni-Frid Lyngstad, Benny Andersson, Björn Ulvaeus, and Agnetha Fältskog) go on to defy expectations by becoming one of the most successful pop groups of all time. Within a month 'Waterloo' will be their first, but certainly not last, UK Number One (it even makes the US Top Ten in August, though the States is a bit slower to take to the band). Abba will go on to notch up 17 UK Top Five singles in the next seven years, nine of which will reach Number One

### JANUARY

• **3RD: AFTER EIGHT YEARS** off the road, Bob Dylan launches into a 39-day US tour with The Band, starting at The Amphitheatre in Chicago, Illinois. The shows are recorded, resulting in the fine double live album *Before The Flood.*
• **8TH: US COMIC-BOOK** glam-rockers Kiss are signed to Casablanca Records.
• **5TH: BROWNSVILLE STATION** earn a US gold record for their only hit single, 'Smokin' In The Boys' Room.'
• **11TH: MRS SUE ROSENKOWITZ** gives birth to the first ever sextuplets, in Cape Town, South Africa.
• **13TH: THE WORLD'S**

**LARGEST** airport opens in Dallas, Texas.
• **16TH: PETER BENCHLEY'S** book *Jaws* is published.
• **23RD: JOHN CUMMINGS** buys a $50 Mosrite guitar at Manny's Guitar Center, 48th Street, New York City. He will put it to good use when he changes his name and becomes Johnny Ramone of The Ramones.
• **24TH: STEVIE WONDER** plays at the Rainbow, London – his first show since his near-fatal accident some months earlier. Audience includes Paul McCartney, Ringo Starr, Bowie, Clapton, and the Staples Singers.

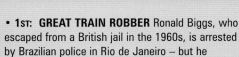

• **JANUARY 5TH: BRITISH PROG-ROCKERS YES** reach Number One on the UK album charts (Number Six in the US) with *Tales From Topographic Oceans.* Reflecting their taste for long, drawn-out pieces, it's a double album with four tracks.

• **31ST: FILM PRODUCER** Sam Goldwyn, co-founder of MGM, home of the Hollywood musical, dies at the age of 91.

## Get Your Coat...

• **FEBRUARY 12TH: ALEXANDER SOLZHENITSYN** is arrested and charged with treason after his book *Gulag Archipelago* is condemned as "slander" by Soviet officials in Moscow. The book details some of the hardships and brutality observed by the dissident author during his own long internment in forced-labour camps. The following day he is expelled from the country, and doesn't return to his homeland until 1994, in the more liberal era after the break-up of the Soviet Union. It does mean he is finally able to collect his 1970 Nobel prize.

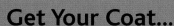

### FEBRUARY

• **1ST: GREAT TRAIN ROBBER** Ronald Biggs, who escaped from a British jail in the 1960s, is arrested by Brazilian police in Rio de Janeiro – but he escapes extradition because he is the father of his Brazilian girlfriend's child.
• **2ND: KEITH EMERSON** of Emerson, Lake & Palmer injures his hands when his piano explodes in San Francisco. A device rigged to blow up the piano as a special effect is triggered too early.
• **4TH: JOHN LENNON** and Yoko Ono separate, for 18 months, during which time Lennon lives with with former assistant May Pang (at Yoko's suggestion, apparently), and also spends much time

socialising with old friends. (It's said he even has a jam with Paul McCartney, which exists on a poor-quality bootleg somewhere.) And there are some notorious hell-raising binges with his mate Harry Nilsson – seen here with John and May Pang – which include being thrown out of The Troubadour in Los Angeles.
• **5TH: NINETEEN-YEAR-OLD** US heiress Patty Hearst is kidnapped from her San Francisco apartment. It is later revealed that she is in the hands of the Symbionese Liberation Army, an extreme left-wing group who want the ransom money used to buy food for the poor. Ten days later Hearst herself is filmed carrying a gun and taking part in a bank raid with her kidnappers.
• **8TH: AFTER 85 DAYS** in the Skylab space station, US astronauts Gerald Carr, Edward Gibson, and William Pogue return safely to earth.
• **14TH: DARYL DRAGON** and Toni Tenille (aka The Captain & Tenille) are married in a Valentine's Day ceremony, shortly after the release of their debut single, 'The Way I Want To Touch You.'
• **15TH: LOU REED** plays in Rome, Italy, and his show is disrupted by fascist group Members Of The Creative Situations. It sparks a riot.
• **20TH: DESPITE A TOTAL LACK** of advertising, Yes sell out their concert at Madison Square Garden, New York City... And Cher files for divorce from Sonny Bono.

## Can't Get Enough Barry

• **FEBRUARY 9TH: THE LOVE UNLIMITED ORCHESTRA,** a 40-piece soul band led by singer/songwriter/producer Barry White, reaches Number One on the US Top 40 with 'Love's Theme.' Throughout 1973-74 Barry is at the peak of his powers, charting five times – topping the US charts with 'Can't Get Enough Of Your Love, Babe,' and the UK charts with 'You're The First, The Last, My Everything.'

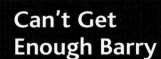

(including 'SOS,' 'Take A Chance On Me,' and 'Dancing Queen,' their only US chart-topper.) And they're still regularly charting when internal wrangles force them to call it quits in early 1982 after their final album, *The Visitors*. (The quartet have formed two couples, married, and divorced, as well as having all the usual band pressures to deal with.) Even their permanent demise (they persistently resist appeals to reform) doesn't stop them selling millions more albums. Quite apart from the music (for which many would say 'Thank you,' like the song says), Abba's other lasting legacy will be the fact that, coming from the previously unknown musical wilds of Scandinavia, they took the notoriously insular US/UK music market by the scruff of the neck in the 1970s, shaking

it vigorously awake, and undoubtedly, although unwittingly, opened up western charts and minds to acts from other 'territories' – at least to some extent. (The fact that they sang in English can't be underestimated.) Abba are of course not without critics – occasionally vituperative – often being accused of churning out predictably 'poppy' and safe music: but in fact many of those Andersson/Ulvaeus compositions are more musically sophisticated than they're given credit for. And besides, it's easy to forget how, that one night on the *Eurovision Song Contest*, dressed in unbelievably glam tight flares and stack-heeled platform boots, they breathed some arctic-fresh air into a very fusty old music industry event.

## MARCH

• **2ND: STEVIE WONDER** collects five Grammy Awards for his album *Innervisions*, plus the singles 'Superstition' and 'You Are The Sunshine Of My Life' .... Meanwhile a US Grand Jury agrees that President Richard Nixon is involved in the Watergate cover-up... But Terry Jacks takes everyone's mind off such depressing matters with his equally depressing death-song 'Seasons In The Sun' (in fact originally recorded by The Kingston Trio).

• **4TH: BRITISH PRIME MINISTER** Edward Heath fails to persuade the Liberal Party to join a coalition with the Tory party, and he resigns. Labour's Harold Wilson will later become Prime Minister for a third time with a narrow majority.

• **9TH: QUEEN'S** second single, Seven Seas Of Rhye, enters the UK chart and gives them their first hit.

• **10TH: A JAPANESE SOLDIER** who still believes the Second World War is being fought is discovered on Lubang Island in the Philippines. He says he was waiting to be relieved by his military.

• **13TH: CHARLES DE GAULLE AIRPORT** in Paris is opened.

• **19TH: JEFFERSON STARSHIP** (formerly Jefferson Airplane) begin their first tour under their new, space-age name.

• **20TH: AN ATTEMPT** is made to kidnap Princess Anne by a gunman in central London. He is later charged with attempted murder, but argues that he only did it to highlight the lack of mental care facilities.

• **23RD: THE GRATEFUL DEAD** introduce their huge new amplification system, the Wall Of Sound, at the Cow Palace, Daly City, California.

• **28TH: ARTHUR 'BIG BOY' CRUDUP**, the blues singer best known for the original versions of Elvis hits 'That's Alright, Mama' and 'My Baby Left Me,' dies at the age of 69.

• **29TH: US MARINER 10** space probe takes close-ups of the red-hot planet Mercury.

• **31ST: TELEVISION** make their debut at CBGB's, New York City. According to punk chronicler Clinton Heylin, 'It was the beginning of a six-month period in which post-glam NY rock'n'roll coalesced into a small but highly active scene.'

• **2ND: THE DOOBIE BROTHERS** are awarded a US gold disc for the album *What Were Once Vices Are Now Habits*.

• **8TH: HANK AARON** slugs his 715th home run, passing the record set by Babe Ruth.

• **10TH: GOLDA MEIR** resigns as Israeli Prime Minister over differences with her Labour Party colleagues. Yitzhak Rabin becomes the new party leader on 22nd April... Meanwhile outside, after a gig at Charlie's Bar, Cambridge, Massachussetts, Bruce Springsteen encounters rock critic Jon Landau for the first time. Landau will later become his manager.

• **13TH: ELTON JOHN** reaches Number One on the US Top 40 singles chart with 'Bennie And The Jets.'

• **22ND: FILMING STARTS** on Ken Russell's movie version of The Who's rock musical *Tommy*.

• **25TH: JIM MORRISON'S** widow Pam dies from a suspected heroin overdose at 27.

• **27TH: EARTH WIND & FIRE** have their first US Top 40 chart entry with 'Mighty Mighty'... And Scottish band The Bay City Rollers have their first UK Top Five with 'Shang-A-Lang.' They're already the biggest homegrown act since The Beatles, with a swelling mass of 'teenybopper' fans...

• **APRIL 20TH: STUDIO BAND MFSB** (Mother, Father, Sister, Brother) & The Three Degrees, below, top the US singles chart with 'The Sound Of Philadelphia'.

• **JUNE 8TH:** 'I WILL ALWAYS LOVE YOU,' written and sung by Dolly Parton, reaches Number One on the US country charts. It's a schmaltzy ballad, to be sure, delivered with Parton's customary rural charm – though nowhere near the quivering overblown aria it becomes when Whitney Houston revives it (to even greater success, admittedly) in 1992. Dolly herself doesn't have any mainstream crossover hits until early 1978.

## MAY

• **1ST:** **THE CARPENTERS** perform in the White House, Washington, DC, at the request of President Nixon, during a dinner in honour of West German Chancellor Willy Brandt. Five days later Brandt resigns when it's revealed that his closest aide is working for the East German communists.

• **4TH:** **GRAND FUNK RAILROAD** reach Number One in the US with a new version of Carole King's 'The Loco-Motion'.

• **5TH:** **THE STILETTOS**, later to become Blondie, play their first gig at CBGB's, New York City, as support to Television.

• **8TH:** **UK BLUES** giant Graham Bond dies after falling in front of an underground train at Finsbury Park. It's never established whether it is an accident or suicide.

• **11TH:** **AS MANY** as 20,000 are feared dead after earthquakes in the Sichuan and Yunnan provinces of China.

• **15TH:** **THE FIRST** Rolling Stone solo album, *Monkey Grip*, is released by Bill Wyman.

• **16TH:** **NEIL YOUNG** unexpectedly appears at the Bottom Line, New York City, to showcase his latest album, *On The Beach*.

• **26TH:** **A 14-YEAR-OLD DAVID CASSIDY FAN**, Bernadette Whelan, is crushed to death at a stadium gig in London.

• **31ST:** **RICK WAKEMAN'S SECOND** solo album, *Journey To The Centre Of The Earth*, becomes his most successful, reaching Number One on the UK album charts and Number Three in the US. The flamboyant virtuoso keyboard player, fast becoming renowned for his extravagant live shows, quits Yes this summer to tour this album around the States, having debuted it in January at the London Festival Hall, complete with orchestra and choir. At the end of the tour, Wakeman has a heart attack, though he will recover to record *King Arthur*, and then to rejoin a new incarnation of Yes in 1976.

## Bruce Off And Running

**M**AY 9TH: THE FIRST known performance of Bruce Springsteen's *Born To Run* takes place during a show at Harvard Square Theatre, Cambridge, Massachusetts. John Landau reviews the show for *The Real Paper*, saying "I saw rock'n'roll future and its name is Bruce Springsteen." Bruce records the song on August 1st, but it'll be more than a year before the album is released, by which time the world is ready for The Boss.

• AUGUST 8TH: RICHARD M. NIXON is the first (and so far, only) President of the US to resign. Even though, as he says in his resignation speech, it goes against "every instinct in my body ... I have never been a quitter," he is forced to do so because of his proven participation in the Watergate affair and subsequent cover-up, and the very real danger of being impeached. The following day, vice-president Gerald R. Ford becomes the 38th US president – the first completely unelected US president, as he also replaced Spiro Agnew as vice-president mid-term.

• MAY 18TH: 'THE STREAK,' by Ray Stevens, becomes the novelty Number One of the summer (in both the US and UK), reflecting the currently popular craze for stripping off and running down busy streets or through sports events for no particular reason...

**JUNE**

## No Choke

• JUNE 14TH: DR HENRY M. HEIMLICH first reveals his lung compression maneuver to prevent choking by expelling trapped items from the windpipe. Dr Heimlich is seen here demonstrating the maneuver himself, presumably with a consenting partner.

• 1ST: A REPORT REVEALS that major changes in the US housing market have been brought about by house buyers' preferences for condominium housing... Meanwhile Alanis Morissette is born in Ottawa, Canada.
• 2ND: IN CALGARY, CANADA, a 13-year-old boy dies accidentally by hanging himself at a 'hanging party' inspired by Alice Cooper's mock scaffold routine, which he has seen on a tv show.
• 5TH: MORE THAN 10,000 PEOPLE are thought to have died in the smallpox epidemic sweeping India.... And Sly Stone of Sly & The Family Stone marries Kathy Silva on the stage at Madison Square Garden, New York City.
• 13TH: ELTON JOHN enters the record books as his new contract with MCA gives him an unprecedented 28 per cent royalty and guarantees him £8m ($13m) in advances over a five-year period.
• 15TH: BO DONALDSON & The Heywoods reach Number One on the US Top 40 singles chart with 'Billy Don't Be A Hero.' The song was first a hit in the UK earlier in the year for the band Paper Lace.
• 17TH: THE IRA SUCCEED in planting a bomb in a section of the UK Houses Of Parliament, injuring 11 people in the blast.
• 29TH: AS A RESULT of her husband's illness, Isabel Perón, second wife of Juan Perón, is sworn in as president of Argentina,
• 30TH: SOVIET-BORN BALLET DANCER Mikhail Baryshnikov defects to the West while on tour in Canada with the Kirov Ballet.

• JULY 8TH: STEELY DAN, led by Walter Becker and Donald Fagen (right), have their biggest hit single with 'Rikki Don't Lose That Number' from their first US Top Ten album, *Pretzel Logic*. They've also just announced their retirement from live work, so they can focus on their smart songwriting and polished recordings.

**JULY**

• 1ST: JUAN PERON dies... And UK fashion designer Laura Ashley opens a shop in San Francisco, her first outlet in the US.
• 6TH: ROCK YOUR BABY by George McCrae reaches No1 in the US R&B singles chart.
• 10TH: THE FIRST OF TWO NIGHTS of shows at the Tower Theater, Philadelphia, Pennsylvania, for David Bowie, during which he records his album *David Live*.
• 13TH: RUFUS, featuring vocalist Chaka Khan, have their first US singles chart entry with 'Tell Me Something Good', written by Stevie Wonder.
• 20TH: UNDER THE TITLE of "The Bucolic Frolic," the first ever *Knebworth Festival* is held at Knebworth House, Stevenage, Hertfordshire, UK, featuring the Allman Brothers Band, Van Morrison, The Doobie Brothers, Mahavishnu Orchestra, The Sensational Alex Harvey Band, and Tim Buckley.
• 25TH: THE RIGHT WING Portuguese regime of Atonio Slazar (in place since 1933), comes to an end after a relatively bloodless coup by army officers (only three people were killed).
• 27TH: LIGHTNING SLIM, Louisiana blues guitarist, dies at the age of 61... And Dutch band Golden Earring peak at Number 13 on the US chart with their song 'Radar Love' – already a hit in the UK at the start of the year.
• 29TH: CASS ELLIOTT, ex-Mamas & Papas, dies after suffering a heart attack in her London flat – the 'choking on a sandwich' theory is dismissed by the pathologist and coroner.

**AUGUST**

• 1ST: PETE TOWNSHEND rounds off a jamming session with Eric Clapton in Atlanta by playfully smashing a ukulele over his head.
• 5TH: US ALL-GIRL rock band The Runaways is formed.
• 10TH: ROBERTA FLACK reaches Number One on the US Top 40 singles with 'Feel Like Makin' Love.'
• 16TH: THE RAMONES begin a residency at the small but trendy

CBGB's Club, in New York City.
• 24TH: LYNYRD SKYNYRD enter the US Top 40 singles chart for the first time with 'Sweet Home Alabama.'
• 26TH: CHARLES A. LINDBURGH, the first pilot to fly non-stop across the Atlantic, dies at the age of 72.
• 31ST: AT THE ANNUAL READING FESTIVAL in the UK, Traffic make their last live appearance together.

• MAY 25TH: JAZZ LEGEND Duke Ellington dies from lung cancer at the age of 75. One of the 20th century's greatest composers and band-leaders, he performed, toured and recorded for over 50 years.

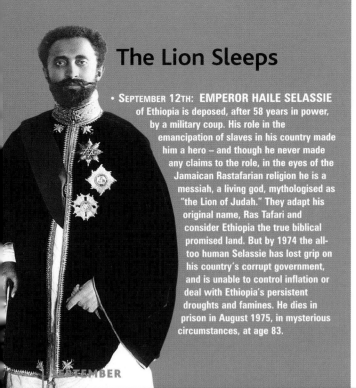

## The Lion Sleeps

• **SEPTEMBER 12TH: EMPEROR HAILE SELASSIE** of Ethiopia is deposed, after 58 years in power, by a military coup. His role in the emancipation of slaves in his country made him a hero – and though he never made any claims to the role, in the eyes of the Jamaican Rastafarian religion he is a messiah, a living god, mythologised as "the Lion of Judah." They adapt his original name, Ras Tafari and consider Ethiopia the true biblical promised land. But by 1974 the all-too human Selassie has lost grip on his country's corrupt government, and is unable to control inflation or deal with Ethiopia's persistent droughts and famines. He dies in prison in August 1975, in mysterious circumstances, at age 83.

## Picking Up The Pieces

**SEPTEMBER 23RD: ROBBIE McINTOSH,** drummer with Scottish funky soulsters Average White Band (AWB), dies at a party in the Hollywood Hills, Los Angeles, after taking a heroin overdose, believing it to be cocaine. The tragedy happens just as their Atlantic debut album hits Number One on the US chart (Number Six back home in the UK). After the initial shock of losing their 24-year old friend and colleague, the band decide to carry on and eventually bring in Steve Ferrone on drums. Their tightly-crafted, Isley Brothers-influenced soul-funk with close-harmony vocals will continue to be more popular in the States than in Britain. But after their single 'Pick Up The Pieces' is a US Number One in February 1975, and the subsequent album Soul Searching reaches Number Eight, they never have another Top Ten on either side of the Atlantic. The individual members go on to play with the likes of Eric Clapton and Paul McCartney, and AWB will re-form a couple of times in the 1980s and 1990s.

**OCTOBER**

• **2ND: SCIENTISTS** in Mexico breed a more disease-tolerant and protein-rich strain of maize and wheat.
• **4TH: THE JACKSON FIVE** go on a month-long tour of South America.
• **12TH: BOB DYLAN** begins recording his next album *Blood On the Tracks* at A&R Recording, New York City.
• **6TH: GEORGE HARRISON** launches Dark Horse Records.
• **7TH: THE 101ERS** make their debut at the Telegraph Club in London's Brixton. The band features a selection of upcoming stars including future Clash mainman Joe Strummer, Richard Dudanski (Raincoats) and Clive Timperly (Passions).
• **8TH: PRESIDENT**

**NIXON** is pardoned for his actions in the Watergate affair by President Ford.
• **14TH: ERIC CLAPTON** reaches No1 in the US Top 40 singles with his version of the Bob Marley song 'I Shot The Sheriff' (from The Wailers' 1973 album *Burnin'*). It will be Clapton's biggest solo hit.
• **15TH: URIAH HEEP** bass player Gary Thain survives a serious electric shock in Dallas, but the rest of the tour has to be cancelled. Sadly Thain will subsequently die two years later from a drug overdose.
• **19TH: BAD COMPANY** are awarded a US gold disc by the RIAA for their eponymous debut album.
• **20TH: CYCLONE 'FIFI'** hits Honduras, leaving over 10,000 dead in its wake.

• **22ND: IN KINSHASA**, Zaire, a music festival known as the Black Woodstock is held. Funded by Zaire's dictatorial president Mobutu, the festival features James Brown, B.B.King, Pointer Sisters, Bill Withers, Sister Sledge, Miriam Makeba and The Spinners.
• **25TH: IT'S DISCOVERED** that freon gas, which is used to power spray from aerosol cans, and the Chloro-FluroCarbons (CFCs) used in fridges and air-conditioners, can damage the earth's protective ozone layer, making it thinner. At the time it all seems too much like science fiction for most people, so little is done. A hole in the ozone layer is confirmed in 1985.

## War And Peace

• **NOVEMBER 13TH: PLO LEADER** Yassir Arafat makes an impassioned plea at the UN in New York for a new Palestinian state in which Christians, Jews and Muslims could live peacefully together. "I have come bearing an olive branch and a freedom fighter's gun," he declares. "Do not let the olive branch fall from my hands."

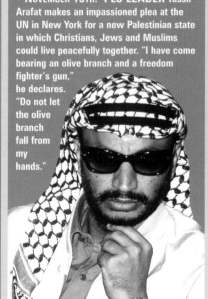

• **1ST: THE FIRST McDONALD'S** opens in London as the UK embraces the fast food revolution. It's some 26 years since the original McDonald brothers 'Speedee Service' restaurant opened in San Bernadino, California (advertising "custom-made hamburgers" for 15 cents), and exactly 20 years since Ray Kroc launched the McDonalds franchise operation, before buying out the McDonald brothers and expanding his fast-food empire.
• **2ND: ROCK GUITARIST** Ted Nugent wins the US National Squirrel-Shooting Archery Contest, taking out a furry little fellow at 150 yards.
• **5TH: FIVE DIE** and 65 are injured in an IRA attack on two pubs in Guildford, UK... And 16 months after it was first released, Mike Oldfield reaches Number One on the UK album charts with *Tubular Bells*.

• **13TH: US SHOWBIZ** legend Ed Sullivan dies of cancer of the oesophagus, at 72.
• **18TH: SOUL STAR AL GREEN'S** girlfriend Mary Woodson bursts into his Memphis, Tennessee, home and scalds him with hot grits from the stove before killing herself with his revolver ...
• **19TH: BILLY PRESTON** reaches No1 in the US Top 40 singles with 'Nothing From Nothing'... And The Three Degrees release 'When Will I See You Again' in the US – it's already been Number One in the UK, and will be their biggest hit on both sides of the Atlantic.
• **TALENTED BUT TROUBLED** UK folk singer-songwriter Nick Drake joins the 1970s 'death by drug overdose' toll, after taking a fatal dose of his own prescribed anti-depressants, perhaps by accident.
• **29TH: STEVE WINWOOD** walks out on Traffic during a US tour.

• **OCTOBER 30TH: MUHAMMAD ALI** (32) defeats the favorite George Foreman (25) to regain the World Heavyweight boxing title in Kinshasha, Zaire. Ali famously lets Foreman punch him freely till big George exhausts himself, and then floors him in the eighth round. The event, known as The Rumble In The Jungle, is later immortalised in the song 'In Zaire,' a UK hit for Johnny Wakelin in 1976.

• **NOVEMBER 28TH: JOHN LENNON** joins Elton John on stage at Madison Square Garden, New York City, where they perform three songs together, including their brand new Number One single, 'Whatever Gets You Through The Night.' Unbeknown to Lennon or the rapt crowd, this will be the ex-Beatles last ever live performance.

**NOVEMBER**          **DECEMBER**

- **1ST: THE FRENCHIES**, a band featuring Chrissie Hynde - later to form The Pretenders - make their debut at L'Olympia, Paris, France, opening for the Flaming Groovies.
- **2ND: IN VANCOUVER**, Canada, George Harrison begins his first North American tour since the break-up of The Beatles.
- **8TH: QUEEN RELEASE** their third album, *Sheer Heart Attack*, which will be their most successful yet – reaching Number 12 in the US and Number Two in the UK. It contains their first US hit single, 'Killer Queen.'
- **9TH: BACHMAN-TURNER** Overdrive reach Number One on the US Top 40 with 'You Ain't Seen Nothing Yet.'
- **21ST: THOUGH HE'S SWORN** never to play with them again, Marty Balin re-joins Jefferson Starship during a gig at Winterland, San Francisco.
- **23RD: BILLY SWAN** reaches Number One in the US with his only hit single, 'I Can Help.'

- **DECEMBER 7TH: CARL DOUGLAS** reaches Number One on the US Top 40 with 'Kung Fu Fighting.' The song, which cashes in on the latest martial arts craze, has already topped the UK charts in September this year.

- **12TH: GUITARIST MICK TAYLOR** officially leaves The Rolling Stones during early recording sessions for the album *Black And Blue* in Munich, Germany. They toy with the idea of getting Jeff Beck to join, and he travels over to Munich to jam with the band. But by mutual agreement, it seems, they decide against it. The eventual replacement, ex-Faces man Ronnie Wood, will complete the album with the Stones, and stay on.
- **14TH: ALL FOUR BEATLES** have singles in the US Top 40: Paul McCartney – 'Junior's Farm;' Ringo Starr – 'Only You;' John Lennon – 'Whatever Gets You Through The Night;' and George Harrison – 'Dark Horse.'
- **18TH: LYNYRD SKYNYRD** earn a US gold disc for their debut album, *Pronounced Leh-nerd Skin-nerd*.
- **21ST: AN ANONYMOUS** caller warns of a bomb explosion at Harrods store in London just ten minutes before it detonates – the second bomb to explode in London's West End in three days.
- **24TH: JONI MITCHELL**, Linda Ronstadt, Carly Simon, and James Taylor sing Christmas carols in the streets of LA.
- **25TH: MARSHALL FIELDS** crashes his car through a White House gate in Washington, DC, and holds off police, who believe he is carrying explosives, for four hours before finally surrendering.
- **29TH: ALMOST 5,000** are killed after earthquakes rock Pakistan.
- **31ST: HARRY CHAPIN** gets a gold disc for his first and last US Number One single, 'Cat's In the Cradle.'

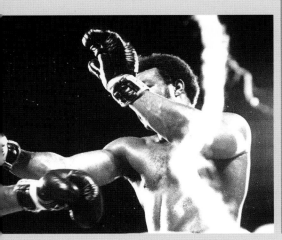

# 1975

## DON'T YOU WORRY ABOUT STEVIE

In August 1973, Stevie Wonder was nearly killed while traveling to a concert in North Carolina when the car in which he was a passenger collided with a timber transport truck, and Stevie was crushed by falling logs. Horrific for anyone, but perhaps doubly traumatic if you're blind. He was in a coma for two days, and brain damage was feared, but apart from losing his sense of smell, he seems to have made a quick and full recovery. It certainly hasn't stemmed his flow of musical ingenuity (although sadly that does seem to desert him later in the 1980s.) Between 1973 and 1976, multi-instrumentalist Stevie crafts four era-defining albums – *Talking Book*, *Innervisions*, *Fulfillingness' First Finale*, and *Songs In The Key Of Life* – which contain some of the most thought-provoking, moving, uplifting, catchy, and downright funky music of all time – just think of songs like 'Superstition,' 'Higher Ground,' 'Living For The City,' 'He's Misstra Know-It-All,' 'All In Love Is Fair,' 'You Haven't Done Nothin','' 'I Wish,' 'As' (later covered by George Michael & Mary J. Blige), 'Pastime Paradise' (which will become Coolio's 'Gangsta's Paradise'), 'Isn't She Lovely,' and 'Don't You Worry 'Bout A Thing.' He is already held in the highest esteem by his peers and wider community, not just for his music but his work with various charities and human rights causes. He's just been honoured by a 'Stevie Wonder Day' in Los Angeles, and of course has been recipient of numerous Grammys and other awards. Always busy, arguably Motown's greatest ever talent, 1975 will be the first year Stevie hasn't released an album since 1962. At the following year's *Grammy Awards* ceremony, winner of the Best Album prize, Paul Simon, will point out in his acceptance speech, half-jokingly, that he'd, "like to thank Stevie Wonder for not releasing an album last year."

# 1975

## January–April

## Fahren Fahren Fahren

APRIL 15TH: 'AUTOBAHN' by Kraftwerk enters the US Top 40 singles chart. An edited version of a hypnotic 20-minute album track, with the only lyrics being "Fahren, fahren, fahren auf der Autobahn" ("Drive, drive, drive on the freeway"), the single makes the US Number 25. It will be the secretive German act's only Top 40 hit in the States. The *Autobahn* album makes US Number Five – their only album to chart in America. In the UK, Kraftwerk have more commercial success – amazingly enough for such a determinedly non-commercial band, who do few interviews and just as few photo sessions (even sending out robots in their place in later years). They will have seven Top 40 UK hits spread over the next 25 years. including the 1982 Number One double A-side 'Computer Love/The Model'. Pop hits or not, Kraftwerk are hugely

## JANUARY

• **JANUARY 4TH: LYNYRD SKYNYRD** enter the US Top 40 with their second single, 'Freebird,' which will peak at 19.

• **1ST: FLEETWOOD MAC** takes on two new members, Lindsey Buckingham and Stevie Nicks – and so the second stage of the band's career begins, with a more US-centred, adult-oriented rock (AOR) focus. And very popular it will be, too...

• **1ST: PARTICIPANTS** in the Watergate affair, John Ehrlichman, John Mitchell, and HR Haldeman are all found guilty of obstructing the course of justice... Meanwhile in the UK, writer PG Wodehouse is

knighted in the honours list, but lives for only one more month ... It's also the first day of International Woman's Year.

• **2ND: THE BEE GEES** arrive at Criteria Studios, Miami, Florida, to begin work on their next album, *Main Course*.

• **5TH: THE WIZ**, a pop musical update of the *Wizard Of Oz*, opens on Broadway, New York. The show will eventually be turned into an ill-advised film starring Michael Jackson and Diana Ross.

• **10TH: AL GREEN** earns his 12th US gold disc for the album *Al Green Explores Your Mind*.

• **12TH: DOOBIE BROTHERS**, (whose new member Jeff 'Skunk' Baxter, see left, has just been

recruited from Steely Dan), plus Little Feat, Montrose, Tower Of Power, Bonaroo, and Graham Central Station, set off on the nine-city, 18-show *Warner Brothers' European Tour*.

• **17TH: BOB DYLAN** releases the album *Blood On The Tracks* in the US.

• **24TH: THREE STOOGES'** Larry Fine dies. His old mate Moe will re-join him in May.

• **24TH: BARRY MANILOW** has his first hit, and first US Number One, with the teary ballad 'Mandy.'

• **26TH: THE OLDEST-KNOWN** rock (3,800 million years-of-age) is discovered in Minnesota.

## FEBRUARY

## Status Who?

• **JANUARY 18TH: STATUS QUO** enjoy their biggest UK hit when 'Down Down' reaches the top of the singles chart. Surprisingly little-known in the US, except for their late 1960s dabbling in psychedelic acid rock on 'Pictures Of Matchstick Men,' Quo are by now established as a wildly successful, no-nonsense head-banging hard rock band in Britain for the 1970s and beyond. Although this is their only Number One, Quo will go on to hold the record for the most UK chart entries for any band (it's well over 50 by 2003).

• **4TH: LOUIS JORDAN**, known as "the Father of Rhythm & Blues," dies at home in Los Angeles of a heart attack.

• **8TH: THE OHIO PLAYERS** reach Number One in the US Top 40 singles with 'Fire,' and Number One in the album chart with the album of the same name.

• **11TH: MARGARET THATCHER** becomes the first female leader of a British political party, in this case the Conservative Party.

• **13TH: UNANNOUNCED**, John Lennon walks into WNEW-FM radio in Manhattan and does a live three-hour broadcast with DJ Scott Muni, mainly to promote his new album *Rock'n'Roll*.

• **15TH: A BOSTON-BASED** doctor (Kenneth Edelin) is found guilty of the manslaughter of a foetus during an abortion... And Linda Ronstadt gets her first and only US Number One with 'You're No Good.'

• **21ST: DAVID BOWIE** releases a new single, 'Young Americans,' in the US. Having been through his Ziggy Stardust, Aladdin Sane and recent scary Thin White Duke phases, Bowie is now hitting his white soul-boy stride, and the 'Young Americans' era is an important stepping stone for his career in the US.

• **25TH: ELIJAH MUHAMMED**, the spiritual leader of the Black Muslims, dies at age 80.

• **25TH: LED ZEPPELIN** release the album *Physical Graffiti*.

• **26TH: TODD RUNDGREN** is awarded a US gold disc by the RIAA for his hit double album *Something/Anything?*

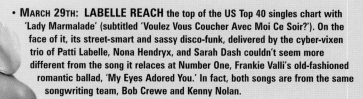

• **MARCH 29TH: LABELLE REACH** the top of the US Top 40 singles chart with 'Lady Marmalade' (subtitled 'Voulez Vous Coucher Avec Moi Ce Soir?'). On the face of it, its street-smart and sassy disco-funk, delivered by the cyber-vixen trio of Patti Labelle, Nona Hendryx, and Sarah Dash couldn't seem more different from the song it relaces at Number One, Frankie Valli's old-fashioned romantic ballad, 'My Eyes Adored You.' In fact, both songs are from the same songwriting team, Bob Crewe and Kenny Nolan.

influential pioneers of machine-driven music, which essentially means all modern dance music post-1975, and much more besides. They introduced the vaguely threatening idea that you don't need to have a glamorous front person to have a group, or even any human focus at all – the music can speak for itself – and you can harness the power of electronic technology to do more than math: you can make people dance with it. Kraftwerk's music and ideas will be endlessly copied, sampled, and built upon by future music scenes such as techno, house, and hip-hop.

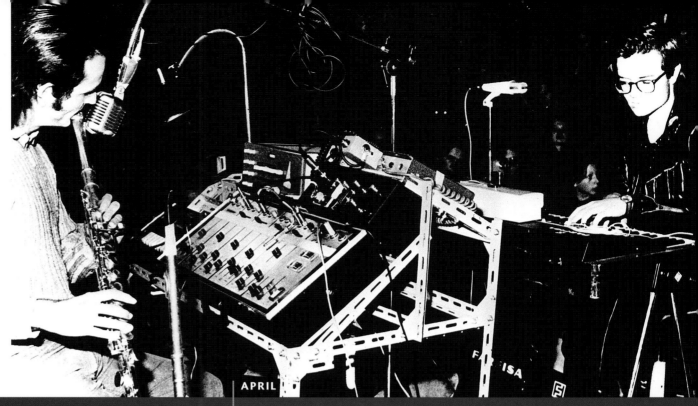

## MARCH

• **1ST:** **THE EAGLES** have their first US No1 single with 'The Best Of My Love.'
• **3RD:** **A MILLION DOLLAR** rubber factory in Connecticut is blown up by three people claiming to be The Weathermen – a breakaway group from the Students for a Democratic Society (SDS), who named themselves after the line 'You don't need a weatherman to know which way the wind blows' from Bob Dylan's 'Subterranean Homesick Blues.'
• **4TH:** **CHARLES CHAPLIN** is knighted at Buckingham Palace.
• **5TH:** **AT A PARTY** thrown by Joni Mitchell in Los Angeles, Rod Stewart meets Britt Ekland, with whom he will soon begin a much-publicised affair.
• **15TH:** **THE DOOBIE BROTHERS** reach No1 in the US Top 40 singles with 'Black Water'... And Greek shipping tycoon Aristotle Onassis dies, making Jacqueline Kennedy Onassis a widow for the second time in 12 years.

• **16TH:** **BLUES GUITARIST** T. Bone Walker, whose show-stopping performing techniques, such as playing the guitar behind his head and cavorting around the stage, are an influence on Jimi Hendrix, dies at the age of 64... And the Rainbow concert hall in north London closes its doors, more or less for good.
• **18TH:** **THE HOWARD HUGHES**-built and CIA-funded deep sea salvage ship Glomar Explorer recovers part of a Soviet submarine from the Pacific Ocean bed.
• **22ND:** **THE BAY CITY ROLLERS** reach No1 in the UK singles chart with 'Bye Bye Baby,' for the first of six weeks.
• **23RD:** **BOB DYLAN**, The Band, and Neil Young are the surprise live guests at promoter Bill Graham's SNACK benefit in Kazar Stadium, Golden Gate Park, San Francisco. Other acts on the bill include the Grateful Dead, Jefferson Starship, Carlos Santana, and The Doobie Brothers.
• **29TH:** **ALL SIX LED ZEPPELIN** albums appear on the U.S album chart.

• **1ST:** **FRANKIE VALLI** is awarded a US gold disc by the RIAA for the hit single 'My Eyes Adored You'... Meanwhile, over 30,000 people come to see the Freedom Train at its first port of call in Delaware. The train, a travelling museum of Americana, is part of the forthcoming bicentennial celebrations. During its 21 months traversing the country, it'll have 7 million visitors and 40 million more spectators lining the tracks.
• **3RD:** **ANATOLY KARPOV** becomes world chess champion, at the age of just 23, when Bobby Fischer fails to attend their match in Manila... Meanwhile Chinese nationalist leader Chiang Kai-Shek dies of a heart attack at **87**, in exile in Taiwan.
• **7TH:** **RITCHIE BLACKMORE**, guitarist of Deep Purple, leaves to form Rainbow. He is replaced by Tommy Bolin.
• **16TH:** **CAMBODIA FALLS** to the Communist Khmer Rouge when the capital, Phnom Penh, surrenders.
• **19TH:** **'THE HUSTLE'** by Van McCoy enters the US R'n'B and Pop singles charts, both of which it will subsequently top.
• **27TH:** **DISASTER STRIKES** the Spanish Grand Prix when four spectators are killed after Rolf Stommelon's car crashes into the crowd.... Later today, Pink Floyd play the last of five nights at the Sports Arena, Los Angeles, California. Over the five days of show, 511 dope smokers have been arrested by over-zealous police.

### APRIL

•**APRIL 5TH:** **MINNIE RIPERTON**, a former Stevie Wonder backup singer with a five-octave vocal range, reaches Number One on the US Top 40 with 'Lovin' You.' It's her only hit. In 1976 she is diagnosed with cancer, and though he she keeps working, she finally succumbs in 1979, at the age of 31.

## Computer World

• **MARCH 8TH:** **CONSIDERED BY MANY** to be the first microcomputer (though this is hotly disputed by other tech-head historians), the MITS Altair 8800 is certainly one of the earliest commercially available personal computers. With a name derived from science fiction – the planet Altair was the home of Robby The Robot in *Forbidden Planet* (and also features in Star Trek), it's based on a 2MHz Intel 8080 chip with 256 bytes of RAM (that's bytes, not Megabytes). The computer is sold for $395 as a kit and $495 assembled. The main drawback is you have to write your own software as you go along – plus there is no keyboard, so you have to enter everything in binary code via switches on the front of the machine. Even so, interest is such that within three months 4,000 people will have ordered one, and it inspires Paul Allen and Bill Gates (a student at Harvard) to write a programming language to run on it. What they create is a scaled-down version of BASIC. At the same time they lay the foundations for a new company, which Gates and Allen will call Microsoft.

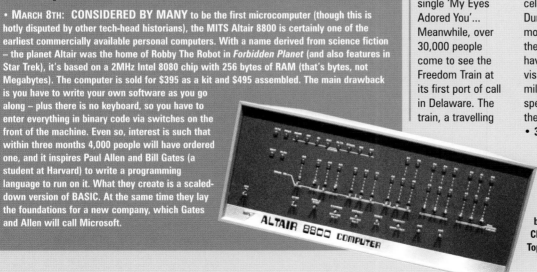

ALTAIR 8800 COMPUTER

• **MARCH 29TH:** **QUEEN**, the UK hard rock band fronted by larger-than-life, camper-than-Christmas singer Freddie Mercury, enter the US Top 40 for the first time with 'Killer Queen.'

• JUNE 12TH: 10CC peak at US Number Two with their biggest hit, and former UK chart-topper, 'I'm Not In Love.' The quartet will split in 1976, with Graham Gouldman and Eric Stewart continuing as 10cc, and Kevin Godley and Lol Creme focusing more on studio and video production.

# New Birds In Town

JUNE 14TH: THE EAGLES enter the US singles chart with 'One Of These Nights,' which will peak at Number One. Following on from the chart-topping 'Best Of My Love,' it's the start of the band's new life in the music biz fast lane. Their latest album, also called *One Of These Nights*, is the first of three Number One albums in the next two years. As Linda Ronstadt's backing band, the Eagles are the band everyone wants to sign. When they sign with David Geffen's fledgling, Asylum label, LA songwriter Jackson Browne and band member Glenn Frey pen their debut single 'Take It Easy'. Thereafter the main song writing partnership of Frey and Don Henley generates most of the group's material with Bernie Leadon – a talented and versatile bluegrass musician – providing traditional acoustic instrumentation. Concept album *Desperado* is seen as the crystalization of country-rock, with Browne

• **1ST:** STYX earn their first US gold disc, for the 1973 album *Styx II*.
• **10TH:** STEVIE WONDER plays for 125,000 fans at the Washington Monument, Washington DC, as part of Human Kindness Day.
• **16TH:** JUNKO TAKEI, a 35-year-old climber from Japan, becomes the first woman ever to reach the summit of Mount Everest.
• **17TH:** ELTON JOHN earns a US platinum disc for the album *Captain Fantastic & The Brown Dirt Cowboy* on its day of release – the first time such a thing has happened.
• **19TH:** A PLOT TO KILL Fidel Castro is unearthed in an investigation into CIA activities.
• **24TH:** THE BEE GEES release their new album, *Main Course*, in the US. It will put them back on the road to success, after three years without a US or UK hit – especially with the release of the first single, 'Jive Talkin'.'
• **29TH:** JOHNNY THUNDERS' Heartbreakers play their first ever gig, in Queens, New York City.

• **MAY 26TH:** US STUNTMAN Evel Knievel suffers serious spinal injuries when he crashes while attempting to leap over 13 double-decker buses in the UK.

• **2ND:** PROSTITUTES in France occupy a church in Lyons to protest at the heavy-handed tactics of local police.
• **3RD:** BRAZILIAN SOCCER genius Pelé signs a three-year contract with the New York Cosmos for $7m.
• **5TH:** PRESIDENT SADAT of Egypt re-opens the Suez Canal.
• **4TH:** THE ROLLING STONES become the first rock band to receive record royalties from the USSR.
• **6TH:** TAMMY WYNETTE'S 'Stand By Your Man' comes to the end of a three-week run at Number One on the UK pop charts – it's something the First Lady Of Country Music never achieves in the US, although she does top the separate Country Music charts a fair few times (as she did with this song in 1969). In November 1975, Scottish comedian Billy Connolly will have a Number One in the UK with his parody of Tammy's 'D.I.V.O.R.C.E.'
• **12TH:** THE O'JAYS are awarded a US gold album for *Survival*.
• **14TH:** IN THE UK, Nazareth enter the charts with 'My White Bicycle' – previously a hit for 1960s band Tomorrow, whose line-up included guitarist Steve Howe, later of Yes.
• **20TH:** THE TALKING HEADS debut at CBGB's, New York City, as support to The Ramones.
• **22ND:** MOSCOW ACCUSES China of trying to interfere in the running of Taiwan – China insists it simply plans to establish diplomatic relations.
• **23RD:** ALICE COOPER breaks six of his ribs falling from a stage in Vancouver, Canada.
• **24TH:** US MUSIC INDUSTRY executives, including Clive Davis of Arista, and Kenny Gamble and Leon Huff of Philadelphia International, are

## Country Boy

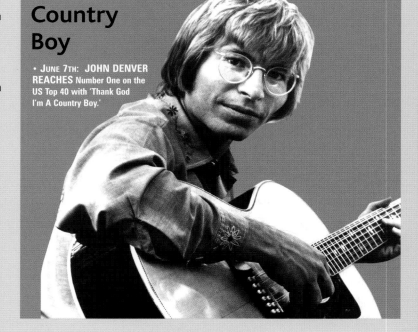

• **JUNE 7TH:** JOHN DENVER REACHES Number One on the US Top 40 with 'Thank God I'm A Country Boy.'

indicted in Newark, New Jersey, on charges ranging from payola to income tax evasion – charges are later dropped... Meanwhile the US and Soviet Union try and reach agreement over the banning of weather alteration for military purposes.
• **26TH:** INDIRA GHANDI is convicted of "corrupt election practices."
• **29TH:** YET ANOTHER HEROIN overdose. This one claims 28-year-old Tim Buckley in Santa Monica (although there are entirely unsubstantiated mutterings that he was killed by his record company, such was the

paranoia of the time).
• **30TH:** CHER MARRIES Greg Allman, only to leave him ten days later. They then get back together again, but only for a short time, and so on and so

• **JUNE 26TH:** THE MOVIE *JAWS* is released, with a gut-churningly scary, minimalist score by Steven Spielberg's favourite soundtrack composer, John Williams. Who'd have thought a cello could make people think of a huge man-eating shark coming at you through the water...

co-writing 'Doolin Dalton,' but still they have yet to break internationally. That process starts when they support Neil Young and Crazy Horse on a seven-date tour of the UK, in 1973. By April 1974, the Eagles are playing in front of 200, 000 at the 'California Jam', east of LA. However as they become more successful, with albums like *On The Border* (1974) and *One of These Nights* (1975) the players' dislike for one another increases. In 1976 Bernie Leadon leaves, to be replaced by Joe Walsh. The Eagles are now solidly AOR: their 'Hotel California' perched at the top of the US charts in January 1977, but the band soon drifted apart. Several reunions later, their *Greatest Hits 1971-1975* would become the biggest selling album in the US ever, eclipsing the record previously held by Michael Jackson's *Thriller*.

**JULY**

**AUGUST**

- **1ST: HAVING EXPELLED ALL ASIANS** from the country in 1972, Uganda's president Idi Amin has now threatened to kill all UK residents living there.
- **3RD: IT'S AGREED**, in principle at least, that the Church Of England will admit women priests. No one will say when this might happen, exactly.
- **5TH: PINK FLOYD**, The Steve Miller Band, and Captain Beefheart play at the Knebworth Festival in the UK. Floyd's typically understated set opens with two World War II Spitfires flying overhead... Meanwhile, Arthur Ashe becomes the first black man to win Wimbledon's singles championship when he beats his US compatriot Jimmy Connors.
- **7TH: KEITH RICHARDS** of The Rolling Stones is charged with reckless driving and possessing an unauthorised weapon, in Arkansas, USA.
- **9TH: RICHARD NIXON** insists that South Vietnam would never have fallen into Communist hands had he remained president.
- **16TH: THE FESTIVAL OF UNRECORDED ROCK TALENT** begins at CBGB's, New York City. Acts appearing today are The Ramones, Tuff Darts,

Blondie, Talking Heads, and White Lightning.
- **17TH: US ASTRONAUTS** and Soviet cosmonauts shake hands after crossing over from their docked spacecraft at an altitude of 140 miles above Earth.
- **18TH: BOB MARLEY & THE WAILERS** play at The Lyceum, London. The show is recorded and released later this year as the album *Live!* – which includes the UK hit and future Marley favorite, 'No Woman, No Cry.'
- **20TH: BRUCE SPRINGSTEEN'S** *Born To Run* tour opens at the Palace Theatre, Providence, Rhode Island, US.
- **26TH: PROTO-PUNK** band The London SS are rehearsing in London, with a line-up that includes future members of The Clash, The Damned, and Generation X.
- **31ST: IRISH OUTFIT** the Miami Showband are returning from a gig in Belfast, Northern Ireland, when their minibus is flagged down near Newry at what appears to be a military roadblock. The band are then attacked by Unionist terrorists (from an illegal group called the UVF) and three shot dead.

## Red Army

- **JULY 11TH: OVER 6,000 LIFE-SIZED** terracotta figures of warriors are unearthed near the ancient Chinese capital of Xian. It's estimated that the red-clay army was made around 206BC to guard the tomb of the first Ch'in dynasty emperor – the same one responsible for starting construction on the Great Wall of China.

- **AUGUST 11TH: AEROSMITH** get a gold disc for US sales of the album *Toys In The Attic*. It includes the track 'Walk This Way', which reaches Number Ten in 1976, but will be an even bigger hit when covered by Run-DMC in 1986.

- **1ST: THE WEST** and the USSR sign the Helsinki 'Human Rights' Agreement, which states 'The participating states will respect human rights & fundamental freedoms, including the freedom of thought, conscience, religion, or belief ... without distinction as to race, sex, language, or religion.'
- **5TH: IT'S ANNOUNCED** at a Los Angeles press conference that Stevie Wonder has renewed his Motown record contract for an estimated $13m... Meantime all-girl rock outfit The Runaways are put together by Kim

Fowley (one of the brains behind The Archies). But the band fail to set the world alight in their short career – except in Japan, where they are a sensation. Guitarist Joan Jett will go on to have solo success with her own band, The Blackhearts.
- **8TH: JAZZ SAX GREAT** Cannonball Adderly dies from a stroke at age 46.
- **9TH: 'JIVE TALKIN''** by The Bee Gees is the new Number One single in the US.
- **10TH: RUSSIAN COMPOSER** Dmitri Shostakovich dies in Moscow, at 68.
- **13TH: STARTING**

A SERIES of five twice-nightly shows at The Bottom Line, New York, Bruce Springsteen begins his transition from cult hero to internationally acclaimed rock star. One show makes the cover of the *New York Times*. They are said to be the most talked-about gigs in a decade.
- **16TH: PETER GABRIEL** publicly announces his decision to leave Genesis.
- **23RD: JOHN LYDON** – soon to find fame as Johnny Rotten – auditions for the Sex Pistols at Sex, their manager Malcolm McLaren's shop in the King's Road, London.
- **23RD: PAUL KOSSOFF**, formerly of Free and then Back Street Crawler, has a heart attack that stops his pulse for over half-an-hour. Remarkably he survives – though only for a few more months.
- **30TH: KC & THE SUNSHINE BAND** top the US singles charts with 'Get Down Tonight.' It's their first of five US Number Ones.

# 1975
## September–December

- **OCTOBER 10TH: RICHARD BURTON** and Elizabeth Taylor re-marry in a remote village in Botswana, southern Africa. Having divorced in the early 1970s – then reconciled and separated several times – they will divorce yet again in 1976.

## Bo Rhap

**O** CTOBER 31ST: QUEEN'S 'Bohemian Rhapsody' is released. The most adventurous single yet delivered by the band (and perhaps by anyone), this magnificently overblown opus climbs steadily to the top of the UK charts, where it will stay for an amazing nine weeks, all over the Christmas and New Year holidays. In the US, the response is more muted – it will peak at Number Nine in February next year. But it is a historic record for several reasons. Firstly, it's the longest single ever to top the

### SEPTEMBER

- **1ST: THE ALBUM** *Born To Run* by Bruce Springsteen is released in the USA, where it will peak at Number Three.
- **2ND: A CROWD OF 500,** armed with rocks and bottles, attempts to storm the gates of the *Great American Music Fair* in Syracuse, New York. The event features Jefferson Starship, the Doobie Brothers, and New Riders

Of The Purple Sage. The crowd is attempting to turn it into a free festival, but only achieves a fruitless riot and 60 arrests.
- **5TH: LYNETTE 'SQUEAKY' FROMME** (so called because of her voice) attempts to assassinate President Gerald Ford. Another disciple of Charles Manson, she apparently fails to load the gun properly, and is easily subdued by the Secret Service... A couple of weeks later, in a bad month for President Ford, yet another attempt is made on his life, this time by mother-of-four Sarah Jane Moore, apparently seeking to impress her radical friends. Ford is saved by a bystander who grabs Moore's arm when he sees the gun.
- **7TH: IN LOS ANGELES,** a new endurance record for guitar-playing is set when 22-year-old Steve Anderson plays for 114 hours & seven minutes non-stop.
- **9TH: 18-YEAR-OLD TENNIS PLAYER** Martina Navratilova defects from Czechoslovakia and seeks political asylum in the US. She will go on to become the most successful ever female tennis player.
- **10TH:** *STARSKY & HUTCH,* a new fast-moving buddy-cop TV show (left), starts in the US. It runs for nearly four years and makes stars of Paul Michael Glaser and David Soul – although Soul already had a bizarre earlier TV incarnation as the mysteriously-masked singer on *The Merv Griffin Show*, known only as The Covered Man. He takes up singing again, without the mask, during the *S&H* run.
- **13TH:** *THE HEAT IS ON* by The Isley Brothers is the new US Number One album.
- **14TH: ELIZABETH ANN BAYLEY SETON** becomes the first US saint when she's canonized by Pope Paul VI.
- **15TH: PINK FLOYD** release their much-anticipated new album, *Wish You Were Here*.
- **20TH: JANIS IAN** reaches US Number Three, strumming the heart-felt teen-angst ballad 'At Seventeen.' The track comes from her US Number One album *Between The Lines*.

- **SEPTEMBER 19TH: THE BBC SCREENS** the first episode of *Python* star John Cleese's comedy classic *Fawlty Towers*.

### OCTOBER

- **1ST: AL JACKSON,** drummer for Booker T & The MGs, is shot dead by an intruder at his home in Memphis, Tennessee. He is just 39.
- **2ND: THERE IS A BOMB** scare at the Uptown Theatre, Milwaukee, where Bruce Springsteen is playing a show. The singer returns to the Hotel Pfister and has a few drinks. On the drive back to the hall, Springsteen rides on the roof of the car.
- **7TH: JOHN LENNON** wins his fight to stay in America when the US Court of Appeals rules that his 1968 UK marijuana bust is not a valid reason for deporting him. He explains later that he likes it in New York because no one bothers him in the street.
- **15TH: THE RAMONES** sign a recording contract with Sire Records. The Sire label, run by Seymour Stein, will become one of the most insightful and influential US labels of the new wave and punk era and beyond, with major signings that include Talking Heads and Madonna.
- **17TH: MARSHALL MATHERS III** is born in Kansas City, Missouri. In the 1990s he will find notoriety as white rap artist Eminem.
- **30TH: BOB DYLAN'S** *Rolling Thunder Review* plays its first show, at the War Memorial Auditorium, Plymouth, Massachusetts.

- **12TH: ROD STEWART** & The Faces play their last live show, in Long Island. Rod officially leaves the band in December, and continues with a successful solo career; Ronnie Wood becomes a full-time Rolling Stone; and Kenny Jones will later take over from Keith Moon in the Who.
- **20TH: THE US SUPREME COURT** rules that individual states may allow spanking of children at schools, with or without the consent of a parent.
- **22ND: RUSSIAN SPACECRAFT** Venera 9 sends back live pictures from Venus.

### NOVEMBER

- **NOVEMBER 20TH: SPANISH DICTATOR** General Franco, who has ruthlessly ruled the country since its bloody civil war ended in 1939, dies at age 83. Two days later, King Juan Carlos is crowned, and signals a move back towards democracy.

- **1ST: KAREN CARPENTER** of The Carpenters, now weighing a mere 90 pounds, begins two months of rest, in the hope of recovering from anorexia. A planned UK tour is cancelled.
- **2ND: ITALIAN DIRECTOR,** screen writer, essayist, poet, and novelist Pier Paolo Pasolini, is murdered
- **6TH: SEX PISTOLS** play their first live gig, at St Martin's School Of Art, London. After ten minutes, the college social secretary pulls the plugs.
- **8TH: 'LOW RIDER'** by War is the new Number One on the US R&B singles chart.
- **9TH: IN THE UK'S** *New Musical Express*, critic Charles Shaar Murray reviews a gig by Blondie at the Performance Studio in New York City. "Sadly," he concludes, "Blondie will never be a star, simply because she ain't good enough."
- **11TH: UNABLE TO GET** his budget plans through the Canberra parliament, Australian prime minister Gough Whitlam refuses to call a general election. He is consequently dismissed by Sir John Kerr, the governor-general, who represents the British crown in Australia.
- **17TH: KC & THE SUNSHINE BAND'S** 'That's The Way (I Like It)' is US Number One.
- **27TH: ONE OF THE TWIN BROTHERS** behind the *Guinness Book Of Records,* Ross McWhirter (the other is Norris), is murdered by the IRA.
- **28TH: BRUSH FIRES IN CALIFORNIA** rage over 100 square miles and cause damage costing millions
- **30TH: BRITISH GRAND PRIX** racing champion Graham Hill dies in a plane crash.

charts, at just under six minutes: in fact, neither the US nor UK record labels want to release it at all, until it gets picked up by some respected DJs in both territories and played to death. Plus it's widely regarded as the record that makes pop videos popular. It represents the first high-profile use of video technology in a music promo, complete with primitive special effects (pop promos were previously just short movies shot on standard film stock). And because the song is practically impossible to play live – until the band eventually work out ways of using backing tracks for the multi-layered vocal parts – the video for 'Bo Rhap,' as it's affectionately known, is an indispensible part of its promotion and success, rather than an optional extra. Other bands will soon follow suit, and before you know it, we have MTV... In the UK, 'Bohemian Rhapsody' will consistently be voted favorite single whenever such random polls are conducted – and it gets an unexpected reprise when featured, very amusingly, in a sequence in the 1992 movie *Wayne's World*.

• SEPTEMBER 10TH: *KISS ALIVE!* is released in the US – a double in-concert album that propels the heavily-made-up New York four-piece into the realm of stadium rock stars, and recruits further hordes of willing volunteers for their growing 'Kiss Army' of fans. Kiss are formed in 1973 by bass player/vocalist Gene Simmons (a former teacher, who soon adopts the stage persona of the long-tongued Demon Lizard) and guitarist Paul Stanley (Star Lover). They add drummer Peter Criss (Cat Man), and second guitarist Ace Frehley (Space Man), and quickly become known for their pyrotechnic stage shows. They will be one of the biggest live draws of the late 1970s.

## DECEMBER

• 4TH: **FLEETWOOD MAC** earn a US gold disc by the RIAA for the album *Fleetwood Mac*.

• 6TH: **PAUL SIMON** hits Number One on the US album charts with *Still Crazy After All These Years*.

• 11TH: **THE BRITISH HOUSE** Of Commons defeats a Conservative move to restore the death penalty for terrorists.

• 16TH: **THE BAY CITY ROLLERS** receive their first US gold disc for the single 'Saturday Night.'

• 20TH: **BERNIE LEADON** officially leaves The Eagles, and Joe Walsh joins. Walsh's first studio work with the band will be on the 1976 album *Hotel California*... Also, Bob Marley and his new line-up of The Wailers (without Bunny Wailer or Peter Tosh), releases the *Live!* album.

• 21ST: **PRO-PALESTINIAN** terrorists break into OPEC headquarters in Vienna, kill three people and take a further 11 oil ministers hostage. They will give themselves up and free their hostages two days later at an airport in Algiers, but ask for, and receive, political asylum in Libya.

• 27TH: **THE SEX DISCRIMINATION** and Equal Pay Acts are passed in Britain at the end of International Women's Year.

• 30TH: **FOURTEEN PEOPLE ARE KILLED** and a further 70 injured after a bomb explodes at New York's La Guardia airport.

• 31ST: **ELVIS PRESLEY** plays at the Silver Dome, Pontiac, Michigan, in front of 60,000 people. He's clearly overweight these days, but the voice is usually still strong. and he keeps up a punishing schedule of live shows.

# 1976

## January–April

JANUARY

## Mouth Music

• **JANUARY 16TH: ON THE DAY** that he releases his live double album, *Frampton Comes Alive*, Peter Frampton starts a US tour at the Civic Centre, Charleston, West Virginia. Five days later he puts out 'Show Me the Way,' which will be his first solo hit single, most notable for its use of a 'Talk Box' mouth-operated guitar effect (though such a device has been used before, as far back as George Harrison's *All Things Must Pass* album in 1970). In the 1960s, while Frampton was a member of jazzy-psychedelic group The Herd, he was voted 'The Face Of '68' by a UK pop magazine. He then went on to form Humble Pie with Steve Marriott from the Small Faces, before venturing solo.

• **1ST: FLEETWOOD MAC** release 'Go Your Own Way,' which goes on to become their first Top Ten single in the US.

• **5TH: MAL EVANS**, the Beatles' former roadie and general assistant, is shot dead in Los Angeles by police, who claim Evans has threatened them with a rifle. It is later discovered the rifle is unloaded.

• **7TH: A RECORD COMPANY** executive, Kenneth Moss, is imprisoned for four months for the involuntary manslaughter of Average White Band member Robbie McIntosh in 1974. He is found to have supplied the drummer with heroin instead of his preferred cocaine.

• **10TH: BLUES LEGEND** Howlin' Wolf (left) dies of cancer in Hines, Illinois, at 65... And C.W. McCall's 'Convoy,' a truck-driving, spoken-word monologue about CB radio, is the new Number One single in the US (in the UK it reaches Number Two).

• **12TH: MYSTERY** writer Agatha Christie dies, age 85.

• **13TH: GREG ALLMAN** of the Allman Brothers is subpoenaed during US grand jury investigations into a drugs ring.

• **21ST: BOTH UK AND FRENCH** supersonic Concordes make their inaugural passenger flights – from London to Bahrain, and from Paris to Rio.

• **23RD: A YOUNG UK BAND** called Malice have their first rehearsal. They will eventually evolve into The Cure.

• **24TH: A 270,000-TON OIL TANKER**, the Olympic Bravery, runs aground off France. It's the largest shipwreck ever recorded. On March 13th the ship will break into two parts.

• **30TH: KISS EARN A PLATINUM** album award in the US for *Kiss Alive*.

• **JANUARY 23RD: POLITICAL ACTIVIST** and inspirational bass-baritone singer Paul Robeson (right) – whose socialist views and connections brought him to the attention of Senator Joseph McCarthy's anti-Communist campaigns – dies at 77 years old.

## High Rollers Take All

THE BAY CITY ROLLERS, with their boyish looks, teen-oriented pop tunes, and tartan-trimmed sawed-off pants, take the US by storm with the Number One single 'Saturday Night.' Named after Bay City, Michigan – though they've never been near the place, hailing instead from Edinburgh, Scotland – they've already had seven Top Ten singles in the UK. Although they do mostly play their own instruments, unlike subsequent boy bands, the group owe a great deal to songwriters Bill Martin and Phil Coulter, who wrote their UK hits 'Remember (Sha La La),' 'Shang A Lang,' 'Summerlove Sensation,' and 'All of Me Loves All of You.' UK Rollermania reaches its zenith on May

3, 1975 when the album *Once Upon A Star* enters the UK charts at Number One. A couple of weeks later, in an open air event at Mallory Park in Leicestershire, 40 fans – of 47,000 in attendance – are rescued from an ornamental lake as they try to swim out to the island where the Bay City Rollers are enjoying the hospitality before going on stage. Four go to hospital, and the Rollers pack up and go home without playing. After their US success, they are mired in controversy when lead singer Les McKeown is charged with reckless driving after knocking down and killing an elderly woman. Then guitarist Eric Faulkner nearly dies after taking barbiturates at the manager's house and by the end of 1978 the group have become a footnote in pop history. Except, that is, in Japan where they will continue to have a huge fan-base, encouraging periodic reunions and tours.

**FEBRUARY**

- **4TH: AN EARTHQUAKE** in Guatemala, Central America, kills more than 23,000 people and leaves millions homeless.

- **7TH: BOB DYLAN'S ALBUM** *Desire* reaches Number One on the US album charts. It's Bob's third US Number One album – all of them since 1974. In the UK, interestingly, Bob has had five Number One albums, but all of them *before* 1971.
- **8TH: AN ENQUIRY** is ordered by the Dutch government into allegations that Prince Bernhard, husband of Queen Juliana of the Netherlands, has received bribes of around £555,000 from the US aircraft company Lockheed.
- **12TH: ACTOR SAL MINEO**, who starred with James Dean in the genre-creating 1955 teen movie *Rebel Without A Cause* – is stabbed to death outside his Hollywood home.

- **13TH:** *PIONEER*, the magazine of Central High School, Minneapolis, prints an interview with Prince Nelson, a senior at the school, who plays with the local band Grand Central Corporation... Meanwhile in the UK, The 101ers, featuring future Clash frontman Joe Strummer, play at Hampstead Town Hall, north London.
- **15TH: FLEETWOOD MAC** begin recording the album *Rumours* at the Record Plant, Sausalito, California
- **18TH: THE RACE RELATIONS ACT** is passed in the UK, making it illegal to incite racial hatred.
- **19TH: EX-TOWER OF POWER** vocalist Rick Stevens is arrested for the murder of three men in San Jose, California. (He is eventually found guilty.)
- **21ST: AN ORIGINAL MEMBER** of The Supremes, Florence Ballard, dies in poverty of a coronary thrombosis, at the age of 32.
- **21ST: THE SEX PISTOLS** tell the *NME* that, "We're not into music, we're into chaos." A week later they are kicked off a tour supporting Eddie & The Hotrods.

**MARCH**

- **7TH: DURING THE LAST** concert of Carole King's three night stint at New York City's Beacon Theatre, Bruce Springsteen joins her on-stage for a storming version of her early song 'The Loco-Motion.'
- **8TH: NAZI-HUNTER** Simon Wiesenthal insists that there are more than 60 World War II war criminals living in the US.
- **10TH: THE JACKSON FIVE'S** record contract with Motown expires, leaving them free to move to the CBS label.
- **17TH: RUBIN CARTER** is granted a retrial over his murder conviction after a high-profile campaign, which has included Bob Dylan's single 'Hurricane.' But he will be found guilty once again – and it's not until February 1988 that the 22-year-old indictment will finally be dismissed.
- **19TH: PAUL KOSSOFF** (right), the 26-year-old guitarist with Free and latterly Back Street Crawler, dies of a drug-induced heart attack aboard a plane from New York to London.
- **21ST: DAVID BOWIE** and Iggy Pop are arrested in a hotel room in Rochester in the US for possession of drugs.
- **22ND: US PRESIDENTIAL CANDIDATE** Jimmy Carter reveals that his inspirations include The Beatles, Led Zeppelin, and Bob Dylan.
- **24TH: ISABEL PERÓN** is deposed as President of Argentina in a bloodless coup
- **29TH AT THE 48TH** Academy Awards, Jack Nicholson picks up a Best Actor Oscar for his role as a rebellious inmate in a psychiatric hospital in *One Flew Over The Cuckoo's Nest*, the movie adaptation of Ken Kesey's book. It is also Best Film.

**APRIL**

- **1ST: GERMAN-BORN** dada/surrealist artist Max Ernst dies, just one day short of his 85th birthday.
- **1ST: THIEVES BREAK** into the home of Pink Floyd's Dave Gilmour and steal guitars worth $12,000.
- **5TH: ECCENTRIC RECLUSE** Howard Hughes dies, leaving more than $1.5 billion and an emaciated, long-fingernailed body.
- **11TH: FRANK SINATRA** is photographed in the company of two known Mafia members Carlo Gambino and Paul Castellano at a concert in Westchester.
- **14TH: BAY CITY ROLLER** Eric Faulkner narrowly escapes death after overdosing on a cocktail of drugs. He insists he didn't know what he was doing as he was very tired.

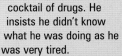

- **17TH: A RE-RELEASE** of the 1957 flop 'Jungle Rock', by Hank Mizell, reaches the UK singles Top Five. A dumbfounded Mizell declares, "It only sold 100 copies originally. I don't even own one."
- **20TH: TIMOTHY LEARY**, the drug guru, is paroled from prison.
- **22ND: HAVING SOLD** over two million copies, 'Disco Lady' by Johnnie Taylor is declared the first platinum single.
- **25TH: ENGLISH FILM DIRECTOR** Carol Reed, who made *The Third Man* (1949), *Our Man in Havana* (1959), and the movie of Lionel Bart's musical *Oliver!* (1968) – and is the uncle of actor Oliver Reed – dies at 69.
- **27TH: DAVID BOWIE** has a collection of Nazi books confiscated at the Russian/Polish border. He apparently then tells Polish custom officials that the UK would benefit from a fascist leader. He will later refer to these pronouncements as "drug induced" aberrations.
- **29TH: AFTER A SHOW** at Ellis Auditorium in Memphis, Tennessee, Bruce Springsteen endeavours to meet his idol Elvis Presley, by the unorthodox method of scaling the walls of Graceland. He is ejected by a security guard.

- **APRIL 8TH: FOLK SINGER PHIL OCHS** hangs himself at his sister's house in Far Rockaway, New York. He has been suffering from manic depression, and is frustrated not only by severe writer's block but also damage done to his vocal cords in an assault some time earlier. Though he never had chart success (his ironically titled 1970 album *Phil Ochs' Greatest Hits* was in fact an eclectic collection of new ideas), he was an important figure on the protest music scene of the 1960s, with pithy and astute views on civil rights, poverty, and Vietnam. Later, his unique idea of combining two great icons, Elvis Presley and Che Guevara, saw him touring in a gold lamé suit, singing a mixture of protest songs and 1950s rock'n'roll. It did not go down too well in most places. His brother Michael, once his manager, becomes a leading rock and pop archivist. This shot of Phil is from Michael's archive, as are many others in this book.

MAY | JUNE

• 1ST: **THE ALBUM** *Presence* by Led Zeppelin hits Number One in the US. It's their fifth album to do so in seven years.

• 2ND: **THE WORLD'S LONGEST** non-stop commercial flight is completed by Pan Am, flying over 8,000 miles in thirteen-and-a-half hours.

• 4TH: **'WALTZING MATILDA'** is adopted as the Australian national anthem, but only lasts until it is superseded by 'Australia Fair' in 1986.

• 11TH: **SEX PISTOLS** begin a Tuesday night residency at the 100 Club, London.

• 14TH: **EX-YARDBIRD** Keith Relf is electrocuted while tuning his guitar – he's been in the process of forming a new band called Illusion.

• 15TH: **A MASSED MARIJUANA-**smoking demonstration staggers through New York, stopping regularly for snacks.

• 19TH: **HAVING CRASHED** his car into the central barrier on a freeway 60 miles north of London, Keith Richards of the Rolling Stones is arrested when police find a silver cylinder full of cocaine in the vehicle.

• 23RD: **BOB DYLAN'S** *Hard Rain* TV special is recorded at a performance by his Rolling Thunder Review in Fort Collins, Colorado.

• 28TH: **THE ALLMAN BROTHERS BAND** call it a day because the other members feel they can no longer share a stage with Greg Allman, who recently testified in a drug case against the band's roadie Scooter Herring.

• 29TH: **'LOVE HANGOVER'** by Diana Ross reaches Number One on the US singles chart. It's the first of Ross's lucrative spate of 'disco' hits.

• 31ST: **THE WHO** enter the *Guinness Book Of Records* as the loudest band in the world: during a concert at Charlton soccer ground in London, the 76,000 watt PA system is clocked at 120db – and that's at 50 metres from the stage. Guitarist Pete Townshend later develops ear problems as a result of excessive sound levels on stage and in the studio.

• 3RD: **QUEEN ARE** awarded a US gold disc for the single 'Bohemian Rhapsody.'

• 4TH: **THE ALBUM** *Live At CBGB's* is recorded over this weekend in the home venue of New York punk, featuring Blondie, Laughing Dogs, Manster, Talking Heads, The Shirts, Mink de Ville, and Tuff Darts.

• 6TH: **BILLIONAIRE** John Paul Getty dies at 83. He leaves over $4 billion, and a priceless collection of artworks.

• 10TH: **PAUL McCARTNEY** and Wings (below) perform in Seattle, Washington, and the show is filmed for release as the

in-concert movie *Rockshow*. It also sets the record for the largest attendance at an indoor concert: 67,100.

• 16TH: **THE BLACK TOWNSHIP** of Soweto near Johannesburg, South Africa, takes to the streets to rebel against the teaching of the Afrikaans language in its schools.

More than 1,000 people die before security forces control the uprising. This date will henceforth be known as Soweto Day in South Africa.

• 19TH: **EDDY ARNOLD** enters the US country charts with the single 'Cowboy,' becoming the first artist to have notched up 100 Country Chart hits.

• 26TH: **'SOMETHING** He Can Feel' by Aretha Franklin reaches Number

• **JUNE 21ST: A HUGE MONKEY** (in fact a 110-foot model of King Kong) is dropped from the top of the World Trade Center in New York during filming of an updated version of the old movie classic.

One on the US R&B Singles chart... And singer Bryan Ferry leaves Roxy Music, shortly after the band achieve their only US hit single – a Number 30 placing for 'Love Is The Drug.' They'll enjoy something of a revival when they reform in 1979.

• 27TH: **WHEN ELVIS PRESLEY** plays at the Capitol Center, Largo, Maryland, Elton John visits him during the intermission... Meanwhile, six Palestinians hijack a French plane leaving Athens, with 280 passengers on board, and force the pilot to fly to Entebbe, in Uganda. There they demand the release of 33 Palestinians held in Israel. The stand-off is broken early in July by Israeli commandos, who fly 2,500 miles, land three large transport planes in the dark, kill the hijackers, three hostages, and the Ugandan troops guarding them, destroy much of the Ugandan airforce, and fly home.

• **JUNE 5TH: THIN LIZZY** enter the US charts with what will be their biggest American hit, 'The Boys Are Back In Town,' which peaks at Number 12. In the UK, they'll have nine Top 20 singles, and seven Top Ten albums, before singer/bass player Phil Lynott's death in 1986.

# Gabba Gabba Hey!

- **MAY 10TH:** **FIRST OF TWO** nights for The Ramones at the Bottom Line club, New York City. Cartoon rockers The Ramones started life in 1974 as vocalist Joey, guitarist Johnny, bass player Dee Dee (later C.J.) and, variously, drummers Tommy, Marky, and Richie. Their live sets comprise less than 20 minutes of lightning quick songs with gloriously daft titles like 'Beat On The Brat' and 'Now I Wanna Sniff Some Glue,' all of which tend to begin 'Wun, two, free, faw,' avoid unnecessary solos, and shudder to a halt less than three minutes later. The inevitable consequence is a 1976 debut album, *Ramones*, containing 14 tracks and totalling less than 30 minutes. They will proceed to plough the same furrow for much of the next 20 years. The Ramones don't finally run out of steam until singer Joey Ramone dies, on April 15, 2001, of lymphatic cancer. He was 49 years old.

# God Bless America

**T**HIS JULY 4TH, INDEPENDENCE DAY, the USA celebrates its 200th birthday as a self-governing nation, rather than a colony. Great Britain, like an estranged parent trying to think of a suitable gift, presents the US with the Magna Carta (the 13th century English bill of rights) especially for the bicentennial. Just on loan, of course – Britain wants it back after the celebrations... Meanwhile, on July 20th, US sporting legend Hank Aaron (left) slugs his final home run, playing for the Milwaukee Brewers at the age of 42. Its the 755th home run in his remarkable 23-year career – an astonishing world record total. Boxer Muhammad Ali once said of Hank Aaron that he was "the only man I idolize more than myself."

# 1976
May–August

## JULY

- **3RD:** **ASPIRING POP STAR** Stuart Goddard meets Andy Warren and they form the B-Sides, who eventually mutate into Adam & The Ants.
- **5TH:** **DURING A FLAMING GROOVIES/RAMONES** gig at Dingwalls, London, a glass of beer is thrown at Joey Ramone on stage. The thrower is Glen Matlock of The Sex Pistols.
- **10TH:** **AFTER AN EXPLOSION** at a chemical factory fills the sky with a poisonous cloud, the Italian town of Seveso is evacuated – but crops are ruined, thousands of animals die, and there will be a huge rise in abnormal births locally... Meanwhile, The Starland Vocal Band reach Number One on the *Billboard* US Top 40 with the 'sexy' song 'Afternoon Delight.'
- **12TH:** **IAN DURY** and Chas Jankel leave Kilburn & The High Roads and record *New Boots & Panties,* then form a new band called The Blockheads.
- **19TH:** **AFTER MONTHS** of speculation about relations within the band, it's announced that Deep Purple have broken up.
- **20TH:** The Buzzcocks play their first gig, supporting the Sex Pistols in Manchester.
- **27TH:** **BRUCE SPRINGSTEEN** starts a legal action in the US district court, aimed at severing all business ties with his manager Mike Appel.
- **31ST:** **THE BLUE OYSTER CULT** release a new single, 'Don't Fear The Reaper,' in the US. Taken from their Top 30 album *Agents Of Fortune*, the track will become the hard rock band's signature tune.

## AUGUST

- **1ST:** **139 DIE** in a flash flood in Colorado, US.
- **5TH:** **VAN MORRISON** joins Eric Clapton on stage at the Odeon, Birmingham, UK, to perform 'Kansas City.' During this gig, Clapton makes a controversial speech, seeming to support the anti-immigration policies of English politician Enoch Powell.
- **7TH:** **MORE THAN 20,000 WOMEN**, both Protestant and Catholic, march for peace in Northern Ireland. Many of them have lost family members in the escalating violence in Ulster.
- **10TH:** **GEORGE BENSON** earns a US platinum album award for his album *Breezin'*... And Elton John plays the first of

a ten-night residency in Madison Square Garden in New York.
- **11TH:** **ELEKTRA RECORDS** announces that it has signed New York 'new wave' band Television.
- **13TH:** **THE CLASH** play a showcase for the press at rehearsal rooms in London's Chalk Farm. Two weeks later they play their first public gig, at a favorite Sex Pistol haunt, the Screen On The Green cinema in Islington, London.
- **15TH:** **ONE HUNDRED AND EIGHTY-EIGHT** fans are arrested, mostly on drugs charges, at a Jethro Tull gig in the Coliseum, Los Angeles.
- **16TH:** **CLIFF RICHARD** begins a tour of Russia. He's also just released a new single, 'Devil Woman,' in the US, which will give him his biggest ever hit there. It is his first US chart entry since 1964, despite a phenomenal success rate in the UK, where's he's notched up over 40 Top Tens by 1976.
- **17TH:** **A MASSIVE EARTHQUAKE** and tidal wave takes the lives of more than 8,000 in the Philippines.
- **21ST:** **THE FIRST EUROPEAN** Punk Rock Festival is staged at

Mont De Marsan, near Bordeaux, France. Acts on the bill include The Damned, Count Bishops, Nick Lowe, Pink Fairies, Eddie & The Hot Rods, Tyla Gang, and Hammersmith Gorillas... And Renee Richards wins her first tournament as a women tennis player in the US. She was previously a male navy officer called Richard Raskind.
- **24TH:** **FUTURE PRESIDENT** Jimmy Carter is booed by the American Legion after he announces his intention to pardon all draft dodgers.
- **27TH:** **THE EUROPEAN COMMISSION** Of Human Rights accuses the UK of torture in Northern Ireland.
- **29TH:** **NEIL YOUNG** joins the briefly re-formed Californian psychedelic band Spirit, on stage at the Civic Center, Santa Monica, for a performance of 'Like A Rolling Stone.' Spirit's guitarist, Randy California, does not recognise Young at first, and tries to have him thrown off.
- **29TH:** **BLUESMAN JIMMY REED** dies at 50. He influenced many white R&B acts.

- **JULY 23RD:** **AT THE MONTREAL** Olympics, 14-year-old Nadia Comaneci becomes the first gymnast to score ten out of ten (leaving the Olympic scoreboards very confused). She goes on to win three gold medals, a silver and a bronze for her country, Romania.

- **AUGUST 2ND:** **GERMAN MOVIE DIRECTOR** Fritz Lang dies at the age of 75. His best known film is the futuristic silent classic *Metropolis*, which he made in 1927, and which influenced every science fiction film from then on. Excerpts will also be used in the video for Queen's 1984 single 'Radio Ga-Ga.'

# 1976

September–December

## The First Pogo

**S**EPTEMBER 20TH: **THE FIRST DAY** of the *100 Club Punk Festival* takes place in central London, featuring The Sex Pistols, The Clash and the debut of Siouxsie & The Banshees (with Sid Vicious, later bassist with The Sex Pistols, on drums). The second night features The Damned, the Buzzcocks, and the Vibrators (but is marred by a glass-throwing incident, attributed to Vicious). The heated debate over the origins of punk rock will continue as long as there's a fan of the genre still willing to pogo for the cause. In the US, The Neon Boys (later Television) and The Ramones certainly formed as far back as 1973/74, but they in turn were influenced by Sixties 'garage,' and bands like The Stooges and The Dictators. But it was midway through 1976 in the UK that punk truly began to spit and snarl into a life of its own. On October 8th, The Sex Pistols sign a £40,000 ($70,000) contract with EMI Records and release 'Anarchy In The UK,' the single which will quickly propel them to international infamy.

## SEPTEMBER

• **SEPTEMBER 17TH: THE SPACE SHUTTLE is** unveiled. As the world's first reusable space-craft, it is designed so it can be launched like a rocket then return from space and land like an airplane. The shuttle Enterprise is used for test purposes and demonstrations only, and will end up in the Smithsonian Institute in Washington DC, without ever having been in space.

• **1ST: LOU ADLER**, president of Ode Records, is kidnapped from his home in Malibu, California, and released the same day, after handing over $25,000 to the kidnappers.

• **4TH: STEVE MILLER** enters the US Top 40 singles chart with 'Rock'n Me,' which will peak at Number One.

• **6TH: IN NEW YORK CITY**, punk pioneers Richard Hell & The Voidoids are recording their first tracks.

• **7TH: FORMER BEATLE** George Harrison is found guilty of having subconsciously plagiarised the 1963 Chiffons' hit 'He's So Fine' when composing his song 'My Sweet Lord.'

• **8TH: HEART** are awarded a US gold disc for their debut album, *Dreamboat Annie*.

• **9TH: MAO TSE-TUNG** dies at the age of 82. A power struggle immediately erupts in China.

• **13TH: CALIFORNIA** approves a law which offers terminally ill patients the right to die.

• **18TH: THE SECOND ANNUAL ROCK MUSIC AWARDS** are held at the Hollywood Palladium. Fleetwood Mac win Best Group and Best Album. Peter Frampton is Rock Personality Of The Year.

• **27TH: THE SOUNDTRACK** to the movie *Dawn: Portrait Of A Teenage Runaway* features the song 'Cherry Bomb,' the debut release from appropriately named all-female rock band The Runaways, who've recently supported Television and Talking Heads at CBGB's in New York. Written by producer/manager Kim Fowley and rhythm guitarist Joan Jett, the single achieves lots of hype but limited success in terms of sales, though it does inspire a new generation of girls to take up music-making instead of just music-buying. After belting out five albums, the band splits in 1979.

## Killer On The Loose

• **SEPTEMBER 29TH: A BAD FEW MONTHS** for heavy-drinking Jerry Lee 'Killer' Lewis as he turns 41... First of all, he accidentally shoots his bass player, Norman Owens, in the chest, twice. He later apologises – he either didn't know the gun was loaded, or was aiming at something else, depending on which story you hear – and although Owens sues, no criminal charges are brought. A few weeks later, on November 28th, Jerry Lee crashes his Rolls-Royce in Memphis, Tennessee, before checking into a hospital for treatment on his ulcers. Then the next day, waving a Derringer pistol, he drives to Graceland, home of Elvis Presley, and demands that Elvis come out to speak with him. Elvis declines. Jerry Lee is shown off the premises by security guards, and goes home.

## OCTOBER

• **OCTOBER 8TH: STEVIE WONDER** releases a new double album, *Songs In the Key Of Life*, in the US. Generally regarded as perhaps the last album of his 1970s creative peak, it will also be his last Number One LP.

• **1ST: MORE THAN 2000 DIE** and 14,000 are injured when Hurricane Lizzie hits Mexico.

• **2ND: JOHN BELUSHI** does a telling impersonation of Joe Cocker on US TV comedy show *Saturday Night Live*, with Joe Cocker partnering him on the song 'Feeling Alright.' As well as Belushi, *Saturday Night Live* will launch the careers of Dan Aykroyd (who later partners Belushi in the movie *The Blues Brothers*), Chevy Chase, Bill Murray, Mike Myers, Eddie Murphy, Harry Shearer, Christopher Guest, Robert Downey Jr, and Chris Rock.

• **11TH: MAO TSE-TUNG'S** widow, Jiang Qing, is arrested in Beijing, China, along with the rest of the 'Gang Of Four' who rose to power during the Cultural Revolution (1966-1976) and dominated Chinese politics during the early 1970s. They will be given lengthy prison terms.

• **14TH: SCIENTISTS** finally identify the disease that has killed more than 300 people in Zaire – it's a viral infection they call Green Monkey Fever.

• **15TH: FLEETWOOD MAC** release the album *Rumours*.

• **15TH: ROD STEWART'S** latest single, 'Tonight's the Night,' is banned by RKO-owned radio stations in the US because the lyric is deemed "suggestive"... And another ship, this time carrying 37 passengers, apparently disappears in the so-called Bermuda Triangle.

• **16TH: ROCK BAND** Boston's debut album enters the US charts on its way to Number Three. Mostly the work of studio wizard Tom Scholz, it includes the enduring hit single 'More Than A Feeling,' and seen in retrospect as a blueprint for the coming boom in 'soft' adult-oriented rock (AOR).

• **22ND: THE FIRST BRITISH** punk single, 'New Rose' by The Damned, is released.

• **29TH: AT THE MUNICIPAL AUDITORIUM**, New Orleans, George Clinton and Parliament debut their massive Mothership stage set.

## The Last Waltz

• **NOVEMBER 25TH:** **THE BAND** play their farewell show at the Winterland ballroom, San Francisco, with assistance from rock's aristocracy, including Bob Dylan, Neil Young, Joni Mitchell, Emmylou Harris, Muddy Waters, Stephen Stills, Paul Butterfield, Dr John, Eric Clapton, Ronnie Hawkins, Ronnie Wood, Van Morrison, Neil Diamond, The Staple Singers, and Ringo Starr. The event is filmed by Martin Scorsese and released as the movie *The Last Waltz* and as a great triple live album. It's a grand swansong for the group, who made their debut as Ronnie Hawkins's backing band in 1963. After the album is released, guitarist Robbie Robertson, bassist Rick Danko, and drummer Levon Helm start solo careers. Then, on March 6th, 1986, pianist Richard Manuel takes his own life, at the age of 40. The Band will re-form in the 1990s, although without Robbie Robertson. In 1999, Rick Danko dies, at age 56.

• **NOVEMBER 21ST:** **ROCKY** premieres in Philadelphia, where the film is set. Its little-known star, Sylvester Stallone, has been paid a relatively meagre $23,000 for his performance. The Rocky series of movies will go on to make close to $1 billion at the box office over the next few years.

## NOVEMBER

• **1ST:** **NEIL YOUNG** and his band Crazy Horse begin a US tour at the Dorothy Chandler Pavilion, Los Angeles.

• **2ND:** **PEANUT FARMER** and former governor of Georgia Jimmy Carter is elected the 39th President of the US. His successful campaign is also the first to use electronic mail, or 'email,' to aid communications. It's around this time too that Queen Elizabeth of Great Britain sends her first email – perhaps she and Jimmy Carter start their own chat room. Using false names, of course...

• **5TH:** **GARY GILMORE** insists on receiving the death penalty just over three months after he was arrested for the murders of two men. He is tried, convicted, and sentenced to death – though the execution isn't carried out until January 1977 by which time he'll have tried to take his own life.

• **6TH:** **'ROCK'N'ME'** by The Steve Miller Band (above) reaches Number one on the US pop singles chart.

• **18TH:** **DADAIST PAINTER**, photographer, and film-maker Man Ray dies at age 86.

• **20TH:** **AT THE MEMORIAL AUDITORIUM**, Sacramento, California, Joni Mitchell, John Sebastian, Country Joe McDonald, and Fred Neil take part in California Celebrates The Whales Day.

## DECEMBER

• **1ST:** **ON UK PRIME-TIME TV**, the Sex Pistols unleash several four-letter words during an interview with host Bill Grundy – and overnight become the most talked-about band in Britain. Next day, Grundy is suspended by his bosses for encouraging the outbursts.

• **4TH:** **BOB MARLEY** is shot and wounded at his home in Kingston, Jamaica. His wife Rita and manager Don Taylor are also shot... And former Deep Purple guitarist Tommy Bolin dies of a drug overdose.

• **8TH:** **THE EAGLES** release their new album, *Hotel California*, in the US.

• **10TH:** **GENERATION X**, a new band formed by UK punk rocker Billy Idol, play their first gig, at the Central College of Art, London.

• **11TH:** **ACE FREHLEY** of Kiss is knocked out by an electric shock during a show at the Civic Center, Lakeland, Florida. During the same show, Gene Simmons's hair catches fire, but the band finishes the performance.

• **27TH:** **BLUES GUITAR LEGEND** Freddie King dies at age 42.

• **31ST:** **THE CARS** make their live debut at Pease Air Force Base, New Hampshire.

# 1977

## ZEPPELIN DEFLATING

The coming year will turn out to be something of a low-point in the dazzling, seemingly unstoppable career of Led Zeppelin – the undisputed world heavyweight champions of Seventies rock. They encapsulate the perfect rock combination: Plant's strutting, blueswailing vocals, Page's stylistically eclectic virtuoso guitar work, and the solid groove of rhythm section Jones & Bonham. After six Number One albums in a row since 1969, the most recent of which was the rather severe, relatively unadventurous *Presence* (ignoring the re-tread live collection on *The Song Remains The Same*), Led Zeppelin is still the biggest stadium draw anywhere. They will even break their own concert attendance record with a crowd of 76,000 at Michigan in May. But illness, bad luck, reckless behaviour, and personal tragedy combine to take the band off the road by the end of this year. Rumours of a permanent break-up abound, although after a recuperative period, Zeppelin will make a triumphant, if temporary, return in 1979 – just before more disaster strikes.

# 1977

## January–April

## Rumours & Dreams

**F**EBRUARY 19TH: THREE WEEKS AFTER the group's founder and former frontman Peter Green is committed to an institution on mental health grounds (having threatened his accountant with a rifle), the new-look Fleetwood Mac release their multi-million selling album *Rumours*. A Number One on both sides of the Atlantic, the album also provides them with three huge hit singles: 'Go Your Own Way,' 'Don't Stop,' and 'Dreams,' and arguably represents the pinnacle of 1970s Adult-Oriented Rock. It's also exactly the kind of slick and laid-back record the punks love to hate...
But 'Mac' have the material reward of seeing it become one of the five best-selling albums of all

### JANUARY

- **1ST: LONDON'S FIRST** full-time punk venue, The Roxy, opens in Neal St, Covent Garden. The Clash play at the opening.
- **2ND: JAZZ PIANIST** Erroll Garner (composer of jazz standard 'Misty') dies, age 53.
- **6TH: EMI DROPS** the Sex Pistols, writing off the advance the label paid them just three months earlier – essentially a $60,000 golden handshake.
- **9TH: WHEN FORMER** Curved Air drummer Stewart Copeland meets former Last Exit bassist Sting in London, they form a relationship that will result in the creation of The Police.
- **10TH: UNESCO BEGINS** an appeal to save the Acropolis in Athens, which is in a very poor state after years of punishment from car emissions and souvenir hunters with chisels.
- **11TH: ROLLING STONE** Keith Richards is fined £750 after being found guilty of possessing cocaine (found in his car after an earlier accident).
- **14TH: THREE HIGH-PROFILE** deaths today: French-born American writer Anais Nin (73), UK statesman and former Prime Minister Anthony Eden (79), and British actor Peter Finch (60) –

**• JANUARY 15TH: DAVID BOWIE** releases the album *Low* – the first of a trilogy in collaboration with former Roxy Music man Brian Eno, which will see Bowie explore the potential of electronic music.

who has only just finished work on the movie *Network*, a performance which will win him a posthumous Best Actor Oscar.
- **17TH: DOUBLE MURDERER** Gary Gilmore is killed by firing squad. He is the first person to be executed in the US since the reintroduction of the death penalty last year. Following his request for his body to be used for medical purposes, his corneas are reportedly transplanted later today – inspiring The Adverts' song '(Looking Through) Gary Gilmore's Eyes.'
- **22ND: ABBA ENTER** the US Top 40 singles chart with Dancing Queen, which will peak at Number One.
- **23RD: HAVING NOTCHED UP** 302 weeks on the US album charts, *Tapestry* by Carole King sets a new record for chart longevity... Meanwhile, punk artist Patti Smith breaks several bones in her neck when she falls from a stage in Tampa, Florida...

### FEBRUARY

- **1ST: THE ULTRA-MODERN** Pompidou Centre, designed by Englishman Richard Rogers and Italian Renzo Piano, brings hi-tech architecture and a vibrant arts scene to the old Marais region of Paris, France. Its 'let it all hang out' design philosophy will shock some and delight many in years to come.
- **4TH: US TV ROCK SHOW** *American Bandstand* celebrates 25 years on air with an ABC TV special, hosted by founding father Dick Clark, and featuring an all-star band that includes Chuck Berry, Junior Walker, Johnny Rivers, The Pointer Sisters, Gregg Allman, Charlie Daniels, Seals & Crofts, and most of

Booker T & the MGs.
- **10TH: THE CLASH** arrive at CBS Studios, London, to start work on their debut album.
- **12TH: THE POLICE** record their first single, 'Fall Out,' at Pathway Studios, London.
- **14TH: THE B-52S** play their first gig, at a Valentine's Day event in a greenhouse in Athens, Georgia.
- **19TH: TELEVISION** release their debut album *Marquee Moon*. In their US home market, its edgy, slightly artsy rock doesn't sell well at all, though hip 'new wave' critics love it. Meanwhile, in the UK it reaches Number 28 on the album chart, and

generates two Top 30 singles, 'Marquee Moon' and 'Prove It.'
- **20TH: THE U.S BEGINS** testing windmill power at Rocky Flats, Colorado.
- **25TH: UGANDAN PRESIDENT** Idi Amin detains 240 U.S citizens after being denounced by President Carter. They are, however, released by March 1st ... In the UK, Polydor sign The Jam, fronted by Paul Weller.
- **26TH: BLUES LEGEND** Bukka White dies in a Memphis hospital... 'And New Kid In Town' by The Eagles is US Number One. On the same day, they release their new single, 'Hotel California.'

### MARCH

- **4TH: TONIGHT'S GIG** at El Mocambo, a 300-capacity club in Toronto, Canada, is advertised as featuring local band April Wine. In fact, the Rolling Stones play unannounced, and record their album *Love You Live*.
- **5TH: BASS PLAYER** Glen Matlock gets his marching orders from the Sex Pistols because, it is claimed, he liked the Beatles. He goes on to form the Rich Kids and is replaced on bass by Sid Vicious (who cannot play, but looks the part).
- **8TH: THE U.S ARMY** admits to performing more than 200 open air germ warfare tests.
- **10TH: SEX PISTOLS** sign to A&M – they are dropped nine days later, $115,000 better off...
- **11TH: THE SLITS** (the all-girl punk outfit who would soon be joined by future Banshees drummer Budgie) make their live debut supporting The Clash in Harlesden, north London.
- **12TH: MOVIE DIRECTOR** Roman Polanski, whose

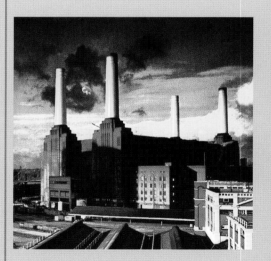

**• MARCH 10TH: PINK FLOYD** are awarded a US platinum disc by the RIAA for their latest album, *Animals*, released only a month ago. The photo shoot for the album sleeve used a large inflatable pig. (It's really there above the power station, not just painted in. That would have been easier, but less fun.) Unfortunately, it broke loose from its moorings and floated away, finally being tracked down more than 50 miles away...

time. Recorded during the emotional turmoil arising from divorce proceedings between both Buckingham and Nicks and the two McVies, the resulting tracks seem to have benefited from the tension, creative and otherwise. The band will never again reach quite these heights, though they still manage a few Number One albums in the US and UK, amid splits, kiss-and-tell biographies, reformations, more splits, and endless line-up changes. In total, over the next 25 years, Fleetwood Mac will shift more than 100 million albums worldwide, establishing them as one of the most popular bands ever.

APRIL

• **MARCH 26TH: DARYL HALL & JOHN OATES** get their first Number One in the US singles chart with Hall's song 'Rich Girl.' It will be three more years before they repeat the feat.

• 6TH: **ALLEN KLEIN**, former manager of both The Beatles and The Rolling Stones, is indicted in New York City on charges of income tax evasion.

• 7TH: **THE CLASH** release their first album, *The Clash,* in the UK.

• 11TH: **ALICE COOPER** is placed under house arrest in Sydney, Australia, following a local promoter's accusation that Cooper owes him Australian $59,632 ($33,000 US) for breach of contract back in 1975.

• 12TH: **THE CHAIRMAN** of Wrigley chewing gum, Phillip K Wrigley, dies at 82.

• 15TH: **HAVING LAUNCHED** the first Apple computer last August, Steves Jobs and Wozniak introduce the Apple II.

• 17TH: **WHEN SOUTHSIDE** JOHNNY plays at the Stone Poney, Asbury Park, New Jersey, he is joined onstage by Bruce Springsteen.

• 23RD: **SIOUXSIE & THE BANSHEES** play at The Roxy, London, and are seen by The B-Sides, who decide to pursue a new direction, and re-emerge as Adam & The Ants.

• 24TH: **SANTANA** and Joan Baez play a free concert for the inmates at Soledad prison in California.

• 26TH: **A NEW DISCOTHEQUE**, Studio 54, opens its doors for the first time on West 54th Street, New York City. It rapidly becomes the most fashionable East Coast nightspot – renowned for its sex and drugs as much as its music – and inspiration for many classic dancefloor hits, not least those of recently formed Chic. Studio 54's original owners, Steve Rubell and Ian Schrager, will be arrested two years later and charged with tax and drugs offences. They go to prison for a year and the club changes hands, but it's heyday is gone, and it closes for good in 1986.

• 28TH: **TWO BAADER-MEINHOF TERRORISTS** are jailed for "life plus 15 years" in Germany.

wife Sharon Tate was slain by the Manson 'family,' is arrested for the statutory rape of a 13-year-old girl in Los Angeles. He is held for psychiatric tests, but, fearing a long prison sentence, he flees the country. He never returns, and 36 years later will still feature on the FBI's wanted list.

• 14TH: **RICHARD HELL** & The Voidoids begin three weeks of recording their debut album, *Blank Generation*, at Electric Lady Studios in New York City.

• 18TH: **THE CLASH** release 'White Riot,' their debut single.

• 24TH: **A SAN FRANCISCO** judge orders five members of the Moonie cult (The Unification Church of the Reverend Sun Myung Moon) to be returned to their families.

• 25TH: **ELVIS COSTELLO** releases his first UK single, 'Less Than Zero,' a searing attack on British fascist leader Oswald Mosley, who had been imprisoned during the World War II for his Nazi sympathies. •

27TH: **A PAN-AM** 747 collides with a KLM jumbo that had began its take-off without clearance at Tenerife airport, killing 574 people. It will emerge that the world's worst air disaster is caused by a misunderstanding about which aircraft is taking off, compounded by fog on the runway, an unusual occurrence in Tenerife.

• 31ST: **THE FIRST PUBLISHED** picture of Tori Amos appears under the headline "Top Teens In Talent Contest" in the *Montgomery Journal* in Maryland. It seems that Miss Ellen Amos (13) has won a first prize of $100, singing her own composition, 'More Than Just A Friend.'

• **APRIL 2ND: CHARLOTTE BREW** becomes the first female jockey to ride in the British Grand National. Her mount (Barony Fort) makes it all the way to the 27th fence before taking a tumble. The eventual winner is Red Rum, seen below scoring his legendary third Grand National win – the only horse ever to achieve this.

## The King Is Dead...

**A**UGUST 16TH: **ELVIS AARON PRESLEY** collapses and dies at home in Graceland, Memphis, Tennessee. He is found on the floor of a bathroom by his girlfriend Ginger Alden, and rushed to the city's Baptist Memorial Hospital, where at 3.30am he is officially pronounced dead. Though traces of drugs are found in his body, the cause of death is heart failure. He is buried next to his mother in a Memphis cemetery, but after apparent attempts to steal Elvis's corpse, both are moved to the grounds of Graceland. They will be joined there by Elvis's father, Vernon, in two years' time. In the hours after the announcement of Elvis's death, the media pack and fans quickly descend on Memphis. As Elvis lies in state, more than 25,000 fans file past his coffin to pay their last respects. President Carter offers his own tribute: "Elvis Presley was a symbol to people the world over of the vitality, rebelliousness and good humor of this country." Though he has an immediate posthumous Number One in the UK with 'Way Down,' Elvis's recent musical output has not matched that of his younger, epoch-forming self: asked to comment on Presley's death, John Lennon famously remarks, "Elvis died when he went into the army." All the same, no one can argue with 114 Top 40 hits in 21 years.

- **2ND: MORE THAN** 1,000 demonstrators are arrested by police as they attempt to disrupt the construction of a nuclear power station in Seabrook, New Hampshire .
- **3RD: THE FIRST** World Badminton Championships are held in the city of Malmö, Sweden.
- **5TH: BILL DRUMMOND** and Holly Johnson form Big In Japan. (Both later top the UK charts: Drummond in KLF, and Johnson in Frankie Goes To Hollywood.)
- **7TH: A CROWD OF 57,000** sees the Day On The Green concert at Oakland Stadium, California, featuring Fleetwood Mac, The Doobie Brothers, Gary Wright, and Steve Gibbons.
- **10TH: THE EAGLES** file a damages suit against their former manager, David Geffen, with intent to get back their song copyrights.
- **14TH: LEO SAYER** has his second US Number One in a row, following up the manic falsetto of 'You Make Me Feel Like Dancing' with the low-key ballad 'When I Need You.'
- **19TH: THE ORIENT EXPRESS** is taken out of service after 94 years... And Kenya bans wildlife hunting.
- **22ND: MICK JAGGER** of the Rolling Stones meets and takes a fancy to a blonde

- **MAY 28TH: A CROWD OF ALMOST** 41,000 fans attends a soul extravaganza at Arrowhead Stadium, Kansas City, Missouri, featuring The Isley Brothers, Parliament/Funkadelic, Rufus featuring Chaka Khan, Bootsy's Rubber Band, The Brothers Johnson, and disco-funk band Rose Royce (above), who've recently had a US Number One hit with 'Car Wash.'

Texan. "He pressed his knee next to mine, and I could feel the electricity," says Jerry Hall later.
- **24TH: EMERSON, LAKE & PALMER** embark on a US tour, said to be the most expensive in history. Their entourage includes a 70 piece orchestra. ELP are another act despised by punk and new wave devotees for indulging in what they see as the overblown excesses of many superstar rock groups.
- **29TH: NIGEL SHORT** from the UK, just 11 years old, qualifies as the youngest ever competitor in a national chess championship (the previous youngest was 12).

- **JUNE 7TH: JUBILEE CELEBRATIONS** begin, to mark Queen Elizabeth II's 25 years as British monarch. Street parties are organised around the UK (and unbridled fun is had by all, as you can see below). In July, UK tennis player Virginia Wade duly wins the women's singles championships at Wimbledon, the first Briton to do so – and in the championship's centenary year too. The Sex Pistols, meanwhile, do their bit by releasing the single 'God Save The Queen' (next line, "She ain't no human being"). It is banned by the BBC, and denied the Number One position in the charts, despite reputedly outselling its closest rival, Rod Stewart's version of 'I Don't Want To Talk About It.' The Pistols also stage their own jubilee party, performing on an open boat on the river Thames in central London, which results in the arrest of manager Malcom McLaren. A few days later, Pistols' singer Johnny Rotten and drummer Paul Cook are attacked in separate incidents, supposedly by 'patriots.'

- **MAY 25TH: *STAR WARS* IS RELEASED** – the original movie, later to be known as *Episode IV*, starring Alec Guinness as an older Ewan McGregor, seen here chewing the Force with Mark Hamill, plus of course Carrie Fisher, Harrison Ford, and the rest of the stellar cast...

# Long Live Elvis II

**J**ULY 26TH: ELVIS COSTELLO (real name Declan MacManus) is arrested for busking outside the London Hilton hotel, where global CBS record executives are meeting. But his publicity stunt works. He persuades the company to release his debut album, *My Aim Is True*, in the US as well as the UK. Emerging alongside 'punk' in the UK, Elvis Costello's abrasive song-writing style makes subsequent albums *This Year's Model* and *Armed Forces* enduring records of their era. Later, with *Get Happy!* and 1981's *Trust*, he develops his more soulful and lyrical side, all the while regularly visiting the UK charts with such varied hits as 'Alison', 'Watching The Detectives', 'I Don't Want To Go To Chelsea', 'Oliver's Army,' and 'I Can't Stand Up For Falling Down.' It becomes clear that what Costello most fears is being pinned down. In May 1981, he will travel to Nashville to make *Almost Blue* with country producer Billy Sherrill, but it does not mark a serious bid to find a new audience. Subsequent albums such as *Imperial Bedroom*, *Punch The Clock* and 1984's *Goodbye Cruel World* will see bitter and sweet halves of Costello's musical personality continuing to battle it out.

## JULY

- **4TH: THE JACKSONS** – formerly the Jackson Five (the rights to the original name were retained by Berry Gordy when the band jumped ship from Motown to CBS/Epic) enter the UK singles chart with 'Show You The Way To Go,' which will go all the way to Number One, having peaked at 28 in the US.
- **13TH: ALICE COOPER** holds auditions in Century City, California, to find a new boa constrictor to take part in his stage show. The previous holder of the lead snake role died earlier in the month.
- **15TH: ADOLFO SUAREZ** wins the first democratic elections in Spain for 41 years...
- **17TH: WHEN JIMMY HELMS** cancels a gig at a college in Egham, Surrey, UK, a member of student committee rushes along to Elton John's house in nearby Windsor. Elton agrees, on the spur of the moment, to fill in for that night's performance.
- **25TH: PRINCE SIGNS** his first recording contract with Warner Brothers Records.
- **26TH: GAY RIGHTS** protestors find themselves on the wrong end of a hail of rubber bullets in Barcelona... And Elvis Presley performs what turns out to be his last live concert at the Market Square Arena, Indianapolis, Indiana.
- **30TH: MARVEL COMICS** launches the Kiss comic book.

- **3RD: WILLIE NELSON** (below) Waylon Jennings, Lynyrd Skynyrd, Jessi Colter, Jerry Jeff Walker, and Asleep At The Wheel pull 57,000

locals to Expos Square Speedway, Tulsa, Oklahoma.
- **6TH: WHEN PINK FLOYD'S** Animals tour ends at the Olympic Stadium, Montreal, Canada, a noisy fan becomes so irritating that Roger Waters spits at him – and then gets the idea of building a wall across the front of the stage...
- **8TH: SEX PISTOLS** release 'Pretty Vacant' and, for the first time, a Pistols record is accepted for sale in the UK's three leading High Street record retailers.
- **9TH: THE CAFÉ RACERS** play their last gig in Deptford, London, UK. They will shortly change their name to Dire Straits.

- **14TH: A POWER CUT** in New York is finally fixed after 3,300 people have been arrested for looting.
- **16TH: 'DA DOO RON RON'** by actor Shaun Cassidy (son of actors Jack Cassidy and Shirley Jones, and half-brother to David Cassidy), is the new US Number One single... And Hot Chocolate, fronted by Errol Brown, begin their third week at Number One in the UK with 'You Win Again.' In August it will be their fourth US Top 40 hit.
- **22ND: WHEN TONY ORLANDO** & Dawn play at the South Shore Music Circus, in Cohasset, a small town in Massachusetts, Orlando stuns audience and band by announcing his retirement from show business. He has, in effect, suffered a nervous breakdown on stage and will spend six months in a New York psychiatric hospital.
- **25TH: ANDY SUMMERS** plays his first gig as a member of The Police at the Music Machine, London.
- **26TH: ROBERT PLANT'S** son Karac (6) dies from respiratory failure while his father is on tour in the US.

## AUGUST

- **1ST: ERIC CLAPTON** charters a yacht, the Welsh Liberty, to travel from Cannes, France, to Ibiza for a gig at the Bull Ring.
- **6TH: 'STRAWBERRY LETTER NUMBER 23'** by The Brothers Johnson, produced by Quincy Jones, is the new Number One R&B single in the US. The flip-side is called 'Get The Funk Out Ma Face.' Bass player Louis Johnson will go on to work with Jones on Michael Jackson's *Off The Wall* and *Thriller*. He will play the bassline on 'Billie Jean.'
- **10TH: SON-OF-SAM** serial killer David Berkowitz is arrested, but is initially declared unfit to stand trial. He claims he is ordered to kill young women by a demon called Sam who speaks to him via howling dogs, though the real motive is suspected to be sexual resentment. "The defendant is as normal as anyone else," argues the prosecution's forensic psychiatrist, adding, in rather understated fashion, "maybe a little neurotic." Berkowitz pleads guilty to multiple murders, and is sentenced to 365 years in prison. Berkowitz subsequently announces that he has turned to God. At his first parole hearing, in 2003, he asks not to be considered for parole.
- **13TH: GENERATION X**, a punk band fronted by Billy Idol (above), sign to Chrysalis Records in the UK.
- **17TH: SOVIET NUCLEAR-POWERED** icebreaker the Artika becomes the first ever boat to reach the North Pole... And Phil Oakey auditions to become vocalist of The Human League at The Workshop, Devonshire Lane, Sheffield, UK.

- **19TH: GROUCHO MARX** finally joins a club that will have him as a member when he dies at 77.
- **20TH: ANDY GIBB** is replaced after four weeks at US Number One with 'I Just Want To Be Your Everything' by the Emotions, whose 'Best Of My Love' will now stay at the top for a total of five weeks.
- **22ND: INSPIRED BY** the release of the various artists album, *Let's Clean Up The Ghetto*, Mayor Tom Bradley of Los Angeles declares a 'Let's Clean Up The Ghetto Week.' The album features Billy Paul, Teddy Pendergrass, Lou Rawls, The O'Jays, The Three Degrees and others.
- **26TH: 'SEX & DRUGS & ROCK & ROLL'** is released by Ian Dury & the Blockheads. It doesn't make much impact on the charts, anywhere, but it's never forgotten by anyone who hears it.

- **MAY 25TH: WOODY ALLEN** & Diane Keaton star in the new movie Annie Hall.

## Once In A Lifetime

• **DECEMBER 8TH: NEW YORK'S TALKING HEADS** release their classic single, 'Psycho Killer.' Talking Heads first came to people's attention in the mid 1970s when they opened for The Ramones at CBGB's. Formed by David Byrne, Tina Weymouth and Chris Frantz at the Rhode Island School Of Design (former Modern Lover Jerry Harrison wouldn't join until 1976), the band would record ten original albums over 11 years, exploring electronics, funk and world music. At the same time, they would create further fine singles, including 'Once In A Lifetime,' 'Road To Nowhere,' and 'Burning Down The House.' And *Stop Making Sense*, their 1984 tour, movie and album collaboration with the film director Jonathan Demme, may be the best – and certainly the most innovative – document of a live show ever made. By 1991, however, internal tensions would all but destroy the band. In 1996, they would appear briefly as The Heads, without Byrne, who was now committed to solo projects in a Latin vein through his Luaka Bop label. Weymouth and Frantz, meanwhile, would have some success with their Tom Tom Club.

**SEPTEMBER**

**OCTOBER**

• **SEPTEMBER 9TH: DAVID BOWIE** is a guest on Marc Bolan's British television show, *Marc*. It's the only time the two will appear on screen together. A week later, barely a month after the death of his hero Elvis, Bolan is killed in his girlfriend Gloria Jones's car when it hits a tree on Barnes Common, south London. (The couple are seen here together, the previous Christmas.) Bolan, now 29, has recently been starting a comeback, making his new TV show and touring with the likes of The Damned.

• **1ST: BLONDIE SIGN** their first major label recording contract with Chrysalis Records.
• **3RD: WITH RECORD SALES** fuelled by his death, Elvis Presley has his biggest international success for nearly five years, with his final album *Moody Blue* and the single 'Way Down,' which hits Number One in the UK. It is less appreciated at home, hitting 18 on the chart.
• **8TH: U.S ACTOR** Zero Mostel dies aged 52, after falling ill during troubled rehearsals for a new Broadway play.
• **9TH: A STUDY** in the U.S discovers that the leading cause of death for black American males is murder.
• **10TH: THE ALBUM** *Oxygene* by Jean-Michel Jarre reaches Number Two in the UK charts, and the single 'Oxygene Part 4' makes the Top Five UK singles.
• **12TH: SOUTH AFRICAN** student leader Steve Biko dies in police custody. The subsequent official inquest into his death finds the 30-year-old did not die as a result of police brutality. It admits, however, that Biko was left shackled and naked for two days and that his head had 'collided with walls and tables,' causing brain injuries, during his five day interrogation.
• **16TH: OPERA SINGER** Maria Callas dies, age 53.
• **24TH: THE BEE GEES** release a new single, 'How Deep Is Your Love,' in the US.
• **26TH: CHEAP** international flights begin when Freddie Laker's Skytrain leaves London Gatwick for New York. The tickets cost just £59 ($90), not including food.

• **SEPTEMBER 5TH: SPACE PROBE VOYAGER I** is launched, 16 days *after* Voyager II. Yes, that's the order in which they're sent. Who knows why... Perhaps it's to do with the space-time continuum?

• **OCTOBER 7TH: THE DAVID BOWIE** album *Heroes*, with electronics by Robert Fripp and Brian Eno, is released in the US.

• **2ND: PETER GABRIEL**, formerly singer with Genesis, releases the first of his solo *Peter Gabriel* albums in the US.

• **15TH: YOU LIGHT UP MY LIFE** by Debby Boone (daughter of entertainer Pat) is the new Number One single in the US.
• **18TH: IN GERMANY**, an anti-terrorist squad storms a hijacked Lufthansa aircraft at Mogadishu Airport, Somalia, killing three of the four Palestinian hijackers and freeing all the hostages.
• **19TH: DR HANS MARTIN SCHLEYER**, a director of Daimler Benz in West Germany, is found dead in the trunk of a green Audi in Eastern France. He had been kidnapped by members of the Baader Meinhof gang, seeking the release of their colleagues in the Red Army Faction terrorist group. Then, when some of the

## Goodbye To Bing

• **OCTOBER 14TH: BING CROSBY DIES**, at the age of 73, after collapsing on a golf course near Madrid – though not until he's finished his game, naturally. His last recording session was just three days ago when he performed eight songs for BBC radio in London, the day after what turns out to be his final concert, in Brighton, Sussex. A giant of 20th century popular music (seen below with Louis Armstrong), Crosby was a pioneer of laid-back crooning, made possible by the development of microphones and public address equipment in the 1920s. He also took a keen interest in recording technology, and owned one of the first multi-track tape machines.

# Heart Like A Wheel

**D**ECEMBER 3RD: AFTER A RECORD 29 weeks at Number One, Fleetwood Mac's *Rumours* is knocked off the top of the US album chart by Linda Ronstadt's *Simple Dreams*, which includes the Top Five singles 'It's So Easy' and 'Blue Bayou.' Her first hit was back in 1968, when her band The Stone Poneys covered the Michael Naismith song 'Different Drum;' then she struck out on her own, eventually putting together a slick band that included Glen Frey, Don Henley, and other proto-Eagles. In early 1975 she had a Number One single with 'You're No Good,' and a chart-topping album in *Heart Like A Wheel*, following these up with 15 Top 40 singles before 1983.

• DECEMBER 14TH: THE FILM *SATURDAY NIGHT FEVER*, starring John Travolta, and with a Bee Gees-dominated soundtrack, opens in New York City. It will quickly bring international interest in the disco craze to fever pitch.

---

**NOVEMBER**

gang's leaders killed themselves in a German prison, those outside decided to kill Schleyer as a form of revenge. They ordered him to kneel and then shot him three times in the head. Then they sent a letter to a French newspaper boasting that they had ended his "miserable and corrupt existence."

• 20TH: A PLANE CRASH in a wood near Gillsburg, Mississippi, kills Lynyrd Skynyrd members Ronnie Van Zant, Steven Gaines and Cassie Gaines.

• 23RD: THE REMAINS OF what are believed to be the earth's earliest life forms are discovered in South African rocks. The one-celled microscopic cells are believed to be 3.4 billion years old.

• 28TH: WHEN JOURNEY play the last of three nights at the Old Waldorf, San Francisco, California, they are joined during the encore by new vocalist Steve Perry, making his debut.

• OCTOBER 28TH: THE SEX PISTOLS release *Never Mind The Bollocks* in the US. Three days later they will release it in the UK, but within a week it is removed from British record stores under the 1889 Indecent Advertisements Act.

## NEVER MIND THE BOLLOCKS
### HERE'S THE
# Sex Pistols

• 4TH: READER'S DIGEST is ordered to stump up $1,375,000 in back pay for female employees. It is the biggest case of sex discrimination the U.S has ever seen.

• 5TH: VOCALIST OZZY OSBOURNE quits Black Sabbath, but will return within a few weeks.

• 9TH: 'I FEEL LOVE' by Donna Summer is certified a gold disc in the US. Its stunning production, by Italian-born Giorgio Moroder, ushers in a new era of synthesizer-driven dance music that will persist into the next century.

• 11TH: A THREE-DAY-LONG free event, the Miami Music Festival of the Arts, begins in Florida. It will be attended by 125,000 fans, who will see acts including Neil Young, Dr Hook, the Ozark Mountain Daredevils, Lake, Tight Squeeze, Point Blank, Mark Farner and the Outlaws... Meanwhile, the censorship of films is abolished in Spain, as it adjusts to democracy after the Franco dictatorship.

• 17TH: Steven Spielberg's *Close Encounters Of The Third Kind* is released.

• 18TH: PRESIDENT SADAT becomes the first Egyptian leader to visit Israel and address the Knesset, the Israeli parliament. He calls for an end to the war between Egypt and Israel.

• 19TH: U.S ROCKERS The Tubes enter the UK charts with 'White Punks On Dope.'

• 20TH: 10,000 DIE when a cyclone hits Andhra Pradesh in India.

• 23RD: SIX STURDY Clydesdale horses carry singer Lou Rawls into the Hellinger Theatre on Broadway, New York City, at the start of his two-week season of concerts.

• 30TH: DAVID BOWIE appears on television, duetting with Bing Crosby on 'The Little Drummer Boy.' Crosby's 42nd Christmas special was filmed in September, and is now screened posthumously.

**DECEMBER**

• 7TH: PETER CARL GOLDMARK, the Hungarian-born inventor of the LP record dies just five days after his 71st birthday... And UK pop newspaper *NME* describes the debut single by teenage Scottish punk outfit Johnny & The Self Abusers as a "drab parade of New Wave cliches." The band will re-group, re-think, and re-appear as Simple Minds.

• 10TH: RANDY NEWMAN'S provocative 'Short People' gets short shrift from many individuals under 5'2" in the US, and is widely censored. But it still enters the top 40: a rare feat for this artist.

• 22ND: AFTER ALLEGEDLY running amok on a flight from Los Angeles, Rod Stewart disembarks at Heathrow with a glass of brandy still in his hand. The first-class cabin is awash with empty bottles and scraps of food.

• 24TH: 'HOW DEEP IS YOUR LOVE' by The Bee Gees becomes the first of six singles on RSO Records to consecutively hit the US No1 slot. It is followed by Player's 'Baby Come Back,' The Bee Gees' 'Stayin' Alive,' Andy Gibb's 'Love Is Thicker Than Water,' The Bee Gees' 'Night Fever,' and finally, 'If I Can't Have You' by Yvonne Elliman. Impressario Robert Stigwood's label dominates the chart for five months.

• 24TH: 'UPTOWN TOP RANKING' by Jamaican school-girls Althea & Donna is released. It will be UK Number One in February, despite its delightfully impenetrable lyrics.

• DECEMBER 25TH: CHARLIE CHAPLIN dies in Switzerland, aged 88. The 'little tramp,' self-exiled from America since the McCarthy era, was not only a performer and director of genius, he composed the songs and incidental music for most of his own films. But he was no musician, calling himself a "hummer" and using an assistant to write down his tunes. Even so, he won the 1972 best music Oscar for his theme for *Limelight*.

# 1978

## January–April

- **12TH:** **THE EXECUTORS** of the will of Lady Churchill, recently-deceased widow of wartime British leader Sir Winston Churchill, admit she burnt Graham Sutherland's uncompromising portrait of him in 1956. That was only 18 months after the House of Commons had proudly presented it to him as an 80th birthday present. Churchill loathed the painting, describing it dryly as "a remarkable example of modern art."
- **13TH:** **SIX WOMEN** are selected by NASA as mission specialists. They are its first female astronauts, 15 years after Valentina Tereshkova orbited the earth for the USSR... Meanwhile The Police move in to Surrey Sound Studios, Leatherhead, to begin recording the songs that will become their debut album.
- **14TH:** **KATE BUSH** (right) releases her debut single, an interpretation of Emily Brontë's *Wuthering Heights*. Her record company, EMI, has very little hope of commercial success. But it goes to Number One in the UK and stays there for four weeks, by which time Kate (originally discovered by Dave Gilmour of Pink Floyd) has become a household name and an instantly recognisable performer... Meanwhile the Sex Pistols' US tour comes to an end, at the Winterland Theatre in San Francisco. Johnny Rotten leaves the audience with this: "Ever get the feeling you've been cheated?" Within days he will have left the band, and although they limp on, with the increasingly deranged Sid Vicious (see far right) on vocals, in reality the Sex Pistols are finished after this show.

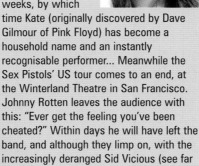

- **17TH:** **SIMPLE MINDS** play their first gig, supporting reggae act Steel Pulse at Satellite City, Glasgow, Scotland.
- **20TH:** **23 INCHES** of snow fall on Boston in one day.
- **23RD:** **TERRY KATH**, guitarist/vocalist of the group Chicago, kills himself in Woodland Hills, California, by accidentally discharging a pistol he is holding to his head in a mock game of Russian roulette.
- **27TH:** **MEMBERS** of the National Socialist Party of America – US Nazis – learn from the Illinois Supreme Court that they have a constitutional right to display swastikas in their march through the (mainly Jewish) Chicago suburb of Skokie.
- **28TH:** **MACHO** rocker Ted Nugent signs an autograph on a fan's arm – with a knife.
- **29TH:** **STEVE CLARKE** has his first rehearsal with Def Leppard in Sheffield, UK. He auditions with 'Freebird.'

- **APRIL 21ST:** **FORMER FAIRPORT CONVENTION** singer Sandy Denny dies, at the age of 37, after falling down some stairs. Denny was one of the leading lights of the UK folk music scene in the late 1960s and early 1970s. Her recordings live on.

- **1ST:** **BOB DYLAN'S** *Renaldo & Clara* movie, nearly four hours long, is premiered in Los Angeles.
- **2ND:** **US ROCKERS** Van Halen sign to Warner Brothers... And metal band Judas Priest release their *Stained Glass* album, which will later land them in court, accused of causing the suicide of an American teenage fan.
- **4TH:** **'STAYIN' ALIVE'** by The Bee Gees reaches Number One on the US Top 40 singles chart.
- **5TH:** **A PIECE OF RADIOACTIVE** Soviet satellite, which plunged to Earth last week, is found in Canada.
- **11TH:** **PIONEERING UK PUNK** fanzine *Sniffin' Glue* folds after 18 months.
- **15TH:** **US BLUES GUITARIST** Mike Bloomfield is found dead in his car in San Francisco, having apparently overdosed on heroin.
- **17TH:** **AS TENSIONS RISE** between China and Vietnam, thousands of people (some say up to 1,000 a month) flee by boat. The 'boat people' are so desperate to get away, whole families are taking to the oceans in anything that will float.
- **23RD:** **THE EAGLES'** 'Hotel California' scoops the Grammy for Record of the Year. The Bee Gees win Best Pop Vocal Performance for 'How Deep Is Your Love'. Fleetwood Mac get album of the Year for *Rumours*.
- **24TH:** **PRESERVED BY** a layer of volcanic lava, the earliest known footprint of man's ancestors is found at the bottom of an Africa watering hole.
- **28TH:** **BOB DYLAN** records his album *Live At Budokan* at the Budokan Hall, Tokyo, Japan.

- **MARCH 17TH:** **US SUPERTANKER** the Amoco Cadiz breaks in two off the coast of France and spills around 200,000 gallons of oil, much of which washes up on the coastline of Brittany and the Channel Islands.

- **4TH:** **ANDY GIBB** gets a US Number One single with '(Love Is) Thicker Than Water.'
- **6TH:** **BILLY JOEL** is awarded a US platinum disc for his single 'Just The Way You Are.'
- **16TH:** **LARRY FLINT, THE OWNER** of US porn magazine *Hustler*, is critically wounded when he is shot after testifying at an obscenity trial in Lawrenceville, Georgia. This and other events in Flint's life later inspire *The People v Larry Flint*, a movie starring Woody Harrelson and Courtney Love. Flint, in a wheelchair since the shooting, will appear in the movie as the conservative trial judge.
- **18TH:** **POPULAR LOCAL BAND** U2 win the Harp Lager Talent Contest in Limerick, Ireland. The prize is £500, plus a chance to audition for CBS Records. CBS signs them, but only for Ireland – the UK division isn't too keen, so Island sign them instead.
- **22ND:** **THE POLICE** sign to A&M Records in the UK... And Beatles spoof *The Rutles* is shown on NBC in the US. It features Monty Python star Eric Idle, ex-Bonzo Dog bandmember Neil Innes, ex-Beach Boy Ricky Fataar, and ex-Patto man John Halsey as the "Pre-fab Four," Dirk, Ron, Stig, and Barry. The show also features guest appearances by Mick Jagger, Paul Simon, and George Harrison.
- **24TH:** **BRITISH COURTS** grant record companies the right to seize bootleg and pirate recordings of their products.
- **30TH:** **THE UK TORY PARTY** calls in the advertising agency Saatchi & Saatchi to give their image a makeover – not to mention their new leader, Mrs Margaret Thatcher.

## All Meat – A Real Treat

FEBRUARY 20TH: MEAT LOAF'S *Bat Out Of Hell* is released in the UK, where it becomes an even bigger hit than it was in the States.

The album never quite makes it to the top spot, but it will still be in the UK charts when its follow-up, *Deadringer*, arrives in 1981. Though he's recorded one earlier album, as part of the duo Stoney & Meat Loaf, and also starred in musicals like *Hair* and *The Rocky Horror Show* (on stage and screen), *Bat Out Of Hell* puts the mountainous Texan and his passionate theatricality squarely on the map. Written by his old Broadway colleague Jim Steinman, *Bat Out Of Hell* is produced by multi-instrumentalist Todd Rundgren – an inspired, if unlikely choice – who even supplies the motorbike noises, using fuzzed guitar. It is the first of a long, and loud, run.

**APRIL**

- 1ST: **ELVIS COSTELLO** releases *This Year's Model*.
- 2ND: *DALLAS IS FIRST* broadcast in the US. Screened by CBS at 10pm on a Sunday night, the ratings are nothing spectacular at first, but in 1979 it will be moved to 9pm Friday, rapidly becoming a TV phenomenon for most of the next decade.
- 5TH: **DURAN DURAN** play their first live date, at Birmingham Polytechnic, Birmingham, UK.
- 7TH: **IN NEW YORK** a record price is achieved for a book. *The Gutenberg Bible*, printed in Mainz, Germany, around 1454-5, was the first major book printed in the west. It goes for $2 million… Meanwhile, Prince releases his debut album, *For You*.
- 8TH: **THE DAMNED** split up for the first time. It will by no means be the last.
- 14TH: **WHEN ELVIS COSTELLO** & The Attractions play at Rafters Club, Manchester, UK, bassist Bruce Thomas cuts his hand on a broken bottle, requiring 18 stitches.
- 19TH: **MORE THAN 40** rock'n'roll artists, including Bruce Springsteen, Jackson Browne, Carly Simon, James Taylor, The Doobie Brothers, and Tom Petty, sign a petition to US President Jimmy Carter to end America's commitment to nuclear power.
- 19TH: **KRAFTWERK RELEASE** their album *Man Machine*.
- 22ND: **GERRY RAFFERTY** releases 'Baker Street,' his new single, in the US. He has already had a Top Five UK hit with the song. Rafferty's last band, Stealer's Wheel, had a worldwide hit with 'Stuck In The Middle' in 1973. The song will later be used to shocking effect on the soundtrack of Quentin Tarantino's bloodthirsty movie *Reservoir Dogs*. Raffert, was once in a folk duo called the Humblebums, with a shipyard worker called Billy Connolly, who will later become something of a comedian.

- APRIL 23RD: **THE NOTORIOUS** video for Sid Vicious's cover version of Sinatra's 'My Way' is filmed as part of the upcoming movie *The Great Rock & Roll Swindle*. At the end of it, Vicious is shown pulling a gun and slaughtering the audience, No doubt there are some nervous moments among cast and crew during the sequence. You never really know with Sid – as events in the near future will prove.

## Tapping Into The Times

**M**AY 24TH: VAN HALEN'S debut album *Van Halen* is awarded a US gold disc. The band take their name from their founder, the innovative and highly influential guitarist Eddie Van Halen (seen left in typical on-stage pose). They are fronted by the impossibly glamorous and vocally dextrous David Lee Roth – pictured below right in a typical gold lamé shirt - and steadied by Eddie's brother Alex on drums and Michael Anthony on bass. Discovered in 1977 by Kiss's Gene Simmons, while playing a club in Los Angeles, the band had already built a reputation over the previous three years due to vocalist Roth's energetic showmanship and Eddie's astonishing guitar skills. The debut album demonstrates this to a wider audience, especially its second track,

'Eruption.' This 1 minute 42 second firestorm of awe-inspiring, histrionic fretwork harnesses raw power to overloaded sonic aggression, before segueing into one of the all-time great rock riffs as the band cover the Kinks' 'You Really Got Me.' Legions of guitarists immediately begin practising two-handed tapping and working on their pull-offs, creating a generation of slavish copyists who fail to grasp the fact that speed and technique aren't all that's required. Although they'll become more widely known in 1984 with stadium -straddling anthems like 'Jump,' in 1978 Van Halen are a new, vibrant rock band, reviving the genre at a time when punk is threatening to make rockers seem old-hat.

- **1ST: NAOMI UEMURA** becomes the first person to reach the North Pole alone using only a dog sled. He's also the first Japanese climber to scale Mount Everest, but will die on Alaska's Mount McKinley in 1984, one day after becoming the first person to climb it in winter.
- **7TH: WITH MUCH** bad blood between the two teams, The Eagles play a game of softball against the staff of *Rolling Stone* magazine, to determine whether or not the band should submit to being interviewed for the publication. The Eagles win 15-8. No interview.
- **9TH: FORMER ITALIAN** Prime Minister Aldo Moro's body is found in the trunk of a small car in central Rome after government officials repeatedly refuse to release 13 members of the Red Brigade on trial in Turin.
- **13TH: EURO-DISCO** group Boney M (below)

reach Number One on the UK singles chart with 'Rivers Of Babylon.' It will also be their only US hit. Their producer and main writer, Frank Farian, will later go on to become infamous for creating Milli Vanilli.
- **17TH: HAVING BEEN** stolen on March 2nd, Charlie Chaplin's coffin turns up intact, just ten miles from its original resting place in a cemetery in Vevey, Switzerland.... And Lou Reed begins a week of shows at the Bottom Line, New York City, some of which are recorded for his live album *Take No Prisoners*.
- **23RD: BRUCE SPRINGSTEEN'S** 118-date *Darkness On The Edge Of Town* tour opens at Shea Theatre, Buffalo, New York.
- **31ST: THE GO-GO'S** play their debut performance at a going-away party for The Dickies at The Masque, a Los Angeles club

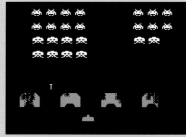

- **JUNE 16TH: THE ELECTRONIC GAME** Space Invaders is demonstrated by Taito Corporation of Tokyo. It'll quickly become an international craze... The other big new trend taking hold this summer will be jogging. Already established in New York and LA, soon every street will be pounded by track-suited fitness freaks. (If they're not home playing Space Invaders.)

- **3RD: THE NEW** post-Peter Gabriel Genesis, now with drummer Phil Collins on lead vocals, enters the US Top 40 singles chart for the first time with 'Follow You, Follow Me.'
- **8TH: SIR FRANCIS CHICHESTER'S** record for sailing solo around the world is beaten by Naomi James, who completes her round-the-world voyage two days faster.
- **12TH: THE HUMAN LEAGUE** play their first ever live gig, at the Bar 2, Sheffield, UK.
- **15TH: DIRE STRAITS** release their debut album, *Dire Straits*, in the UK.
- **16TH: THE UNDERTONES** record the EP *Teenage Kicks* on a miserable wet day in Belfast, Northern Ireland...

- **20TH: US BEAUTY QUEEN** (and 1973 Miss World contender) Joyce McKinney is sentenced to one year in prison, in her absence, for abducting Mormon Kirk Anderson from the Ewell Church of the Latter Day Saints in Epsom, UK, and then unlawfully imprisoning him at a hideaway in Devon, only releasing him when he agrees to marry her. McKinney has in fact fled Britain, posing as a deaf-mute mime artist, and subsequently turns up in Georgia, US, disguised as a nun.
- **28TH: AT A CEREMONY** backstage in Madison Square Garden, New York City, US band Kansas are nominated by UNICEF, the UN's children's fund, as Deputy Ambassadors of Goodwill.

- **JUNE 16TH: IN NEW YORK**, it's the glamorous premiere of the *Grease*, starring Olivia Newton-John and John Travolta, the highest-grossing movie musical ever made. The stage version already holds the record for longest Broadway run, having first opened in 1972.

## Another Stage, Another Show

•JUNE 21ST: *EVITA*, THE ANDREW LLOYD WEBBER/TIM RICE musical starring Elaine Paige (left), Joss Ackland, and David Essex, opens at the Prince Edward Theatre, London. Following the phenomenal success of *Jesus Christ Superstar*, Rice has turned to the life of Eva Peron, who rose from poverty to become the wife of President Juan Peron of Argentina. Though both writers go on to have major successes elsewhere, this is the last collaboration between Lloyd Webber and Rice until their Oscar-winning song, 'You Must Love Me,' which they add to the score for Alan Parker's screen adaptation of *Evita* in 1996. It stars Madonna, whose performance in the title role is not much admired, and Antonio Banderas.

**JULY**

**AUGUST**

• 8TH: **COMEDIAN/ACTOR** Steve Martin has his first and only musical hit, when 'King Tut' makes it into the US Top 40, rising to Number 17.

• 10TH: **MAX ROBINSON** becomes the first African-American news anchor on US national TV when *World News Tonight* airs on ABC.

• 11TH: **THE TOURISTS**, led by Annie Lennox and Dave Stewart, who will later become The Eurythmics, play at The Marquee, London.

• 14TH: **TALKING HEADS** release their second album, *More Songs About Buildings And Food*. The title is unusually accurate.

• 22ND: **THE ALBUM** *Dire Straits* takes the band of that name onto the UK LP chart for the first time.

• 24TH: *THE SERGEANT PEPPER'S Lonely Hearts Club Band* movie, featuring the Bee Gees and Peter Frampton, premieres in New York. It is both a critical and commercial failure.

• 25TH: **JOHN LYDON** (formerly Johnny Rotten of the Sex Pistols), announces his new band PiL, short for Public Image Ltd.

• 26TH: **THE WORLD'S** first 'test-tube' baby, Louise Joy Brown, is born in a hospital in Oldham, UK. She weighs a healthy 5lb 12oz. The 'in vitro fertilization' technique gives hope to the childless.

• 29TH: **WHEN GUITARIST** Lindsey Buckingham collapses before a gig in Philadelphia, Pennsylvania, Fleetwood Mac cancel upcoming concerts in Pittsburgh and Cleveland.

• **AUGUST 25TH: THE TURIN SHROUD** is displayed for the first time in St John's Cathedral in Turin. Claimed by the Vatican to display the image of the crucified body of Jesus Christ, carbon dating tests on the cloth later suggest it's around 1,000 years too new to be authentic. But fire damage and possible insect contamination leave enough uncertainty to keep both doubters and believers busy for years to come.

• JULY 5TH: **THE NEW ROLLING STONES** album *Some Girls* is threatened with lawsuits by some of the celebrities whose crudely cut out and bewigged faces appear on the sleeve's mock-advertising collage – they include Raquel Welch, Lucille Ball, Sophia Loren, and Farrah Fawcett from the *Charlie's Angels* TV show. From the next print-run, and all subsequent pressings, the sleeve will be changed to feature anonymous faces... Though not exactly flavor-of-the-month among feminists, the Stones are in a musically productive period: during the five months of studio sessions for the *Some Girls* album, they've recorded almost 40 songs, only ten of which actually make it onto the finished LP, including the US Number One 'Miss You.'

• 9TH: **MUDDY WATERS** plays a set at the White House Lawn Picnic, at the request of President Jimmy Carter. Shortly aftwerwards the 63-year-old blues legend moves into a new home of his own in the Chicago suburbs, with his 25-year-old wife.

• 12TH: **THE FUNERAL** of Pope Paul VI is attended by 200,000 people. He is succeeded by Pope John Paul I, who lives for less than a month, who is in turn followed by Polish-born Cardinal Karol Wojtyla – the first non-Italian pope for over 400 years – who takes the name John Paul II.

• 13TH: **US POLICE** burn 100 tons of marijuana... And Bill Nelson's clever rockers Be-Bop Deluxe split (the two events are not thought to be linked).

18TH: **THE LAST OF** the first wave of UK punk acts, Siouxsie & The Banshees, release their debut single 'Hong Kong Garden.' It'll be 13 years before the band achieve even a minor hit in the US, by which time Siouxsie will have reached the UK Top 40 no fewer than 16 times.

• 21ST: **BRUCE SPRINGSTEEN** plays his first headlining gig at Madison Square Garden, New York City. Two more follow on subsequent nights.

• 25TH: **A PUNK RIOT** explodes at the *Reading Festival*, Reading, UK, when drunken Sham 69 fans run wild.

• 26TH: **FRANKIE VALLI** takes the US Number One single spot with 'Grease,' the theme from the new hit movie.

## First Time For Lionel

• JULY 8TH: **THE COMMODORES**, fronted by singer/saxophonist/keyboard player Lionel Ritchie, enter the US Top 40 with his song 'Three Times A Lady,' which will be the group's first Number One (US and UK).

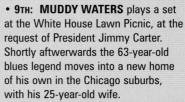

# Police Chase Success Across States

**O**CTOBER 20TH: NEWLY LANDED in New York City, The Police race across town in a cab in order to make it onto the stage at the legendary CBGB's club on time. It is the start of their first American tour. Interestingly, it was in the States, earlier this year, that they acquired their bleached-blond punky image. They took on the look for a Wrigley's chewing gum advert, and decide to keep it. Signed to A&M, they release *Outlandos d'Amour*, which sits comfortably in the burgeoning punk/new wave market (thanks to the hair and the reggae influence) but fails to chart at first. But it gradually picks up, reaching Number 23 in the US in early 1979 and then Number Six in Britain. Over their next three albums, *Regatta De Blanc*, *Zenyatta Mondatta*, and *Ghost In The Machine* their reputation grows, and they notch up a string of hit singles, from 'Roxanne' and 'Message In A Bottle' to 'Don't Stand So Close To Me' and 'De Do Do Do, De Da Da Da.' Up to 1982, their most successful single is the ultra-poppy 'Every Little Thing She Does Is Magic,' but then in 1983 they release the deep-thinking, multi-levelled *Synchronicity*, with its haunting Number One single 'Every Breath You Take.' Things now take a more serious turn for for The Police, in more ways than one. As we'll see...

SEPTEMBER

• **SEPTEMBER 8TH: KEITH MOON** of The Who is found dead in his London apartment from an overdose of Heminevrin, a drug normally prescribed to help people deal with the symptoms of alcohol withdrawal or epilepsy. In a state of shock, his three Who bandmates are unsure what to do next, having lost not just a great friend but a unique and crucial musical element of the band. They agree that Moon is "irreplaceable."

• **1ST: A BOOK** called *Jogging With Jesus* is published, cashing in on the thriving audience for both religious evangelism and the keep-fit kick. It's written by C.S. Lovett, author of other spiritual/physical improvement manuals such as *Help Lord – The Devil Wants Me Fat!*

• **7TH: FORMER** Sex Pistols' bassist Sid Vicious plays a woefully poor show backed by ex-New York Dolls Jerry Nolan and Arthur Kane and the Clash's Mick Jones at Max's Kansas City.

• **9TH: JACK WARNER**, who co-founded Warner Brothers, dies at 86... And A Taste Of Honey reach

• **SEPTEMBER 18TH: PRESIDENT CARTER** succeeds in bringing together Israel's [rime minister Menachem Begin and Egypt's president Anwar Sadat at Camp David, the presidential mountain retreat in Maryland. The following month the Nobel Prize Committee announces that the next peace prize, to be awarded on December 10th, will go to Sadat and Begin for their efforts. Soviet foreign minister Andrei Gromyko spoils the party by calling the announcement "something of a joke."

Number one on the US Top 40 singles chart with the disco floor-filler 'Boogie Oogie Oogie.'

• **11TH: GEORGI MARKOV**, a Bulgarian defector, is assassinated in London by a Bulgarian secret agent who stabs him with a poisoned umbrella. Markov falls into a coma and dies four days later.

• **14TH: THE GRATEFUL DEAD** play the first of three gigs at the Sound and Light Amphitheatre, in the shadow of The Great Pyramid in Egypt.

• **16TH: AT LEAST 25,000** die in a massive earthquake in Iran.

• **20TH: MARVIN GAYE** signs a new seven-year deal with Motown, worth more than $3m.

• **21ST: RUSSIAN ASTRONAUTS** set an endurance record of 96 days in space.

• **SEPTEMBER 2ND: SOUL CROONER** Teddy Pendergrass performs a show 'For Women Only' at Avery Fisher Hall in New York City. White chocolate lollipops shaped like teddy bears are given to the audience.

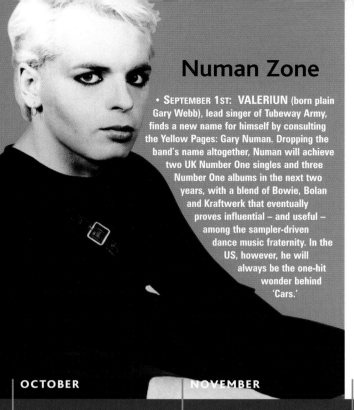

## Numan Zone

- **SEPTEMBER 1ST: VALERIUN** (born plain Gary Webb), lead singer of Tubeway Army, finds a new name for himself by consulting the Yellow Pages: Gary Numan. Dropping the band's name altogether, Numan will achieve two UK Number One singles and three Number One albums in the next two years, with a blend of Bowie, Bolan and Kraftwerk that eventually proves influential – and useful – among the sampler-driven dance music fraternity. In the US, however, he will always be the one-hit wonder behind 'Cars.'

## Feel The Rhythm

NOVEMBER 18TH: CHIC enter the US Top 40 with 'Le Freak,' which goes to Number One by the end of the year, stays for six weeks, and sells two million copies. Formed by three former session musicians – guitarist Nile Rodgers, bass player Bernard Edwards and drummer Tony Thompson – Chic's crisp, note-perfect disco-funk is a cut above the rest. Rodgers and Edwards are soon in great demand as producers (for Sister Sledge, Debbie Harry, and David Bowie, among others), and remain a dance-floor inspiration for the next 25 years.

**OCTOBER**  **NOVEMBER**  **DECEMBER**

- **5TH: MICK JAGGER** of the Rolling Stones apologises to the Rev Jesse Jackson for the racially offensive lyrics of *Some Girls*, but doesn't remove them.
- **9TH: DURING A US TOUR**, Jethro Tull play a gig at Madison Square Garden, New York City, which is broadcast live by satellite to an estimated global audience of 400 million.
- **9TH: BELGIAN SINGER-SONGWRITER** Jacques Brel dies of cancer at age 42.
- **12TH: WITH PUNK** still the UK's ruling rock ethic, a curious duo take the stage at a club called Eric's, in Liverpool. The pair litter the stage with synthesizers and signal generators. They call themselves Orchestral Manoeuvres In The Dark... Meanwhile, Sid Vicious is arrested in New York City for the murder of his girlfriend Nancy Spungen, found dead in her room at the Chelsea Hotel. Sid attempts to commit suicide while being detained at Rikers Island Prison in New York.
- **15TH: IRENE MILLER** and Vera Komakova become the first women to reach the summit of the Annapurna in the Himalayas.
- **22ND: NEIL YOUNG** & Crazy Horse play at the Cow Palace, San Francisco, where most of the in-concert album *Live Rust* is recorded. It includes 'My, My, Hey, Hey (Out Of The Blue),' dedicated to Johnny Rotten, of whom Young notes "It's better to burn out than it is to rust."
- **25TH: A POLL IN THE UK** reveals that one in three people feel the Royal family is out of touch with reality.

- **1ST: AFTER A FAIRLY DISASTROUS** first experience, unsigned Irish band U2 go into a demo studio for the second time, determined to do better.
- **7TH: ELTON JOHN** is rushed to a clinic in Harley Street, London, suffering from chest pains believed to be related to exhaustion caused by overwork.

- **11TH: DONNA SUMMER'S** disco re-working of 'MacArthur Park,' originally by Richard Harris, tops the US charts. It's the first of four Number Ones for Summer (above).
- **15TH: BUCKINGHAM PALACE**, London, vibrates to the sound of disco as the Three Degrees perform live for Prince Charles on his 30th birthday. They're his favorite group.
- **16TH: A SENSATION** is caused at Queen's Madison Square Garden gig in New York City when a stream of naked women cycle across the stage during 'Fat Bottomed Girls.'
- **18TH: HAVING MURDERED** three visiting newsmen and a US congressman, who had come to investigate the Guyana base of his religious cult, the 'Reverend' Jim Jones then orders his 900 followers, men, women and children, to commit mass suicide by swallowing a soft drink laced with cyanide.

- **6TH: NOW OUT ON BAIL**, Sid Vicious attacks Todd Smith (brother of singer Patti), pushing a beer glass in his face, and is re-arrested the following day.
- **7TH: THE US MILITARY** begin reviewing their policy that forbids homosexuals from serving in the armed forces.
- **8TH: ISRAEL'S FIRST WOMAN** prime minister, Golda Meir, dies from hepatitis at age 80.
- **14TH: THE FBI** raids the ultra-exclusive Studio 54 discotheque in New York City, confiscating the accounts, and seizing two ounces of cocaine. No one knows how much may have been quickly flushed down the toilets beforehand.
- **15TH: MAGNAVISION**, part of the giant Philips/MCA group, launches the DiscoVision system, storing moving pictures on a 12" optical disk. It flops ... And the movie version of *Superman* is released, with Christopher Reeve as star.
- **16TH: CHUCK BROWN** & The Soul Searchers make their US chart debut with the single 'Bustin' Loose,' regarded as one of the first hits in the funky dance style later known as Go Go.
- **19TH: COCA-COLA** says it will be on sale in China next year.
- **22ND: FORMER FACES** and Small Faces drummer Kenney Jones is invited to join The Who, to replace Keith Moon in the studio and on tour.
- **27TH:** **CHRIS BELL** of Big Star is killed, at 27, when his car hits a telegraph pole near his home in Memphis, Tennessee.
- **31ST: ROCK PROMOTER** Bill Graham closes down his Winterland venue in San Francisco with a final concert featuring The Grateful Dead and The Blues Brothers.

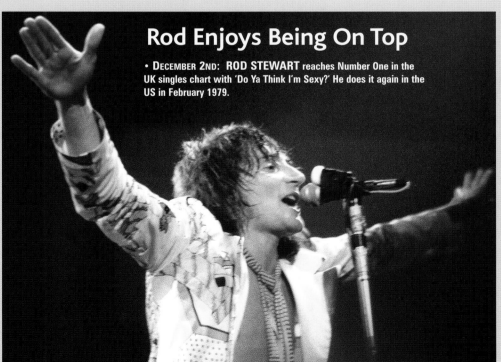

## Rod Enjoys Being On Top

- **DECEMBER 2ND: ROD STEWART** reaches Number One in the UK singles chart with 'Do Ya Think I'm Sexy?' He does it again in the US in February 1979.

# 1979

## BEE GEES FEVER

Robin, Barry, and Maurice Gibb are currently at their commercial peak, in the middle of a run of six consecutive US Number One singles, and three Number One albums. Things will start going a bit quiet in the 1980s – though even then they'll enjoy indirect success penning and producing hits for the likes of Barbra Streisand, Dionne Warwick, Diana Ross, Kenny Rogers & Dolly Parton. But for those who have been following the group's career since the 1960s, the 'disco' incarnation is something of an anomaly, albeit a very lucrative one, in a long and prolific career. Born in Manchester in the north of England, the brothers moved to Australia when Barry was ten and twin brothers Robin and Maurice eight. They'd already started performing before they left (both parents were musicians too), and soon attracted attention in their new adopted homeland as a talented trio of kids – with perhaps a self-deprecating humour, as illustrated by the inset photo. (A long way from the apparent machismo and chest-hair flaunting of the Seventies.) Evolving into adolescent pop stars in Australia, they started attracting a similar hysterical reaction to that experienced by the Beatles in the UK. In 1967 they returned to Britain, and had their first hit within weeks with 'New York Mining Disaster (Have You Seen My Wife, Mr Jones?),' a Top 20 single in both the US and UK. Masterful pop songs like 'Words,' 'Massachusetts,' 'World,' 'To Love Somebody,' and 'I Started A Joke,' cemented their reputation as skilled writers and vocal harmonizers into the early 1970s, but it was only when they made the unexpected move into dance-floor beats and falsetto voices – starting with 'Jive Talking' and 'You Should Be Dancing,' that their career took on a new life. The disco explosion was fuelled by 1977's *Saturday Night Fever* movie, for which The Bee Gees provided most of the music, selling over 30 million soundtrack albums worldwide. Despite 1978's flop *Sgt Pepper* movie, 1979 will bring more award-winning chart-toppers like 'Too Much Heaven,' 'Tragedy,' and 'Love You Inside Out.' This really is the Bee Gees' golden age – quite literally.

# 1979

## January–April

### Don't Let Me Be Misunderstood

**M**ARCH 15TH: **AFTER A GIG** at the Agora Club, Columbus, Ohio, Elvis Costello and his bassist, Bruce Thomas, retire to the bar of the local Holiday Inn for a chat. During their rambling discussion, overheard by Steven Stills and Bonnie Bramlett, Costello uses a string of insulting terms, one of them racial, about the singer Ray Charles. Bramlett immediately attacks Costello, knocking him to the ground. Costello later claims his remarks have been taken out of context. He says he was being deliberately offensive during a drunken conversation, to provoke an outraged reaction, and that what he said was not his real opinion. (He has been a stalwart of the UK's Rock Against Racism movement.) But the controversy rumbles on. Costello seemed to have been on the brink of a breakthrough, but that is now looking less likely.

• **FEBRUARY 17TH: WHEN THE CLASH'S** American tour (*Pearl Harbor '79*) arrives at The Palladium, New York City, they open the set with 'I'm So Bored With The USA.' Celebrities gathered backstage include Paul Simon, Carrie Fisher, Bruce Springsteen, Andy Warhol, Debbie Harry, Nico, and John Cale.

### JANUARY

• **1ST: SIMPLE MINDS** sign to the independent Zoom Records label in Edinburgh, Scotland... Meanwhile, The Invaders play a show at the London Filmmakers Co-op – the next time they play it will be as Madness. They take their new name from a ska track by Jamaican artist Prince Buster.

• **5TH: PRINCE** makes his debut as a solo artist at the Capri Theatre, Minneapolis, Minnesota... And legendary jazz bassist Charles Mingus dies in Mexico at age 57.

• **7TH: CAMBODIAN DICTATOR** Pol Pot's regime is overthrown as Vietnamese troops capture Phnom Penh in Cambodia.

• **11TH: A REPORT** from the surgeon general in the US removes all doubt that smoking causes lung cancer.

• **13TH: SOUL SINGER** Donny Hathaway falls (or jumps) from a 15th floor hotel room window in New York. He is just 33. His last hit, 'The Closer I Get To You,' was just nine months ago. It was one of three he made with old friend Roberta Flack.

• **22ND: THE JACKSONS** begin a world tour to promote their *Destiny* album, starting in Bremen, West Germany.

• **26TH: NELSON ROCKEFELLER**, former US Vice

•**JANUARY 4TH: BLONDIE, FRONTED BY DEBBIE HARRY,** release a controversial dance re-mix of their song 'Heart Of Glass.' It will on to be the group's first US and UK Number One, despite being denounced by new wave purists as as a surrender to commercialism.

President, dies of a heart attack at 70.

• **31ST: THE UK GRINDS** to a halt due to a series of public service strikes which will become known as the "winter of discontent." The disruption, and the lack of action to end it, will ultimately lead to the downfall of Prime Minister James Callaghan.

• **JANUARY 16TH: KING OF IRAN** since 1941, Shah Mohammad Reza Pahlavi is forced to flee before he is overthrown. He has been blamed for Iran's political repression and social divisions. In two weeks, Ayatollah Khomeini will return from 14 years of exile in France, to lead a new Iranian Islamic republic. The Shah settles in Egypt, where he dies in July 1980.

FEBRUARY

• **JANUARY 6TH:** **VILLAGE PEOPLE** top the UK singles chart with 'YMCA.' Though they were initially put together by producer Jacques Morali to entertain the gay community in New York City (and would probably look rather out of place in most rural English communities), the guys are actually more successful in the UK than the US – with seven Top 40s, including some 1990s remixes. Their UK-only hit 'Go West' is later an even bigger smash for the Pet Shop Boys.

MARCH

# Great Pretenders

**F**EBRUARY 10TH: THE PRETENDERS make their UK chart debut at Number 34 with the old Kinks' song 'Stop Your Sobbing,' in a new version produced by Nick Lowe. The following year, US-born Pretenders singer Chrissie Hynde meets the song's writer, Ray Davies, one of her childhood heroes, and soon afterwards they start a four-year relationship, during which they have a child together. The mid 1980s will be a busy period for Hynde and the band in the US, but they don't begin to match their UK tally of 11 Top 40 hits, including a 1980 Number One with 'Brass In Pocket.'

APRIL

• **2ND:** **PATTY HEARST**, released from prison yesterday, plans to marry her bodyguard. Her seven-year sentence was commuted to 22 months by President Carter... And former Sex Pistols bassist Sid Vicious dies in New York City of a heroin overdose while on bail, awaiting trial for the murder of his girlfriend, Nancy Spungen.

• **9TH:** **A HUMAN LEAGUE** gig at Notre Dame Hall, London, is cancelled, when the vicar of a nearby church raises objections on moral grounds.

• **12TH:** **LONG BEFORE** she finds fame as a pop star, Madonna Louise Ciccone poses nude for photographer Martin Schreiber in a New York City photography college. She earns $30.

• **13TH:** **FRENCH FILM DIRECTOR** Jean Renoir – son of French Impressionist painter Auguste Renoir – dies at the age of 84.

• **15TH:** **THE ANNUAL** run up the Empire State Building (using the stairs, rather than the Spiderman/ King Kong route up the outside) is won by Jim Rafferty for the men and Nina Kuscsik for the women. The race was initiated in 1978. In February 2003, a new record of 9 minutes and 33 seconds will be set by Australian Paul Crake. (Belinda Soszyn's 1996 women's record of 12 minutes 19 seconds still stands, by the way).

• **15TH:** **AT THIS YEAR'S** Grammy Awards, The Bee Gees collect five Grammys for their 'Saturday Night Fever' soundtrack album. Billy Joel gets Song Of The Year, and Record Of The Year for 'Just The Way You Are.'

• **17TH:** **DIRE STRAITS** debut single 'Sultans Of Swing' enters the US charts, on its way to Number Four.

• **21ST:** **BREAKING FIVE** world records in the process, former astronaut Neil Armstrong, now an aviation executive, takes a LearJet Longhorn business jet to 50,000 feet in just over 12 seconds.

• **26TH:** **THE TRIAL** of painter Tom Keating's trial at the Old Bailey criminal court in London – he is accused of forging old masters – is halted due to the defendant's ill health. Keating later goes on to present a television series on painters, and becomes a celebrity in his remaining years.

• **1ST:** **THE POLICE** embark on a 29-date US tour, starting at The Whisky in Los Angeles.

• **10TH:** **ACTOR LEE MARVIN'S** ex-girlfriend, Michelle Triola Marvin, sues Marvin for 'palimony' – alimony without having been maried – demanding half the $3.6m he has made during the time they lived together. She will eventually only receive $104,000.

• **10TH:** **AS 'I WILL SURVIVE'** by Gloria Gaynor reaches Number One on the US Top 40, nine out of the top ten hits are disco-oriented.

• **14TH:** **OUTRAGEOUS** New York City quartet The Plasmatics, fronted by former porn star Wendy O. Williams, make their vinyl debut with a three-track EP featuring 'Butcher Baby,' 'Fast Food Service,' and 'Concrete Shoes.'

• **24TH:** **BRITISH BAND** Supertramp release a new single, 'The Logical Song.' Taken from their Number One album *Breakfast In America*, it's their big US breakthrough – though in 1974 they had a Top Five UK album with *Crime Of The Century*.

• **28TH:** **THE THREE MILE ISLAND** nuclear power station in Pennsylvania is discovered to have a badly damaged reactor. The authorities initially decide against evacuation, even though the building is badly contaminated, but later relent and move thousands away. Defective equipment and operating errors are blamed.

• **29TH:** **UGANDAN PRESIDENT** Idi Amin flees the country as the opposition Uganda National Liberation Front captures Entebbe airport and lays siege to Kampala.

• **MARCH 17TH:** **RICKIE LEE JONES** releases her debut album, which makes the Top Five in the US charts in April, as does her first single, 'Chuck E's In Love,' written about LA musician friend Chuck E. Weiss. Jones's laid-back 'bohemian jazz' is markedly at odds with the current pop chart diet of rock, new wave and disco – and all the more refreshing for it. She never quite recaptures this level of commercial success again.

• **2ND:** **ISRAELI** Prime Minister Begin meets President Sadat in Cairo, and becomes the first Israeli leader to visit Egypt.

• **3RD:** **KATE BUSH** performs live as a solo act for the first time, at The Empire, Liverpool, in the UK.

• **11TH:** **BBC TV** in the UK broadcasts the first annual *British Rock & Pop Awards*, which will eventually become known as *The Brit Awards*, or *Brits*. The first edition includes Dave Dee, Georgie Fame, Mary Hopkin, Hank Marvin, and Dusty Springfield – all pretty much old-timers, even in 1979, it must be said.

• **14TH:** **THE DOOBIE BROTHERS** reach Number One on the US Top 40 singles chart with 'What A Fool Believes.'

• **15TH:** **BRUCE SPRINGSTEEN** injures his leg in a motorcycle crash, so recording of his new album is halted for several weeks.

• **20TH:** **PRESIDENT CARTER** is attacked by a rabbit while taking a few days off in Plains, Georgia, to go fishing from a canoe. A later press account insists that the rabbit swam towards him, "hissing menacingly, its teeth flashing and nostrils flared." The Secret Service, caught flatfooted, leave the president to fend off the furry assailant with an oar. (Carter is seen below with Israel's Moshe Dayan, perhaps laughing off the incident, or swapping animal-fighting stories.)

• **25TH:** **THE MOVIE** *Rock'N'Roll High School* opens in Los Angeles, starring The Ramones as themselves.

• **26TH:** **ROCK MANAGER** Allen Klein is convicted by a New York jury of falsifying income tax returns relating to undeclared sales of Beatles' promotional records on the Apple label. He is sentenced to two months in prison with a $5,000 fine, but lodges an appeal.

• **29TH:** **ON 'SOLIDARITY SUNDAY,'** 100,000 join a protest march through New York, in support of persecuted Jews in the Soviet Union.

• JULY 13TH: **THE BOOMTOWN RATS**, fronted by Bob Geldof, release a new song. It tells the story of California girl Brenda Spencer (16), who shot dead the principal and caretaker of an elementary school and wounded several small children. When asked why, she replied, "I don't like Mondays." The single is the band's second UK Number One and Bob's defining pop moment – until 1985...

## Walk This Way

**J**ULY 1ST: SONY introduces the first Walkman, the TPS-L2 portable personal cassette player. It is the brainchild of company bosses Masaru Ibuka and Akio Morita. The name is a cause for concern. Chosen by the young design team because of its 'superhero' connotations, Walkman is thought to sound too 'Japanese,' and several alternatives are suggested for international use (including 'Soundabout' in the US). Sony will sell almost 200 million Walkmans, and there will be countless copies. Soon half the population is humming along to a vague percussive noise, while the other half seethes.

**MAY**

**JUNE**

• 1ST: **BOB DYLAN** is in Muscle Shoals Sound Studio, Sheffield, Alabama, working on the album *Slow Train Coming*, with Mark Knopfler of Dire Straits on guitar.
• 2ND: **THE WHO** play their first live show without Keith Moon... and the mod-centred movie based on Pete Townshend's latest concept album *Quadrophenia* premiers in London.
• 3RD: **THE SPECIALS** (later known as The Special AKA) are seen by Roy Eldridge, A&R man for Chrysalis Records, when they play at The Moonlight Club, London. Eldridge will sign them to the company, but allows them to keep their own label, 2-Tone. It was created by Specials founder Jerry Dammers, and will be used to launch other bands operating in a similar ska-based, racially integrated vein – including The Selecter and The (English) Beat.
• 5TH: **PEACHES AND HERB** reach Number One in the US Top 40 singles with 'Reunited.'

• MAY 4TH: **THE TOURISTS**, fronted by Annie Lennox, release their debut single, 'Blind Among The Flowers,' in the UK.

• 11TH: **LEGENDARY** bluegrass banjo star Lester Flatt, of Flatt & Scruggs, dies at 64.
• 12TH: **KATE BUSH** plays a benefit concert for Billy Duffy, her lighting engineer, who died during an accident at a concert on April 20th. Peter Gabriel and Steve Harley lend support.
• 16TH: **JOURNEY** play the first of five nights at the Aragon Ballroom, Chicago, Illinois.
• 18TH: **KAREN SILKWOOD**, a worker in a US nuclear plant, wins $10.5 million for suffering nuclear

contamination, four years after she's died in a car accident. The figure is ultimately reduced to $1.3 million, but the Kerr-McGee nuclear fuel plant will close in 1975, and in 1983 Karen Silkwood's story will become a movie, in which she is played by Meryl Streep.
• 19TH: **ERIC CLAPTON** marries Patti Boyd, ex-wife of George Harrison and subject of Eric's songs 'Layla' and 'Wonderful Tonight,' at his home, Hurtwood Edge, Surrey, UK.
• 24TH: **A BOTTLE** of 1860 Chateau Lafite claret sells for a record $28,000.
• 25TH: **A DC10** wide-bodied jet crashes just after take-off from Chicago. A total of 272 people are killed.
• 26TH: **'BOOGIE WONDERLAND,'** by Earth Wind & Fire with female vocal group The Emotions, dances into the US charts. EWT are at the start of a run of five Top Ten singles in a row and a string of best-selling albums.
• 29TH: **BISHOP ABEL MUZOREWA** becomes the first prime minister of what is now called Zimbabwe Rhodesia. In less than a year, it will be plain Zimbabwe, under Robert Mugabe.

### Who's That Lady?

• MAY 4TH: **53-YEAR-OLD RIGHT-WINGER** Margaret Thatcher becomes the UK's first woman Prime Minister, following the Conservative Party's election win.

• MAY 25TH: **RELEASE OF** the Ridley Scott movie *Alien*, starring Sigourney Weaver (right), John Hurt, and, of course, an HR Giger alien.

• 1ST: **THE KNACK** release their debut album, *Get The Knack*, in the US. Their 'power-pop' single 'My Sharona' goes to Number One in August, stays there for six weeks, and becomes America's top-selling record of 1979.
• 2ND: **POPE JOHN PAUL II** returns to his homeland of Poland for a visit, and in the process becomes the first pope ever to visit a communist country.
• 8TH: **UK SINGER** songwriter Gilbert O'Sullivan sues ex-manager Gordon Mills over royalty payments.
• 11TH: **ACTOR JOHN WAYNE** dies from cancer – "the Big C," as he calls it – at 72.
• 12TH: **'BORN TO RUN'** by Bruce Springsteen is adopted by the New Jersey State Legislature as its "Unofficial Youth Rock Anthem."
• 15TH: **MALAYSIA** refuses entry to 70,000 boat people and sends them back out to sea.
• 16TH: **'RING MY BELL,'** by part-time schoolteacher Anita Ward, reaches No1 on the UK singles chart and the US R&B singles chart simultaneously. In two weeks, it will do the same on the mainstream *Billboard* chart. Written and produced by Frederick Knight, the song becomes famous not just for its suggestive lyrics but also for its gimmicky use of primitive synthesized drums.

• 18TH: **PRESIDENT CARTER** and USSR premier Brezhnev sign the SALT II agreement (Strategic Arms Limitation Treaty II) in Vienna. It will not be ratified by the US, because the Soviets invade Afghanistan.
• 21ST: **THE GLASTONBURY FESTIVAL** opens in Pilton, Somerset, UK. Now a three-day event for the first time, it welcomes 12,000 people who pay £5 each to see Peter Gabriel, Steve Hillage, the Alex Harvey Band, and many others.
• 29TH: **LOWELL GEORGE**, ex-Frank Zappa sidekick, founder of Little Feat, singer-songwriter, slide guitar player, and troubled soul, dies in Washington, DC, from a heart attack brought on by drugs and obesity.
• 30TH: **THE ANNUAL** *ROSKILDE FESTIVAL* is held in Roskilde, Denmark. Artists appearing include Talking Heads, Peter Tosh, Taj Mahal, Jeff Beck, Tom Robinson, and Lindisfarne.

## Napalm In The Morning

**M**AY 24TH: FRANCIS FORD COPPOLA'S *Apocalypse Now* emerges with the top prize from this year's *Cannes Film festival*, where it's been premiered. Starring Martin Sheen, Marlon Brando, and Robert Duvall (seen here entertaining his troops), the movie takes a hallucinogenic trip through the drug-hazed horrors of Vietnam, accompanied by a suitably atmospheric soundtrack that includes The Doors, Creedence Clearwater Revival – and a bit of Wagner.

**JULY**

**AUGUST**

• **1ST: POPULARITY POLLS** indicate that Senator Ronald Reagan is now more popular than President Jimmy Carter.

• **6TH: SONGWRITER/ARRANGER/PRODUCER** and disco star Van McCoy – best known for the 1975 track 'The Hustle' – dies of a heart attack in a New Jersey hospital at the age of 38.

• **7TH: 'GOOD TIMES'** by Chic enters the US Top 40 singles chart, where it will peak at Number One.

• **10TH: CHUCK BERRY** gets four months in jail for tax evasion.

• **11TH: SKYLAB** returns to earth after six years in orbit. As it reaches the Earth's atmosphere, the 79-ton structure burns up and scatters over Western Australia, creating a spectacular firework effect, but thankfully no damage.

• **14TH: JEAN MICHEL JARRE'S** first live concert, at the Place de la Concorde, Paris, France, draws an audience of one million people.

• **16TH: GUITARIST RAY ROGERS** of Ohio finds a place in the record books when he begins a guitar solo that lasts more than 253 hours.

• **17TH: AFTER MONTHS** of tension between the Nicaraguan government and Sandinista rebels – and additional pressure from the US – General Anastasio Debayle Somoza resigns as president and takes sanctuary in the US.

• **23RD: THE AYATOLLAH KHOMEINI** tells a mass gathering of his subjects in Teheran that, "Music is no different from opium. Music affects the human mind in a way that makes people think of nothing but music and sensual matters ... Music is a treason to our country, a treason to our youth, and we should cut out all this music and replace it with something instructive."

• **27TH: SINGER TEDDY** Pendergrass is awarded a US platinum disc for his album *Teddy*.

• **4TH: DEF LEPPARD** sign to Vertigo Records, a UK subsidiary of Phonogram.

• **9TH: A 'WHITE RIGHTS'** march from Selma to Montgomery is undertaken by Ku Klux Klansmen.

• **14TH: THOSE SUSPECTED** of being homosexual are no longer officially barred from entering the US.

• **15TH: SEBASTIAN COE** breaks his third world record in three weeks at the 1500 metres in Zurich. He also broke the record for the Golden Mile and the 800 metres and becomes the first athlete to simultaneously hold all three records at once

• **18TH: NICK LOWE** marries Johnny Cash's step daughter Carlene Carter.

• **19TH: EVIDENCE** is uncovered of the genocide practiced by Pol Pot's Khmer Rouge party in Cambodia. It is thought to have claimed millions of lives since 1975.

• **21ST: THE CHARLIE DANIELS BAND** is awarded a US gold disc by the RIAA for the hit single 'The Devil Went Down To Georgia.'

• **24TH: B.B. KING** celebrates 30 years in music with a concert at The Roxy, Los Angeles. The 53-

• **AUGUST 11TH: DR HOOK** (above) have their third million-seller when 'When You're In Love With A Beautiful Woman' peaks at Number Sox in the US.

year-old 'Blues Boy' has a new record deal too, with MCA, and his new album, *Take It Home*, will be his first to reach the UK charts.

• **30TH: THE SPATE** of bank robberies in New York totals 137 this month alone.

• **AUGUST 18TH:** *Monty Python's Life Of Brian*, the most controversial film of the summer, opens in New York.

• **JULY 4TH: AT BUDOKAN**, the new live album from Cheap Trick reaches Number Four on the US charts, while the single 'I Want You To Want Me' climbs to Number Seven. They are also huge in Japan.

# 1979

## September–December

**S**EPTEMBER **16**TH: often named as the first rap single, The Sugarhill Gang's 'Rapper's Delight' is released in the US, where it will peak at Number 36. (In the UK it reaches Number Three.) Having seen the popularity of amateur DJs and MCs at Bronx block parties in New York, Sugarhill Records founder Sylvia Robinson (one half of the former pop duo Mickey & Sylvia) has

---

### SEPTEMBER

- **1ST: PIONEER 11** flies past Saturn, spotting two new mini moons and taking some nice snaps along the way. In 1995, after 22 years and four billion miles of space exploration, Pioneer 11 will reach the end of its useful life. It may still be transmitting – but we won't be able to pick up the signals any more.
- **8TH: ACTRESS JEAN SEBERG** dies of a barbiturate overdose at 40... And Alecia Moore is born in Philadelphia, Pennsylvania. She will find fame in 20 years' time as singer-songwriter Pink.
- **15TH: BOB DYLAN** releases his new album, *Slow Train Coming,* in the US.
- **20TH: JEAN BEDEL BOKASSA** is removed from power in the Central African Republic by his nephew David Dacko. Bokassa, who is said to have eaten some of his enemies, declared himself emperor for life almost three years ago. He is sentenced to death for his crimes, but this is commuted to life imprisonment, and he is released in 1993.
- **21ST: BRUCE SPRINGSTEEN**, Jackson Browne, Tom Petty, and Crosby Stills & Nash headline the *No Nukes* concert at Madison Square Garden, New York City.
- **22ND: GARY NUMAN** has his second UK Number One, with 'Cars,' the follow-up to 'Are Friends Electric.' 'Cars' will be Numan's only US hit, when it is released next spring
- **27TH: BBC TV'S QUESTION TIME** is first broadcast. It is presented by a bow-tied Torquemada called Robin Day, who will stay with the show for its first ten years.

- **OCTOBER 20TH: BUGGLES REACH NUMBER ONE in the UK with the single 'Video Killed The Radio Star.'** Formed by former session musicians Geoff Downes and Trevor Horn (below), Buggles never again have such a hit – it also reaches US Number 40 at the end of the year. The track will be best known in the States as the first to be played on MTV when it is launched in 1981. Downes and Horn later join Yes, before Downes forms Asia, and Horn returns to his first love, studio production. He will turn out distinctively action-packed records for Yes, Art Of Noise, and Frankie Goes To Hollywood.

---

### OCTOBER

- **DECEMBER 10TH: THE NOBEL PEACE PRIZE is** awarded to Mother Teresa of Calcutta for her charitable work with the poor and sick

- **1ST: ROY HARRIS**, the composer of 'When Johnny Comes Marching Home,' dies at age 81... And Elton John plays the first of eight successive nights at Madison Square Garden, New York City.
- **8TH: THE NEW FLEETWOOD MAC** album *Tusk* is released a week early in the US, after tracks are played without authorization on US radio stations.
- **11TH: FIDEL CASTRO** sets foot on US soil for the first time since 1960 to address the UN on the subject of Third World aid.
- **12TH: PIL RELEASE** their album *Metal Box* – packaged, rather appropriately, in a round metal canister.
- **19TH: THE SPECIALS**, Madness, and Selecter set off on the 2-Tone label's first tour of the UK.
- **20TH: ON US TV** show *Saturday Night Live*, Bob Dylan makes the surprising revelation that he has become a born-again Christian.
- **21ST: GRETE WAITZ** of Norway becomes the first woman to run a marathon in under two-and-a-half hours.
- **23RD: NEIL YOUNG'S** house on Zuma Beach burns down while he and Crazy Horse play at Inglewood Forum, Los Angeles.
- **24TH: PAUL McCARTNEY** is awarded a rhodium disc by the *Guinness Book Of Records* for record breaking sales. (Rhodium is a silvery white with a higher melting point and lower density than platinum.) He's also just bought the copyright to Buddy Holly's song catalogue.
- **29TH: 1,045 ANTI-NUCLEAR** protestors are arrested trying shut down the New York Stock Exchange.

---

### NOVEMBER

- **2ND: UK SECURITY FORCES** capture £500,000 worth of weapons, supplied to the IRA by US sympathizers.
- **3RD: DRIVING DOWN** Hollywood Freeway to meet a cocaine dealer, teen pop idol and actor Leif Garrett turns his Porsche over. His passenger, Roland Winkler, is paralyzed from the waist down and later receives $4.3 million in damages.
- **4TH: IRANIAN STUDENTS** storm the US Embassy in Tehran, holding more than 60 staff and US Marines hostage.
- **6TH: PINK FLOYD** finish recording their album *The Wall* in Los Angeles.
- **10TH: THE EAGLES** reach Number One on the US Top 40 chart with 'Heartache Tonight.'
- **20TH: ANTHONY BLUNT**, Surveyor of the Queen's Pictures, is stripped of his knighthood after admitting to spying for the Soviet Union and owning up as the Fourth Man in the Burgess, Maclean and Philby espionage scandal.
- **22ND: THE BBC** Year Of The Child concert is staged at Wembley Arena, London, featuring Wishbone Ash, Cat Stevens, Gary Numan, and David Essex.
- **23RD: MARIANNE FAITHFULL** is arrested for possession of marijuana at Oslo airport, Norway.
- **24TH: IT'S REVEALED** that thousands of troops have been exposed to Agent Orange, a plant defoliant used during the Vietnam war in an attempt to clear jungle and expose the enemy.
- **27TH: JOHN GLASCOCK**, bass player with Jethro Tull, dies in London at the age of 26 from complications arising from a tooth abscess – infection spreads and he dies after emergency heart surgery. Dave Pegg of Fairport Convention takes his place in the band.
- **30TH: ADAM & THE ANTS** release their debut album, *Dirk Wears White Sox*, in the UK.

cannily brought together local rappers Master Gee, Wonder Mike, and Big Bank Hank as The Sugarhill Gang, cutting 'Rappers Delight' over the instrumental backing of Chic's recent hit 'Good Times.' The is not exactly a 'sample': the technology doesn't exist yet, so the Sugarhill session band of Skip McDonald, Doug Wimbish and Keith LeBlanc (later to form Tackhead) reproduce the parts. Even so, Chic's Nile Rodgers and Bernard Edwards are not best pleased, and the ensuing court battle for royalty payments (which Chic eventually win) is perhaps the first of its kind. Though the Sugarhill Gang by no means invent rap (as we've seen, it's been around since the early 1960s, with acts like the Watts Prophets from LA, and their East Coast counterparts The Last Poets), 'Rapper's Delight' is acknowledged as the first time rap is commercially exploited: the single will sell more than eight million copies, bringing the international audience a taste of New York's black underground music, and terms like 'rap' and 'hip-hop,' for the first time. In the process, it launches a massive worldwide industry.

## Goths In The Haus

- **SEPTEMBER 3RD:** **BAUHAUS** release the single 'Bela Lugosi's Dead,' widely considered the track that ushers in the era of 'gothic' or 'goth' rock. Typified by black hair, black clothes, and deathly white complexions – a cross between The Doors and The Munsters – it will include among its devotees such bands as The Cult, Mission, and Fields Of The Nephilim (who add to the haunted-house look by dusting their frock coats with talcum powder). All forerunners of goth-metal acts, including Marilyn Manson.

## DECEMBER

- **3RD:** **ELEVEN FANS** die in a crush at a Who concert in Cincinnati, Ohio.
- **5TH:** **THE DOLLY MIXTURES** play at the Rock Garden, Covent Garden, London, supported by young Irish hopefuls U2.
- **8TH:** **STYX** reach Number One on the US Top 40 with 'Babe.' It's their first and only Number One single, though they're a perennially big-selling album band in the States.
- **9TH:** **BOTH** the deposed Shah of Iran and the current Khomeini administration are charged with human rights abuses by Amnesty International.
- **14TH:** **WHILE OUT JOGGING** in preparation for an upcoming six-mile race, former pop idol Dion has a vision – "a revelation of the Lord" – and is re-born as a deeply committed Christian.
- **15TH:** **JACKIE BRENSTON DIES** of a heart attack in a Veteran's Administration hospital in Memphis, Tennessee. His 1958 US R&B chart-topper, 'Rocket 88,' is regarded by many as the first rock'n'roll record... And Pink Floyd reach Number One on the UK singles chart with 'Another Brick In the Wall' for the first of five weeks.
- **15TH:** **A PICTURE EDITOR** on the *Montreal Gazette,* Chris Haney, and sports writer Scott Abbott come up with the idea for a game called Trivial Pursuit. It will be manufactured in 1982 and will sell 45 million copies worldwide in its first five years – making the two 30-year-old Canadians very rich indeed.
- **21ST:** **A BENEFIT** for presidential candidate and California Governor Jerry Brown is arranged by his girlfriend Linda Ronstadt, who ropes in The Eagles and Chicago... Meanwhile Frank Zappa's movie *Baby Snakes* premieres in New York City.
- **24TH:** **SOVIET TROOPS** invade Afghanistan as the Kabul government falls, seeking to shore up their interests in the region and prevent civil war.
- **29TH:** **FOUR CONCERTS** for the boat people of south-east Asia come to an end: performers include Paul McCartney, Elvis Costello, Robert Plant, The Clash, and The Who.
- **30TH:** **EMERSON, LAKE & PALMER** announce that the group has officially split.

- **DECEMBER 30TH:** **RICHARD RODGERS,** the composer of many much-loved musicals, including *South Pacific, Oklahoma,* and *The Sound Of Music,* and the partner of such celebrated lyricists as Lorenz Hart and Oscar Hammerstein II, dies at the age of 77. Even an abbreviated list of his songs is truly awesome: 'My Funny Valentine,' 'You'll Never Walk Alone,' 'My Favourite Things,' 'The Lady Is A Tramp,' 'Bewitched, Bothered And Bewildered,' 'Some Enchanted Evening,' 'Happy Talk,' 'Blue Moon,' 'Oh What A Beautiful Morning.' A true genius of the first great age of popular music, his like simply won't be seen again.

# The Eighties

# 1980

## January–April

• FEBRUARY 7TH: **PINK FLOYD** debut their concept show *The Wall* at The Sports Arena in Los Angeles, at the start of a brief US tour.

• JANUARY 2ND: **RUBIK'S 'MAGIC' CUBE**, an ingenious geometrical puzzle, first appeared in toyshops in Budapest, Hungary, in 1977, but it has now started creating such a stir around Europe that the Ideal Toy Company in the UK is persuaded to place an order for one million of the things – which will quickly followed by four million sales in the US in a single year. By 1982, Rubik's Cube will even make it onto the dictionary, and ensure that Erno Rubik (who wisely patented the design) is Hungary's richest private citizen – a millionaire at 35.

• 5TH: **KC & THE SUNSHINE BAND** reach Number One on the US Top 40 with 'Please Don't Go.'

• 7TH: **US VOCALIST** Larry Williams, famed for hits like 'Bonie Moronie' and 'Short Fat Fannie,' dies five days after shooting himself at home in Los Angeles... Meanwhile, Hugh Cornwell, singer with UK punk band The Stranglers, is sentenced to two months in prison for drug possession... And writer Henry Miller dies at age 87.

• 16TH: **PAUL McCARTNEY** is arrested in Tokyo, Japan, when customs officials find half a pound of marijuana in his luggage. He is released nine days later and booted out of Japan.

• 18TH: **SOUTHERN BOOGIE LABEL** Capricorn Records, home of the Allman Brothers Band, files for bankruptcy in Macon, Georgia... And Plasmatics vocalist Wendy O. Williams is arrested for simulating masturbation on-stage in Milwaukee

• 19TH: **THE PRETENDERS** reach Number One on the UK singles chart with 'Brass In Pocket,' and also release their debut album.

• 21ST: **WHEN TOM PETTY** & The Heartbreakers play a low-key club date at The Whisky A Go Go in Hollywood, Los Angeles, guests include Britt Ekland, Robin Zander of Cheap Trick, Eddie Van Halen, Dave Lee Roth, and Todd Rundgren.

• 29TH: **U.S COMEDIAN** Jimmy 'Schnozzola' Durante dies at the age of 86. His best-known musical number is his 1940s recording of 'The Man Who Found The Lost Chord.'

• 30TH: **PROFESSOR LONGHAIR**, the influential New Orleans R&B piano player (real name Henry Byrd), dies at age 62. Having gone into semi-retirement after a stroke in the 1950s, he made a comeback in the 1970s, before this heart attack.

• 2ND: **FBI AGENTS** posing as Arab sheikhs arrest Senator Harrison Williams and seven other US Representatives for accepting bribes. Williams of New Jersey will later become the first US senator since 1905, and the third in US history, to be convicted of criminal offences while in office.

• 8TH: **DAVID AND ANGIE BOWIE** divorce. David gets custody of son Zowie – who, perhaps wisely, will grow up using the name Duncan.

• 9TH: **DR ANDREI SAKHAROV'S** wife pleads with the West to help free her dissident husband from jail in the Soviet Union.

• 11TH: **WHEN A CONCORDE** delay strands George Harrison at London's Heathrow Airport, Bee Gee Maurice Gibb lends him his private jet.

• 12TH: **THE CLASH** release a new single, 'Train In Vain,' in the US. It will give them their first Top 30 entry, peaking at Number 23.

• 14TH: **UK PRIME MINISTER MARGARET THATCHER** halves state benefits to striking miners.

• 15TH: **PRINCE** makes his New York City debut appearance, playing the first of two nights at the Bottom Line.

• 16TH: **THE CAPTAIN & TENNILLE** reach Number One on the US Top 40 with 'Do That To Me One More Time.'

• 22ND: **MALCOLM McLAREN** steals Adam Ant's first backing band to form Bow Wow Wow with Annabella Lwin (after originally trying Boy George as a frontperson).

• 23RD: **QUEEN ACHIEVE** their first US Number One with 'Crazy Little Thing Called Love.' The single is a taster for this summer's album, *The Game*, which also features 'Another One Bites The Dust,' and will be the band's first (and only) Number One album in the US.

• 29TH: **BUDDY HOLLY'S GLASSES** – the pair he was wearing the night he died – are found in police files in Iowa.

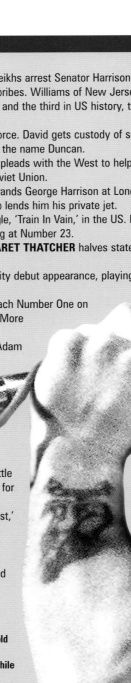

• FEBRUARY 19TH: **BON SCOTT**, 33-year-old singer with Australian-based (but largely Scottish-born) hard-rock band AC/DC, dies while sleeping overnight in someone's car after a drinking binge in London. After a period of mourning and reflection, the band replace him (in March) with Newcastle-born singer Brian Johnson, and continue for another two decades.

# Good Evening, And Goodbye

• APRIL 29TH: **MASTER FILM MAKER** Alfred Hitchcock dies at the age of 80. Despite being enormously influential, in a career dating back to the silent era, he never won an Oscar as Best Director. But he was nominated five times (for *Rebecca*, *Lifeboat*, *Spellbound*, *Rear Window*, and *Psycho*), and made many more classics such as *Strangers On A Train*, *Rope*, *Vertigo*, *Dial M For Murder*, *North By Northwest*, and *The Birds*. In 1967 the Academy finally did the decent thing and gave him an Irving Thalberg Memorial Award for direction. His movies did decline in quality during the 1960s (not helped by the departure of his favourite soundtrack composer, Bernard Herrmann), but Hitchcock's TV appearances, in his long-running series of thrillers and macabre tales, immortalised his public image as a ghoulish MC.

**MARCH**

**APRIL**

• 1ST: **'AND THE BEAT GOES ON'** by The Whispers reaches Number One on the US R&B singles chart.

• 11TH: *SCARSDALE DIET* author Dr Herman Tarnower is shot dead at his Westchester County home by Mrs Jean Harris, 56-year-old headmistress of a prestigious Virginia girls' school.

• 15TH: **CLASH MOVIE** *Rude Boy* premieres in London.

• 20TH: **TO CELEBRATE** their 11th wedding anniversary, John Lennon buys a heart-shaped diamond and 5000 gardenias for Yoko Ono. She buys him a Rolls Royce.

• 22ND: **THE PRESIDENTIAL** elections in Turkey are postponed after no candidates are put forward... And Pink Floyd begin a four-week run at the top of the US singles chart with 'Another Brick In the Wall.'

• 23RD: **U2 ARE SIGNED** to a recording contract by Island Records – as legend has it – in the ladies' toilet at The Lyceum Ballroom, London.

• 24TH: **OUTSPOKEN HUMAN RIGHTS** activist Archbishop Oscar Romero is shot by right-wing paramilitary gunmen while saying mass in San Salvador

• 29TH: **CHICAGO ANTIQUE DEALER**/musician Ronald Selle files suit against the Bee Gees alleging that their hit 'How Deep Is Your Love' plagiarises two sections of his song, 'Let It End.' While giving evidence in court, Maurice Gibb is played a section of a melody which he identifies as their own song, but turns out to be Selle's. The jury is convinced, but an appeal judge later reverses their decision.

• 29TH: *DARK SIDE OF THE MOON* moves ahead of Carol King's *Tapestry* as the longest-lasting album on the chart – it's in its 303rd week.

• 5TH: **AT A BIRTHDAY PARTY** in the former St Mary's Episcopal Church at 394 Oconee Street, Athens, Georgia, 300 teenagers dance at the debut gig of a band formed just weeks earlier – they're called Twisted Kites, and will later become R.E.M.

• 14TH: **THE FIRST FULL-LENGTH** music video offered for sale to the public is Gary Numan's *The Touring Principle*.

• 15TH: **JEAN-PAUL SARTRE** existentialist thinker and writer, dies at the age of 74.

• 17TH: **BOB MARLEY** calls it "the greatest honour of my life" when he and The Wailers perform and are state guests at Zimbabwe's Independence Festival. The former British colony of Rhodesia has chosen its first president, Dr Canaan Banana, and prime minister, Robert Mugabe.

• 19TH: **FOR THE FIRST TIME EVER**, female performers (Crystal Gayle, Dottie West, Debbie Boone, Emmylou Harris, and Tammy Wynette), hold the top five positions in *Billboard*'s country singles chart.

• 24TH: **PRESIDENT CARTER'S** efforts to free 53 US hostages held in the American Embassy in Tehran, Iran, end in disaster when eight servicemen die when their helicopter crashes into a transport plane full of fuel during the rescue attempt... In the UK, Duran Duran place an advert in pop paper *Melody Maker*, looking for a 'live-wire guitarist.' It will be answered by Andy Taylor, who gets the job. It means there are now three Taylors in the band, none of them related. They also

audition drama student Simon Le Bon, who gets the gig despite – or perhaps because of – his pink leopard-skin trousers.

• 26TH: **NEW YORK DISCO** night-club Studio 54 is closed down for licensing law violations.

• 29TH: **BOB SEGER** & The Silver Bullet Band's album *Against The Wind* is certified platinum in the US, and will soon spend six weeks at Number One.

• 30TH: **McVICAR**, a film starring Roger Daltry as career criminal John McVicar, has its premiere in London.

## Who's The Boss?

• MARCH 5TH: **BRUCE SPRINGSTEEN** fails to win the Best Female Vocalist award in *Rolling Stone* magazine's reader's poll. He can manage only Artist Of The Year, Band Of The Year, Best Album, Best Single, and Best Songwriter. There is no award for best bandana.

# Lost Control

**MAY 18TH: IAN CURTIS,** singer and songwriter with Joy Division, hangs himself at his home in Manchester, UK. In their tragically short career the band have been critically acclaimed and a powerful influence on numerous introspective post-punk outfits who follow in their wake. This they owe in no small part to the disturbed lyrics and deranged stage presence of vocalist Curtis, an epileptic, who has been known to suffer grand mal seizures on stage. The rest of the group – guitarist Bernard Albrecht (later Sumner), bassist Peter Hook, and drummer Stephen Morris, are technically barely competent, but create beautifully bleak and spare musical backing. The band's use of Nazi imagery (a 'Joy Division' was a brothel in a concentration camp) has caused controversy but their 1979 debut, *Unknown Pleasures,* was still lauded, and they were soon being chased by major American labels. They are about to start their first US tour, having finished recording their second album, *Closer*, when Curtis takes his life. The band continue, changing their name to New Order.

• **2ND: WHEN BLACK CHILDREN** in South Africa adopt 'Another Brick In The Wall' by Pink Floyd as their anthem, censorship rears its ugly head, and the single is banned by the apartheid regime.

• **4TH: MARSHALL TITO,** Yugoslavia's great reformer – or Socialist tyrant, depending on your view – dies at 87. There are now concerns that without Tito (born Josip Broz), the bond holding the six republics together will disappear and hostilities between ethnic Serbians and Croatians may resurface. Which is almost exactly what happens.

• **6TH: POPE JOHN PAUL II** learns that nine people were trampled to death two days previously when 1.5 million thronged to hear him preach at the plaza of the people's palace in Zaire, central Africa.

• **8TH: THE WORLD HEALTH ORGANISATION** announces that the smallpox virus no longer exists. The virus was previously thought to be extinct in 1977, but a strain escaped from a laboratory in Birmingham UK and caused several deaths.

• **14TH: INXS RELEASE** their debut single, 'Simple Simon,' in their homeland of Australia.

• **16TH: TREVOR HORN** (and Geoff Downes, both formerly with Buggles), join Yes – a move that's controversial to say the least among traditional fans of the ageing prog-rockers. Downes is with them less than a year, before forming the 'supergroup'

Asia with Steve Howe, John Wetton, and Carl Palmer. Horn stays on to produce Yes, and will provide them with their only big hit single, in 1983... Meanwhile, Earvin 'Magic' Johnson, in his rookie year at the LA Lakers, helps them win the NBA title by scoring a record-breaking 42 in the final against Philadelphia.

• **21ST: JOE STRUMMER** is arrested for hitting an audience member in Hamburg, Germany.

• **23RD: U2 RELEASE** their first single for Island Records, '11 O,Clock Tick Tock,' in the UK.

• **31ST: THE NEW NUMBER ONE** single in the US (Number Two in the UK) is the electro-funk dancefloor fave 'Funkytown' by Lipps Inc – essentially US musician Steven Greenberg.

• **JULY 10TH: US COMEDIAN** Richard Pryor is severely burned after a 'freebase' mix of ether and cocaine explodes in his face. Revered for his painfully honest and fearless observations of black and white culture, and a major influence on Eddie Murphy, Robin Williams, and Chris Rock, Pryor will suffer further troubles when he is diagnosed with multiple sclerosis in 1986.

• **JULY 26TH: ABBA** release 'The Winner Takes It All' in the UK, which will give them their eighth, and penultimate, Number One there. In the US the song will make Number One on the Adult Contemporary chart. The two couples, Bjorn & Agnetha (far left) and Benny & Frida have been having severe marital problems, and the end is apparently nigh.

• **1ST: CNN,** the world's first 24-hour news channel, is launched in the US by entrepreneur Ted Turner... Meanwhile John Lennon sails from New York City to Bermuda, where, after a creative dry spell, he begins writing songs again.

• **5TH: THE GRATEFUL DEAD'S** 15th Anniversary Celebration gig is at Compton Terrace, Phoenix, Arizona.

• **7TH: TWENTY THOUSAND FANS** turn out for the 11th Crystal Palace Garden Party, south London, where they see Bob Marley & The Wailers, Joe Jackson, Average White Band, and Q-Tips (fronted by singer Paul Young).

• **9TH: WHEN LARRY CORYELL** plays at the Plaza de Toros de las Arenas, Barcelona, Spain, he is joined by

Carlos Santana for several numbers .

• **14TH: UK PUNK COMBO** Splodgeness-abounds enter the UK charts with 'Two Pints Of Lager And A Packet Of Crisps.' Needless to say, this is not a hit in the US.

• **17TH: ROADIE DAY** is proclaimed in Los Angeles, recognising the work-horses without whom no rock show could happen...

Coincidentally, the new Meat Loaf movie, called *Roadie*, opens across the US.

• **21ST: THE STRANGLERS** are arrested in Nice, France for inciting a riot... And early Beatles producer (in their German days) Bert Kaempfert dies at age 51. Kaempfert led his own 'easy-listening' orchestra, and had a US Number One in 1960 with 'Wonderland By Night.'

• **JUNE 16TH:** *THE BLUES BROTHERS* movie has its premiere in Chicago. It will open in New York in two days' time. Written by its stars, John Belushi and Dan Aykroyd, it is based on characters the pair created on the *Saturday Night Live* TV show, Jake and Elwood Blues, but is really just a good excuse to sing lots of old R&B numbers, invite some very special guest musicians to appear, and film some outrageous car chases. The songs include 'Everybody Needs Somebody To Love' and 'Sweet Home Chicago,' and the musical guests are James Brown, Ray Charles, Aretha Franklin, Cab Calloway, and of course the 'Blues Brothers Band,' featuring none other than the old Stax/MGs team of guitarist Steve Cropper and bass player Donald 'Duck' Dunn (seen inset). Directed by John Landis, the movie soon creates a cult following. Belushi will die, tragically young, in 1982, but two decades later Dan Aykroyd will resurrect the act with John's brother Jim Belushi for some live shows and the *Blues Brothers 2000* movie.

## JULY

• **MAY 16TH:** *FAME*, THE MOVIE MUSICAL directed by Alan Parker, is released in the US. It launches a worldwide craze for leggings and dancing on cars.

• **2ND:** **GRATEFUL DEAD** members Bob Weir and Mickey Hart, plus manager Danny Rifkin, are arrested when they intervene in a drug-related arrest at the Sports Arena, San Diego, California.

• **5TH:** **WHEN DURAN DURAN** play at the Edinburgh festival, Scotland, they appear for the first time with the line-up that will become famous.

• **7TH:** **THE POLICE** begin recording the album *Zenyatta Mondatta* at Wisseloord Studios, Hilversum, Holland.

• **11TH:** **U2 PLAY** their first sell-out show in England – at the Half Moon pub, Herne Hill, south London.

• **14TH:** **BRITISH PUNK/REGGAE** reggae outfit The Ruts – a largely underrated band – lose their vocalist Malcolm Owen to a heroin overdose.

• **16TH:** **ADAM & THE ANTS** are signed to CBS Records in London.

• **19TH:** **BILLY JOEL** reaches Number One on the US singles chart with 'It's Still Rock'N'Roll To Me'... And David Bowie takes to the stage in Denver as *The Elephant Man*, which will transfer to New York in September.

• **23RD:** **ACTOR PETER SELLERS**, the UK-born comedy legend, dies after a heart attack at 54.

• **25TH:** **DAVID KNOPFLER**, brother of Mark, quits Dire Straits mid-way through recording *Making Movies*.

## AUGUST

• **1ST:** A HAND-PICKED CREW of session players begin rehearsals at The Hit Factory, New York City, with producer Jack Douglas, unaware that the album they are preparing for will be John Lennon's comeback.

• **3RD:** A TOTAL OF 65 COUNTRIES, including the US, boycott the Moscow Olympics as a protest against the Soviet invasion of Afghanistan. The UK team attends, against the wishes of its government.

• **4TH:** **PINK FLOYD BEGIN** a six-night stint at Earl's Court, London, performing *The Wall* live in the UK for the first time.

• **8TH:** **TONIGHT'S GIG** by US shock-rockers The Plasmatics, at Hammersmith Odeon, London, is cancelled by the Greater London Council – not so much on moral grounds this time, but more because of the band's tendency to blow up cars on stage.

• **12TH:** **MEXICO** is home to the first Panda cub born in captivity.

• **15TH:** **FIRST OF TWO DAYS** of the URGH! new wave festival in Santa Monica, California, features Pere Ubu, X, Dead Kennedys, Dead Boys, and others... And George Harrison's autobiography *I, Me, Mine* is published (this is the limited leather-bound edition, costing £148 – the paperback follows later).

• **16TH:** **MUSICAL DIFFERENCES** abound today as Jah Wobble leaves PiL, Cozy Powell departs Rainbow, Jools Holland jumps ship from Squeeze, and Bill Ward runs screaming from the ranks of Black Sabbath.

• **30TH:** **CHRISTOPHER CROSS** reaches Number One in the US with 'Sailing'... Meanwhile the single 'Xanadu' by Olivia Newton-John and Electric Light Orchestra enters the US charts, drawn from the new fantasy musical movie featuring Newton-John and legendary veteran Hollywood actor/dancer Gene Kelly. The music proves more popular than the film, which one critic describes as, "the most dreadful, tasteless movie of the decade ... probably of all time."

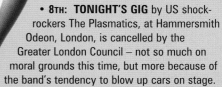

• **JUNE 19TH:** **DISCO GODDESS** Donna Summer is the first artist to sign to Geffen Records, owned by music business mogul David Geffen.

## Dream Is Over

**D**ECEMBER 8TH: **JOHN LENNON** is shot dead outside the Dakota Building, New York City, as he and Yoko Ono return home from the recording studio. His killer, Mark Chapman, a deranged fan, has been stalking him for several days – he was even happy to be photographed getting Lennon's autograph earlier in the day – and is waiting as the couple arrive home just before 11pm. As Yoko gets out of the car, Chapman says hello to her, than lets Lennon walk past before pulling the gun, calling out "Mr Lennon?" and shooting him four times at point-blank range as the ex-Beatle turns (a fifth bullet misses). The bullets puncture Lennon's lungs, sever his windpipe, and cause massive loss of blood. He's rushed to hospital in a police car, but dies soon after arrival. Chapman, meanwhile, has not attempted to leave the crime scene,  but instead taken

## SEPTEMBER

• 3RD: **ABBIE HOFFMAN**, a fugitive for six years (undergoing plastic surgery and suffering a breakdown while in hiding), finally gives himself up to authorities in New York. A political activist, radical counter-cultural icon of the 1960s, and self-styled 'Yippie,' his classic 1971 work, *Steal This Book,* was turned down by dozens of publishers before it finally, ironically, became a best-seller.
• 5TH: **A STATUE** of Buddy Holly is unveiled in his home town, Lubbock, Texas.
• 10TH: **THE WORLD'S LONGEST** tunnel (ten miles) opens in Switzerland.
• 12TH: **ACCORDING TO LEGEND,** this is the day Van Halen singer David Lee Roth trashes the facilities at a gig in Colorado (or perhaps New Mexico, depending on the version you believe), causing $12,000 worth of damage, just because the band's concert rider has not been met. They have a clause in their contract which specifies there must be no brown M&Ms anywhere in the backstage area, and Roth has found some. They claim later it's a way of checking whether the complex document has been well-read, to avoid technical problems with stage equipment – but Roth admits to having a bit of fun in the process.
• 15TH: **JAZZ PIANIST** Bill Evans dies at age 51.
• 17TH: **BETTE MIDLER'S** *Divine Madness* concert movie premieres in Los Angeles.
• 18TH: **INDEPENDENT** trade union Solidarity, led by Lech Walesa, is founded in Poland.
• 23RD: **IRAQI SOLDIERS** destroy oil refineries in Iran.
• 29TH: **STEVIE WONDER** releases *Hotter Than July.*

## Diana's Way

•SEPTEMBER 6TH: **DIANA ROSS** begins four weeks at Number One on the US Top 40 with 'Upside Down.' The Chic-produced track is her first chart-topping single in four years, and her biggest solo hit – but only after Ross has remixed it, and the rest of the album, to make her voice more prominent.

• SEPTEMBER 25TH: **JOHN 'BONZO' BONHAM**, titanic drummer with Led Zeppelin, dies at the home of bandmate Jimmy Page, in Windsor, UK. It follows a heavy vodka-drinking session – not his first by any means, but sadly his last. Ten weeks later, unable to face continuing without their unique colleague, and after a decade as the world's biggest rock band, Zeppelin officially disband.

out a book and started to read. It is his favourite novel, J.D. Salinger's *The Catcher In The Rye*, about a teenager who goes to New York and has a nervous breakdown, while decrying the 'phonies' that make up the adult real world. Chapman will be diagnosed as a paranoid schizophrenic, who later admits to having a list of possible targets whose celebrity lifestyle he detests – he never expected to succeed with his first choice. But he refuses to plead insanity, and will be sentenced to 20 years in prison. Lennon has been recording his first new material for over five years, having recently struck a verbal deal with David Geffen (Elton John's new label boss), who offered to release anything Lennon recorded.

## Catch A Fire

• **SEPTEMBER 21ST: REGGAE SUPERSTAR** Bob Marley collapses while jogging in Central Park, New York. He's been in town playing support to The Commodores, hoping finally to crack the American market, which has remained curiously oblivious to his appeal – unlike the UK, where he's had seven hits in the past five years. But his health has been troubling him for some time; indeed he almost blacked out during a recent show. Three years earlier, an examination of a toe injury (sustained while playing soccer) revealed a previously undiscovered melanoma cancer on his foot, but Marley's Rastafarian beliefs would not permit surgery at the time. Now, doctors find that the cancer has spread to his stomach, lungs and brain. They give him only weeks to live. Despite this, on September 23rd, Marley travels to Pittsburgh and plays what will be his last concert, before reluctantly cancelling the rest of his tour. He also agrees to be babtized into the Ethiopian Orthodox Christian Church, taking the name Berhane Selassie. After undergoing limited conventional cancer treatment, he flies to the Bavarian holistic therapy centre of Dr Josef Issels, who against all the odds keeps him alive for more than six months, but eventually concedes defeat. Marley plans to return to Jamaica, but dies in Miami, where his mothers lives, on May 11th 1981, at the age of just 36.

### OCTOBER

• **1ST: PAUL SIMON'S** movie, *One Trick Pony*, opens in New York City. The cast includes Lou Reed, The Lovin' Spoonful, Sam & Dave, The B-52s and Tiny Tim.
• **2ND: THOUSANDS** are reportedly heading to the Brazilian Amazon after more than $50 million in gold nuggets are found in the Serra Pelada and numerous other mines.

• **3RD: BRUCE SPRINGSTEEN'S** tour to promote *The River* opens at Crisler Arena, Ann Arbor, Michigan. During 'Born To Run,' Springsteen forgets the lyrics.
• **4TH: GEORGE BENSON** has his biggest US hit when 'Give Me The Night' hits Number Four.
• **6TH: THE BEE GEES** instigate legal proceedings against former manager Robert Stigwood ... and

• **OCTOBER 25TH: BARBRA STREISAND** achieves her fifth US Number One single with the Barry & Robin Gibb song 'Woman In Love.' A technically impeccable singer, Streisand has been famous since she starred in the show *Funny Girl* in 1964. But her pop breakthrough only came in 1973, with the Number One 'The Way We Were,' taken from the hit movie in which she co-starred with Robert Redford.

John Lydon is arrested on assault charges, later dropped.
• **8TH: TALKING HEADS,** bolstered for the first time by session musicians, release the album *Remain In Light* in the US.
• **10TH: 17,000 DIE** in an earthquake in Algeria.
• **13TH: U2 RELEASE** their debut album, *Boy* (left) in the UK... Meanwhile *Back In Black* by AC/DC is certified as a US double platinum album by the RIAA.
• **25TH: THE POPE** tells divorced and remarried Catholics that they can only receive communion if they do not have sex with their new partner.
• **28TH: MARK CHAPMAN** boards a flight from Hawaii to New York City, carrying the gun he will use to murder John Lennon.

### NOVEMBER

• **1ST: VOCALIST GRAHAM BONNETT** leaves Rainbow to pursue a solo career... And Stevie Wonder tops the US R&B singles chart with 'Master Blaster (Jammin')' – later to become a favorite of *Simpsons* Police Chief Wiggum.
• **7TH: DEXY'S MIDNIGHT RUNNERS** split. They'll be back.
• **8TH: IT'S REPORTED** in the UK music press that Martyn Ware and Ian Craig Marsh are leaving The Human League to form British Electric Foundation, whose main project will be the group Heaven 17.
• **10TH: MICHAEL FOOT** takes over from James Callaghan as leader of the UK Labour Party.
• **18TH: THE B-52s** from Athens, Georgia, collect a US gold disc for their debut album.

• **21ST: OVER 80 DIE** in a fire at the MGM Grand Hotel in Las Vegas... Meanwhile a naked 16-year-old girl, found in the Los Angeles home of Eagles member Don Henley, has to be treated for drug intoxication. Henley is arrested and charged with possession of marijuana, cocaine and quaaludes, plus contributing to the delinquency of a minor.
• **22ND: MAE WEST,** the Madonna of the 1920s-30s, dies at the age of 87. In 1926, her Broadway show *Sex* got her arrested for obscenity, and the follow-up, *Drag*, was banned because of its 'sexual deviancy.'
• **23RD: THE BIGGEST EARTHQUAKE** to hit Europe in 65 years claims more than 3,000 lives in Italy.
• **26TH: PRINCE** releases a new single, 'Dirty Mind,' from the album of the same name... And the movie *Wings Over America* premieres in New York.

## Gipper Wins

• **NOVEMBER 4TH: RONALD REAGAN** beats Jimmy Carter by a landslide (44 out of 50 states), to become the 40th President of the US, at the age of 69.

### DECEMBER

• **NOVEMBER 7TH: US ACTOR STEVE McQUEEN,** dies from cancer at age 50.

• **1ST: U2 SUPPORT** Talking Heads at London's Hammersmith Palais venue.
• **2ND: A JONI MITCHELL** TV special, *Shadows And Light*, airs on Showtime TV in the US.
• **6TH: A SOLAR-POWERED** aircraft (the MacCready Solar Challenger) covers almost 18 miles between Tucson and Phoenix before cloud cover brings it back down to earth
• **23RD: JOHN McVIE** of Fleetwood Mac is arrested for cocaine possession at his home in Honolulu, Hawaii.
• **29TH: FOLK SINGER/SONGWRITER** Tim Hardin is found dead after a heroin overdose in his LA home.
• **31ST: YEAR-END SALES FIGURES** for the recording industry in the US and UK show a major slump, blamed mainly on the demise of disco. In the US, record sales will start to pick up again in the mid 1980s, largely due to UK imports, but the UK itself continues on this downward trend until the mid 1990s.

# 1981

## January–April

**B**ORN AS A DIRECT response to the dour, iconoclastic punk movement, with its plain black clothing held together with safety pins, the 'new romantics' positively celebrate the importance of image and glamor, embracing ostentatious clothing and hedonistic behaviour. Initially based around a few select London clubs, the movement draws inspiration from David Bowie's more androgynous incarnations, prompted especially by the recent video for his UK Number One single 'Ashes To Ashes,' in which the star, heavily made up and outlandishly attired, appears as several characters, like a one-man fancy-dress party. Its lasting influence on fashion is big hair, wide shoulders, and baggy trousers, while the music itself is initially very synthesizer-led, typified by

## JANUARY

- **1ST: THE FIRST** Number One of the new year is John Lennon's 'comeback' single, the poignantly-named '(Just Like) Starting Over.' It stays top for five weeks, making it his biggest ever solo hit. In the UK Lennon has three (almost consecutive) Number Ones in the weeks following his murder: 'Starting Over' tops the charts at Christmas, then his re-released 'Imagine' spends four weeks there from 10th January, followed by 'Woman,' from the new Double Fantasy album. The only interruption to the run comes (in typically eccentric British fashion) from St Winifred's School Choir singing 'There's No One Quite Like Grandma.'
- **2ND: FORMER PLATTERS** vocalist David Lynch dies.
- **5TH: PETER SUTCLIFFE**, the man believed to be the Yorkshire Ripper, is arrested in the UK.
- **10TH: AS OF TODAY** it is no longer against the law to use obscene language in front of women in Alabama.

- **12TH: THE RECORD INDUSTRY** Association Of America (RIAA) donates 8000 albums to the White House music library, including the Sex Pistols and Kiss.
- **17TH: MÖTLEY CRÜE'S** line-up is completed when lead singer Vince Neil joins the band.
- **18TH: WENDY O. WILLIAMS** of The Plasmatics is seen on-stage, according to a police report, "fondling herself" and also "simulating sexual intercourse." She is arrested but charges are later dropped.
- **21ST: AFTER 444 DAYS** of captivity, and a failed rescue attempt, the final 52 American hostages who were seized in Iran are released.
- **26TH: BLONDIE IS AWARDED** a platinum disc for the album *Autoamerican*.
- **29TH: BARRY KRAMER,** publisher of US rock magazine *Creem*, dies at 37.
- **31ST: THE INDIAN POINT** nuclear plant in New York is closed after leaks are discovered... And Justin Timberlake, later of boy-band *NSync, is born in Tennessee.

- **JANUARY 22ND: RUPERT MURDOCH** (below left) gains control of *The Times* newspaper in London, UK. In the US he already owns the *San Antonio Express News*, the *New York Post*, *The Village Voice*, and *New York Magazine*. And he has a few more ideas up his sleeve...

## FEBRUARY

- **FEBRUARY 14TH: 'VIENNA' BY ULTRAVOX** peaks at Number Two on the UK singles chart. It's the biggest hit for the group, now fronted by former teen idol Midge Ure, who has replaced the intense John Foxx. In the US, success must wait for 1983's *Quartet*, produced by George Martin.

- **2ND: DURAN DURAN** release their debut UK single, 'Planet Earth.'
- **6TH: HUGH MONTENEGRO**, who had a hit in 1968 with Ennio Morricone's theme from *The Good The Bad & The Ugly*, dies at age 55.
- **7TH: KOOL & THE GANG** reach Number One on the US Top 40 singles with 'Celebration.'

- **8TH: R.E.M. TRAVEL** to Joe Perry's Bombay Studios in Atlanta, Georgia, where they record 'Radio Free Europe' and other songs.
- **9TH: IN THE GRIP OF** alcoholism, and suffering bouts of paranoia, Bill Haley dies of a heart attack, in Harlingen, Texas, at age 56.
- **13TH: ONE PLUS ONE,** a

cassette tape format with one side pre-recorded and the other side blank, is launched by Island Records.
- **15TH: BLUES-ROCK** guitarist Mike Bloomfield dies from a drug overdose, at 39.
- **20TH: KURT COBAIN**, future leader of Nirvana, turns 14 and gets his first guitar.
- **24TH: IN THE UK**, Buckingham

Palace announces the engagement of Prince Charles, heir to the British throne, and Lady Diana Spencer, 13 years his junior.
- **25TH: CHRISTOPHER CROSS** wins four Grammy Awards, for Best New Artist, Song Of The Year ('Sailing'), Record of the Year ('Sailing') and Album Of The Year (*Christopher Cross*).

groups like Visage (led by Steve Strange, below right), Classix Nouveaux, and Ultravox (see February) It even includes proto-synth-pop bands of the day, like Depeche Mode and Soft Cell. A few of the acts make a successful transition across the Atlantic – for instance Adam Ant (opposite page, left) – though in some cases it's not until they've shed most of their new romantic trappings, give or take the odd frilly shirt, and adopted a more traditional pop sound – as is the case with Duran Duran and Spandau Ballet (above). Although short-lived, the new romantics do leave a lasting legacy, and throw up some intriguing characters, such as David Sylvian, who forms Japan and later works with Ryuichi Sakamoto, and Boy George, later of Culture Club – nominally a new romantic, he soon proves something quite unique. In the mid 1990s there's a half-hearted new romantic revival, called 'romo.'

## Bear Down

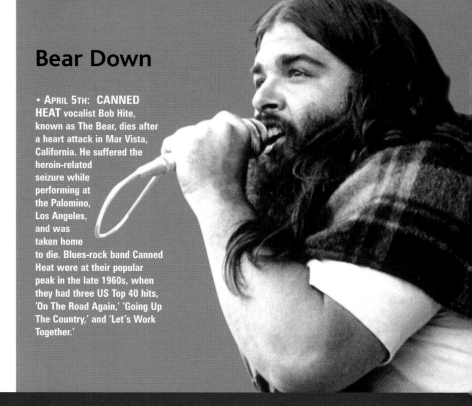

• **APRIL 5TH: CANNED HEAT** vocalist Bob Hite, known as The Bear, dies after a heart attack in Mar Vista, California. He suffered the heroin-related seizure while performing at the Palomino, Los Angeles, and was taken home to die. Blues-rock band Canned Heat were at their popular peak in the late 1960s, when they had three US Top 40 hits, 'On The Road Again,' 'Going Up The Country,' and 'Let's Work Together.'

---

**MARCH**

**APRIL**

• **MARCH 14TH: BLEEDING ULCERS** cause Eric Clapton to be hospitalized in St Paul, Minnesota, forcing him to cancel the remaining dates of his massive US tour, which he's booked to promote his album *Another Ticket* (above). In a month's time, Eric will be back in hospital after a minor car crash.

• **3RD: THE ROD STEWART** album *Foolish Behaviour* is certified as a US platinum disc.

• **5TH: PRESIDENT REAGAN** tries to end Legal Aid for the poor and to link welfare payments to availability for work.

• **20TH: ISABEL PERON**, former Argentine president, is jailed for corruption... And Prince plays for 300 people at Bowen Field House, Eastern Michigan University, Ypsilanti, Michigan.

• **21ST: REO SPEEDWAGON** reach Number One on the US Top 40 with 'Keep On Loving You.'

• **26TH: THE SDP** (Social Democratic Party) is launched in the UK by four high-profile defectors from the Labour party, dubbed the Gang Of Four by the press. An ad in the next day's paper offers "an invitation to join the SDP." Cost? Just £9 ($14).

• **27TH: THE GRATEFUL DEAD** play the first of four nights at The Rainbow Theatre, London.

• **30TH: DEWITT WALLACE** dies in Mount Kisco, New York at the age of 91. In 1922, with his wife Lila, he set about publishing and distributing a new kind of magazine, consisting of condensed articles from other sources, and abridged fiction. He called it *Reader's Digest*. This simple but visionary concept now has a circulation of 30 million.

• **7TH: FORMER WHO** manager Kit Lambert falls down stairs and dies... Meanwhile in Chicago, Illinois, Steve Marriott (of Small Faces and Humble Pie fame) crushes his fingers in a door, and it's said his guitar-playing days may be over. They're not.

• **9TH: THE US-BASED** Sam Goody chain of record shops is convicted of dealing in pirate tapes, after Billy Joel testifies that he cannot distinguish between a bootleg version of his LP, *The Stranger*, and the official CBS release.

• **11TH: DARYL HALL & JOHN OATES** reach Number One on the US Top 40 with the single 'Kiss On My List.'

• **12TH: THE RE-USABLE** Space Shuttle Columbia lifts off, heralding the start of a new era of spaceflight.

• **15TH:** *THE WASHINGTON POST* admits fabricating a Pulitzer Prize-winning article (written by 26-year-old reporter Janet Cooke) about an eight-year-old heroin addict.

• **18TH: A NEW MUSIC-PLAYING** device, a Compact Disc (CD) player, is demonstrated for the first time, in Europe, by Philips & Sony.

• **23RD: JOHNNY CASH**, Jerry Lee Lewis and Carl Perkins record *The Survivors* in Stuttgart Germany.

• **25TH: DENNY LAINE** leaves Wings, and Paul McCartney disbands the group for good. Though obviously never as critically acclaimed as The Beatles (quite a hard act to follow), the solo Paul McCartney & Wings have nevertheless had 26 US Top 40 singles in the last decade, including seven Number Ones – the most recent being a live version of 'Coming Up' (recorded in Glasgow, Scotland), which topped the charts last summer.

• **APRIL 4TH: DEPECHE MODE** enter the UK charts with their debut single 'Dreaming Of Me.' At this stage the band still includes Vince Clarke, later of Erasure, seen here gazing enviously at singer Dave Gahan's healthy, if strangely fringed, head of hair.

## Gun Law

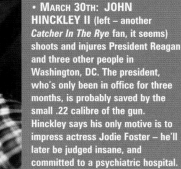

• **MARCH 30TH: JOHN HINCKLEY II** (left – another *Catcher In The Rye* fan, it seems) shoots and injures President Reagan and three other people in Washington, DC. The president, who's only been in office for three months, is probably saved by the small .22 calibre of the gun. Hinckley says his only motive is to impress actress Jodie Foster – he'll later be judged insane, and committed to a psychiatric hospital.

## Big Time Sheena

**M**AY 1981: LONG BEFORE the *Pop/American Idol* TV show concept, a 1980 BBC series called *The Big Time* has been documenting the efforts of an unknown 20-year-old singer from Scotland as she endeavors to become a 'star.' Her name is Sheena Easton, and much to the surprise of almost everyone concerned with the show, she makes it – and not only in her native UK. Within a year of becoming a household name in Britain, Sheena has not only been asked to sing the new James Bond movie theme song ('For Your Eyes Only'), she's also topping the US charts with her debut single 'Morning Train (Nine To Five),' which she follows up with a dozen more hits in the following decade – including several which result from a spell of sexually explicit collaboration with Prince.

## Go Girls

**JULY 7TH: THE GO-GO'S RELEASE** their debut album, *Beauty And The Beat*, which will climb all the way to Number One in the US – though it takes all of eight months to get there. Before that, the all-female quintet's first taste of success will be with their Top 20 single 'Our Lips Are Sealed,' which guitarist Jane Wiedlin has co-written with Terry Hall (formerly of The Specials, now of Fun Boy Three). Keen to capitalize on their success, the former punks-turned-streetwise surf-popsters will release their second album, *Vacation*, in 1982,

## MAY

- **2ND:** **TOM PETTY & THE HEARTBREAKERS** score their first US Top 40 singles chart entry with 'The Waiting,' which will peak at Number One and remain there for six weeks.
- **5TH:** **IT'S ANNOUNCED** that Bobby Sands, an IRA hunger striker and recently elected member of parliament, has died. The hunger strikes began when Irish Republican prisoners demanded to be treated as political prisoners rather than criminals.
- **9TH:** **RICK SPRINGFIELD** releases a new single, 'Jessie's Girl,' in the US.
- **13TH:** **MEHMET ALI AGCA** barely escapes with his life after shooting the Pope four times in St Peters Square, Rome. Although badly injured, the Pope will recover. Agca's motives are unclear.
- **15TH:** **A RIOT BREAKS OUT** at The Ritz in New York City when PiL (Public Image Ltd) play a show entirely from behind a screen. The audience – who have waited for hours in the rain to watch their heroes perform – see only silhouettes, interspersed by filmed footage. Guitarist Keith Levene calls it "live video." It might be novel and intriguing at first, but matters are not helped by John Lydon berating the audience for paying "$12 for this." The show has to be stopped when fans at the front are hit by bottles thrown from the back of the hall.
- **16TH:** **KIM CARNES** reaches Number One on the US Top 40 singles chart with 'Bette Davis Eyes.' It stays there for five weeks.
- **22ND:** **THE YORKSHIRE RIPPER,** Peter Sutcliffe, is sentenced to life in prison for killing 13 women in the north of England. Sutcliffe has claimed to be on a divine mission to eliminate prostitutes.
- **26TH:** **THE ENTIRE ITALIAN CABINET** resigns after hundreds of government officials are linked to illegal masonic lodge P-2... Meanwhile, The Clash begin 17 nights of gigs at Bond's International Casino, New York.

## JUNE

- **4TH:** **THE PSYCHEDELIC FURS** release a new single, 'Pretty In Pink.'
- **7TH:** **AN IRAQI NUCLEAR** plant is destroyed by Israeli war planes... And a new medical report finds rare types of pneumonia, and later cancers, in the gay community. No one knows the cause.
- **8TH:** **WHEN THE CURE** begin a European tour at the Stadthalle, Freiburg, Germany, only 40 fans turn up.
- **10TH:** **SUPERGROUP ASIA** is formed with Carl Palmer (Atomic Rooster, ELP), Steve Howe (Tomorrow, Yes), John Wetton (Roxy Music, King Crimson), and Geoff Downes (from... Buggles).
- **13TH:** **A 17-YEAR-OLD YOUTH** fires six pistol blanks at Queen Elizabeth during the 'Trooping The Colour' ceremony in London. Marcus Sarjeant, from Folkestone in Kent, will be jailed for five years. The court heard that he had first tried to obtain a real gun, and wanted to be famous. Meanwhile, Smokey Robinson (above) reaches

which makes Number Eight. The third album, 1984's *Talk Show*, is the last before Wiedlin leaves for a solo career (the peak of which is 1998's 'Rush Hour'). She is briefly replaced by Paula Jean Brown, but by then both vocalist Belinda Carlisle and bass guitarist Kathy Valentine will be having drug problems, and the band breaks up in 1985. Belinda Carlisle (centre in main photo) soon gets herself together to launch her own successful solo career – initially with help from the band's lead guitarist Charlotte Caffey – quickly producing a string of Top Ten singles such as 'Mad About You,' 'Heaven Is A Place On Earth' (a Number One in both the US and UK), 'I Get Weak,' and 'Circle In The Sand.' Unlike The Go-Go's, Carlisle's profile will be stronger in the UK than in the US... The Go-Go's will reform briefly in 1990, and again at various points throughout the Nineties, and beyond, for gigs and occasional recording.

## JULY

## AUGUST

## Here Come The Planes

• JUNE 5TH: NEW YORK CITY avant-garde artist Laurie Anderson makes her debut on record with the eight-minute long single, 'O Superman.'

Number One in the UK (Two in the US) with 'Being With You,' his biggest hit since 'Tears Of A Clown' in 1970

• 15TH: THE POLICE begin recording their fourth album, *Ghost In The Machine*, at George Martin's studios on the Caribbean island of Montserrat. Producer Hugh Padgham recalls that the band's manager Miles Copland (brother of Police drummer Stewart) offered him the job over the phone, asking just two questions: "Did I want to produce it? I said yes. Did I take drugs? I said no. He said, 'OK, you're hired.'"

• 19TH: THE NATIONAL MUSEUM OF AMERICAN HISTORY admits losing George Washington's gold and ivory dentures.

• 20TH: THE DISCO-POP medley craze begins with 'Stars On 45' by Star Sounds – a segue of Beatle songs, curiously introduced by 'Venus' and 'Sugar Sugar,' all set over a constant disco beat. It will be followed, in the US and/or UK, by similar treatments of The Rolling Stones and Stevie Wonder, and even more novelty items like 'Punk On 45,' 'Stars Over 45,' and 'Christmas On 45.'

• 21ST: WAYNE B. WILLIAMS, a music promoter and talent scout, is arrested and charged after the most recent of 28 murders of black children and young adults in Atlanta... And Steely Dan split when founder members and songwriters Donald Fagen and Walter Becker announce they are going their separate ways.

• 23RD: ROBERT FRIPP proclaims the reformation of King Crimson, which has lain dormant for seven years.

• 26TH: THE ALBUM *Arc Of A Diver* by Steve Winwood is certified platinum in the US by the RIAA. It's also provided him with a Top Ten single, 'While You See A Chance.'

• 27TH: BRITISH BAND MOTORHEAD release their live album *No Sleep Till Hammersmith*, which will become their only Number One, opening with their best-known track, 'Ace Of Spades.'

• 1ST: JERRY LEE LEWIS is in a critical condition in hospital in Memphis, having been rushed there yeasterday with stomach pains, caused by a perforation in his stomach. After major surgery, he will recover enough to resume performing in a few months.

• 2ND: BRUCE SPRINGSTEEN plays the first of six shows to open the 21,000 capacity Brendan Byrne Arena, New Jersey.

• 3RD: A RIOT BREAKS OUT in the predominently Asian area of Southall, London, after a gig by Oi! band the 4 Skins. Oi! represents the second wave of lumpen aggressive punk outfits like Cock Sparrar, Angelic Upstarts, and Argy Bargy.

• JULY 29TH: DOUBTLESS AWARE of the money-making potential of today's royal wedding between the Prince of Wales and Lady Diana Spencer, which will be watched by 700 million on TV, a series of tacky cash-in records is released to coincide with the event – including 'Lady D' by Typically Tropical, 'Charlie's Angel' by Mini & The Metros, 'Diana' by Mike Berry, and numerous others.

• 9TH: THE JACKSONS, including Michael, begin their 36-date *Triumph* tour in Memphis, Tennessee. The tour will gross $5.5m.

• 11TH: THE SPECIALS reach the UK Number One slot with 'Ghost Town,' a song which reflects the depressed mood in parts of the UK, where racial tensions and youth riots are becoming alarmingly common... Later in the month, prime minister Margaret Thatcher announces new measures intended to combat unemployment, which is thought by many to be the root cause of the rioting, while ex-Tory leader Edward Heath insists Thatcher's own policies breed crime and race hatred.

• 13TH: DURAN DURAN release a new single, 'Girls On Film,' worldwide.

• 16TH: US SINGER-SONGWRITER Harry Chapin dies from a massive heart attack, brought on when a tractor crashes into his car in Jericho, New York state.

• 17TH: TWO CONCRETE and metal walkways in Hyatt Regency Hotel in Kansas City collapse, leaving at least 111 dead and almost 200 injured.

• 25TH: AIR SUPPLY – Australian 'soft-rockers' – reach Number One on the US Top 40 singles chart with 'The One That You Love'... Meanwhile Journey are about to have their biggest hit to date with 'Who's Crying Now.'

• 1ST: MTV, a new 24-hour video music channel, is transmitted for the first time on US cable TV. The video carefully chosen to open the broadcast is 'Video Killed The Radio Star' by Trevor Horn's Buggles.

• 5TH: THE CARTOON MOVIE *Heavy Metal* premieres, with music from such unlikely 'metal' stalwarts as Devo, Journey, and Stevie Nicks. It does however feature some real heavy metal, courtesy of Black Sabbath.

• 6TH: PRESIDENT REAGAN fires 12,000 US air traffic controllers whose three-day strike has grounded about half of the 14,000 daily airline flights.

• 7TH: THE EUROPEAN ECONOMIC COMMUNITY (EEC) orders the destruction of one million tons of fruit to maintain price levels.

• 8TH: RESPECTED SOUL back-up singer Luther Vandross begins his solo career, as his debut single, 'Never Too Much,' enters the US R&B charts en route to Number One.

• 15TH: AT THE ROSE BOWL in Pasadena, California, Stevie Wonder headlines the Black Family Fair, drawing 50,000 fans.

• 19TH: CHRIS LOWE meets Neil Tennant, browsing in a musical instrument shop in King's Road, London. The pair go on to form Pet Shop Boys.

• 22ND: *THE MONSTERS OF ROCK* festival at Castle Donington, UK, is headlined by AC/DC, in front of an audience of 65,000... And the brand new US Number One album is *4* by rockers Foreigner.

# The DJ's The Star

**S**EPTEMBER 3RD: 'THE MESSAGE' by New York DJ Grandmaster Flash & The Furious Five – with the memorably stark refrain, 'It's like a jungle sometimes, it makes me wonder how I keep from going under" – enters the UK Top 40, where it will peak at Number Eight. Though it will only reach 62 in the US, the record is nonetheless a crucial milestone in the history of DJ-ing and hip-hop music, demonstrating many of the techniques DJs will use for the next 20 years. In the early days of recorded music, the disc jockey was seen as little more than a live jukebox, a conduit for music which already existed – the only skill required was lifting a needle onto a record. But that began to change with the sound systems of Jamaica in the late 1950s and 1960s, when local DJs, operating bass-heavy mobile sound-systems, began talking, or 'toasting' over the records, while a 'selector' spun a selection of US black R&B tunes for people to dance to. In 1967, DJ Kool Herc (Clive Campbell) moved from Jamaica to New York, bringing recorded music to open-air venues, incorporating 'breaks' from various

## SEPTEMBER

- **1ST: 'SPASTICUS AUTISTICUS'** by Ian Dury (himself a polio sufferer), is banned in the Year Of The Disabled by radio stations who singularly fail to grasp the record's message.

- **5TH: THE NEW NUMBER** One album in the US is *Bella Donna* by Stevie Nicks of Fleetwood Mac fame.
- **15TH: DURAN DURAN** fly to New York City to begin their first US headlining tour.

- **20TH: BELIZE**, the last British colony in the Americas, gains independence.
- **25TH: THE ROLLING STONES** begin their tenth US tour with the first of two

dates in front of 90,000 fans at JFK Stadium, Philadelphia. The support act are Journey. In a ground-breaking commercial deal, the tour is sponsored by Chicago-based perfume company Jovan Inc.

- **SEPTEMBER 19TH: SIMON & GARFUNKEL** perform live (for the first time in nine years) in Central Park, New York, in front of 400,000 fans. Having resolved old differences, the pair stay together for further touring, and even start recording, before another rift in 1983.

## OCTOBER

- **1ST: WHEN MARTIN CHAMBERS** of The Pretenders accidentally cuts tendons and arteries in his hand on a broken window, the band is forced to end its current US tour.
- **2ND: THE UK'S LEADING** 2-Tone band, The Specials, decide to split, with some members going on to form the Fun Boy Three.
- **3RD: THE HUNGER STRIKE** in Belfast's Maze prison is finally called off, but not until ten people have died.
- **4TH: LEE HARVEY OSWALD'S** body is exhumed after doubts are expressed as to who, if anyone, is in the grave. Conspiracy theorists are disappointed to discover it is Oswald.
- **5TH: PRINCE** and his band play a 'secret' gig at Sam's, Minneapolis, Minnesota, under the name Controversy.
- **6TH: PRESIDENT ANWAR SADAT** of Egypt is assassinated by one of his own soldiers.
- **10TH: THE POLICE** enter the US chart with the future Number One, 'Every Little Thing She Does Is Magic.'
- **16TH: ISRAELI SOLDIER-STATESMAN** Moshe Dayan dies at

66 from a heart problem.
- **17TH: FORMER DOOBIE BROTHERS** roadie Christopher Cross tops the US Hot 100 with 'Arthur's Theme (The Best That You Can Do)'... And tonight is the first of two nights for The Rolling Stones at Candlestick Park, San Francisco – the gig attracts 146,000 fans, the biggest-ever audience for an open-air show in that city. The Stones are currently enjoying massive support in the US – their new, back-to-basics album *Tattoo You* has topped the US charts for nine weeks.

- **19TH: DEBBIE HARRY OF BLONDIE** is awarded a US gold disc for her solo album *Koo Koo,* produced by Nile Rodgers and Bernard Edwards of Chic.
- **30TH: THE HEAD** of UK euthanasia group EXIT, Nicholas Reed, is jailed for two-and-half years for "aiding and abetting" a suicide.

records, and inspiring later innovators like Grandmaster Flash. Flash, whose real name is Joseph Saddler, will further refine DJ arts like 'cutting' (sliding from one record to another without missing a beat), 'back-spinning' (manually pulling back records and repeating sections – as distinct from the more manic back-and-forth 'scratching' (invented by Grand Wizard Theodore) – and 'phasing' (manipulating playback speed for effect). He also pioneers what later becomes known as cross-fading, using a throw switch to flip blindingly fast between two turntables – hence the name Flash. The 'scratch wars' of early hip-hop in the Bronx follow. Movements like Chicago house, Detroit techno, and London rave (not to mention dub, garage, and drum & bass) will all be DJ-led. A Technics turntable will be as much a musical instrument as a guitar or keyboard, and DJs like Frankie Knuckles and Paul Oakenfold will be superstars – as celebrated, and well paid, as any pop or rock performer.

DECEMBER

## Vince & Alf

**DECEMBER 1ST: KEYBOARDIST/ SONGWRITER** Vince Clarke quits Depeche Mode. He says he doesn't feel comfortable in a band situation. He soon forms a duo with old acquaintance Alison Moyet, a big-voiced ex-punk blues singer who likes to go by the name of Alf. They call themselves Yazoo, taking the name from a US vintage blues label.

## NOVEMBER

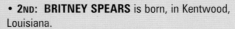

- **1ST: RCA RECORDS** in the US raises the price of 45rpm singles from $1.69 to $1.99.
- **4TH: THE ALBUM** *Private Eyes* by Daryl Hall & John Oates is certified platinum in the US... And Dr Nick (George Nichopoulus) is acquitted after being charged with over-prescribing addictive drugs to Elvis Presley.
- **16TH: AT THE CIVIC HALL**, in Wolverhampton, UK, Eric Clapton plays a one-off testimonial gig for British soccer player John Wile.
- **16TH: HOLLYWOOD STAR** William Holden dies, at age 63.
- **18TH: VAN HALEN** earn a US platinum disc for the album *Fair Warning*.
- **19TH: PAUL McCARTNEY** bids £21m ($32m) to gain full control of the publishing firm Northern Songs, which holds the Lennon-McCartney song catalogue. His bid is rejected by the current owner, Sir Lou Grade's ATV company.
- **22ND: MICK JAGGER**, Keith Richards, Ronnie Wood, Buddy Guy, and Muddy Waters jam at Chicago's Checker Board Lounge.
- **27TH: THE BPI** (British Phonographic Industry) launches its controversial 'Home Taping Is Killing Music' campaign.
- **29TH: ACTRESS NATALIE WOOD** drowns off the California coast, at the age of just 43.

- **DECEMBER 26TH: THE ALBUM** *For Those About To Rock (We Salute You)* by AC/DC – with school-uniform-wearing lead guitarist Angus Young, right – reaches Number One in the US.

- **2ND: BRITNEY SPEARS** is born, in Kentwood, Louisiana.
- **3RD: FOLLOWING RECENT** concessions gained by trade union Solidarity, Polish Premier General Jaruzelski imposes martial law, blaming the country's dreadful economic situation. The union will soon find itself outlawed and its leader Lech Walesa imprisoned.
- **5TH: 'DON'T YOU WANT ME'** by The Human League enters the UK charts on its way to Number One.
- **18TH: THIRTY FIVE MILLION PEOPLE** worldwide are estimated to be watching the satellite broadcast of a Rod Stewart concert from the Forum, Los Angeles, also featuring Tina Turner and Kim Carnes.
- **27TH: HOWARD 'HOAGY' CARMICHAEL**, legendary composer of 'Stardust,' dies at age 82.

- **NOVEMBER 14TH: AMERICA GOES** down under, as Australian musicians hold a record four spots on America's Top Ten : Air Supply with 'Here I Am (Just When I Thought I Was Over You);' Little River Band with 'The Night Owls;' Rick Springfield with 'I've Done Everything for You;' and Olivia Newton-John with 'Physical,' which stays at Number One for an exhausting ten weeks.

- **25TH: THE US STATE DEPT** is criticised for its decision to block a visit to the States by Ulster loyalist MP Rev Ian Paisley (above). The ban has come about due to pressure from members of Congress sympathetic to Irish unification... Meanwhile the J. Geils Band plays a Christmas gig for the inmates of Norfolk Correction Center, Massachusetts.

# 1982

## January–April

**F**EBRUARY 24TH: THE 1981 GRAMMY AWARD winners are announced. They include: Kim Carnes (right), winning Record Of The Year and Song Of The Year for 'Bette Davis Eyes'; John Lennon & Yoko Ono, winning Album Of The Year (*Double Fantasy*); Sheena Easton, Best New Artist; and Quincy Jones, Producer Of The Year. Former Monkee Michael Nesmith gets the first Video Of The Year award for his innovative long compilation, *Elephant Parts*. The Police get Best Rock Vocal Performance By A Group for 'Don't Stand So Close To Me,' and also Best Rock Instrumental Performance for 'Behind My Camel,' a track from the album *Zenyatta Mondatta*.

### JANUARY

- **JANUARY 14TH: THE ALBUM** *CONTROVERSY* **by Prince is awarded a US gold disc by the RIAA.**

- **1ST: THE LAST ABBA** concert, in Stockholm, Sweden.
- **3RD: AT HOME** in Holmdel, New Jersey, Bruce Springsteen begins recording demos which will become his album *Nebraska*.
- **9TH: LOS ANGELES GIRL-GROUP** The Bangs are compelled to change their name because another group already have that one. They become The Bangles.
- **11TH: MARK THATCHER**, son of the British prime minister, disappears in the Sahara while on the Paris-Dakar rally. He is later spotted by a search plane and rescued... And The Eurythmics play their first ever concert, at the Barracuda Club, London.
- **17TH: 'HI-HEEL SNEAKERS' MAN** Tommy Tucker dies at 48, after being overcome with fumes while renovating a floor at home.
- **21ST: B.B. KING** donates his huge record collection (from his DJ days) to The University Of Minnesota.
- **29TH: UK ELECTRONIC-ROCKER** Gary Numan emergency-lands his Cessna light aircraft on an English public highway near Winchester – but escapes unhurt.
- **30TH: SAM 'LIGHTNING' HOPKINS** dies at age 70.

- **JANUARY 20TH: AFTER HE BITES** the head off a bat thrown on stage by a fan, Ozzy Osbourne is hospitalized in Des Moines, Iowa, with suspected rabies. Ozzy claims later that he believed it was a rubber toy bat, not a real one... Later, on March 19th, Ozzy's guitarist Randy Rhoads will be killed when the tour plane crashes – apparently when a game of 'dive-bombing the tour bus' goes badly wrong.

## Keeping The Funk...

• APRIL 1982: GEORGE CLINTON, narrowly escaping the same fate as the increasingly drug-addled Sly Stone, has signed a solo record deal with Capitol Records in the US, at the age of 40. In his junior high school days Clinton was in a five-man doo-wop band with some classmates, which they called The Parliaments. After graduating, they opened a barber shop, where they straightened hair in the front and rehearsed in the back, and eventually managed a Top 20 hit in 1967 with '(I Wanna) Testify.' After a legal dispute with another similarly-named band, they became simply Parliament, while their backup band were known as Funkadelic, adding keyboard virtuoso Bernie Worrell and later several former members of James Brown's band, such as horn players Maceo Parker and Fred Wesley, and super-funky bassist Bootsy Collins. Funkadelic become ever more experimental and innovative – as on the sci-fi funk of *Mothership Connection* – and Clinton, with aliases like Dr Funkenstein, becomes a larger-than-life cartoon ringmaster to the whole circus. He will also be a major influence on the 'P-Funk' hip-hop scene, which liberally samples his music.

## FEBRUARY

• 4TH: ALEX HARVEY, underrated Scottish rocker, leader of The Sensational Alex Harvey Band, and popular live draw, dies of a heart attack in Belgium at the end of a European tour.
• 6TH: THE J. GEILS BAND reach Number One on the US Top 40 singles chart with 'Centerfold,' on the same day that their album *Freeze-Frame* reaches Number One... And Kraftwerk become the first German act ever to top the UK charts, with their re-released single, 'The Model.'
• 8TH: THE ALBUM *LOVERBOY* by Loverboy is awarded a US platinum disc.
• 13TH: PINK FLOYD'S *Dark Side Of The Moon* notches up its 402nd week on the *Billboard* Top 100, making it the longest-charting rock album ever.
• 14TH: FRANCOIS MITTERRAND, president of France, begins carrying out his campaign promises to nationalise banks and industry. Business groups call the take-overs "costly, useless, and dangerous."
• 15TH: 84 DIE when the Ocean Ranger oil platform sinks off the coast of Newfoundland.
• 17TH: JAZZ PIANO GREAT Thelonious Monk dies at 64.
• 18TH: JOHN SHARPLES of Preston, UK, sets a new world record by disco dancing for 371 hours.
• 19TH: JOHN DE LOREAN'S Belfast car company goes into receivership, ending the entrepreneur's attempt to start the first major car company in decades. The car he created will, however, be immortalised in the *Back To The Future* movies in a few years. De Lorean himself will be arrested in Los Angeles in October, for possession of 59 pounds of cocaine.

• 21ST: DJ MURRAY THE "K" KAUFMAN, who liked to call himself the fifth Beatle because he was the first US DJ to play their records – dies, age 60.
• 25TH: EUROPEAN COURT Of Human Rights upholds the ban on corporal punishment in UK schools.

## MARCH

• 1ST: VIRGIN SIGN UK band Culture Club.
• 5TH: US COMIC ACTOR John Belushi dies from a drug overdose at just 33.
• 6TH: *BEAUTY AND THE BEAT* by The Go-Go's reaches Number One on the US album chart, where it will remain for six weeks.
• 16TH: CLAUS VON BULOW is found guilty of the attempted murder of his wife, Martha, who is in a coma induced by a double injection of insulin. Von Bulow stood to inherit $14 million. He is sentenced to 30 years, but later acquitted when his legal team successfully argue that there were inconsistencies in the medical and scientific evidence at the trial.
• 17TH: US SOUL STAR Teddy Pendergrass is paralysed from the waist down when his Rolls-Royce hits a tree in Philadelphia, Pennsylvania.

• MARCH 1ST: DAVID BOWIE begins work on the film *The Hunger*, with Catherine Deneuve (below). Next day he's seen on British TV, starring in Berthold Brecht's *Baal*.

• MARCH 12TH: ELVIS PRESLEY'S former manager, Col Tom Parker (seen above with Elvis in happier times), files a lawsuit in Las Vegas, challenging the Presley Estate for control of the deceased singer's assets.

• 19TH: IN THE SOUTH ATLANTIC, an Argentinean scrap metal dealer lands at South Georgia in the Falkland/Malvinas islands and raises the Argentinean flag. He will be followed by troops on April 2nd, when Argentina invades.
• 24TH: UK POP DUO WHAM! sign a recording contract with Innervision Records.
• 26TH: THE FIRST TEST TUBE TWINS are born in hospitial in Cambridge, UK
• 27TH: HARRIET ADAMS, who wrote under various pen-names, but was author of *Nancy Drew*, *The Hardy Boys*, and *Tom Swift Jr*, dies at 89. She has apparently suffered a heart attack while watching *The Wizard Of Oz*.
• 28TH: DAVID CROSBY is arrested and charged with possession of drugs and firearms. Two weeks later he is re-arrested when police find cocaine in his dressing room at a Texas night club, and a gun hidden nearby.

## APRIL

• 6TH: REPRESENTING an athletic dorm at Oklahoma State University, aspiring singer Garth Brooks wins the $50 first prize in a student talent show.
• 7TH: IRON MAIDEN'S new album *The Number Of The Beast* goes to the top of the UK charts, and reaches 33 in the US.
• 7TH: THE ENVIRONMENT in and around the South Pole in Antarctica is now protected by international agreement.
• 14TH: PAUL McCARTNEY and Michael Jackson begin recording together at Westlake Studios, Los Angeles, California, with Quincy Jones producing.
• 15TH: BILLY JOEL is hurt in a motorcycle accident in New York.
• 17TH: THE MOVIE SOUNDTRACK *Chariots Of Fire* by Vangelis reaches Number One on the US album chart..
• 20TH: BIOLOGISTS DISCOVER forms of life 8,500 feet below sea level off the coast of California, surviving on little more than volcanic activity.
• 21ST: THE RECORDING INDUSTRY ASSOCIATION OF AMERICA (RIAA) tells a Senate Judiciary Committee that, "Home taping has exploded – it threatens the very livelihoods of thousands of retailers, distributors, suppliers and manufacturers who make the industry work."
• 24TH: JOHN COUGAR's single 'Hurts So Good' enters the US Hot 100 at 82, the first of his hits.
• 26TH: ROD STEWART is mugged on Sunset Boulevard, LA.
• 30TH: MUSIC JOURNALIST Lester Bangs dies of a heart attack at the age of 33.

## Planet Dance

JUNE 12TH: PIONEERING hip-hop/dance track 'Planet Rock' by New York DJ Afrika Bambaataa & The Soulsonic Force, produced by Arthur Baker, enters the US charts. It will peak at only Number 48 (53 in the UK), but its influence is almost incalculable. Essentially all strands of modern dance and club-oriented music will be traced back to here. Similar experiments with electronic sounds and looping beats to create music for the dancefloor will be taking place in Detroit and Chicago, but this is the first time it's appeared on record in such a striking way – the clearest glimpse yet in the mainstream of what's happening in underground dance clubs. 'Planet Rock,' itself rooted in Kraftwerk's 1977 single 'Trans-Europe Express,' spawns a million imitations, as well as galavanizing many new talents, from hip-hop to house and techno.

• MAY 22ND: **SOFT CELL** enter the US Top 40 with the old Gloria Jones soul favorite 'Tainted Love.' Though it'll be the band's only US hit, it's an enduring one, staying in the *Billboard* Top 100 for a record-breaking 108 weeks, and popping in and out of the UK charts five times over the next ten years.

• 6TH: **FORMER BAY CITY ROLLERS** manager Tom Paton is sentenced to three years in prison for acting in a "shameless and indecent manner" with ten teenage boys.

• 8TH: **NEIL BOGART** dies of cancer at the age of 39. A bubblegum music producer, he was the founder of Casablanca Records, home to Kiss, Donna Summer, and the Village People, and the man behind the solo success of Joan Jett.

• 8TH: **VANGELIS REACHES** Number One on the US Top 40 with the theme from the movie *Chariots Of Fire*.

• 12TH: **POPE JOHN PAUL II** escapes yet another assassination attempt, this time narrowly avoiding a knife attack in Portugal.

• 15TH: **'EBONY & IVORY'** by Paul McCartney & Stevie Wonder reaches Number One on the US singles chart.

• 18TH: **STING REVEALS** his annoyance that The Police song 'Don't Stand So Close To Me,' which he wrote, is being used in a Body Mist deodorant commercial on TV.

• 21ST: **CULTURE CLUB** release their debut single, 'White Boy,' in the UK.

• 23RD: **APPARENTLY** worried that drum machines and synthesizers could put musicians out of work, the UK Musicians Union puts forward a resolution to ban these new devices from recording studios.

• 24TH: **DRUMMER** Topper Headon leaves The Clash due to drug problems. Joe Strummer will later say that this was the point when The Clash should have called it a day.

• 27TH: **DURING A GIG** in Strasbourg, Robert Smith of The Cure has a fight with bassist Simon Gallup, which results in both of them leaving the band – temporarily.

• 28TH: **ARGENTINEAN DIEGO MARADONA** becomes the world's most expensive soccer player when he is sold to Barcelona for $8 million. Within 20 years, the record signing for one player will be more than ten times this amount.

• 28TH: **THE ALAN PARSONS PROJECT**, led by former Abbey Road engineer, who worked with the Beatles and Pink Floyd, has its biggest hit with the album 'Eye In The Sky.' The single even reaches US Number Seven.

• 2ND: **AT THE UNIVERSITY OF BERKELEY** in California, Professor Diogenes Angelokos is seriously injured by a bomb – the FBI begins its hunt for the Unabomber... Meanwhile the band Asia are awarded a US platinum disc by the RIAA for the album *Asia*.

• 5TH: **SOPHIA LOREN** leaves Italy after serving 17 days of a 30-day prison sentence for tax fraud, in the city of Caserta.

• 8TH: **PRESIDENT REAGAN** goes riding with Queen Elizabeth, has lunch with Margaret Thatcher, and makes the first speech to the British Parliament by a US President – but the speech is boycotted by nearly 200 members of the opposition Labour party.

• 10TH: **THE SHIRELLES' MICKI HARRIS** dies of a heart attack while performing in Los Angeles, at age 42... And The Clash release a new single, 'Should I Stay Or Should I Go,' in the US.

• 13TH: **FIFTEEN MEMBERS** of the Black Leopards Karate Club demolish a house in Alberta, Canada, with their bare hands and feet. Fortunately the owners have consented to the destruction.

• 14TH: **TEN WEEKS OF CONFLICT** on the Falkland Islands ends when British troops recapture the capital, Port Stanley, after the Argentine garrison surrenders. The islands, known to the Argentines as the Malvinas, lie 300 miles east of Argentina and 8,000 miles from the UK. A British colony since 1833, they were invaded by the Argentines in April after years of failed negotiations about sovereignty.

• 16TH: **JAMES HONEYMAN-SCOTT** of The Pretenders dies from a drug overdose, having taken a cocktail of heroin and cocaine.

• 19TH: **THE STEVE MILLER BAND** enter the US Top 40 singles chart with 'Abracadabra,' which will peak at Number One.

• 21ST: **THE PRINCESS OF WALES** gives birth to Prince William Arthur Phillip, making him second in line to the British throne.

• 26TH: **SURVIVOR RELEASE** 'Eye Of The Tiger,' the Sly Stallone-commissioned theme from *Rocky III*, which will spend several weeks at Number One in the US and UK, and be the band's biggest hit.

• 30TH: **AN EXTRA LEAP** second is added to the end of the day to bring the clock into alignment with solar time. It's the eleventh such adjustment since 1972.

• JUNE 11TH: **STEVEN SPIELBERG'S** movie *ET – The Extra-Terrestrial,* with atmospheric music by trusty adventure-epic composer John Williams, has its US premiere. Two of its stars are seen here watching for flying lawn-chairs...

## He's A Man

- **JUNE 30TH:** **ERIC CLAPTON** is joined onstage by Muddy Waters, at the climax of a US tour in Miami, Florida. Sadly, it'll be Muddy's last stage appearance – he dies, after a brief retirement, in April 1983. Born McKinley Morganfield in Mississippi in 1915, Waters was the father of electric blues – he started playing blues on the electric guitar back in the mid 1940s – an important precursor of rock'n'roll, and certainly of the British blues and R&B boom in the late 1950s and early 1960s. Without Muddy Waters there would be no Rolling Stones (who even took their name from his 1950 debut Chess single), no Yardbirds, no Eric Clapton, maybe no Hendrix. In the 1960s and 1970s Waters was involved in some ill-advised 'modern' projects, but found a blues soul-mate in Johnny Winter, who produced some of his best later work, including a hit reworking of 'Mannish Boy.'

**JULY**

- **JULY 3RD:** **'DON'T YOU WANT ME'** by the revamped Human League – now with backup singers Joanne Catherall and Susanne Sulley joining Phil Oakey, and musicians such as Jo Callis on guitar – reaches Number One on the US Top 40. The second British Invasion has begun...

- **4TH:** **OZZY OSBOURNE** marries his manager, Sharon Arden, in Maui, Hawaii. She is the daughter of notorious UK rock manager/impresario Don Arden.
- **5TH:** **BILL JUSTIS**, session saxophonist best known for the 1950s instrumental hit 'Raunchy' on Sun Records, dies at 55.
- **7TH:** **AT THE PRINCE'S TRUST GALA**, in London's Dominion Theatre, Phil Collins plays drums with Jethro Tull for three songs.
- **8TH:** **A PAN AMERICAN AIRWAYS** jetliner crashes in a residential area near New Orleans, killing all 145 on board and at least four people on the ground.
- **9TH:** **IN BUCKINGHAM PALACE**, London, the Queen wakes to find a strange man sitting at the end of her bed, dressed in jeans and a dirty T-shirt, cradling a broken ashtray and dripping blood from a cut hand. The intruder, 31-year-old Michael Fagan, had apparently planned to commit suicide in the Queen's bedroom, but decided it wasn't "a nice thing to do" once there. After they spend ten minutes talking, a chambermaid enters

the Queen's quarters and raises the alarm.
- **13TH:** **NEIL YOUNG'S** *TRANS* **TOUR** begins with a warm-up date at Catalyst, Santa Cruz, California.
- **15TH:** **MORE THAN 4,000 FOLLOWERS** of the Reverend Sun Myung Moon (commonly known as Moonies) are married in a mass ceremony at Madison Square Garden, New York City. Moon, South Korean founder of the Unification Church, was convicted only two months earlier of filing false US income tax returns.
- **16TH:** **THE FIRST** *WOMAD* (World Of Music And Dance) Festival, founded by Peter Gabriel, begins in Shepton Mallet, UK, featuring Drummers Of Burundi, Echo & The Bunnymen, Musicians Of Tthe Nile, Ustad Amjad Ali Khan, The Beat and Prince Nico Mbarga.
- **17TH:** **STEVIE RAY VAUGHAN** (right) and his band Double Trouble play a show at the *Montreux International Jazz Festival*, where they are seen by David Bowie, who will subsequently help propel Vaughan to international stardom when he invites him to play on his hit album *Let's Dance*.
- **23RD:** **US ACTOR VIC MORROW** (51) and

two Vietnamese children, age six and seven, are killed when a helicopter crashes during the shooting of the movie *The Twilight Zone*. One of the children is crushed, while Morrow and the other child are decapitated by the helicopter's blades. Director John Landis is among those charged with involuntary manslaughter, but later acquitted. Warner Brothers will pay several million dollars in compensation to the families involved.

## Chair Lift – Strange But True...

- **JULY 2ND:** **IN A RADIO MESSAGE** to the control tower at Los Angeles airport, the startled pilot of a TWA airliner reports that he's just seen a man in a large chair floating past his plane at 16,000 feet. This turns out to be 33-year-old truck driver Larry Walters, who's got there by attaching 40 large helium-filled weather balloons to his garden lawn-chair. He's always had an ambition, he explains later, to drift across his neighbourhood and out into the desert. And it starts as a fairly well-organised, if ill-conceived trip: he packs plenty of supplies, a two-way radio to keep in touch with friends and local air authorities, a parachute in case he has to bail out, some water-filled cannisters as ballast, and a BB gun to burst the balloons when he wants to come down. But when he untethers the chair, he suddenly rockets up thousands of feet into the air, and only manages to shoot a few balloons before he drops his gun. Several hours later, half-frozen, he gradually descends enough to get entangled in some power lines and is rescued. When the Federal Aviation Administration works out exactly what to charge him with, Walters receives a fine of $1,500. It also says it would revoke his pilot's license, except he doesn't have one.

**AUGUST**

- **6TH:** **PINK FLOYD'S** *The Wall* premieres in New York.
- **7TH:** *MIRAGE* by Fleetwood Mac is the new Number One album in the US.
- **11TH:** **THE ALBUM** *VANITY 6* is released in the US. Although all the songs are credited on the album cover to the band, Vanity 6, seven of the eight tracks are actually written by their famous mentor, Prince.
- **12TH:** **HENRY FONDA** dies aged 77. It is rumoured that shooting his final film, *On Golden Pond*, hastened his demise.
- **13TH:** **JOE TEX** dies of a heart attack, at age 49, in Navasota, Texas.
- **14TH:** **MOTHER THERESA** rescues 37 children from a badly shelled mental hospital in Beruit.
- **23RD:** *EYE OF THE TIGER* by Survivor is certified as a platinum album in the US.
- **28TH:** **AMID RUMOURS** that Blondie are to split, UK rock newspaper NME reports that the band's upcoming British tour has been cancelled... Meanwhile 'The Message' by Grandmaster Flash and the Furious Five enters the UK singles chart, where it will peak at Number Eight.
- **29TH:** **INGRID BERGMAN**, the Swedish actress who captivated audiences throughout the 1940s, loses her seven-year battle with cancer, age 67.
- **31ST:** Israel invades the Lebanon after the PLO move out of Beirut.

## Jam Today...

**O**CTOBER 30TH: **PAUL WELLER** announces that The Jam will be splitting. This is a surprise to both fans and bandmates, as the group are one of the most successful in the UK (though criminally under-acknowledged in the US). The trio – Paul Weller (vocals/guitars), Bruce Foxton (bass), and Rick Buckler (drums) – were snapped up in 1977 by Polydor, keen to get a punk band on its books. But their mod-styled sharp suits and hook-laden pop had more in common with 1960s bands like The Who, Kinks, Beatles, and Small Faces, and The Jam in fact proved more influential, and more popular, than the Pistols, Clash, and the rest. They attempted a couple of US tours in the late 1970s, one of which bizarrely paired them with The Blue Oyster Cult. Weller now goes on to form soul band The Style Council, and will later be revered as the father-figure of 'Britpop.'

## SEPTEMBER

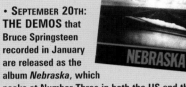

• SEPTEMBER 20TH: **THE DEMOS** that Bruce Springsteen recorded in January are released as the album *Nebraska*, which peaks at Number Three in both the US and the UK.

• 2ND: **KEITH RICHARDS'** Redlands home, in Sussex, England, is badly damaged by fire, almost ten years after it was rebuilt following an earlier blaze.

• 3RD: **CULTURE CLUB** release their third single, 'Do You Really Want To Hurt Me,' in the UK. Within a few months, it will become their big breakthrough international hit.

• 10TH: **PETER GABRIEL** releases his fourth solo album. Like the previous three, it is called *Peter Gabriel*... And Pablo Picasso's Spanish civil war painting *Guernica* returns to Madrid after 40 years in the USA.

• 11TH: 'HARD TO SAY I'M SORRY' by jazz-rock giants Chicago reaches Number One on the US Top 40 singles chart.

• 13TH: **GENERAL WILLIAM C. WESTMORELAND**, former US commander in Vietnam, sues CBS for $120 million, claiming the network libeled him in its recent documentary *The Uncounted Enemy: A Vietnam Deception.*

• 14TH: **PRINCESS GRACE** of Monaco (formerly actress Grace Kelly) dies when her car leaves the road and falls 120 feet. Her daughter Stephanie miraculously survives the crash.

• 15TH: **POPE JOHN PAUL II** outrages Israel by giving Yasser Arafat a private audience at the Vatican. The meeting helps solidify international recognition of the PLO as the official voice of the Palestinian people.

• 20TH: 'I LOVE ROCK'N'ROLL' by Joan Jett (left) & The Blackhearts is certified as a US platinum single.

## OCTOBER

• 1ST: **DUTCH-BASED** electronics giant Philips and Japan's Sony Corporation finally keep their four-year-old promise to release a marketable compact disc and appropriate hardware, launching the Sony CDP-101 player and 112 different CD albums – including Billy Joel's new *Nylon Curtain* and his 1978 Number One *52nd Street*, Simon & Garfunkel's *Bridge Over Troubled Water*, REO Speedwagon's *Hi Infidelity*, and Michael Jackson's *Off The Wall*. Soon consumers will be repurchasing albums they already own...

• 4TH: **GLENN GOULD**, the gifted Canadian pianist best known for his recordings of the works of Bach, and for humming along to his own playing, dies at the age of 50... And The Smiths play their first gig, at The Ritz, Manchester, UK, supporting Blue Rondo A La Turk.

• 5TH: **THE MANUFACTURER** of pain-reliever Tylenol recalls all capsules after hearing of the eighth case of strychnine poisoning caused by deliberate contamination of the pills.

• 7TH: **AFTER BEING** found guilty of cocaine possession, former Led Zeppelin guitarist Jimmy Page gets a 12-month conditional discharge and is fined £100.

• OCTOBER 27TH: **PRINCE RELEASES** the album *1999* in the US.

• OCTOBER 1ST: **JACK AND DIANE**, by John Cougar (not yet reverted to his given name of Mellencamp) is the new US Number One single.

• 11TH: **KING HENRY VIII'S** flagship, the Mary Rose, sunk during an engagement with the French in 1545, is raised from the sea-bed off the coast of Portsmouth in the UK. Most of its oak frame is intact, and complex preservation efforts begin.

• 12TH: **THE CLASH** support The Who during one of the latter's many farewell tours, at Shea Stadium, New York.

• 23RD: 'I RAN' BY A FLOCK OF SEAGULLS (best remembered for singer/keyboard player Mike Score's outlandish, lacquered fringe) enters the US Top Ten singles. It's further evidence of the invasion of British techno-pop on the US charts, hot on the heels of The Human League and Soft Cell.

• 26TH: **PRESIDENT REAGAN** awards 73-year-old singer Kate Smith the Medal Of Freedom for inspiring the nation with her rendition of Irving Berlin's 'God Bless America.'

• 29TH: **AT A PETER FRAMPTON** gig in Houston, Texas, one fan is shot dead, one stabbed to death, and another wounded.

## NOVEMBER

• 5TH: **FRENCH FILM DIRECTOR** and comedy actor Jacques Tati dies at 74.

• 6TH: **JOE COCKER** & Jennifer Warnes reach Number One on the US Top 40 singles chart with 'Up Where We Belong,' the love theme from *An Officer & A Gentleman.* Cocker's only previous Number One was his 1968 UK cover of The Beatles' 'A Little Help From My Friends.'

• 8TH: **SUFFERING** from anorexia nervosa, Karen Carpenter leaves the Manhattan Hospital, New York City, after a short stay. The following month she makes what will be her last live appearance, singing Christmas carols at Buckley School, Sherman Oaks, California. The show is attended by her godchildren.

• 10TH: **LEONID BREZHNEV**, leader of the Soviet Union for the past 18 years, dies at age 75. Two days later, 68-year-old Yuri Andropov is named as new General Secretary. He will only live for another 15 months.

• 16TH: **A NEW NATIONAL** economic survey confirms that the US is still in the depths of a severe recession. Indeed, figures show that unemployment in both the US and UK is at its highest level since World War II.

• 21ST: **JONI MITCHELL** marries her bass player, Larry Klein, in Malibu, California, at the home of Mitchell's manager Elliott Roberts.

• 24TH: **FRANKIE GOES TO HOLLYWOOD** record their first session for the BBC – four tracks recorded live for the John Peel radio show.

• **NOVEMBER 3RD: US EXPERIMENTAL-POP BAND DEVO** present what they describe as the first "video-synchronized" rock concert in Minneapolis, Minnesota, at the start of a US tour. For much of the show, the band, founded in Akron, Ohio, perform in front of, and interact with, a huge rear-projection screen showing animation, computer-graphics, song lyrics, and filmed sequences.

## DECEMBER

• **25TH: THE JAMAICA WORLD MUSIC FESTIVAL** begins in Montego Bay. Over the three days, acts

include Aretha Franklin, Peter Tosh, Gladys Knight, The Clash, Black Uhuru, Joe Jackson, The (English) Beat, Rita Marley, Rick James, and Squeeze.

• **27TH: TONI BASIL** (left), former actor/choreographer, is almost at the end of her two-year wait for her song 'Mickey' to become a major hit. Originally released in 1980, the track only really took off after the advent of MTV, with its TV-friendly promo video. It reached Number Two in the UK, and will top the US charts in just two weeks...

• **3RD: DURAN DURAN** release a re-mixed version of their current single, 'Hungry Like The Wolf,' in the US. It's this new version that effectively launches the band in America.

• **2ND: BARNEY B. CLARK** becomes the first person to receive a permanent artificial heart, in a seven-and-a-half-hour operation performed by a surgical team headed by Dr William DeVries at the University of Utah Medical Centre in Salt Lake City.

• **5TH: IN AIR STUDIOS**, Montserrat, The Police start work on their album *Synchronicity*. It'll be their final recording together.

• **8TH: COUNTRY SINGER** Marty Robbins dies from a heart attack, at 57.

• **9TH: THE LIONEL RICHIE** album *Lionel Richie* is awarded a US platinum disc by the RIAA.

• **12TH: 20,000 WOMEN** protest outside Greenham Common air-force base, near Newbury, UK. They are opposing the presence of US cruise missiles.

• **17TH: BIG JOE WILLIAMS** (best known for writing 'Baby Please Don't Go') dies at 79.

• **19TH: PIANIST ARTHUR RUBINSTEIN** dies peacefully in his Geneva home at 95 years of age... And Axl Rose leaves his home town of Lafayette, Indiana, and moves to Los Angeles, where he will form Guns N' Roses.

• **29TH: THE BOB MARLEY** stamp is issued in his home country of Jamiaca.

• **DECEMBER 1ST: MICHAEL JACKSON** releases the album *Thriller*. Impeccably produced by Quincy Jones, who has as usual assembled a team of top session musicians to help bring Jackson's inspired ideas to life, the album will go on to become the biggest-selling pop record ever, by some margin. (One of the statistics thrown around is that it will pass one million sales *in Los Angeles alone*.) It doesn't happen overnight, though: the first single from the album, the Paul McCartney duet 'The Girl Is Mine,' peaks at US Number Two (UK Number 10); it's the next single that will be the biggy...

# 1983

## CULTURE SHOCK

Having decided against boxing, the chosen profession of his father and two brothers, George O'Dowd (now known as Boy George) has been a colorful feature of the London club scene since 1978, initially attracting media attention for his exotic dress-sense and gender-defying make up, long before he gave any indication of musical talent. After a brief taste of band life with Malcom McLaren's post-Pistols project Bow Wow Wow, George formed his own group, initially called In Praise Of Lemmings, becoming Culture Club in 1981. Rejected by EMI, they signed for Virgin (following the same route as the Sex Pistols before them), and got together with producer Steve Levine. After a couple of false starts, they will release five Top Ten US hits in 1983, including the transatlantic Number One 'Karma Chameleon' – the video for which is astutely filmed, in period costume, aboard a Mississippi steamboat. Their smash-hit album *Colour By Numbers* is only held off the top of the US album charts by Michael Jackson's unstoppable *Thriller*. Ably backed by Mikey Craig on bass, Jon Moss on drums, and Roy Hay on guitar (seen right with George), it's undeniably the singer's charisma and unique image that sells – though it's perhaps surprising how keenly the relatively conservative US mainstream market embraces the act. It will be suggested, maybe unfairly, that many people start buying the records thinking the singer is a glamorous female, though many more become hooked simply by the easy reggae-pop of the music and O'Dowd's winning way with a melody. An unfortunate drop in support will begin in late 1984, when the group's 'War Song' is viewed as overly simplistic and trite, and the singer's own personal decline is capped in 1986 by the media revelation of his heroin addiction. A long, slow recovery will see George return as a club DJ, remixer, and solo performer, before Culture Club eventually reform for some triumphant and money-spinning global comeback concerts in 1998.

# 1983

## January–April

- **JANUARY 8TH:** 'SEXUAL HEALING,' the 'comeback' single from Marvin Gaye (left), becomes the first record in 20 years to rack up ten weeks at Number One on the US R&B singles chart. (The last was 'I Can't Stop Loving You' by Ray Charles.) It also makes the main Top Five in both the US and UK. Sadly Gaye's revival is short-lived – after a financially unsuccessful tour, later this year, he retreats to the netherworld of drug addiction, and moves back to live in his parents' house in LA.

- **1ST:** U2 RELEASE a new single, 'New Year's Day,' in the UK – it'll be their first big hit.
- **2ND:** NORWEGIAN pop band A-Ha move their base of operation from Oslo to London.
- **7TH:** *DAYLIGHT AGAIN*, the first album in five years from Crosby, Stills & Nash, goes platinum in the US.
- **13TH:** THE AMERICAN MEDICAL ASSOCIATION calls for a ban on boxing after new evidence suggests that chronic brain damage is prevalent in fighters.
- **15TH:** AUSTRALIAN band Men At Work have their second US Number One (their first in the UK) with 'Down Under.'
- **15TH:** CULTURE CLUB enter the US Top 40 singles chart with 'Do You Really Want To Hurt Me,' which will peak at Number Two.
- **22ND:** THE CLASH have their biggest US hit when 'Rock The Casbah' peaks at Number Eight... Meanwhile, following the recent demise of The Jam, their UK record company re-issues all of their 18 singles and, over the next four weeks, 14 of them re-enter the charts.
- **25TH:** WWII NAZI KLAUS BARBIE, known in France as "the butcher of Lyon," is arrested in Bolivia, before being returned to France to face trail.
- **26TH:** NEW ORDER debut their new single, 'Blue Monday,' at The Hacienda, a celebrated club in Manchester, UK.
- **29TH:** WIVES RECEIVE equal rights in the home in Greece... Meanwhile, not in Greece, Stevie Nicks of Fleetwood Mac marries Warner Brothers Records promotions man Kim Anderson.

- **4TH:** IN LOS ANGELES, Karen Carpenter of The Carpenters dies at 32, after complications arising from her anorexia nervosa.
- **5TH:** A MANUSCRIPT is authenticated as being written by Mozart, a symphony written when he was just nine years old... Meanwhile, Toto reach Number One on the US singles chart with 'Africa.' Later this month, this collection of former session musicians receive five Grammys for their album *Toto IV*.
- **8TH:** GIOVANNI VIGLIOTTO is found guilty of bigamy, after admitting to marrying more than 105 women in 33 years – spreading his activities around the US and a dozen other countries. He was arrested after making off with $36,000 after just two weeks of marriage to his latest victim.
- **9TH:** WEARING A TUXEDO, Frank Zappa conducts the San Francisco Music Players at the War Memorial Opera House in a concert of works by Varese and Webern. MC for the night is Grace Slick of Jefferson Starship.
- **12TH:** RAGTIME musician Eubie Blake (best known for 'I'm Just Wild About Harry') dies at the grand age of 100... And Rev Richard Czachor, director of the Catholic Youth Center, Scranton, Pennsylvania, cancels a planned show by Ozzy Osbourne because of the artist's recent behaviour, such as biting heads off bats and urinating on the Alamo.
- **15TH:** HEAVY METAL hopefuls Metallica move from Los Angeles to San Francisco.
- **25TH:** PETER PAUL & MARY reform after a 16-year hiatus.

- **1ST:** THE SWATCH watch is introduced in Zurich by Swiss company Asuag-SSIH. At first it comprises 12 colourful, thin, plastic, hard-wearing, and, most importantly, cheap models. This revolution in watch production will shift one million units within a year, 50 million within five years, and well over 200 million by the end of the century.
- **3RD:** A CLEVELAND HELL'S ANGEL tells a Senate Judiciary Panel that the California Angels have had a contract on the life of Rolling Stones vocalist Mick Jagger since the 1969 Altamont concert, after which a biker was jailed for killing an audience member... Meanwhile, Hergé (Georges Remi) the creator of Tintin, dies of anemia.
- **4TH:** HAVING PHONED a TV station in Jacksonville, Alabama, and let it be known he intends to set fire to himself, a very drunk Cecil Andrews proceeds to do just that, live on television... Elsewhere, Neil Young collapses from exhaustion on tour.
- **8TH:** PRESIDENT REAGAN refers to the Soviet Union as "the focus of evil in the modern world." The Soviets respond by insisting he has a "pathological hatred of communism and socialism." Two weeks later Reagan proposes a space-based laser weapons system called the Strategic Defence Initiative, or 'Star Wars' to the press.
- **15TH:** TOP UK RECORD PRODUCER Trevor Horn is listening when the Radio One's Kid Jensen show transmits four live tracks by unsigned Liverpool quartet Frankie Goes To Hollywood, including 'Relax.' Horn decides to sign the band to his new label, ZTT.
- **21ST:** IN CHINA, the People's Music Press publishes a guide entitled, *How To Distinguish Decadent Music*, singling out Elvis Presley as an example of the "expression of confused, blind excitement" and directing Chinese music-lovers to such wholesome home-grown songs as 'The Nightsoil Collectors Are Descending The Mountain.'

- **MARCH 7TH:** ELTON JOHN records 'I Guess That's Why They Call It The Blues' at AIR Studios on the island of Montserrat. His new album, which will be called *Too Low For Zero*, will be the first full album he's written with lyricist Bernie Taupin since they ended their seven-year rift.

## Brits Are Back

**M**ARCH 26TH: **DURAN DURAN** enter the UK singles chart at Number One with 'Is There Something I Should Know.' In the US, meanwhile, the band are having their first big hit with 'Hungry Like The Wolf.' It's the first of 13 US Top 40 singles between now and the end of the decade, two of which will make Number One ('The Reflex' in 1984 and 'A View To A Kill' the year after). The band, who took their name from a villain in the movie *Barbarella* (mis-spelling Durand-Durand), are never a favourite with the critics. The UK music press in particular, still deeply mired in the grime of punk, takes great exception to what it sees as a prime example of Thatcher's 'I'm all right Jack' Britain. The group initially lock into the increasingly commercialized new romantic scene, helped by their bouffant, pin-up poster boy image, but the synthesized leanings of the first album are soon replaced by a very efficient pop-rock outfit with a penchant for extravagant videos and exotic locations...

In 1983 there's a dramatic increase in the number of UK acts in the US Top Ten – 34 in all, the biggest tally since the height of Beatlemania in 1965. Some are well-established in Britian, like The Human League, ABC, and Culture Club, while others are more successful in the US than they at home. For instance, few people in Britain would know The Fixx, or Naked Eyes, yet they'll have four US Top 40 hits in this period: keyboardist/writer Rob Fisher will have more UK success when he forms Climie-Fisher. Other popular UK acts are little more than one-hit wonders in the US, including the likes of Soft Cell, Haircut 100, Kajagoogoo, and Dexy's Midnight Runners...

**APRIL**

• **APRIL 4TH: US ACTRESS** Gloria Swanson, silent movie queen and later star of the classic *Sunset Boulevard*, dies at the age of 86.

• **1ST: GLORIA STAVERS** dies of cancer at 51. Editor, writer and photographer for teen magazine *16*, Stavers is also credited with discovering Jim Morrison.

• **5TH: US INTERIOR SECRETARY** James Watt announces that rock bands like The Beach Boys and The Grass Roots are to be banned from playing at the annual Fourth Of July celebrations in Washington, DC, because they attract "the wrong element." The attack on the Beach Boys, almost a symbol of America by this stage, is universally condemned. In a year's time, Watt will no longer be in office and First Lady Nancy Reagan will personally invite the

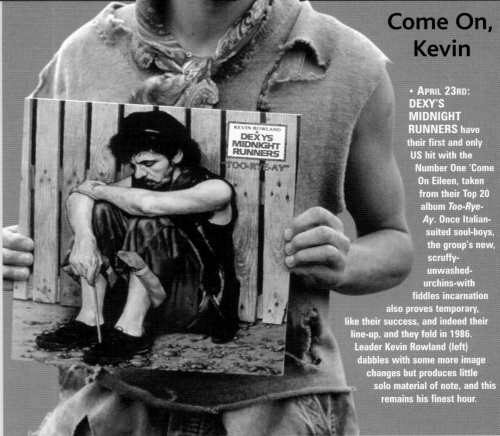

## Come On, Kevin

• **APRIL 23RD: DEXY'S MIDNIGHT RUNNERS** have their first and only US hit with the Number One 'Come On Eileen,' taken from their Top 20 album *Too-Rye-Ay*. Once Italian-suited soul-boys, the group's new, scruffy-unwashed-urchins-with fiddles incarnation also proves temporary, like their success, and indeed their line-up, and they fold in 1986. Leader Kevin Rowland (left) dabbles with some more image changes but produces little solo material of note, and this remains his finest hour.

## Billie Jean... King Of Pop

• **MARCH 5TH: MICHAEL JACKSON** begins a seven-week run at Number One in the US Top 40 singles with 'Billie Jean' – the track that will transform his already thriving career into something previously undreamt of. It's the makings of the King Of Pop... And it's not just his music that's attracting fans – his slick dance moves are said to be admired by no lesser hoofers than Gene Kelly and Fred Astaire.

band to come back and headline the free show in the grounds of the Washington Monument.

• **11TH: BOB DYLAN** begins recording sessions at The Power Station, New York City for his upcoming album, *Infidels*. Among the players on the record, welcomed as a return to form, is Mark Knopfler of Dire Straits.

• **14TH: HAVING RECENTLY** been fired from The Pretenders because of his drug problems, Pete Farndon is found dead in his bath after an overdose. It is only a year since the band's guitarist,

James Honeyman-Scott went the same way.

• **16TH: DEF LEPPARD** emerge from the so-called New Wave of British Heavy Metal to achieve their first US Top 40 singles chart entry with 'Photograph,' which will peak at Number 12. The album from which it is taken, *Pyromania* saw them emphasizing melody over metal and making the most of the promotional opportunities offered by MTV.

• **17TH: FELIX PAPPALARDI** (43) of US heavy rock band

Mountain, is shot dead in his New York aparment by Gail Collins, his wife and songwriting partner.

• **18TH: THE US EMBASSY** in Beirut is attacked by a suicide bomber, killing at least 40 people.

• **21ST: THE ONE-POUND** coin comes into circulation in Britain.

• **22ND: GERMAN MAGAZINE** *Stern* announces the discovery of Hitler's diaries – but they turn out to be fake.

• **24TH: TIMOTHY LEARY** is back at Harvard lecturing for the first time in 20 Years.

## Getting Serious

- **MAY 21ST:** **DAVID BOWIE** tops the US charts with his new single 'Let's Dance,' having just done the same in the UK. It's his first US Number One since 'Fame' in 1975.

**MAY**

## James's Shadow

**A**UGUST 2ND: AT 9PM, legendary Motown bassist James Jamerson (right) dies in USC County Hospital, Los Angeles, of complications arising from cirrhosis of the liver, heart failure and pneumonia. Throughout the 1960s and into the early 1970s, Jamerson was at the heart of the Motown sound, his melodic and forceful basslines a central element in the so-called Funk Brothers, the team of top-notch local musicians assembled by Berry Gordy when he set up his Hitsville studio in Detroit. His bass work drives tracks by everyone from The Supremes and Martha Reeves to The Four Tops and Marvin Gaye, and he's been an inspiration to countless bass players – including Paul McCartney – and other musicians who admired his work . Allan Slutsky's biography of Jamerson, *Standing In The Shadows Of Motown*, will later be filmed.

**JUNE**

- **4TH: PRESIDENT REAGAN** admits that the Contras, fighting the left-wing Sandinista government in Nicaragua, have been receiving covert aid from the CIA. But he insists they are "freedom fighters."
- **5TH: PILOT RICHARD BODDY** manages to miraculously land a Lockheed L-1011 at Miami airport after both engines fail.
- **12TH: OWING**

**MORE THAN $1M**, Meat Loaf is declared bankrupt in New York City.
- **13TH: UK BAND THE SMITHS** release their debut single, 'Hand In Glove.' It fais to chart.
- **14TH: 'CANDY GIRL'** by New Edition – the teenage group featuring Bobby Brown – is the new US Number One R&B single. Two weeks later the song will also hit Number One on the UK pop

chart.
- **14TH: KONRAD KUJAU**, the forger behind the 'Hitler Diaries,' gives himself up to police. Both *Stern* magazine and the London *Sunday Times* have recently published extracts, convinced they were the genuine article.
- **16TH: DJ RICK SOMMERS** of WBLI in Long Island, New York state, finds himself unwittingly

embroiled in a hostage situation when a former teacher kidnaps 12 children and uses Sommers as an 'on air' go-between. After having his demands read out – and having some of his favorite songs played – the kidnapper surrenders... Later tonight, the star-studded Motown 25 celebration is broadcast by NBC TV in the US, bringing The Temptations, Four Tops, Michael Jackson, The Jacksons, Diana Ross, Marvin Gaye, Stevie Wonder, Smokey Robinson, Linda Ronstadt, Adam & The Ants, and more together on

one stage.
- **28TH: DAVID BOWIE**, Van Halen, Judas Priest, Motley Crue, Quiet Riot, Ozzy Osbourne, Triumph, The Clash, The Pretenders, U2, Stray Cats, and the Scorpions are among acts at the US '83 Festival in Glen Helen Park, San Bernardino, California, which runs for the next three days. Bowie and Van Halen each net $1.5m for their appearances.
- **30TH: ELTON JOHN** arrives in Beijing to accompany English soccer club Watford FC, of which he is chairman, on a three-match tour of China.

- **MAY 7TH: HAVING SIGNED** a new record deal with Capitol Records in the US, Iron Maiden – pioneers of the New Wave Of British Heavy Metal – release the Top 20 album *Piece Of Mind*.

- **MAY 23RD: THE ALBUM** *The Final Cut* by Pink Floyd is awarded a US platinum disc by the RIAA. It's the last Floyd album to feature founder member and chief songwriter Roger Waters, who quits the band at this time – and may well expect that to spell the demise of the band. But he'll turn out to be mistaken...

## More Stars In Heaven...

- **JULY 29TH: DASHING** British actor David Niven, an old drinking pal of Errol Flynn, dies at the age of 74... And on the same day, provocative Spanish film director Luis Bunuel – who once famously said, "Thank God I'm an atheist" – passes away at 83.

- **3RD: ACUTELY PARANOID** as a result of drug abuse, Jim Gordon, rock drummer and co-writer of Eric Clapton's Layla, beats his mother to death with a hammer.
- **9TH: THE BIRTHDAY PARTY** play their final concert at the Seaview Ballroom, Melbourne, Australia. Their songwriter and vocalist Nick Cave will go on to a lasting solo career.
- **9TH: MARGARET THATCHER** is re-elected as Prime Minister of the UK.
- **10TH: METALLICA** begin recording their first album, *Kill 'Em All*, in New York City.
- **11TH: R.E.M.** are in Los Angeles, supporting The Human League at the Palace Theatre, when singer Michael Stipe is struck with an idea for a song which will eventually become 'So. Central Rain.'
- **13TH: 11 YEARS** into its journey Pioneer 10 becomes the

first spacecraft to leave the solar system.
- **25TH: THE POLICE'S** new (and final) album *Synchronicity* enters the UK album chart at Number One – it quickly makes the top spot on the US charts too. In two weeks' time, the first single from it, 'Every Breath You Take,' begins an eight-week stay at Number One in America (though it only manages a meagre four weeks at the top in the UK).
- **29TH: THE APOLLO THEATER** in Harlem, New York City, is designated a landmark site by the city's Landmarks Preservation Commission. As "the premier performance hall for practically every major black American performer," it has played its part in the careers of James Brown, Aretha Franklin and hundreds more. When it first opened, in 1914, the theater was not open to black people.

# Rapid Ear Movement

**M**AY 1ST: R.E.M. RELEASE their first album, *Murmur*. The foursome began life in the early 1980s when University of Georgia student Michael Stipe (vocals) met record store clerk Peter Buck (guitar) and formed a band with fellow students Mike Mills (bass) and Bill Berry (drums). They made their debut live appearance in April 1980, at a party in Stipe and Buck's apartment in an abandoned church. Short tours in the south-east of the US followed, building a fan-base, and in May 1982 R.E.M. signed to small independent label IRS Records, which released the *Chronic Town* EP – a hit with college radio stations. The debut album, *Murmur*, wins acclaim from *Rolling Stone*. It is followed in April 1984 by *Reckoning*, gaining more critical praise and college airplay but little commercial success. By 1985's *Fables Of The Reconstruction,* the band's grassroots approach will finally bear fruit, with the album selling several hundred thousand copies with little radio play. But the real breakthroughs come with 1986's *Life's Rich Pageant,* which goes gold, and then 1987's *Document,* which reaches the Top 10 and goes platinum, thanks to its single, 'The One I Love.' In 1988 R.E.M., now with Warner Bros, release *Green*. Highly influential on record, they also become a huge live act worldwide.

## JULY

- **1ST: AN OPINION POLL** conducted today finds that most US citizens have no idea who the US supports in Central America.
- **6TH: JEAN-MICHEL JARRE** releases his new album, *Music For Supermarkets*, in a limited edition of one copy, which is sold at auction to a French collector for 69,000 francs (about $12,000).
- **12TH: CHRIS WOOD**, former saxophone player with Traffic, dies of liver failure, age 39.
- **19TH: THE FOSSILISED** remains of a new breed of carnivorous dinosaur is discovered in a clay pit in darkest Surrey, UK... Meanwhile Simon & Garfunkel begin their latest reunion tour at the Rubber Bowl, Akron, Ohio.
- **21ST: MARTIAL LAW** is finally lifted in Poland, where it has been in force since December 1981 in a

crackdown against trade union Solidarity... In New York, torrential rain causes Diana Ross to abandon a free concert she is giving in Central Park after only a few songs. (She returns to finished the set the following day.)
- **23RD: AFTER THEIR SHOW** at Villa Park, Birmingham, UK, Duran Duran hold a party at The Rum Runner club, where John Taylor meets Robert Palmer and they discuss the possibility of working together. The result will be the band Power Station.
- **27TH: MORE THAN 100 PEOPLE DIE** after fighting between Sri Lanka's Sinhalese and Tamil communities, following the Tamils' demand for a separate state.

## AUGUST

- **3RD: PRINCE DEBUTS** his song 'Purple Rain' at First Avenue, Minneapolis, Minnesota.
- **5TH: TEXAN JUDGE** Pat McDowell sentences David Crosby to five years in jail for a 1982 drugs and firearms offence.
- **16TH: PAUL SIMON** marries actress Carrie Fisher (who played Princess Leia in *Star Wars*)

in a traditional Jewish ceremony in the singer's apartment overlooking Central Park, New York City.
- **16TH: THE WHITE HOUSE** admits the US helped Nazi war criminal

Klaus Barbie escape to Bolivia after the war. Barbie, currently on trial in France for war crimes, worked as an anti-communist spy for the US.
- **18TH: THE POLICE**, Joan Jett and R.E.M, play to 70,000 people at Shea Stadium, New York City.

- **24TH: TWO MONTHS AFTER** their marriage, Jerry Lee Lewis, fifth wife, Shawn, is found dead in their Mississippi home from an accidental overdose of prescribed drugs.

- **MAY 28TH: BRITISH BAND MADNESS** – whose ska-derived tunes and manic videos have already brought more than a dozen Top 20 hits back home – enter the US charts for the first time with their biggest transatlantic track, 'Our House,' which will peak at Number Seven.

# 1983
## September–December

SEPTEMBER

OCTOBER

- **1ST: A RUSSIAN FIGHTER** plane shoots down a Korean 747, flight number KAL-007, which accidentally strays over a military base on Sakhalin Island. All 269 passengers are killed, including a US congressman. The incident is initially covered up by the Soviets, and becomes the subject of years of conspiracy theory... Meanwhile The Clash announce that founder-member Mick Jones is to be sacked.
- **8TH: A CYCLIST FROM CZECHOSLOVAKIA** floats his family of four – plus his bicycle – over the Iron Curtain to freedom, using an air-balloon made of stitched-together raincoats filled with helium.

- **SEPTEMBER 3RD: EURYTHMICS REACH** Number One on the US Top 40 singles chart with 'Sweet Dreams (Are Made Of This).'

- **18TH: KISS APPEAR** for the first time without their trademark make-up, on MTV.
- **20TH: ERIC CLAPTON**, Jimmy Page, Jeff Beck, Steve Winwood, Bill Wyman, Kenney Jones, Charlie Watts, and others, take part in a fund-raising benefit at the Royal Albert Hall, London, in aid of former Faces bassist Ronnie Lane, who suffers from multiple sclerosis.
- **26TH: AUSTRALIAN YACHT** Australia II becomes the first non-American boat to win the Americas Cup for 132 years
- **27TH: AT HIS HOME** in St Catherine's, Jamaica, reggae artist Prince Far I is shot dead by gunmen.

- **OCTOBER 1ST: BONNIE TYLER REACHES** the top of the US singles chart with 'Total Eclipse Of The Heart,' making her the first Welsh artist to have a US Number One – even Tom Jones only ever made Number Two.

- **3RD: THE SINGLE** 'Say, Say, Say,' a duet featuring Paul McCartney and Michael Jackson, is simultaneously released in the UK and US.
- **5TH: POLISH TRADE UNION LEADER** Lech Walesa wins the Nobel Peace prize.
- **6TH: R.E.M.** make their US national TV debut, performing 'Radio Free Europe' and 'So. Central Rain' on NBC's *David Letterman Show.*
- **10TH: UK ACTOR** Ralph Richardson dies at age 80.
- **18TH: THE POLICE** play to an audience of 70,000 at Shea Stadium, New York City.
- **20TH: LEGENDARY COUNTRY** guitarist/songwriter Merle Travis dies of a heart attack in Nashville, Tennessee, aged 65.
- **22ND: A QUARTER OF A MILLION** people attend an anti-nuclear rally, organised by CND (Campaign for Nuclear Disarmament) in London. Similar protests take place in Belgium, Netherlands, West Germany, France and the U.S... And Culture Club notch up one million sales of 'Karma Chameleon,' making it only the third platinum single in the UK in the 1980s.
- **25TH: PRESIDENT REAGAN** orders troops into Grenada to remove the left-wing government put in place by a recent coup. The UN criticise the move as a violation of international law.
- **29TH: KENNY ROGERS** and Dolly Parton reach US Number One with 'Islands In The Stream,' written and produced by Barry Gibb of the Bee Gees.
- **31ST: TV NEWS PRESENTER** Christine Craft, who was awarded $500,000 in a recent sex discrimination case, sees her award overturned when a Federal judge rules that her employers were justified in sacking her because she was "too informal, too opinionated and lacking in warmth."

# Charmers

**N**OVEMBER 12TH: BRITISH BAND The Smiths have their first hit when 'This Charming Man' enters the Uk charts... Occasionally a band will happen along who are so much more than the sum of their influences, and so separate from any transient scenes, that it's hard to imagine how – or indeed why – they existed at all. The Smiths, formed in 1982, are just such a group, having nothing in common with the self- aggrandizing obsessions of the new romantic scene and being totally removed from the nihilistic thrashings of punk. Overnight, The Smiths all but invent the UK's alternative rock scene. They marry guitarist Johnny Marr's masterful, and varied, guitar compositions – no flash, solo-heavy posturing here – to (Stephen Patrick) Morrissey's off-kilter vocals, which deliver deeply intimate, introverted and angst-filled lyrics. All this is reliably underpinned by a steadfast engine-room rhythm section of Andy Rourke on bass and Mike Joyce on drums, The Smiths are a breath of fresh air for music fans more interested in words and music than Max Factor or grunting violence. Denounced as fey, miserable, and/or asexual by some, The Smiths are in fact inspired songwriters, trading in intelligent, thoughtful and timeless rock music. They are also, to their fans at least, definitely sexual – Smiths' shows are always awash with fans throwing themselves wildly at their hero Morrissey (right), desperate to touch the man who has so deeply touched them. In the five years that follow The Smiths will produce five exceptional albums, before stuttering to an untidy close in the late 1980s amid nasty litigation.

## NOVEMBER

• **NOVEMBER 12TH: LIONEL RICHIE** begins four weeks at Number One in the US Top 40 singles chart with 'All Night Long (All Night).'

• **3RD: RCA RECORDS** signs a $30m recording deal with Puerto Rican teen sensations Menudo. The boy group are famous for

having a perpetually changing line-up – whenever one member gets too old, he is simply replaced, but the group itself always continues.

• **3RD: JESSE JACKSON** announces his intention to run as Democratic Presidential candidate First African-American ever to do so.

• **10TH: MICROSOFT** announce Microsoft Windows 1.0, an extension of the MS-DOS operating system that will provide a Macintosh-style graphical operating environment for IBM-compatible PC users. Bill Gates wants to call it Interface Manager, but is persuaded against. It is planned to go on sale in 1984, but, it doesn't actually appear in the shops until November 1985.

• **13TH: IN DALLAS**, Texas, at a

Police concert in the Reunion Arena, fan Paula Lewellen sustains a broken arm. She later sues the band for $300,000.

• **19TH: TOM EVANS**, 36-year-old former bass player with Badfinger, is found hanged at his home in Surrey, UK.

• **26TH: SIX ROBBERS** break into the Brinks-Mat warehouse at Heathrow Airport, London, expecting to find £3 million ($4.8m). Instead, they find 6,800 bars of gold bullion, worth £26 million ($41m).

• **28TH: ANOTHER RONNIE LANE** benefit concert, with a similar line-up to the London gig, this time in Dallas, Texas.

• **30TH: THE JACKSONS** hold a press conference at Tavern On the Green, New York City, to announce their upcoming *Victory Tour*, sponsored by Pepsi.

• **NOVEMBER 21ST: MICHAEL JACKSON'S *THRILLER* VIDEO**, costing over $1m and directed by Jon Landis, celebrated for his recent *An American Werewolf in London*, is premiered at the Metro Theater, Westwood, California.

## DECEMBER

• **DECEMBER 3RD: WOMEN PEACE PROTESTORS** break into the Greenham Common military base in Berkshire in the UK, where US nuclear cruise missiles are stationed... Meanwhile DeBarge reach Number One on the US R&B singles chart with 'Time Will Reveal.'

• **1ST: NEIL YOUNG** is sued by Geffen Records for $3m. The label claims that his album, incongruously titled *Everybody's Rockin'* is "not commercial in nature and musically uncharacteristic of his previous albums."

• **6TH: WHEN ASIA PERFORM** at the Budokan Stadium, Tokyo, Japan, the show is broadcast live on MTV to 20 million viewers in Japan and America.

• **8TH: ANNIE LENNOX** of Eurythmics flies to Vienna, Austria, to see a throat specialist, after experiencing

problems during a show at the Lyceum, London.

• **10TH: MADONNA** achieves her first US Top 40 single with 'Holiday', which will peak at Number 16.

• **14TH: NEW PHOTOS** from the Very Large Array radio telescope in New Mexico reveal a 'black hole,' 2.6 times the mass of the Sun, at the heart of the Milky Way.

• **16TH: A HEAVY METAL** football match is played between Def Leppard and Iron Maiden, in Dortmund, Germany... And The Who officially split up, but will later reconvene for Live

Aid and further tours.

• **17TH: AN IRA CAR BOMB** kills six Christmas shoppers outside Harrods department store in London.

• **18TH: JAMES BROWN** guitarist Jimmy 'Chank' Nolan dies at the age of 47.

• **20TH: FORMER PRESIDENT GERALD FORD** makes a cameo appearance on U.S soap *Dynasty*.

• **28TH: BEACH BOYS' DRUMMER** Dennis Wilson – the band's only real surfer – drowns while swimming off his boat at Marina Del Rey, California. He was 39.

# 1984

## January–April

- **2ND: APPLE COMPUTER** releases the Macintosh, the first affordable computer to be based entirely around a 'graphical user interface,' meaning windows, icons and a mouse. Even so, at $2,495, it's still not very affordable. Using the new Motorola 68000 chip, significantly faster than previous processors, and running at 8MHz, the Mac comes in a small beige case with a built-in black & white monitor, and has a keyboard, a mouse, and a built-in floppy drive that takes 400k 3.5" disks – the first personal computer to do so.

- **JANUARY 28TH: FRANKIE GOES TO HOLLYWOOD** goes to Number One in the UK with 'Relax,' the song that launched a million 'Frankie Says...' T-shirts. The song will become a belated US hit a year later, reaching Number Ten. The group take their name from an old newspaper headline about Frank Sinatra going to Hollywood to make a movie, and will inspire several copycat bandnames, including Pepe Goes To Cuba, and Bonzo Goes To Washington.

- **7TH: PINK FLOYD'S** *Dark Side Of The Moon* notches up its 500th consecutive week in the Billboard Top 200 albums.
- **10TH: CYNDI LAUPER** becomes the first female singer since Bobbie Gentry to be nominated for five Grammy Awards (Best Album, Best Record, Best Song, Best Vocal Performance and Best New Artist).
- **10TH: THE US** and the Vatican establish diplomatic relations for the first time in 100 years.
- **11TH: KENNY LOGGINS** releases 'Footloose,' the title song from the movie of the same name, which stars Kevin Bacon, in his first big role, as a boy who moves to la town where rock music and dancing are banned. The song will go on to reach Number One in the US.
- **14TH: THE MAN BEHIND** the expansion of the McDonalds hamburger empire, Ray A. Kroc, dies at the age of 81. Kroc was promoting a milkshake machine when he visited the McDonald brothers at their sole hamburger stand in California in 1954. He persuaded them to let him start a chain that went on to have branches in 31 countries. Eating will never be the same again... And tonight, when US TV show *Saturday Night Live* asks viewers to phone in their choices for the US

- **JANUARY 20TH: ACTOR JOHNNY WEISSMULLER,** Olympic swimmer famous for playing Tarzan, dies at age 79.

Democratic candidate, 131,384 votes are cast for ZZ Top.
- **17TH: THE SUPREME COURT** rules it is legal for people to tape television programs for their own use.
- **21ST: BRITAIN'S FIRST** test-tube triplets, a girl and two boys, are born to a couple in London.
... And Jackie Wilson, who never recovered after his 1975 collapse, dies in a New Jersey nursing home.
- **27TH: WHILE FILMING** a TV commercial for Pepsi Cola, Michael Jackson's hair is set alight.

- **8TH: THE 14TH WINTER OLYMPIC** games opens in Sarajevo, Yugoslavia (later Bosnia-Herzegovina). Some 1,579 athletes from 50 nations participate. Sadly the Olympic facilities will mostly be destroyed during the war in Bosnia.
- **9TH: SOVIET LEADER** Yuri Andropov dies. A former chief of the KGB, Andropov succeeded Leonid Brezhnev in late 1982 and was in power for less than 15 months. He will be replaced by Konstantin Chernenko... And at the British record industry awards in London, Culture Club are Best Group, David Bowie is Best Male Artist, and Paul Young

is Best Newcomer.
- **14TH: ELTON JOHN** marries Renate Blauel, a German sound engineer, in Sydney, Australia.
- **16TH: JERRY LEE LEWIS** surrenders to US Federal Authorities who are pursuing him on charges of tax evasion. After posting bail of $100,000 he is released.
- **22ND: DAVID,** known as the Boy In The Bubble (as mentioned in Paul Simon's song), dies after a failed bone marrow transplant. He has spent just 15 days of the last 12 years outside of sterile isolation, after being born with combined immune deficiency.
- **25TH: VAN HALEN** reach Number One in

the US Top 40 singles chart for the first of five weeks with 'Jump.'
- **28TH: BOB DYLAN** and Stevie Wonder induct nominees at the Grammy Awards Ceremony in Los Angeles, California. Michael Jackson scoops a remarkable eight Grammys. The Police get Song Of The Year and Best Pop Performance By A Group With Vocal (phew) for 'Every Breath You Take,' and also Best Rock Performance By A Group With Vocal for 'Synchronicity 2,' apparently inspired by Carl Jung.
- **29TH: CANADIAN PRIME MINISTER** Pierre Elliott Trudeau announces his retirement.

## Lucky Star?

• **April 14th:** 'BORDERLINE' BY MADONNA enters the US singles chart, where it will be her first Top Ten entry (her first UK hit will be 'Holiday,' although not until it's re-released in 1985). She is still a few years away from establishing herself as the most famous female pop star ever – which will be due as much to her astute business and promotional sense as her skill with a song. Madonna Louise Veronica Ciccione, born August 16th, 1958, wanted to be a ballerina as a child, until the lure of drama at Rochester Adams High School opened her eyes to performance. Hoofing with various dance troupes through the late 1970s and early 1980s, she only found a clear direction after signing to Sire in 1982, with debut single 'Everybody' and follow-up 'Physical Attraction' making more than a few ripples in the clubs and dance charts. Then, after the release of her debut album *Madonna* in 1983, 'Holiday' crossed over to the mainstream US charts, beginning an extraordinary run of 17 consecutive Top Ten hits – most of which were helped on their way by a series of undeniably sexy videos. Her second album, 1985's *Like A Virgin*, kick-starts Madonna-mania with a vengeance, as hordes of young girls begin dressing like their idol, and young boys find their heads filled with impossible fantasies – not to mention a few exceptionally catchy pop songs.

## Against All Odds

• **April 21st:** PHIL COLLINS, the former Genesis drummer, reaches Number One on the US Top 40 with his solo single 'Against All Odds (Take A Look At Me Now).' It's the first of a string of 13 US Top 10 hits between now and 1990, making Collins one of the more unlikely contemporary adult pop stars of the 1980s, a decade in which image became at least as important as talent. Certainly not known for his dashing good looks, he began his entertainment career as a child actor (appearing in a stage production of *Oliver* in 1964), before joining progressive rockers Genesis in 1970, while maintaining a separate career as drummer with jazz-rockers Brand X. Promoted to the front of the stage after Peter Gabriel jumped ship in 1974 (and only after the band had auditioned as many as 400 other singers), Collins launched his parallel solo career in 1981 with the album *Face Value* and hit single 'In The Air Tonight,' followed swiftly by *Hello I Must Be Going*. Collins will successfully balance Genesis with his other projects (including acting) throughout the 1980s, but his success begins to cause friction within the group, and he will eventually go entirely solo in 1996.

---

**MARCH** | **APRIL**

• **3rd:** LEGENDARY REGGAE rhythm section Sly Dunbar and Robbie Shakespeare celebrate ten years together with a concert in Kingston, Jamaica.

• **5th:** IRAN ACCUSES IRAQ of using chemical weapons.

• **5th:** CBS RECORDS reports that the Michael Jackson album *Thriller* has now sold 19.4m copies in the US alone, and 30.9m worldwide.

• **12th:** THE NATIONAL UNION of Mineworkers in the UK begins a 51-week strike over pit closures, clashing directly with the political agenda of the Thatcher government.

• **15th:** THE THREE SURVIVING Beatles (Paul McCartney, George Harrison and Ringo Starr) are named as freemen of the city of Liverpool, UK, a great honor from a city that had often officially ignored its most famous sons. McCartney arranged to receive the award in Liverpool before the premiere of his film *Give My Regards To Broad Street*.

• **17th:** DOMINIC 'MAD DOG' McGLINCHEY, top of the list of most wanted Irish terrorists, is captured after a 90 minute gun battle in County Clare, Ireland. McGlinchey was chief of the Irish National Liberation Army, who admitted responsibility for more than 200 shootings and 30 deaths.

• **20th:** 'EVERY BREATH YOU TAKE' by The Police is chosen as Song Of The Year at the Fifth Annual National Music Publishers Association Song Awards in Beverly Hills, California.

• **22nd:** GEORGE MICHAEL and Andrew Ridgeley, two school friends from Hertfordshire, UK, calling themselves Wham!, are signed to Epic Records.... And Andrew Lloyd Webber marries singer/dancer Sarah Brightman.

• **28th:** MICK FLEETWOOD of Fleetwood Mac files for bankruptcy in California, with $3.7m in debts and assets of only $2.4m.

• **4th:** IN GEORGE ORWELL'S prophetic novel *1984*, Winston Smith begins his secret diary.

• **6th:** SATIRICAL DOCUMENTARY or, if you will, 'rockumentary' *This Is Spinal Tap* has its US premiere, in New York City. Featuring a group of American comedy actors as a British heavy metal act enduring a disastrous tour and the long slide into obscurity, it becomes an enduring cult.

• **6th:** SOUTH AFRICAN athlete Zola Budd is granted UK citizenship, thanks to her British grandfather. This decision means she can now compete in the Olympic games from which, as a South African citizen, she has been banned.

• **11th:** THE ROLLING STONES sue former manager Allen Klein to reclaim song copyrights from before 1972.

• **23rd:** THE DISCOVERY of HIV, the virus which may cause AIDS, the fatal disease sweeping the world, is hailed as a breakthrough in medical research. Even so, by 1997 AIDS will still have killed over two million people, and 30 million people will still be believed to be carrying the virus.

• **April 26th:** JAZZ LEGEND COUNT BASIE dies of pancreatic cancer in a Florida hospital, at the age of 79.

# 1984

May–August

## Let's Hear It For The Ectoplasm

• **August 11th:** 'GHOSTBUSTERS' BY RAY PARKER JR reaches Number One on the US Top 40 singles chart. Taken from the soundtrack of the spectral-slime-slaying movie, starring Dan Aykroyd and Bill Murray, it's not the only hit this year to come straight from a movie: *Footloose* provides chart-toppers for Kenny Loggins (the theme tune) and Deniece Williams ('Let's Hear It For The Boy'), while Gene Wilder's *The Woman In Red* helps 'I Just Called To Say I Love You' become one of Stevie Wonder's best sellers, if not exactly one of his artistic high-points.

## His Name Is Prince

• **June 25th:** PRINCE RELEASES the album *Purple Rain* in the US, and it sells 1.3m copies on its first day. Its first single, 'When Doves Cry,' will also become his first Number One, staying at the top for five weeks this summer. Often overshadowed by the less prolific, and some would say less talented, Michael Jackson, Prince may not benefit from as much hype as Jacko, but he'll produce a back-catalogue that's a wonder to behold. Fusing funk with hi-octane rock, and possessing a natural ear for a pop hook, Prince is also downright dirty, which gives the whole package even more allure. While earlier efforts lacked the pop-funk edge, *Purple Rain* qualifies him for deity status, complete with a preposterously overblown movie. Next year he'll shake psychedelia by the scruff of the neck on *Around The World In A Day*, before throwing everything into 1997's pivotal *Sign O The Times*.

### MAY

• **1st:** THE CLASSIC Deep Purple line-up of Richie Blackmore, John Lord, Ian Paice, Roger Glover and Ian Gillan (the latter fresh from a nine-month stint with Black Sabbath), reconvene for the first time since they parted company in 1976. The reunion will result in a new album *Perfect Strangers*, followed by another split, then another reunion, another split and...

• **4th:** 'DANCING IN THE DARK' is released, giving Bruce Springsteen his biggest single yet, reaching Number Two on the US charts. (It will only reach Number Four in the UK.)

• **5th:** CHRISSIE HYNDE of The Pretenders marries Jim Kerr, frontman of Simple Minds, in Central Park, New York City.

• **7th:** THE ALBUM *She's So Unusual* by Cyndi Lauper is awarded a US platinum disc by the RIAA.

• **8th:** THE USSR boycotts the Los Angeles Olympics, which comes as no real surprise, because the US boycotted the 1980 Moscow Olympics.

• **16th:** LAWYERS acting on behalf of Michael Jackson obtain an injunction in New York City preventing the sale of unauthorised merchandise bearing his likeness.

• **18th:** PRESIDENT REAGAN has a small non-malignant polyp removed from his colon.

• **23rd:** SOME $17,000 WORTH of box office receipts are stolen while The Clash are on stage at Michigan State University.

• **23rd:** THE SURGEON GENERAL C. Everett Koop announces that there is now solid evidence that non-smokers can suffer lung damage from other people's smoke. But the effects of passive smoking are dismissed by the Tobacco Institute, the smoking industry's lobbying organization, as negligible.

• **28th:** BOB DYLAN plays his first show in two-and-half-years in Verona, Italy, at the start of a European tour. This is reckoned by some Dylan scholars to have been his worst concert ever.

• **29th:** BRITISH COMEDIAN Eric Morecambe dies, age 58. With his partner Ernie Wise, he had dominated UK TV comedy in the 1970s.

### JUNE

• **1st:** THE ALBUM *Break Out* by The Pointer Sisters is awarded a US gold disc by the RIAA... Meanwhile, Box Of Frogs, featuring ex-Yardbirds Chris Dreja, Jim McCarty and Paul Samwell-Smith (plus former Medicine Head man John Fiddler), release their debut single 'Back Where I Started'.

• **7th:** POLYGRAM'S CD factory in Hanover, Germany, produces its ten millionth compact disc since opening in 1982.

• **8th:** DONALD DUCK is awarded an honorary membership of the Screen Actors' Guild to mark his 50th birthday.

• **16th:** EX-10CC MEMBERS Godley and Crème raise eyebrows when they direct a video for the new Frankie Goes To Hollywood single 'Two Tribes.' It features lookalikes of Ronald Reagan and Soviet Premier Chernenko fighting hand to hand in a wrestling ring.

• **18th:** AT A JUDAS PRIEST concert in Madison Square Garden, New York, rioting fans tear up hundreds of seats.

• **22nd:** RICHARD BRANSON'S Virgin Atlantic Airways, the first airline owned by a record business mogul, is launched.

• **June 4th:** BRUCE SPRINGSTEEN'S album *Born In The USA* is released worldwide. It will spend four weeks at Number One in America, and eight months later it will reach Number One in the UK, where it will log a serious 128 weeks on the chart.

## Loose Talk

AUGUST 11TH: PRESIDENT REAGAN, during what he believes is an unrecorded voice test into a microphone in a radio studio, makes an impromptu speech: "My fellow Americans, I am pleased to tell you today that I have signed legislation that will outlaw Russia forever. We begin bombing in five minutes." The distasteful joke is picked up and heard by millions of people. Thankfully nuclear carnage is narrowly avoided, but the incident shaves seven percentage points off Reagan's popularity.

## Smooth Operator

• JULY 9TH: SADE RELEASE their debut album, *Diamond Life*, in the UK. The group, fronted by Nigerian-born, UK-based singer Sade Adu, will have two hit singles from the album: 'Your Love Is King' and 'Smooth Operator.' That one will also reach Number Five in the US nine months from now (Number One on the Adult Contemporary chart). Sade's smooth, jazzy grooves have wide cross-cultural appeal, and prove perfect for mid-1980s audiences. The album is appreciated by authentic soul fans of all ages, and also looks good on the coffee tables and CD racks of the aspiring *nouveau riche* – a new class of young, upwardly-mobile urban professionals, known as 'Yuppies.' Sade will do well with future albums, such as *Promise* and *Stronger Than Pride*, before splitting. Sade herself returns with another seamless groove on *Love Deluxe* in 1992, followed in 2000 by *Lovers Rock*, a Top Five hit in both US and UK.

## JULY

• 5TH: **MICHAEL JACKSON** announces that he will donate all of his earnings from The Jacksons' *Victory* tour to charity. This year will turn out to be his last with The Jacksons, and from now on he will concentrate on solo work.

• 7TH: **THE BOB DYLAN/CARLOS SANTANA** tour of the UK arrives at Wembley in London, where guests onstage include Eric Clapton, Van Morrison and Chrissie Hynde.

• 12TH: **GERALDINE FERRARO** becomes the first woman ever to run for vice president, as running mate to Democratic presidential hopeful Walter Mondale.

• 14TH: **PHILIPPE WYNNE**, 43-year-old lead vocalist with The Spinners (known as The Detroit Spinners in the UK) dies of a heart attack after leaping from the stage during a nightclub performance in Oakland, California.

• 20TH: **JAMES FIXX**, author of *The Complete Guide To Running* (who once remarked, "The qualities and capacities that are important in running – such factors as will power, the ability to apply effort during extreme fatigue and the acceptance of pain – have a radiating power that subtly influences one's life'), dies after suffering a heart attack while jogging.

• 21ST: **UK ROCK LEGENDS** Status Quo play what is billed as their last gig, at Milton Keynes Bowl. They will, however, reform to play Live Aid, and resume touring in 1986.

• 23RD: **MISS WORLD** winner Vanessa Williams – the first black woman to win the title – is stripped of her crown when it is discovered she had posed nude for *Penthouse* magazine. Runner-up Suzette Charles, who is also black, accepts the position.

• 25TH: **RUSSIAN ASTRONAUT** Svetlana Savitskaya becomes the first woman to walk in space... And blues singer Willie Mae 'Big Mama' Thornton, dies at the age of 57.

• 28TH: **THE 23RD OLYMPIC GAMES** open in Los Angeles... And a Free Nelson Mandela benefit concert is staged at Crystal Palace Bowl, London, featuring Jimmy Cliff, Aswad, Gil Scott-Heron, Hugh Masakela, Benjamin Zephaniah and others. A song called 'Free Nelson Mandela,' by Jerry Dammers and The Specials, has just reached Number Nine in the UK.

## AUGUST

• 1ST: **STEVIE WONDER** releases a new single, 'I Just Called To Say I Love You,' in the US.

• 4TH: **'CARELESS WHISPER,'** the first solo single by George Michael of teen idols Wham!, enters the UK chart on its way to Number One.

• 5TH: **BRITISH ACTOR** Richard Burton dies from a stroke, at the age of 59, shortly after finishing the movie *1984*.

• 6TH: **THE VIDEOCASSETTE** of Pink Floyd's *The Wall* is certified gold in the US.

• 10TH: **RUNNER ZOLA BUDD**, born in South Africa but running for the UK, accidentally trips American Mary Decker, the favorite, during the 3,000m race at the Olympics. Decker falls and is out of the race, while Budd limps home seventh. Afterwards, a distraught Decker refuses to accept Budd's apology.

• 14TH: **MICROSOFT** releases MS-DOS version 3.0, an operating system designed to accompany IBM's new, more powerful AT personal computer.

• 15TH: **BRITISH NOVELIST J.B. PRIESTLEY** dies just short of his 90th birthday.

• 16TH: **JOHN DELOREAN**, the man behind the De Lorean car that was intended to be produced in Northern Ireland, is acquitted of cocaine smuggling charges after the jury decides he was entrapped.

• 18TH: **AROUND 65,000 FANS** attend the Monsters Of Rock festival at Castle Donington, UK. They see and hear AC/DC, Van Halen, Ozzy Osbourne, and Motley Crue.

## Fries With That Shake?

• AUGUST 28TH: **TINA TURNER** honors a commitment to play at a McDonalds convention in Ottawa, Ontario, Canada. The gig was arranged before her return to major success with 'What's Love Got To Do With It,' which is about to be declared America's new Number One single. It'll be Turner's biggest hit, and her first US Top 20 entry since 1971.

# 1984

September–December

## Brighton Rocked

**O**CTOBER 12TH: **THERE IS A BOMB** attack on the British government while its members are taking part in the annual Conservative party conference in Brighton, on the South Coast. The town's Grand Hotel is partly destroyed by a bomb that explodes at 2.40 am, killing five and injuring more than 30, including two senior Cabinet ministers. Prime Minister Margaret Thatcher and her husband Denis narrowly escape injury. In 1986, Irish Republican Army bomber Patrick Magee will be jailed for 35 years for the attack. He will be released early, in 1999, as part of the Northern Ireland peace process.

## SEPTEMBER

- **5TH: AT A PRESS CONFERENCE** in Los Angeles, Michael Jackson's manager Frank DiLeo reads a statement from the troubled star refuting allegations about cosmetic surgery and his sexual orientation.
- **8TH: BILLY OCEAN** reaches Number One on the US R&B singles chart with 'Caribbean Queen.'
- **14TH: DRESSED AS A BRIDE** and singing 'Like A Virgin,' Madonna hi-jacks the first MTV Video Awards, in Radio City Music Hall, New York City, by simulating sexual activity on the stage.
- **19TH: PRESIDENT REAGAN** declares that Bruce Springsteen's ironic 'Born In The USA' represents, "Hope ... and helping make those dreams come true is what this job of mine is all about."
- **20TH: MARVIN GAYE'S FATHER** pleads 'no contest' to charges of voluntary manslaughter of his son. He will receive five years probation.
- **26TH: BRITAIN AND CHINA** sign an agreement to return the Hong Kong colony to China in 1997

- **SEPTEMBER 20TH: FIRST SHOWING OF THE COSBY SHOW**, starring comedian Bill Cosby. Frustrated by persistent stereotyping on TV (where the black guy is either a drug dealer or pimp) and noting the lack of any entertainment shows depicting a typical 1980s middle-class family who happen to be African-American, Cosby decides to create one of his own. The Cosby Show quickly becomes a massive hit, and its star becomes not only a US institution, but the highest-paid actor on TV.

## OCTOBER

- **1ST: US SCIENTISTS** warn that global warming is on the increase, due to the burning of fossil fuels and release of 'greenhouse' gases... And U2 release their album *The Unforgettable Fire*.
- **2ND: YET ANOTHER RECORD** is set after Russian astronauts return from a 237 day orbital space flight.
- **4TH: ELAINE YADWIN, 61**, lands her husband's Piper Cherokee light aircraft after he dies from a heart attack while it is in flight. She has no flying experience, and has to be talked down by an instructor.
- **5TH: THE LARGEST** space flight crew in history take off in Challenger... Meanwhile, Queen play the first of eight days at Sun City Super Bowl, Bophuthatswana, a black 'homeland' created by the South African government.
- **11TH: HAVING COLLAPSED** from exhaustion in his dressing room, Elton John is forced to cancel a show in Charlotte, North Carolina.
- **13TH: MICK JAGGER OF THE ROLLING STONES** and wife Jerry Hall throw a party at their New York City home, with guests including Jack Nicholson, Andy Warhol, Whoopi Goldberg, Mike Nichols and Art Garfunkel.
- **26TH: DR LEONARD L. BAILEY** implants a baboon's heart into a 15-day old infant at Loma Linda University Hospital in California. However, the procedure proves unsuccessful and baby Fae dies after only 20 days.
- **26TH: ARNOLD SCHWARZENEGGER** stars in *The Terminator*, the start of a long-running franchise.
- **27TH: DURING A GIG** in Berkeley, California, the Grateful Dead set aside an area for fans who want to bootleg the show.
- **30TH: GEORGE HARRISON** announces that, unlike Paul McCartney, he has declined the Freedom of the City of Liverpool, an honor bestowed by his home town.
- **31ST: INDIAN PRIME MINISTER** Indira Gandhi is killed by two of her own bodyguards. They are Sikhs, avenging the storming of their sacred Golden Temple in Amritsar last June. She is succeeded by her son, Rajiv Gandhi.

## Beach Bums

- **DECEMBER 17TH: WHAM! REACH** Number One on the US Top 40 with 'Wake Me Up Before You Go Go.'

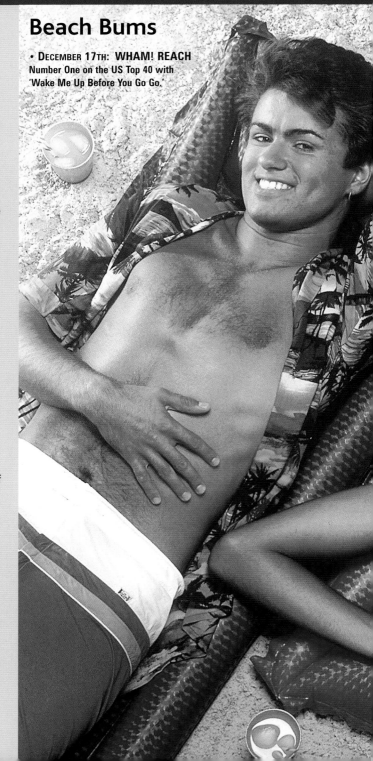

## Wounded Leppard

• NOVEMBER 9TH: **WES CRAVEN'S** original *Nightmare On Elm Street* movie is released, making an instant star of pizza-faced, blade-fingered, stripy-sweatered anti-hero Freddy Krueger.

• DECEMBER 31ST: **RICK ALLEN** (right), drummer with heavy rockers Def Leppard, badly injures his arm in a car wreck. Several days later it will be amputated — but the band refuse to replace the 20-year-old drummer (who's been with them since he was 15), deciding to wait until he is well enough to perform again. Allen has to learn new techniques requiring only one arm, and will employ special equipment and later digital technology to once again master the full drum kit.

**NOVEMBER**

**DECEMBER**

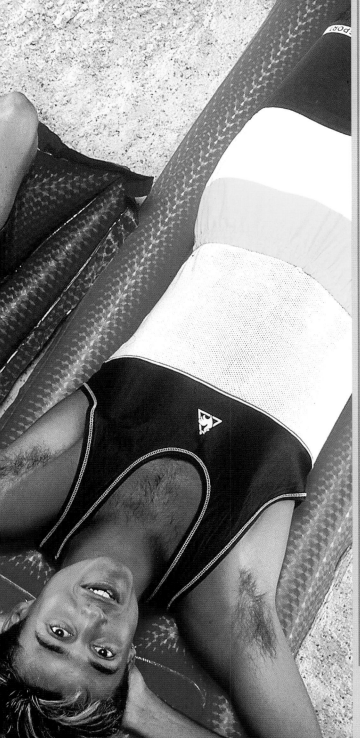

• 2ND: **VELMA BARFIELD**, a 52-year-old grandmother who had murdered four people, becomes the first woman to be executed in America since 1962, the first since the re-introduction of the death penalty in 1976, and the first woman to be executed by lethal injection.
• 4TH: **PRINCE BEGINS** his Purple Rain tour with seven sold-out shows at the Joe Louis Arena, Detroit, Michigan.
• 6TH: **PRESIDENT REAGAN** is re-elected in the greatest Republican landslide in history, winning 49 states against Democrat Walter Mondale.
• 10TH: **THE DEBUT ALBUM** by Frankie Goes To Hollywood, called *Welcome To The Pleasuredome*, enters the UK chart at Number One. It features their three consecutive Number One singles, 'Relax,' 'Two Tribes,' and 'The Power Of Love,' which together keep them at the top of the charts for 15 weeks in 1984.
• 19TH: **500 PEOPLE** are killed when a liquid petroleum gas plant explodes in Mexico.

• NOVEMBER 25TH: **RECRUITED BY FORMER BOOMTOWN RATS** leader Bob Geldof (above), nearly 40 pop stars gather in SARM Studios, London under the name Band Aid, to record a charity single in aid of Ethiopian famine relief. The song is 'Do They Know It's Christmas' (with the chorus of "Feed The World"). Artists giving up their time include Sting, George Michael, Culture Club, Duran Duran, Spandau Ballet, Frankie Goes To Hollywood, and Bananarama, with Phil Collins on drums. The single will quickly make Number One in the UK, and stay there for five weeks over the holiday period.

• 20TH: **MICHAEL JACKSON** is awarded a star on Hollywood's Walk of Fame.
• 24TH: **FOREIGNER** release the single, 'I Want To Know What Love Is,' which will be their first, and only, Number One.

• 3RD: **MORE THAN 2,000 PEOPLE DIE** from poison gas emissions in Bhopal, India. As many as 200,000 more will go on to suffer blindness, kidney or liver failure as a result of the leak at the Union Carbide pesticide factory outside the town.
• 8TH: **VINCE NEIL** of Mötley Crüe is charged with manslaughter and drunk driving, relating to an incident in which he lost control of his Pantera car on Redondo Beach, California, resulting in the death of Nicholas 'Razzle' Dingley, drummer of Hanoi Rocks. He is eventually sentenced to 30 days in jail and must pay $2.6m compensation.
• 10TH: **SOUTH AFRICAN BISHOP** Desmond Tutu is awarded the Nobel Peace prize just three days after meeting Ronald Reagan to discuss US policy on South Africa.
• 12TH: **THE US WITHDRAWS** from the United Nations Educational, Scientific and Cultural Organisation (UNESCO) charging the organisation with mismanagement, politicisation and "endemic hostility."
• 15TH: **SOVIET PRESIDENT** Mikhail Gorbachev, second in command in the Soviet Union, visits London and has 'positive' talks with Margaret Thatcher.
• 22ND: **MADONNA** reaches Number One on the US Top 40 singles with 'Like A Virgin.'
• 26TH: **THE SONGS** 'COCAINE' (by Eric Clapton) and 'Sister Morphine' (by the Rolling Stones) are banned at a festival in Indonesia for promoting drugs.
28TH: **US MOVIE** director Sam Peckinpah dies at 59.

# 1985

## THE WORLD IS WATCHING

The largest television audience of all time will tune in on Saturday July 13th this year to watch the great and the good of the rock and pop world perform for free in the world's biggest fund-raising musical extravaganza. It would be easier to try and think who isn't at *Live Aid* than who is – see p196 for a list of the better-known participants, many of whom are personally cajoled by Bob Geldof into appearing at either the London or Philadelphia event. In one memorably enterprising stunt, Phil Collins will contrive to perform at both concerts, thanks to a supersonic ride on Concorde and some private helicopters. A few minor technical gremlins aside (negligible faults considering the technological scale of the broadcast), the event is an unparalleled triumph for Geldof and the production team, but the central message is always repeated – viewers are implored to donate much-needed cash to combat famine in Ethiopia and similarly drought-stricken and economically-desperate nations. And so they will, by the sack-load. (Not that it solves the world's problems, but it does help alleviate a few temporarily.) The sheer scale of the project, and improbable logistics – like finding a schedule that would screen as many big names as possible at peak times around the world, and include snippets from the many other concerts on the day, from Australia to Russia – coupled with the raw enthusiasm and single-minded ambition of Geldof, and the goodwill towards such a novel idea, make *Live Aid* a unique event. It also makes it hard to envisage it ever happening again... Which is a shame. But on the other hand, if it were to become an annual event, it would surely lose its impact. There may be future global fund-raising events, but could there be another *Live Aid*?

# 1985

## January–April

### REO / AOR / FM

MARCH 9TH: REO SPEEDWAGON hit Number One on the US Top 40 singles with 'Can't Fight This Feeling.' It's a prime example of the Eighties AOR 'power ballad', but because the band have been toying with this particular track for around ten years before it's released, they know it as "that stupid ballad" – at least until it becomes a hit. Other classic examples from this era are Foreigner's 'I Want To Know What Love Is,' Cutting Crew's '(I Just) Died In your Arms Tonight,' 'Broken Wings' by Mr Mister, and Boston's 'Amanda.' It's a great sound for ever-expanding FM radio stations – nicely produced, clean but full-bodied, laid-back but powerful... Multi-million-selling REO Speedwagon (who got their name from an old fire engine, if you wondered) even appeared in the 1978 movie *FM*, as if to prove the point.

### JANUARY

- **1ST: DUSTY HILL** of ZZ Top is accidentally shot in the stomach by his girlfriend, Jane Ellen Henderson. She is pulling his boots off when his gun falls to the floor and goes off.
- **2ND: PAUL McCARTNEY** turns down a £1m ($1.5m) offer to appear as a wealthy British landowner in eight episodes of US TV soap *Dallas*.
- **7TH: PRINCE'S ALBUM** *Purple Rain* is confirmed as America's biggest seller since *Thriller* by Michael Jackson.
- **18TH: GRATEFUL DEAD** leader Jerry Garcia is caught freebasing in a car in Golden Gate Park, San Francisco, and is sentenced to enter a drug-aversion program and play a benefit concert.
- **21ST: RONALD REAGAN** has to be sworn into office twice, once for real and once for the Super Bowl football audience whose game clashed with the ceremony.
- **23RD: THE THIRD LEG** of U2's massive Unforgettable Fire tour begins at the Drammenshalle, Drammen, Norway.
- **28-29TH: ENCOURAGED** by the Band Aid effort in the UK, the USA For Africa single 'We Are The World' is recorded at A&M Studios, Los Angeles, with Michael Jackson, Lionel Richie, Bob Dylan, Stevie Wonder, Bruce Springsteen, Ray Charles, and Diana Ross. It will top the US charts for four weeks when it's released in March. (It also makes Number One in the UK for two weeks.)
- **29TH: OXFORD UNIVERSITY** lecturers vote against offering Margaret Thatcher an honorary degree.

- **MARCH 1ST: TEARS FOR FEARS** release their second album, *Songs From The Big Chair*. Although they've already had a Number One album in the UK with 1983's *The Hurting*, *Big Chair* will be a major breakthrough for them in the US, reaching the top of the album charts and delivering two US Number One singles, 'Shout' and 'Everybody Wants To Rule The World.'

FEBRUARY     MARCH     APRIL

- **1ST: GLENN FREY** of the Eagles makes his acting debut in US TV show *Miami Vice*. The episode is based on Frey's song 'Smuggler's Blues.'
- **2ND: SPANDAU BALLET** announce their intention of suing their label Chrysalis for not supporting them.
- **5TH: TERRY WAITE**, a Church of England envoy, secures the release of four Britons, who have been held hostage in Libya for nearly nine months.
- **7TH: NEW YORK CITY** mayor Ed Koch announces that Frank Sinatra's 'New York New York' has been adopted as the official musical anthem of the city.
- **8TH: FRENCH RESEARCHERS** report that they have had "significant results" with a new anti-AIDS drug called HPA-23.
- **12TH: THE BAND** playing under the name 'Hornets Attack Victor Mature' at the Uptown Lodge, Athens, Georgia, is actually R.E.M.
- **16TH: GEORGE MICHAEL** reaches Number One on the US Top 40 singles with 'Careless Whisper.'
- **23RD: THE SMITHS** achieve their first UK Number One album with *Meat Is Murder*.
- **26TH: WHEN THE GRAMMY AWARDS** are held at the Shrine Auditorium, Los Angeles, Bruce Springsteen collects his first Grammy, for Best Male Vocalist on 'Dancing In The Dark.' At the same ceremony, veteran rocker Chuck Berry is given a Lifetime Achievement Grammy.

## Two Virgins

- **JANUARY 10TH: 'LIKE A VIRGIN'** by Madonna is certified as a gold single in the US. A month later the album of the same name begins a three-week stint at Number One on the US album charts.

- **MARCH 3RD: STRIKING UK COAL MINERS** finally call it a day after almost a year of industrial action. Within two more days, more than 85 per cent are back at work. But not necessarily for very long…

- **2ND: THE FBI** arrest more than 20 neo-Nazis in the US. Known variously as The Order or The Silent Brotherhood, they are thought to be behind the murder of talk-show host Alan Berg and a plot to overthrow the government.
- **6TH: IN THE BRITISH HOUSE OF COMMONS**, Conservative MP Ivan Lawrence speaks for 4 hours 23 minutes on fluoridation of water – the longest speech this century.
- **11TH: MOHAMMED AL FAYED** buys Harrods, the upmarket London department store.
- **13TH: MIKHAIL GORBACHEV** becomes head of the Soviet Union, following the funeral of Konstantin Chernenko. At 54, he is the youngest ever member of the ruling Politburo.
- **16TH: US JOURNALIST** Terry Anderson is kidnapped in Beirut; he will not be released until December 4th, 1991, after being

held in captivity for 2,454 days.
- **21ST: BRUCE SPRINGSTEEN** begins his first ever Australian tour with five nights at the Entertainment Centre, Sydney, Australia.
- **23RD: BEN HARDWICK**, Britain's youngest liver transplant patient dies in hospital aged just three… And Billy Joel marries blonde model Christie Brinkley, who appeared in his 'Uptown Girl,' aboard a yacht in New York City harbor.
- **25TH: PRINCE WINS** an Oscar for Best Original Song Score in his movie *Purple Rain*. At the same ceremony, Stevie Wonder gets the Best Song award for 'I Just Called To Say I Love You.' He dedicates his award to Nelson Mandela.
- **29TH: PAUL SIMON** begins two weeks in South Africa working with local musicians, to create tracks for his comeback album *Graceland*.

- **2ND: PRINCE** issues a statement declaring that he is about to stop live performances.
- **5TH: WHAM!** arrive in Peking, China, to begin a brief tour – the first ever by a Western pop band. They visit the Great Wall and are honoured with a banquet by the Chinese Youth Federation. During the tour, the band's trumpet player Raul De Oliviera suffers a breakdown during a flight to Canton and tries to stab himself with a penknife.
- **9TH: 300 PEOPLE** are fighting fires on the Galapagos Islands – the archipelago that inspired Charles Darwin's 'Origin Of The Species' – and attempting to

rescue some of the giant tortoises too cumbersome to escape the blaze.
- **11TH: THE ROLLING STONES** assemble at Pathé Marconi studios in Paris, France, to begin recording a new album, which will become 1986's *Dirty Work*… Meanwhile, scientists on Hawaii measure the distance between the earth and moon to within one inch, rather than the previous, rougher calculation of 240,000 miles.
- **15TH: THE JAPANESE** population are encouraged to buy foreign goods by Prime Minister Yasuhiro Nakasone, to help with the looming trade crisis.
- **29TH: COCA-**

**COLA** has a new recipe for Coke, after 99 years pushing the same formula. Pepsi immediately invites the press to a conference where they can taste "the REAL real thing." Public pressure ensures that 'Classic' coke is soon reintroduced, and Coca-Cola never changes again.
- **30TH: PC MAKER ATARI** is preparing to release its new ST range, having demonstrated a prototype at the Las Vegas electronics show in January. With a 16-bit processor, built-in MIDI ports, and clear graphics, it will become first choice with computer music-makers, and remain so for many years to come.

## Get Your Money Out

**J**ULY 13TH: ARGUABLY the rock event of the decade, the massive, all-day *Live Aid* charity concert starts at Wembley Stadium, London, and continues at JFK Stadium, Philadelphia. It's an extension of Bob Geldof's Xmas Band Aid project. In seven months, Geldof has bullied almost every major act on the planet into performing for free: Bob Dylan, Paul McCartney, Elton John, The Rolling Stones, David Bowie, Eric Clapton, Sting, Queen, Santana, Madonna, Crosby, Stills & Nash, Neil Young, Simple Minds, Judas Priest, Bryan Adams, U2, The Beach Boys, Phil Collins, Dire Straits, The Who, Tina Turner, Lionel Richie, The Four Tops, B.B. King, Black Sabbath, Run DMC, and even a re-formed Led Zeppelin. They will be watched by 1.5 billion people, in the biggest live broadcast ever. It raises around $70m for emergency food and long term development.

• **4TH: BILL COSBY** hosts the recording of a three-hour NBC TV concert, *Motown Returns To The Apollo*, celebrating a $10.4m renovation of the legendary venue in Harlem, New York. Artists appearing include Stevie Wonder, Smokey Robinson, Diana Ross, Temptations, Four Tops, Drifters, Manhattans, Commodores, Cadillacs, Martha Reeves, Mary Wells, Patti LaBelle, Rod Stewart, George Michael, Boy George, and Joe Cocker. The show is transmitted on 19th May.
• **13TH: IN A SECRET** midnight ceremony at Our Lady Of The Lake Catholic Church, Lake Oswego, Portland, Oregon, Bruce Springsteen marries model Julianne Phillips.
• **21ST: THE WASHINGTON WIVES**, a pressure group formerly known as PMRC (Parents Music Resource Center), petition the music business to introduce a rating system to warn buyers about violent or sexually explicit lyrics.
• **24TH: THE US**, West Germany, and Israel announce plans to joins forces to hunt down Nazi war criminal Dr Josef Mengele, the world's most wanted man (with a price of $4 million on his head).

On June 6th, a body believed to belong to Dr Mengele is located in Sao Paolo, Brazil, and exhumed for tests to ensure its identity.
• **25TH: BANGLADESH** is hit by a cyclone which will claim over 10,000 lives.
• **29TH: THIRTY-NINE SOCCER FANS**, mostly Italian, are crushed or trampled to death and more than 400 people are injured in riots involving Liverpool and Juventus supporters at the European Cup Final at the Heysel stadium in Brussels. As a direct result, English clubs are banned from European competitions by the governing body UEFA.

• **JUNE 29TH: DAVID BOWIE** and the Stones' Mick Jagger record a version of the Martha & The Vandellas classic 'Dancing In The Street' at Westside Studios, London, as part of their contribution to the upcoming Live Aid event.

• **MAY 18TH: SIMPLE MINDS** reach Number One on the US Top 40 with 'Don't You (Forget About Me),' their first single to get anywhere near the US charts. This, and their performance at *Live Aid*, solidifies their new career path as stadium rockers, though many of their long-time fans, and initially the band itself, are unsure about this change of direction. But you can't argue with success, can you?

• **1ST: THREE HUNDRED PEOPLE** are arrested when police clash with 'new age travelers' on an annual midsummer pilgrimage to Stonehenge. The UK's National Trust has insisted no one is any longer allowed access to the site or indeed to touch the ancient stone circle... And Prince reaches Number One on the US album charts with *Around The World In A Day*.
• **6TH: THE DEFINITIVE** line-up of Guns N' Roses plays together for the first time, in the Troubadour, Los Angeles.
• **22ND: THE LONGEST DAY** concert at Milton Keynes Bowl in the UK is headlined by U2, but also features R.E.M., The Ramones, Billy Bragg, Faith Brothers, and Spear Of Destiny.
• **22ND: BRYAN ADAMS** gets his first US Number One with 'Heaven.' Canadian born Adams — who used to be in a band called Sweeney Todd — has already had a US Number Six hit this year with 'Run To You,' and will follow up 'Heaven' with another career-establishing hit, 'Summer Of 69.'
• **23RD: A BOMB DESTROYS** an Air India Boeing 747 120 miles west of Ireland. 329 die as a result of the explosion.
• **29TH: JOHN LENNON'S** psychedelic 1966 Rolls Royce Phantom V — with artwork by The Fool — fetches $2.2m at an auction held in New York City.

# Rise Of The Machines

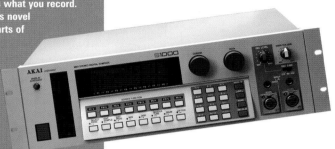

• MAY 11TH: **PAUL HARDCASTLE** begins five weeks at Number One in the UK with '19.' (Later in the summer it will hit Number 15 in the US). The track, whose title is a reference refers to the average age of a combat soldier in Vietnam, is significant not just for its harrowing theme, but because it's one of the first hit singles to make extensive use of digital sampling technology. It shows that the rhythmic repetition of a snippet of sound can be used to great effect, a simple theme repeated, expanded upon, and a new kind of music crafted around it. All this is achieved using innocuous-looking machines like the Akai S1000 (pictured right) – in its way as significant a technological development as the electric guitar in the 1930s and 1940s. A digital sampler is a sonic camera: it is to music what the Polaroid camera is to photography. It lets a musician accurately capture and play any sound. Though there's controversy about the use of digital music technology in general (with its tendency to sound less 'warm' and 'full' than traditional analog equipment – in these early days at least – the sampler itself doesn't have an identifiable sound: it depends what you record. This new technology is more often than not used to 'steal' (literally at first, as copyright law is unprepared for this novel development) older, admired recordings, which are then used as the basis for a new track. The idea of reusing parts of old songs has been around for centuries, especially in the oral tradition of folk and urban street-music, but with samplers, everything is now up for grabs – at least it will be until the record companies demand their cut. A thoroughly groundbreaking combination of sampling and tape-cutting work (which itself dates back to The Beatles 'Tomorrow Never Knows' from 1966's *Revolver* album) could be heard on *My Life In The Bush Of Ghosts*, produced in 1981 by Brian Eno (formerly of Roxy Music) & David Byrne (of Talking Heads). But it's within hip-hop and dance music in general that the role of sampling becomes central, with wholesale 'borrowing' of sections of other records, endlessly cut up and repeated for rappers to throw down their skills over the top. This is illustrated brilliantly by such landmark albums as Public Enemy's *It Takes A Nation Of Millions To Hold Us Back* in 1988, or De La Soul's more approachable *Three-Feet High And Rising* in 1989.

## JULY

## AUGUST

• JULY 4TH: **DIRE STRAITS**, whose new album *Brothers In Arms* has gone to Number One in both the UK and the US, begin a ten-night stand at Wembley Arena, London, leading neatly up to Live Aid, at which they also appear. It's the band's biggest year so far.

• JULY 7TH: **TENNIS PLAYER BORIS BECKER** becomes the youngest man to win the Wimledon Men's Singles Championship, at just 17. He's also the first unseeded player to win, and the first German.

• 3RD: **THE MOVIE** *Back To The Future* is released.

• 6TH: **PHIL COLLINS** reaches Number One on the US singles chart with 'Sussudio,' just one of seven US Number Ones he achieves in the 1980s. From his art-rock beginnings in Genesis, Collins has now come to typify mid-1980s 'adult-oriented' soft-rock.

• 8TH: **TAMPONS** are now freely available in China.

• 14TH: **WHEN EUROPEAN** singing star Demis Roussos flies from Athens, Greece, to Rome, Italy, with his girlfriend Pamela, the plane is hijacked and Roussos is held hostage for five days in Beirut, Lebanon.

• 15TH: **PRESIDENT REAGAN** has a cancerous tumour removed from his intestine.

• 16TH: **WHEN THE ROLLING STONES** begin mixing their new album in Los Angeles, Led Zeppelin's Jimmy Page drops in to overdub some guitar parts... Meanwhile, seven youths from

• JULY 10TH: **GREENPEACE** flagship Rainbow Warrior is blown up in Auckland Harbour, New Zealand and one of the 11 crew members, Portuguese photographer Fernando Pereiro, killed. Investigations later reveal the explosions were caused by limpet mines placed by French secret agents Major Alain Mafart and Captain Dominique Prieur. The French Government initially deny any involvement but the scandal ultimately leads to French defence minister Hernu resigning and France paying New Zealand $7m compensation.

New Jersey bite off more than they can chew when they hack into the Pentagon computer system and subsequently find the police on their doorsteps.

• 20TH: **TREASURE HUNTERS** find the Spanish galleon, Nuestra Senora de Atocha, which sank during a hurricane off the coast of Key West, Florida, in 1622. The ship contains more than $400 million in coins and silver ingots.

• 24TH: **IT'S ANNOUNCED** that

Michael Jackson is to star in a 3D science-fiction musical film, Captain EO, to be shown exclusively at Disney's theme parks throughout the world.

• 27TH: **PAUL YOUNG** reaches Number One on the US singles chart with 'Every Time You Go Away.' The old Hall & Oates song is just one of five US Top 40 hits for British singer Young in an eight-year period, before throat problems put his career on hold.

• 5TH: **BOWING TO DEMANDS** from the moral pressure group Parents Music Resource Centre, also known as the Washington Wives, Stan Gortikov, President of the Recording Industry Association Of America, announces that 19 record companies have agreed to sticker potentially offensive albums with the words "Parental guidance – explicit lyrics." At last, kids can instantly identify the records they want in a store without having to listen to them.

• 11TH: **DURAN DURAN** vocalist Simon Le Bon nearly drowns when his yacht, Drum England, sinks, two miles off the British coast... And 135 residents in Charleston, West Virginia, are treated for eye, throat and lung irritation after toxic chemicals escape from a nearby Union Carbide plant.

• 16TH: **THE WEDDING** of Madonna and Sean Penn takes place at 6970 Wildlife Rd, Point Dume, the $6.5m Malibu clifftop home of real estate developer Kurt Unger.

• 17TH: **IN THE MIDDLE** of their Reconstruction tour, at Barrymore's Club, Ottawa, Canada, a somewhat the worse for drink R.E.M. abandon their planned set and play an unscheduled evening of impromptu cover versions.

• 18TH: **MICHAEL JACKSON** and CBS Songs pay $40m to acquire the ATV Music catalogue, which includes most of the Lennon & McCartney songbook, formerly owned by British TV mogul Lew Grade.

• 24TH: **HUEY LEWIS & THE**

**NEWS** reach Number One on the US Top 40 singles chart with 'Power Of Love.'

• 15TH: **VIRGIN ATLANTIC CHALLENGER** capsizes in heavy seas off the south-west of England, foiling an attempt at the fastest-ever Atlantic crossing. It is just 140 miles (224km) short of its target, the Isles of Scilly, off Cornwall. Richard Branson, the man behind Challenger, veteran sailor Chay Blyth and all other crew members are reported safe and well. In 1986, Branson will realize his dream when Virgin Atlantic Challenger II completes the trip in three days, eight hours and 31 minutes.

• 21ST: **THE US** accuses Moscow of using Spy Dust. Against all the odds, this turns out to be a genuine counter-intelligence device: it later transpires the KGB has been using the chemical marking compound, also called METKA, to keep tabs on the activities of its targets.

• 22ND: **THREE AVIATION ACCIDENTS** make this month one of the scariest in the history of air travel, with a total of 710 deaths. Today, 55 die at Manchester airport, UK, in a fire on takeoff. Earlier in the month, 520 died in the Japanese crash, when a Japan Air Lines 747 crashed into Mount Otsuka – though remarkably four people survived. And before that 135 died at Dallas, Texas, when a jet crash landed. The British Civil Aviation Authority says this is the worst year in the history of commercial flights, with 15 crashes and 1400 deaths.

# 1985

## Game On

IT HAS BEEN an important year for computers, and computer games in particular, after a low-point in 1983-84 when the embryonic games industry nearly disappeared. Indeed, several large companies bailed out at that stage because they couldn't see a big enough market – how silly will they feel in a few years time? Apple Computer's launch of the graphics-based Macintosh computer in 1984 has been followed by several more major introductions during 1985: Atari has produced its ST range, which will prove popular for graphic designers, publishing, and music creation, thanks to the introduction of MIDI sockets that allow the interconnection of digital synthesizers and drum machines. Commodore, meanwhile, has taken over production of the sophisticated Amiga computer, and will target it largely towards video editors and gamers. Then in November, Bill Gates's Microsoft company will belatedly introduce Windows 1.0, a graphic-based operating system for the PC. This is a major advance over the text-led MS-DOS. On the games front, the well-established Japanese company Nintendo – it began manufacturing playing cards in the last century – will wait until December to test-market a new computer games console for the domestic market. It is called The Nintendo Entertainment System (or NES). Nintendo has already had some success in the video games market, producing arcade and hand-held 'Game & Watch' novelties like Donkey Kong. Now the 'human' star of that game, originally called 'Jumpman,' becomes a miniature superhero (and occasional plumber) called Super Mario. Mario and his brother Luigi – with help from their creator, Shigeru Miyamoto – launch a revolution in video games, suggesting computers can be leisure tools, too.

## SEPTEMBER

### New Heights

- **SEPTEMBER 28TH: KATE BUSH**, who has now had four hit albums in the UK, releases her fifth collection, *Hounds Of Love*. It contains her only US hit, 'Running Up That Hill.'

- **1ST: A JOINT US** and French expedition finally locates the wreck of the Titanic, 560 miles off the coast of Newfoundland.
- **7TH: 'ST ELMO'S FIRE'** by John Parr hits Number One on the US singles chart. It's the theme from the 'brat-pack' movie of the same name, which stars Emilio Estevez, Demi Moore, and Rob Lowe.
- **13TH: ON A PARTICULARLY** unlucky Friday 13th, President Mitterand of France watches horrified as Ariane III, his nation's unmanned satellite-launching mission craft, bursts into flames just nine minutes into its flight... (Fear of the number 13, incidentally, is known as triskaidekaphobia.)
- **16TH: BRITAIN AND RUSSIA** get into a tit-for-tat round of expulsions involving claims and counter claims of spying. Both countries kick out 25 people, and

then Margaret Thatcher ups the ante and removes another six... Meanwhile in Nice, France, Prince starts filming his second movie, *Under The Cherry Moon*.
- **17TH: FASHION DESIGNER** Laura Ashley dies after a fall.
- **21ST: A MASSIVE EARTHQUAKE** rocks Mexico, causing millions of dollars worth of damage, and leaving many thousands dead or homeless... And after almost a year on the UK album chart, *Like A Virgin* by Madonna finally reaches the Number One spot.
- **22ND: BOB DYLAN**, Willie Nelson, Neil Young, John Cougar Mellencamp, Lou Reed, Billy Joel, Foreigner, Joni Mitchell, Ry Cooder, and others, perform at the fund-raising *Farm Aid* concert in Champaign, Illinois. They raise $10m for America's hard-pressed dustbowl farmers.
- **22ND: BULGARIAN ARTIST** Christo takes his passion for wrapping things to extremes when he (or rather his 300 workers) envelopes the Pont Neuf bridge over the River Seine in Paris, France, in 40,000 square meters (450,000 square feet) of woven polyamide fabric. He will later do something similar to the Reichstag in Berlin, and some trees in Switzerland.
- **28TH: RIOTS BREAK OUT** in Brixton, London, after police shoot and wound Cherry Groce while trying to arrest her son.
- **29TH: THE LIST OF WESTERN** governments imposing sanctions against South Africa, in opposition to its apartheid policies, grows to 12.

## OCTOBER

- **1ST: THE FAR CORPORATION** (a band made up of various members of Toto and Foreigner) release a cover version of Led Zeppelin's 1971 epic 'Stairway To Heaven,' whose guitar-picking introduction has become a favorite among apprentice guitarists. Later cover versions will include light-hearted deconstructions by Frank Zappa, Rolf Harris and Dread Zeppelin (a Led Zeppelin cover band fronted by an Elvis impersonator). In 1992 a whole album, entitled *Stairways To Heaven*, will feature 12 different interpretations.
- **2ND: BRUCE SPRINGSTEEN'S** *Born In The USA* tour comes to an end at The Coliseum, Los Angeles.
- **2ND: ROCK HUDSON** dies from AIDS-related illnesses, at the age of 59.
- **7TH: PALESTINIAN HI-JACKERS** seize the cruise ship Achille Lauro, with more than 400 passengers and crew, and demand that Israel frees 50 Palestinian prisoners. After killing a 69-year-old wheelchair-bound tourist, they are promised safe passage, but their plane is forced to the ground and they are held.
- **8TH: MUSICAL *LES MISERABLES*** opens at The Barbican Theatre in London. Written by a relatively unknown French songwriting team of Alain Boublil and Claude-Michel Schönberg, it transfers to the West-End's Palace Theatre in December 1985, and stays there for the rest of the century – making it the third longest running musical in history, behind Andrew Lloyd Webber's *Cats* and *Phantom Of The Opera*.
- **12TH: ACTOR AND DIRECTOR** Orson Welles dies at 70... And Bono of U2 records the track 'Silver And Gold' for the anti-apartheid *Sun City* album, with Keith Richards and Ron Wood of The Rolling Stones on guitars, at Right Track Studio, New York City.
- **13TH: RICKY WILSON** of the B-52s dies of AIDS.
- **16TH: INTEL INTRODUCES** the 32-bit 80386 computer chip.
- **19TH: A-HA** reach Number One on the US Top 40 singles chart with 'Take On Me.'
- **20TH: ERIC CLAPTON**, Phil Collins and Carl Perkins play an unannounced gig in the Civic Hall, Guildford, UK.
- **26TH: WHITNEY HOUSTON** has her first Number One single with 'Saving All My Love For You' (this month in the US, December in the UK).

- **OCTOBER 10TH: ACTOR YUL BRYNNER**, star of *The Magnificent Seven*, *Westworld*, and *The King & I* (below), dies at the age of 65.

## Gorby & Ron

- **NOVEMBER 9TH: THE INCREASINGLY** error-prone President Reagan refers to the Princess Of Wales as Princess David at a state banquet. Two weeks later he meets Soviet leader Mikhail Gorbachev in Geneva: the summit ends in optimism but with no agreement on the Star Wars space defence system.

**NOVEMBER**

**DECEMBER**

- **NOVEMBER 12TH:** Former DJ Norman Cook (second from left) – real name Quentin, and later to become known as Fatboy Slim – replaces Ted Key as bass player in The Housemartins, the self-styled "fourth-best band in Hull."

- **1ST: FORMER CLASH** member Mick Jones releases *This Is Big Audio Dynamite*, the first album by his new band, B.A.D.
- **2ND: STEVIE WONDER** reaches Number One on the US singles chart with 'Part-Time Lover' – the first song ever to top the pop, R&B, adult contemporary, and dance/disco charts in the US.
- **7TH: RUBIN 'HURRICANE' CARTER** is finally freed when Judge H. Lee Sarokin of the Federal District Court Newark, New Jersey overturns the second trial convictions, finding them based on "racism rather than reason and concealment rather than disclosure." All indictments are officially dismissed in 1988.
- **11TH: THE ALBUM** *Single Life* by Cameo is certified gold in the US by the RIAA.
- **13TH: NEVADO DEL RUIZ,** Columbia's long dormant volcano (which last caused trouble some 140 years ago) erupts while people in four nearby towns are asleep. At least 25,000 are feared dead and more than 100,000 are now homeless.
- **16TH: STARSHIP** (dropping Jefferson) reach Number One on the US Top 40 singles chart with 'We Built This City.'
- **25TH: A CALIFORNIA JUDGE** orders that Cathy Smith is arrested and charged with first-degree murder for her role in the injection of the drugs that killed *Blues Brothers* actor/comedian John Belushi. She later bargains this down to manslaughter and spends 18 months behind bars.
- **29TH: AFTER A LENGTHY** court battle, Dick James of music publishers DJM is ordered to pay £5m ($8m) in unpaid royalties to the songwriting team of Elton John and Bernie Taupin. The pair fail, however, to recover the copyrights on 169 of their songs.

- **3RD: ZZ TOP** start out on their epic globe-spanning 212-date *Afterburner* tour in Toronto, Canada.
- **7TH: MR MISTER** reach Number One on the US Top 40 singles chart with their one hit, 'Broken Wings.'
- **12TH: IAN STEWART,** former roadie and keyboardist with The Rolling Stones, often described as the sixth Stone, dies of a heart attack. Bassist Bill Wyman has said, "Without him there would have been no Rolling Stones."
- **13TH: GENERAL ELECTRIC** pays $6.3 billion for RCA.
- **16TH: PAUL CASTELLANO,** head of the Gambino family, one of the most powerful mafia families in New York, is shot and killed by three gunmen in Manhattan.
- **19TH: ON THE LAST NIGHT** of Elton John's nine-day stint at Wembley Arena, London, he is joined on stage by Rod Stewart and George Michael.
- **21ST: THE GREATER LONDON COUNCIL** (soon to be closed down by Margaret Thatcher), holds a Christmas party for the unemployed in Finsbury Park, north London, with performances by Madness, Ian Dury, Marc Almond, and the Frank Chickens – a Japanese duo largely responsible for introducing karaoke to the UK.
- **23RD: IN RENO,** Nevada, after listening to Judas Priest records, heavy metal fans Raymond Belknap and Jay Vance attempt suicide with a sawn-off shotgun. Belknap dies instantly. Vance surivives but is seriously disfigured.

- **31ST: RICK NELSON,** his fiancee and five bandmembers are killed in a plane crash in Texas.
- **31ST: AT A NEW YEAR'S PARTY** held by former Eagles member Don Henley at his ranch in Aspen, Colorado, US presidential candidate Gary Hart first meets Donna Rice, who will later become embroiled in a scandal with him.

- **NOVEMBER 4TH: SIR CLIVE SINCLAIR,** the inventor behind the groundbreaking ZX Spectrum computer, has all but ruined his reputation with the failure of the ill-fated C5 electric cycle-car. Today TPD, the company producing the vehicle, crawls into liquidation.

# 1986

## January–April

## JANUARY

• **4TH: PHIL LYNOTT** of Thin Lizzy dies in hospital in Salisbury, Wiltshire, UK, from heart failure, pneumonia, and other conditions relating to years of drug abuse.

• **12TH: LUTHER VANDROSS** (right) is seriously injured when his Mercedes Benz goes out of control and crashes on Laurel Canyon Boulevard, Los Angeles, California, killing his passenger. Vandross is charged with manslaughter.

• **13TH: JOHN LYDON**, Steve Jones, Paul Cook, and Mrs Beverly (Sid Vicious's mum), sue Malcolm McLaren and his Glitterbest company for £1 million ($1.5m).

• **16TH: THE PARENTS** of young suicide victim John McCollum begin a legal action against Ozzy Osbourne, claiming Ozzy's song 'Suicide Solution' drove the boy to kill himself.

• **20TH: THE UNITED STATES** celebrates the first holiday in honour of civil rights leader Martin Luther King Jr... And France and Britain finally decide to undertake the Channel Tunnel project, promising that trains will run under the Channel by 1993.

• **24TH: VOYAGER II** passes within 81,593km of the planet Uranus, and in doing so discovers two moons.

• **25TH: THE RED WEDGE** tour – a left-wing musician-based pressure group set up to encourage debate and to politicize the UK's apathetic youth – starts in Manchester, featuring sets from The Style Council, Billy Bragg, Junior, and The Communards.

• **26TH: THE ALBUM *BOY IN THE BOX*** by Corey Hart reaches the one million sales mark in Canada, making him only the second Canadian artist (Bryan Adams was the first) to reach this figure.

• **28TH: THE US SPACE SHUTTLE** Challenger explodes, just 73 seconds after lift-off, killing the crew of five men and two women. The next shuttle will not fly until September 1998.

• **28TH: SOVIET PARTY** Secretary Mikhail Gorbachev announces radical reforms and restructuring ('perestroika') in economic policy. He also talks about 'glasnost' – Soviet openness about its past.

• **JANUARY 7TH: HAVING BEEN MARRIED** for just three months, Janet Jackson files for divorce from James DeBarge. Shortly afterwards, she has her first hit with 'What Have You Done For Me Lately,' followed closely by the Number One album, *Control*. Emerging from the shadow of her world-famous older brothers was never going to be easy – indeed Janet first took to acting instead, on programs like *Different Strokes* and *Fame*. Then from 1982, with a deal of heavy-handed prompting from her father (keen to have another million seller in the family), she released a couple of average-selling albums, before being put on a strict diet, given dancing lessons, and matched up with top producers Jimmy Jam & Terry Lewis. The first fruit of this new regime, *Control*, will go on to sell 14 million copies...

## FEBRUARY

• **2ND: WOMEN IN LIECHTENSTEIN** are allowed to vote for the first time today.

• **5TH: A COMBINED WORLD TOUR** featuring Bob Dylan and Tom Petty & The Heartbreakers begins in Athletic Park, Wellington, New Zealand.

• **6TH: THE MOTHER** and sister of ex-Undertones vocalist Feargal Sharkey are held hostage by terrorists – fortunately their four-hour ordeal ends without anyone getting hurt.

• **7TH: HAITIAN DICTATOR** 'Baby Doc' Duvalier – who, with his father 'Papa Doc', ruthlessly ruled Haiti for over 28 years – flees to France to avoid a national uprising. He manages to take more than $150m with him.

• **10TH: THE FIFTH ANNUAL BRIT AWARDS** ceremony is held at the Grosvenor House Hotel, London. Wham! win the Outstanding Contribution To British Music Award. Elton John picks up an Outstanding Achievement Award for his recent Russian dates.

• **15TH: WHITNEY HOUSTON** reaches Number One on the US Top 40 singles chart with 'How Will I Know?'

• **19TH: USSR LAUNCHES** the Mir space station into orbit.

• **21ST: METALLICA RELEASE** their third album, *Master Of Puppets*, in the US.

• **26TH: AFTER A SERIES** of rigged elections, President Marcos of the Philippines is deposed and Mrs Corazon Aquino becomes president. A mob later ransacks the palace after Marcos and his shoe-loving wife Imelda flee the country.

## I've Got The Brains...

• **JANUARY 11TH: THE PET SHOP BOYS** reach Number One on the UK singles chart with 'West End Girls.' It will top the US chart in May. Chris Lowe and Neil Tennant met in London in 1981 while Neil was working at *Smash Hits,* a pop magazine, and Chris was studying architecture. In 1983, on a trip to New York to interview The Police, Tennant approached legendary disco producer Bobby O, who agreed to produce the duo's first single, 'West End Girls,' inspired by 'The Message' by Grandmaster Flash. Some 18 months later (having slipped out of the Bobby O contract) the Stephen Hague re-recording of 'West End Girls' is released on Parlophone, swiftly followed by debut album *Please.* Combining thought-provoking but unashamedly commercial pop with theatrical live events, high-profile collaborations, and astute marketing, The Pet Shop Boys will, as they predict, make lots of money.

## Tough Enough?

• **FEBRUARY 8TH: BILLY OCEAN** reaches Number One on the UK singles chart (Number Two in the US) with 'When The Going Gets Tough, The Tough Get Going.' It's taken from the movie The Jewel Of The Nile, the stars of which, Kathleen Turner, Michael Douglas (seen together, below), and Danny DeVito, appear as backing vocalists in the video for the song. This causes controversy, by all accounts, because they are not members of the Musicians' Union.

**MARCH**

**APRIL**

• **3RD: CHUCK BERRY** is inducted into the Songwriters' Hall Of Fame, at the 17th annual awards dinner, at the Hotel Plaza, New York City... Meanwhile, in the southern hemisphere, Queen Elizabeth II signs the Australia Bill in Canberra, formally severing Australia's remaining constitutional ties with the UK.

• **4TH: RICHARD MANUEL**, pianist in The Band, hangs himself from a shower curtain rod in a motel room in Winter Haven, Florida, after a reunion show in the Cheek To Cheek lounge.

• **8TH: 'CHAIN REACTION'** by Diana Ross (above), written and produced by Barry Gibb of the Bee Gees, reaches Number One on the UK singles chart. Surprisingly, while she carries on having solo hits in the UK until the end of the century, Ms Ross fails to trouble the US Top 40 after 1985.

• **12TH: HAVING JUMPED** ship from Pepsi, Michael Jackson now holds a press conference to announce a sponsorship deal with Coca-Cola.

• **13TH: THE RUSSIANS** launch Soyuz T-15, intended to establish a permanent human presence in space when docked with the Mir space station, launched three weeks ago... On the same day, Halley's comet is photographed in astonishing detail by the European Space Agency's Giotto craft.

• **17TH: OZZY OSBOURNE'S** father-in-law, fearsome pop impresario Don Arden, finds himself in court for physically attacking a former business partner. Arden, who has worked with Gene Vincent, The Animals, The Nashville Teens, The Small Faces, Amen Corner, The Move, ELO, and of course Ozzy, once famously hung Robert Stigwood out of a fourth-floor window... Meanwhile, unsigned pop songstress Tiffany now signs a contract with manager George Tobin, giving him absolute control over her career. Will they never learn?

• **25TH: GUNS N' ROSES** sign a recording contract with the Geffen Records label.

• **1ST: NEW KIDS ON THE BLOCK** release their eponymous debut album in the US. Give them a couple of years and they'll be huge, you wait and see.

• **5TH: THE BIGGEST AUDIENCE** ever to have attended a free outdoor musical – 1.3 million people – turn up to see Jean-Michel Jarre's live son-et-lumiere event at Rendezvous Houston, in Texas.

• **11TH: HEAVY METAL CHARITY** record 'Stars' by Hear'N'Aid is released. With contributions from Ted Nugent, Ronnie James Dio, and members of Judas Priest, Iron Maiden, Blue Oyster Cult, and even Spinal Tap, the worthy aim behind this frightening assemblage of poodle-perms and spandex is to raise funds for African famine victims.

• **13TH: WHEN WELSH ROCKERS** The Alarm visit Disneyland in Los Angeles, Snow White and Pluto ask to have their pictures taken with singer Mike Peters.

• **14TH: US AIRCRAFT** attack Libya in response to the bombing of a Berlin discotheque. Four days later two Britons and an American are murdered in retaliation by Libyan revolutionaries.

• **15TH: TWO WEEKS** after The Dead Kennedys have been publicly targeted by the PMRC (Parents' Music Resource Center), frontman Jello Biafra's house in San Francisco is raided by police.

• **17TH: BRITISH JOURNALIST** John McCarthy is kidnapped by Islamic Jihad in Beirut. He will not be released for four-and-a-half years.

• **19TH: PRINCE REACHES** Number One on the US Top 40 singles chart with his unique-sounding 'Kiss.' Its minimalist production stands out against the rock norm of the time.

• **25TH: VAN HALEN REACH** Number One in the US on the Billboard album chart with *5150*. The album title (which is police code indicating "maniac on the loose") is later borrowed for a range of Peavey musical equipment, which Eddie Van Halen endorses.

• **APRIL 26TH: THE WORLD'S WORST NUCLEAR** accident occurs at Chernobyl power station, north of Kiev in Ukraine, part of the Soviet Union. Staff have been testing reactor Number Four without proper safety precaution. The reaction goes out of control and blows the top off the reactor, sending out a cloud of radioactive material that spreads as far as the UK. Some 30 people are killed immediately. But the Soviet authorities say nothing, even to the local population, until after a four-day holiday. Then 116,000 are evacuated, and 200,000 more will leave the area in the next ten years. The long-term health effects will not be known until the next century, but the UN calculates that three million people will die prematurely.

• **APRIL 8TH: CLINT EASTWOOD IS ELECTED** Mayor of Carmel, California, without firing a single shot.

## Talk This Way

• **JULY 15TH: THE ALBUM** *Raising Hell* by Run-DMC is awarded a US platinum disc by the RIAA – the first rap record to achieve this. It contains 'Walk This Way, ' shortly to become their first big hit single and the first hip-hop/rock mainstream crossover track. (Purists, however, consider their 1983 release 'It's Like That' the seminal hip-hop breakthrough.) A cover version using samples from Aerosmith's 1976 rock original, 'Walk This Way' spawned a video featuring Aerosmith themselves, dueling with Run-DMC from an adjoining rehearsal studio. As a result, the rock band's own career is revived after a ten-year slump. Of all the rap acts to emerge in the 1980s, Run-DMC – Jam Master Jay (Jason Mizell), Joseph 'Run' Simmons, and MC Darryl 'D' McDaniels – set the agenda with their spare beats and rock samplings. And though they are tough and street savvy, they avoid sensationalist gangsta posturing. Their music is seen by later generations as prime 'old skool' hip-hop.

## MAY

• **3RD: ROBERT PALMER** reaches Number One on the US singles chart with 'Addicted To Love.' (It makes UK Number Five.)
• **5TH: IT'S ANNOUNCED** that a Rock'N'Roll Hall Of Fame is to be built in Cleveland, Ohio.
• **10TH: TWO SHOWBIZ WEDDINGS** this week: Tommy Lee of Mötley Crüe marries actress Heather Locklear, while in the UK Toyah Wilcox marries Robert Fripp, of King Crimson.
• **14TH: THE MUSICAL *CHESS*,** written by ex-Abba men Björn Ulvaeus and Benny Andersson with lyricist Tim Rice, opens at the Prince Edward Theatre in London.
• **19TH: THE PINK POP FESTIVAL** in Holland features The Cure, The Waterboys, The Cult, Fine Young Cannibals, Stevie Ray Vaughan, and many more.
• **31ST: PETER GABRIEL** enters the US Top 40 singles chart with 'Sledgehammer,' which will peak at Number One. Its innovative animated video is widely acclaimed... And

James Brown (above) whose 'Living In America' has just given him his first Top Ten hit single since 1968, is working *Gravity*, on his first new album in three years.

• **MAY 8TH: CAMEO HAVE** their biggest hit when 'Word Up' climbs to Number Six on the US chart – it'll make Number Three in the UK later in the year. Originally known as the New York City Players when they formed back in 1974, this soul-funk trio is fronted by some-time drummer Larry Blackmon, whose choice of stagewear – particularly his bright red plastic codpiece – helps cement the band in the public mind. The song's extremely catchy electro-funk does the rest.

## JUNE

• **4TH: AMNESTY INTERNATIONAL** launches a two-week worldwide tour, entitled *A Conspiracy Of Hope*, beginning at the Cow Palace, San Francisco. It features U2, Sting, Bryan Adams, Peter Gabriel, Jackson Browne, Lou Reed, Joan Baez, and The Neville Brothers.
• **7TH: MADONNA** reaches Number One in the US with the single 'Live To Tell.'
• **8TH: KURT WALDHEIM** is elected Austrian president, despite his war-time record as a member of a German army unit that committed atrocities in Yugoslavia. Waldheim insists he is not to blame.
• **9TH: WHAM!** release their final single, 'The Edge Of Heaven,' with Elton John playing piano.
• **12TH: THE ALBUM** Whitney Houston is awarded a US six-times platinum disc by the RIAA. Even a video of her hits goes platinum.
• **16TH: THE SMITHS** release *The Queen Is Dead*, their fourth album if you include a compilation, to predictable tabloid outrage.
• **20TH: PAUL McCARTNEY,** Elton John, Eric Clapton, Tina Turner, Phil Collins, Midge Ure, Paul Young, Mark Knopfler, Level 42, and others, play live at the Prince's Trust Concert in Wembley Arena, London.
• **24TH: HARD-LINE ULSTER UNIONIST** leader, the Reverend Ian Paisley, says that Northern Ireland is on the verge of civil war and calls on Protestants to mobilize for action.
• **27TH: THE UNITED STATES** is found guilty of violating international law by supporting armed Contra rebels against the left-wing Sandinista government in Nicaragua. The International Court of Justice later rules that the US should compensate the country. But the Reagan administration, which has boycotted the case, ignores the verdict. Proceedings are finally dropped, at the Nicaraguan government's request, in 1991.

## JULY

• **2ND: PRINCE'S NEW** movie *Under The Cherry Moon* opens nationally in the US, but the critics hate it and box office receipts are poor.
• **3RD: DEAD KENNEDY'S** vocalist Jello Biafra is charged with "distributing harmful material to minors" after a free poster, 'Penile Landscape' by H.R. Giger, is given away with their album *Frankenchrist*.
• **4TH: RUDY VALLEE** dies of throat cancer at the age of 85. As a big-band vocalist in the 1930s he pioneered the crooning style taken up by Bing Crosby and later Frank Sinatra. Often to be seen singing through a megaphone on-stage, he attracted an enormous following, and it's said that, long before Tom Jones, female fans used to throw their underwear at him during concerts.
• **5TH: BILLY OCEAN** reaches Number One again in the US with 'There'll Be Sad Songs.'
• **10TH: JERRY GARCIA** of The Grateful Dead falls into a diabetic coma at home in San Rafael, California. He is rushed to Marin General Hospital where he remains in a coma for five days before recovering.
• **12TH: BOY GEORGE** is arrested in London on heroin charges... Meanwhile, in Northern Ireland, dozens are injured in the second consecutive night of violence in Portadown, Armagh. Violence flared when Orangemen converged on the town yesterday evening, after their annual marches to commemorate the Battle of the Boyne in July 1690.
• **16TH: DOLLY PARTON** opens her own theme park, Dollywood, in Tennessee.
• **23RD: PRINCE ANDREW,** second son of Queen Elizabeth II, marries Lady Sarah Ferguson at Westminster Abbey, in front of 500 million TV viewers. They divorce in 1996.

## Arise Sir Bob

**J**UNE 10TH: IT'S ANNOUNCED that Bob Geldof is to receive an honorary British knighthood for his humanitarian work as organiser of Live Aid. Since he's not actually a British citizen, this requires the blessing of the Irish government. A year on from Live Aid, Bob is still busy with spin-off projects (in fact he never loses interest in aid work from then on). This May, he's been involved in a 'Self-Aid' concert in Dublin, Eire, raising cash for the unemployed, alongside U2, Elvis Costello, Van Morrison, The Pogues, etc; and on May 25th the Geldof-promoted Race Against Time gets more than 30 million people around the world running for the Sport Aid charity. In August, Sir Bob even finds time to marry TV presenter Paula Yates (right).

## AUGUST

• **MAY 15TH: TOM CRUISE**, Kelly McGillis, and Val Kilmer star *Top Gun*, one of the biggest box office successes of the 1980s. One of the songs from the movie, 'Take My Breath Away,' becomes an international Number One for Berlin – though this electro-pop track, written and produced by Georgio Moroder, is not in the group's chosen style.

• **1ST: NEW YORK CITY** hard rock station WAPP is replaced by a new station, WQHT HOT 103, the first in the city to program specifically dance & club music in the genre known as freestyle. The first song played on HOT 103 is 'Point Of No Return' by Nu Shooz.
• **5TH: A 27-YEAR-OLD** session musician, Michael Rudetsky, is found dead from a drug overdose in Boy George's Hampstead home in London.
• **9TH: QUEEN** headline the UK's annual Knebworth Festival in Hertfordshire, UK, alongside the likes of Status Quo and Big Country. No one knows it, but this will be Queen's last show.
• **14TH: TONIGHT**, in London, when Prince plays the last of three nights at Wembley Arena, he is joined by Ron Wood of the Rolling Stones and Sting for a version of 'Miss You.'
• **16TH: MADONNA'S** self-produced album *True*

*Blue* begins a five-week stay at Number One in the US, where it will eventually sell more than five million copies. On the same day, 'Papa Don't Preach' goes top of the US singles chart.
• **21ST: A HUGE GLACIER** in Alaska is threatening to cause an ecological disaster in the area, as it starts moving after millennia of inactivity. (Talk of global warming is still dismissed by the authorites as hot air.)
• **23RD: FARLEY 'JACKMASTER' FUNK** brings Chicago house music to the British mainstream when his version of Isaac Hayes's 'Love Can't Turn Around' enters the UK charts and rises to Number Ten – even though it barely registers outside of the club scene back home in the US.
• **29TH: BRITAIN'S OLDEST TWINS**, May and Marjorie Chavasse, both receive telegrams from the Queen on their 100th birthday.

## Another Country

• **PERHAPS ONE OF THE MOST INFURIATING** traits of the modern music industry, or more often the music media, is the insistence on giving everything a name. Every slight deviation from what's been heard before has to be packaged up and put in a labeled box. The trendier music papers, especially in the UK, are particularly prone to this 'naming' disease, tying themselves in knots to think up new genres and 'scenes.' At one low-point, in the early 1990s, the even came up with the laughably meaningless idea of "The scene that celebrates itself." In the US, country music is almost certainly the worst offender, with dozens of pernickety sub-divisions within what almost everyone else hears as simply 'country.' By 2003 the *All Music Guide* will list a dizzying 42 variants, among which the main strands might be identified as: *old-time* (acoustic banjos, fiddles, Jimmie Rodgers, etc); *honky-tonk* (Hank Williams (above), Ernest Tubbs, steel guitars); *Bakersfield* (early electric country, a little bit rock'n'roll, Telecasters, Buck Owens); *Nashville* (Chet Atkins, Patsy Cline, strings, choirs, and its 1960s off-shoot, *Countrypolitan* – basically the country mainstream, such as Eddy Arnold, Don Gibson, Tammy Wynette, Jim Reeves, George Jones); *progressive* (1960s long-hairs, Kris Kristofferson, Willie Nelson, Jimmie Dale Gilmore); *outlaw* (Nelson's 1970s Texas mavericks, Waylon Jennings, Merle Haggard etc); *neo-traditionalist* (modern honky-tonk revivalists, Rosanne Cash (right) and the like); *new-traditionalist* (younger honky-tonkers with electric guitars, Dwight Yoakam, Randy Travis, Ricky Skaggs, George Strait, Steve Earle – who's also been described as more of a 'neo-Outlaw,' just to confuse things further); *alternative* country adds some punky/new wave attitudes (as with kd lang, Earle, The Handsome Family); and of course *contemporary* country, which is essentially country-pop-rock, and encompasses household names like The Eagles, Alabama, Garth Brooks, Shania Twain, Vince Gill, LeAnn Rimes, Faith Hill, and The Dixie Chicks. It was in the 1980s, though, that the idea of *new* country first emerged, directly prompted, it's suggested, by the John Travolta movie *Urban Cowboy* (1980), in which traditional country styles such as honky tonk were depicted on the soundtrack as a diluted country rock, incensing true fans of the music's roots. It's the sense that country music has been losing touch with its past, its rich traditions and integrity, that has prompted the likes of Strait, Yoakam (left), Travis, Earle, and bands like Uncle Tupelo, etc, to attempt to reinvigorate this great American genre – however it might be sub-labelled.

P A U L · S I M O N
G R A C E L A N D

## Under African Skies

• OCTOBER 4TH: **PAUL SIMON** releases his African-influenced album *Graceland*. Having emerged from a slight creative hiatus that included the well-received, if water-treading, Simon & Garfunkel reunion and the commercially unsuccessful *Hearts And Bones* album of 1983, Paul Simon has rediscovered his muse in the sounds of South Africa. Paying no heed to the anti-apartheid cultural boycott (the African National Congress and UN will later forgive him), he's spent several weeks recording in Johannesburg with the likes of local superstar vocal group Ladysmith Black Mambazo. The *Graceland* album will be enormously successful, reaching Number Three in the US and topping the charts in the UK, where he also has a Top Five hit with the single, 'Call Me Al.' It's Simon's most successful solo period since the early 1970s, but the momentum isn't maintained. 1990's *Rhythm Of The Saints* will attempt much the same thing with Brazilian influences, but Simon's long breaks from recording and performing mean he is rarely in the public eye after 1990. In 1992, he will marry singer Edie Brickell, leader of The New Bohemians.

## Oh-Way-Oh

• DECEMBER 20TH: **THE BANGLES** reach Number One on the US Top 40 singles chart with 'Walk Like An Egyptian.' They've already had a Number Two hit this year with 'Manic Monday,' which Prince wrote for them under the pseudonym Christopher. Back in April, he even joined the band on stage in San Francisco for an encore of the song. Jules Shear's cryptic 'If She Knew What She Wants' is less successful, but 'Walk Like An Egyptian' takes The Bangles to the top of the charts over Christmas. Their second album, *Different Light,* will outsell contemporaries The Go-Go's. A cover of Simon and Garfunkel's 'Hazy Shade Of Winter,' produced by Def Jam label supremo, Rick Rubin, for the soundtrack of the film *Less Than Zero,* brings them a US Number Two. The next album, *Everything,* fares less well initially, but singles 'In Your Room' and 'Eternal Flame' keep up the momentum. In 1989, the Bangles split. Guitarist/vocalist Susanna Hoffs subsequently works with former Go-Go Jane Wiedlin and Bangles colleague Charlotte Caffey and appears in *Austin Powers: International Man Of Mystery* (1997).

### SEPTEMBER

## Hail Chuck

• OCTOBER 16TH: **TO CELEBRATE** Chuck Berry's 60th birthday, Keith Richards of the Rolling Stones organises a special concert at the Fox Theatre, St Louis, Missouri. As well as Richards, Berry's backing band includes Eric Clapton, Etta James, Julian Lennon, and Linda Ronstadt.

• 1ST: **THE UK'S** most successful 2-Tone band, Madness, announce their split.
• 2ND: **SCHOOLGIRL DEBBIE GIBSON** signs worldwide to Atlantic Records.
• 5TH: **THE DRONGOS** record an entire album live on the sidewalks of Manhattan, New York City. It goes on to achieve top five status on the US college radio charts.
• 7TH: **BISHOP DESMOND TUTU** becomes the first black head of the Anglican church in South Africa when he is made the Archbishop of Capetown.

• 10TH: **AT THE BUDOKAN**, Tokyo, Japan, Cyndi Lauper sets off on her 56-date long *True Colors* tour.
• 15TH: **AFTER A GAP OF 28 YEARS**, Europe wins golf's Ryder Cup, beating the US at The Belfry in Sutton Coldfield, UK.
• 22ND: **THE WORLD'S YOUNGEST** heart transplant patient, a two-and-a-half-month-old baby from north-west London, is given the heart of a five-day-old Belgian boy by one of the world's leading heart specialists, Dr Magdi Yacoub, at the Harefield Hospital, UK.

• SEPTEMBER 27TH: **CLIFF BURTON** (below left), bass player for Metallica, dies when the band's tour bus crashes on icy roads near Ljungby, Sweden, during a European tour.

**OCTOBER**  **NOVEMBER**  **DECEMBER**

• **SEPTEMBER 6TH: BANANARAMA** reach Number One on the US Top 40 singles chart with 'Venus.' The trio are the UK's most successful girl group to date. Original member Siobhan Fahey (above right), later marries Dave Stewart of Eurythmics, then leaves the group in 1988, and forms Shakespear's Sister with former Eric Clapton band vocalist Marcella Detroit.

• **2ND: THE EVERLY BROTHERS** are awarded a star on the Hollywood Walk Of Fame.
• **13TH: NICK CAVE** spends two days in jail in New York City, having been arrested during a police swoop to clear the streets of vagrants.
• **24TH: THE UK GOVERNMENT** breaks off diplomatic relations with Syria, after it's discovered that a bomb intended to blow up an El Al airplane was constructed at the Syrian Embassy in London.
• **26TH: NOVELIST** and member of the UK parliament Jeffrey Archer stands down as deputy chairman of the Conservative party after reports in a Sunday newspaper allege he tried to pay a prostitute to go abroad to avoid a scandal. In 14 years' time, Archer will be found guilty of perjury and sentenced to four years in prison.
• **31ST: ROGER WATERS** instigates legal proceedings in London to prevent his former colleagues David Gilmour and Nick Mason from using the name Pink Floyd. He fails.

• **OCTOBER 25TH: CYNDI LAUPER** (above) achieves her second Number One in the US with the single 'True Colors.'

• **2ND: UK SINGER-SONGWRITER** Billy Bragg, known for his protest songs and political leanings, is arrested in Norfolk, UK, and charged with criminal damage because he cut the wire fence around an air base during a demonstration.
• **8TH: BOSTON** reach Number One in the US with 'Amanda,' their first hit single for more than seven years... Over in the UK tonight, when blues guitarist Robert Cray plays at The Mean Fiddler, London, Eric Clapton makes an appearance on several numbers.
• **12TH: THE WAY IT IS** by Bruce Hornsby & The Range (right) is awarded a US gold album by the RIAA.
• **15TH: FOR THE FIRST TIME** in British chart history, the top five slots are held by female vocalists. In ascending order they are: Corinne Drewery of Swing Out Sister ('Breakout'), Mel & Kim Appleby ('Showing Out'), Susannah Hoffs leading The Bangles ('Walk Like An Egyptian'), Kim Wilde ('You Keep Me Hanging On'), and Terri Nunn with Berlin ('Take My Breath Away').

• **17TH: THE HEAD** of the Renault car company, Georges Besse, is assassinated in Paris, France, by Nathalie Menigon and Joelle Aubron, female members of anti-capitalist terror group Action Directe.
• **22ND: MIKE TYSON**, at age 20, becomes the youngest world heavyweight boxing champion in history when he knocks out Trevor Berbick in Las

Vegas after two explosive rounds.
• **24TH: HI INFIDELITY** by REO Speedwagon is awarded a US seven-times platinum album by the RIAA.

• **NOVEMBER 29TH: BON JOVI'S** 'You Give Love A Bad Name' is the band's first US Number One single.

• **3RD: A LEGAL SUIT** begins against Judas Priest, following the death of fan Raymond Belknap and the injury of his friend James Vance, who shot themselves after listening to the Priest album *Stained Class*.
• **6TH: PETER CETERA** & Amy Grant have a US Number One single with 'The Next Time I Fall.'
• **9TH: ELTON JOHN** collapses on-stage as he begins a six-night run at the Entertainment Centre, Sydney, Australia.
• **14TH: DICK RUTAN** and Jeana Yeager take off from Edwards Air Force Base in California on the first ever non-stop, non-refueling flight around world, in an aircraft called Voyager, described as a "flying fuel tank" In fact it has 17 fuel tanks, carrying more than 7,000 pounds of fuel for the 25,000-mile trip, which they complete in nine days (with just 100 pounds of fuel to spare).
• **16TH: DENNY LAINE**, a former member of the Moody Blues and Paul McCartney's Wings, is declared bankrupt in London, with debts running to more than £76,000.
• **21ST: MICK JAGGER** of The Rolling Stones flies to the island of Mustique for Christmas with Jerry Hall; later they will be joined by David Bowie.
• **25TH: LINKED BY SATELLITE** via the British Telecom tower, Cliff Richard in London sings a duet of the song 'Slow Rivers' with Elton John in Australia, as part of the BBC's seasonal *Christmas Morning With Noel Edmonds* variety show. God bless us, every one...

# 1987

## BELIEVE THE HYPE

Early this year, Public Enemy will sign to Russell Simmons & Rick Rubin's Def Jam organisation – joining the likes of Run-DMC and The Beastie Boys – and they will quickly become one of the label's most polemical and headline-grabbing acts. At the *29th Annual Grammy Awards*, on February 24th, The Beastie Boys will be invited to present an award (to singer Robert Palmer), and while using the opportunity for a bit of shambolic clowning, they'll hold up a boom-box and play an impromptu taster of Public Enemy's 'Timebomb,' a track from the as-yet-unreleased debut album *Yo! Bum Rush The Show*. Word-of-mouth promotion and unconventional publicity methods will be crucial in Public Enemy's early advancement: chief wordsmith for the band, Chuck D (described by Spike Lee as, "one of the most politically and socially conscious artists of *any* generation"), is also more than usually willing to give interviews to the press, making him almost the de-facto spokesperson for hip-hop. The group takes stage presentation seriously too, ensuring the visual elements are in place to hook an audience and hold its attention in what could otherwise be viewed as a bludgeoning lyrical tirade. This may include a full-on light show, or the Security Of The First World with their uniforms and martial arts moves, or eccentric Flavor Flav (seen here with Chuck) as a comic foil to sweeten the pill administered by the straight-talking straight man. Then there's the British angle: Chuck is an admirer of the radical stance of UK agit-punk band The Clash, and well aware of the value of the 'cool' factor on the UK music scene, coupled with the genuine enthusiasm for something new – and also how influential the music press there can be if they choose to champion a cause. It's in the UK that Public Enemy will make their first impact, initially as the new 'bad-boy' anti-heroes of the alternative music scene, but soon translating this into significant record sales. The group will score several hits on the Top 40 in the UK over the next few years, before their 1990 *Fear Of A Black Planet* album finally makes Public Enemy a widely recognised name in the States.

# 1987

## January–April

• **FEBRUARY 22ND: ANDY WARHOL DIES**, at 55.

• **2ND: THE PUBLISHERS** of Enid Blyton's Noddy books bow to pressure groups and retire the increasingly controversial Golliwog character.

• **6TH: FOLLOWING THROAT SURGERY**, Elton John cancels all live performances for the next year... Meanwhile, astronomers sight a new galaxy believed to be some 12 billion light years away.

• **8TH: WHEN ERIC CLAPTON** plays the last of three nights at the Royal Albert Hall, London, he is joined by Steve Winwood and Sting for a couple of numbers. Mark Knopfler of Dire Straits is the other guitarist in Clapton's band.

• **10TH: THE BANGLES** equal the longest run at the top of the US singles chart by a girl group, when 'Walk Like An Egyptian' notches up its fourth week at Number One. This feat has previously been achieved by The Chiffons, The Supremes and The Emotions.

• **11TH: TWENTY-FIVE PEOPLE** are lashed in public for staging an unofficial car race in Jeddah, Saudi Arabia.

• **20TH: TERRY WAITE**, special envoy to the British Archbishop of Canterbury, is last seen at around 7pm in Beirut, before being kidnapped.

• **21ST: TODAY'S INDUCTIONS** to the Rock'N'Roll Hall of Fame include Hank Williams, The Coasters, Eddie Cochrane, Bo Diddley, Aretha Franklin, Marvin Gaye, Bill Haley, Louis Jordan, B.B. King, Leiber & Stoller, Clyde McPhatter, Rick Nelson, Roy Orbison, Carl Perkins, Smokey Robinson, Big Joe Turner, T-Bone Walker, Muddy Waters, Jackie Wilson, Ahmet Ertegun, and Jerry Wexler.

• **22ND: BUDD DWYER**, the State Treasurer for Pennsylvania, calls a press conference to proclaim himself innocent of bribery charges. He then shoots himself dead.

• **23RD: HERE'S A MORE** encouraging tale: the current US Number One is 'Shake You Down' by Gregory Abbot, whose career, and studio, was initially bankrolled by some New York investment bankers he met while he was earning some cash working as a researcher on Wall Street.

• **JANUARY 26TH: AT THE *14TH ANNUAL AMERICAN MUSIC AWARDS*** in the Shrine Auditorium, Los Angeles, California, Whitney Houston gets Favourite Female Artist (Soul/R&B and also Pop/Rock), Favourite Video Single (Soul/R&B), and Favourite Album (Soul/R&B and also Pop/Rock). Madonna has to content herself with the Favourite Female Video Artist award. Whitney – a cousin of Dionne Warwick – is in the middle of an astonishing run of seven US Number One singles in just three years.

## Party Animals

- **JANUARY 24TH:** '(YOU GOTTA) FIGHT For Your Right (To Party)' by white rap-rockers The Beastie Boys enters the US singles chart, where it will peak at Number Seven (Number 11 in the UK). In March, their debut album *Licensed To Ill* becomes the first rap album to top the US chart, where it remains for seven weeks. Adam Horovitz (King Ad-Rock), Adam Yauch (MCA), and Michael Diamond (Mike D) embrace the bad-boy machismo of hip-hop, while embracing the have-a-go ethos of punk/new wave. They encourage middle-class white juveniles to start rapping (over overtly metal backing) and to misbehave. It's even claimed that some kids in Washington DC burn down their house trying to re-enact the band's 'Party' video. Tabloid fury is inevitable – not least for the spate of Volkswagen hood badges stolen to match the group's medallions – and with the credibility gained from intuitive producer Rick Rubin and his Def Jam label, the Boys' influence is assured. Their music becomes more adventurous, and their appeal endures into the Nineties and beyond.

**FEBRUARY**

**MARCH**

**APRIL**

- **2ND: THE ALBUM** *Bruce Springsteen & The E-Street Band Live 1975-85* is awarded a US triple platinum disc by the RIAA.
- **7TH: MADONNA** achieves her fifth US Number One single with 'Open Your Heart.'
- **9TH: FIVE STAR** are named Best British Group at the BRIT Awards in the Grosvenor House Hotel, London.
- **16TH: THE TRIAL** of John Demjanjuk, a 66-year-old Ukrainian who settled in Ohio after WWII, begins in Israel. Demjanjuk is alleged to be 'Ivan the Terrible,' a guard at the Treblinka death camp. He is later found guilty of murdering 870,000 Jews in 1943,

and sentenced to death.
- **17TH: A GROUP** of Tamil men strip to their underwear at London's Heathrow Airport in an attempt to prevent being returned to Sri Lanka. The ploy doesn't work.
- **19TH: BOB DYLAN,** George Harrison and John Fogerty, former leader of Creedence Clearwater Revival, put in a guest appearance at a Taj Mahal show, at the Palomino Club, Hollywood, California.
- **24TH: STEVE WINWOOD'S** 'Higher Love' wins Record Of The Year at the Grammy Awards. Robert Palmer is Best Male Vocalist. Janet Jackson performs 'What Have You Done For Me Lately,' but does not win any awards. The Beastie Boys are also in attendance.

- **MARCH 20TH: TV EVANGELIST** Jim Bakker (above) – a favourite target for Frank Zappa – insists he was tricked into having sex with a woman in Florida, shortly before resigning his post... In the same week, evangelist Oral Roberts' on-air insistence that he will die if his fund-raising goals aren't met, prompts one gullible Florida millionaire to hand over $1.3 million. Ozzy Osbourne sends Roberts $1, "for psychiatric treatment."

- **3RD: RAPPER EAZY-E** meets Jerry Heller at a record-pressing plant in Hollywood, California. The pair will soon become partners, launching their own record label, Ruthless Records. A founder member of Niggaz With Attitude (NWA), Eazy-E – real name Eric Wright, son of soul-funk man Charles Wright – will have a hit solo album of his own in 1993, but dies from AIDS two years later.
- **6TH: THE HERALD OF FREE ENTERPRISE,** a British ferry carrying cars and passengers, capsizes just outside Zeebrugge

harbour, Belgium. She has set out to sea with her bow doors open, allowing water to pour in, only 90 seconds into her voyage. Nearly 200 passengers and crew drown.
- **8TH: AT JOE LOUIS HALL,** Detroit, Michigan, Bob Seger finishes what he claims will be his last tour.
- **10TH: THE VATICAN** condemns surrogate parenting, test tube babies, and artificial insemination.
- **12TH: NO DOUBT** make their official live debut at Fender's Ballroom, Long Beach, California. Their previous shows were all at private parties.
- **16TH: THE POPULATION CRISIS COMMITTEE** publishes its "Best place to live" chart, with Switzerland topping the league, the US in fifth position, and Mozambique coming last out of 130 countries.
- **23RD: AT THE FIRST EVER** *Soul Train Music Awards* in the Civic Center, Santa Monica, California, Cameo win the Best Album and Best Single (Group) Of The Year. Janet Jackson gets Album Of The Year (Female) and Best New Video.
- **29TH: THE IRON LADY** goes behind the Iron Curtain. British Prime Minister Margaret Thatcher visits Moscow, and receives a warm reception.

- **4TH: U2'S ALBUM** *The Joshua Tree* goes straight on to the US album chart at Number Seven, becoming the highest new album chart entry since 1980. It'll also firmly establish U2 as superstars in the States.
- **6TH: THE ALBUM** *Control* by Janet Jackson is awarded a US four-times platinum disc.
- **6TH: A B.B. KING** television special is recorded at The Ebony Showcase Theater, Los Angeles, featuring the veteran bluesman with a stellar cast of guests, including Paul Butterfield, Eric Clapton, Phil Collins, Dr John, Etta James, Chaka Khan, Albert King, Gladys Knight, Billy Ocean, and Stevie Ray Vaughan.
- **17TH: CARLTON BARRETT,** famed as drummer for Bob Marley & The Wailers, is shot dead by his wife and her lover at his home in Kingston, Jamaica.
- **18TH: 'I KNEW YOU WERE WAITING (FOR ME)'** by Aretha Franklin & George Michael is the new US Number One single. It gives George his fourth of ten US Number Ones, and Aretha her first since 1967.
- **29TH: THE MUSICAL** *CABARET* is performed without music at the Strand Theatre in London after the orchestra go on strike due to five of its members being sacked. The show is performed for a further two nights without music before being suspended.

- **FEBRUARY 4TH: LIBERACE,** piano-playing showman, and favorite of elderly ladies and candelabra-makers, dies from AIDS at the age of 57.

- **FEBRUARY 21ST: CROWDED HOUSE** have their first US hit single with 'Don't Dream It's Over,' which reaches Number Two.

## Astaire Way To Heaven

• **JUNE 22ND: BELOVED** veteran entertainer Fred Astaire – one of the screen's greatest dancers – dies at the age of 88. In the same way that the Beatles were turned down by Decca's Dick Rowe, Astaire was rejected at an early Hollywood audition, with the memorably blunt put-down, "Can't sing. Can't act. Balding. Can dance a little."

## U2 Find What They're Looking For

**M**AY 13TH: THE ALBUM *The Joshua Tree* by U2 is awarded a US double-platinum disc by the RIAA. Three days later the band achieve their first US Number One single, 'With Or Without You,' which is followed to the top in August by 'I Still Haven't Found What I'm Looking For.' Though they've already had two Number One albums in the UK, this is the US breakthrough they've been aiming at. Yet few who first encountered the young, earnest, god-fearing, mullet-sporting Irish quartet in 1978 would have imagined they were in the presence of a future world-straddling colossus, with access to the ears of presidents, prime ministers, and pontiffs. U2 began life at Mount Temple School in Dublin, Ireland, when Bono (vocals), the Edge (guitars, piano), Larry Mullen Jr (drums), and Adam Clayton (bass) began playing tiny local venues. After five years of transatlantic grind, their live album *Under A Blood Red Sky*, recorded at Red Rocks Amphitheatre in Colorado, prompted *Rolling Stone* to vote them Band Of The Year 1983. Now their link-up with former Roxy Music/Talking Heads muse Brian Eno, first heard on 1985's *The Unforgettable Fire* and now on *The Joshua Tree*, has given new depth and ambience to the band's music, and cemented their appeal.

**MAY**

**JUNE**

• **4TH: IN THE KITCHEN** of his North Hollywood apartment, influential Chicago blues harmonica player and bandleader Paul Butterfield dies of intestinal problems related to years of drug and alcohol abuse.
• **6TH: IN BELGRADE**, Yugoslavia, Miroslav Milhailovic begins a 54-hour joke-telling marathon. Milhailovic claims to know over 287,000 jokes, but doesn't guarantee they're all good.
• **15TH: FORMER HOLLYWOOD** movie pinup Rita Hayworth dies after a long battle with Alzheimer's disease.

• **16TH: WHEN DAVID CROSBY** marries Jan Dance, guests include Stephen Stills, Roger McGuinn, Chris Hillman, Paul Kantner, Jackson Browne, and Warren Zevon. At the same ceremony, Graham and Susan Nash renew their vows on their tenth anniversary.
• **23RD: WET WET WET** achieve their first week in the UK Top 20 singles chart with 'Wishing I Was Lucky.'
• **28TH: MATHIAS RUST**, a 19-year-old West German, flies his Cessna plane through heavily-defended Soviet air space from Helsinki to Moscow, then lands in Red Square. He is arrested and sentenced to eight years in prison, but will be released after 18 months. He later opts to become a shoe salesman in Moscow.
• **29TH: A BID OF $50,000** by Michael Jackson to buy the remains of 'Elephant Man' John Merrick is rejected.
• **31ST: ADAM HOROVITZ** of The Beastie Boys is arrested at The Portobello Hotel in London, for allegedly causing "grievous bodily harm" to a fan the previous night.

• **2ND: LINDY CHAMBERLAIN**, the mother in the Australian 'dingo baby' case, who was five years ago found guilty of the murder of her disappeared nine-week-old daughter Azaria, is finally pardoned. Newly found clothing indicates that a wild dog did, in all likelihood, snatch the baby and kill her, as Chamberlain had insisted. In 1988 her story will become a movie, starring Meryl Streep.
• **3RD: CLASSICAL GUITARIST** Andres Segovia dies, age 94. He is buried in Madrid, Spain, but will later be moved to Linares in his home province of Jaen.
• **5TH: THE FIRST DAY** of this year's Prince's Trust Concerts takes place at Wembley Arena, London, featuring George Harrison, Eric Clapton, Phil Collins, Ringo Starr, Ben E. King, Mark King of Level 42, Bryan Adams, Midge Ure, and Spandau Ballet.
• **11TH: MARGARET THATCHER** becomes the first British Prime Minister in 160 years to win a third consecutive term in government.
• **13TH: MÖTLEY CRÜE'S** single 'Girls Girls Girls' enters the US Top 40, just as their future Number One album of the same name is released.
• **16TH: THE GRATEFUL DEAD** release a new

• **JUNE 6TH: 'YOU KEEP ME HANGING ON'** by Kim Wilde peaks at Number One on the US Top 40 singles chart. Daughter of veteran British rock'n'roller and songwriter Marty Wilde, Kim later retreats from the music business to become a gardener.

single, 'Touch Of Grey,' in the US. It will give them their only Top Ten hit. In July, Ben & Jerry's agree to donate 50 per cent of profits from their Cherry Garcia flavor ice cream, to the Rex Foundation, founded by Dead leader Jerry Garcia himself. Named after the band's former road manager Rex Jackson, who died in 1976, it supports community arts and services, in the generous "spirit of the Sixties," as well as encouraging new musicians and bands. It will give away more than $5m in the next decade.
• **19TH: GUNS N' ROSES** make their European debut with a gig at The Marquee, London. They'll be back home in August to shoot their first video, for 'Welcome To The Jungle,' in Los Angeles.
• **22ND: THE *DEF JAM* TOUR**, hip-hop's first package event, starts in Richmond, Virginia, with LL Cool J, Public Enemy, Stetsasonic, Eric B & Rakim, Whodini, Doug E. Fresh & The Get Fresh Crew.
• **23RD: THE US SUPREME COURT** supports the use of hypnosis on a woman accused of shooting her husband when he tried to prevent her going out to buy a burger. Under hypnosis, she says the gun went off accidentally and is acquitted.
• **27TH: *WHITNEY*,** by Whitney Houston becomes the first album by a female artist to debut at US Number One, where it will stay for 11 weeks.

• **MAY 1ST: PUBLIC ENEMY** release their blistering debut album, *Yo! Bum Rush The Show*. Formed by rapper Chuck D and producer Hank Shocklee, soon joined by wisecracking, clock-wearing Flavor Flav, DJ Terminator X, and Professor Griff (later sacked for his anti-semitic remarks), they're described by manager Bill Stephney as "the Black Panthers of rap," and have been eagerly signed up by Rick Rubin and Russell Simmons' Def Jam label.

# 1987
May–August

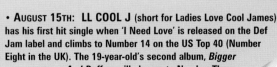

JULY

- **1st: THE ALBUM** *1984* by Van Halen is awarded a US six-times platinum disc by the RIAA.
- **3rd: LOS LOBOS** decide not to pursue legal action against Paul Simon who, they allege, simply added lyrics to one of their tracks in order to create the song 'The Myth Of Fingerprints' on his album *Graceland*.
- **4th: FORMER SS OFFICER** Klaus Barbie, now 73 years old, starts a life sentence for war crimes committed in France during World War II. In Barbie's case, life turns out to mean only four years, as he will die from leukemia in a prison hospital in Lyon, France, in September 1991.
- **5th: MARTINA NAVRATILOVA** wins the Wimbledon tennis title in the UK for a record sixth time after beating Steffi Graf in the final.

- **7th: SIX FORMER TECHNICIANS** from Chernobyl face trials relating to last year's disastrous accident at the nuclear power station. Three will later receive ten year prison sentences.
- **8th: MARINE COLONEL OLIVER NORTH** admits lying at the so-called 'Iran-Contra' hearings, and being a willing scapegoat for the Reagan administration. It transpires that North and his boss, National Security Adviser John Poindexter, were indeed secretly selling arms to the fundamentialist regime in Iran to help it fight Iraq (at the same time as the US was selling chemical and biological weapons to Saddam Hussein). The proceeds from this trade were then used to fund the Contra rebels in their action against the left-wing

Sandinista government in Nicaragua.
- **11th: HEART** reach Number One on the US singles chart with 'Alone.' It will remain there for three weeks.
- **18th: ROAD RAGE** comes to California, with a vengeance, as the first of nine different freeway shootings in the state this month takes place.
- **20th: PAUL MCCARTNEY** begins a two-day recording session in London, making an album of rock'n'roll oldies, for release in the Soviet Union only. It is called *Choba B CCCP*, translated as *Back In The USSR*.
- **24th: HULDA CROOKS**, of California, climbs Mount Fuji at 91 years of age, becoming the oldest person to conquer Japan's highest peak.

## The Talent Scout

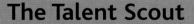

- **July 10th: LEGENDARY US RECORD** producer/A&R man John Hammond dies in New York City, at age 76. During a remarkable 50-year career, Hammond 'discovered' or helped establish many young and soon-to-be-significant artists, from Bessie Smith, Robert Johnson, and Billie Holiday to Pete Seeger, Bob Dylan, Aretha Franklin, and Bruce Springsteen. He was also instrumental in helping break down the color/race barrier in big-band jazz in the 1930s, encouraging Benny Goodman to hire musicians like Lionel Hampton, Teddy Wilson, and Charlie Christian. In the late 1930s Hammond organized the groundbreaking *Spirituals To Swing* concert, and helped launch the first non-segregated night club, Cafe Society. His son, also John Hammond, is a respected blues musician.

- **2nd: LUIS REINA** becomes the first matador to enter a bullring with advertising on his suit. The ad is for Akai, a Japanese electronics company.
- **11th: *ROLLING STONE*** magazine selects *Sgt Pepper's Lonely Hearts Club Band* by The Beatles as the best of the preceding 20 years.
- **13th: CHRIS MARSHALL** becomes the youngest pilot to fly round-trip across the U.S. He is ten years old.
- **19th: SIXTEEN PEOPLE** are killed and 14 wounded in Hungerford, Hertfordshire, UK, when 27-year-old Michael Ryan goes on a shooting spree. The worst civil massacre in modern British history only ends when Ryan shoots himself.
- **20th: VOCALIST/GUITARIST/SONGWRITER** Lindsey Buckingham leaves Fleetwood Mac after 12 successful years.
- **22nd: 'LUKA'** provides Suzanne Vega with her first major hit single, reaching US Number Three, and earning her a Grammy nomination. She generally has more luck in the UK, with five Top 40 entries...
- **26th: A BUSY EVENING** for Bruce Springsteen, who joins Jah Love on stage for three songs in the Key Largo club, Belmar, New Jersey, then wanders over to the Columns club, Avon, New Jersey, where he plays two songs with The Cherubs.
- **29th: US ACTOR** Lee Marvin dies, at the age of 63 (though he seemed older). In 1970, growling the *Paint Your Wagon* song 'Wandrin' Star,' he topped the UK charts for three weeks (though it seemed longer).

- **August 15th: LL COOL J** (short for Ladies Love Cool James) has his first hit single when 'I Need Love' is released on the Def Jam label and climbs to Number 14 on the US Top 40 (Number Eight in the UK). The 19-year-old's second album, *Bigger And Deffer*, will also go to Number Three on the US album chart.

## A Journey Into Sound

OCTOBER 3RD: 'PUMP UP THE VOLUME' by M/A/R/R/S reaches Number One on the UK singles chart (it'll become a Top 20 US hit early in 1988). This short-lived collaboration between two bands on the 4AD label, Colourbox and AR Kane, is musically significant because it introduces the pop mainstream to techniques previously only common in hip-hop and underground dance music circles – namely the use of sampling to create collages of 'rare-groove' beats, sampled from old funk and soul tracks, popularly James Brown and George Clinton, and vinyl scratching, as demonstrated here by top DJ/mixer CJ Mackintosh.

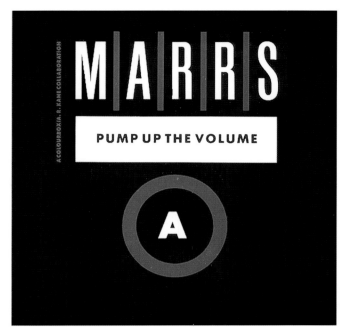

M|A|R|R|S

PUMP UP THE VOLUME

A

### SEPTEMBER

- **1ST: STEVIE WONDER** plays the first of five nights at Wembley Arena, London.
- **2ND: PHILIPS INTRODUCE** CD-video, which combines digital sound with high-definition visuals on a standard Compact Disc.
- **9TH: PINK FLOYD** begin their *Momentary Lapse Of Reason* tour in Ontario, Canada – in spite of persistent protests from Roger Waters over their use of the band name. Years later guitarist Dave Gilmour will dismiss the controversy, saying: "It's just a pop group, isn't it? ... It had happened before – Syd had left, Roger left, we carried on. It didn't seem to be a major decision."
- **11TH: FOUR ANIMAL RIGHTS** protesters are arrested for plotting to steal a dolphin (worth $35,000) from Marineland in Morecambe, UK.
- **11TH: PETER TOSH**, founder member of The Wailers alongside Bob Marley, is shot dead in Jamaica, at age 42.
- **16TH: TWENTY SEVEN**

**COUNTRIES** make an agreement to protect the world's atmosphere by controlling their CFC emissions.
- **17TH: THE US CONSTITUTION** is 200 years old today... And tonight, the video for Peter Gabriel's single 'Sledgehammer' wins ten of the 20 awards at the MTV Video Awards ceremony.
- **20TH: BONO OF U2** dislocates his arm during a gig at RFK Stadium, Washington, DC, when he slips on the wet stage during the song 'Exit.'
- **26TH: *BAD* BY MICHAEL JACKSON** reaches Number One on the US album chart for the first of six weeks.
- **30TH: BRUCE SPRINGSTEEN** plays rhythm guitar as part of an all-star band backing Roy Orbison during filming of the Cinemax special Roy Orbison & Friends. Other members include Elvis Costello, Tom Waits, Elvis Presley guitarist James Burton, k.d. lang, and Jackson Browne.

- **OCTOBER 15TH: THE WORST HURRICANE** to hit Britain since records began strikes in the early hours of the morning, devastating southern England and causing at least 17 deaths.

### OCTOBER

- **1ST: GRUNGE PIONEERS** Soundgarden release their debut recording, an EP entitled *Screaming Life*, on Seattle's independent Sub Pop label... Meanwhile, further down the west coast (but probably not connected), LA is hit by a 6.1 magnitude earthquake.
- **7TH: GEFFEN RECORDS** agrees to end its recording contract with Neil Young, who has been trying to get out of the deal for some time.
- **8TH: CHUCK BERRY** is awarded a star on the Hollywood Walk Of Fame.
- **11TH: THE LATEST ATTEMPT** to find the Loch Ness Monster fails after a huge sonar sweep of the Loch comes up blank.
- **14TH: THE BEASTIE BOYS** are hit with a "breach of copyright" lawsuit by members of the Jimmy Castor Bunch, who allege that a portion of their 1967 hit 'The Return Of Leroy' has been used without permission on the Boys' 'Hold It, Now Hit It.'
- **17TH: 'LOST IN EMOTION'** by Lisa Lisa & Cult Jam reaches Number One on the US Top 40 singles chart.
- **18TH: A US COMPANY** announces it is shipping 12 million pairs of chopsticks to Japan because of a shortage of timber there.
- **19TH: WORLDWIDE STOCK MARKETS** crash on what will become known as Black Monday. On Wall Street, share values fall by half a trillion dollars (the New York Post calls it "a bloodbath"), while in London stocks drop a record 508 points. The crash is thought to be

triggered by general lack of confidence, due to trade deficits and high interest rates, compounded by insider trading scandals. The sums of money involved are greater than those in the 1929 crash that ushered in the Great Depression.
- **23RD: LESTER PIGGOTT**, the former British champion jockey, and now a top trainer, is jailed for three years for tax evasion... Fortunately for Lester, he doesn't try the same trick as a burglar in San Antonio, Texas, who

receives a seven-year prison sentence today. He decides to complain to the judge that seven is his unlucky number: the judge obligingly raises the sentence to eight years.
- **29TH: THOMAS 'HIT MAN' HEARNS** wins the world middle heavyweight title, making him the first boxer to win a world title at four different weights.
- **31ST: US BAND GREEN RIVER** break up, but bandmember Stone Gossard will go on to form Pearl Jam.

### Big Hopes

- **NOVEMBER 7TH: SIXTEEN-YEAR-OLD TIFFANY** (who chooses not to use her surname – Darwisch) becomes the youngest female to top the US singles charts, with a mostly-in-tune cover version of the Tommy James & The Shondells classic 'I Think We're Alone Now.' She follows it up in a couple of months with another Number One, 'Could've Been.'

# True Faith

- **DECEMBER 5TH: NEW ORDER** have their first US hit with 'True Faith,' accompanied by an eye-catchingly surreal video by French choreographer Philippe Decouflé. It's a colorful, and brave, departure for a band whose image has previously reflected the more austere and industrialized side of their northern English background.

## NOVEMBER

- **2ND: DENG XIAOPING** retires from the Central Committee in China.
- **8TH: TODAY IS THE 100TH ANNIVERSARY** of Emile Berliner obtaining US patent number 372,786 for his new invention – the gramophone.
- **11TH: WHEN U2 PLAY** a free open air concert at the Embarcadero Center, San Francisco, Bono climbs onto a modern sculpture by Armand Vaillancourt, and spray-paints it with the words "Rock And Roll"

and "Stop The Traffic." The city of San Francisco issues a warrant for his arrest and fines him for vandalizing public property.
- **12TH: VAN GOGH'S IRISES** – painted while he was a patient at the St Rémy lunatic asylum – is sold for a world record $45 million (£30.2m).
- **13TH: WHEN AEROSMITH PLAY** at the Brendan Byrne Arena, Meadowlands, New Jersey, Bon Jovi joins them for a rendition of 'I'm Down.'

- **15TH: DIRE STRAITS'** album Brothers In Arms become the first in history to sell three million copies in the UK alone.
- **17TH: MORE THAN SEVEN MONTHS** after hearings began into the Iran-Contra scandal, the US Senate & House Commission finds Ronald Reagan responsible – but it's unclear whether it's for lying or simply having no idea what was going on.
- **18TH: THE WORST FIRE** in the history of the London Underground kills 30 people – the blaze begins below a wooden escalator at King's Cross Underground tube station, probably caused by a discarded match. A smoking ban is immediately introduced on public transport.
- **19TH: A 1931 BUGATTI ROYALE** is sold for £5.5 million ($8.25m) at an auction at the Royal Albert Hall, London – it's a record fee for a car.
- **20TH: ELTON JOHN SELLS HIS SHARE** in English soccer club Watford FC to media magnate Robert Maxwell.
- **26TH: A JURY AT THE OLD BAILEY** in London decide that drawings of English banknotes by US artist James Boggs are works of art, and not illegal forgeries of currency.

## DECEMBER

- **3RD: RUSH PRODUCTIONS**, the management company for Run-DMC, sues the group's record label, Profile, alleging a $7m underpayment of royalties for the album Raisin' Hell.
- **4TH: MADONNA** files for divorce from Sean Penn in Malibu – only to change her mind a week later.
- **5TH: BELINDA CARLISLE**, formerly of The Go-Go's, scores her first US Number One with 'Heaven Is A Place On Earth.'
- **8TH: PRESIDENTS GORBACHEV** and Reagan sign the first-ever treaty to reduce USSR and US ground-based intermediate-range missiles – though the INF (Intermediate Nuclear Forces) treaty will not be fully agreed until June 1988.
- **9TH: THE FIRST PICTURE** CDs are issued by CBS, featuring Michael Jackson, Bruce Springsteen, George Michael, and Terence Trent D'Arby.
- **11TH: CHARLIE CHAPLIN'S** cane & bowler hat are sold at Christie's, London, for $125,000, and his boots for $60,000.
- **16TH: ITALY'S BIGGEST MAFIA TRIAL** convicts 13 Mafia bosses to life sentences, 22

- **DECEMBER 19TH: IVAN BOESKY**, the 'King of Arbitrage' is beginning a three-year prison term for insider dealing on the US stock exchange. Boesky is believed to be the model for the Michael Douglas character, Gordon "Greed Is Good" Gekko, in Oliver Stone's new movie Wall Street.

months after the trial opened. More than 1300 people have testified, and of the 474 defendants, two have been shot while out on bail.
- **18TH: THE MYSTERY SURROUNDING** Prince's unreleased, untitled 'Black' album intensifies when, despite having denied its existence earlier in the month, Warner Brothers now admits that several hundred copies of the album were in fact pressed, but immediately withdrawn.
- **20TH: A PHILIPPINES FERRY**, the Dona Paz, with more than 1,500 passengers on-board, sinks in shark-infested waters south of Manila, after colliding with an oil tanker. More lives are lost than when the Titanic sank.
- **23RD: SANTA CLAUS**, by arrangement with the Finnish Tourist Board, has an audience with the Pope to prove that, "the Finnish Santa is the genuine article."
- **26TH: SLASH OF GUNS N' ROSES** is partying at the LA home of Motley Crue's Nikki Sixx, when Sixx collapses and turns blue – he is revived by paramedics.

## New Faith

- **NOVEMBER 6TH: GEORGE MICHAEL** releases Faith, his first album since the demise of Wham!. It enters the UK chart at Number One, though it's out-sold by the Paul McCartney compilation All The Best. Faith also gets to Number One on the US albums chart, and spawns four US Number One singles for stubbly George.

# 1988
## January–April

## New Sensation

**JANUARY 30TH: INXS** have their first and only US Number One with 'Need You Tonight,' aided by an intriguingly uncluttered production and a cleverly edited video, which MTV predictably puts on heavy rotation. The band follows this with 'Devil Inside,' 'New Sensation,' and 'Mystify Me,' which reach Numbers Two, Three and Seven respectively this year. All four tracks come from the impressively assured, and astutely promoted, *Kick*. It's the first time many people are aware of the band, though it's actually their sixth album; and they're already stars in their native Australia, where they formed back in 1977. Based around the Farriss brothers, Andrew, Tim, and Jon, plus of course drop-dead handsome frontman Michael Hutchence, they have taken a long tough road from outback gigs in mining camps to LA glitz, but INXS have finally arrived. It's all good news – for the next few years...

## G-L-O-R-I-A

• **MARCH 26TH: GLORIA ESTEFAN** & The Miami Sound Machine enter the US Top 40 singles chart with 'Anything For You,' which will give them their first Number One. Based around Cuban-born Gloria and her husband Emilio, the group initially record in Spanish only, but soon decide to start releasing English language singles and albums as well, efficiently spreading the band's infectious Latin rhythms to international audiences.

• **1ST: BONEY M** producer Frank Farian invites breakdancers Rob Pilatus and Fabrice Morvan to his studio in Frankfurt, Germany. They sign a contract, which will result in the creation of a carefully manufactured pop duo – Milli Vanilli.

• **2ND: A NEW YORK** accountant finally claims his $3 million lottery jackpot, won 45 days earlier. He's waited until the New Year in order to save about $15,000 in taxes.

• **4TH: MTV EDITS OUT** semi-naked girls fondling phallic crucifixes from Billy Idol's 'Hot In The City' video (made to promote the re-released single), so Idol refuses to let them air it at all. He's just had a Number One single with a live version of 'Mony Mony,' and is at the peak of his career. Sadly for him, it's all downhill from here on...

• **4TH: MEANWHILE,** Indian moustache-growing champion Karni Bheel dies, taking his 7'10" lip-hair with him.

• **7TH: SANTANA,** The Eagles, and Fleetwood Mac are the latest to be inducted to The Rock & Roll Hall Of Fame.

• **19TH: CHRISTOPHER NOLAN,** a 22-year-old Irish writer, wins the £20,000 Whitbread Book Of The Year Award for his autobiography, *Under The Eye Of The Clock*. Nolan is completely paralyzed, and used a 'unicorn' attachment on his forehead to write the novel, painfully slowly.

• **21ST: U2 ARE NOW** the biggest concert attraction in America, having grossed $35m from US gigs in 1987.

• **23RD: KURT COBAIN,** later to lead Nirvana, records several demos at Reciprocal Recording Studios, Seattle, Washington.

• **JANUARY 16TH: QUIET BEATLE** George Harrison ascends to Number One in the US with his comeback single, a cover of James Ray's 1962 song 'Got My Mind Set On You.' It's George's first chart-topper since he released 'Give Me Love (Give Me Peace On Earth)' in 1973.

• **FEBRUARY 8TH: AT THE BRIT** Awards in the Royal Albert Hall, London, George Michael wins Best British Male Artist; Pet Shop Boys are Best Band; Alison Moyet is Best Female Singer; Rick Astley's 'Never Gonna Give You Up' is Best Single; and Sting's Nothing Like The Sun is Best Album; and Best British Newcomers are Wet Wet Wet. Of all these acts, the one who's most successful in the US this year is Rick Astley (above), a former drummer and tape operator at Pete Waterman's PWL studios, who eventually ends up singing on a string of Stock, Aitken & Waterman hits, including two US Number Ones.

• **1ST: THE CARS** announce that they have decided to disband.

• **4TH: US ROCK CRITIC** Chuck Eddy serves a $500,000 lawsuit on the Beastie Boys for "commercial appropriation of his image." They'd thrown a bucket of water over him while he slept, then used the image in one of their videos.

• **6TH: CONTROVERSIAL RAP** band Public Enemy make their

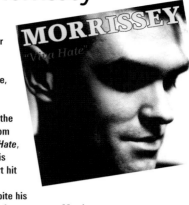

## Viva Morrissey

• **FEBRUARY 27TH: EX-SMITHS** singer Morrissey releases his debut solo single, 'Suedehead,' which reaches Number Five in the UK. It comes from his album *Viva Hate*, which will be his biggest US chart hit to date, solo or otherwise. Despite his relative lack of chart success, Morrissey attracts a fanatical cult following in the States, which gradually becomes his second home. Indeed it eventually becomes his base, as this apparent epitome of British wit and culture becomes an enthusiastic resident of Los Angeles, with a mansion in the Hollywood Hills.

**MARCH**

**APRIL**

first appearance on the US singles charts with 'Bring The Noise.'

• **10TH: SIR JOHN GIELGUD** makes theatrical history when, just weeks away from his 84th birthday, he plays Sydney Cockerell in Hugh Whitmore's play *The Best Of Friends*, the longest role ever for an actor of his age.

• **20TH: EXPOSÉ** reach Number One in the US with 'Seasons Change' – the fourth Top Ten hit from their debut album.

• **23RD: MICHAEL JACKSON** opens the US leg of his Bad tour at the Kemper Arena, Kansas, Missouri... And the 15th Winter Olympic Games opens in Calgary, Canada. English plasterer and occasional ski-jumper Eddie Edwards, who stays at a psychiatric home in Finland while training, becomes the surprise sensation of the Games. The fearless, bespectacled skier comes last, but gains headlines around the world, and the nickname 'Eagle.'

• **25TH: US TV EVANGELIST** Jimmy Swaggart (a piano-playing cousin of Jerry Lee Lewis) is suspended by the elders of his church, the Assemblies Of God, for his descent into immorality. Swaggart admits he's been spending time with a prostitute in New Orleans, although he claims they did not have sex – he just liked to watch her undress. He tearfully pleads for forgiveness (and more funds) on TV, and is back within months. As Swaggart himself asserts, "God loves a sinner."

• **2ND: THE 30TH ANNUAL GRAMMY AWARDS** are held in Radio City Music Hall, New York City. Bruce Springsteen's album *Tunnel Of Love* scoops Best Rock Solo Vocal Performance. Whitney Houston gets Best Pop Vocal Performance (Female). U2's album *The Joshua Tree* gets two Grammies. Paul Simon gets Record Of The Year for *Graceland* – which is curious, as he won with the same album a year ago.

• **3RD: RUN-DMC** lose their legal battle to sever their contract with Profile Records, and find themselves signed up to the label – which they claim has ripped them off to the tune of $7m – for another ten years. The dispute has also

• **MARCH 8TH: SOAP OPERA** writers in the US go on strike, threatening shows such as *Dallas* and *Dynasty* (below).

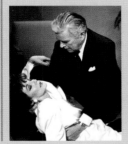

delayed the release of their fourth album, 'Tougher Than Leather,' and other hip-hop bands have muscled into their territory in the meantime. Although they continie to be respected as 'Old Skool' pioneers, their career will never quite hit the same heights again – at least for ten years.

• **9TH: THE MOTHER** of teenage pop star Tiffany files a missing person report on her daughter, who disappeared the previous day. Simultaneously, Tiffany files for legal emancipation with LA Juvenile Court...

• **10TH: ANDY GIBB**, the singing Gibb brother who was not in the Bee Gees, dies of heart failure in Oxford, UK, at age 29. He had eight Top 20 hits, including three Numbers Ones, from 1977 to 1980.

• **12TH: DIAMOND MINE** owners De Beers, unveil a 599-carat diamond, second only in size to the one in the British royal sceptre, and worth tens of millions of dollars.

• **19TH: MICHAEL JACKSON** buys Sycamore Ranch in the Santa Ynez Valley, California, for no less than $28 million.

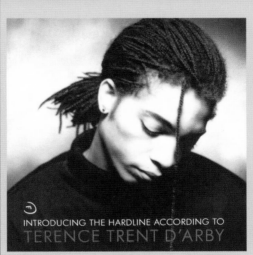

INTRODUCING THE HARDLINE ACCORDING TO TERENCE TRENT D'ARBY

• **APRIL 19TH: THE ALBUM** *Introducing The Hardline According To Terence Trent D'Arby,* by UK-based American singer Terence Trent D'Arby, is certified as a platinum disc in the US by the RIAA. His debut single, 'Wishing Well,' is also on its way to Number One on the US singles chart.

• **APRIL 30TH: CELINE DION** wins the *Eurovision Song Contest,* in Dublin, Eire, with 'Ne Partez Pas Sans Moi.' Though French-Canadian, she is representing Switzerland.

• **8TH: R.E.M.** sign a $6m record contract with Warner Brothers, a step on the road to world fame.

• **9TH: 'GET OUTTA MY DREAMS, GET INTO MY CAR'** by Billy Ocean, once a Ford worker in the UK, reaches Number One on the US Top 40 singles chart.

• **10TH: THE WORLD'S LONGEST** double-decker bridge opens to cars and trains. The 7.6 mile (12.2 km) Great Seto Bridge in Japan crosses the Inland Sea and links the islands of Honshu and Shikoku. It's taken ten years to build at a cost of $8 billion.

• **11TH: GUNS N' ROSES** shoot the video for their single 'Sweet Child O' Mine' in a ballroom at Huntington Park, California.

• **19TH: CHINA RADIO** begins broadcasting western pop music for the first time, ranging from Glenn Miller to Madonna. 'Roll Over Beethoven' is banned, however, as being disrespectful to the composer.

• **23RD: KANELLOS KANELOPOULOS** sets three world records for human-powered flight when he stays in the air for four hours and travels 74 miles in his pedal-powered aircraft Daedalus... Meanwhile Whitney Houston overtakes The Beatles and The Bee Gees when 'Where Do Broken Hearts Go' gives her seven consecutive US Number One singles.

• **30TH: NEW KIDS ON THE BLOCK**, whose debut album last year has sold only 5,000 copies, audition for US teen star Tiffany in her dressing room, and earn themselves the opening slot on her upcoming tour.

# Fast Car, Fast Track

**A**UGUST 27TH: **TRACY CHAPMAN'S** self-titled debut is the US Number One album. It's been a rapid rise to stardom for the 24-year-old singer-songwriter, triggered in particular by one event this summer – her appearance at the Nelson Mandela 70th Birthday Tribute Concert in June (see below), which was broadcast on TV across the globe. Such is the impact of her performance that her previously modestly-selling album shifts 12,000 copies in the UK in just two days. Within two months, she has topped the charts on both sides of the Atlantic. The single 'Fast Car' is equally successful, and Chapman is invited to participate with Bruce Springsteen, Peter Gabriel, Youssou N'Dour, and Sting on the Human Rights Now Tour, on behalf of Amnesty International, which starts in London in September and ends up in Buenos Aires, Argentina. But her suddenly elevation to rock's élite is difficult for her to sustain, and while her next album, 1989's *Crossroads*, makes Number One in the UK, it stalls at Number Nine in the US. And 1992's *Matters Of The Heart* (Number 19 in the UK) is all but ignored in her homeland. But she will be called upon to perform 'The Times They Are A-Changin' at a 30th Anniversary Dylan tribute in New York in 1992.

## MAY

- **5TH: THE FIRST LIVE BROADCAST** from the summit of Mount Everest is transmitted by Japanese television.
- **7TH: BOB DYLAN**, George Harrison, Roy Orbison, Tom Petty, and Jeff Lynne get together at Dylan's home in Malibu, California, to start work on the first Traveling Wilburys album... Meanwhile the first gathering of people claiming to have been abducted by aliens takes place in Boston, Massachusetts.
- **8TH: NANCY REAGAN'S** reliance on an astrologer (Joan Quigley) and the extent of her influence on President Reagan are revealed when *Time* magazine publishes the first extract from the memoirs of former chief of staff, Donald Regan... And Madonna makes her stage debut on Broadway in David Mamet's play *Speed The Plow*. Critics are less than enthusiastic about her thespian accomplishments. One says her performance is a "a joke, but not a funny one."
- **14TH: ATLANTIC RECORDS** celebrates its 40th anniversary with a concert in Madison Square Garden, New York City. The line-up features Led Zeppelin, Yes, Genesis, Iron Butterfly, The Rascals, Crosby, Stills & Nash, Foreigner, Paul Rodgers, Bob Geldof, Booker T. Jones, Wilson Pickett, The Coasters, The Spinners, Peabo Bryson, Roberta Flack, Manhattan Transfer, Debbie Gibson, The Bee Gees, Ruth Brown, LaVern Baker, Ben E. King, and Vanilla Fudge.
- **15TH: SOVIET TROOPS** begin leaving Afghanistan after eight years of occupation, which had cost 13,000 soldiers' lives.
- **16TH: THE RED HOT CHILI PEPPERS** release their *Abbey Road* EP, whose cover features the band striding across the famous London pedestrian crosswalk, naked except for socks over their penises.
- **29TH: SPEEDING OUT** of their brains, unknown pop fans Noel and Liam Gallagher go to the International Two venue in Manchester to see The Stone Roses supporting James.
- **31ST: A MALE NORWEGIAN** soldier wins the right to wear earrings on parade. Two female judges declare it would be sexual discrimination to order him to take them off.

## JUNE

- **JUNE 11TH: NELSON MANDELA'S 70TH BIRTHDAY** is celebrated (in his absence, as he's still in prison) with a star-studded ten-hour concert at Wembley Stadium in London. A crowd of 72,000 turn up, while close to a billion watch the televised event around the world. The line-up includes Simple Minds, Whitney Houston, Dire Straits (with guest Eric Clapton), Sting, George Michael, Al Green, The Eurythmics, Natalie Cole, Joe Cocker, Paul Young, Bryan Adams, The Bee Gees, Wet Wet Wet (whose guest backing band includes Midge Ure, Phil Collins, and Johnny Marr of The Smiths), UB40 with Chrissie Hynde (below), Jerry Dammers, South African stars Hugh Masakela and Miriam Makeba, Peter Gabriel, Stevie Wonder, 'Little Steven' Van Zandt, Tracy Chapman (see above), and opera singer Jessye Norman. There are also non-musical contributions from actors and comedians like Billy Connolly, Harry Belafonte, Whoopi Goldberg, Michael Palin, and Richard Gere... Also today, Nirvana record their debut single, 'Love Buzz,' at Reciprocal Recording Studios, Seattle, Washington.

- **JUNE 25TH: SALT-N-PEPA** re-release the single 'Push It' in the UK – having already reached Number 19 in the US earlier on the year – and end up with a Number Two hit.

- **1ST: THE ALBUMS** *Bad* and *Off The Wall* by Michael Jackson are both awarded US six-times platinum discs by the RIAA... Meanwhile inmates inside Oregon penitentiary begin pacing their exercise yard in the first sponsored walk to take place in a prison. They will ultimately walk 3,400 miles for charity.
- **5TH: AFTER SIX MONTHS** at sea, lone yachtswoman Kay Cottee sails into Sydney Harbour, Australia, becoming the first woman to circumnavigate the world non-stop, in her 35 foot yacht First Lady. It has taken her 189 days.
- **6TH: THREE GIANT** Snapping Turtles are found inside a Bronx sewage treatment plant in New York City. Weighing about 50 pounds each, they've probably been unwanted pets, flushed down the toilet when quite small.
- **7TH: BOB DYLAN** begins his *Never Ending Tour* at Concord Pavilion, Concord, California, supported by The Alarm. Neil Young shows up and plays during Dylan's electric set.
- **10TH: SUCCESSFUL UK BAND** The Housemartins split. Singer Paul Heaton will form The Beautiful South, while Norman Cook will evolve into Fatboy Slim.
- **17TH: DENNIS LOBAN**, a street vendor and ex-convict, is found guilty of the murder of reggae star Peter Tosh in Kingston, Jamaica, during a robbery.
- **25TH: DEBBIE GIBSON** reaches Number One on the US Top 40 singles chart with 'Foolish Beat.'
- **26TH: HILLEL SLOVAK**, 26-year-old guitarist with The Red Hot Chili Peppers, dies alone in his apartment after a heroin overdose. His body will not be discovered for two days.

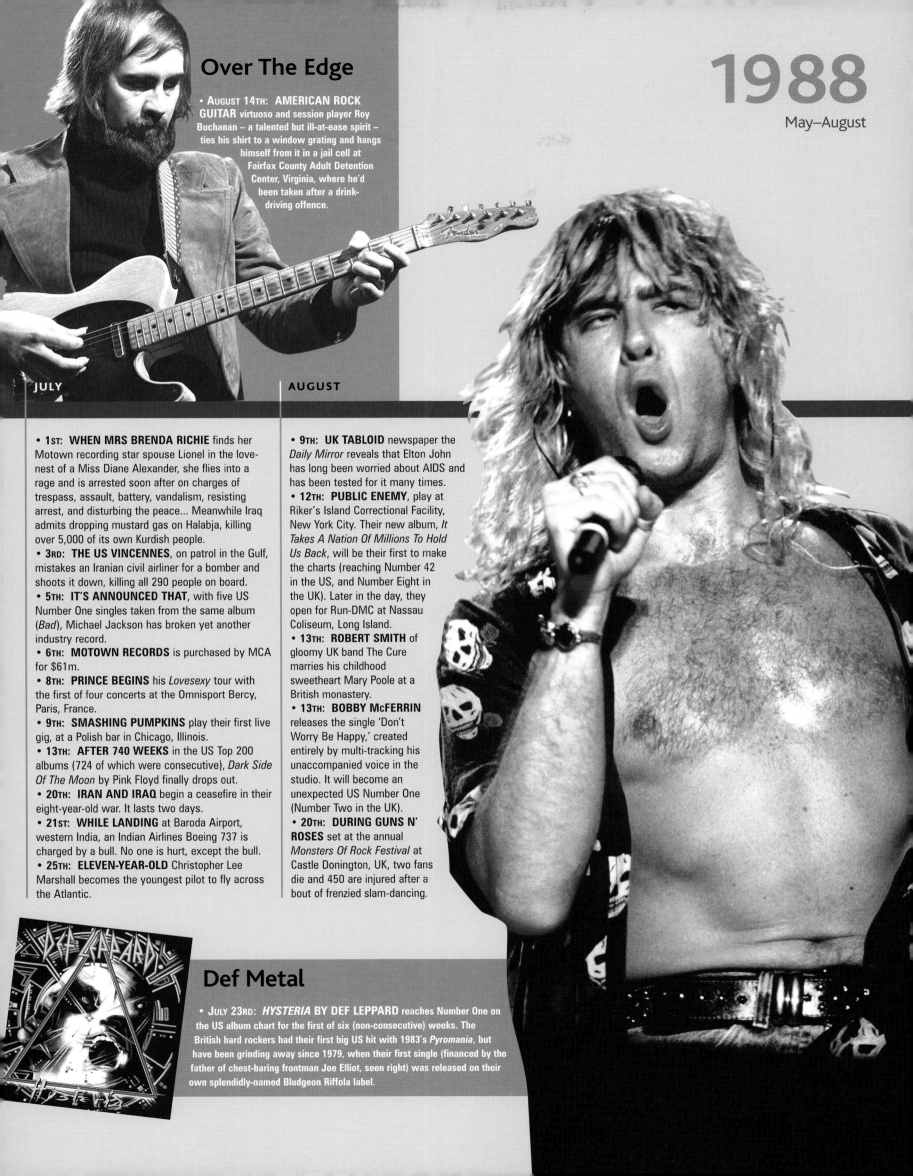

## Over The Edge

- **August 14th:** **AMERICAN ROCK GUITAR** virtuoso and session player Roy Buchanan – a talented but ill-at-ease spirit – ties his shirt to a window grating and hangs himself from it in a jail cell at Fairfax County Adult Detention Center, Virginia, where he'd been taken after a drink-driving offence.

### JULY

- **1st:** **WHEN MRS BRENDA RICHIE** finds her Motown recording star spouse Lionel in the love-nest of a Miss Diane Alexander, she flies into a rage and is arrested soon after on charges of trespass, assault, battery, vandalism, resisting arrest, and disturbing the peace... Meanwhile Iraq admits dropping mustard gas on Halabja, killing over 5,000 of its own Kurdish people.
- **3rd:** **THE US VINCENNES**, on patrol in the Gulf, mistakes an Iranian civil airliner for a bomber and shoots it down, killing all 290 people on board.
- **5th:** **IT'S ANNOUNCED THAT**, with five US Number One singles taken from the same album (*Bad*), Michael Jackson has broken yet another industry record.
- **6th:** **MOTOWN RECORDS** is purchased by MCA for $61m.
- **8th:** **PRINCE BEGINS** his *Lovesexy* tour with the first of four concerts at the Omnisport Bercy, Paris, France.
- **9th:** **SMASHING PUMPKINS** play their first live gig, at a Polish bar in Chicago, Illinois.
- **13th:** **AFTER 740 WEEKS** in the US Top 200 albums (724 of which were consecutive), *Dark Side Of The Moon* by Pink Floyd finally drops out.
- **20th:** **IRAN AND IRAQ** begin a ceasefire in their eight-year-old war. It lasts two days.
- **21st:** **WHILE LANDING** at Baroda Airport, western India, an Indian Airlines Boeing 737 is charged by a bull. No one is hurt, except the bull.
- **25th:** **ELEVEN-YEAR-OLD** Christopher Lee Marshall becomes the youngest pilot to fly across the Atlantic.

### AUGUST

- **9th:** **UK TABLOID** newspaper the *Daily Mirror* reveals that Elton John has long been worried about AIDS and has been tested for it many times.
- **12th:** **PUBLIC ENEMY**, play at Riker's Island Correctional Facility, New York City. Their new album, *It Takes A Nation Of Millions To Hold Us Back*, will be their first to make the charts (reaching Number 42 in the US, and Number Eight in the UK). Later in the day, they open for Run-DMC at Nassau Coliseum, Long Island.
- **13th:** **ROBERT SMITH** of gloomy UK band The Cure marries his childhood sweetheart Mary Poole at a British monastery.
- **13th:** **BOBBY McFERRIN** releases the single 'Don't Worry Be Happy,' created entirely by multi-tracking his unaccompanied voice in the studio. It will become an unexpected US Number One (Number Two in the UK).
- **20th:** **DURING GUNS N' ROSES** set at the annual *Monsters Of Rock Festival* at Castle Donington, UK, two fans die and 450 are injured after a bout of frenzied slam-dancing.

## Def Metal

- **July 23rd:** **HYSTERIA BY DEF LEPPARD** reaches Number One on the US album chart for the first of six (non-consecutive) weeks. The British hard rockers had their first big US hit with 1983's *Pyromania*, but have been grinding away since 1979, when their first single (financed by the father of chest-baring frontman Joe Elliot, seen right) was released on their own splendidly-named Bludgeon Riffola label.

# 1988
## September–December

# House Vs Techno

**B**Y 1998, TWO NEW musical forms are appearing in the mainstream, spreading from the dance clubs of the bigger cities of the US and UK, and beginning to make an impact on the charts. House music is a natural descendent of disco, but stripped down to its rhythmical basics, with minimal lyrics and vocals, often using the crucial ability of newly-developed digital sequencers to supply tirelessly repetitive beats and loops. Though originating in the clubs of New York (mainly on the gay scene at first), it was taken to Chicago in the early 1980s by New York DJ (and former bass player) Frankie Knuckles, who started a club called called The Warehouse, giving the new style a name: '(Ware)house music.' Knuckles would mix disco, funk, and soul with tracks from European synthesizer outfits like Depeche Mode and Soft Cell, and in doing so he inspired numerous copyists. At the same time, Farley Jackmaster Funk was spreading the word about house on his groundbreaking Chicago radio show on WBMX. Techno, an even more minimalist, intense and experimental off-shoot of house, first appeared in Detroit, also in the early 1980s. It was created by pioneers like Juan Atkins, Kevin Saunderson and Derrick May. May famously explained techno by saying, "It's like George Clinton and Kraftwerk are stuck in an elevator, with only a sequencer to keep them company." Electronic music was going through a boom period at this time, with equipment prices falling dramatically and options expanding, thanks to products from

## SEPTEMBER

• **SEPTEMBER 10TH: GUNS N' ROSES**, led by singer Axl Rose and guitar player Slash (left), have their first big hit when the single 'Sweet Child O' Mine' lands at Number One in the US. In the UK it doesn't make the Top Ten until it's reissued in summer 1989.

• **2ND: BRUCE SPRINGSTEEN**, Sting, Peter Gabriel and others kick off a worldwide charity tour at Wembley Stadium in London. The intention is to raise funds for the human rights organization Amnesty International.

• **3RD: IN LOS ANGELES**, Madonna starts work with producer, pianist and songwriter Patrick Leonard on what will become the *Like A Prayer* album.

• **5TH: NEARLY TWO THIRDS** of Pakistan (including the capital Dhaka) is now underwater, after extensive flooding leaves over 20 million people homeless.

• **15TH: MARK KNOPFLER** announces that Dire Straits are being disbanded after 11 successful years to enable him to pursue a solo career.

• **16TH: FROM TODAY** you can own your own Elvis Presley credit card, with a limit of $3,500, issued in the US by a Memphis finance house in conjunction with Elvis's estate. Thousands of people apply.

• **24TH: HAVING JUST DISRUPTED** an insurance seminar by brandishing a sawn-off shotgun and demanding to know "Who used my restroom?", James Brown is arrested in Augusta, Georgia after an interstate car chase. He gets a six year jail sentence, but is released on parole after serving two.

• **26TH: SPRINTER BEN JOHNSON** is stripped of his 100 metres gold medal after failing a drugs test at the Seoul Olympics in South Korea.

• **30TH: FIVE ASTRONAUTS** return to Earth in the space shuttle Discovery, completing the first manned space flight since the Challenger disaster in 1986.

## OCTOBER

• **OCTOBER 15TH: REGGAE TOPS THE US** chart for the first time with UB40's version of Neil Diamond's 'Red Red Wine.'

• **4TH: BAVARIAN ENVIRONMENT** minister Alfred Dick appeals to people not to yodel in the Alps as the noise is scaring off the rare wildlife.

• **6TH: THE ALBUM** *Whitney Houston* is declared a US nine-times platinum album by the RIAA.

• **8TH: THE BIZARRE PARTNERSHIP** of Queen's Freddie Mercury and opera diva Montserrat Caballe launch their duet single 'Barcelona,' in the Spanish city of that name.

• **11TH: A BRIEF BUT HISTORIC REUNION** of former Cream stars Eric Clapton and Jack Bruce takes place when they jam at the Bottom Line Club in New York City.

• **17TH: BEETHOVEN'S** lost *10th Symphony* is performed for the first time, in London, as a result of researcher Barry Cooper piecing together fragments of manuscript discovered in Berlin. Critics insist it should be called the *Excerpts & Snippets' Symphony*.

• **18TH: BRITISH HOME SECRETARY**, Douglas Hurd, bans all spoken broadcasts by IRA or Sinn Fein spokespeople. They can still be seen on TV, but their voices must be dubbed by actors.

• **25TH: THE ALBUM** *The Traveling Wilburys Volume One* is released by a supergroup comprising Bob Dylan, George Harrison Roy Orbison, Jeff Lynne, and Tom Petty.

• **30TH: KURT COBAIN** of Nirvana smashes his first guitar onstage, at the Evergreen State Dorm Party, Olympia, Washington.

Japanese companies like Roland, Akai, Korg, and Yamaha. The technology may have been primitive by later standards, but a surprising amount of modern dance music will be produced on these relatively unsophisticated machines for many years to come. Early techno depends largely upon the use of a succession of punchy-sounding Roland drum machines and bass generators (whose model numbers, like 101, 303, 606, and 808, will crop up in various track titles and artist names), along with crudely-sampled drumbreaks from old funk records, horn stabs, strings, and vocals. Unlike the house sound coming out of Chicago, Detroit techno is originally all about minimal percussive loops and hypnotic string arrangements. New York DJs like Joey Beltram and Frankie Bones then pick up on the sound with their own leaner, tougher versions, and soon Germany and the UK are clamoring for acts like Jeff Mills, Plastikman, and Hardfloor. In 1986, acid house makes its first appearance, with the sonic emphasis on manipulating the 'squelchy' filters on the Roland TB-303 bass synth, thanks to the lead shown by experimenters like DJ Pierre, his colleague Spanky, remixer Marshall Jefferson, and acid's key populariser, Warehouse DJ Ron Hardy. (Jefferson later goes on to specialise in a more soulful "deep house.") The first big mainstream breakthroughs for the new

US underground club sounds are, ironically, in the UK, where Raze's 'Jack The Groove' breaches the Top 20 at the end of 1986, and 'Jack Your Body' becomes a Number One hit for Chicago DJ Steve 'Silk' Hurley in January 1987. The hugely influential 'Acid Trax,' released in 1988 by Pierre & Spanky under the name Phuture, leads to a thriving acid house culture in the UK, where the scene is subjected to a media assault because of its associated drug use. The originators of the music insist that the 'acid' in the name has nothing to do with drugs, but the nature of the scene, with its all-night 'rave' parties and loved-up atmosphere (and 'smiley face' logos) becomes inseparable from the growth in sales of a newer drug, ecstasy. For the next few years, organisers of secret, illegal raves, in empty warehouses or large fields, play cat-and-mouse with police intent on stopping them. Acid house will eventually turn into hardcore, and plays a part in spawning newer breeds of dance music like jungle and gabba.

## NOVEMBER

- **1ST: UK TV POP CHART SHOW** *Top Of The Pops* bans any record that includes the word "acid." At the same time, the UK's Mecca ballroom chain bans acid house music events (see top panel story)... Meanwhile, after 48 years as Batman's sidekick, Robin is blown up by the Joker in this month's edition of DC Comics' *Batman* (Number 428). The Boy Wonder's demise comes in response to a readers' poll which voted he should go.
- **5TH: TWENTY-TWO YEARS** after their last US chart-topping single, 'Good Vibrations,' The Beach Boys return to Number One with the single 'Kokomo.'
- **6TH: IT'S DISCOVERED** that a computer virus which crippled more than 6,000 US Defense Department computers was in fact spread by a 23-year-old graduate whose father heads the US's computer security agency.
- **7TH: SONGWRITER** John Fogerty is cleared of plagiarism, following a bizarre lawsuit in

- **NOVEMBER 21ST: CROSBY STILLS NASH & YOUNG** release *American Dream*, their first studio album since *Deja Vu*, 18 years earlier.

which Fantasy Records claimed that Fogerty's 1985 US Top Ten solo single 'The Old Man Down The Road' copied the 1970 song 'Run Through The Jungle' — which Fogarty himself had written while a member of Creedence Clearwater Revival.
- **8TH: GEORGE BUSH SR** beats Mike Dukakis for presidency of the USA.
- **11TH: RUSSIAN COSMONAUTS** Vladimir Totov and Musa Manarov spent their 326th record-breaking day in space.
- **12TH: 'ORINOCO FLOW'** by Enya starts its third week at Number One in the UK singles chart. The multi-layered vocals of the former Clannad singer will eventually reach the bottom half of the US Top 40 next spring.
- **14TH: THE POGUES** become the first musical victims of a British government ban on broadcasting statements by terrorists or their supporters when their song 'Birmingham Six' (about those accused, wrongly as it is later proved, of the bombing of a pub in the Midlands city) is blacklisted.
- **16TH: FORMER BEACH BOYS** manager Steve Love (brother of singer Mike and cousin of the Wilson brothers) is sentenced to five years' probation for embezzling more than $900,000 from the group.
- **17TH: FRANZ KAFKA'S** manuscript of The Trial is sold at Sotheby's in London for £1 million ($1.5m), a world record for a modern literary text. It does little for Kafka, however, who died in poverty in 1924.

## DECEMBER

- **DECEMBER 24TH: HARD ROCK BAND POISON,** fronted by Bret Michaels, get the Christmas Number One with the power ballad 'Every Rose Has Its Thorn.'

- **1ST: BENAZIR BHUTTO** is named the first female Prime Minister of a Muslim country when the PPP (Pakistan Peoples Party) wins the first democratic elections held in Pakistan for 11 years... And Canadian singer-

songwriter Sarah McLachlan is signed to Arista Records in the US.
- **4TH: LORIN MAAZEL** conducts all of Beethoven's nine symphonies in one day at the Royal Festival Hall, London, using three orchestras.
- **6TH: ROY**

**ORBISON** dies at home in Nashville, Tennessee, having suffered a heart attack while visiting his mother.
- **7TH: A SEVERE EARTHQUAKE** hits Armenia causing widespread destruction, up to 45,000 people die and

a further 500,000 are left homeless.
- **10TH: IT'S REPORTED** in UK rock weekly the *NME* that the British Phonographic Industry (BPI) is expecting sales of compact discs to overtake sales of vinyl before the end of the year.
- **21ST: IN MANCHESTER,** UK, aspiring rock star Noel Gallagher

auditions for the job of vocalist in The Inspiral Carpets, at Mill Street Studio, South Street, Ashton-under-Lyme. He is turned down, but is kept on as the band's roadie.
- **23RD: KURT COBAIN** of Nirvana is completing lyrics for the songs he will begin recording

tomorrow, which will become the basis of the band's first album, *Bleach*.
- **28TH: NOT HAVING** had a very merry Christmas, Madonna files assault charges against actor husband Sean Penn at the sheriff's office in Malibu, California. It is reported – and denied – that he had tied her to a chair.

- **DECEMBER 21ST: THIRTY-EIGHT MINUTES** after take-off, a US Pan-Am jumbo jet blows up in mid-air and falls onto the Scottish town of Lockerbie. (Parts of the aircraft are retrieved from miles around, as seen below.) The plane, which was en route to New York, contained a bomb hidden in a radio-cassette player. In total 259 people aboard the flight and 11 on the ground die. Two men accused of being Libyan intelligence agents are eventually charged with planting the bomb: Abdelbaset Ali Mohmed al-Megrahi is jailed for life in January 2001, following an 84-day trial, but his alleged accomplice, Al Amin Khalifa Fhimah, is found not guilty.

# 1989

## STILL ON TOP

Prince has just completed the American leg of his *Lovesexy* tour, his first run of US dates since the *Parade/Hit & Run* concerts in 1986. A prolific composer and multi-instrumentalist, with insatiable appetites for funk, pop, and sex – guess which one attracts the most media attention – he's a fascinatingly complex writer and performer: a consummate showman who's also intensely private and protective of both his personal and professional life. Though he's tough on journalists – persistently refusing interviews, or else demanding vetting rights, and even banning tape recorders in his presence – Prince is known to be generous with his time to fellow artists and fans. He's recently signed one of his own boyhood heroes, George Clinton, to his Paisley Park record label, and has been working again with Sheena Easton, as well as with Madonna and, according to rumour, an ailing Miles Davis. He has a penchant for unannounced, after-hours performances wherever he happens to be touring, and regularly sets up benefit concerts, often unpublicized, for causes close to his heart. But the next couple of years will see his popularity peak, before a dip later in the decade. This year's *Batman* album, written for the Tim Burton movie – and enthusiastically embraced as a pet project by Prince – will be his first to reach Number One in the US since *Around The World* in 1985 (surprisingly his classic *Sign Of The Times* stuck at Number Six), and it'll be his first ever to top the UK charts.

# 1989

## January–April

### Song & Dance Girl

FEBRUARY 11TH: PAULA ABDUL'S 'Straight Up' becomes the first of three consecutive US Number One singles for the former choreographer. Previously best known for providing Janet Jackson with some slick dance moves, she has also works with less obvious clients such as ZZ Top, Warren Zevon, and Duran Duran. Abdul will notch up six US Number Ones in all, before concentrating on more choreography and acting, and later becoming a celebrity judge on the *American Idol* TV show.

**JANUARY**

### Jazzie Soul

• MARCH 18TH: **SOUL II SOUL**, the brainchild of producer/vocalist/songwriter/DJ and clothes designer Jazzie B (above), enter the UK charts with 'Keep On Movin'. The track will launch the group around the world, helped by vocals from Caron Wheeler and production by Nellee Hooper – later to work with Massive Attack, Bjork, Madonna, and U2. The follow-up, 'Back To Life,' does even better, making Number One in the UK, and Number Four in the US. Soon recognized as one of the most creative and influential dance/R&B outfits of the day, Soul II Soul will soon undergo the departure of Wheeler and Hooper, resulting in increasingly fewer future sales.

• **3RD: IT IS ANNOUNCED** that Prince is to split from his long-time management team of Cavallo, Ruffalo and Fargnoli. He now signs up with Albert Magnoli, who directed his movie *Purple Rain*.
• **9TH: JAPAN GOES** into mourning with the news that the Imperial Son of Heaven, Emperor Hirohito, has succumbed to stomach cancer at the age of 82. He is succeeded by Crown Prince Akihito.
• **13TH: THE 'FRIDAY** The 13th' computer virus threatens hard disks worldwide.
• **14TH: GENESIS-OFFSHOOT** band Mike & The Mechanics enter the UK singles chart with 'The Living Years,' which will peak at Number Two, before becoming an international best-seller, topping the US chart in March.
• **16TH: A GROUP OF US RAPPERS**, including Public Enemy, KRS-1, Kool Moe Dee, Stetsasonic, and MC-Lyte, release a joint single, 'Stop The Violence,' intended to combat the association of rap with violent behaviour.
• **20TH: GEORGE BUSH SR** is inaugurated as 41st President of the US, with Dan Quayle becoming 44th Vice President.
• **21ST: AN ALL-STAR CONCERT** is held at the Convention Center,

Washington DC, to celebrate the success of new President George Bush. Those taking the stage include Bo Diddley, Percy Sledge, Willie Dixon, Eddie Floyd, Dr. John, Carla Thomas, Albert Collins, Billy Preston, Ron Wood, plus Steve Cropper and Duck Dunn of The MGs.
• **24TH: TED BUNDY**, notorious serial killer responsible for the deaths of at least 22 women, dies in the electric chair in Florida.
• **29TH: THE ARTIFICIAL LEG** that belonged to World War II RAF pilot Sir Douglas Bader is up for sale. His widow is selling memorabilia to raise money to buy a house.

• JANUARY 21ST: ***DON'T BE CRUEL*** by former New Edition singer Bobby Brown tops the US album chart.

• JANUARY 14TH: **MUSLIMS IN THE UK** ritually burn a copy of Salman Rushdie's book *The Satanic Verses*. This is the first serious protest in Britain about the book, which has already been banned as blasphemous in some Muslim countries. Next month, Iranian leader Ayatollah Khomeini will issue a 'fatwa' or religious instruction calling on all Muslims to kill Rushdie, and breaks off diplomatic relations with Britain over the matter.

**FEBRUARY**

• **2ND: F.W. DE KLERK** replaces President Botha as South Africa's Nationalist Party leader.
• **6TH: THE SKY** satellite TV service is launched for UK viewers by Rupert Murdoch. He has by now become a US citizen, taken over 20th Century Fox, and launched Fox Television.
• **7TH: IT RAINS** sardines over the Australian town of Ipswich, 30 miles inland from Brisbane, after a violent storm causes up-draughts to drag the fish into the sky from the coastal waters.
• **8TH: LOL TOLHURST**, a founding member of The Cure, is ejected from the band. His drinking problem is given as the reason.
• **10TH: KID ROCK** – real name Robert Ritchie – signs a contract entitling his business associate Alvin Williams to half of his earnings. The contract will become the source of a lawsuit after Kid Rock rockets to international fame and fortune.
• **17TH: MICHAEL JACKSON** sacks Frank Dileo, his manager for the past five years. "I lived before Michael," says Dileo, "I'll live after Michael."
• **18TH: 'WILD THING'** by Tone Loc becomes the US's highest-charting rap single to date when it hits Number Two on the Hot 100. Even more than 20 years later, it remains one of the biggest selling rap singles.
• **21ST: TWO MEMBERS** of Winnie Mandela's bodyguard ('Mandela United Football Club'), in Soweto, South Africa, are charged with the abduction, assault and murder of 14-year-old Stompie Moeketsi.

• MARCH 25TH: **THE EXXON VALDEZ** oil tanker runs into a reef, spilling 11 million gallons of crude oil into the remote and previously unspoilt Prince William Sound, Alaska, and creating a major environmental disaster.

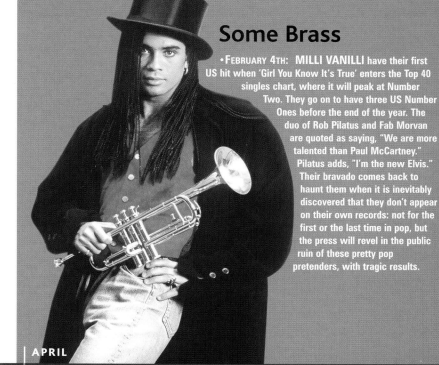

## Some Brass

• FEBRUARY 4TH: **MILLI VANILLI** have their first US hit when 'Girl You Know It's True' enters the Top 40 singles chart, where it will peak at Number Two. They go on to have three US Number Ones before the end of the year. The duo of Rob Pilatus and Fab Morvan are quoted as saying, "We are more talented than Paul McCartney." Pilatus adds, "I'm the new Elvis." Their bravado comes back to haunt them when it is inevitably discovered that they don't appear on their own records: not for the first or the last time in pop, but the press will revel in the public ruin of these pretty pop pretenders, with tragic results.

## Got The Look...

• APRIL 8TH: **ROXETTE REACH** Number One on the US Top 40 with 'The Look.' Despite cutting a deal with EMI shortly after getting together in 1984, singer Marie Fredriksson and guitarist Per Gessle didn't take off until 1988's *Look Sharp!*. The record was initially not released in the US, but a Minneapolis radio station picked up on it after getting a copy from a European student. The album will sell more than eight million copies.

• 1ST: **RUMOURS** by Fleetwood Mac, released 12 years ago, is certified as a 13-times platinum album in the US.
• 3RD: **ITALIAN TV** refuses to broadcast Madonna's relatively demure Pepsi commercial, based on 'Like A Prayer,' after the Vatican objects to her sacriligious cavortings in the video for the same song. Pepsi drops the ad and cancels its sponsorship of her concert tour, but Madonna keeps her $5m advance.
• 4TH: **'LOST IN YOUR EYES'** by singer/songwriter/producer Debbie Gibson reaches Number One on the US Top 40 singles chart. This will be her last Number One single, but Gibson later goes on to

star in the Broadway production of the popular musical *Les Miserables*.
• 4TH: **TIME INC** and Warner Communications announce plans to merge, thus becoming the world's largest media/entertainment conglomerate.
• 21ST: **AUSTRALIAN PRIME MINISTER** Bob Hawke cries on television after confessing to adultery... Meanwhile Dick Clark is to stand down as host of US TV institution American Bandstand, after 33 years. His replacement is David Hirsh.
• 29TH: **AS THE PRIZE** in a competition, Crowded House play live in the home of film student Grant Harvey, who lives in Calgary, Canada.

• 1ST: **'ETERNAL FLAME'** by The Bangles hits Number One in the US singles chart.
• 2ND: **NWA'S** 'Straight Outta Compton' video is reported to have been banned from MTV for showing police rounding up inner city gangs.
• 7TH: **A SOVIET NUCLEAR-POWERED** submarine, the Konsomolets, catches fire and sinks off the coast of Norway carrying nuclear warheads. More than 40 crew members are lost.
• 8TH: **THE LONGEST** single-movement piece of classical music in Western musical history, a symphony called *Odyssey*, by Nicholas Maw, receives its first complete performance in London. It lasts 100 minutes.
• 14TH: **POLICE IN HUDDERSFIELD**, UK, reveal that violent prisoners are being put into a bright pink cell, which seems to have a calming effect. Try it at home.
• 20TH: **SCIENTISTS ADMIT** that the Earth only narrowly missed being struck by an asteroid weighing 400 million tons.
• 21ST: **MORE THAN 100,000** Chinese students pour into Peking's Tiananmen

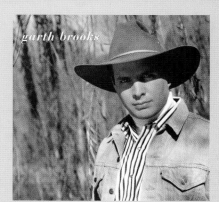

*garth brooks*

• APRIL 13TH: **GARTH BROOKS** releases his self-titled debut album in the US.

Square, ignoring government warnings of severe punishment.
• 28TH: **JON BON JOVI** marries his childhood sweetheart Dorothy Hurley on the steps of Graceland Chapel, Las Vegas, Nevada.
• 30TH: **ITALIAN MOVIE DIRECTOR** Sergio Leone dies at the age of 60.

• APRIL 12TH: **ANDREW LLOYD WEBBER'S** *Cats* is performed for the 3,358th time at the New London Theatre, Drury Lane, making it Britain's longest running musical.

# Wave Of Inspiration

**M**AY 13TH: THE PIXIES' ALBUM *Doolittle* becomes their first to chart, climbing to Number Eight in the UK, though only scraping to Number 98 in the Boston-based quartet's home country. The word "influence" is regularly bandied around in musical circles (this book uses it a few times too). But truly innovative and influential performers, the complete one-offs you find dotted about each generation, are rare indeed. The Pixies – namely Black Francis (real name Charles Thompson, later to become Frank Black) on guitar and vocals, Joey Santiago on guitar, David Lovering on drums, and Kim Deal on bass and vocals (who responded to a 'musicians wanted' ad that said, "must be into Hüsker Dü and Peter, Paul & Mary") have exploded,

pretty well literally, onto the US alternative rock scene. They produce five astonishingly accomplished, goosebump-inducing albums (half-album *Come On Pilgrim*, *Surfer Rosa*, *Doolittle*, *Bossanova*, and *Trompe Le Monde*) between 1986 and 1992. Their intuitive blend of pop melody and raw agression is unsurpassed. Kurt Cobain will later admit that Nirvana's 'Smells Like Teen Spirit' is a straightforward Pixies knock-off. Indeed, like the Velvet Underground before them, far more people will claim to have loved The Pixies than ever buy their records. And has there ever been a more feral piece of vocal-cord shredding than Black Francis on 'Tame'? Francis, now Frank Black, goes solo in 1993, and The Pixies are over.

---

**MAY**

• **MAY 13TH: HUNDREDS OF STUDENTS** camping in Tiananmen Square, Beijing (Peking), China, begin a hunger strike to draw attention to their peaceful protest for democratic reforms. By May 17th, hundreds of thousands of people have assembled in the square. Prime Minister Li Peng meets student leaders in televised talks, but the students say his attitude only proves how out of touch the leaders are with the people. On the 20th, Li Peng declares martial law, though at first human barricades prevent troops from entering the city centre. On June 4th, however, the army will start firing into the crowd, and street battles continue for days. The authorities claim 200 citizens are killed, but the true figure may be more than 2000. On June 5th, the world witnesses the unforgettable image of a lone protester halting the progress of a line of tanks by standing in front of them, clearly unarmed. The US suspends sales of arms to China.

• **2ND: IN A JEWELLER'S SHOP** in a Californian shopping mall, Michael Jackson is detained by a security guard for "looking suspicious." He is wearing a wig, a false moustache and fake teeth. Later, Jackson signs autographs for the guard and his colleagues.

• **6TH: TEDDY RILEY**, founder of the style known as 'new jack swing,' achieves his first US chart entry as part of the group Teddy Riley & Guy, with 'My Fantasy.'

• **14TH: LED ZEPPELIN** play a one-off reunion at Madison Square Garden, with Jason Bonham, son of deceased drummer John, taking his father's place.

• **20TH: PAULA ABDUL** takes the US Number One single slot with 'Forever Your Girl.'

• **31ST: A ROW** over who owns the name Yes ends in a compromise when the current line-up of Anderson, Squire, White, Howe, Kaye & Wakeman agree to tour under the name Yesshows.

---

**JUNE**

• **4TH: GAS FROM** a leaking pipeline explodes, engulfing two packed passenger trains on the Trans-Siberian railway. Some 575 people are killed and more than 600 injured in the world's second-worst rail disaster.

• **5TH: IN POLAND**, Solidarity defeats the Communists in the first free elections since the end of the Second World War.

• **9TH: A McDONALDS RESTAURANT** in the UK is firebombed – setting off a lengthy legal war between the burger chain and high-profile vegetarian Chrissie Hynde of the Pretenders, who joked just days earlier that she had once firebombed a branch of the fast food outlet.

• **14TH: THE GAMEBOY** (above) is launched by Nintendo. It is the first hand-held, pocket-sized video console with replaceable game cartridges. Priced at $169,

it comes with a copy of Tetris, a highly addictive new game.

• **15TH: NIRVANA** release their debut album *Bleach* in the US. It's acclaimed on the underground alternative rock circuit, but makes no impact on the charts at this stage.

• **16-18TH: 65,000 FANS** make the annual pilgrimage to Glastonbury Festival, Somerset, UK, where a £28 ($40) ticket

gives them the opportunity to enjoy The Wonderstuff, Elvis Costello, Van Morrison, The Pixies, and Suzanne Vega

• **17TH: FRANCE CELEBRATES** the 100th birthday of the Eiffel Tower, which critics originally claimed was ugly and unsafe.

• **19TH: MEMBERS OF NWA** are arrested for performing their track 'F*** Tha Police' on-stage.

• **30TH: SPIKE LEE'S** acclaimed and contentious movie *Do The Right Thing* is released. It deals with such sensitive subjects as politics, racism, and violence, with music playing a central role. The soundtrack includes Public Enemy's 'Fight The Power.'

• **JUNE 3RD: FINE YOUNG CANNIBALS'** album *The Raw And The Cooked* reaches Number One in the US, where it will remain for seven weeks. On July 8th they score a second Number One with 'Good Thing.' They also have several hits, though no Number Ones, in their native UK.

## Block Busters

- JUNE 17TH: 'I'LL BE LOVING YOU (FOREVER)' gives New Kids On The Block their first Number One on the US Top 40 singles chart. Essentially the first of the new 'boy band' species, NKOTB were dreamt up by producer Maurice Starr to be a white version of his group New Edition, with slickly choreographed routines and well-crafted but formulaic pop that sells by the million. The concept spreads, and soon there's a tidal wave of copy-cat 'manufactured' outfits, who in turn sweep away the older generation. By 1992, it's all over for NKOTB.

**JULY**

**AUGUST**

- JUNE 2ND: ROLLING STONES BASS PLAYER Bill Wyman marries Mandy Smith. He is 53, she is 19 – and the affair began some six year ago. It doesn't last. Soon she'll be too old for him.

- 4TH: **FAITH NO MORE** release the album *The Real Thing*.
- 5TH: **TIN MACHINE**, the new band formed by David Bowie, have peaked at Number Three on the UK album chart. In the US the experimental project proves even less popular, only reaching Number 28, while the follow-up album doesn't chart at all. A defiant Bowie perseveres with the band for three years.
- 13TH: **THE MOSCOW MUSIC PEACE FESTIVAL**, in Russia, features hard rock acts Bon Jovi, Ozzy Osbourne, Mötley Crüe, The Scorpions, Skid Row, and Cinderella. All of which certainly stretches the definition of the word "peace."
- 17TH: **THE FIRST** commercial non-stop flight from London to Sydney is cleared for take-off.
- 19TH: **IN POLAND**, Solidarity's Tadeusz Mazowiecki becomes Prime Minister, making Poland the first Eastern Bloc country to end one-party rule.
- 22ND: **THE WORLD'S FIRST** pocket phones – small handsets which operate within 100 yards of a base station – are introduced by British Telecom.
- 27TH: **WHEN THE VOYAGER 2** leaves the solar system, Chuck Berry's 'Johnny B. Goode' is included among the craft's examples of music from planet Earth, along with works by Bach, Beethoven and others.
- 31ST: **THE ROLLING STONES'** Steel Wheels tour begins, appropriately enough, at Veterans Stadium, Philadelphia, Pennsylvania.

- 1ST: **THE GROUP** calling themselves the Band Du Lac at a charity event in Wintershall, Surrey, UK, feature Phil Collins on drums, guitarists Eric Clapton, Mike Rutherford of Genesis, and Andy Fairweather Low, Steve Winwood on keyboards, and Gary Brooker of Procol Harum on keyboards and vocals.
- 12TH: **IN A COURT** in Cleveland, Ohio, a woman who has been convicted of stealing jewellery repeatedly shouts at the judge. She is ordered to have her mouth taped shut.
- 14TH: **SIXTEEN-YEAR-OLD** Claire Leighton dies in the UK's trendiest club, The Hacienda in Manchester, after taking Ecstasy.
- 15TH: **DESPITE OBJECTIONS** from the local council, which claims that the volume of the music could damage the city's historic buildings, Pink Floyd play at The Grand Canal, Venice, Italy.
- 18TH: **WHEN NIRVANA** play at the Pyramid Club, New York City, as part of the New Music Seminar, guitarist Jason Everman quits the group. They will carry on as a three-piece, comprising Kurt Cobain, Krist Novoselic, and drummer Chad Channing.
- 21ST: **DURING A 'LIVE' GIG** in Bristol, Connecticut, the backing track playing pop duo Milli Vanilli's vocals gets stucks, repeating 'Girl, you know it's...' some 15 times. The game is almost up.

- AUGUST 5TH: **'BATDANCE' BY PRINCE** reaches Number One on the US Top 40 singles chart. It's taken from Tim Burton's new live-action *Batman* movie, in which Jack Nicholson's Joker character (below) dances to the song.

# 1989

September–December

## Miracle Cure

**O**CTOBER 21ST: **THE CURE** reach US Number Two with the single 'Love Song,' having appeared on the recent MTV Video Music Awards. Sporting bad hair and unnerving make-up (later perfected by Marilyn Manson), leader Robert Smith took the black & white goth look and smeared it with unexpected colour. The same goes for The Cure's music, where what you expected was seldom what you got. From the hypnotic and moody *Pornography* (1982) to jaunty pop songs like 'Love Cats' and 'Why Can't I Be You,' the Cure seldom plough the same furrow for long. Formed in Crawley, UK, in 1976, by schoolmates Smith (vocals/guitar), Paul 'Porl' Thompson (guitar), Michael Dempsey (bass) and Lawrence 'Lol' Tolhurst (drums), they frequently change line-up and disappear, popping up when least expected.

## SEPTEMBER

- **2ND: OZZY OSBOURNE** is arrested and charged with threatening to kill his wife/manager, Sharon. On receiving his promise to stay away from her, she decides not to press charges.
- **3RD: THE US BEGINS** shipping military aircraft and weapons worth $65 million, to help Colombia in its fight against drug lords.
- **6TH: THE PITTSBURGH STEELERS**, four-time Super Bowl winners, are banned from practising at their Three Rivers Stadium because The Rolling Stones are rehearsing there for their upcoming concert.
- **7TH: LEGISLATION** is approved by the US Senate that prohibits discrimination against the disabled in employment, public accommodation, transportation, and communications.
- **8TH: AFTER A STRUGGLE** with his addiction to crack cocaine, Cowboy (Keith Wiggins) of Grandmaster Flash & The Furious Five dies.
- **9TH: 'HANGIN' TOUGH'** by New Kids On the Block is the new US Number single.
- **10TH: HUNGARY OPENS** its borders to the West, an unexpected move which angers the East German government, because thousands of East German refugees take the opportunity to leave for the West.
- **16TH: THE ALBUM** *Mother's Milk* by The Red Hot Chili Peppers enters the US album charts, where it will remain for eight months – although never reaching higher than Number 52.

- **18TH: TINA TURNER** releases a new album, *Foreign Affair*, which includes the hit singles 'Steamy Windows' and 'The Best.'
- **21ST: HURRICANE HUGO** sweeps across South Carolina and Georgia in the US, causing a great deal of damage ($8 billion) and many deaths.
- **25TH: BILLY JOEL** uses a court in New York City to file a $90m damages suit for fraud against his manager, Frank Weber.

## OCTOBER

- **1ST: SEVENTEEN-YEAR-OLD** Geri Halliwell, later to become Ginger Spice of The Spice Girls, loses her virginity to a boy called Toby, described in her autobiography as "a grey and sickly looking ex-public schoolboy."
- **5TH: THREE VERY DIFFERENT** events today: the Dalai Lama is named the winner of the Nobel Peace Prize; US TV Evangelist Jim Bakker is found guilty of fleecing his followers of some $158 million, and in Paris, France, the Moulin Rouge club celebrates its centenary.
- **7TH:** *FOREVER YOUR GIRL* by Paula Abdul reaches Number One on the US album chart.
- **11TH: MICHAEL JACKSON'S** former school, Gardner Street Elementary, in Gary, Indiana, inaugurates the Michael Jackson Auditorium.
- **18TH: EAST GERMAN** leader Erich Honecker is replaced by Egon Krenz, in response to the failing economy and mass exodus of young East Germans across the border.
- **20TH: SUB POP** labelmates Nirvana and Tad leave Seattle, Washington, to fly to London to begin their first European tour.
- **21ST: HERB ALPERT'S** A&M Records is bought by Polygram for around $500m.
- **27TH: LONDON CALLING** by The Clash tops the *Rolling Stone* magazine critics' list of the Top 100 Albums Of The 1980s (although it was first released in the UK in 1979).

- **OCTOBER 17TH: THE WORST US** earthquake since 1906 shakes the entire San Francisco Bay area. Centred near Santa Cruz, 50 miles (80 km) south of San Francisco, it kills 67 people and injures more than 600.

## NOVEMBER

- **NOVEMBER 9TH: EAST GERMANY** opens all its border points, following demands for political reform from its citizens – essentially lifting the 'iron curtain' and allowing free travel through the Berlin Wall. Soon after the announcement, many thousands of jubilant East Berliners swarm through the crossing points into West Berlin, and citizens from both sides join in the enthusiastic destruction of the wall, using anything that comes to hand. The following day bulldozers move in and begin the official demolition of the 28-year-old barrier.

- **3RD: 'MISS YOU MUCH'** by Janet Jackson is certified platinum in the US.
- **4TH: 'LISTEN TO YOUR HEART'** by Roxette reaches Number One on the US Top 40.
- **7TH: SONY**, having already acquired CBS Records for $2bn, adds Columbia & Tri-Star Pictures to its haul, paying the Coca-Cola Company $3.4bn in the deal.
- **8TH: THE BEATLES'** legal battle with EMI Records over royalty payments, which has dragged on for 20 years, is finally settled when the record company agrees to pay the group many millions of pounds – the precise amount remains undisclosed…

- **13TH: NEWSWEEK** runs an item stating that Bruce Springsteen has fired the E-Street band.
- **24TH: THE CZECHOSLOVAKIAN** communist party leadership resigns following huge and violent protests in Prague and elsewhere in the country. In only a months' time, leading playwright and former political dissident Vaclav Havel will become the new president of Czechoslovakia.
- **26TH: NEIL YOUNG**, Crosby, Stills & Nash, Steve Miller Band, the Chambers Brothers and Santana appear at the Cow Palace, San Francisco, in a fund-raising TV concert for victims of the recent California earthquake.

- **11TH: SONGWRITER** Dianne Warren becomes the first female to have written the Number One and Number Two records in the US singles chart. The songs in question are 'When I See You Smile' by Bad English and 'Blame It On The Rain' by Milli Vanilli.

**DECEMBER**

• SEPTEMBER 16TH: **MÖTLEY CRÜE**
release the best-selling album, *Dr Feelgood*.

• **1ST:** **SLY STONE** is sentenced to 55 days in jail for driving under the influence of cocaine... Meanwhile Pope John Paul II and Mikhail Gorbachev end 70 years of hostility between the Roman Catholic Church and the Soviet Union by meeting in Rome.

• **5TH:** **LOU REED** begins legal action against the promoters of one of his recent gigs. In the course of the event he broke his ankle when a metal step collapsed.

• **12TH:** **BILLIONAIRE LEONA HELMSLEY**, who once remarked, "Only the little people pay taxes," is fined $7 million and sentenced to four years' imprisonment for tax evasion. Little people everywhere smile.

• **16TH:** *STORM FRONT* by Billy Joel makes its way to Number One on the US album charts.

• **20TH:** **LISA MARIE PRESLEY**, 21-year-old daughter of Elvis Presley, inherits his $100m estate – although it will be managed by a trust until 1998... Meanwhile, US troops invade Panama and overthrow the government of Manuel Noriega. Noriega, wanted on drug charges, takes refuge in the Vatican mission but is finally arrested, tried, found guilty of 'genocide' by a military court, and executed.

• **22-25TH:** **NICOLAE CEAUSESCU**, teh son of a peasant who rose to become communist dictator in Romania for over 20 years, is overthrown and executed, along with his wife, during a public revolt.

• **27TH:** **CHUCK BERRY** finds himself the subject of a civil suit for invasion of privacy, brought against him by Hosana A. Huck, a cook at a restaurant which Berry owns. She claims that he secretly installed video cameras in the ladies' toilets for his own erotic titillation. No fewer than 200 other women who've visited the restaurant will follow suit.

• **26TH:** **SAMUEL BECKETT**, author of the acclaimed play *Waiting For Godot*, dies in Paris at the age of 83.

• **DECEMBER 9TH:** **GARTH BROOKS** scores his first US Number One country hit with the single 'If Tomorrow Never Comes.'

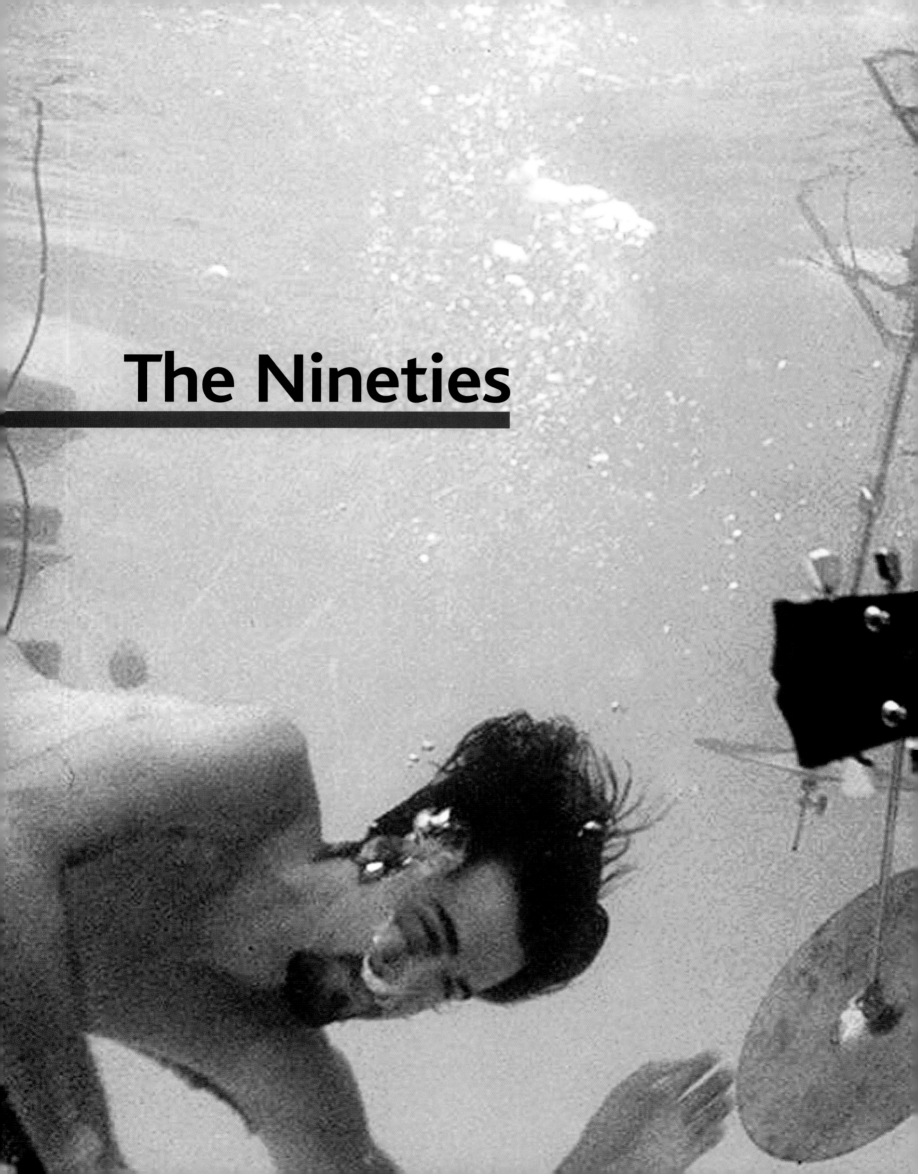

# The Nineties

# 1990

## January–April

## The Paths Of Rhythm

**A**PRIL 14TH: **A TRIBE CALLED QUEST,** from the jazzier end of the hip-hop spectrum, release their debut album, *People's Instinctive Travels And The Paths Of Rhythm*, on the Jive label. It contains their first two hit singles, 'Bonita Applebum,' and 'Can I Kick It?' A remix of the latter, blending samples from the likes of Lou Reed ('Walk On The Wild Side') and Ian Dury & The Blockheads ('What A Waste'), with a laidback groove and cool rap, will give them their biggest mainstream success when it gets to Number 15 in the UK early next year. The trio's frontman Q-Tip is also in demand as a remixer and/or rapper on recordings by the likes of Deee-Lite (he appears on 'Groove Is In The Heart'), Tony! Toni! Tone! (working as producer), and

## JANUARY

• **JANUARY 6TH:** *BUT SERIOUSLY* by Phil Collins reaches Number One on the US albums chart. The former Genesis drummer has enjoyed an unbelievably lucrative five years since his last album, *No Jacket Required*, with no fewer than 13 US Top Ten hits, either solo or with Genesis. Seven of them have been Number Ones.

• **1ST: DAVID DINKINS** is sworn in as New York City's first black mayor.
• **2ND: THE WORLD POPULATION** passes five billion. In 1960 it was three billion.
• **3RD: MANUEL NORIEGA** surrenders to US forces in Panama, ten days after taking refuge in the Vatican's diplomatic mission.
• **7TH: THE LEANING TOWER** of Pisa in Italy is closed to the public when an increase in 'leaning' raises fears for the safety of visitors.
• **10TH: MEDIA GIANTS** Warner Communications and Time Inc complete a $14 billion merger. The new company, Time Warner, is now the world's largest entertainment company.
• **12TH: BOB DYLAN**

starts the new decade with a small club date at Toads, New Haven, Connecticut, where he plays a set lasting no less than four hours.
• **17TH: AT THE WALDORF-ASTORIA** hotel, New York City, legendary songwriting team Carole King and Gerry Goffin are inducted into the Rock'N'Roll Hall Of Fame.
• **18TH: MAYOR MARION BARRY** of Washington, DC, is arrested by FBI agents after being videotaped smoking crack cocaine in a hotel room. He will serve six months.
• **21ST: THE FIRST MTV** *UNPLUGGED* show is broadcast (it was recorded late last year), featuring UK band Squeeze, Elliot Easton of The Cars, and female singer Syd Straw.
• **31ST: THE FIRST MCDONALDS** burger outlet opens in Moscow, Russia. It's also the world's biggest.

• **JANUARY 20TH: SINEAD O'CONNOR** releases a new single, 'Nothing Compares 2 U,' written by Prince, with a tearjerking face-only video. It hits Number One in the UK in February, and by April does the same in the US, where it will be certified platinum.

## FEBRUARY

• **FEBRUARY 2ND: SOUTH AFRICAN** President F.W. de Klerk lifts the ban on the ANC (African National Congress) and promises to release Nelson Mandela. Nine days later, he keeps his word, and Mandela is freed after 27 years in prison.

• **6TH: AFTER SUSTAINING INJURIES** when crashing his Harley-Davisdon into a car, Billy Idol undergoes surgery in Los Angeles.
• **7TH: SOVIET LEADERS** agree to free elections, surrendering the Communist Party's 72 year power monopoly.
• **9TH: SINGER DEL SHANNON** dies of self-inflicted gunshot wounds, at home in Santa Clarita, Los Angeles.
• **10TH: 'OPPOSITES ATTRACT'** by Paula Abdul with The Wild Pair reaches Number One on the US Top 40 singles chart.
• **16TH: IKE TURNER** is sentenced to four years in prison on cocaine charges... Meanwhile Pink Floyd's *Dark Side Of The Moon* is certified as eleven-times platinum in the US.
• **17TH: THE B-52s** (right) veterans of leftfield pop, have been having their most commercially successful period, with 'Love Shack' hitting US Number Three late last year, and now 'Roam' doing the same.
• **18TH: THE NINTH ANNUAL** BRIT Awards are held at the Dominion Theatre, London. Fine Young Cannibals are chosen as Best British Group, while their album *The Raw & The Cooked* is Best Album by a British Artist.
• **21ST: AT THE 32ND ANNUAL GRAMMY AWARDS,** jazzy R&B singer Anita Baker collects three Grammys. At the same ceremomony, manufactured pop duo Milli Vanilli are named Best New Artist, no doubt encouraging one half of the duo, Rob Pilatus, to share his "new Elvis" boast with *Time* magazine a few days later.
• **26TH: CORNELL GUNTER** of the Coasters is murdered in Las Vegas at the age of 53.

De La Soul (guesting on 'Me Myself And I'). De La Soul (left) broke the mold of rap groups, rejecting the usual macho posturing and death threats in favour of, well, everything else. Like Tribe, they are also members of the Africa-centric Native Tongues Posse, founded by The Jungle Brothers, Queen Latifah, and the inspirational Afrika Bambaataa. De La Soul (who've just had their biggest hit with 'The Magic Number' – a UK Number Seven) also make the news because they're being sued by 1960s band The Turtles for using a sample without permission. In future, all samples will have to be legally cleared with their owners before they can be used.

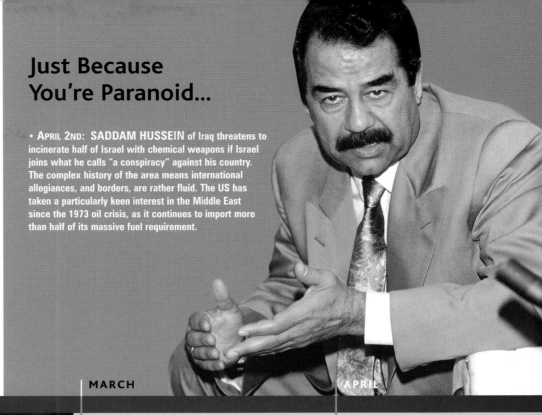

## Just Because You're Paranoid...

• **APRIL 2ND:** SADDAM HUSSEIN of Iraq threatens to incinerate half of Israel with chemical weapons if Israel joins what he calls "a conspiracy" against his country. The complex history of the area means international allegiances, and borders, are rather fluid. The US has taken a particularly keen interest in the Middle East since the 1973 oil crisis, as it continues to import more than half of its massive fuel requirement.

**MARCH** | **APRIL**

• **JANUARY 2ND: AT THE NATIONAL** Exhibition Centre, Birmingham, UK, Paul McCartney begins his first UK tour since the death of John Lennon nine years ago. It's part of his massive ten-month world tour, covering 13 countries, and performing for around three million fans.

• **MARCH 24TH:** 'BLACK VELVET' by Alannah Myles reaches Number One the US singles chart.

• **1ST: JANET JACKSON** begins her first ever tour, Rhythm Nation, in Miami, Florida.

• **6TH: THE SOVIET PARLIAMENT** approves a law that gives private citizens the right to own the means of production: they can now buy property and start businesses.

• **9TH: POLICE SEAL OFF** Brixton in south London after another night of protest against the Conservative government's imposition of what has been dubbed the 'Poll Tax.' Protests have been taking place throughout Britain in the last week after local councils set the new tax rates. On the 21st, a massive demonstration in central London turns into a riot, with 417 people injured and 341 people arrested.

• **10TH: AMERICAN JENNIFER CAPRIATI,** aged just 13 years and 11 months, becomes the youngest player ever to reach the final of a professional tennis tournament in Florida.

• **15TH: MIKHAIL GORBACHEV** is elected Executive President of the USSR.

• **18TH: EAST GERMANY** holds its first free elections since the state was formed after World War II.

• **20TH: GLORIA ESTEFAN'S** back is broken when a tractor rams her tour bus during a freak snowstorm outside Scranton, Pennsylvania.

• **24TH: IN THE WAKE** of his widely reported anti-Jewish remarks, Professor Griff of rap band Public Enemy announces his departure.

• **25TH: AFTER BARING HIS BUTT** at the crowd during a concert in Augusta, Georgia, Mötley Crüe drummer Tommy Lee is arrested and charged with indecent exposure.

• **28TH: STEVEN ADLER,** drummer with Guns N' Roses, agrees to quit the band in the next month.

• **7TH: NICK OF TIME** by Bonnie Raitt reaches Number One on the US albums chart... Meanwhile, at Cincinnati's Contemporary Arts Centre a display of Robert Mapplethorpe's controversial photographs goes on display. The centre's director is indicted on obscenity charges.

• **12TH: JAMES BROWN** is released from his South Carolina jail cell on work furlough after serving 15 months of a six-year sentence for aggravated assault.

• **13TH: THE SOVIET UNION** finally owns up, accepts responsibility, and apologizes for the murder of thousands of imprisoned Polish officers in the Katyn Forest during World War II. The massacre was previously blamed on the Nazis... Meanwhile, Madonna's 54-date worldwide Blonde Ambition tour opens in Tokyo, Japan.

• **16TH: NELSON MANDELA** appears at Wembley Stadium, London, as part of the Nelson Mandela Birthday Tribute Concert, featuring Peter Gabriel, Neil Young, Aswad, Simple Minds, Bonnie Raitt, and others.

• **22ND: THE NINTH MTV UNPLUGGED** show to be transmitted features a live acoustic performance by former Eagles man Don Henley.

• **25TH: THE HUBBLE SPACE TELESCOPE** is launched from the Space Shuttle.

• **27TH: AXL ROSE OF GUNS N' ROSES,** ever the romantic, goes to girlfriend Erin Everly's house at 4am and tells her he has a gun in his car and if she doesn't marry him he'll kill himself. Despite his history of abuse, she agrees.

# 1990
## May–August

# Hammer Won't Hurt 'Em

**J**UNE 9TH: *PLEASE HAMMER DON'T HURT 'EM* by MC Hammer (left) reaches Number One on the US album chart, the start of a run lasting a record-breaking 21 (non-consecutive) weeks. With its pop-friendly samples and a snappy video featuring a loon-panted Hammer showing off his gymnastic dance routines, this represents the non-threatening face of rap culture, and is lapped up by teens and parents alike. One person who is less than impressed is Rick James, whose 1981 hit 'Super Freak' is shamelessly sampled by Hammer to create his biggest hit, 'U Can't Touch This.' James will sue, and Hammer has to settle out of court, agreeing belatedly to give James a credit and a royalty. Hammer's real name is Stanley K. Burrell: apparently the nickname comes from his resemblance to baseball legend 'Hammerin'' Hank Aaron. He rides the wave of popularity for 18 months or so, then just as quickly slides out of the picture. Critics suggest that this happens after he stops using so many well-known samples. Hammer dabbles in heavier R&B, and even gangsta-rap, but can't halt the decline. Despite numerous awards in the early days, Hammer is seen by serious hip-hop and dance devotees as, at best, an irrelevance – or more likely an embarrassment. But for many white pop kids, he is nonetheless an entrée to the world of rap.

**MAY**

- **11TH:** *I DO NOT WANT WHAT I HAVE NOT GOT* by Sinead O'Connor is certified as a double-platinum album in the US by the RIAA.
- **15TH:** **VINCENT VAN GOGH'S** *Portrait of Doctor Gachet* is sold for $82.5 million, setting a new world record.
- **19TH:** **'VOGUE' BY MADONNA** is the Number One single in the USA.
- **19TH:** **UK AGRICULTURE MINISTER** John Gummer feeds a hamburger to his five-year-old daughter, in front of the world's media, in an effort to counter rumours about the spread of Mad Cow Disease, properly known as Bovine Spongiform Encephalopathy (BSE), and the likelihood of its transmission to humans.
- **20TH:** **THE HUBBLE SPACE TELESCOPE**, the world's first optical telescope in space, sends back its first photographs.
- **21ST:** **MAFIA-LINKED RECORD COMPANY** boss Morris Levy dies of cancer in Ghent, New York. He was the owner of such labels as Roulette, Gee, Rama and Tico.
- **22ND:** **MICROSOFT** releases Windows 3.0.
- **24TH:** **AXL ROSE** and Erin Everly file for divorce. They have been married less than a month.
- **26TH:** **THE TOP FIVE US** singles are all by female artists – behind Madonna come Sinead O'Connor, Heart, Wilson Phillips, and Janet Jackson.
- **26TH:** **ANGIE BOWIE** begins a legal suit against her former husband David Bowie, seeking to lighten his wallet by $56m.
- **30TH:** **THE 20TH ANNUAL SONGWRITERS' HALL OF FAME AWARDS** ceremony is held in the New York Hilton. Whitney Houston inducts Smokey Robinson to the Hall, and goes on to win the Hitmaker Award herself.

## Move Over, Whitney

- **AUGUST 4TH:** MARIAH CAREY tops the singles chart for the first of four weeks with 'Vision Of Love.' It's the start of a run of five consecutive Number Ones, leading to a total of 14 throughout the 1990s, making her America's biggest star of the decade. Presumably influenced by her opera-singing voice-coach mother, Carey has a love-it-or-loathe-it range-straddling vocal style (apparently spanning five octaves) that stands her in good stead as a pop diva. Her career prospects aren't harmed, either, by the fact that her boyfriend (later husband) is Tommy Mottola, president of Sony Music in the US.

## Step Right Up

- **MAY 8TH:** TOM WAITS WINS $2.5 million when a Los Angeles court rules that snack giants Frito-Lay unlawfully used a Waits sound-alike in its Doritos ads.

**JUNE**  **JULY**  **AUGUST**

---

- **3RD:** MICHAEL JACKSON is admitted to St. John's Hospital in Santa Monica after complaining of chest pains. Tests show he has bruised his ribs during an extended bout of dance practice.
- **9TH:** THE SINGLE 'HOLD ON' by Wilson Phillips – a trio comprising various daughters of The Beach Boys and The Mamas & The Papas – reaches US Number One.
- **10TH:** BULGARIA'S FORMER Communist Party wins the country's first free elections in more than four decades... Meanwhile, back in the old free world, members of rap group 2 Live Crew are arrested on obscenity charges in Florida for performing tracks from their album *As Nasty As They Wanna Be*.
- **11TH:** OLIVIA NEWTON-JOHN becomes a United Nations environmental ambassador.
- **15TH:** THE VELVET UNDERGROUND, reformed for an Andy Warhol retrospective in Paris, France, perform a 15-minute version of 'Heroin.'
- **21ST:** LITTLE RICHARD DAY is declared in Los Angeles, California. The celebration is held in City Hall, with guests including Arnold Schwarzenegger, and telegrams from Michael Jackson, David Bowie, and Bon Jovi. In the evening, Little Richard performs live on the *Arsenio Hall Show*.
- **22ND-24TH:** THE 20TH ANNIVERSAY GLASTONBURY FESTIVAL, in Pilton, Somerset, UK, attracts 70,000 fans who pay £38 each to see The Cure, Happy Mondays, Sinead O'Connor, Aswad, and World Party.
- **25TH:** THE US SUPREME COURT upholds a court verdict that an individual has the right to refuse life-sustaining medical treatment. This comes just three weeks after Dr Jack Kevorkian lets a terminally ill woman, Janet Adkins, use his "suicide machine." This crude but effective device allows people to give themselves a controlled dose of fatal drugs. In the next few years, Kevorkian will be involved in more 100 assisted suicides. He has his medical license revoked and is arrested and tried on four occasions. But he escapes conviction, often receiving praise for his compassion. Then in 1998, one of the suicides is taped and shown on national TV. Kevorkian (or Dr Death, as he will have become known) gets 20 years in jail. He won't be due for parole until 2007, but the debate goes on.

- **1ST:** EAST AND WEST GERMANY merge currency and economies, paving the way for full reunification.
- **2ND:** REPRESENTATIVES of the Italian Catholic Church announce they will attempt to halt Madonna's concerts in Rome because of her inappropriate use of crucifixes and sacred symbols.
- **4TH:** PAUL STANLEY OF KISS suffers neck injuries in a car crash in Pelham, New York, forcing him to cancel some upcoming shows.
- **10TH:** MIKHAIL GORBACHEV wins re-election as the leader of the Soviet Communist Party.
- **16TH:** JUDAS PRIEST go on trial in Reno, Nevada, accused of placing subliminal messages in their *Stained Class* album and causing two teenage fans to shoot themselves, one fatally.
- **21ST:** 'SHE AIN'T WORTH IT' by Glenn Medeiros & Bobby Brown is the new US Number One single.
- **25TH:** ROSANNE BARR sings the National Anthem in San Diego before a baseball game and is roundly booed for her performance.
- **26TH:** GRATEFUL DEAD pianist Brent Mydland dies outside his Lafayette, California, home, from a morphine/cocaine overdose.
- **29TH:** PAUL MCCARTNEY'S World Tour, which began in Oslo, Norway, ten months earlier, ends in Chicago, Illinois.
- **31ST:** PRACTICAL JOKERS create elaborate crop circles in Wiltshire in the UK and leave a ouija board behind as evidence of their work.

- **JULY 21ST:** FORMER PINK FLOYD songwriter Roger Waters, with help from guest acts like Sinead O'Connor and Thomas Dolby, stages an epic performance of *The Wall* in front of 200,000 people at Potzdamer Platz in Berlin, Germany, to mark the fall of the Berlin Wall.

- **AUGUST 5TH:** WHEN HBO BROADCASTS Madonna's Blonde Ambition concert in the US, it becomes the cable station's most widely viewed presentation ever.

- **2ND:** IRAQ INVADES and occupies Kuwait. It claims that Kuwait has driven down oil prices by exceeding production quotas set by OPEC. The invasion precipitates the (first) Gulf War.
- **10TH:** THE US'S MAGELLAN SPACECRAFT arrives at Venus after a 15-month journey. It is placed in an elliptical orbit around the planet's poles and will begin mapping the surface, carrying on until 1994.
- **13TH:** SOUL STAR CURTIS MAYFIELD is paralyzed from the neck down when a lighting rig collapses on him at an outdoor show in Brooklyn, New York City.
- **15TH:** IN THE HONEYSUCKLE a pub in Poolstock, near Wigan, UK, an un-named band plays its first gig. It will be six months before they play again, by which time they are called The Verve.
- **18TH:** THE FIRST SHOTS are fired by the US in the Persian Gulf, when the USS Reid, a guided-missile frigate, fires rounds across the bow of an Iraqi oil tanker that refuses to alter its course.
- **22ND:** ANGRY SMOKERS blockade a street in Moscow to protest about the summer-long cigarette shortage. But they soon get tired and need to have a rest.
- **24TH:** SINEAD O'CONNOR sparks controversy when she says she won't perform today's show at the Garden State Arts Center, Holmdel, New Jersey, if the US national anthem is played, as is traditional. A patriotic uproar ensues which leads to several radio stations banning her music.
- **27TH:** HOT-SHOT TEXAN GUITARIST Stevie Ray Vaughan dies in a freak helicopter crash after a concert in East Troy, Wisconsin. The 35-year-old has only recently made a comeback after long-term drink and drugs problems. Pilot error is blamed for the accident.

# 1990

September–December

## Give The Drummer Some

**T**HIS IS THE AGE of the drum sample, and the most commonly pilfered of all is taken from James Brown's 'Funky Drummer' track. It is famously 'borrowed' by Public Enemy for 'Rebel Without A Pause,' as well as by the likes of LL Cool J, The Beastie Boys, Dr Dre, Ice Cube, Ice T, De La Soul... In fact almost every hip-hop act has probably used it at one time or other, whether knowingly or not: sometimes they have sampled it off each other's records. By 1990, the idea has moved into the UK's 'alternative' guitar-band market, thanks to its use on tracks like 'Fool's Gold' by The Stone Roses. Suddenly it's everywhere – you can't move for pale white guitar bands, for whom the concept of a funky rhythm was previously alien, strumming over the top of crudely-sampled funk breakbeats. Or you find rock drummers making a stuttering attempt at the 'Funky Drummer' pattern. (The other big favourite for an 'instant groove' is John Bonham's intro to Led Zeppelin's 'When The Levee Breaks.') Even Sinead O'Connor jumps on the bandwagon. In the meantime, Clyde Stubblefield, the original musician who laid down the beat on James Brown's 'Funky Drummer' in 1969 (as well as on tunes like 'Cold Sweat' and 'I Got The Feeling'), is

## SEPTEMBER

- **1ST: 'IF WISHES CAME TRUE'** by Sweet Sensation reaches Number One on the US Top 40 singles chart.
- **6TH: TOM FOGERTY**, former guitarist with Creedence Clearwater Revival dies, age 48, in Scottsdale, Arizona. He was suffering from respiratory failure brought on by tuberculosis.
- **10TH: PRINCE'S NUDE** tour comes to an end at Yokohama Stadium, Yokohama, Japan, having drawn a worldwide audience of over one million people.
- **15TH: BRUCE HORNSBY** begins filling in on keyboards for The Grateful Dead, following the death of Brent Mydland.
- **18TH: BANKER CHARLES H. KEATING** is jailed in Los Angeles on criminal fraud charges concerning saving-and-loans.
- **19TH: ZZ TOP'S** 1983 album *Eliminator* is certified as a US seven-times platinum album by the RIAA.
- **25TH: AT THE DUTCHMAN** rehearsal room, Seattle, Washington, Dave Grohl (formerly with Scream) auditions to become the new drummer in Nirvana. He is successful.
- **29TH: THE SINGLE** '(Can't Live Without Your) Love And Affection' by Nelson – the sons of Rick Nelson – reaches Number One in the US.

- **SEPTEMBER 10TH: WILL SMITH** makes his debut in US TV sitcom *The Fresh Prince Of Bel-Air*, which will run until 1996. Smith first emerged as his Fresh Prince alter-ego, rapping with his friend DJ Jazzy Jeff (Jeff Townes), in the mid-1980s. The duo had a UK hit as far back as 1986, and their first US hit in 1988 with 'Parents Just Don't Understand.' Their biggest successes will be 1991's 'Summertime' and 'Boom! Shake The Room,' a huge Number One pop hit in 1993, after which Smith finds even greater fame as a solo artist and actor.

## OCTOBER

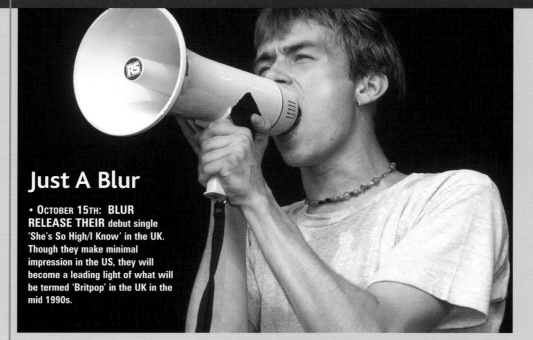

### Just A Blur

- **OCTOBER 15TH: BLUR RELEASE THEIR** debut single 'She's So High/I Know' in the UK. Though they make minimal impression in the US, they will become a leading light of what will be termed 'Britpop' in the UK in the mid 1990s.

- **3RD: AFTER THE SIGNING** of agreements by the USA, UK, France, and the USSR, the two halves of Germany, East and West, are finally reunited after 43 years of division.
- **5TH: A JURY** in Cincinnati, Ohio, acquits the city's Contemporary Arts Centre and its director of obscenity charges stemming from the exhibit of sexually graphic photographs by Robert Mapplethorpe.
- **6TH: 'CLOSE TO YOU'** by Maxi Priest is the new Number One single in the US. This makes Maxi only the second British reggae act to top the US charts (after UB40).
- **8TH: PEARL JAM** start work in Seattle, Washington, on demos which will become their debut album, *Ten*.
- **10TH: JETHRO TULL** are inducted into the Hall Of Fame of the National Association of Brick Manufacturers in New York City, because their Number One 1972 album *Thick As A Brick* has raised public awareness of the product.
- **15TH: MIKHAIL GORBACHEV**, the Soviet President, is awarded the Nobel Peace Prize.
- **18TH: THE CITY OF LOS ANGELES** declares today Rocky Horror Picture Show Day.
- **20TH: THREE MEMBERS** of 2 Live Crew,

- **OCTOBER 14TH: COMPOSER AND CONDUCTOR** Leonard Bernstein dies at the age of 72. His most loved popular music work is *West Side Story*.

playing Top 40 covers and Motown classics with his Blue Monday Band in clubs and bars around his home in Madison, Wisconsin, US, oblivious to the impact his 20-year-old drum part is having. What's more, he's not making a cent from the record sales his sound is generating. All this is unknown territory for copyright law, and the availability of cheap digital sampling technology makes its proliferation hard to control. Several high-profile lawsuits (like the De La Soul case mentioned already) come and go before music lawyers agree how samples can be used and royalties shared – or sometimes diverted competely. Even Stubblefield (right) gets to make his own drum-sample CD, another 1990s musical phenomenon, with the idea that people can use his patterns with a cleaner conscience. (As a postscript, Stubblefield will be diagnosed with cancer in 2002. He has no insurance and little funds, but some money is raised from grateful fans via the Internet to help support his medical expenses.)

## NOVEMBER

the rap band, are acquitted of charges of obscenity arising from their performance in Fort Lauderdale, Florida. But a storeowner is found guilty of distributing obscene material and fined $1,000, after selling a copy of their album *As Nasty As They Wanna Be*.

• **29TH: WHEN TOM PETTY** throws his 40th birthday party at his home in Encino, California, his guests include Bruce Springsteen, Roger McGuinn, and Jeff Lynne.

• **30TH: AXL ROSE** of Guns N' Roses is arrested for hitting a neighbour with a bottle in a fight about the volume of his stereo.

• **OCTOBER 20TH: DEEE-LITE ENTER** the US Top 40 with their single 'Groove Is In The Heart,' which has already been given the American three-piece a Number Two hit in the UK. As well as a rap from Q-Tip of A Tribe Called Quest, the song also includes the welcome return to the limelight of William 'Bootsy' Collins, former bass-slapping sidekick of both James Brown and George Clinton, and leader of his own Rubber Band. On 'Groove Is In The Heart' his bass part reproduces a seriously funky line from Herbie Hancock's 1966 *Blow-Up* score.

• **6TH: ABOUT 20 PER CENT** of the Universal Studios back-lot in southern California is destroyed after an arson attack.

• **9TH: MARY ROBINSON** becomes the first woman to be elected president of the Republic of Ireland... The next day, Chandra Shekhar is sworn in as India's new prime minister.

• **10TH: THE AMBITIOUSLY TITLED** *To The Extreme* by Vanilla Ice reaches Number One on the US albums chart for the first of a mind-numbing 16 weeks. His single 'Ice Ice Baby,' built on a sample from 'Under Pressure' by Queen and David Bowie, will also bring him a Number One hit in both the US and UK.

• **12TH: ROLLING STONE** Ron Wood is injured when he is hit by a car near London.

• **14TH: THE WHO'S** Pete Townshend tells an interviewer that he is bisexual. He will later claim he was misquoted.

• **16TH: BRUCE SPRINGSTEEN** plays his first concerts without the E Street Band, at The Shrine Auditorium, Los Angeles.

• **18TH: PAUL McCARTNEY'S** birth certificate is auctioned for $18,000.

• **19TH: MILLI VANILLI** are ordered to return their Grammy Awards, now that their producer/manager, Frank Farian, has publicly admitted that they did not actually sing on their records. Ten days later, one half of the duo, Rob Pilatus, attempts suicide in the Mondrian Hotel, Sunset Strip, Los Angeles, by taking an overdose of pills and then slashing his wrists.

• **21ST: MADONNA** is sued by her next door neighbour because her hedge blocks his view.

• **22ND: MARGARET THATCHER** resigns as UK Conservative party leader and prime minister.

• **23RD: ROALD DAHL** dies in an Oxford hospital. He's best known as author of *Charlie & The Chocolate Factory*, *The Witches*, and *The BFG*.

• **25TH: LECH WALESA** wins Poland's first free election and becomes president.

• **27TH: JOHN MAJOR** wins the second ballot for leadership of the Conservative party, and becomes the UKs new prime minister.

## DECEMBER

• **DECEMBER 1ST: WHITNEY HOUSTON** reaches Number One on the US singles chart with 'I'm Your Baby Tonight'... Meanwhile, after a gig at Louisville Gardens, Kentucky, Poison's guitarist C.C. DeVille spends six hours in jail charged with public drunkenness and criminal mischief... Oh yes, and in Europe, engineers digging the railway tunnel under the English Channel break through, joining Britain to mainland Europe for the first time since the Ice Age.

• **9TH: SLOBODAN MILOSEVIC** becomes the president of Serbia, one of the republics making up the troubled state of Yugoslavia.

• **10TH: THE FIRST BILLBOARD MUSIC AWARDS** is held, with 'Nothing Compares 2 U' by Sinead O'Connor chosen as Top Worldwide Single. Janet Jackson picks up eight of the other awards.

• **14TH: AFTER 30 YEARS** in exile, ANC president Oliver Tambo returns to South Africa.

• **15TH: ROD STEWART** marries blonde model Rachel Hunter in Beverley Hills, California.

• **26TH: ROMANIA** expels ex-King Michael only 12 hours after he returns from 43 years of exile (he was originally was forced to abdicate when the Romanian people's republic was proclaimed in 1947).

• **31ST: YEAR-END STATISTICS** reveal that The Grateful Dead have played to over 1.5m people and grossed over $30m.

• **DECEMBER 8TH: R.E.M. MEMBERS** Peter Buck, Mike Mills, and Bill Berry release the side-project album *Hindu Love Gods*, with singer-songwriter Warren Zevon (right) as the frontman.

# 1991

## January–April

**M**ARCH 1ST: THE FILM biography of The Doors opens in the US. Directed by Oliver Stone, with Val Kilmer (left) taking the role of 'Lizard King' Jim Morrison, it renews interest in the band's music to such an extent that, in the UK at least, there will be three successful single reissues this year – 'Break On Through,' 'Riders On The Storm,' and 'Light My Fire,' which gets as high as Number Seven on the charts. In the US, the movie soundtrack album will reach Number Eight.

---

### JANUARY

### Every Cloud...

• **MARCH 14TH: DOC POMUS**, the lyric-writing half of Pomus & Shuman, one of rock & roll's great creative teams, dies at the age of 65. Together, Doc and Mort penned songs like 'His Latest Flame,' 'Can't get Used To Losing You,' 'Suspicion,' and 'Teenager In Love.' Pomus is also the first non-African-American to receive a Pioneer Award from The Blues Foundation. At his star-studded funeral, following Pomus's wishes, his friend Jimmy Scott (left) sings the Gershwin song 'Someone To Watch Over Me.' Scott is semi-retired, but was once Billy Holiday's favourite singer. His delicate soprano voice is a side-effect of a childhood illness. The entire congregation is reduced to jello at the performance, and Sire Records boss Seymour Stein offers 65-year-old Scott a recording contract on the spot.

• **5TH: MADONNA'S NEW SINGLE**, 'Justify My Love,' co-written with Lenny Kravitz, reaches Number One in the US.
• **8TH: STUDENT JEREMY WADE DELLE** shoots himself in a Texas classroom. His death will inspire the song 'Jeremy' by Pearl Jam... And Steve Clark, guitarist for Def Leppard, dies from a cocktail of drugs and alcohol at his home in London, UK.
• **12TH: ALTHOUGH** she has not actually appeared in a film, Whitney Houston receives a distinguished achievement award from the American Cinema Award Foundation in Los Angeles... And country singer Johnny Paycheck, best known for his 1997 song 'Take This Job And Shove It,' is released from an Ohio prison after serving two years of a seven-year sentence for a shooting offence.
• **15TH: SEAN LENNON** remakes his father's 'Give Peace A Chance' with updated lyrics to coincide with the United Nation's midnight deadline for Iraq to withdraw from Kuwait... The ultimatum deadline passes, and the White House announces the start of Operation Desert Storm. The US bombing of Iraq begins, and continues for over a month.
• **18TH: THREE TEENAGERS** die in the crush during an AC/DC gig at Salt Palace Arena, Salt Lake City, Utah.
• **27TH: NWA RAPPER** Dr Dre gets into a physical confrontation with Dee Barnes, host of Fox TV rap video show *Pump It Up*, at a party in Los Angeles. As a result, Barnes will file criminal charges against Dre for assault and battery, and begin a $22.7 million lawsuit against Dre and NWA. The case is eventually settled out of court... And veteran rockers Styx have their first US Top 40 hit in seven years when their song 'Show Me The Way,' climbs the charts to Number Three. It has been picked up by US radio stations, which use it as a Gulf War anthem.

### FEBRUARY

• **1ST: ONE AIRPLANE** lands on top of another at Los Angeles International Airport and 35 people are killed. An investigation showed a flight controller had forgotten about the small plane on the runway.
• **5TH: ON US TV'S DONOHUE SHOW**, Peter Criss of Kiss exposes an impostor who has successfully impersonated him for a newspaper interview.
• **6TH: THIS DATE** is declared Bob Marley Day in Jamaica: it's Bob's birthday.
• **7TH: THE IRA** launch a mortar bomb attack on the UK prime minister's residence at 10 Downing Street, London, during a cabinet meeting. The three bombs, fired from a van on a nearby street corner, land in the back garden, 40 feet from the building.
• **10TH: FLAVOR FLAV** of Public Enemy is arrested on a charge of assaulting his girlfriend. He will spend 20 days in jail.
• **20TH: THE 33RD ANNUAL GRAMMY AWARDS** are held at Radio City Music Hall, New York City. Public Enemy have boycotted the event because the rap award is not going to be presented during the live TV ceremony. Mariah Carey wins Best Pop Vocal Performance (Female) for 'Vision Of Love,' and Best New Artist. Sinead O'Connor gets Best Alternative Music Performance for 'I Do Not Want What I Have Not Got,' though she is also boycotting the ceremony.
• **25TH: PEARL JAM** begin rehearsals for their contributions to the soundtrack album of the movie *Singles*, along with several other Seattle bands.
• **26TH: SADDAM HUSSEIN** announces on Baghdad Radio that Iraqi troops are being withdrawn from Kuwait. A ceasefire is declared the next day.
• **27TH: JAMES BROWN** is paroled from prison after serving two years of his six-year sentence.
• **28TH: CURTIS MAYFIELD DAY** is held in Los Angeles, in honor of the paralyzed artist.

• **FEBRUARY 9TH: EN VOGUE reach** Number One on the US R&B singles chart with 'You Don't Have To Worry.'

### MARCH

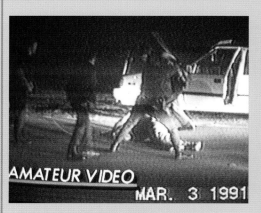

AMATEUR VIDEO MAR. 3 1991

• **MARCH 3RD: RODNEY KING** is severely beaten by Los Angeles police officers. The incident is captured, unknown to them, on a nearby camcorder.

• **2ND: AFTER 36 WEEKS** on the charts, Mariah Carey's debut album finally reaches Number One, on its way to six platinum awards.
• **8TH: LL COOL J** makes his movie debut, as an undercover cop in *The Hard Way*.
• **12TH: SMASHING PUMPKINS** sign a recording contract with Virgin Records.
• **11TH: IN SOUTH AFRICA** a curfew is imposed on black townships after fighting between political gangs leaves 49 dead.
• **13TH: EXXON PAYS $1 BILLION** in fines for the oil spill caused when the Exxon Valdez ran aground on the coast of Alaska in 1989.
• **14TH: IN THE UK, THE BIRMINGHAM SIX** are freed after 16 years of wrongful imprisonment for an IRA pub bombing. One of the six, Paddy Hill, tells a waiting crowd: "We have been used as political scapegoats. The police told us from the start they knew we hadn't done it. They didn't care who had done it."
• **16TH: SEVEN MEMBERS** of country singer Reba McEntire's band and her road manager are killed when their plane crashes after a gig. McEntire is on a separate aircraft.
• **20TH: CONOR CLAPTON**, the four-year-old son of Eric Clapton, falls from the 53rd floor window of a New York apartment block and dies.

# Like Father, Like Son

• **APRIL 26TH: AT A MUSICAL TRIBUTE** to singer-songwriter Tim Buckley at St Anne's Church, Brooklyn, New York, his 24-year-old son Jeff turns up, unannounced, to pay his own respects to the father he barely knew: "It bothered me that I hadn't been to his funeral – that I'd never been able to tell him anything," he says. To a hushed and gripped audience, Jeff sings two songs from his father's 1967 *Goodbye And Hello* album: 'I Never Asked To Be Your Mountain,' and 'Once I Was.' In the process, he unexpectedly kick-starts his own music career.

• **APRIL 23RD: JOHNNY THUNDERS,** formerly of The New York Dolls and The Heartbreakers, dies of an overdose in St Peter's House Hotel, New Orleans, Louisiana, at 38.

## APRIL

• **21ST: LEO FENDER,** inventor of the Telecaster and Stratocaster guitars, dies at age 82, at home in Fullerton, California.

• **23RD: JANET JACKSON** signs a $16m, three-album deal with Virgin Records.

• **27TH: DONNIE WAHLBERG** of New Kids On The Block is arrested after setting fire to a vodka-soaked hotel carpet in Louisville, Kentucky. He later agrees to tape a series of public service messages warning against drugs, driving drunk, and starting fires, in return for having his sentence reduced.

• **1ST: THE US SUPREME COURT** rules that jurors can no longer be barred from serving on the grounds of their race.

• **3RD: ONE OF THE ODDEST** double-acts in history makes its debut when Dweezil Zappa and Donny Osmond perform the Bee Gees song 'Stayin' Alive.' Dweezil has been looking for someone to sing this track on his album *Confessions*, and it seems his first choice, Ozzy Osbourne, is unavailable. So he asks Donny Osmond (the names sounds similar, right?) to fill in... Meanwhile, at a Grateful Dead show in Atlanta, Georgia, police confiscate 4,856 acid tabs, plus crack cocaine, nitrous oxide, marijuana, and magic mushrooms.

• **10TH: R.E.M.** record an MTV *Unplugged* concert at Chelsea Studios, New York City.

• **13TH: 'I'VE BEEN THINKING ABOUT YOU'** by Londonbeat reaches Number One on the US Top 40 singles chart.

• **14TH: TWENTY PAINTINGS** are stolen from the Van Gogh Museum in Amsterdam, Holland, but are recovered 35 minutes later when they are discovered in an abandoned car.

• **15TH: *PLEASE HAMMER DON'T HURT 'EM*** by MC Hammer is certified as a ten-times platinum album in the US.

• **17TH: NIRVANA PLAYS** 'Smells Like Teen Spirit' live for the first time at the OK Hotel, 212 Alaskan Way, Seattle, Washington.

• **20TH: STEVE MARRIOT** of the Small Faces is killed in a house fire, at the age of 44.

MAY       JUNE

• **MAY 11TH:** 'JOYRIDE' by Roxette reaches Number One on the US Top 40 singles chart... And Pearl Jam begins recording the album *Ten*, at London Bridge studios, Seattle, Washington.

• **2ND: NIRVANA BEGIN RECORDING** the album *Nevermind* at Sound City Studios, Van Nuys, California.

• **3RD: ANDY WILLIAMS** (age 60) and Debbie Haas (age 36) are married.

• **4TH: PHIL COLLINS** and Al Jarreau receive honorary music degrees from Berklee College of Music, Boston, Massachusetts.

• **5TH: CARNEGIE HALL** in New York marks its 100th anniversary.

• **6TH: IN BED WITH MADONNA**, a revealing and controversial documentary movie, has its premiere in Los Angeles.

• **7TH: A COUPLE FROM MACON**, Georgia, fail to prove that their son was inspired to attempt suicide by Ozzy Osbourne's music.

• **10TH: BUSHWICK BILL**, of rap group Geto Boy, loses his right eye after being shot by his girlfriend.

• **15TH: FOLLOWING A GIG** at Norwich Arts Centre, Norwich, UK, Welsh band The Manic Street Preachers are interviewed by Steve Lamacq of the *NME*. To convince the doubting journalist of their sincerity, guitarist Richey James Edwards carves the words '4 Real' into his own forearm using a razor.

• **15TH: EDITH CRESSON** becomes the first woman prime minister of France

• **16TH: QUEEN ELIZABETH II** becomes the first British monarch to address the US Congress.

• **21ST: FORMER INDIAN PRIME MINISTER** Rajiv Gandhi, campaigning for re-election, is killed in Madras, India, by a bouquet of flowers that contains a bomb.

• **1ST: IN PHILADELPHIA**, Pennsylvania, a crack cocaine overdose takes the life of Temptations' lead vocalist David Ruffin.

• **3RD: WILLIE NELSON** releases his *Who'll Buy My Memories – The IRS Tapes* album. The record is made up of songs that have been taken by the US government to go towards paying off his $16 million tax bill.

• **8TH: 'MORE THAN WORDS'** by Extreme, from their album *Pornograffiti*, reaches Number One on the US Top 40 singles chart.

• **8TH: A VICTORY PARADE** is held in Washington to honor veterans of the Gulf War... Meanwhile, in LA, Bruce Springsteen marries backing vocalist Patti Scialfa in "a romantic sunset ceremony" on the lawn of their Beverly Hills mansion.

• **12TH: AFTER THE PEOPLE** of Russia win an earlier referendum to have their own president (as opposed to the Soviet Union president, Mikhail Gorbachev), Boris N. Yeltsin is elected to the post.

• **17TH: THE PARLIAMENT OF SOUTH AFRICA** repeals the Population Registration Act – the act that required all South Africans to be classified by race at birth.

• **21ST: OUTSIDE** a Los Angeles supermarket, rapper Vanilla Ice and his bodyguard are arrested for carrying concealed weapons.

## Gangsta Paradise

• **JUNE 3RD: IN A RAID** under the UK's Obscene Publications Act, police seize 13,000 copies of Los Angeles rap act NWA's second album, *Efil4zaggin*. A few weeks later it becomes the first 'gangsta rap' album to reach Number One on the US *Billboard* charts. Up until the late 1980s the US hip-hop scene was more or less an East Coast phenomenon. But underground activity was stirring on the West Coast in the form of gangsta rap, courtesy of the likes of Ice-T (main photo, left) and NWA (Niggas With Attitude, inset). NWA's *Straight Outta Compton* album and notorious 'F*** Tha Police' track created outrage: even the FBI complained vociferously about the band's lyrical content. (Acts like Philadelphia's Schooly D could also lay claim to any 'granddaddy of gangsta' tag.) Needless to say, the furore over NWA simply helped sell millions more copies of the album, and launched the solo careers of Ice Cube (below), Eazy-E, and soon-to-be G-Funk supremo Dr Dre (later to be the man behind white gangsta-wannabe money-machine Eminem). By the early 1990s, the list of OGs (original gangstas) has grown, and the likes of Snoop Doggy Dog, The Wu-Tang Clan, and Mobb Deep are lining up to relate stories of violence, misogyny, drugs, and rampant consumerism – filling an obvious void created by the pop-pap alternative. They become the biggest music thing to hit the US music scene in decades, but sadly not without the loss, and ultimately pointless waste, of several young lives.

# Shiny, Happy, Beardy, Bingo

• **JUNE 18TH:** *OUT OF TIME* BY R.E.M. reaches Number One on the US album charts. Having just finished a low-key tour under the pseudonym Bingo Hand Job, the band now enter the commercial big-time with this transatlantic Number One album, and its two major hit singles, 'Losing My Religion' and 'Shiny Happy People.'

Featuring distinctive backing vocals by Kate Pierson of the B-52s, 'Shiny Happy People' is a huge radio and MTV favourite and is played to death over the summer of 1991, establishing the band as mainstream pop superstars with stadium-filling appeal. But rather than taking the easy route to fame and fortune by continuing to churn out more shiny, happy pop songs, R.E.M. will typically take a step back and start work on the much more intense *Automatic For The People*. They might not have another huge-selling single, but it does no harm to their album sales. Their next three albums reach Two, One, and Two respectively in the US. All three are Number Ones in the UK.

• **AUGUST 22ND:** *SHAKE YOUR MONEY MAKER* by the Black Crowes is certified as a US triple-platinum album. An all-American band with strong similarities to UK acts like The Faces and The Rolling Stones, the Crowes will do even better with their next album release, 1992's *The Southern Harmony And Musical Companion* – a future US Number One and UK Number Two.

## JULY

• **JULY 27TH: GRAVEL-LARYNXED** Canadian rocker Bryan Adams reaches Number One on the US singles chart for the first of seven weeks with his ten million-selling ballad '(Everything I Do) I Do It For You,' taken from the soundtrack of the Kevin Costner movie *Robin Hood: Prince Of Thieves*. In the UK the song stays at Number One for a teeth-grindingly long 16 weeks.

• **4TH: A RIOT BREAKS OUT** after Axl Rose of Guns N' Roses attacks a fan for taking photographs during a gig in Maryland Heights, St. Louis, Missouri. Two weeks later the band's former drummer, Steve Adler, files suit in Los Angeles against his ex-bandmates, claiming they pressured him to use heroin, and then dropped him after he entered a rehabilitation program.

• **5TH: REGULATORS** shut down the Pakistani-managed Bank of Credit and Commerce International (BCCI) in eight countries, for fraud, drug money laundering and illegal infiltration of the US banking system.

• **9TH: US PRESIDENT GEORGE BUSH** gives country star Roy Acuff the National Medal Of Art.

• **10TH: PRESIDENT BUSH** lifts US economic sanctions against South Africa, thanks to its progress towards racial equality.

• **17TH: THE FIRST LOLLAPALOOZA** travelling tour begins – featuring Jane's Addiction, Nine Inch Nails, Ice-T, Living Colour, and others.

• **22ND: THE BAND ON A FRIDAY** (later to become Radiohead) play their first after-graduation gig at the Hollybush, Oxford, UK... meanwhile in the US, Desiree Washington, a Miss Black America contestant, accuses boxer Mike Tyson of rape in an Indianapolis hotel room. Tyson is later convicted and will do three years in prison.

• **23RD: POLICE CHARGE** Jeffrey Dahmer with 17 counts of murder after finding the remains of 11 victims in his apartment in Milwaukee yesterday. Dahmer confesses to all 17 murders and will be sentenced to life in prison.

• **31ST: PRESIDENT BUSH** and President Gorbachev sign the Strategic Arms Reduction Treaty.

## AUGUST

• **2ND: FUNK STAR RICK JAMES** is arrested and charged with torturing a woman during a bizarre three-day orgy at his Hollywood home.

• **8TH: JOHN McCARTHY**, a British television producer, is finally released by Lebanese kidnappers after being held captive for more than five years. Three days later, American Edward Tracey is released by his Shiite Muslim kidnappers after almost five years.

• **15TH: 750,000 FANS** turn out for the final date of Paul Simon's Born At The Right Time tour, in Central Park, New York City.

• **17TH: THE MONSTERS OF ROCK** festival at Castle Donington in the UK convinces 72,500 fans to part with £22.50 ($33) to see AC/DC, Metallica, Mötley Crüe, Queensryche, and The Black Crowes.

• **20TH: RIOT GRRRLS** arrive big time, with the International Pop Underground Convention in Olympia, Washington, featuring six days of performances mostly by women, including Seven Year Bitch, Jean Smith, and Bikini Kill.

• **24TH: THE PRODIGY'S** second single, 'Charly' (using samples from a televised public safety campaign featuring a cartoon cat of that name) becomes their first hit, reaching Number Three on the UK charts. Favourites on the underground rave scene, it will be six years before the group, led by musical innovator Liam Howlett, spread their brand of ultra-heavy techno as far as the US mainstream – but when they do, it happens in a big way.

• **31st: METALLICA** by Metallica (below) reaches Number One on the US album chart, for the first of four weeks. It only manages a week at the top in the UK (curiously squeezed between Pavarotti and *Joseph & The Amazing Technicolor Dreamcoat*, starring singing soap star Jason Donovan), but the lead single, 'Enter Sandman,' rises even higher in the UK than in the States. Of all the metal sub-genres, speed-metal attracts the biggest following, and Metallica (James Hetfield, Kirk Hammett, Lars Ulrich, and Jason Newstead replacing the late Cliff Burton) are its godfathers. Their 1983 album *Kill 'Em All* laid out the blueprint for speed-metal (and indeed off-shoots like thrash, although the more 'satanic' lyrical content of black and death metal was influenced more by Venom), and the scene was quickly populated by the likes of Megadeth (right), formed by ex-Metallica man Dave Mustaine), the fearsome Slayer, South American outfit Sepultura, and New Yorkers Anthrax.

## Entertain Us

SEPTEMBER 24TH: Nirvana release the multi-million-selling album *Nevermind* in the US. They back it up with some stunning live shows, delivered with an unflinching ferocity and an estimable disregard for the health and safety of either themselves or their equipment. In the UK they win over virtually a whole generation with jaw-slackening performances at the Reading festival and on national TV show *The Word*. Though it seems to come as a shock, and eventually has a disastrous effect, this success is something they've worked hard for. Nirvana's roots lie in the underground hardcore scene of the mid 1980s when Cobain, then playing drums, formed the Stiff Woodies with Krist Novoselic (bass), before moving to vocals and guitar in 1987, adding drummer Chad Channing and

• DECEMBER 27TH: **THE RED HOT CHILI PEPPERS** begin a US tour at Los Angeles Sports Arena, supported by Nirvana and Pearl Jam. The Chili Peppers are enjoying their most high-profile period since first getting together (originally as Anthem) eight years ago: their current album *Blood Sugar Sex Magik*, their first for their new label Warners, will reach Number Three in the US (25 in the UK), and provide the hit single 'Under The Bridge.'

## SEPTEMBER

• 4TH: **COUNTRY SINGER** Dottie West dies at the age of 58 from injuries received in a car accident five days ago. West was the first ever female country Grammy winner.

• 5TH: **THE EIGHTH ANNUAL MTV AWARDS** ceremony is held at the Universal Amphitheater, Universal City, California. Mariah Carey performs 'Emotions.' R.E.M. get six awards, including Best Group, Best Video, and even Best Alternative Video.

• 6TH: **THE NAME** St Petersburg is restored to Russia's second largest city. Founded in 1703 by Peter The Great, the city's name was changed to Petrograd in 1914, and to Leningrad in 1924.

• 7TH: **GUITARIST** Izzy Stradlin take his leave from Guns N' Roses.

• 12TH: **THE SPACE SHUTTLE** Discovery takes off on a mission to release an observatory to study the Earth's ozone layer.

• 16TH: **A FEDERAL JUDGE** in Washington dismisses the Iran-Contra charges against Oliver North.

• 17TH: **THE UNITED NATIONS GENERAL ASSEMBLY** opens its 46th session. New members are Estonia, Latvia, Lithuania, North and South Korea, Micronesia, and the Marshall Islands.

• 21ST: ***ON EVERY STREET***, the first new Dire Straits album in six years, enters the UK album chart at Number One. In the US, it makes Number 12. It'll be their final studio album.

• 24TH: **THEODOR SEUSS GEISEL** dies at the age of 87. He is better known as children's author Dr Seuss.

• 28TH: **LEGENDARY JAZZ TRUMPETER** and composer Miles Davis dies, at the age of 65, in Santa Monica, California.

• 28TH: **GARTH BROOKS** scores a new first by debuting at Number One on the US pop and country album charts simultaneously with 'Ropin' The Wind.' The album will go on to notch up a staggering 18 (non-consecutive) weeks at the top of the pop chart.

## OCTOBER

• OCTOBER 5TH: **PRESIDENT GORBACHEV** announces the USSR will cut its nuclear arsenal in response to the arms reduction initiated by George Bush... At the same time, *Use Your Illusion II* by Guns N' Roses reaches Number One on the US album chart, just as it drops off the top slot in the UK.

• 1ST: **MICHAEL JACKSON'S** white crystal-beaded glove is stolen from the Motown Museum in Detroit. MC Hammer offers $50,000 for its return

• 6TH: **ELIZABETH TAYLOR** weds for the eighth time. This time her husband is former builder Larry Fortensky.

• 8TH: **A SLAVE BURIAL SITE**, closed in 1790, is rediscovered by construction workers in lower Manhattan.

• 10TH: **SALT-N-PEPA** have their biggest hit to date with 'Let's Talk About Sex,' which reaches Number Two in the UK, and Number 13 in the US.

• 16TH: **PERRY FARRELL** of Jane's Addiction is arrested in Santa Monica after police find syringes and crack pipes in his hotel room.

recording 1989's debut album *Bleach* (Channing would be replaced by Dave Grohl the following year). But now with *Nevermind*, and the almost blanket coverage on MTV for lead single 'Smells Like Teen Spirit,' Cobain & co are the kings of grunge – and, in a period where rap has taken over at the centre of alternative youth culture, they find themselves hyped as the new saviours of rock. It's not a role Cobain is at all comfortable with. It also starts to attract an element Cobain despises – the "jocks," or mainstream rock "rednecks," the kind of guys who used to beat him up at school. So this creative and commercial peak only increases Cobain's already unstable behaviour – and when he marries Courtney Love next year, things go from bad to wildly out of control...

## NOVEMBER

• **17TH: TENNESSEE ERNIE FORD** dies, 36 years to the day after the release of his biggest hit, 'Sixteen Tons.'
• **19TH: OASIS** play their first gig in their definitive quintet line-up at The Boardwalk, Manchester, UK.
• **25TH: US ROCK IMPRESARIO** Bill Graham, founder of the Fillmore theater in San Francisco, and manager of the Grateful Dead and Jefferson Airplane, dies at the age of 60 – killed in a helicopter crash on the way back from a Huey Lewis gig he's been promoting in California. His girlfriend, Melissa Gold is also killed.
• **25TH: WEARING A RATHER** fetching dress, Kurt Cobain of Nirvana is interviewed on MTV.

• **2ND: NEIL YOUNG'S** fifth Bridge School Benefit concert is held at Shoreline Amphitheater, Mountain View, California, featuring John Lee Hooker, Don Henley (of The Eagles), Willie Nelson, Sonic Youth, Tracy Chapman, and others.
• **3RD: ISRAELI** and Palestinian representatives hold their first-ever face-to-face talks, in Madrid, Spain.
• **4TH: RONALD REAGAN** opens his presidential library in California. The dedication ceremony is attended by President Bush and former US presidents Carter, Ford and Nixon. It's the first such gathering of five ex-US presidents... Meanwhile some legendary musical names are elected to the Rock'n'Roll Hall Of Fame in Cleveland, Ohio, today, such as Jimi Hendrix, Booker T & The MGs, The Isley Brothers, Johnny Cash, Sam & Dave, The Yardbirds, and Bobby 'Blue' Bland.
• **5TH: CZECH-BORN** Jan Ludvik Hoch (better known as UK media magnate Robert Maxwell) falls from his luxury yacht and drowns. Investigations into his death later reveal misappropriation of company pension funds.

• **NOVEMBER 30TH: PM DAWN** hold the US Number One position with their single 'Set Adrift On Memory Bliss,' based on a sample from Spandau Ballet's 1983 hit 'True.'

• **7TH: TWO SHOCK** medical announcements today: Frank Zappa has been diagnosed with prostate cancer, and basketball player Magic Johnson announces he has tested positive for AIDS and is retiring from the game... Meanwhile, in Florida, actor Paul Reubens, better known as Pee Wee Herman, pleads 'no contest' to charges of indecent exposure, having been arrested for being rude in a cinema.
• **11TH: THE US STATIONS** its first diplomat in Cambodia for 16 years to help the nation arrange democratic elections.
• **18TH: SECTIONS OF MICHAEL JACKSON'S** *Black Or White* video, which includes crotch-grabbing and car smashing scenes, are edited out after TV viewers protest.
• **19TH: MADONNA** dresses in drag to see an all-male revue at the Gaiety Theatre in Manhattan, New York City. Wearing a pants suit with a baseball cap, she manages to gain admittance to the men-only club.
• **23RD: TAKE THAT**, the first of the Britsh breed of boy-bands – following the example of the US's New Kids On The Block – enjoy their first UK chart entry with the single 'Promises,' which peaks at Number 38.

## DECEMBER

• **2ND: THE US SUPREME COURT** rules that The Shirelles, B.J. Thomas, and Gene Pitney are owed $1.2 million in unpaid royalties.
• **3RD: IN THE SECOND ANNUAL BILLBOARD MUSIC AWARDS**, Mariah Carey wins Hot 100 Singles Artist, Top Pop Artist, Top Pop Album, and Top Adult Contemporary Artist. Whitney Houston wins Top R&B Artist, Top R&B Singles Artist, Top R&B Album and Top R&B Album Artist. Was it worth anyone else turning up?
• **4TH: ASSOCIATED PRESS** correspondent Terry Anderson is released after nearly seven years in captivity in Lebanon... Meanwhile Pan American World Airways, better known as 'Pan Am', ceases operations due to financial problems.
• **5TH: BRIAN WILSON** of the Beach Boys is legally obliged to sever links with his controversial therapist/business adviser Dr Eugene Landy.
• **13TH:** *LUCK OF THE DRAW* by Bonnie Raitt is certified as a US double platinum album.
• **18TH: A LONG-RUNNING** legal dispute between the family of Bob Marley and MCA Music about control of the singer's estate is decided in favour of the Marley family.
• **26TH: THE SOVIET UNION'S** parliament formally votes the country out of existence.

• **DECEMBER 7TH:** *ACHTUNG BABY* by U2 enters the US album chart at Number One – their third US chart-topping album in a row. It's their most experimental album to date, not just musically, but also in terms of the band's more adventurous dressing-up and stage act. But it will still sell more than four million copies in the US alone.

## Showstopper

• **NOVEMBER 24TH: FREDDIE MERCURY** of Queen dies in London, at the age of 45. Only two days ago he released a public statement confirming, for the first time, media speculation that he was dying of AIDS. He's spent his last few precious months working in the studio as much as his health would allow, including on his final single, 'The Show Must Go On.' But the show can't go on, really. Although the three remaining members will reunite in 1994 to record music around some of Mercury's final vocal tracks, Queen performing live without the strutting, preening, master showman would be unthinkable.

• FEBRUARY 24TH: **COURTNEY LOVE & KURT COBAIN**, leaders of Hole and Nirvana respectively, are married in Hawaii.

**JANUARY**

## Hmmm, Pop Stars

• **JANUARY 9TH: STING MAKES** a guest appearance in *The Simpsons* (helping to free Bart from a well). He's one of many pop stars who lend their image and voices to the show (including Paul McCartney, Tom Jones, Aerosmith, The Chili Peppers, Ringo Starr), although series creator Matt Groening (right) says his own tastes are less commercial, preferring "totally uncompromising weirdos."

• **8TH:** *TOO LEGIT TO QUIT* by MC Hammer is certified as a triple platinum album in the US... And President George Bush collapses during a state dinner in Tokyo. White House officials say he is suffering from stomach flu.

• **11TH: NIRVANA TOPPLE** Michael Jackson's Dangerous from the US Number One album spot with *Nevermind*... And Paul Simon begins a tour of South Africa – the first international star to perform there following the end of the UN cultural boycott.

• **13TH: JAPAN APOLOGIZES** for forcing tens of thousands of Korean women to serve as sex slaves for Japanese soldiers during World War II.

• **21ST: WILLIE DIXON**, great Mississippi blue man, whose songs were inspirational to The Rolling Stones and Led Zeppelin, among others, dies at age 76.

• **22ND: MARIAH CAREY'S** stepfather, Joseph Vian, files suit against her in Manhattan Federal Court. He alleges that she has not fulfilled an agreement to repay him for his financial and emotional support when she was trying to become a star.

• **24TH: A MUSIC PROFESSOR** at the University of Massachusetts, Greg McPherson, files a $21 million lawsuit against New Kids On The Block manager Maurice Starr, alleging he was not paid for his work on the group's *Hangin' Tough Live* album. McPherson also claims the group only sing 20 per cent of the album, and lip-synch in their concerts.

• **25TH: 'ALL 4 LOVE'** by Color Me Badd reaches Number One on the US Top 40 singles chart.

• **27TH: IT'S MADE PUBLIC** that C.C. DeVille has left Poison, apparently to form the C.C. DeVille Experience.

• **30TH: BRUCE SPRINGSTEEN** hosts a party at Tipitina's in New Orleans, Louisiana, to preview the long-awaited *Human Touch* and *Lucky Town* albums for Columbia Records executives.

**FEBRUARY**

• **10TH: VINCE NEIL**, singer with Mötley Crüe, shows up hours late for practice to find that he's been fired. The band claim he doesn't "share their determination and passion for music." Neil's version of the story is that he quits to spend more time on his alternative career as a racing car driver... The band will reunite five years later on the American Music Awards.

• **15TH: THE VILLAGE OF KRINJABO** in Ivory Coast, west Africa, names Michael Jackson 'King Of The Sanwis.'

• **16TH: MICK JAGGER** of The Rolling Stones is refused entry into Japan because of drug-related criminal convictions.

• **25TH: AT THE 34TH ANNUAL GRAMMY AWARDS**, in Radio City Music Hall, New York City, Natalie Cole walks off with Best Traditional Pop Performance. At the end of last year she had a hit by duetting 'Unforgettable' with her deceased father, Nat King Cole, using the vocal track from Nat's

• **FEBRUARY 14TH: THE** *WAYNE'S WORLD* movie is released, based on the characters created by Mike Myers and Dana Carvey (left) on the TV show *Saturday Night Live*. They play two innocent, ageing adolescent rock fans in the US Midwest with their own cable access show. It will ultimately spawn two films (one good, one not so), and will even help to revitalise Queen's career in America, thanks to the famous scene involving head-banging to 'Bohemian Rhapsody' in a small, crowded car. It will also litter the world with some new and amusingly inane catchphrases. These include "Not!" (added to the end of a statement to negate its effect, and still heard a decade later in less hip circles), "schwing" (uttered on spying an attractive "babe," and accompanied by a sudden lurch forward in the pants department), "We're not worthy" (directed at the awe-inspiring, but bafflingly tedious figure of Alice Cooper in the movie); and the disbelieving "shaw... and monkeys might fly out of my butt." Party on, Wayne. Party On Garth. Wherever you are. Excellent.

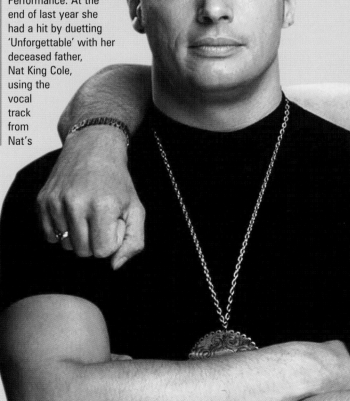

## Completely Justified

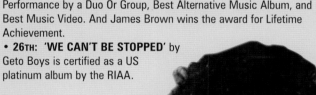

**F**EBRUARY 11TH: After the KLF perform '3AM Eternal' at the *11th Annual BRIT Awards* in London, they leave a dead sheep at the door to the aftershow party, with a note attached stating, "I died for you." (Other highlights of the night include R.E.M. collecting Best International Group award.) KLF, consisting of Bill Drummond and Jimmy Cauty, both experienced music business veterans with a wickedly anarchic streak, had a Top Five US hit last year with '3AM Eternal' (a former UK Number One), and have now just released their latest, typically unpredictable offering – a duet with revered county diva Tammy Wynette. The song, 'Justified and Ancient,' is probably as perplexing to Tammy, good sport that she is, as it is to the listeners (all the stuff about driving an ice-cream van, for instance), but even so, the cult status of the band, and the force of their personalities, and perhaps a few misled country music fans, take the record to US Number 11 (Number Two in the UK). It'll be Tammy's first pop chart hit for 23 years.

## Elton & Sun

• **F**EBRUARY **1**ST: GEORGE MICHAEL & ELTON JOHN have a joint Number One with their duet of Elton's old song, 'Don't Let The Sun Go Down On Me.'

**MARCH**

**APRIL**

1961 recording of the song. Meanwhile R.E.M. collect Best Pop Performance by a Duo Or Group, Best Alternative Music Album, and Best Music Video. And James Brown wins the award for Lifetime Achievement.

• **26**TH: **'WE CAN'T BE STOPPED'** by Geto Boys is certified as a US platinum album by the RIAA.

• **1**ST: **BOSNIAN SERBS** begin sniping in Sarajevo, after Bosnian Croats and Muslims vote for Bosnian independence. In a month's time, on 6th April, the siege of Sarajevo begins.

• **6**TH: **THE COMPUTER VIRUS** Michelangelo begins popping up.

• **11**TH: **FORMER US PRESIDENT** Richard Nixon accuses the Bush administration of not giving enough economic aid to Russia.

• **16**TH: *TIME, LOVE, AND TENDERNESS* by Michael Bolton is certified a five-times platinum album in the US... And Milli Vanilli are ordered by a Californian court to refund the purchase price of CDs to fans who bought them under false impressions.

• **17**TH: **CALIFORNIAN HEAVY SKA** band No Doubt release their self-titled debut album. It is widely ignored.

• **18**TH: **WHITE SOUTH AFRICANS** vote for constitutional reforms that give legal equality to blacks.

• **20**TH: **JANICE PENNINGTON** is awarded $1.3 million for an accident on the set of US TV show *The Price is Right*, when she was knocked into Contestants' Row by a wayward camera. She received over 100 stitches on her right shoulder, resulting in it being one inch shorter than the other.

• **21**ST: **'SAVE THE BEST FOR LAST'** by Vanessa Williams reaches Number One on the US Top 40 singles chart. Williams first came to fame as the first Africa-American woman to win the Miss America beauty pageant, though she was pressured to give up the title because she had appeared nude in *Penthouse* magazine.

• **24**TH: **THE ROLLERCOASTER TOUR,** planned as a British version of Lollapalooza, sets off from the Apollo, Manchester. Acts on the bill are The Jesus & Mary Chain, Dinosaur Jr, My Bloody Valentine, and Blur.

• **24**TH: **EN VOGUE** release the album *Funky Divas* in the US.

• **F**EBRUARY **8**TH: **'I'M TOO SEXY'** by Right Said Fred (or R*S*F, as they're cryptically known in the States) reaches Number One on the US Top 40 singles chart. One-hit wonders in the US, the trio, based around shaven-headed brothers Fred and Richard Fairbrass, will have four Top Five UK hits over the next couple of years.

• **1**ST: **THE RED HOT CHILI PEPPERS'** album *Blood Sugar Sex Magik* is certified as a US platinum disc... And the band Mighty Joe Young, from San Diego, California, are signed to Atlantic Records. They will shortly change their name to Stone Temple Pilots.

• **2**ND: **JOHN GOTTI,** known to the media as the 'Teflon Don' is found guilty of the death of Mafia boss Paul Castallano.

• **3**RD: **PRINCE** sets off on his extravagantly staged Diamonds & Pearls World Tour from the Tokyo Dome in Japan.

• **9**TH: **JOHN MAJOR,** a Conservative, is elected UK Prime Minister.

• **12**TH:

**MICKEY MOUSE** moves to Europe when the Euro Disney Theme Park opens just outside Paris, France.

• **18**TH: **THE NEW ALBUM** *DIVA*, by Annie Lennox, formerly of The Eurythmics, enters the UK chart at Number One.

• **20**TH: **MADONNA** signs a re-negotiated seven-year contract with Warner Brothers for $60m... And Tori Amos begins a US tour at the Bottom Line, New York City.

• **29**TH: **A CALIFORNIA JURY** acquits the Los Angeles policemen involved in last year's Rodney King beating. The worst violence and looting in US history follows, and at least 50 die.

## Men & Boyz

**A**UGUST 15TH: BOYZ II MEN reach Number One on the US Top 40 singles chart with 'End Of The Road.' It remains at the top for 13 weeks (a mere three weeks in the UK). The laidback Motown R&B vocal group from Philadelphia will have 14 US Top 40 hits in the 1990s, including five Number Ones. That made them Motown's best-selling act ever. What's more, they'll go on to achieve the remarkable feat of spending longer at the top of the US charts than any group since The Beatles.

• **3RD: FIVE DAYS** of rioting and looting end in Los Angeles.
• **4TH: DUDU MNTOWAZIWAYO NDLOVU** (Dudu Zulu), a member of Johnny Clegg's band Savuka, dies of a gunshot wound in Zululand, South Africa, at age 33.
• **7TH: IMMEDIATELY BEFORE A GIG** in Tokyo, guitarist John Frusciante tells the rest of the Red Hot Chili Peppers he is

• **MAY 19TH: USING A SAMPLE** from the Jackson Five, 'Jump' by Kris Kross is the new US Number One single. It's in the middle of an eight-week run at the top, and has just been certified double-platinum, and confirmed as the fastest-selling US single since the late 1970s. (It's about to reach Number Two in the UK as well.) The rap duo consists of two 13-year-old boys, whose impressively baggy denim pants are worn back-to-front (as are their tops), sparking a new teenage fashion craze.

leaving. Next morning he's gone. But he will return... in 1998.
• **13TH: THE PET SHOP BOYS** play at The Hacienda, Manchester, UK, during the massively influential club's tenth anniversary celebrations.
• **14TH: CHART-TOPPING UK BAND** the KLF issue a press statement announcing that they have "retired from the music business." ... Meanwhile former Soviet president Mikhail Gorbachev appeals to members of the US Congress to pass a bill to aid the people of the former Soviet Union.
• **16TH: WEIRD AL YANKOVIC'S** 'Smells Like Nirvana' hits the lower end of the US Top 40. It's the parody specialist's second hit, following 1984's Michael Jackson take-off, 'Eat It.'
• **20TH: RICHIE KOTZEN** joins Poison, replacing departed guitarist C.C. DeVille.
• **23RD: 'ACHY BREAKY HEART'** by Billy Ray Cyrus, enters the US Top 40, on its way to Number Four.
• **26TH: CHARLES GESCHKE**, president of software giants Adobe Systems, is kidnapped from the company car park in Mountain View, California. His family and business receive a ransom demand for $650,000, but the kidnappers will be apprehended as they attempt to collect the ransom, and Geschke is freed soon after.
• **30TH: *THE SOUTHERN HARMONY AND MUSICAL COMPANION*** by the Black Crowes reaches Number One on the US album chart.

• **JUNE 6TH: DAVID BOWIE** marries Somalian model Iman Abdulmajid in a church in Florence, Italy. They have already had a civil ceremony in Lausanne, Switzerland, in April.

• **4TH: THE ALBUM *HEART*** by Heart is certified as five-times platinum in the US.
• **4TH: THE US POSTAL SERVICE** announces the result of a nationwide vote to decide which image of Elvis should appear on a commemorative stamp. The public preference is for the younger Elvis, rather than the singer in his later, more corpulent, Las Vegas years.
• **10TH: A JUDGE** in Los Angeles throws out a $25 million palimony suit brought by Kelly Emberg against Rod Stewart.
• **12TH: RE-ESTABLISHED** record industry mogul Clive Davis is honoured as Man Of The Year in a special tribute event held at the Friars' Club in the Waldorf-Astoria Hotel, New York City. Whitney Houston and Dionne Warwick sing 'That's What Friends Are For' ... Meanwhile, in a letter to the US Senate, Russian leader Boris Yeltsin admits that in the early 1950s the Soviet Union shot down nine US planes and held 12 American survivors.
• **14TH: A TOTAL OF 178** countries attend the UN conference on the environment in Rio, Brazil. All agreed a 27-point declaration to limit damage to the natural world.
• **16TH: THE MADONNATHON** – the first International Madonna Appreciation Convention, but not the last – takes place in the Holiday Inn in Southfield, Missouri.
• **20TH: MARIAH CAREY** has another US Number One single, her sixth in two years, this time with a cover of the old Jacksons' hit 'I'll Be There.'
• **22ND: FRANK PAUL JONES** is arrested in the grounds of the Jackson family home in Encino, California. The stalker believes himself to be Janet Jackson's husband.

• **AUGUST 22ND: WHEN STING MARRIES** Trudie Styler at his country home, Lake House, in Wiltshire, UK, The Police reform for one night only.

• **JUNE 15TH: US VICE PRESIDENT** Dan Quayle instructs a student to spell potato by adding an 'e' to the end during a spelling bee arranged as a photo-opportunity. Quayle becomes notorious for his foot-in-mouth quotes, such as: "If we don't succeed, we run the risk of failure," and "A low voter turnout is an indication of fewer people going to the polls."

**JULY**

**AUGUST**

## The Jackal Has His Day

• **JUNE 1ST: ILICH RAMIREZ SANCHEZ,** known as Carlos The Jackal – for a long time the world's most wanted man – is sentenced to life imprisonment by a court in France. He's been convicted of shooting two French secret agents and a Lebanese informer, but is also implicated in more than 80 killings and hundreds of injuries during a 25-year campaign of bombings and terrorist attacks for the Palestinian cause. Venezuelan-born Carlos is also suspected of being involved in the Munich Olympics massacre of Israeli athletes, the kidnap of OPEC oil ministers, and the hijacking of the Air France passenger jet which ended in the bloody raid in Entebbe. He was nicknamed The Jackal after the character in Frederick Forsyth's novel *Day Of The Jackal.* Also a successful movie, it featured an elusive and ruthless assassin.

• **2ND: MICK JAGGER** of The Rolling Stones becomes a rock grandad when his daughter Jade gives birth to a daughter, Assissi... And Michael Bolton begins a US tour at the Coca-Cola Starplex Amphitheater, Dallas, Texas, supported by Celine Dion. The show takes $292,174.
• **4TH: SIR MIX-A-LOT** tops the US singles chart with 'Baby Got Back,' which will win him a Grammy award. A musically intriguing artist – mixing everything from Black Sabbath to Kraftwerk and Devo to Public Enemy, Mix-A-Lot also attracts contrtoversy for his sexist lyrics and images (MTV bans the video for 'Baby Got back'). Later his humorous approach will be cited in mitigation.
• **9TH: FRANK ZAPPA,** Luther Campbell of 2 Live Crew, and Joey Ramone of The Ramones are among musicians who condemn today's selection of Al Gore as Bill Clinton's US presidential running mate. Their objections are in fact aimed at his wife, Tipper Gore, founder of the Parents' Music Resource Centre, which forced record labels to put warning stickers on albums with content considered unsuitable for minors.
• **10TH: A FEDERAL JUDGE** In Miami sentences former Panamanian leader Manuel Noriega to 40 years in prison on drug and racketeering charges... And in New York, a jury finds Pan Am responsible for allowing a terrorist to destroy Flight 103 over Lockerbie in 1988, killing 270 people.
• **11TH: A RANGE OF TIES** designed by Grateful Dead leader Jerry Garcia goes on sale at exclusive Bloomingdales, New York City, selling at $28.50 each. Garcia cheerfully reassures his fans that he won't be wearing them himself.
• **12TH: AXL ROSE** of Guns N' Roses is arrested at New York's JFK airport on a warrant from St Louis on charges stemming from a 1991 GN'R concert.
• **14TH: OLIVIA NEWTON-JOHN** announces she has breast cancer, but that doctors expect a full recovery.
• **18TH: LOLLAPALOOZA 2** kicks off at the Shoreline Amphitheater, Mountain View, California, featuring Ministry, Red Hot Chilli Peppers, Soundgarden, and Pearl Jam. It eventually grosses $30m on its cross-country trek... Meanwhile Whitney Houston marries Bobby Brown at her mansion in Mendham, New Jersey. Stevie Wonder sings for them.
• **20TH: VACLAV HAVEL,** the playwright who led the revolution against communism, steps down as president of Czechoslovakia in protest against Slovak demands to split the country in two. In 1992 he will become president of the Czech Republic.

• **AUGUST 7TH: BUCKINGHAM PALACE,** London home of the British Queen, opens its doors for public visits for the first time.

• **1ST: U2 BEGIN** rehearsals for their Zoo TV: Outside Broadcast tour in Hershey, Pennsylvania.
• **3RD: THE US SENATE** votes to restrict and eventually end the testing of nuclear weapons.
• **5TH: FEDERAL CIVIL RIGHTS** charges are filed against the four Los Angeles police officers who assaulted Rodney King. Two of the officers, previously acquitted on California State charges, are later convicted and jailed.
• **9TH: JAMES HETFIELD** of Metallica suffers third-degree burns to his left hand when he accidentally steps in front of a flame jet during a gig at the Olympic Stadium, Montreal, Canada.
• **11TH: THE MALL** of America, the largest in teh US, opens in Bloomington, Minnesota.
• **12TH: THE US,** Canada, and Mexico announce the North American Free Trade Agreement.
• **13TH: 'BABY BABY BABY'** by TLC is certified as a gold single in the US.
• **17TH: THE FBI BEGINS** the Siege of Ruby Ridge when 400 armed federal agents descend on the Weaver family's Idaho mountain home, ultimately killing Randy Weaver's son, wife and dog. The Justice Department's later recommends prosecuting the agents, and the surviving Weavers win $3.1 million in civil damages.
• **18TH: WOODY ALLEN** admits to being romantically involved with Soon-Yi Previn, the adopted daughter of his partner Mia Farrow
• **25TH: MADONNA** reportedly spends $15,000 on having a solid gold tooth fitted into the front of her top row of teeth.

# Stop Whispering

**S**EPTEMBER 21ST: RADIOHEAD release a new single, 'Creep,' on Parlophone Records in the UK, where it becomes the band's first Top Ten hit. When it's released in the US, in summer 1983, it peaks at Number 34 – appealing to the same sort of alienated audience as Kurt Cobain's uneasy listening. Like Nirvana, Radiohead then reject the route of releasing an obvious single follow-up, preferring to work towards a less immediate, more thought-provoking body of work: they expect their audience to do a little work. Believed by some to be the most important band of the Nineties, certainly from the UK, and one of the all-time great rock outfits, Radiohead, made up of Thom Yorke (left) on vocals, keyboards, and guitar, Jonny Greenwood, guitar, keyboards, xylophone, Ed O'Brien, guitar, Colin Greenwood, bass, and Phil Selway, drums, first began playing together in 1987 in their home town of Oxford, UK. They only went full-time when gig attendances began to grow, as word-of-mouth acclaim increased for their intense live shows. 'Creep' marks Yorke out as a forceful, if troubled, writer, but it's not until their next album, *The Bends*, in two years' time, that critics and fans will be convinced of the band's depths.

## SEPTEMBER

• **SEPTEMBER 5TH:** **'EBENEEZER GOODE'** by The Shamen enters the UK singles chart, where it will peak at Number One. Another popular product of the UK rave scene, The Shamen had a minor US hit earlier in the year with 'Move Any Mountain.' But this latest song causes controversy because its repetition of the title is interpreted as containing the phrase "Es are good," widely seen as condoning the use of the drug ecstasy.

• **1ST:** **GLORIA ESTEFAN** and her husband Emilio organize a relief project for victims of Hurricane Andrew, which has killed 15 people in Florida.
• **2ND:** **WHEN GUNS N' ROSES** play at the Citrus Bowl, Orlando, Florida, vocalist Axl Rose launches into a vitriolic rant against 'alternative music,' singling out Kurt Cobain of Nirvana.
• **4TH:** **IT'S ANNOUNCED** that Prince has negotiated a new contract with Warner Brothers, under which he will have his own label on which his name will be denoted only by a symbol.
• **6TH:** **A 35-YEAR-OLD MAN** dies 71 days after receiving a transplanted baboon liver. The liver is still working, but the patient suffers a brain haemorrhage.
• **10TH:** *TEN* **BY PEARL JAM** is certified as a US triple platinum disc by the RIAA.
• **12TH:** **DR MAE CAROL JEMISON** becomes the first African-American woman in space. Also on the same mission is the first Japanese astronaut, Mamoru Mohri, and the first married couple in space – if you don't count the Space Family Robinson.

## Funk Brother

• **SEPTEMBER 18TH:** **EARL VAN DYKE**, known as 'The Chunk Of Funk,' dies of prostate cancer in Detroit, Michigan, at the age of 62. Van Dyke was the keyboardist/leader of Motown's legendary Funk Brothers, the session band of the 1960s and early 1970s who laid down the backing tracks for innumerable artists at Berry Gordy's Hitsville studios in Detroit and LA.

## OCTOBER

## Lang Time

• **OCTOBER 3RD:** **KD LANG** has her first US hit single when 'Constant Craving' enters the Top 40. It's taken from her Top 20 album *Ingenue* (Number Three in the UK). Before this, Canadian-born Kathryn Dawn Lang has been best known in the country charts, and for her exuberant stage-shows, as well as her 1989 duets with Roy Orbison on 'Crying' (another UK Top 20 hit), and 'Blue Bayou.'

• **1ST:** **CARTOON NETWORK** is launched by Ted Turner (who already owns CNN and drama channel TNT), initially as a showcase for the Hanna-Barbera cartoons he's acquired... Meanwhile, the United States Supreme Court upholds a ruling that the First Amendment protects Ozzy Osbourne against lawsuits which seek to prove that his music has encouraged suicide.
• **3RD:** **THE PROMOTERS** of Guns N' Roses upcoming concert tour veto Ice-T's thrash-metal band Body Count as a potential support act, declaring them to be "inappropriate"... Meanwhile, on US TV's *Saturday Night Live*, Sinead O'Connor rips up a photograph of the Pope, declaring him to be "the real enemy."
• **8TH:** **THE US POSTAL SERVICE** announces a commemorative stamp booklet that will include Bill Haley, Elvis Presley, Buddy Holly, Ritchie Valens, Clyde McPhatter, Dinah Washington, and Otis Redding.
• **10TH:** **AUTOMATIC FOR THE PEOPLE** by R.E.M. enters the UK album charts at Number One. In the US it hits Number Two.
• **13TH:** **A COMMERCIAL FLIGHT** record is set by an Air France Concorde supersonic jetliner, which circles the Earth in 32 hours and 49 minutes. Bruce Springsteen crosses a picket line to play at the Tacoma Dome in Washington, Seattle.
• **16TH:** **AN ALL-STAR 30TH ANNIVERSARY** tribute show for Bob Dylan is held at Madison Square Garden, New York City. Performers include The Band (minus Robbie Robertson), Stevie Wonder, Roger McGuinn, Tom Petty, George Harrison, Neil Young, Eric Clapton, Lou Reed, Eddie Vedder of Pearl Jam, and Sinead O'Connor who, because of her previous controversial socio-political statements, is booed off before she can sing.
• **25TH:** **SINGER-SONGWRITER** Roger Miller dies of cancer at age 56. His best-known hit was 1965's chestnut 'King Of The Road,' but he was one of country music's most unconventional writers, penning such intriguing titles as 'Where Have All the Average People Gone,' 'My Uncle Used to Love Me But She Died,' and 'You Can't Roller Skate in a Buffalo Herd.'
• **26TH:** **PEARL JAM** set a new record for first week sales when *Vs* sells some 950,000 copies.
• **31ST:** **FIVE AMERICAN** nuns are killed near Monrovia in Liberia. Rebels loyal to Charles Taylor are blamed for the murders. Taylor will later become the country's president.

• **NOVEMBER 10TH: RAGE AGAINST THE MACHINE**
release the album *Rage Against The Machine*. Led by militant vocalist/rapper Zack De La Rocha and explosive guitarist Tom Morello, the band have a politically aware, anti-capitalist stance that seems at odds with their presence on a major record label like Sony. They explain simply that they want their message heard by as many people as possible. And it works – though whether it changes anything or not is open to debate.

## NOVEMBER

• **3RD: DEMOCRAT BILL CLINTON,** governor of the state of Arkansas, wins the US Presidential election, defeating the incumbent, George Bush, and a third candidate, Ross Perot.

• **14TH: ELTON JOHN** and his lyricist, Bernie Taupin, have a new and improved publishing deal with Warner-Chappell, part of Time-Warner. It guarantees them $39m, placing them ahead of Prince and Madonna in the ever-escalating contract wars.

• **21ST: GEORGE MICHAEL,** currently suing Sony for $75m in a bitter contractual battle, issues a written statement to the press accusing the company of seeing its artists as "little more than software."

• **24TH: WHEN CYNDI LAUPER MARRIES** actor David Thornton, Little Richard performs the ceremony, and Patti LaBelle sings 'A Whiter Shade Of Pale.'

• **28TH: WHITNEY HOUSTON'S** latest single, 'I Will Always Love You,' from the soundtrack of her film The Bodyguard, reaches Number One in the US, and will remain there for 14 weeks. (The UK sees fit to give it ten weeks at the top.) With 399,000 sales in one week, it will become the fastest-selling single in history.

## DECEMBER

• **1ST: 165,000 TICKETS** are sold on the day the dates for the next U2 tour, named Zooropa, are announced.

• **4TH: US TROOPS** land in Somalia, Africa, to protect food shipments from warring factions.

• **7TH: MARIAH CAREY'S** seven track mini-album, *MTV Unplugged*, becomes the first MiniDisc title pressed for commercial release, as Sony begins pushing the new format.

• **9TH: THE SEPARATION** of Prince Charles and Princess Diana is announced by UK Prime Minister John Major... Meanwhile, the Third Annual Billboard Music Awards are held in Universal Amphitheater, Universal City, Los Angeles, California. Michael Jackson scoops awards in four categories, including Hot 100 Singles Artist (Male), and R&B Singles Artist (Male). Mariah Carey gets Hot 100 Singles Artist (Female), and Top Billboard 200 Album Artist (Female).

• **11TH: GLORIA ESTEFAN** turns down a lucrative $5m soft drinks sponsorship deal for her forthcoming tour, pointing out that, "It was only money."

• **15TH: IBM ANNOUNCES** it will lose 25,000 employees in the coming year.

• **20TH: THE FOLIES BERGERE** music hall in Paris closes down, having been open since 1869.

• **26TH: WHEN ICE CUBE** taunts the audience at the Paramount Theatre, Seattle, Washington, violence breaks out. Three people receive gunshot wounds, one is stabbed, and another is run down outside.

## Shining On

• **NOVEMBER 2ND: NEIL YOUNG** reunites the musicians who played on his 1972 classic *Harvest* to create a sequel, called *Harvest Moon*. Young will enjoy a popular revival over the next few years – his next album, with Crazy Horse, goes Top Ten in the US and reaches Number Two in the UK, while the follow-up, *Mirrorball*, will be recorded with Pearl Jam. Pushing 50, the grizzled Young will be adopted as the godfather of grunge.

# 1993

## OOOOOOOHHH... TLC

A timely reminder of the more positive side of hip-hop – proving it's not all gangsters, gold chains, and guns – TLC are a feisty, funky, female trio who capitalize on the prevalent 'new jack swing' sound of the early 1990s, and refashion it as so-called 'new Jill swing.' It's a new blend of rap and soulful R&B, with some upbeat grooves, memorable tunes, and assertive messages, especially for women: looking out for themselves, not taking any crap from their men, and practicing safe sex. The group's name plays on the popular shorthand for Tender Loving Care, but is in fact based on the trio's initials. T is for T-Boz – the boss, here on the right – real name Tionne Watkins, who provides the cool, deep, smooth lead vocals. L is for Left-Eye, also known as Lisa Lopes, the sassy, strident rapper and self-styled 'crazy' one of the three – who's taken to wearing outlandish hats at this point, and a condom over her left-eye. And C is for Chilli – who replaced the original third member Crystal – born Rozonda Thomas, a former dancer, who exudes a smoldering exotic glamor. TLC were initially brought together by former singing star Perri 'Pebbles' McKissack (married at one stage to producer L.A. Reid), who masterminded their 1992 debut album *Oooooooohhh... On The TLC Tip*. An immediate success, this spawned Top Ten hits such as 'Ain't 2 Proud 2 Beg,' and 'Baby-Baby-Baby.' But it will be their next album, 1994's *Crazysexycool*, that will give TLC their first two Number Ones with 'Creep' and 'Waterfalls,' earn them two Grammys, lots of MTV rotation for their entertaining videos, and ensure their fame and fortune... Except of course it doesn't always work that way. The next few years are clogged up by court appearances (you'll read about it later), bankruptcy, frequent personal fall-outs, long-term illness – and that's before the trio are finally separated by a tragic death in 2002, after their big-selling 'comeback' hit 'No Scrubs.' But TLC, for many, define urban soul in the 1990s, and they do it with a wicked humour and zest for life, and some distinctive, memorable music.

## Qualified Success

**M**ARCH 30TH: *Pocket Full Of Kryptonite* by The Spin Doctors (right) is certified as a US double platinum album by the RIAA It contains their big hit single 'Two Princes,' which even people who don't like the band can't help humming, and guitarists everywhere inevitably learn to play. The Spin Doctors' main claim to fame – apart from having a topically astute name, and attempting to bring beards back into pop, probably unwisely – is the fact that they got together at a music college, in their case the New School Of Jazz in New York. This is a relatively new phenomenon in the rock and pop world, dating back only to the 1980s, when the first graduates started to emerge from such courses. The earliest to be widely acknowledged was the Los Angeles Musicians Institute,

---

### JANUARY

- **1ST: CZECHOSLOVAKIA** is peacefully divided into the Czech Republic and Slovakia.
- **3RD: PRESIDENT GEORGE BUSH** and Russian President Boris Yeltsin sign the second Strategic Arms Reduction Treaty (START) in Moscow.
- **6TH: BASSIST BILL WYMAN** announces his intention to leave The Rolling Stones... Meanwhile David Bowie is revealed to have lost more than £2.5m worth of royalties because of a Mafia-linked Italian bootleg operation.
- **10TH: TED NUGENT** is fined $1500 for shooting flaming arrows on stage during a concert in Cincinnati, Ohio.
- **13TH: FOLLOWING A CONCERT** in Augusta, Georgia, Bobby Brown is arrested for simulating sex on stage in front of an under-age audience.
- **18TH: THE MARTIN LUTHER KING** J. holiday is finally observed in all 50 US states.
- **25TH: THE 20TH ANNUAL AMERICAN MUSIC AWARDS** are held at the Shrine Auditorium, Los Angeles, California. Mariah Carey wins Favourite Female Artist (Pop/Rock) and Favourite Album (Adult Contemporary). Pearl Jam are Favourite New Artists in both the Pop/Rock and Heavy Metal/Hard Rock categories.

- **JANUARY 20TH: BILL CLINTON** is sworn in as the 42nd President of the US. The various inauguration balls and events around this time include a brief reformation of Fleetwood Mac's classic *Rumours* line-up for the first time in six years (in response to Clinton's use of their track 'Don't Stop' as a theme during his campaign). Clinton dances a waltz with his wife Hillary to the sound of their music. He also famously plays the saxophone during the televised inauguration celebrations. The members of Fleetwood Mac go their own way again after this – Lindsey Buckingham is particularly uncomfortable about it, and pleased to return to solo work – at least for another decade.

---

### FEBRUARY

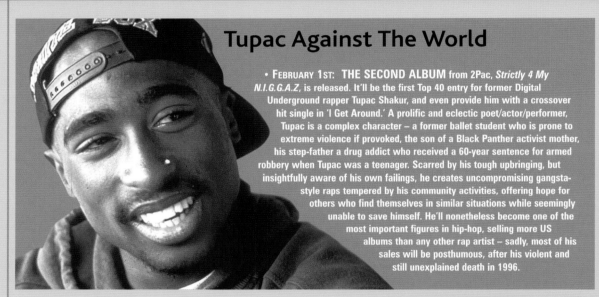

## Tupac Against The World

- **FEBRUARY 1ST: THE SECOND ALBUM** from 2Pac, *Strictly 4 My N.I.G.G.A.Z,* is released. It'll be the first Top 40 entry for former Digital Underground rapper Tupac Shakur, and even provide him with a crossover hit single in 'I Get Around.' A prolific and eclectic poet/actor/performer, Tupac is a complex character – a former ballet student who is prone to extreme violence if provoked, the son of a Black Panther activist mother, his step-father a drug addict who received a 60-year sentence for armed robbery when Tupac was a teenager. Scarred by his tough upbringing, but insightfully aware of his own failings, he creates uncompromising gangsta-style raps tempered by his community activities, offering hope for others who find themselves in similar situations while seemingly unable to save himself. He'll nonetheless become one of the most important figures in hip-hop, selling more US albums than any other rap artist – sadly, most of his sales will be posthumous, after his violent and still unexplained death in 1996.

- **2ND: WILLIE NELSON** and the tax man settle their differences after the government keeps the $3.6 million in assets it has already seized and Nelson agrees to pay $5.4 million of the $13.1 million balance. On April 28th, Nelson and some friends will get together in a TV studio in Austin Texas for a double celebration – it's also his 60th birthday – and the result is screened on CBS in May and released on video in June as *Willie Nelson: The Big Six–0.* The impressive line-up of guests includes Ray Charles, Bob Dylan, B.B. King, Paul Simon, Bonnie Raitt, Waylon Jennings, Emmylou Harris, Kris Kristofferson, Travis Tritt, and Lyle Lovett... Meanwhile rap star Ice-T is dropped by Time-Warner following the controversy over his album *Body Count*, which included the track 'Cop Killer.'
- **3RD: FOLLOWING HIS ARREST** in December for having a

- **FEBRUARY 13TH: SNOOP DOGGY DOG** (born Calvin Broadus) sees his name in the charts for the first time, co-writing and rapping on Dr Dre's new gangsta-rap single 'Nuthin But A 'G' Thang.' By the end of the year Snoop – another former drug dealer and teenage delinquent who sees music as a way out of his problems (though of course it leads to a whole lot of new ones) – will have his own Number One album, *Doggy Style*, and the gangsta-rap movement has a new icon.

- **FEBRUARY 24TH: ERIC CLAPTON** flies to Los Angeles to collect no fewer than six Grammy Awards at the Shrine Auditorium. His *Unplugged* set for MTV, and the resulting Number One album, revived his career at the end of last year – giving him his first chart-topping album for nearly 20 years. He's also had a couple of rare hit singles, an acoustic re-working of 'Layla,' and a melancholy ode to his dead son, 'Tears In Heaven.' Also picking up a Grammy are The Red Hot Chili Peppers for Best Hard Rock Song with 'Give It Away.'

gun in his luggage at New York's Kennedy Airport, singer/piano player/actor Harry Connick Jr makes a plea bargain with the New York authorities and agrees to make public service announcements about carrying guns.

set up in 1977, originally just for guitarists but later for all rock musicians and recording engineers. Previously, musicians would either be self-taught, seek private tuition, or else train formally at a classical music college, but these courses represent an attempt to standardize the art and craft of playing pop, rock or jazz and give it some structure. By the late 1980s/early 1990s, a new strain of confident, note-perfect, multi-disciplined musicians is starting to appear, though very few of these break beyond the realms of the skilled session player, or the funk-fusion club band. The odd exceptions include Paul Gilbert, guitarist with Mr Big, whose 'To Be With You' was a US Number One in 1992, and even Jeff Buckley, who studied at the LAMI. But many industry stalwarts at this time regard the new breed with suspicion, claiming that even though it's obviously possible to teach the mechanics of music, and produce a slick technician, the necessary creativity and hands-on experience can't be bought: these courses also imply a certain level of wealth, at several thousand dollars a term. After all, the opponents argue, many of the best and most innovative things in rock and pop history have happened through happy accidents and sometimes blind experimentation. It becomes common to see self-styled 'cool' bands placing 'Musicians Wanted' ads with the tagline 'No MI graduates.' Proponents of the rock-goes-to-college route, on the other hand, claim it simply enhances the creative spark, and gives them the tools and opportunity to ply their trade effectively, while opening doors in a notoriously impenetrable business. Whichever view you take, the fact is such courses have spread and prospered. One day they may even become the industry norm.

## MARCH

• **4TH: RUSSIAN SCIENTISTS** flash a beam of sunlight across Europe via a giant mirror in orbit – but observers see only a momentary flash.

• **6TH: 'INFORMER'** by white Canadian reggae vocalist Snow enters the US singles chart, where it will lodge at Number One for seven weeks.

• **11TH: IT'S ANNOUNCED** that Guns N' Roses are to be the first rock band ever to play at The Kremlin in Moscow, with a date set for May 22nd.

• **26TH: A BOMB EXPLODES** at the World Trade Center in New York, killing six people and injuring more than 1,000. Less than a week later, Mohammad Salameh is arrested on suspicion of being involved, and will later be convicted.

• **27TH: AFTER 14 STRAIGHT WEEKS** at the US Number One spot, Whitney Houston's 'I Will Always Love You' is America's longest-running chart topper.

• **28TH: THE BRANCH DAVIDIAN** fundamentalist religious cult led by David Koresh (aka Vernon Howell), based outside Waco, Texas, is visited by the Treasury Department's Alcohol, Tobacco & Firearms Unit (ATF) after reports of child abuse. Four ATF officers are killed, Koresh is wounded, at least two of his followers killed. A stand-off ensues, lasting 51 days, at the end of which the compound is burned to the ground, killing 86 people, including 17 children.

• **28TH: IN MEXICO,** Metallica complete a five-day stint at the Sports Palace, Mexico City.

• **MARCH 6TH: RADIOHEAD RELEASE** their debut album, *Pablo Honey*, in the UK.

• **1ST: THE US GOVERNMENT** announce that 26.6 million low-income families are now receiving food stamps. (In 1969 it was under three million.)

• **3RD: WHEN VAN HALEN** play a 'secret' gig at the Whisky A Go Go, Los Angeles, to mark their 15th anniversary as Warner recording artists, so many fans turn up and throng the neighbouring streets that riot police have to be called in.

• **5TH: BEN JOHNSON,** the canadian sprinter who was stripped of his gold medal at the 2988 Olympics, is banned from racing for life by the Amateur Athletic Association after testing positive for banned performance-enhancing drugs a second time.

• **8TH: ANIMATED MUSIC CRITICS** and headbanging cartoon morons Beavis & Butthead premiere on MTV. Yes, we said butt. Uhuh, uhuh.

• **11TH: JANET RENO** becomes the first female attorney general of the US... Meanwhile North Korea withdraws from the Nuclear Non-Proliferation Treaty after refusing to open their sites for inspection.

• **20TH: J. MASCIS,** leader of grunge pioneers Dinosaur Jr, announces that he is taking a break from the band to recover from tendonitis, but he is soon back, steering the band towards ever greater accessibility and commercial success.

• **21ST: THE 22ND ANNUAL JUNO AWARDS** are held in Toronto, Ontario, Canada. As well as hosting the ceremonies, Celine Dion picks up four awards, including Single Of The Year and Female Vocalist Of The Year.

• **MARCH 2ND: CAT STEVENS,** now known as Yusuf Islam, is awarded libel damages against satirical British magazine *Private Eye,* which claimed he used charity funds to buy weapons for Afghan rebels. A devout Muslim, Yusuf's only recorded work in the last 15 years has been a tape of Islamic talks and chants – though he will gradually start recording more, and even eventually re-do his old hit 'Peace Train.'

## APRIL

## Dirty Mode

• **APRIL 3RD: DEPECHE MODE'S** *Songs Of Faith & Devotion* is the Number One album in both the US and UK. It's the first time the band have topped either chart in their 13-year career. Fronted by the now-tattooed and lived-in Dave Gahan, their image has changed somewhat since their early, clean-cut synth-pop days, particularly since 1990's *Violator* album.

• **5TH: MARKY MARK WAHLBERG** has assault charges against him dropped when he reaches an out-of-court settlement with the man he allegedly attacked in 1992.

• **7TH: FORMER FRANKIE GOES TO HOLLYWOOD** frontman Holly Johnson reveals publicly that he has the HIV virus that causes AIDS.

• **12TH: ACTRESS LISA BONET** files for divorce from Lenny Kravitz.

• **16TH: EX-VAN HALEN VOCALIST** David Lee Roth is arrested for buying marijuana in Washington Square Park, New York City.

• **19TH: BRIAN LITTRELL,** a student at Tate's Creek High School, Lexington, Kentucky, auditions over the phone to join the Backstreet Boys, his big cousin Kevin's group. He gets the gig.

• **23RD: BLACK TEENAGER** Stephen Lawrence is murdered while waiting for a bus in a suburb of London, UK. A vigorous campaign by the victim's family and sections of the media ensures the case retains a high profile, and a later official enquiry into the lack of convictions concludes that the police force is guilty of "institutional racism."

• **27TH: PRINCE ANNOUNCES** his retirement from studio recording. But he'll be back.

• **30TH: US TENNIS PLAYER MONICA SELES,** currently world number one, is stabbed in the back during a tennis match in Hamburg, Germany. The assailant, a fan of sporting rival Steffi Graf, is later convicted of causing grievous bodily harm and receives a suspended sentence... Meanwhile *Breathless* by Kenny G, soft-focus alto saxophonist, is certified as a four-times platinum in the US.

• **APRIL 29TH: MICK RONSON,** guitarist for Bowie in his Ziggy years of the 1970s (see p89), and latterly for Bob Dylan's Rolling Thunder Review band, dies from cancer.

- **JULY 28TH: THE 10,000 MANIACS** play their last show with lead singer/songwriter Natalie Merchant, who is leaving the group after 12 years to pursue a solo career.

# Blood On The Tracks

**A**UGUST 10TH: **TOM WAITS** provides guest vocals on an extended musical piece by British experimental composer Gavin Bryars, called *Jesus' Blood Never Failed Me Yet*. The 75-minute work is based on a tape loop of a tramp singing a burst of a hymn in a railroad station. Bryars gradually brings in a string quartet and then Waits' gruff vocals, duetting with the original tramp's, to unexpectedly moving effect. Surprisingly, the record is one of ten chosen to be put forward for the forthcoming Mercury Music Award in the UK. This is a new, annual prize for Album Of The Year, chosen by a small but select panel of judges. The Bryars/Waits collaboration fails to win, but is certainly heard more widely than it would otherwise have been.

- **JUNE 9TH: *CORE*,** last year's debut album by Stone Temple Pilots, is certified as platinum in the US by the RIAA. It peaked at Number Three on the US album chart, but next year's follow-up, Purple, will go all the way to the top.

**MAY**  **JUNE**  **JULY**

- **1ST: 'FREAK ME'** by Silk reaches Number One on the US Top 40 singles chart.
- **3RD: JEWEL KILCHER** makes her first live solo radio appearance on *Loudspeaker*, a show on 99XFM radio in San Diego, California.
- **8TH: THE BACKSTREET BOYS** perform their first professional show, at Seaworld, Orlando, Florida, to an audience of 3,000.
- **13TH: YOUNG BRITNEY SPEARS**, from Kentwood, Louisiana, makes her first TV appearance, as a Disney Mouseketeer.
- **18TH: JANET JACKSON** releases a new album, simply called *Janet*. To promote it, she famously appears topless on the cover of Rolling Stone magazine, with her boyfriend's hands covering her breasts. On July 23, she will be seen in her big-screen acting debut, *Poetic Justice*, which also stars Tupac Shakur. It is directed by an old school friend of hers, John Singleton, who also made the influential 1991 gang movie *Boyz In The Hood*.
- **22ND: THE BEASTIE BOYS** help out at record store counters in New York, to raise funds to assist victims of HIV and AIDS.
- **31ST: CREATION RECORDS** owner Alan McGee sees Oasis play at King Tut's Wah Wah Hut in Glasgow, Scotland (as support to Boyfriend, 18 Wheeler, and Sister Lovers) and immediately offers them a record deal.

## Web Master

- **MAY 10TH: STUDIES REVEAL** the rapid growth of the Internet, now regularly used by millions of people daily, mostly in the US. Originally based on the ARPAnet military network, launched in 1969 to link only universities, government bodies and defense agencies, the Internet has now evolved into thousands of linked networks. And thanks to the development of the World Wide Web, by Tim Berners-Lee (above) in 1990, information is easily shared between users, using point-and-click 'hyperlinks.' In 1993 there are fewer than 100 web servers in the world. Ten years later there will be over 30 million.

- **JUNE 27TH: LYLE LOVETT**, the 'new country' maverickm and actress Julia Roberts are married. They will divorce in 1995, quoting irreconcilable mouths.

- **2ND: RONALD RAY HOWARD'S** murder trial began in Texas. Howard, who killed a state trooper after listening to Tupac Shakur's *2Pacalypse Now*, will be convicted and sentenced to death.
- **4TH: KURT COBAIN** of Nirvana is arrested following a fight with his wife, Courtney Love, at home in Seattle, Washington.
- **5TH: MARIAH CAREY** marries Tommy Mottola, president of Sony Music, at St Thomas Episcopal Church, Manhattan. Guests include Bruce Springsteen, Ozzy Osbourne, Billy Joel, Barbra Streisand, and Robert de Niro.

- **7TH: A CEREMONY** of ground-breaking is held for the new Rock And Roll Hall Of Fame, Cleveland, Ohio. The foundation-laying is witnessed by stars from several generations, such as Chuck Berry, Sam Phillips, Sam Moore, Billy Joel, and Pete Townshend.
- **9TH: THE LOS ANGELES POLICE** arrest well-connected Hollywood madame Heidi Fleiss.
- **10TH: SCIENTISTS** announce that genetic material has been extracted from an insect that lived when dinosaurs roamed the Earth. Oddly enough, the Steven Spielberg movie *Jurassic Park*, based on the very same idea, goes on general release in the US tomorrow.
- **21ST: ENGLISH**

**MATHEMATICIAN,** Andrew Wiles proves Fermat's last theorem after spending seven years working on a 200-page document that solves the 350-year-old problem. Later someone finds a mistake in the proof, but Wiles is able to fix it.
- **26TH: SON THOMAS**, last of the traditional Delta bluesmen, dies at age 67.

- **JUNE 8TH: *PORK SODA*** by Primus enters the US album charts, where it will reach Number Seven.

- **7TH: MIA ZAPATA** of The Gits is found strangled in Seattle, at the age of just 27.
- **10TH: KENYAN RUNNER** Yobes Ondieki becomes the first man to run 10,000 meters in less than 27 minutes
- **13TH: 'LOSER,'** a single by obscure singer-songwriter Beck, receives its first airplay from DJ Chris Douridas on KCRW radio, Los Angeles.
- **13TH: WHEN PHIL COLLINS** and Art Garfunkel start to sing at a friend's late night wedding reception in Los Angeles, annoyed neighbours call in the LAPD to shut them up.
- **23RD: IN A NEW YORK CITY HOTEL**, Kurt Cobain of Nirvana overdoses on heroin and passes out. He is due onstage at the New Music Seminar later that day. Courtney Love revives him by injecting a drug to counter the effect. He manages to go on stage and perform.
- **24TH: CYPRESS HILL'S** 'Insane In The Brain' becomes their only US hit single, entering the Top 40 on its way to Number 19. It's from their Number One stoner-gangsta album, *Black Sunday*... Meanwhile, 'Can't Help Falling In Love' by UK reggae artists UB40 tops the US singles chart.
- **29TH: THE ISRAELI SUPREME COURT** clears John Demjanjuk (accused of being Ivan The Terrible) of war crimes, his death sentence is thrown out, and he is set free to return to his home in Cleveland, Ohio. And Elton John auctions his entire record collection, with all proceeds to AIDS charities.

# My Name Is... Unpronounceable

**1993**

May–August

• JUNE 7TH: **ON HIS 35TH BIRTHDAY,** Prince announces he is changng his name to an unpronounceable symbol, and promptly becomes known in the music press as TAFKAP (The Artists Formerly Known As Prince), or simply 'Symbol' or 'Glyph.' MTV substitutes a puff of air whenever his name is mentioned. He claims that this is some kind of spiritual development. It's not until almost seven years later, when his publishing contract with Warner-Chappel expires, that Prince explains that the true intention had been to disassociate himself from Warner Brothers (he was on the Warners record label at the time too). He felt they were stealing his name and stifling his progress as an artist. It's also the reason he will inscribe the word 'Slave' on his face at one stage.

## AUGUST

• 2ND: **BY SELLING** more than 200,000 copies in its first week of release, U2's ambitious *Zooropa* becomes the year's fastest-selling album in the UK.

• 10TH: **A WHITE**-supremacist plot to assassinate Ice-T and Ice Cube, uncovered by the FBI, is revealed in UK rock weekly *NME*, following the firebombing of the offices of the National Association For The Advancement Of Colored People in Tacoma, Washington.

• 12TH: **THE RED HOT** Chili Peppers replace guitarist Arik Marshall with Jesse Tobias. In three months' time Tobias will be replaced by Dave Navarro, a founder member of Los Angeles band Jane's Addiction.

• 14TH: **PAULA ABDUL** has won a court battle in the US, refuting claims that her voice was enhanced by uncredited backing vocalist Yvette Marine on the multi-million-selling *Forever Your Girl* album.

• 23RD: **POLICE RAID** Michael Jackson's homes in California after allegations of child abuse. This is the beginning of the long-running Jordan Chandler scandal which will irreparably blight Jackson's reputation.

• JULY 17TH: **'PRAY' BY** Take That (including a young Robbie Williams, far right) goes straight in at Number One on the UK singles chart, giving the New Kids-style UK boy-band their first chart-topper.

# 1993

## September–December

• OCTOBER 18TH: *VS*, THE SECOND album from Pearl Jam (whose Jeff Ament & Eddie Vedder are seen right), has gone straight to the US Number One slot on release, and become the fastest-selling album ever in the United States.

## SEPTEMBER

• SEPTEMBER 13TH: SMASHING PUMPKINS (below) release a new single, 'Today,' taken from their Top Ten album *Siamese Dream*. Growing up in Chicago, Billy Corgan (guitar/vocals) met future Pumpkins James Iha (guitar), D'Arcy Wretzky (bass), and Jimmy Chamberlin (drums) and released the 1990 debut *Gish* on indie label Caroline. *Siamese Dream* is their critical and commercial breakthrough (it goes triple-platinum) and, along with Nirvana's *Nevermind*, drags the word alternative back into populist rock music. Follow-up double album *Mellon Collie & The Infinite Sadness* (1994) will be less well reviewed, though still sells well, but then egos and drug problems will ensure the band tread water creatively until their messy demise after the final album *Machina: The Machines of God* in 2000.

• 11TH: MARIAH CAREY'S single 'Dreamlover' ascends to the US Number One slot and stays for a solid eight weeks.
• 13TH: ISRAELI PRIME MINISTER Yitzhak Rabin and Palestine Liberation Organization chairman Yasser Arafat shake hands after signing an historic peace agreement.
• 15TH: "PAPA'S GOT A BRAND NEW BRIDGE!" declares Godfather Of Soul James Brown at the opening ceremony of the newly constructed James Brown Soul Centre Of The Universe Bridge in Steamboat Springs, Colorado. Some locals object to the name.
• 16TH: GRACE SLICK'S home in Marin County, California, is destroyed by fire, apparently caused by welders fixing a

• SEPTEMBER 14TH: COUNTING CROWS release their debut album, *August And Everything After*, which peaks at Number Four in the US (16 in the UK).

"Danger: Fire Area" sign.
• 18TH: WHILE GENESIS are playing at Cowdray Park, Sussex, UK, Phil Collins decides it is time to quit the group.
• 22ND: 47 PEOPLE ARE KILLED when an Amtrak passenger train derails in Alabama.
• 30TH: KATE PIERSON of the B-52s is arrested at a sit-in at the New York offices of *Vogue*, against fur in clothing and ads.

## OCTOBER

• 5TH: CHINA SETS OFF an underground nuclear explosion.
• 8TH: US SCIENTISTS report they have successfully cloned a human embryo.
• 19TH: *BIGGER, BETTER, FASTER, MORE!* by 4 Non Blondes is certified as a US platinum album by the RIAA. It contains the hit single 'What's Up,' which reached US Number 14, and UK Number Two, earliere in the year.
• 20TH: ATTORNEY GENERAL Janet Reno warns the TV industry that it must limit violence in its programs.
• 21ST: GEORGE MICHAEL'S battle to free himself from his Sony contract moves to the High Court in London.
• 22ND: OASIS ARE SIGNED to a six-album deal by Creation Records, with a £40,000 advance.
• 26TH: CATHOLIC CHURCHES in San Juan, Puerto Rico, urge residents to tie black ribbons around trees to protest against Madonna's first concert there.
• 30TH: AMERICA'S FIRST space-veterinarian, Martin Fettman, performs the first – and possibly last – animal dissections in space, on the space shuttle Columbia.
• 31ST: WHEN ACTOR River Phoenix collapses from a drug overdose outside the Viper Club, Los Angeles, Flea of The Red Hot Chili Peppers accompanies him to hospital... Meanwhile rap star Tupac Shakur is arrested after being involved in an incident in Atlanta, Georgia, in which two off-duty police officers are shot. The charges will be dismissed.

smashing pumpkins • siamese dream

# The Sincerest Form Of Flattery

THERE'S A NEW PHENOMENON starting to spread around the music world – the tribute band. Musicians have always covered other people's songs, sometimes in fastidious detail, and bands have always enjoyed dressing up – from 1950s leathers to glam to 21st century trainers & 'bling.' But this is something new: a deliberate attempt to recreate a live show as performed by a famous act, living or dead. In fact, it's not quite so new. Predictably, the first target for such a homage were The Beatles. Back in the 1970s, in Los Angeles, there was a band called Rain who took it upon themselves to learn and reproduce every note of every record The Beatles ever made, and perform it all live – which, of course, is something the Beatles themselves didn't attempt after 1966. Then there were Broadway and London musicals based on the music of The Beatles, with bewigged musical actors playing the parts. These spawned UK bands like The Bootleg Beatles, and off-shoots like The Counterfeit Stones. In the 1990s, though, it explodes: Sheer Heart Attack are a Queen tribute act from Los Angeles, Bjorn Again a pioneering Abba tribute from Australia, and soon almost anyone you can think of is being recreated on-stage – sometimes badly, sometimes well. At least some of the names will be entertaining: Motorheadache, Alanis Moreorless, Shania's Twin... There's even be an Irish band called The Gardai: that's Gaelic for The Police.

## NOVEMBER

• **SEPTEMBER 2ND: AFTER ACTING AS A PRESENTER** at the MTV Music Awards in Universal Amphitheater, Universal City, Los Angeles, Snoop Doggy Dogg turns himself in to police who have been seeking him in connection with a murder that happened in Los Angeles last month.

• **1ST: IN EUROPE**, the Maastricht Treaty comes into effect, turning the European Economic Community into the European Union.
• **1ST: US RAPPER** Flavor Flav is arrested and charged with attempted murder. Allegedly paranoid because of crack cocaine use, he imagined that his girfriend was having sex with a neighbour. To resolve the issue, he barged into the neighbour's apartment but, failing to find his girl, chased the unfortunate man down the hall firing a pistol at his feet.
• **6TH: 'I'D DO ANYTHING FOR LOVE (BUT I WON'T DO THAT)'** by Meat Loaf reaches Number One on the US Top 40 singles chart, where it will rest its impressive frame for five weeks. Over in the UK, the song stays top of the charts for seven weeks, only to be replaced by a spotty pink singing blancmange going by the name of Mr Blobby. Sad but true.
• **10TH: THE US HOUSE OF REPRESENTATIVES** passes the Brady Bill, which calls for a five-day waiting period before a handgun can be purchased.
• **11TH: IN WASHINGTON**, a bronze statue is unveiled, honoring the 11,000 or more women who served in the Vietnam War.
• **13TH: NIRVANA RECORD** an *Unplugged* session for MTV, which will be released as an album.
• **12TH: MICHAEL JACKSON** cancels a world tour, insisting he has developed a dependence on painkillers. But as child-abuse investigations continue against him, Pepsi cancels its nine-year multi-million dollar sponsorship deal.
• **25TH: COUNTRY MUSIC** radio is reported to be America's leading format, with 77.3m listeners – some 42 per cent of all adults – regularly tuning in.

## DECEMBER

• **2ND: PABLO ESCOBAR**, boss of the Medellin cocaine cartel in Colombia, is killed in a shoot-out as police try to arrest him.
• **5TH: RECOVERING ALCOHOLIC** Doug Hopkins of The Gin Blossoms dies by shooting himself with a .38 calibre pistol.
• **6TH: THE EAGLES**, who split 13 years ago, re-unite briefly to tape a video for country singer Travis Tritt's version of their song 'Take It Easy,' which forms part of a 'various artists' tribute album of Eagles' covers.
• **7TH: GUNS N' ROSES** announce they will keep the tune 'Look At Your Game Girl,' written by Charles Manson, on their covers album *The Spaghetti Incident?* after the band learn that the royalties will go to the son of one of Manson's victims.
• **9TH: RUMOURS** by Fleetwood Mac is certified as a 14-times platinum album in the US... Meanwhile, 90,000 people jam into Tokyo Dome to see U2 play the first of two nights in Japan, at the end of their 157-date Zoo TV tour.
• **10TH: THE CREW OF THE SPACE SHUTTLE** Endeavour send the newly repaired Hubble space telescope back out into Earth's orbit.
• **11TH: 'AGAIN' BY JANET JACKSON** is the new US Number One single.
• **15TH: UK PRIME MINISTER** John Major and the Republic Of Ireland prime minitser Albert Reynolds both sign the Downing Street declaration, the basis for trying to achieve peace in Northern Ireland.

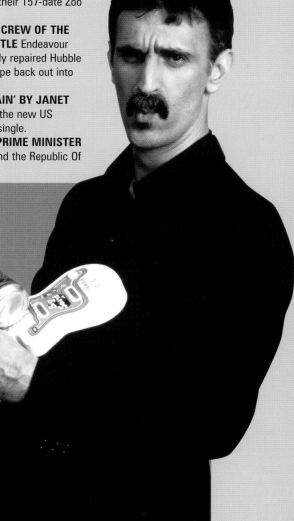

## Viva Zappa

• **DECEMBER 4TH: FRANK ZAPPA** dies of prostate cancer, at the age of 53. Zappa was a genius (a word used often but seldom correctly) and a total original. Equally at home as social satirist, entertainer, musical innovator or anti-censorship campaigner, he even became Czechoslovakia's cultural liaison officer with the West in 1991, thanks to his friendship with President Vaclav Havel. Picking musical threads from sources as diverse as Edgard Varèse and Johnny 'Guitar' Watson, Zappa artfully mixed convoluted soundscapes with any populist musical form that grabbed his attention, peppering most of the results with acerbic, pomposity-deflating humour, and creating a body of work most of his contemporaries could only dream of.

# 1994

## January–April

## Oldest Swinger In Town

**M**ARCH 1ST: At this year's Grammy Awards, Whitney Houston's 'I Will Always Love You' wins Record Of The Year and Best Female Pop Vocal, Toni Braxton is Best New Artist, and Aretha Franklin receives the Lifetime Achievement Award. But Frank Sinatra receives a special Legends Award from Bono of U2, who comments that "Frank is living proof that God is a Catholic." Bono recently appeared on Sinatra's *Duets* album, singing 'I've Got You Under My Skin' with the legendary

## Me And A Piano

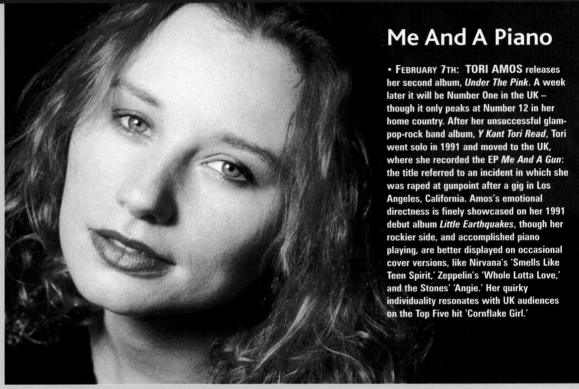

• **FEBRUARY 7TH: TORI AMOS** releases her second album, *Under The Pink*. A week later it will be Number One in the UK – though it only peaks at Number 12 in her home country. After her unsuccessful glam-pop-rock band album, *Y Kant Tori Read*, Tori went solo in 1991 and moved to the UK, where she recorded the EP *Me And A Gun*: the title referred to an incident in which she was raped at gunpoint after a gig in Los Angeles, California. Amos's emotional directness is finely showcased on her 1991 debut album *Little Earthquakes*, though her rockier side, and accomplished piano playing, are better displayed on occasional cover versions, like Nirvana's 'Smells Like Teen Spirit,' Zeppelin's 'Whole Lotta Love,' and the Stones' 'Angie.' Her quirky individuality resonates with UK audiences on the Top Five hit 'Cornflake Girl.'

• **1ST: THE NORTH AMERICAN FREE TRADE AGREEMENT** (NAFTA) comes into effect.

• **8TH: TONYA HARDING** wins the US Ladies Figure Skating Championship in Detroit, but is stripped of the title when it's discovered she is implicated in an attack on rival skater Nancy Kerrigan, two days before the final. Four men, including Harding's ex-husband, will eventually be sentenced to prison for the assault.

• **11TH: TINA WOLFE**, a devoted fan of country 'hat act' Vince Gill, starts lining up for tickets for his upcoming North Carolina concert, despite the fact that they won't be on sale until February 24th: "I promised Mama front row seats," she explains... Meanwhile the Irish government announces the end of a 20-year broadcasting ban on the IRA and its political arm, Sinn Fein.

• **16TH: GRAMMY-WINNING** singer-songwriter Harry Nilsson dies, at age 52, at his home at Agoura Hills, near Los Angeles, California.

• **17TH: DONNY OSMOND** fights Danny Bonaduce of the Partridge Family in a charity boxing match in Chicago (picture below left). Donny is in the red shorts, and seems to have the upper hand, but Bonaduce wins on a split decision.

• **19TH: JOHN LENNON**, Duane Eddy, The Animals, Elton John, Bob Marley, Rod Stewart, and The Grateful Dead are inducted into the Rock'N'Roll Hall Of Fame.

• **21ST: ROD STEWART**, Sting, and Bryan Adams reach Number One on the US Top 40 with 'All For Love.'

• **25TH: MICHAEL JACKSON** settles out of court in a civil lawsuit which accuses him of molesting 13-year-old Jordan Chandler during sleepovers at his California ranch.

• **27TH: ROLLING STONE** magazine publishes its annual Readers' Poll, showing Pearl Jam as Best Band, Artist Of The Year, and Brightest Hope.

• **31ST: GERMAN LUXURY** car-maker BMW announces the purchase of Rover from British Aerospace, ending nearly a century of independent mass car production in Britain.

• **5TH: SERBS FIRE ARTILLERY SHELLS** into a Sarajevo market, leaving 68 dead and more than 200 injured. On the 28th, US warplanes will shoot down four Serb aircraft over Bosnia, in the first NATO use of force in the troubled area.

• **10TH: TUPAC SHAKUR** is convicted in Los Angeles of beating up a music video director.

• **12TH: *JAR OF FLIES*** by Alice In Chains reaches Number One in the US album chart (UK Number Four).

• **13TH: PRINCE'S LOVESEXY** tour ends at the 9,000 seat Osakajo Hall, Osaka, Japan. In eight Japanese concerts over two weeks he's been seen by 140,000 fans, and earns enough money to wipe out losses he has made in the early part of the tour.

• **17TH: AN EARTHQUAKE** measuring 6.7 on the Richter scale in the Northridge area of Los Angeles leaves 57 dead.

• **19TH: CRASH TEST DUMMIES** enter the US charts with 'Mmm Mmm Mmm Mmm.'

• **20TH: "SOME SONGS** ask profound questions about life," explains British vicar Steve Croft, when he hires a room in a bar in Halifax, West Yorkshire, to deliver a sermon based on Meat Loaf's *Bat Out Of Hell 2*.

• **22ND: POLICE ARE CALLED** to deal with a dispute between Lisa 'Left Eye' Lopes of TLC and her boyfriend Andre Rison at his house. Having caught him with another woman, she set fire to the teddy bears he had given her, and he then felt obliged to hit her.

• **24TH: IN GLOUCESTER**, UK, local police begin excavations at the Cromwell Street home of Frederick and Rosemary West. Four days later the couple are arrested and charged with 12 murders. Fred West will commit suicide while awaiting trial; his wife receives ten life sentences.

• **26TH: GREEN DAY** release the album *Dookie*, which will peak at US Number Two.

crooner, although the two didn't meet at the time. The *Duets* album, 78-year-old Sinatra's first studio recording for ten years, used modern recording technology to bring the increasingly frail singer together with several generations of established artists in various locations and singing in different keys. That was something else the technology had to cope with, digitally manipulating the voices to fit Frank's range. The duets feature the likes of Aretha Franklin, Tony Bennett, Natalie Cole, Anita Baker, Gloria Estefan, Julio Iglesias, Liza Minnelli, Carly Simon, Barbra Streisand, and Luther Vandross. The album's success will mean that Sinatra has, uniquely, had hit records in every decade since the 1930s. He follows it up later this year with *Duets II*, this time featuring Willie Nelson, Lena Horne, Chrissie Hynde, Neil Diamond, and Antonio Carlos Jobim, the great Brazilian singer-songwriter who originally collaborated with Sinatra on a classic Latin swing album. back in 1967.

## All Apologies

• **APRIL 8TH: KURT COBAIN**'s body is found at his home in Seattle, Washington. Cause of death is given as a self-inflicted shotgun wound. It's thought he has lain undiscovered for three days. There have been clear warning signs about his state of mind. On March 4th, he was hospitalised in a coma in Rome, Italy, after overdosing on alcohol and prescription drugs. On March 18th, Courtney Love called the police, claiming Cobain was suicidal, and they removed guns and ammunition from the house. On April 1st, Kurt checked out of a rehab centre near Los Angeles, and travelled back to Seattle, leaving Courtney in Los Angeles: she apparently asked friends to find him. It's the last time he's seen. As usual, rumors of foul play abound, but the gut-wrenching note found by his body confirms the depth of his unease with celebrity, referring to his envy of people like Freddie Mercury who relish the "adoration of the crowd." Kurt says he feels a fake, and though he thanks his fans, the note concludes that everyone – including, it seems, his baby daughter – will be better off without him.

**MARCH**

**APRIL**

• **MARCH 5TH: BECK ENTERS THE US** Top 40 singles chart for the first time with 'Loser.' It'll be a rare US hit for the 'slacker' icon, though in the UK he'll have nine Top 40 entries before 2000. Musical magpie Beck Hansen creates a lo-fi mix of folk, blues, hip-hop, rock'n'roll, country, even disco: and his almost unheard-of contract with DGC Records lets him release albums on other labels if DGC rejects them.

• **3RD: THE MEXICAN GOVERNMENT** reach a peaceful agreement with the Chiapas rebels.
• **4TH: FOUR MUSLIM FUNDAMENTALISTS** are found guilty of the 1993 World Trade Center bombing in New York, and each sentenced to 240 years in prison.
• **5TH: GRACE SLICK** is arrested for pointing a shotgun at police at her home in Tiberon, California.
• **7TH: IN RESPONSE** to music press ads, the original five Spice Girls meet for the first time... Meantime the US Supreme Court rules that parodies which poke fun at an original work can

be considered 'fair use,' and do not require permission from the copyright holder. This must come as a relief to Weird Al Yankovic.
• **10TH: WHITE HOUSE** officials begin testifying about Whitewater, a controversial real estate transaction by Bill and Hillary Clinton in Arkansas.
• **12TH: A PHOTO OF THE LOCH NESS MONSTER** by Marmaduke Wetherell is confirmed to be a hoax. It is, in fact, a toy submarine with a head and neck attached.
• **19TH: 160,000 EGGS** are used in the largest omelette in the world in Yokohama, Japan.
• **22ND: MORRISSEY'S** releases his fifth solo album, *Vauxhall And I*, which will become his most successful in the

• **MARCH 12TH: ACE OF BASE**, the latest Scandinavian pop sensation, reach Number One on the US Top 40 singles chart with 'The Sign,' having already had a UK Number One last May with 'All That She Wants.'

States – with or without the Smiths – reaching Number 18. It's also his

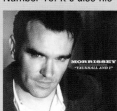

first UK Number One since 1985.
• **31ST: A SKULL** of Australopithecus afarensis, humankind's earliest ancestor, has been found in Ethiopia... And Madonna says the f-word 13 times on *The Late Show With David Letterman*.

## Mr Self-Destruct

• **MARCH 8TH: NINE INCH NAILS** release the album *Downward Spiral*, recorded in the house in Los Angeles where the Manson Family murders took place. NIN main-man Trent Reznor insists he was unaware of this when he rented the house and installed a studio there, but the album does include some oddly Manson-esque titles, like 'Piggy.' With trademark angry slabs of noise, Trent is responsible for introducing a wider audience to the joys of industrial electronica (bands like Ministry and Skinny Puppy being just too scary for populist tastes), as well as offering a leg up to the likes of Marilyn Manson.

• **4TH: NETSCAPE COMMUNICATIONS,** one of the big names of the Internet revolution, is founded.
• **7TH: IT'S REPORTED** that the reason why The Bee Gees cancelled a European tour in February was indeed an ailment afflicting Barry Gibb. But it was not a heart condition as first thought, it was arthritis.... Meanwhile, civil war erupts in Rwanda, central Africa, between the Patriotic Front rebel group and government soldiers. Hundreds of thousands will die in the following months fighting
• **9TH: 'BUMP'N'GRIND'** by R. Kelly is the new US Number One single. It's the rapper's first chart-topping single
• **13TH: BILLY JOEL** and his Uptown Girl, Christie Brinkley, announce their separation.
• **15TH: GLOBAL COMMERCE FORUM** The World Trade Organization is established.
• **16TH: FORMER CLASH** leader Joe Strummer makes his first live appearance in two years when he joins Czech band Dirty Pictures on-stage in a concert in Prague.
• **19TH: A LOS**

**ANGELES** jury awards $3.8 million to Rodney King for the violation of his civil rights (not to mention being beaten up by the police).
• **25TH: SNOOP DOGGY DOGG** is named Rap Artist of The Year at the inaugural Source Hip-Hop Awards in New York. A Tribe Called Quest pick up the Group Of The Year award.
• **26TH: THE FIRST MULTI-RACIAL** elections are held in South Africa.
• **27TH: THE FILLMORE CLUB** reopens in San Francisco.... Elsewhere, Ace Of Base singer Jenny Berggren is threatened by knife-wielding 21-year-old Manuela Behrendt, a German fan/stalker who breaks into her home in Gothenburg, Sweden, to get an autograph. Behrendt is overpowered and arrested, and will later be sentenced to a year in jail. Berggren writes a song about the incident, which appears on the group's second album.
• **28TH: FORMER CIA** official Aldrich Ames, who gave US secrets to Russia, pleads guilty to espionage and tax evasion and is sentenced to life in prison.

# 1994

May–August

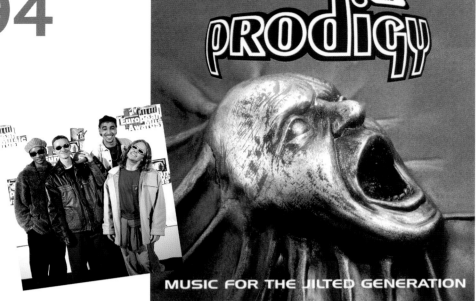

MUSIC FOR THE JILTED GENERATION

## Full Throttle

**J**ULY 16TH: The Prodigy's second album *Music For The Jilted Generation*, reaches Number One in the UK, though it fails to chart in the US. It features the rave hits 'One Love' and 'No Good (Start The Dance).' Originally a stage name for keyboardist/DJ Liam Howlett, The Prodigy enhance their appeal through the strong visual impact of dancers/vocalists Keith Flint, Leeroy Thornhill, and MC Maxim Reality, setting the group apart from its more static rivals. *Music For The Jilted Generation* meshes techno, guitars, quirky samples, and hip-hop breakbeats – ingredients which will be cooked to perfection in the bug-eyed melting pot of their 1997 follow-up.

## MAY

- **1ST: AYRTON SENNA**, three times world Formula One racing champion, dies after a high-speed crash in the San Marino Grand Prix.
- **2ND: A LOS ANGELES** jury decides that Michael Bolton has plagiarised 'Love Is A Wonderful Thing' by The Isley Brothers...
- **6TH: PEARL JAM** take on Ticketmaster by filing a memorandum with the Department of Justice claiming that the ticketing company operates a monopoly.
- **7TH: BLUR'S ALBUM** *PARKLIFE* enters the UK album charts at Number One, the start of an 84-week residency in the chart. Again, it makes no impression on the US charts... Unlike Warren G, whose single 'Regulate' becomes his first hit, entering the US Top 40 today on its way to Number Two.
- **10TH: AFTER SOUTH AFRICA'S** first fully democratic election, Nelson Mandela becomes the country's first black president, following more than 300 years of white rule.
- **19TH: JACQUELINE KENNEDY ONASSIS** dies in New York, at age 64.
- **26TH: MICHAEL JACKSON** secretly marries Lisa Marie Presley, Elvis's daughter, in the Dominican Republic.
- **27TH: THE EAGLES** begin their massive re-union tour, Hell Freezes Over, at Irvine Meadows Amphitheater, California.
- **31ST:** Members of Primal Scream, support band on Depeche Mode's current US tour, are arrested for swimming naked in the San Antonio river.

## JUNE

- **2ND: TORI AMOS** – a victim of rape – becomes the first artist to receive a Visionary Award from the Washington DC Rape Crisis Center.
- **3RD: EDDIE VEDDER** of Pearl Jam marries his girlfriend, Beth Liebling, in Rome, Italy.
- **4TH: WET WET WET** reach Number One on the UK singles chart with their version of the old Troggs hit 'Love Is All Around,' which will stay top for all of 15 weeks. After that, it's voluntarily withdrawn by the band. It's also the Wets' highest-placed US single, reaching 41. For the song's writer, Reg Presley, it's a welcome reminder (financially as well as nostalgically) of the heady days of the 1960s when The Troggs topped the charts with 'Wild Thing,' and took their own version of 'Love Is All Around' to Number Seven in the US. Presley admits he will use some of the proceeds to fund his latest obsession: crop circles.
- **9TH: LISA 'LEFT-EYE' LOPES** of TLC fails to live up to her band's name again, this time setting fire to the house of her boyfriend, Andre Rison of the Atlanta Falcons.
- **14TH: HENRY MANCINI** dies at the age of 70. He was the composer of 'Moon River,' themes for *The Pink Panther*, *Love Story*, Romeo & Juliet (a Number One in 1969), Peter Gunn (a hit for Duane Eddy in 1960), and many more. He won 20 Grammy awards (nominated for 72) and four Academy Awards out of 18 Oscar nominations.
- **17TH: FORMER FOOTBALL**

star turned actor O.J. Simpson is arrested for the murder of his ex-wife Nicole and her new boyfriend Ron Goldman, after a dramatic car chase and a 90-minute stand-off at his home, all broadcast live on TV. Simpson will later be acquitted in a criminal trial, but is found liable in a civil suit.
- **21ST: GEORGE MICHAEL** loses his long-running court battle against Sony Music, in which he was disputing the terms of his contract... Meanwhile Colombian soccer

player Andres Escobar accidentally scores an own goal in an important World Cup match against the USA, contributing to his country's unexpectedly early exit from the competition. Ten days later, at home in Medellin, he is shot 12 times and killed, allegedly by hit-men working for drug cartels who have lost a heavy bet on the match.
- **25TH: ON THE SECOND DAY** of the normally peaceful Glastonbury Festival in Pilton, Somerset, UK, five festival goers are shot by a crazed gunman.

- **JULY 21ST: OASIS (BELOW)** play their first US gig, at the New Music Seminar, Wetlands Hall, Brooklyn, New York City. They're just about to release their debut album *Definitely Maybe*, which will head straight to the top of the UK charts, and quickly be seen as the most significant and influential British rock release for years – although it will peak at a sluggish 58 in the US when it's released there next year. The volatile relationship between the band's leaders, the Gallagher brothers, writer Noel and singer Liam, will at one stage cause the abrupt curtailment of a US tour.

## Music Club

• **AUGUST 27TH:** **SHERYL CROW** releases a remixed version of 'All I Wanna Do,' from her 1993 album *Tuesday Night Music Club*, and will suddenly have an international Top Five single on her hands (and a Number One on the US Adult Contemporary chart). Already known as a writer and back-up singer – with Michael Jackson, among others – Crow recorded the loose, ramshackle yet charming *TNMC* album after informal weekly writing sessions with colleagues like David Baerwald, Kevin Gilbert, and Bill Botrell (with a cameo from her father, trumpeter Wendell Crow). But the album's success antagonizes her associates, who believe Crow has hogged the limelight for herself and not given them adequate credit.

## Those Were The Days, My Friend...

• **JULY 21ST:** **TONY BLAIR** is confirmed as the new leader of the Labour Party, after the sudden death of John Smith. Fresh-faced 41-year-old Mr Blair, an attorney by profession, is the youngest leader of the party since WWII. He was famously the singer in a rock band called Ugly Rumours while a student at Oxford in the early 1970s.

**JULY**

**AUGUST**

• **5TH:** **FOLLOWING A DRUG OVERDOSE** at his Hollywood Hills home, Billy Idol is admitted to hospital.
• **6TH:** **'STAY (I MISSED YOU)'** by Lisa Loeb & Nine Stories reaches Number One on the US Top 40 singles chart. It is taken from the soundtrack of the movie *Reality Bites*.
• **10TH:** **THREE MEN** are arrested at Munich airport, Germany, after being caught smuggling Russian plutonium into the country.
• **21ST:** **JEWEL BEGINS** recording her first solo album, *Pieces Of You*, at Broken Arrow Ranch studio, Woodside, California.
• **26TH:** **ARTHUR CORNHILL** is given the world's first battery-operated artificial heart in a pioneering operation in the UK. Unfortunately, he will die in nine months' time from kidney failure.

• **31ST:** **R. KELLY DUPES** 15-year-old Aaliyah into marrying him at the Sheraton Gateway in Rosemont, Illinois. The marriage is annulled a few weeks later... And a ceasefire is declared by the Irish Republican Army after 25 years of bloodshed in Northern Ireland.... At the same time, Russia officially ends its military presence in the former East Germany after a half-century.

• **AUGUST 23RD:** **JEFF BUCKLEY** releases the album *Grace*. It will be his only full-length record.

• **AUGUST 14TH:** **ALTHOUGH TORRENTIAL RAIN** turns the event into a mudbath, Green Day (above) take the honours at *Woodstock '94*, held at Winston Farm, Saugerties, New York State, to mark the 25th anniversary of the original event. The bill also includes The Red Hot Chili Peppers, Santana, Peter Gabriel, Bob Dylan, Nine Inch Nails, Metallica, Sheryl Crow, and Aerosmith. Estimates of attendance vary from 235,000 to 350,000. Popular and hyperactive punk-pop trio Green Day get into the spirit of the day by famously indulging in a massive mud-fight with the festival audience, which culminates in bass player Mike Dirnt losing some of his front teeth.

• **1ST:** **YASSER ARAFAT**, the chairman of the Palestinian Liberation Organisation, returns to the Gaza Strip after 27 years in exile.
• **2ND:** **'BACK AND FORTH'** by Aaliyah peaks at Number Five on the US Top 40 singles chart... And The Fugees debut album, *Blunted On Reality*, enters the US R&B albums chart, where it will stall at Number 62.
• **13TH:** **KISS APPEAR LIVE** on US TV's *Tonight Show*, where they take part in the year's most unlikely duet, playing with Garth Brooks on 'Hard Luck Woman.'
• **23RD:** **AN ASTEROID** orbiting between Mars and Jupiter is named Zappafrank, in honour of late rock musician Frank Zappa.
• **25TH:** **ISRAEL AND JORDAN** end the state of war that has existed between their two countries since 1948.
• **30TH:** **WITH RICHEY EDWARDS** now checked into a rehab clinic suffering nervous exhaustion, Manic Street Preachers are obliged to fulfil performance obligations as a trio of single guitar, bass, & drums.

• **AUGUST 25TH:** **ROBERT PLANT** and Jimmy Page reunite to record their *MTV Unplugged* show *Unledded*.

## Korn Rocks

OCTOBER 11TH: KORN release their self-titled debut album in the US. They immediately attract the hardest of hardcore rock followings, more than willing to subject themselves to Jonathan Davis's harrowing, tormented vocals (and even occasional bagpipe-playing), and the sonic metal barrage from the rest of the band. Though this album only reaches Number 72 in the US, the follow-up, *Life Is Peachy*, will put them in the US Top Three, while the single 'A.D.I.D.A.S.' – nothing to do with sports wear, it stands for 'All Day I Dream About Sex' – reaches Number 22 on the UK charts (one of five Top 40 singles they'll have in Britain before the end of the decade).

### SEPTEMBER

- **3RD: THE SINGLE** 'Wild Night' by John Mellencamp and Me'Shell NdegéOcello peaks at Number Three on the US Top 40.
- **6TH: NICKY HOPKINS**, legendary British session keyboardist who played with Quicksilver Messenger Service, Rolling Stones, The Beatles, and countless others, dies in Nashville, Tennessee, of abdominal and heart problems.
- **9TH: THE US AGREES** to accept 20,000 Cuban immigrants every year in return for a promise from Cuba to halt the influx of refugees.
- **12TH: FRANK CORDER** is killed when he crashes a stolen Cessna light aircraft on the South Lawn of the White House.
- **14TH: THE TEMPTATIONS** are awarded a star on the Hollywood Walk Of Fame.
- **15TH: PRESIDENT CLINTON** tells Haiti's military leaders, "Leave now or we will force you from power." A month later, they do so, averting a US invasion.
- **21ST: THE LOS ANGELES** and Santa Barbara Prosecutors Offices announce that charges of child molestation will not be laid against Michael Jackson, but the case will remain open until 1999.
- **28TH: A CAR AND PASSENGER FERRY** with 950 people on board sinks in the Baltic Sea, in bad weather, on its way from Estonia to Sweden. Fewer than 100 people survive the disaster.
- **30TH: THE FRONT PAGE** of UK tabloid *The Sun* reveals that Phil Collins has been sending what are described as 'hate faxes' to his estranged wife.

### OCTOBER

- **4TH: THE EAGLES'** Hell Freezes Over tour is temporarily stopped because Glen Frey requires urgent stomach surgery.
- **9TH: THE US SENDS TROOPS** and warships to the Persian Gulf in response to Saddam Hussein sending thousands of troops and hundreds of tanks toward the Kuwaiti border.
- **14TH: RAP GROUP PO' BROKE & LONELY** sue rapper/record company owner Eazy-E (formerly of NWA), claiming that his label, Ruthless Records, has interfered with their ability to negotiate with other labels.
- **15TH: THE ALBUM MONSTER** by R.E.M. enters the US album charts where it will peak at Number One.
- **17TH: THE FOO FIGHTERS**, a new band formed by ex-Nirvana drummer Dave Grohl (now on guitar and vocals), is hard at work in Bob Lang Studios, Seattle, Washington.
- **21ST: NORTH KOREA** and the US agree that North Korea will halt its nuclear program.
- **27TH: THE US JUSTICE DEPARTMENT** announces that the prison population has exceeded one million for the first time in American history.
- **28TH: DEPARTURE**, the 1980 album by Journey, is certified as triple-platinum by the RIAA in the US.
- **29TH: FRANCISCO MARTIN DURAN** fires at the White House while standing on Pennsylvania Ave, Washington DC. He is later convicted of trying to kill President Clinton.

### Let It Linger

- **OCTOBER 21ST: THE CRANBERRIES** have a US airplay hit with 'Zombie,' the first single from their Top Ten album *No Need To Argue*. The Irish group, fronted by Delores O'Riordan (left), have already had a US Top Ten single with 'Linger' at the start of the year, and will score even higher in the album charts with 1996's *To The Faithful Departed*.

# Every Breath You Take...

• **SEPTEMBER 2ND:** **MUCH-LOVED BRITISH** entertainer, multi-instrumentalist, and television presenter Roy Castle (right) dies at age 62, after a long fight with lung cancer. Castle is a non-smoker, and attributes the disease to the years he spent gigging in smoke-filled jazz clubs. (He is seen on the left in his prime, with bass player Charles Mingus.)

## NOVEMBER

• **1ST:** **THE LIVE ALBUM** *Nirvana: Unplugged In New York* is released in the US. On a wave of grief after Kurt Cobain's death, it reaches Number One in both the US and UK.

• **5TH:** **THE SOUNDTRACK** album to the movie *Murder Was The Case* reaches Number One on the US album chart. Directed by and starring Dr Dre, alongside Snoop Doggy Dogg and Ice Cube, the storyline concerns a successful rapper who is shot by a jealous gangster, and then makes a deal with the devil to escape death... Meanwhile George Foreman becomes boxing's oldest heavyweight champion at 45 – 20 years after his 'Rumble In The Jungle' with Muhammad Ali – when he knocks out Michael Moorer in Las Vegas... And Former President Reagan announces that he has Alzheimer's disease.

• **15TH:** **THIS YEAR'S INDUCTEES** into the Rock'N'Roll Hall of Fame: Led Zeppelin, Al Green, Allman Brothers, Martha

• **NOVEMBER 8TH:** **SONNY BONO**, of Sonny & Cher fame, is elected to the US Congress.

• **NOVEMBER 30TH:** **TUPAC SHAKUR** is robbed of jewelry and shot five times outside of Quad Studio, Times Square, New York City. He survives, and discharges himself from hospital a matter of hours after surgery. Two days later he's back in court, to be found guilty of sexually abusing a woman, but he's acquitted of more serious sexual and weapons charges.

& The Vandellas, Janis Joplin, Neil Young, and Frank Zappa. Vocal group The Orioles are inducted into the wing that honors early influences in rock.

• **18TH:** **BOYZ II MEN'S** 'I'll Make Love To You' remains at Number One on the US singles chart for its 14th week, equalling the record set by Whitney Houston's 'I Will Always Love You.' ... And Cab Calloway, the ever flamboyant, zoot-suit-wearing, hep-talking bandleader, whose career dates back to the New York Cotton Club of the 1930s, dies at the age of 86, having suffered a stroke in June. Calloway's first film appearance was in 1932: his last was in a Janet Jackson video in 1989.

• **4TH:** **OF THE 400 UN PEACEKEEPERS** being held by Bosnian Serbs, 53 are released – they're hanging on to the rest as insurance against further NATO air-strikes.

• **8TH:** **PRESIDENT CLINTON** fires Surgeon General Joycelyn Elders after she tells a conference that masturbation should be discussed in school as a part of human sexuality classes.

• **9TH:** **REPRESENTATIVES** of the Irish Republican Army and the British government begin peace talks.

• **10TH:** **PLEDGING TO PURSUE** their mission of bringing peace to the Middle East Yasser Arafat, Shimon Peres, and Yitzhak Rabin receive the Nobel Peace Prize.

• **15TH:** **RITCHIE SAMBORA**, guitarist with Bon Jovi, marries actress Heather Locklear in Paris, France. She was previously married to another rocker, Tommy Lee of Mötley Crüe.

• **17TH:** **'HERE COMES THE HOTSTEPPER'** by Jamaican reggae artist Ini Kamoze hits Number One in the US Top 40 singles chart.

• **21ST:** **SNOOP DOGGY DOGG** is arrested on drugs charges in Lake Charles, Louisiana.

• **26TH:** **FRENCH ANTI-TERRORIST POLICE** storm a hijacked jet at Marseille, killing all four Islamic fundamentalist hostage-takers and freeing 170 passengers and crew.

• **30TH:** **IN A SURVEY** carried out by BBC Radio 1 and *The Times Magazine* in the UK, 'Born To Run' by Bruce Springsteen is declared the greatest song ever.

• **DECEMBER 5TH:** *LIVE AT THE BBC* by The Beatles – a compilation of live radio sessions from the 1960s – reaches Number One on the UK album chart.

*Live at the BBC*

• **NOVEMBER 20TH:** **DAVID CROSBY** gets a much needed liver transplant at UCLA's Medical Center.

# 1995

## DEFINITELY MAYBE

Back in 1991, things weren't looking quite so promising for Oasis. They had formed as 061, after the telephone area code for Manchester, their home city, then changed their name to The Rain. Then guitarist Paul 'Bonehead' Arthurs, bass player Paul 'Guigsy' McGuigan, and drummer Tony McCarroll sacked their original singer in favour of stroppy, loud-mouthed Liam Gallagher. Lacking direction, and decent songs, they immediately decided to lumber themselves with a truly terrible band name – Oasis. It conjures up images of a cheesy cabaret band with velvet bow ties and cummerbunds, and a palm tree painted on the bass drum skin, rather than the alternative post-grunge rockers they were. Still, they showed enough promise to tempt Liam's older brother Noel to join them. A serious guitarist, and budding tunesmith, he'd been earning a living as technical roadie for local 'indie' pop heroes Inspiral Carpets. Noel soon took control and hammered the band into shape by enforcing a strict rehearsal regime. Having famously wasted a golden opportunity by arguing on stage at an A&R-studded industry event, they invited Creation Records boss Alan McGee along to an early show in Scotland. Immediately convinced of their potential, he signed them straight away, and by late 1994 their debut album *Definitely Maybe* had gone straight to the top of the UK charts. It takes a slower route in the US, but will eventually reach gold sales figures, due to MTV smashes like 'Live Forever' and 'Supersonic.' From day one, the sibling rivalry of the brothers Gallagher becomes as well-documented as their music – they openly brawl with each other, with other bandmembers (drummer Tony McCarroll will leave in 1995 to be replaced by Alan White), with the press, and even with other bands, notably staunch Britpop 'rivals' Blur. While it makes good headlines, it leaves a trail of cancelled gigs, tours, and TV shows, as well as many missed opportunities – especially in the States, where their antics are less well tolerated. Despite all this turmoil, the band's unshakeable self-belief carries them on, and they'll produce a blistering follow-up with *(What's The Story) Morning Glory*, which again debuts at Number One in the UK while doing slow but sure business in the US. The most popular and influential British rock band of the mid 1990s, they might have done even better to steer a less confrontational path – but then, of course, they wouldn't have been Oasis.

# 1995

## January–April

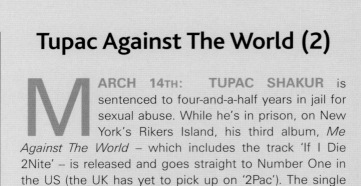

## Tupac Against The World (2)

**M**ARCH 14TH: TUPAC SHAKUR is sentenced to four-and-a-half years in jail for sexual abuse. While he's in prison, on New York's Rikers Island, his third album, *Me Against The World* – which includes the track 'If I Die 2Nite' – is released and goes straight to Number One in the US (the UK has yet to pick up on '2Pac'). The single 'Dear Mama' also goes US Top Ten. Tupac conducts media interviews from prison, during which he apparently renounces his former 'Thug' lifestyle, and he even gets married in jail to his girlfriend Keisha Morris. He does, however, make some allegations about people he believes to be in some way implicated in his shooting – including fellow rapper Biggie Smalls (Notorious BIG). Smalls later denies this.

### JANUARY

• **1ST: ROD STEWART** sets a new concert record when 3.5 million fans see his New Year's Day concert on Copacabana Beach, Rio.

• **2ND: THE MOST DISTANT GALAXY** yet discovered is found by scientists using the Keck telescope in Hawaii. It's estimated to be 15 billion light years away. Perhaps in 15 billion years from now, astronomers in that distant galaxy will be able to watch Rod Stewart in Rio through their own mega-telescopes.

• **3RD: THE US POSTAL SERVICE** raises the price of the first-class stamp to 32 cents.

• **12TH: IN PERTH, AUSTRALIA**, at the start of their mammoth Monster Tour, R.E.M.'s Peter Buck marries Stephanie, the mother of their two daughters, Zoe and Zelda. Grant Lee Buffalo provides the party music.

• **9TH: BREAKING THE RECORD** for the longest continuous time spent in outer space, Russian cosmonaut Valeri Poliakov (51) completes his 366th day aboard the Mir space station.

• **11TH: MICHAEL JACKSON** releases a statement attacking unsubstantiated rumors of a video depicting Jackson fooling around with a young boy. He says "I will no longer stand by and watch reckless members of the media try to destroy my reputation."

• **15TH: LED ZEPPELIN** guitarist Jimmy Page pays his ex-wife Patricia Ecker $6 million in a divorce settlement.

• **18TH: DRIED BLOOD** scraped from a guitar owned by Nirvana's Kurt Cobain is sold at auction in New York.

• **22ND: U2 DISCOVER** they have no legal right to stop a condom manufacturer from selling a brand using their name in Ireland.

• **24TH: UK MUSIC PAPER** the NME holds its annual BRATS Awards at the New Empire, London. Oasis win Best Band, Album Of The Year (*Definitely Maybe*) and Best Single ('Live Forever')... In the States, the O.J. Simpson trial begins, with live television coverage.

• **28TH: 'CREEP' BY TLC** reaches Number One on the US Top 40 singles chart.

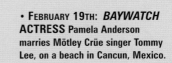

• **FEBRUARY 19TH:** *BAYWATCH* **ACTRESS** Pamela Anderson marries Mötley Crüe singer Tommy Lee, on a beach in Cancun, Mexico.

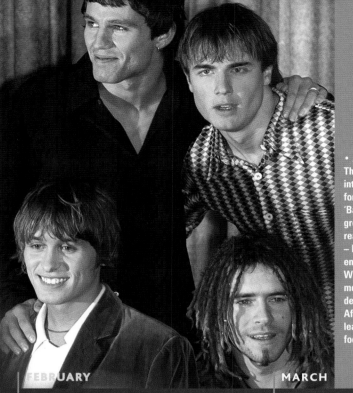

• **APRIL 3RD: UK BOY-BAND** Take That break a record by going straight into the British charts at Number One for the sixth time, on this occasion with 'Back For Good.' This will also be the group's only US hit single, when it reaches Number Seven later in the year – but they don't stay together long enough to capitalise on it. Robbie Williams is first to leave, but after two more UK chart-toppers, the group decide to call it a day, in early 1996. After a couple of Numnber Ones from lead singer Gary Barlow, most of the focus will then shift to Robbie.

FEBRUARY

MARCH

## In A Kobe Minute

**J**ANUARY 17TH: MORE THAN 6,000 people are killed after an earthquake hits Kobe, Japan. It measure 6.9 on the Richter scale, and is the worst to hit the country in over 70 years. The quake lasts only 20 seconds, but in such a highly built-up urban area it results in around 300,000 people losing their homes, and many tens of thousands being injured. The financial consequences are estimated at around US $200 billion, making it almost certainly the most expensive natural disaster ever.

APRIL

---

• **1ST: RICHEY EDWARDS** (above) of The Manic Street Preachers walks out of the Embassy Hotel in West London, climbs into his Vauxhall Cavalier car, and is never seen again. Two weeks later police find his car abandoned near the Severn Bridge in Wales.
• **3RD: DA LENCH MOB** rapper JD is jailed for 29 years for killing his girlfriend's room-mate, back in 1993.
• **4TH: AMERICA'S BIGGEST RAP STARS**, including Public Enemy, Snoop Doggy Dogg, Dr Dre and Onyx, are turned into cartoon characters by Marvel Comics.
• **7TH: PINK FLOYD** co-founder Rick Wright announces he is suing Yes frontman Jon Anderson for $1.5 million. The money has mistakenly been moved to Anderson's bank account by Wright's accountant .
• **15TH: THE FBI** arrests Kevin Mitnick and charges him with hacking into some of the nation's most protected computers. He will eventually receive a five-year jail sentence.
• **17TH:**

**RADIOHEAD** release a new double A-sided single, 'High And Dry/Planet Telex' on the Parlophone Records label in the UK.
• **23RD: MELVIN FRANKLIN** of The Temptations, dies of heart failure at 52.
• **25TH: 'TAKE A BOW'** by Madonna reaches Number One on the US Top 40 singles chart... And Lyle Lovett breaks his collarbone when he crashes his motorbike in Mexico.
• **26TH: BRITAIN'S OLDEST** banking firm, Barings, collapses after a 28-year-old dealer called Nick Leeson loses $1.4 billion on Tokyo stock prices. Leeson is arrested four days later.

• **1ST: THE EUROPEAN PARLIAMENT** rejects legislation aimed at allowing biotechnology companies to patent new life forms.
• **3RD: A STALKER** is arrested while trying to break into Roberta Flack's New York apartment... Meanwhile, having recently collapsed on-stage, R.E.M. drummer Bill Berry undergoes life-saving surgery in Lausanne, Switzerland to repair a ruptured aneurysm on the right side of his brain.
• **9TH: RAPPER T-BONE** is acquitted of murder charges in California.
• **14TH: US ASTRONAUT NORMAN THAGARD** becomes the first American to go into space in a Russian spacecraft.
• **15TH: ANGRY NEIGHBOURS** in Glasgow, Scotland, throw rotten eggs at The Artist Formerly Known As Prince

• **MARCH 20TH: IN TOKYO**, 12 people are killed and more than 5,000 hospitalized when the poisonous gas sarin is leaked on five subway trains. A secretive, apocalyptic religious cult, Aum Shinrikyo, is later found to be behind the attacks.

when his all-night party keeps them awake.
• **17TH: GERRY ADAMS** becomes the first leader of Sinn Fein (the political wing of the IRA) to be received at the White House.
• **22ND: GRATEFUL DEAD** guitarist Jerry Garcia launches his own range of psychedelic scuba-diving equipment.
• **25TH: A LIFEGUARD** rescues Pearl Jam's Eddie Vedder from drowning in New Zealand. He was swimming with Crowded House's Neil Finn.
• **26TH: EAZY-E** of gangsta rap group NWA, founder of Ruthless Records, dies of AIDS at the Cedars-Sinai Medical Centre, Los Angeles.
• **28TH: POLICE SUBDUE** an angry crowd when Latoya Jackson refuses to strip nude as specified in her contract at Al's Diamond Cabaret in Pennsylvania.
• **31ST: A FORMER LED ZEPPELIN FAN** is arrested after trying to stab Jimmy Page at a Page & Plant concert.

• **APRIL 15TH: 'THIS IS HOW WE DO IT' by** R&B singer Montell Jordan reaches Number One on the US Top 40 singles chart.

• **5TH: YOLANDA SALDIVAR**, former fan club president of Latin superstar Selena, is charged with Selena's murder a week, after the star was shot in the back. Saldivar will claim the shooting was an accident and that she was trying to shoot herself.

Selena's death, ironically, will lead to her first US hit singles.
• **19TH: A TRUCK** packed with an explosive-fertilizer compound blows up in Oklahoma City, gutting the Alfred P. Murrah federal building (above) and killing 168 people. In two years' time, Timothy McVeigh will be found guilty of the attack and sentenced to death.
• **21ST: MTV ASIA** re-launches its Mandarin-language channel... And Eddie Van Halen is fined $300 and sentenced to a year's probation for carrying a loaded shotgun into an airport in Burbank, California.
• **26TH: BOBBY BROWN** is arrested and charged with assaulting a man outside a Florida nightclub.

• JULY 4TH: **AN INCREASINGLY VOLATILE** Courtney Love thumps Kathleen Hanna of Bikini Kill on the Lollapalooza tour. Love later receives a suspended one-year sentence and is forced to attend anger-management sessions. These obviously don't work very well, because next month, while performing on-stage, she will get into a fight with her own fans, whom she berates for not cheering enough, and has to be carried off-stage by security guards.

• 2ND: **CARLOS SANTANA** is honored with his own postage stamp in the African state of Tanzania.

• 3RD: **AT THE ANNUAL** World Music Awards in Monte Carlo, Monaco, the best-selling artist is Mariah Carey and best-selling pop group are Ace Of Base. The best-selling rock group are Bon Jovi.

• 5TH: **TONE LOC** is sentenced to an anger-management course in Los Angeles, California, after threatening a female friend with a baseball bat.

• 7TH: **JACQUES CHIRAC** wins the French presidential election, beating Socialist opponent Lionel Jospin and ending a 14-year Socialist hold on the French presidency.

• 11TH: **ERIC CLAPTON**, B.B. King, Buddy Guy, Robert Cray and Jimmy Vaughan reunite for a tribute to Stevie Ray Vaughan. All five played with Vaughan at his last show on August 26th 1990, before he was killed in a helicopter crash.

• 13TH: **WHEN JEFF BUCKLEY** plays at The Cabaret Metro, Chicago, Illinois, the show is recorded for the *Live In Chicago* album.

• 15TH: **STONE TEMPLE PILOTS'** Scott Weiland is arrested trying to buy drugs in a motel parking lot in Pasadena, California.

• 16TH: **JAPANESE POLICE** besiege the headquarters of the Aum Shinrikyo cult near Mount Fuji in Japan, following the attack on the Tokyo subway. Cult leader Shoko Asahara is found hidden in a ceiling and arrested.

• 17TH: **REMARKABLY**, Chuck Berry, Little Richard, and Fats Domino appear together on stage for the very first time, in Sheffield, UK.

• 21ST: **VAN MORRISON** agrees to let the British government use his hit 'Brown-Eyed Girl' for a TV commercial promoting peace in Northern Ireland.

• 26TH: **PUBLIC ENEMY'S** Flavor Flav is sentenced to three months in jail for firing a gun at a neighbor.

• 27TH: **CRACKED REAR VIEW** by Hootie & The Blowfish reaches Number One on the US album chart for the first of eight weeks.

• 27TH: **FORMER SUPERMAN** actor Christopher Reeve is paralyzed in Charlottesville, Virginia, after being thrown from his horse during a jumping event.

• 31ST: **BOB DOLE** singles out Time-Warner for "the marketing of evil" in movies and music. He later admits he has not even seen or heard the vast majority of what he has been criticizing.

• 1ST: **DEPECHE MODE** member Alan Wilder, who replaced Vince Clarke back in 1981, quits the group.

• 3RD: **'HAVE YOU EVER REALLY LOVED A WOMAN'** by Bryan Adams heads the US Top 40. It's his fourth Number One since 1985.

• 5TH: **SEAGRAM**, a huge drinks company, buys MCA/Universal from Matsushita (its owners since 1991) for $5.7 billion. In 18 months' time, they will drop the MCA part of the name and relaunch Universal.

• 6TH: **PEARL JAM'S ALBUM** *Ten* is certified by the RIAA as having achieved nine million sales in the US.

• 11TH: **PHIL COLLINS'** touring crew is held at gunpoint by Venezuelan police in a mix-up over tax payments totalling some $900,000.

• 14TH: **CHECHEN REBELS** take 2,000 people hostage in a hospital in Russia.

• 16TH: **MICHAEL JACKSON** apologises publicly for some lyrics on his *HIStory* album, which have been branded as anti-semitic by Jewish groups.

• 18TH: **NOTORIOUS B.I.G.** is arrested in New Jersey on robbery and aggravated assault charges.

• 25TH: **AUDIENCE MEMBER** Kristin Daniel is struck by lightning at a Bob Dylan and The Grateful Dead concert in Washington DC.

• 29TH: **OVER 500 PEOPLE** are killed and almost 1,000 injured when the Sampoong department store suddenly collapses in Seoul, South Korea.

• MAY 13TH: **ALANIS MORISSETTE** releases the album *Jagged Little Pill* on Madonna's Maverick label. It will reach US Number One and win former child performer Alanis four Grammy Awards and a Brit.

# American Wolfman

**J**ULY 1ST: Legendary US DJ Wolfman Jack dies of a heart attack in Belvidere, North Carolina, at age 57. Known as "the world's most famous DJ" (by those in the know), the Wolfman – real name Bob Smith – became famous as a purveyor of uncompromising rock'n'roll and black R&B in the late 1950s and early 1960s, broadcasting mainly from Mexico via a hugely powerful transmitter. More than anyone else, he created the role of the 'personality' DJ, with his instantly distinctive, exaggeratedly raspy, piercing voice and pumped-up between-song chat, which were as crucial to his program's appeal as the undoubtedly heady musical mix he beamed across America, at a time when such music was hard to find on the radio. His eclectic tastes were not popular with everyone – the Ku Klux Klan is reported to have planted a burning cross outside his house, which perhaps encouraged his anonymity and the move to Mexico. The Wolfman's mysterious identity was ultimately revealed in the 1973 movie *American Graffiti*, in which he appeared as himself.

• **JUNE 27TH: ENGLISH ACTOR HUGH GRANT** is arrested in Los Angeles for engaging in 'lewd behavior' with a prostitute in his rented BMW.

## JULY

• **JULY 28TH: JIMI HENDRIX'S FATHER** Al (above right with Jimi in the 1960s) wins back the rights to his son's songs, estimated to be worth $50 million. To fund the action, Al Hendrix, a retired gardener, borrowed $5m interest-free from Microsoft co-founder Paul Allen, a devoted fan of the guitarist's work.

• **2ND: FORBES MAGAZINE** reports that Microsoft's chairman, Bill Gates is worth $12.9 billion, making him the world's richest man (by 1999, this will have increased to $77 billion).

• **3RD: EXCLUSIVE NEW YORK** store Saks Fifth Avenue reveals that it is suing soul legend Aretha Franklin for $263,000 in unpaid bills.

• **11TH: BOSNIAN SERBS** march into Srebrenica, forcing Dutch UN peacekeepers to leave, and precipitating the massacre of 7,000 Muslim men.

• **12TH: R.E.M.'S MIKE MILLS** is recovering from yesterday's emergency intestinal surgery in Germany. Seven shows of the band's European tour have to be cancelled.

• **14TH: THE TOWN COUNCIL** of Vilnius, Lithuania, agrees to erect a statue of outrageous rock musician Frank Zappa in its town centre. The connection? None at all: there's just a strong Zappa fan club in the town, admirers of Zappa's anti-establishment stance. But this is not the country's only link to leftfield musical icons: in 1992 when the Lithuanian basketball team defeated Russia to take the bronze medal at the Barcelona Olympic Games, they received their awards dressed in psychedelic T-shirts donated by The Grateful Dead. The town has also been hosting a rather impressive international jazz festival since 1988.

• **18TH: THE OLDEST KNOWN** musical instrument in the world is found: the 45,000 year-old relic – a hollowed bear bone with four artificial holes along its length – is discovered in the Indrijca River Valley in Slovenia... And Keith Elam, better known as Guru, the incisive rapper from Gang Star, releases the second of his critically acclaimed Jazzmatazz albums, creating more hip-hop/jazz fusion with the help of an impressive list of guest artists, including Donald Byrd, Ronny Jordan, Chaka Khan, Freddie Hubbard, and Courtney Pine.

• **19TH: HAVING MARKETED** a new scent called Get Wild, Prince is sued by Dynasty star Joan Collins, whose own perfume is named Wild.

• **19TH: ELVIS PRESLEY'S** former physician, Dr George Nichopoulos, loses his medical license for being 'too liberal' with his prescription pad... Meanwhile in the UK, in the wake of Robbie Williams leaving top boy band Take That, social workers set up emergency hotlines to calm devastated teenage fans threatening to kill themselves.

• **31ST: HAVING ALREADY** bought Miramax for $80m in 1993, the Walt Disney Company now acquires Capital Cities/ABC for a cool $19 billion.

## AUGUST

• **1ST: WESTINGHOUSE ELECTRIC CORPORATION** announce they intend to buy CBS for $5.4 billion.

• **2ND: CHINA ORDERS** the expulsion of two US Air Force officers who are said to have been caught spying.

• **3RD: MADONNA'S BLACK BUSTIER**, complete with black tassels and gold-sequined nipple-plates, is withdrawn from a London auction after failing to reach its reserve price of $3,750.

• **5TH: DREAMING OF YOU** by Selena reaches Number One on the US album chart, over four months after her death.

• **6TH: THOUSANDS OF GLOWING LANTERNS** are set afloat on rivers in Hiroshima, Japan, on the 50th anniversary of the first atomic bombing.

• **8TH: BECK'S ALBUM** *Mellow Gold* is awarded a US platinum disc by the RIAA... Meanwhile Saddam Hussein's two eldest daughters and their husbands hurriedly leave Iran after displeasing their father.

• **12TH: THE WORLD'S FIRST NUDIST** rock festival is held at Michigan's Turtle Lake Resort, featuring Blue Oyster Cult, Foreigner, Kansas, and Starship. Only the audience is nude, apparently.

• **13TH: THE INCREASINGLY INJURY-PRONE** R.E.M. add Michael Stipe's hernia surgery to the list.

• **14TH: ALISON HARGREAVES**, who became the first woman (and only the second person) to climb Mount Everest without oxygen or the help of sherpas, back in May, is killed by an avalanche while climbing K-2.

• **17TH: DEPECHE MODE** frontman Dave Gahan is hospitalized after a failed suicide attempt at his Los Angeles home.

• **31ST: THE ROCK AND ROLL** Hall Of Fame opens in Cleveland, Ohio.

• **AUGUST 9TH: GRATEFUL DEAD** leader Jerry Garcia dies, a week after his 53rd birthday, from a drugs-related heart attack at a rehabilitation clinic in San Francisco. It effectively means the end of the group after 30 years on the road. Garcia was the focal point and icon in the great, rolling, self-contained sub-culture of The Dead – although veteran members Weir, Lesh, and Hart will reunite in 1999 with guests in an outfit called, knowingly, The Other Ones.

# Hello Goodbye

**S**EPTEMBER 11TH: DESPITE HAVING SPLIT a quarter of a century ago, The Beatles have earned an estimated $130 million gross income in the year 1994-1995, according to today's *Forbes* magazine in the US. If any more proof were needed of the level of interest the band still attracts, in three days' time, at Sotheby's auction house in London, hand-written lyrics for Paul McCartney's *Sgt Pepper* song 'Getting Better' will sell for $249,000. And if that isn't enough, they can expect to earn another $100m or so from the new *Anthology* set: three double CDs containing many previously unheard out-takes and alternate versions of their hits, plus of course some long-awaited 'new' material. Out of the public gaze, the three surviving Beatles, Starr, McCartney, and Harrison (left) have been meeting up secretly over the last year to record two

## SEPTEMBER | OCTOBER | NOVEMBER

- **1ST: THE LOUIS ARMSTRONG** US postage stamp is released.
- **3RD: THE H.O.R.D.E.** tour featuring The Black Crowes, Blues Traveler, Ziggy Marley, Taj Mahal, Wilco, Joan Osborne, and Mother Hips, plays at the Shoreline Amphitheater, Mountain View, California.
- **5TH: THE BACKSTREET BOYS** release their debut single, 'We've Got It Goin' On.' It misses the Top 40 in both the US and UK first

time around, but it will be re-reissued in the UK in August 1996, and reach Number Three, creating a manic teenage following for the band in Europe before they make much impact back home...
- **9TH: COOLIO HITS** Number One on the US with 'Gangsta's Paradise,' a rap cover version of Stevie Wonder's 1976 track 'Pastime Paradise. (The pair are pictured together above.) The song appears on the soundtrack of the movie *Dangerous Minds*, starring Michelle Pfeiffer – Coolio himself appears as a school sex counselor in

the first episode of a TV series spun off from the film later this year.
- **19TH: THE** *WASHINGTON POST* and the *New York Times* publish the Unabomber's 35,000-word manifesto. The Unabomber is currently the most wanted individual in the US, having sent letter bombs to various targets (from universities to airlines and computer stores) on-and-off for 20 years. His manifesto explains in coherent terms that he is against technological progress, industrialisation, and political correctness, which he sees as blights on both the natural world and society. In return for publishing his text, the bomber promises that he will stop his campaign. At least after one more bomb... By agreeing, the publishers and the FBI

hope someone will recognise the writing style – and, in fact, the bomber's brother does just that. Six months later, 53-year-old former university professor Ted Kaczynski is arrested at his remote cabin home near Lincoln, Montana. He eventually pleads guilty, and is sentenced to life in jail.
- **20TH: INDIVIDUAL STATES** are allowed to set their own speed limits after the US House of Representatives votes to drop national controls.
- **22ND: BRANDY WINS** Best Solo Single, Song Of The Year, Album, and New Artist awards at the *Soul Train*'s first Lady Of Soul Awards in Santa Monica.
- **28TH: BOBBY BROWN** escapes unharmed when his sister's fiancé is killed by a gunman spraying Brown's car with bullets in Boston, Massachusetts.

- **SEPTEMBER 24TH: THE ROLLING STONES** announce that their Voodoo Lounge tour took a staggering $313 million was in ticket sales alone, topping the record of $290 million set by the 1989 Steel Wheels tour.

- **1ST: SHEIK OMAR ABDEL-RAHMAN** and nine other defendants are convicted in New York of conspiring to bomb various US buildings as part of a campaign against America's policies in the Middle East... Meanwhile U2 launch a campaign to protect the rights of street buskers in Dublin, Eire.
- **7TH: TONE LOC** is arrested in Los Angeles for taking $80 from a pizza parlor.
- **14TH: TUPAC SHAKUR** is released from prison on $1.4m bail, while he appeals against his four-and-a-half year jail sentence for sexual assault.
- **17TH: STING'S** former financial adviser is sentenced to six years in prison in the UK after being found guilty of embezzling $9.4 million from the musician.
- **20TH: BRITAIN, FRANCE AND THE U.S.** announce a treaty banning atomic tests in the South Pacific.
- **21ST: ON BLIND MELON'S TOUR BUS** in New Orleans, the band's 28-year-old singer Shannon Hoon is found dead after a cocaine overdose. Their biggest hit was 1993's 'No Rain,' and their second album, *Soup*, has just gone into the US Top 40.
- **22ND: DEF LEPPARD** play three gigs in three continents in a single day. First comes Tangier, in Africa, followed by London, in Europe and finally Vancouver, in North America.

- **3RD: AN OUT-OF-COURT SETTLEMENT** is reached by Bob Dylan and Hootie & The Blowfish over the use of Dylan's lyrics in their song 'Only Want To Be With You.'
- **4TH: ISRAELI PRIME MINISTER** Yitzhak Rabin is assassinated by Yigal Amir as he leaves a peace rally in Tel Aviv. Amir will later insist he was acting on God's orders.
- **7TH: RAPPER FLAVOR FLAV** of Public Enemy is arrested (again) on gun and drugs charges.
- **8TH: MICHAEL JACKSON** and Sony combine forces and create the world's third-largest music publishing company with more than 100,000 titles. This will later become a bone of contention between the two parties.
- **9TH: CHAD SMITH**, drummer of The Red Hot Chili Peppers, breaks a wrist while playing baseball, forcing the band to cancel its upcoming tour.
- **11TH: *MELLON COLLIE AND THE INFINITE SADNESS*** by The Smashing Pumpkins reaches Number One on the US album chart.
- **11TH: THE DEBUT ALBUM** from Garbage peaks at US Number 20 and Number Six in the UK.
- **13TH: LEAH BETTS**, an 18-year-old from Essex, UK, collapses four hours after swallowing an ecstasy tablet and dies three days later without regaining consciousness. Her parents will become high-profile anti-drugs campaigners... And Aerosmith release a rock'n'roll-themed computer game, Quest For Fame.
- **16TH: A UN COURT** charges Bosnian Serb leader Radovan Karadzic with genocide.
- **17TH: THREE GENERATIONS** of popular music icons are united in an impromptu sing-song around the piano at Frank Sinatra's house with Bob Dylan, Bruce Springsteen, and Ol' Blue Eyes himself. Two days later they tape a Sinatra 80th birthday tribute.
- **21ST: GREEN DAY** frontman Billie Joe Armstrong is arrested for indecent exposure after baring his backside at the audience during a show in Milwaukee, Wisconsin.

- **OCTOBER 10TH: NO DOUBT** issue the album *Tragic Kingdom* in the US. It's their third album release, but will be their first to register on the charts – and it registers all the way to Number One... In December, when No Doubt support Bush at Universal Amphitheater, Los Angeles, singer Gwen Stefani (right) will meet her future husband, Bush singer Gavin Rossdale.

new tracks based around old demo recordings by John Lennon. They invited their old mentor, the great George Martin, to produce them once again, but he declined. Not only did he not feel up to it (recognizing that his ears are no longer the infallible instruments they once were), but, more importantly, he wasn't sure it was a good idea at all. He did, however, oversee the selection of the archive material on *Anthology*. Harrison's buddy Jeff Lynne (formerly of The Traveling Wilburys and ELO) was hired instead as producer for the new pieces, and long-serving Martin sidekick Geoff Emerick brought back as engineer. The resultant recordings, 'Free As A Bird' and 'Real Love,' could clearly never be described as classic Beatles – in the cold light of day they are fairly plodding and empty songs – but they have a certain charm and undeniable nostalgic resonance for listeners of a

certain age. (Those under 30 must be wondering what the hell all the fuss has been about.) 'Free As A Bird' reaches Number Two in the UK, and Number Six in the US, with 'Real Love' performing slightly less well a few months later. The new songs don't add much to the legacy, but neither do they detract from it, as some doom merchants had predicted at the time: you only have to look at the consistent sales figures to see that. Besides, why shouldn't three old friends get together to make some music, while they still have the chance? They also, indirectly, raise some extra cash for Michael Jackson, who has just acquired the ATV publishing catalog, including 250 Beatles songs – which McCartney tried to buy some years earlier – for a reputed $47 million. A strange idea, one artist owning the rights to another's songs, but that's show business...

## DECEMBER

- **DECEMBER 25TH: DEAN MARTIN,** king of the lounge singers, dies at the age of 78.

- **2ND:** *THE GUINNESS BOOK OF WORLD RECORDS* confirms Ace Of Base's *The Sign* to be the best-selling debut album of all time, with 19 million copies sold.
- **3RD:** **THE RUSSIAN BEER LOVERS** political party offers $17,000 to Michael Jackson to sing at a rally in Moscow. He declines.
- **6TH:** **TLC** win the Artist Of The Year and Best R&B Artists at the Billboard Music Awards in New York City.
- **10TH:** **DARREN ROBINSON** (formerly with the Fat Boys) dies of a heart attack at just 28 years of age.
- **13TH:** **CHINA'S MOST INFLUENTIAL** and well-known democracy activist, Wei Jingsheng, who has already spent 16 years in prison, is sentenced to 14 more.
- **14TH:** **UNDER THE NAME** The Lemmys, Metallica play a set of Motorhead covers at Motorhead leader Lemmy's birthday bash in Los Angeles... Meanwhile The Dayton Peace Agreement is signed in Paris and war in Bosnia formally ends, though localised conflicts continue to erupt sporadically.
- **15TH:** **UK POP TRIO** Eternal perform their latest single 'I Am Blessed' at the Cistine Chapel in Rome before a select audience including Pope John Paul II... And newly released classified documents from the White House reveal that the FBI spied on John Lennon and kept extensive files on his anti-war activities during the early 1970s, possibly in an attempt to have him deported.
- **18TH:** **STEVIE WONDER** leads a singalong in Times Square, New York City, in aid of America's homeless and hungry.

- **DECEMBER 2ND:** *R. KELLY,* by R. Kelly, reaches **Number One on the US album chart.**

# 1996

## January–April

• **FEBRUARY 3RD:** **MARY J. BLIGE** has her biggest US hit to date with 'Not Gon' Cry,' taken from the Whitney Houston movie *Waiting To Exhale*.

### JANUARY

• **2ND: THE ALBUM *ALICE IN CHAINS*** by Alice In Chains is certified platinum in the US by the RIAA
• **3RD: MADONNA TESTIFIES** in Los Angeles against Robert Dewey Hoskins, who has been accused of stalking her and threatening to kill her.
• **4TH: THE GRAMMY NOMINATIONS** are announced: Alanis Morrisette and Mariah Carey get six nominations each, Joan Osborne gets five, Shania Twain gets four. Also among the nominees are D'Angelo, Coolio, Babyface, Michael Jackson, and Hootie & The Blowfish.
• **5TH: YAHYA AYYASH,** thought to be behind a wave of Islamic suicide bombings against Israel, is killed in Gaza by a booby-trapped cellular telephone.
• **7TH: ONE OF THE BIGGEST BLIZZARDS** in US history hits the eastern side of the country, causing more than 100 deaths.
• **8TH: FORMER FRENCH PRESIDENT** Francois Mitterrand dies at age 79.
• **16TH: WAYNE NEWTON** performs his 25,000th Las Vegas show... Meanwhile the Jamaican authorities open fire on Jimmy Buffett's seaplane, carrying Buffet and U2's Bono. They later apologise, explaining they mistakenly thought that the airplane belonged to a drug trafficker.
• **18TH: LISA MARIE PRESLEY** files for divorce from Michael Jackson.
• **22ND: WHITNEY HOUSTON** signs a two-picture contract with Disney subsidiary, Touchstone Films.
• **29TH: VENICE'S OPERA HOUSE** La Fenice (The Phoenix) is destroyed by fire for the second time in its history.

## Media Babylon

• **JANUARY 27TH:** BABYLON ZOO (also known as Jas Mann, left) releases the single 'Spaceman' in the UK, and it immediately goes to Number One, holding that position for seven weeks. It largely owes this success to its use in a Levi's TV commercial in the UK. The track does zip in the US. It's an example of the ever-increasing use of pop and rock tracks in commercials, sometimes making unlikely, if often temporary, stars of otherwise unknown artists. The other favored technique in commercials is to take a song from a well-known act and give it a new lease of life, whether it wants one or not. Whether for cars, clothes, credit cards, burgers, or booze, the game among advertisers soon becomes finding the most unpredictable but catchy track and making it work. The result is a bizarre mix of music, from Louis Armstrong and Dean Martin to They Might Be Giants and The Pet Shop Boys. It becomes a marketing tool that can make or break an ad campaign, but also boosts the fortunes of the bands concerned, as long as they don't mind being permanently associated with that ad. For instance, 'Da da da' by Trio, a defunct group of German minimalists, was a UK hit in 1982 but unknown in the US until used in a VW commercial in 1997 – when people assumed it had been written specially for the ad.

### FEBRUARY

• **4TH: THE NEUROTIC BOY OUTSIDERS** – a bizarre 'supergroup' comprising John Taylor of Duran Duran, Duff MacKagan of Guns N' Roses, and Steve Jones of the Sex Pistols, plays at the Off Ramp, Seattle, Washington... Meanwhile former Milli-Vanilli performer Rob Pilatus is hospitalized after being hit over the head with a baseball bat in Hollywood. Pilatus was apparently attempting to steal a car, and struck by the owner.
• **6TH: THE RED HOT CHILI PEPPERS** begin a US tour at CoreStates Spectrum, Philadelphia, Pennsylvania.
• **9TH: THE IRA CEASEFIRE** ends when a one-ton bomb explodes in London's Canary Wharf district, killing two people.
• **11TH: PAULA ABDUL** makes her adult acting debut on the CBS TV show *Cybill*. The star of the show, former *Taxi Driver* and *Moonlighting* actress Cybill Shepherd, is a singer herself, recording in styles from pop and rock to jazz and cabaret.
• **13TH: SHAKIRA RELEASES** the album *Pies Descalzos* (Bare Feet) in the US.
• **20TH: RAPPER SNOOP** Doggy Dogg and his bodyguard are found not guilty of first-degree murder. The jury is deadlocked on voluntary manslaughter charges, resulting in a mistrial.
• **27TH: ALANIS MORRISETTE** releases a new single, 'Ironic.' Critics enjoy pointing out that many of the supposedly 'ironic' situations in the lyrics, while unfortunate, are not technically ironic at all. Which is rather ironic in itself, isn't it?

### MARCH

• **1ST: FOR THE FIRST TIME** in 20 years, Neil Diamond gives a live performance in a record shop – the Virgin Megastore in Los Angeles.
• **10TH: *THE JUNO AWARDS*** (Canada's equivalent of The Grammys) are held in Hamilton, Ontario, with Alanis Morissette winning awards for Female Vocalist Of The Year, Album Of The Year (Jagged Little Pill), Rock Album, Single Of The Year ('You Oughta Know') and Songwriter, along with co-writer and producer Glen Ballard. Ballard is a veteran industry composer, who co-wrote Michael Jackson's 'Man In The Mirror,' and over his 25-year career works with everyone from Kiki Dee in the 1970s to Christina Aguilera in 2002..
• **12TH: THE CUBAN LIBERTY & DEMOCRATIC SOLIDARITY ACT,** better known as the Helms-Burton Act, is signed into law by President Clinton. The act attempts to restrict trade with Cuba by other nations.
• **13TH: A LONE GUNMAN** goes on a shooting spree at a school in Dunblane, Scotland, killing 16 children and their teacher, before turning the gun on himself. The massacre persuades the British government to ban the sale and use of handguns.
• **14TH: FORMER NIRVANA BASSIST** Krist Novoselic lashes out against the US Communications Decency Act during his keynote address at the music industry's South By Southwest (SXSW) conference in Austin, Texas. Internet users consider the act a threat to freedom of speech.

Fugees
The Score

## Refugee Rap

**J**ANUARY 31ST: The Fugees release the album *The Score*. By this summer it will have been awarded gold, platinum and double platinum disc status in the US, making The Fugees the most successful hip-hop group ever. It'll also have given them two UK Number One singles, 'Killing Me Softly,' a hip-hop cover of the old Roberta Flack hit, and 'Ready Or Not.' Their version of Bob Marley's 'No Woman No Cry' reaches UK Number Two. The Fugees were formed by Haitian cousins Wyclef Jean and Pras Michel, but singer and actress Lauryn Hill has the most immediate solo success when the trio splinters in 1998.

**APRIL**

• MARCH 18TH: **THE SEX PISTOLS** announce they are reuniting for a 20th anniversary tour, with the original line-up of John Lydon, Steve Jones (left), Paul Cook, and once-sacked bass player Glen Matlock. Between June and November they will play around 70 dates in Europe, North & South America, Australasia, and Japan. Though John Lydon points out he will be continuing with his own, relatively non-commercial PIL project, he makes no bones about the financial appeal of this get-together. The reunion jaunt will, appropriately enough, be called *The Filthy Lucre Tour*.

• 16TH: **LONG PAST ITS GLORY YEARS**, London's legendary Marquee club closes down without even a final concert. The last event is a dance club night.
• 19TH: **SARAJEVO** becomes a united city again, after four years, when Moslem-Croat authorities take control of the last district held by Serbs.
• 20TH: **THE BRITISH GOVERNMENT** announces that at least ten people have died from a disease related to BSE in cattle, which is known in the press as Mad Cow Disease.
• 22ND: **WHEN OASIS PLAY** the first of two nights at The Point, Dublin, Eire, vocalist Liam Gallagher has a fight with his girlfriend, Patsy Kensit, then engages in a verbal battle with INXS singer Michael Hutchence in a nearby bar.
• 23RD: **A GOOD DAY** for Celine Dion – her single 'Because You Loved Me' reaches the top of the US Hot 100 at the same time as *Falling Into You* enters the UK albums chart at Number One.

## Manic Design

• MARCH 27TH: **HAVING SOLD** 93,000 copies in its first week of release, 'A Design For Life' by The Manic Street Preachers (right) enters the UK singles chart at Number Two. Formed in Wales in 1988, obsessed with The Clash and Public Enemy, The Manics have survived early media contempt, public vitriol, illness, and the loss of a crucial band member, to emerge defiant and triumphant with the album *Everything Must Go*, which will be a huge commercial and critical success in the UK and Asia.

• 2ND: **LECH WALESA**, the former Solidarity union leader who became Poland's first post-war democratic president, resumes his old job as an electrician at the Gdansk shipyard.
• 4TH: **WILSON PICKETT** is arrested for cocaine possession while out on probation.
• 7TH: **SMASHING PUMPKINS**, Sonic Youth, Afghan Whigs, Garbage, and The Walkabouts play at the WDR Rocknacht, Philipshalle, Düsseldorf, Germany.
• 16TH: **QUEEN ELIZABETH'S** second son, Prince Andrew, and his wife Sarah announce they are to divorce after ten years of marriage... Meanwhile Rage Against The Machine's second album, *Evil Empire*, is released, and makes its way determinedly to Number One on the US album chart (Number Four in the UK).
• 18TH: **BERNARD EDWARDS**, admired and inspirational bass player and songwriter with Chic, dies from pneumonia in a Tokyo hotel room during a Japanese tour. He is 43.
• 23RD: **WHEN IT'S ANNOUNCED** that Eric Clapton, The Who, Bob Dylan, and Alanis Morissette will headline "the biggest rock concert in London's Hyde Park for 20 years," 150,000 tickets are sold in 48 hours.
• 24TH: **MARK KNOPFLER**, formerly of Dire Straits, begins his first solo tour at Liesureland, Galway, Eire... Meanwhile the PLO changes its charter to omit the commitment to destroying Israel.
• 30TH: **THE CRANBERRIES** release their new album, *To The Faithful Departed*, in the US.

• FEBRUARY 19TH: **AT** *THE BRIT AWARDS* ceremony in Earls Court, London, Oasis win the Best British Group, Best Album, and Best Video awards. The headline-grabbing event of the night, though, is when Jarvis Cocker (left) of UK band Pulp invades the stage in the middle of Michael Jackson's messianic performance of 'Earth Song' and performs a parody of Jackson's act. Cocker's band Pulp have recently had a Number One UK album with *Different Class*, their first big success in over 12 years of perseverance.

## Fiction Or Reality?

**M**ARCH 2ND: THE PARENTS of teenage murder victim Elyse Pahler are suing the thrash/speed/death-metal band Slayer, and their record label, Rick Rubin's American Recordings. They contend that the band's lyrics are "satanic" and inspired three boys to rape, torture, and stab their daughter to death, near her home in San Luis Obispo, California. The three admitted murder and are serving prison sentences of at least 25 years, but the Pahler family insists that the band (whose 1994 album *Divine Intervention* was a US Top Ten hit) knowingly marketed and distributed "harmful and obscene" material to minors. Slayer and their label claim they are protected by the First Amendment – the right to free expression.

**MAY**

**JUNE**

- **1ST: THE ALBUM** *Blood Sugar Sex Magik* by The Red Hot Chili Peppers is certified by the RIAA as having sold four million copies in the US.
- **3RD: WHEN THE CAPACITY CROWD** in The Forum, London, learns that rapper Busta Rhymes has pulled out of the show at the last minute, a riot breaks out among the fans, causing upwards of $75,000 worth of damage.

- **4TH: RAGE AGAINST THE MACHINE'S** new album, *Evil Empire*, enters the US album chart at Number One.
- **11TH: WHEN THE SMASHING PUMPKINS** play at The Point Depot, Dublin, Eire, a crush develops in front of the stage. Injured audience member Bernadette O'Brien is pulled out, but dies the following day.
- **18TH: 'THA CROSSROADS'** by Bone Thugs-N-Harmony reaches Number One on the US Top 40 singles chart.
- **28TH: DAVE GAHAN** of Depeche Mode 'dies' in the Sunset Marquis, Los Angeles, after overdosing on a 'speedball' of heroin and cocaine. Miraculously, he is revived by medics after his heart has stopped for several minutes – and then he is immediately arrested.
- **31ST: HOPING TO FIND SUCCESS**, Scottish band Travis move south to live together in a house in north London.

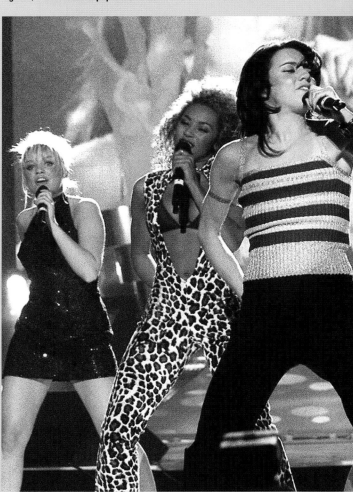

- **MAY 7TH: THE DAVE MATTHEWS BAND release their third album, *Crash*, which takes the group to Number Two on the US album chart.**

- **8TH: CHINA SETS OFF** an underground nuclear test blast
- **13TH: AN 81-DAY STAND-OFF** between the 'Freemen' and the FBI ends in Montana when the anti-government group surrenders.
- **14TH: GUERNSEY**, one of the UK's Channel Islands, votes to legalize abortion. The previous law, from 1910, meant women faced life imprisonment if found guilty of having a termination.
- **15TH: SMASHING PUMPKINS** and Red Hot Chili Peppers play at the Free Tibet Benefit, in Golden Gate Park, San Francisco.
- **18TH: BECK RELEASES** his new album, *Odelay*, worldwide
- **27TH: A WARRANT** is issued for the arrest of Stone Temple Pilots' vocalist Scott Weiland, who has left a drug rehabilitation centre before finishing his required sentence... And tonight, during the Wu-Tang Clan's set at the Hoodshock concert in Harlem, New York City (on a bill with The Fugees, Biggie Smalls, and Total), a member of the audience goes on a gun-shooting spree, and 22 fans end up hospitalized. The Hoodshock concert, arranged by The Fugees, was intended to "bring musicality and an atmosphere of peace, purpose and unity to urban communities," as well as raising money for youth clubs and programs.
- **28TH: IT'S REPORTED** that Sammy Hagar has been fired from Van Halen, to be replaced by the band's original vocalist, David Lee Roth. But the 'reunion' will be shortlived.

- **JUNE 24TH: 'WANNABE,'** the first single by The Spice Girls, is released in the UK. On July 27th it will reach Number One, and remain there for seven weeks. Six months later, defying expectations, 'Wannabe' does the same thing in the US, although only for four weeks. In fact The Spice Girls and their self-styled Girl Power phenomenon prove to a one-off blip in a downward trend of British pop exports to the States: the number of UK acts finding success in the US is at an all-time statistical low. According to the *Guinness Book Of Hit Singles* there have been only nine UK-born Number One artists in the US since 1990 – as opposed to, for example, 12 in 1965 alone, and 13 in 1985 – and only one more British act will top the US charts this decade (and that's Elton John's Diana memorial). Precious few will even make the Top Ten. Still, at least The Spice Girls have done their bit for their country's trade figures, manufactured pop band or not.

## Ali's Flame

- **JUNE 19TH: MUHAMMAD ALI** – displaying the typical shaking symptoms associated with Parkinson's disease – lights the flame that opens the Olympic Games in Atlanta, Georgia. There's barely a dry eye in the house.

## Ash Let It Flow

**JUNE 11TH: NORTHERN IRELAND** band Ash release their second album, *1977*, which will take them to the top of the UK charts (while barely causing a ripple in the States). Blending frenetic fuzz-guitar punk and hooky pop tunes, the album's title represents an important date for the band – not only when the original *Star Wars* movie was made, but also when the band's founder members were born. The CD ends with a truly revolting 'hidden' track, a tape recording of somebody being deliberately, and copiously sick, much to the amusement of his friends.

### JULY

- **1ST: ACTRESS MARGAUX HEMINGWAY** commits suicide in her apartment at Santa Monica, California. Four other members of her family have previously taken their own lives, including her grandfather, writer Ernest Hemingway.
- **12TH: JONATHAN MELVOIN**, backing keyboardist for Smashing Pumpkins and Prince, is found dead in the Regency Hotel, Park Avenue, Manhattan, New York City, after a heroin overdose. Co-band member Jimmy Chamberlin is arrested for using the drug – and is fired from the band a week later... Meanwhile Flea of Red Hot Chili Peppers plays naked at Wembley Stadium, London, relying on his guitar to cover his manly charms.
- **13-14TH: THE ANNUAL T IN THE PARK FESTIVAL** is held in Glasgow, Scotland, with Radiohead, Alanis Morissette, Foo Fighters, Bluetones, Beck, Pulp, Black Grape, Prodigy, Teenage Fanclub, and Manic Street Preachers
- **16TH: DOLORES O'RIORDAN** of The Cranberries accepts an undisclosed settlement from a UK tabloid newspaper that alleged she appeared on-stage without underwear.
- **17TH: BRYAN 'CHAS' CHANDLER** (57) dies at North Tyneside General Hospital, Newcastle, UK, after suffering a heart attack. Chandler had been the bass player with The Animals before going on to discover and manage Jimi Hendrix, and later Slade.
- **29TH: DRUMMER CHAD SMITH** confirms widespread rumours that the Red Hot Chili Peppers have split. In fact, it turns out they're just taking a break to do other things, and are back in action in less than two years.
- **31ST: THE SEX PISTOLS** play their first US date in over 18 years at Red Rocks, Denver, their first of 21 gigs in the US and Canada on the Filthy Lucre Tour.

### AUGUST

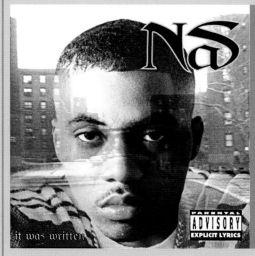

it was written

## Nas Is Coming

- **AUGUST 1ST: NEW YORK** rapper Nas releases his second album, *It Was Written*, which will top the US album chart. Influenced by his jazz musician father, Nas has become a highly acclaimed rap artist, working on his 1994 debut *Illmatic* with the likes of Q-Tip. His much-anticipated 1999 follow-up album, *I Am...*, will also top the US chart, and he'll duet with Puff Daddy, Missy Elliot, and Jennifer Lopez. *Q Magazine* in the UK reckons, "Nas is the only rapper capable of challenging the Wu-Tang Clan's dominance."

- **1ST: MTV LAUNCHES M2**, which is intending to screen non-stop music videos, without interruptions for news, game shows, documentaries and the like.
- **3RD: SPANISH GUITAR DUO** Los Del Rio climb to Number One on the US Top 40 singles chart with a dance remix of their song 'Macarena,' which proves to be a huge international hit.
- **5TH: JOSIA THUGWANE** becomes the first black South African to win an Olympic gold medal, after finishing first in the marathon.
- **6TH: THE RAMONES** play their final live show together, in Los Angeles. Eddie Vedder of Pearl Jam and Lemmy of Motorhead join them for guest slots. Vedder also videotapes the Ramones placing their hands in cement on the Hollywood Rock Walk prior to the show.
- **7TH: BOWING TO PUBLIC PRESSURE** in the wake of child-sex allegations against Michael Jackson, Hyundai pulls its sponsorship from his upcoming concerts in Seoul, South Korea.
- **13TH: DATA SENT BACK** by the Galileo space probe indicates there may be water on one of Jupiter's moons, heightening the possibility it could once have supported a primitive life-form.
- **17TH: ROSS PEROT**, a Texas billionaire, announces he intends to stand as the Reform Party's presidential candidate.
- **20TH: DAVID BYRNE** files a legal suit against his former Talking Heads colleagues, Chris Frantz, Tina Weymouth, and Jerry Harrison, to prevent release of the album *No Talking Just Heads*, which the trio have made under the name The Heads, using various guest vocalists, including Debby Harry, Michael Hutchence, and Shaun Ryder from Happy Mondays. Byrne claims that calling themselves 'The Heads' amounts to "dilution of a protectible trademark in violation of the Lanham Trademark Act 1946." His action fails, and the album is released in November.
- **24TH: WARNER BROTHERS RECORDS** announces that it has re-signed R.E.M. to a new five-album contract, which nets the band a tidy $80m.

# 1996

September–December

## Wired For Sound

**O**CTOBER 21ST: **JAY BARBIERI**, a former executive with Angel, a division of EMI Records, announces the launch of the "first internet record label," J-Bird Records. His idea is to let music-hungry web users act as A&R people, suggesting artists he might sign. He then uses traditional and Internet-based marketing and distribution to promote the roster which, by the end of the decade, will have risen to more 300 artists, including some major names like John Entwistle. But he's not the first to think about using the Internet to help bands promote themselves. It's unlikely you've heard of The Ugly Mugs, but as Internet visionaries, their place in history is assured. In 1993, bandmember Jeff Patterson spotted the potential of the internet for disseminating the band's music, and he set up the Internet Underground Music Archive or IUMA for short (www.iuma.com). This was a year before the Yahoo! directory was launched. IUMA started a new self-help philosophy among new artists. The deal was that listeners could download new music for free, and bands could find an audience, without having to toady to major record labels or radio stations. And, in some cases, without having to be distinctive enough to grab their attention. Over the next few years, many more websites will launch with the same idea, to the extent that the web is soon awash with free music, raising the problem of how to compete without any income. And how will listeners know where to find you? Centralized sites like Peoplesound, Vitaminic, and MP3.com will sell ad space to support the bands they feature, and pay artists depending on how popular their

## SEPTEMBER

- **SEPTEMBER 8TH: TUPAC SHAKUR is shot several times while driving through Las Vegas, Nevada, having just been to watch a Mike Tyson boxing match. Despite being critically injured, he survives in hospital for six days before dying from his injuries. Though Tupac always moved in violent circles, his work has a deeper dimension than his adoption of the phrase 'Thug Life' would initially suggest. 'Thug Life,' he'd explain, stands for 'The Hurt U Give Little Infants F****s Everyone.' His life and music will be the subject of much frenetic interest and discussion, intensified as always by his pointless early death. Needless to say, record sales go through the roof – he'll have more success after his demise than before, particularly in the UK. In coming years, some colleges and universities (including Washington and Harvard) will even offer classes or symposiums on Tupac. His legend and legacy looms large in hip-hop, and the music world in general.**

- **SEPTEMBER 14TH: THE ALBUM *NO CODE* by Pearl Jam enters the US chart at Number One. It's the third chart-topper in a row for the Seattle grunge stars, whose angry, thought-provoking words and wicked riffs have stood them in good stead, despite making powerful enemies (including the press, MTV, and Ticketmaster).**

- **11TH: DAVID BOWIE** becomes the first major artists to release a single ('Telling Lies') that is only available on the Internet.
- **12TH: IT'S REPORTED** that, after 22 years of marriage, Tom Petty's wife Jane has filed for separation, citing irreconcilable differences.
- **14TH: UNDER THE BANNER** of Lilith Fair, Sarah McLachlan organises a concert in Vancouver, British Columbia, Canada, which also features Paula Cole, Lisa Loeb, and Michelle McAdorey. The event will go on to grow into a massively successful annual all-women tour.
- **21ST: JOHN GILLIS** and Megan White, later to find fame as The White Stripes, are married in the county of Oakland, Michigan. They will divorce iin less than three years' time. And throughout, bizarrely, they claim to be brother and sister.
- **24TH: THE WORLD'S MAJOR POWERS** sign a treaty to end all testing and development of nuclear weapons.
- **26TH: SHANNON LUCID** returns to Earth after being in space for 188 days, setting a new record for a US astronaut, and for a woman of any nationality.
- **27TH: THE TALIBAN** seize control of Kabul, the capital of Afghanistan, and kill the former president Najibullah and his brother, publicly hanging their bodies from lamp-posts. Strict Islamic dress becomes become compulsory, including beards for men, while women are obliged to stay indoors.

## OCTOBER

- **7TH: OASIS BEGIN** recording their third album, which will become *Be Here Now*, at EMI's Abbey Road Studios, London.
- **14TH: MADONNA GIVES BIRTH** to a baby girl, Lourdes, at the Good Samaritan Hospital, LA.
- **15TH: TOMMY LEE** is charged with attacking a cameraman who was trying to take pictures of him with his wife Pamela Anderson Lee.
- **19TH: NEIL YOUNG'S** annual Bridge School Benefit Concert is held at the Shoreline Amphitheater, Mountain View, California. Artists performing include David Bowie, Pearl Jam, Neil Young with Crazy Horse, Patti Smith, Cowboy Junkies, and Hayden.
- **23RD: THE CIVIL TRIAL** of O.J. Simpson opens in California.
- **26TH: BABYFACE** has his first hit in over a year with the old Shalamar song 'This Is For The Lover In You,' on which he's backed by the original Shalamar trio plus L.L. Cool J.
- **27TH: R.E.M. TELLS** Warner Bros that Bill Berry has decided to leave the group.
- **29TH: AN AUCTION** is held to sell artwork stolen by the Nazis during the German occupation of Austria during World War II.

- **OCTOBER 5TH: THE ALBUM *FALLING INTO YOU*** by Celine Dion reaches Number One in the US.

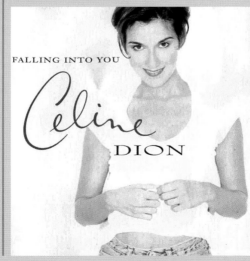

downloads or CD sales are. It soon becomes a serious business in itself: by July 2000, the top earner on MP3.com will be paid $20,000 from a total pot of $1 million shared out among the most popular acts. Like other emerging music sites, MP3.com (which is, perhaps inevitably, later taken over by a multinational music company) will also offer a CD-pressing facility, so it becomes a one-stop shop. CDBaby.com will start doing the same in 1998, and within five years it can claim to be the biggest seller of independent CDs after Amazon.com. They Might Be Giants (above) were one of the first established acts to use the web to communicate with fans, often giving away free goodies as well as selling stuff. In 1999 they will sell 30,000 copies of the Internet-only album 'Long Tall Weekend.' This idea spreads, until even mainstream acts on major labels are using the web for promotional opportunities, offering exclusive content online, but perhaps only to those buying a CD first. Inevitably, the big boys muscle in, but the spirit of free music on the web doesn't die, and will continue to haunt the music establishment.

## Bigmouth Strikes Again

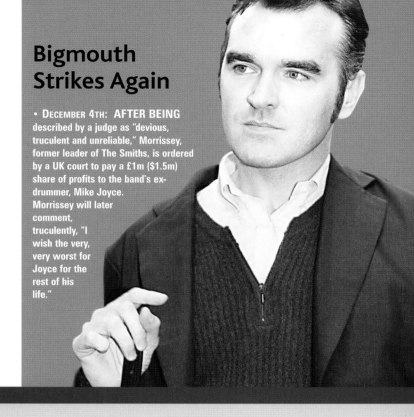

• **DECEMBER 4TH: AFTER BEING** described by a judge as "devious, truculent and unreliable," Morrissey, former leader of The Smiths, is ordered by a UK court to pay a £1m ($1.5m) share of profits to the band's ex-drummer, Mike Joyce. Morrissey will later comment, truculently, "I wish the very, very worst for Joyce for the rest of his life."

## NOVEMBER

• **4TH: MELISSA ETHERIDGE** and her partner Julie Cypher appear on the cover of *Newsweek* magazine, accompanying an article on gay parents.
• **5TH: DEMOCRAT BILL CLINTON** is re-elected US President, defeating Republican Bob Dole.
• **9TH: 'NO DIGGITY'** by Blackstreet featuring Dr Dre reaches Number One on the US Top 40 chart.
• **9TH: JOURNEY'S** first new album in ten years, *Trial By Fire*, enters the US album chart at Number Three in its week of release.
• **11TH: THE VIETNAM VETERANS MEMORIAL FUND** unveils The Wall That Heals, a half-scale replica of the Vietnam Veterans Memorial in Washington, which will tour communities throughout the US.
• **12TH: A WEEK BEFORE** the launch of the first EMI-distributed album by The Artist (better known as Prince), the 3-CD set *Emancipation*, the label flies journalists from all over the world to Minneapolis for a gala party at Paisley Park. Prince and his band, surprisingly, perform a set for MTV with backing tapes.
• **14TH: MICHAEL JACKSON** marries a nurse, Debbie Rowe (who allegedly works for his plastic surgeon), in Sydney, Australia. A few days earlier he announced that he and Debbie are expecting a child, but denied they've used artificial insemination or that Rowe has been paid to carry the baby.
• **23RD: A HIJACKED ETHIOPIAN** passenger jet crashes into the Indian Ocean just 500 metres from land, after running out of fuel. More than 100 people are killed.
• **24TH: NEIL FINN** quits Crowded House after a farewell gig at Sydney Opera House, Australia, attended by over 200,000 fans.
• **27TH: IN A TELEVISED** blind taste test, country legend Kenny Rogers chooses NBC-TV's cafeteria chicken over that provided in his own Kenny Rogers' Roasters restaurant chain.
• **29TH: BOSNIAN SERB** army soldier Drazen Erdemovic is sentenced by a UN court to ten years in prison for his role in the massacre of 1,200 Muslims – the first international war crimes sentence since WWII.
• **30TH: TINY TIM**, the eccentric ukulele-playing entertainer, dies at the age of 71.

## DECEMBER

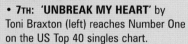

• **4TH: THE SEVENTH ANNUAL BILLBOARD MUSIC AWARDS** are held at the Aladdin Hotel Theatre, Las Vegas, Nevada, with major awards as follows: Artist Of The Year, Alanis Morissette; Album Of The Year, Jagged Little Pill, Alanis Morissette; Single Of The Year, 'Macarena', Los Del Rio; R&B Artist Of The Year, R. Kelly.
• **5TH: THE WALL STREET JOURNAL** reports that, in a ground-breaking move for a rock artist, David Bowie is planning to sell his own $50 million asset-backed bond issue within the next few months.
• **7TH: 'UNBREAK MY HEART'** by Toni Braxton (left) reaches Number One on the US Top 40 singles chart.
• **9TH:** UN Secretary General Boutros-Ghali approves a deal allowing Iraq to resume its exports of oil and easing the UN trade embargo imposed in 1990.
• **10TH: COUNTRY & WESTERN** singer Faron 'Young Sheriff' Young, who shot himself yesterday, dies at age 64.
• **16TH: BRITAIN'S** agriculture minister announces the slaughter of an additional 100,000 cows thought to be at risk of contracting BSE, in an effort to persuade the EU to lift its ban on British beef exports.
• **17TH: THE TUPAC AMARU** guerilla group (the rapper was named after them, not the other way around) take 5000 hostages in the Japanese Embassy in Lima, Peru... Meanwhile Nine Inch Nails' Trent Reznor is being sued for $1.1m by a security guard who was left feeling "sick, sore, lame and disturbed" after being crushed by the crowd at a 1994 New York City gig.

• **DECEMBER 7TH: FUN LOVING CRIMINALS** (below), The Presidents Of The USA, Silverchair, Orbital, Luscious Jackson, Stabbing Westward, and Eels play at the *Deck The Hall Ball*, sponsored by alternative music radio station KNDD in Seattle, Washington.

# 1997

## January–April

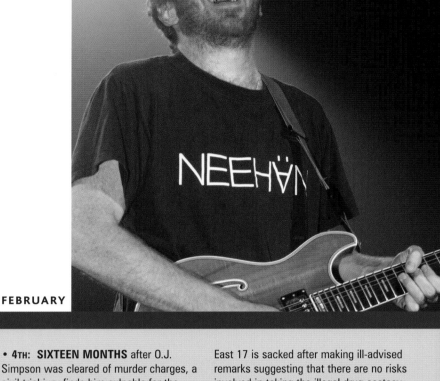

### Hello Hello Dolly

- **FEBRUARY 23RD: SCIENTISTS IN SCOTLAND, UK,** announce they have succeeded in cloning an adult sheep, producing a lamb named Dolly.

- **4TH: RANDY CALIFORNIA**, founding member of experimental West Coast rock band Spirit, disappears after being sucked into the surf off the coast of Molokai, Hawaii.
- **9TH: YACHTSMAN TONY BULLIMORE** is found alive, five days after his boat capsizes in the freezing Southern Ocean, 2,200km off the coast of Australia...

Meanwhile David Bowie stages his 50th birthday concert at Madison Square Garden, New York City, with guests including Foo Fighters, Billy Corgan of Smashing Pumpkins, Robert Smith of the Cure, Sonic Youth, and Lou Reed.
- **10TH: TOM PETTY** & The Heartbreakers begin a 20-night season at The Fillmore, San Francisco.
- **10TH: JAMES BROWN** is awarded a star on the Hollywood Walk Of Fame.
- **17TH: COMEDIAN AND ACTOR** Bill Cosby's only son is murdered while changing a flat tyre on his Mercedes convertible in the early hours of the morning. The body of Ennis William Cosby, age 27, is found near the Santa Monica Mountains, California.
- **20TH: BILL CLINTON** is inaugurated for his second term as President of

the United States.
- **21ST: COL TOM PARKER**, former manager of Elvis Presley, suffers a stroke and dies in Valley Hospital, Las Vegas, Nevada.
- **23RD: RICHARD BERRY**, composer of 'Louie Louie,' dies at home in Los Angeles... And a British woman receives a record £186,000 ($300,000) damages for RSI (Repetitive Strain Injury).

- **29TH: A UK PRESS FURORE** erupts when it's revealed that Noel Gallagher of Oasis has compared taking ecstasy to having a cup of tea. Interestingly, back in the mid 1960s, Oasis heroes The Beatles would apparently talk about "stopping for a cup of tea" as a euphemism for having a quick puff on a joint – though no doubt they enjoyed plenty of cups of tea as well.

- **4TH: SIXTEEN MONTHS** after O.J. Simpson was cleared of murder charges, a civil trial jury finds him culpable for the killings of his ex-wife and her friend and orders him to pay $8.5 million in compensation.
- **5TH: THREE OF SWITZERLAND'S** biggest banks create a 100 million Swiss franc ($71 million) Holocaust Memorial Fund after years of international pressure.
- **6TH: DIANE BLOOD**, 32, wins the right to use her dead husband's sperm to conceive a child in the UK.
- **9TH: THE SIMPSONS** becomes the longest-running prime-time animated series, overtaking *The Flintstones* which had previously held the record.
- **11TH: IT'S REPORTED** that The Fugees are working with Internet company Mediadome to release a computer game based on their hit song 'Ready Or Not.'
- **13TH: TO ANNOUNCE DETAILS** of their upcoming PopMart concert tour, U2 holds a RealAudio press conference in a K-Mart in Manhattan, New York City.
- **18TH: BRIAN HARVEY** of UK boy-band

East 17 is sacked after making ill-advised remarks suggesting that there are no risks involved in taking the illegal drug ecstasy.
- **19TH: A NEW YORK JUDGE** dismisses a $7 million lawsuit filed against Mötley Crüe for the hearing loss apparently suffered by a fan at one of their concerts.
- **20TH: 'WANNABE'** by The Spice Girls hits Number One on the US Top 40 chart.
- **24TH: AT THE BRIT AWARDS** in London, the major award winners are Gabrielle for Best Female, George Michael for Best Male, and Manic Street Preachers for Best Group. But Geri Halliwell of The Spice Girls steals the limelight by appearing in that skimpy mindress made from the British Union Jack flag.
- **26TH: THE 39TH ANNUAL GRAMMY AWARDS** are held in Madison Square Garden, New York City. Album Of The Year is *Falling Into You* by Celine Dion; Record Of The Year is *Change the World* by Eric Clapton; Best Rock Album is *Sheryl Crow* by Sheryl Crow; Best R&B Album is *Words* by The Tony Rich Project; Best Rap Album is *The Score* by The Fugees.

- **MARCH 9TH: RAPPER NOTORIOUS B.I.G.**, aka Biggie Smalls, is shot dead by a drive-by gunman outside the Petersen Automotive Museum, Los Angeles.

## Phish Scoop

**F**EBRUARY 20TH: BEN & JERRY'S ice cream company introduces a new flavour to its range, entitled Phish Food. It's named after the US rock group Phish. Led by guitarist/vocalist Trey Anastasio (in action, far left), Phish have been building up a huge grassroots fan base in the States (though their allure seems limited elsewhere) since the early 1980s, and have acquired the tag of "the new Grateful Dead" – not just for their love of extended instrumental workouts, but also their dogged avoidance of playing the music industry game. They don't rely on image and hit singles, but instead keep a network of fanatical followers happy with their musically eclectic, and very comprehensive live shows, backed up by a regular newsletter, and more recently a website, which has quickly become one of America's most popular band sites. Having said that, they are on a major label, Elektra, and have just enjoyed their first taste of the Top Ten with their album *Billy Breathes*. They're even in the process of releasing a rare single, called 'Free,' which fails to chart – not that they or their fans really care. Why should they, when they can sell out Madison Square Garden in just a few a hours?

## Share Mary

• **APRIL 27TH: MARY J. BLIGE** tops the US album chart with *Share My World*.

### MARCH

• **2ND: GARBAGE** start work on recording their second album.
• **4TH: U2 RELEASE** their new album, *Pop*, in the US.
• **5TH: NORTH KOREA** and South Korea meet for first time in 25 years for peace talks.
• **11TH: FOR HIS SERVICES** to popular music, Paul McCartney is knighted by Her Majesty the Queen, Elizabeth II, once described by Paul in song as "a pretty nice girl" at Buckingham Palace, London. The Queen has also just launched the first official royal website (royal.gov.uk).
• **18TH: JONI MITCHELL** announces she has reunited with Kilauren Gibb, the daughter she gave up for adoption many years earlier.

• **20TH: 'CAN'T NOBODY HOLD ME DOWN'** by Puff Daddy featuring Mase, reaches Number One on the US Top 40 singles chart... Meanwhile the maker of Chesterfield cigarettes settles 22 state lawsuits by admitting the industry has marketed cigarettes to teenagers.
• **21ST: PHIL SPECTOR** wins a UK High Court action to regain the British copyright of his 1958 hit 'To Know Him Is To Love Him' (a song he's said to have written about his father), which was assigned to publishers Bourne Music almost 40 years earlier.
• **27TH: THE BODIES** of 39 members of the Heaven's Gate cult are found after a mass suicide – they apparently hoped to be joining aliens following the Hale Bopp comet.

### APRIL

• **APRIL 7TH: LIAM GALLAGHER** of Oasis marries actress Patsy Kensit. Patsy already has a son by Jim Kerr of Simple Minds, though the couple will have their own son in 1999, who'll be called Lennon.

## Flycatcher

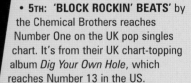

• **MARCH 1ST: THE PRODIGY**, propelled by studio wizard Liam Howlett and fronted by manic dancer/vocalist Keith Flint (seen left, at his most rabid), have their biggest US hit when 'Firestarter,' a former UK Number One, enters the US Top 40, where it peaks at Number 30.

• **5TH: 'BLOCK ROCKIN' BEATS'** by the Chemical Brothers reaches Number One on the UK pop singles chart. It's from their UK chart-topping album *Dig Your Own Hole*, which reaches Number 13 in the US.
• **8TH: MAE BOREN AXTON**, who found her greatest fame as co-author (with her son, Hoyt Axton) of the Elvis Presley hit 'Heartbreak Hotel,' dies at home in Henderson, Tennessee.
• **10TH: A MARILYN MANSON SHOW** in Columbia, South Carolina, is cancelled because State Treasurer Richard Eckstrom is alarmed by reports of Manson's "satanism."
• **12TH: THE UK'S CONSERVATIVE PARTY** asks national broadcasting service the BBC to ban the song 'Things Can Only Get Better' by D:Ream, because it is being used as the campaign song of their opposition, the Labour Party.
• **21ST: THE ASHES** of 1960s LSD guru Timothy Leary and Star Trek creator Gene Roddenberry are blasted into space in the Earth's first space funeral... Meanwhile at the World Music Awards Celine Dion collects trophies as Best Selling Canadian Artist, World's Best Selling Pop Artist, and World's Best Selling Overall Artist.
• **25TH: THE US SENATE** ratifies the global treaty banning the development, production, storage and use of chemical weapons.

## Big In Japan – Part Two

**W**HEN WE LAST LOOKED at the Japanese music scene, back in the mid 1960s, Group Sounds (GS) was the dominant style. By the early 1970s, bands like Led Zeppelin had influenced 'new rock,' and the Japanese pop world became swamped with 'aidoru' (idol) artists: young, pretty and mainly female. These included the legendary Pink Lady, a girl duo who even had a Top 40 hit and a short TV series in the US in 1980, and later reform in 2003. There were also novelty pop acts like Checkers, who wore checked suits, and have been described as a "camp Bay City Rollers." More musically adventurous were pioneering ambient-house-techno-poppers Yellow Magic Orchestra, a band who remain a seminal influence on contemporary electronica today. Band member Ryuichi Sakamoto (right) went on to become probably the best known Japanese musician in the world, and starred in the movie *Merry Christmas, Mr Lawrence* alongside David Bowie. Since the late 1980s the Japanese charts

## MAY

- **3RD: THE CARDIGANS' 'LOVEFOOL'** has been reissued on the strength of its use in the Baz Luhrmann movie *Romeo + Juliet*. It will peak at Number Two on the UK singles chart and the same position on the US airplay chart – it stays in circulation in the States for nine months.
- **3RD: A GROUP INTENT** on gaining the independence of Texas from the US, known as The Republic Of Texas, surrenders to the authorities, ending an armed stand-off in which two people have been held hostage.
- **4TH: THE LABOUR PARTY** wins a landslide victory in the UK general election ending 18 years of Conservative government. Tony Blair will be the new prime minister.
- **6TH: AT THE 12TH** Annual Rock & Roll Hall Of Fame Induction Ceremony in Cleveland, Ohio, inductees include The Bee Gees, Buffalo Springfield, and Crosby, Stills, & Nash. But Neil Young ducks out of the ceremony, declaring it to have, "nothing to do with the spirit of rock'n'roll and everything to do with making money." Elsewhere, four health-care companies agree a settlement of $600 million in payments to haemophilia sufferers who contracted AIDS from infected blood between 1978-1985.
- **17TH: MADONNA** calls UK record producer/recording artist William Orbit to ask if he would like to work on her forthcoming album. As yet un-named, the album will eventually be released as *Ray Of Light*.
- **22ND: 'MMM-BOP'** by Hanson reaches Number One on the US Top 40 singles chart.
- **25TH: BOB DYLAN** is admitted to St John's Hospital, Santa Monica, California, suffering from the potentially fatal heart condition pericarditis, which impairs breathing. He leaves five days later.
- **29TH: JEFF BUCKLEY** drowns in the Mississippi while in Memphis, Tennessee, to record his second album. He had taken an impromptu midnight swim, fully clothed, only to be sucked under by the wash from a passing barge. He was 30 years old. His body was washed up a week later.
- **31ST: NEIL YOUNG** is obliged to cancel European tour dates, having accidentally sliced a finger open while cutting a sandwich in half during a break in rehearsals.

## JUNE

- **JUNE 7-8TH: *THE TIBETAN FREEDOM CONCERT*** takes place at Downing Stadium, Randall's Island, New York. Performers include Foo Fighters, A Tribe Called Quest, Ben Harper, Patti Smith, Porno For Pyros (playing an acoustic set), Noel Gallagher of Oasis, Radiohead, Sonic Youth, Beastie Boys, Blur, Bjork, De La Soul, Lee 'Scratch' Perry (above) with the Mad Professor & The Robotiks Band, R.E.M.'s Michael Stipe & Mike Mills, Pavement, and Taj Mahal. Special guest is Alanis Morissette.

## Life After Death

- **JUNE 12TH: 'I'LL BE MISSING YOU'** by Puff Daddy & Faith Evans, based around The Police's hit 'Every Breath You Take,' and released as a homage to the late Notorious BIG, reaches Number One on the US Top 40 singles chart (and in the UK two weeks later). BIG was a good friend of Sean 'Puffy' Combs, as the rapper movingly makes clear.

- **4TH: FORMER SMALL FACES** songwriter and bass player Ronnie Lane dies at 51, after a long struggle with multiple sclerosis.
- **6TH: UK POP STAR** Robbie Williams enters a rehabilitation clinic to deal with his drug and drink problems.
- **13TH: TIMOTHY MCVEIGH**, recently convicted of the 1995 bombing of a federal building in Oklahoma City, is sentenced to death by a court in Denver, Colorado.
- **19TH: FAST FOOD CHAIN** McDonalds wins a partial victory in its libel trial against two environmental campaigners, Helen Steel and Dave Morris. The longest trial in English legal history ends with judge Justice Bell agreeing that some of the claims made by the duo were unjustified. But McDonalds' victory is widely regarded by commentators as a public relations disaster, costing the company more than $10 million. Steel and Morris represented themselves in court.

- **20TH: LAWRENCE PAYTON**, a founding member of The Four Tops, dies of liver cancer at his Detroit, Michigan, home... Meanwhile William Hague celebrates becoming the youngest leader of Britain's Conservative party in nearly 200 years.
- **30TH: HONG KONG** reverts to Chinese sovereignty after the UK's lease expires, ending more than 50 years of British control.

have been dominated by 'J-pop,' music created, in the main, by impresarios like producer Komuro Tetsuya, one of the richest men in Japan, and the brains behind artists like trf, Amuro Namie, and Kahala Tomomi. Other big names in J-pop at the end of the century include boy-band SMAP, Ayumi Hamasaki, Every Little Thing, and the band with the oddly Japanese-English name, Do As Infinity. And of course there are the usual 'big in Japan' western acts – often female-fronted outfits like The Cardigans (left). Outside of mainstream J-pop, there are interesting homegrown acts like hip-hop rappers Dragon Ash, Thee Michelle Gun Elephant (TMGE), Buffalo Daughter, Seagull Screaming Kiss Her Kiss Her, and The Boom Boom Satellites – following in the 'alternative' footsteps of Shonen Knife, Pizzicato Five, and Cibo Matto, who've taken Western influences, given them a Japanese twist, and re-exported them to the West.

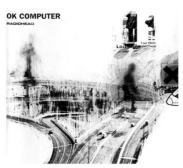

## No Surprises?

**JUNE 16TH: RADIOHEAD** surprise everyone with their 'difficult' third album, *OK Computer*. Two years in the making, it's difficult for listeners too. Sombre and meticulously crafted, there's little in the way of easy pop – but they still get three UK hit singles from it: 'Paranoid Android,' 'Karma Police,' and 'No Surprises.'

## JULY

• **JULY 5TH: THE FIRST *LILITH FAIR*,** organised by singer Sarah McLachlan to celebrate women in music, kicks off at The Gorge, George, Washington State. The first act on-stage is Suzanne Vega, and others include Tracy Chapman, Joan Osborne, Sheryl Crow, Shawn Colvin, Jewel, Paula Cole, Fiona Apple, Mary Chapin Carpenter, Indigo Girls, The Cardigans, and Emmylou Harris (left).

• **3RD: PRESIDENT CLINTON** makes his first formal response to accusations of sexual harassment by Paula Jones. He denies all the charges and asks that the judge dismiss the case.

• **4TH: THE US. PATHFINDER** probe lands on Mars. A roving vehicle named Sojourner is deployed several days later to gather data about the surface of the planet... Meanwhile, back where the action is, the travelling alternative rock tour Lollapalooza arrives at Kingswood Amphitheatre, Toronto, Ontario, Canada. Acts featured on this year's trek include The Marley Brothers, Jes, Tricky, Korn, Snoop Doggy Dogg, Tool, and Orbital. Orbital (right) are not exactly rockers, more ravers, but they are certainly alternative.

• **6TH: SQUEAKY-CLEAN** 1950s pop crooner Pat Boone, clad in a stars & stripes suit, drives a Honda moped down the aisle of the Church On The Way, Los Angeles, before leading the congregation in song. The incident is a dig at his former bosses on the *Gospel America* TV show who fired him after he adopted a heavy metal biker image.

• **8TH: ONE DAY** after being bailed on gun charges, Flesh-N-Bone of Bone Thugs-N-Harmony is re-arrested for threatening a neighbor.

• **9TH: MIKE TYSON** is banned from boxing for biting Evander Holyfield's ear.

• **10TH: SCIENTISTS IN LONDON** discover DNA from a Neanderthal skeleton which supports the theory that all humanity descended from a single woman, dubbed African Eve, between 100,000 and 200,000 years ago.

• **13TH: FOLLOWING A MOTOR BIKE ACCIDENT**, Anthony Kiedis of The Red Hot Chili Peppers undergoes five hours of surgery at Cedars Mount Sinai Medical Center, Los Angeles... Meanwhile the body of Che Guevara is returned to Cuba for burial.

• **15TH: ITALIAN FASHION DESIGNER** Gianni Versace, tailor to the stars, is shot dead outside his Miami beach mansion by Andrew Cunanan. Cunanan himself is found dead eight days later.

• **30TH: UK PRIME MINISTER** Tony Blair hosts a private party at Number 10 Downing Street, London, to celebrate the success of the UK music industry, with guests including Oasis and the Pet Shop Boys.

• **31ST: POLICE IN NEW YORK CITY** intercept five bombs believed to be intended for use in terrorist attacks on city subways.

## AUGUST

• **2ND: FELA KUTI** (right), a hugely influential musician and political activist in his homeland of Nigeria, Africa, dies at age 58. A multi-instrumentalist and bandleader, pioneer of Afro-beat and a new African jazz, he finally succumbs to AIDS. It's said hundreds of thousands of people attend his funeral.

• **3RD: LAURYN HILL** of The Fugees gives birth to a six-pound, nine-ounce baby, Zion David, in New York City.

• **6TH: APPLE COMPUTERS** and Microsoft agree to share technology in a deal that gives Microsoft a stake in Apple's survival.

• **15TH: OVERTURNING AN INJUNCTION** by Creedence Clearwater Revival leader John Fogerty, a US court decides in favour of his former bandmates Doug Clifford and Stu Cook, allowing them to continue performing under the name Creedence Clearwater Revisited... Meanwhile Tony Nicole from Tony Records files suit against Gene Simmons and Paul Stanley of Kiss for alleged "intentional interference" with Kiss drummer Peter Criss's contract with the label.

• **16TH: ROD STEWART**, Jon Bon Jovi, Steve Winwood, kd lang, Seal, Mary J Blige, Robert Palmer, Toni Braxton, and Chaka Khan appear in the Songs And Visions concert at Wembley Stadium, London.

• **20TH: THE GOVERNOR OF ALABAMA** joins the mayors of Montgomery and Georgina to dedicate a 50-mile stretch of Interstate 65 to Hank Williams renaming it the Hank Williams Memorial Lost Highway.

• **21ST: IN THE LARGEST** food recall in US history, Hudson Foods Inc closes a plant in Nebraska, after recalling 25 million pounds of ground beef potentially contaminated with E coli bacteria.

• **22ND: THE ROLLING STONES** arrive at Pearson International Airport, Toronto, Canada, at the start of three weeks of rehearsals for their upcoming Bridges To Babylon tour.

• **25TH: A COURT IN BERLIN** sentences former East German leader, Egon Krenz, to six years in prison for the shoot-to-kill policy employed by border guards against people trying to flee East Germany

• **28TH: 'MO MONEY MO PROBLEMS'** by the late Notorious BIG. reaches Number One on the US Top 40 singles chart.

• **31ST: DIANA, PRINCESS OF WALES** is involved in a car wreck in a tunnel in Paris, France, where the princess's car hits a pillar while being pursued by photographers on motorbikes. She is taken to hospital in the early hours of Sunday morning but dies soon afterwards. Dodi Al Fayed, with whom she's been romantically linked, and the vehicle's driver are also killed. The death affects the music industry in many ways. Michael Jackson, Wet Wet Wet, and many other artists cancel gigs as a mark of respect. Kylie Minogue decides to change the title of her upcoming album Impossible Princess, and, most famously, Elton John and Bernie Taupin re-write 'Candle In The Wind' to make it refer to Diana.

## Wu-Tang Knock-Out

**O**CTOBER 2ND: **WU-TANG CLAN** members Rza, Method Man, and Redman, along with the University of Pennsylvania, are sued by Juanita Evans, who claims that, while watching their gig on the campus, she was distracted by Redman and so did not see Method Man when he leapt off-stage, accidentally knocking her out. The Wu-Tang Clan have just had their biggest hit yet, reaching Number One in the US and the UK with their second album *Wu-Tang Forever*. Fans of kung-fu films, martial arts in general – the name Wu-Tang is derived from a battle with swords practised by Shaolin monks – and the teachings of Islam, Wu-Tang Clan revolutionized hip hop in the early 1990s with their slowed-down hardcore beats, surreal minimalism, and menacing raps. (They also say they are keen chess players, insisting the game sharpens their warfare skills and killer instincts.) Forming around cousins Rza and Gza, who encouraged other like-minded performers to join up, including Ol' Dirty Bastard, Method Man, Raekwon the Chef, Ghostface Killah, U-God, Masta Killer, and Inspecta Deck (there are numerous other extended Wu-Family members, such as Redman), their single 'Protect Ya Neck' soon had labels lining up to sign them. Loud/Sony won, after agreeing that all Clan members would be able to make their own records. The group's debut *Enter the Wu-Tang: 36 Chambers* was an instant critical and commercial success, paving the way for five hit solo albums, plus clothing and comic merchandise. *Wu-Tang Forever*, a double CD, makes them global stars.

### SEPTEMBER

- **1ST: DIANA – THE AFTERMATH.** The French prosecutor's office announces that the driver of the car in which Princess Diana was killed was over the legal alcohol limit. On January 4th, at the annual MTV Awards in New York City (where No Doubt collect the Best Group Video trophy for their hit 'Don't Speak'), Madonna delivers a speech lamenting the death of Princess Diana.
- **5TH: MOTHER TERESA**, the Nobel Peace Prize winner who devoted half a century to helping the sick and the poor, dies at the age of 87. But her passing goes largely unnoticed, due to the continuing Diana coverage. Tomorrow, more than one million people will line the route of Diana's funeral procession in London, and almost 2.5 billion will watch on television.
- **9TH: WHEN THE US** financial magazine *Forbes* publishes its annual list of the richest entertainers, David Bowie appears in 16th place with $63 million gross income for the year 1996/97, much of it earned as a result of his innovative stock market share issue, the Bowie Bond... Meanwhile Sinn Fein, the IRA's political wing, formally renounces violence and take its place in talks on Northern Ireland's future. They're joined there shortly by Northern Ireland's main Unionist party – the first time all the major players meet around one table.
- **11TH: SCOTLAND VOTES** for its own parliament – though it won't be called that – after 290 years of union with England.
- **13TH: PRINCE TURNS UP** on *The Muppets Tonight*.
- **14TH: AN ENGLISH HERITAGE** plaque, marking the house where Jimi Hendrix once lived, is unveiled at 23 Brook Street, London.
- **19TH: CONTEMPORARY CHRISTIAN** singer-songwriter Rich Mullins dies in a car accident with fellow artist, Mitch McVicker. All memorial donations received are forwarded to Compassion International, a foundation that supports Native American ministries.
- **22ND: BBC TV** in the UK begins running an innovative self-promotional campaign based on the Lou reed song 'Perfect Day.' It features a superstar-studded line-up of artists, each singing just one or two lines from the song, including U2's Bono, Elton John, Tom Jones, Dr John, Robert Cray, David Bowie, Emmylou Harris, M People, The Lightning Seeds, and of course Lou Reed himself.
- **24TH: STUDENT BARRY LOUKAITIS** of Frontier Junior High, Moses Lake, Washington, is convicted of having shot dead two of his fellow students and one teacher. His lawyers had claimed that he committed the murders in emulation of the Pearl Jam video for the song 'Jeremy.'

- **SEPTEMBER 20TH: ELTON JOHN** reaches Number One on the UK singles chart with the re-written 'Candle In The Wind 1997,' which he performed at the memorial service for Diana, Princess Of Wales. The song does the same in the US in October, after massive pre-release orders. In fact, it will rapidly become become the world's biggest-selling single – including 11 million sales in the US alone, where it stays at the top of the charts for 14 weeks. Its global sales approach 30 million copies within a month.

### OCTOBER

- **OCTOBER 5TH: THE UK'S *EXPRESS ON SUNDAY MAGAZINE*** prints an article falsely alleging Tom Cruise and Nicole Kidman are gay and that their marriage is a sham. The magazine's owners will later pay damages estimated at £100,000 ($160,000) to each of them to settle their libel action. They also received a public apology in the High Court in London.

- **4TH: THE FUND-RAISING** event An Intimate Celebration is held at the MGM Grand Garden, Las Vegas, Nevada. Stars attending include Elton John, Celine Dion, Lionel Richie, Ray Romano, Clint Black, Jay Leno, and David Foster.
- **12TH: JOHN DENVER** dies at the age of 53 when the experimental airplane he's flying crashes into Monterey Bay, California... Meanwhile, a Backstreet Boys concert in Madrid, Spain, is cancelled by local police because too many fans have poured into the streets of the town in advance of the show.
- **15TH: PATRICIA RICHARDSON** sues Snoop Doggy Dogg and Death Row Records for allegedly tricking her into transporting marijuana to a venue.
- **19TH: GLEN BUXTON**, original guitarist for Alice Cooper, dies of illnesses exacerbated by years of multiple drug/alcohol abuses, which have caused his immune system to break down.
- **22ND: THE BEE GEES** walk out in the middle of *Clive Anderson – All Talk*, a UK TV show, when their famously rude host makes some unflattering observations.
- **27TH: BILL BERRY**, drummer and co-writer with R.E.M., leaves the group. He says he's "kind of ready to not be a pop star any more."
- **31ST: A BOSTON JURY** finds British au pair Louise Woodward, age 19, guilty of second-degree murder of eight-month-old Matthew Eappen who died in her care. Woodward will later have her conviction reduced to manslaughter and is freed from jail after serving 279 days.

• **DECEMBER 2ND:** **A PHILADELPHIA RECORD STORE** files a class-action lawsuit against the six major US record distributors, claiming that Sony, Warners, Universal, EMI, Bertelsmann Music Group (BMG), and Polygram have conspired, "to raise, fix, and maintain at artificially high and non-competitive levels the wholesale prices" of CDs. The record industry has always been extremely competitive, with large sums of money to be won or lost, so aggressive business practises have been common, from payola onwards. But now it's easy for the more paranoid among the smaller players to feel they're being gradually squeezed by the multi-nationals – never a comfortable feeling. In fact, by the end of the 1990s, roughly 80 per cent of all the music we hear and buy will be owned by just five huge companies: Time Warner, Sony, Vivendi/Universal, BMG, and EMI (with talk of this becoming four, if EMI joins Time Warner, who will already have share links with Vivendi). Even labels that listeners assume to be 'independent' are often owned, and almost always distributed, by major record companies: they include Sub Pop, Sire, Maverick (all Warners); Def Jam, Death Row (Vivendi/Universal), Silvertone, LaFace (BMG). And older label names like Philips, A&M, Island, and Motown, have simply been subsumed into larger conglomerates. The fear is that these majors now have unrivaled power to force retailers, and even artists, to do things their way, under pain of being left out of the money-spinning loop.

## NOVEMBER

• **5TH:** **IN A MOVE** widely seen as signalling the end of their golden period, The Spice Girls sack their manager Simon Fuller.

• **6TH:** **PAUL RICARD**, France's King of Pastis and one of the country's richest and most influential men, dies at the age of 88. His Pastis de Marseilles is sold in 150 countries and is the world's third favorite alcoholic drink.

• **8TH:** **CHINESE ENGINEERS** divert the Yangtze River to make way for building work on the Three Gorges Dam.

• **12TH:** **THE BAND** advertised as the Honking Seals and appearing tonight at The Catalyst, Santa Cruz, California, are actually Pearl Jam.

• **13TH:** **IRAQ EXPELS** six UN arms inspectors after yesterday's UN Security Council imposed sanctions due to constraints being placed on inspectors.

• **14TH:** **THE BEE GEES** play their first One Night Only concert at the MGM Grand Hotel, Las Vegas, Nevada. The show, including a duet with Celine Dion, is filmed for international TV broadcast.

• **21ST:** **COOLIO** and members of his band are arrested and charged with theft and assault in Boblingen, Germany. All eight are charged with assaulting a female clerk in a clothing store and stealing goods worth $2,000.

• **23RD:** **DURING PUFF DADDY'S** No Way Out Tour, the tour bus transporting rapper Jay-Z is destroyed by fire near Dayton, Ohio. Jay-Z is unhurt, but unable to make the next tour date in Richmond, Virginia. A few days later Jay-Z pulls out of the tour, after a show at Madison Square Garden, New York City, claiming he has been treated unfairly by the tour's promoters, and saying he now intends to concentrate on running his own record label, Roc-A-Fella, in partnership with Damon Dash.

• **NOVEMBER 1ST:** **'BARBIE GIRL' BY AQUA**, pumped-up Scandinavian Euro-popsters, reaches Number One on the UK pop singles chart, their first of three chart-toppers in a row there. The track reaches Number Seven in the US.

## DECEMBER

• **3RD:** **JOHN FOGERTY**, former leader of Creedence Clearwater Revival, receives the Lifetime Achievement Award from the National Academy Of Songwriters, in Los Angeles... Meanwhile, more than 120 countries are present in Ottawa, Canada to sign a treaty prohibiting the use and production of anti-personnel land mines. The United States, China and Russia refuse to sign.

• **9TH:** **THE RIAA IN AMERICA** certifies that the Celine Dion album *Falling Into You* has sold over ten million copies.

• **11TH:** **SINN FEIN LEADER** Gerry Adams becomes the first political member of the IRA to meet a British leader in 76 years, when he visits Prime Minister Tony Blair in London... Elsewhere more than 150 countries, meeting in Kyoto, Japan, agree to control the Earth's greenhouse gases.

• **13TH:** **'TELETUBBIES SAY EH-OH'** by The Teletubbies reaches Number One on the UK pop singles chart. When the *Teletubbies* children's show is launched in the US early next year, some right-wing Christian groups will condemn the purple-colored Tinky Winky character because he carries a handbag, therefore promoting a gay lifestyle to toddlers. A BBC spokesperson says: "Tinky Winky is simply a sweet, technological baby with a magic bag."

• **17TH:** **IN THE SPACE** of one day, Garth Brooks makes coast-to-coast promotional appearances in four cities in Canada, flying by jet from Montreal to Toronto, Calgary, and Vancouver.

• **18TH:** **PUBLICIST KEN PHILLIPS** acknowledges that Red Hot Chili Peppers' guitarist Dave Navarro is back on hard drugs.

• **31ST:** **THE KENNEDY FAMILY** suffer yet another tragedy when Michael Kennedy, 39-year-old son of the late US senator Robert, is killed in an accident while skiing on Aspen Mountain in Colorado.

• **NOVEMBER 22ND:** **AT 11.50AM, INXS** singer Michael Hutchence is found dead, hanging by a leather belt from the back of his hotel room door in the Ritz Carlton, Sydney, Australia. The coroner later concludes he took his own life after consuming drugs and alcohol. Although friends insist he wasn't suicidal, he's known to have been under stress from media coverage of his relationship with Paula Yates, ex-wife of Bob Geldof.

# 1998

## INDEPENDENT WOMEN

Just as TLC dominated the urban soul scene in the US in the 1990s, so Destiny's Child, with sales of around 40 million albums, will be one of the top-selling acts of the new century. Formed in 1990 in Houston, Texas, as a pre-teen singing/rapping group, Destiny's Child started with Beyoncé Knowles (seen here second from the right) and her cousin Kelly Rowland (second left), both of whom had sung together since they were small children. They were joined originally by LaTavia Roberson and then, from 1993, by LeToya Luckett. Managed by Beyoncé's father (her mother was in charge of the fashions), the group appeared on TV show *StarSearch*, before contriving to get some high-profile opening slots for acts such as SWV. Signing to Columbia, they made their recording breakthrough on the *Men In Black* soundtrack, but in 1997 their own debut album, *Destiny's Child*, with its R&B grooves and soulful vocals, starts selling by the truckload – the eight years of work and waiting have finally paid off. Helped by guest appearances and production from the likes of The Fugees' Wyclef Jean, the album also provides them with their initial hit single, 'No, No, No (Part 2),' which they'll follow up in 1999 with their first Number One, 'Bills, Bills, Bills.' Then comes the second multi-million-selling album, *The Writing's On The Wall*. Despite the acclaim, or perhaps because of it, there will be the usual 'creative differences,' which lead to LeToya and LaTavia leaving the group early in 2000 (there will later be an out-of-court settlement in their favor). Beyoncé and Kelly will then settle into a trio with new member Michelle Williams and, if anything, the group's success escalates, particularly abroad. With their 2000 hit 'Independent Women (Part I),' they'll become the first American all-female group ever to debut at Number One on the UK charts – and the first to get to the top there since The Bangles in 1989. And by the time of 2001's *Survivor*, the fastest-selling record ever on Columbia, the group will be everywhere – together and solo – from working on movies to picking up so many awards and platinum discs they could fill a house with them. You just can't escape Destiny's Child.

# 1998

## January–April

### Bitter Sweet Tales

FEBRUARY 9TH: AT THE *BRIT AWARDS* this evening in the London Arena, Chumbawamba vocalist Danbert Nobacon empties a bucket of water over the UK's Deputy Prime Ministerm John Prescott. Meanwhile, on-stage, All Saints collect two awards each, and Robbie Williams duets with Tom Jones. The Verve (right) also pick up two *BRITS*: the band

## JANUARY

- **1ST: A NEW ANTI-SMOKING LAW**, prohibiting people from lighting up in bars, comes into effect in California.
- **2ND: RUSSIA RELEASES** new roubles in effort to keep inflation in check.
- **3RD: SWEDISH POLICE** arrest a total of 314 people following a neo-Nazi concert near Stockholm by US group Max Resist.
- **5TH: SONNY BONO**, of Sonny & Cher fame, dies in a skiing accident at South Lake Tahoe's Heavenly Ski Resort after colliding with a tree on an intermediate slope.
- **7TH: MONICA LEWINSKY**, a former White House intern, signs an affidavit denying that she had an affair with President Clinton... Meanwhile, the Rock & Roll Hall of Fame inducts Santana, The Eagles, Fleetwood Mac, The Mamas & The Papas, Jelly Roll Morton, Allen Toussaint, Gene Vincent, and Lloyd Price, in a ceremony at New York's Waldorf-Astoria.
- **8TH: SCIENTISTS ANNOUNCE** their discovery that the galaxies are accelerating and moving apart at ever faster speeds.
- **22ND: WHEN R&B DIVA** Toni Braxton files for bankruptcy, her record label claims the move is simply a ploy to secure herself a more favourable contract.
- **26TH: PRESIDENT CLINTON** tells reporters, "I did not have sexual relations with that woman, Miss Lewinsky."... Later tonight, The Spice Girls dominate the American Music Awards, winning Favorite Band, Favorite Album, and Favorite New Artist (Pop/Rock) awards.
- **29TH: PAUL SIMON'S** long-awaited musical, *The Capeman*, finally opens in New York City to very mixed reviews.

- **JANUARY 15TH: 'TRULY MADLY DEEPLY'** by Savage Garden reaches Number One on the US Top 40 singles chart. Meanwhile, James Brown is admitted to a hospital for an addiction to painkillers.

are about to have their first US hit with the former UK Number Two, the appropriately-titled 'Bitter Sweet Symphony.' Despite the record's success, The Verve will not see a penny of its royalty income, because they've used a sample from an Andrew Loog Oldham Orchestra recording of the Rolling Stones track 'The Last Time.' They'd actually cleared the sample with Oldham himself, but not with the owner of the song's copyright, fearsome lawyer Allan Klein, who later demands that 100 per cent of the copyright be forfeited. The group eventually makes something from the track by licensing it for use in a Nike commercial. The follow-up, 'The Drugs Don't Work,' earns Richard Ashcroft and the band a UK (but not US) Number One.

## FEBRUARY

- **5TH: TIM KELLY** of Slaughter dies in a car accident in Arizona, at just 34.
- **6TH: BEACH BOYS** vocalist/guitarist Carl Wilson dies of lung cancer, at age 51. The middle Wilson brother, Dennis, drowned in 1993. Carl's death leaves Brian Wilson the last surviving brother, and he is no longer a Beach Boy.
- **17TH: DESTINY'S CHILD** release their debut album, *Destiny's Child*, in the US.
- **24TH: MÖTLEY CRÜE** drummer Tommy Lee is arrested for abuse of his wife, *Baywatch* star Pamela Anderson, and their children... Meanwhile Larry Flynt, publisher of porn magazine *Hustler* is acquitted of defaming the character of Jerry Falwell. He's been supported by various media groups, afraid the case would set a precedent limiting freedom of the press.
- **25TH: AT THE 40TH ANNUAL GRAMMY AWARDS**, Bob Dylan takes Best Album honors for *Time Out Of Mind*, while Shawn Colvin wins Song and Record Of The Year for 'Sunny Came Home.'
- **27TH: VINCE NEIL** of Mötley Crüe announces an agreement with the Internet Entertainment Group and Vivid Video to distribute an hour-long home video of him having sex with two models in Hawaii.

- **FEBRUARY 14TH: *TITANIC*,** starring Kate Winslet and Leonardo Di Caprio, is also a colossal success for Celine Dion. Her theme song, 'My Heart Will Go On,' achieves a US record of 116 million plays in a single week.

## MARCH

- **MARCH 3RD: MADONNA** releases the album *Ray Of Light*, widely perceived as her artistic rebirth.

- **2ND: IMAGES** from the spacecraft Galileo reveal that Jupiter's moon Europa has a liquid ocean and a source of interior heat.
- **3RD: RAPPER C-BO** is arrested for parole violation, the violation being his use of lyrics that encouraged violence against the police.
- **6TH: ZEELAND HIGH SCHOOL**, Zeeland, Michigan, suspends a student, Eric VanHoven, for wearing a T-shirt bearing the name of the band Korn. The band then serves a writ on the school's assistant principal and the school district.
- **11TH: BUSINESSMAN** Carl Legault files a $2.8m lawsuit claiming Celine Dion has broken a deal with him to market lingerie bearing her name.
- **19TH: GODFATHER OF FUNK** James Brown is ordered to undertake a three month drug treatment programme by a South Carolina judge.
- **20TH: THE ROC-A-FELLA RECORDS** tour sets off from Studio 652, Buffalo, New York State, featuring Jay-Z, Noriega, Akinyele, Sauce Money, Memphis Bleek, Diamonds in Da Ruff, Christion and Rell and DJ Clue.
- **21ST: THE SPICE GIRLS**, latest single, 'Stop!', stalls at Number Two in the UK.
- **24TH: US BOY BAND 'N SYNC** release their self-titled debut album.
- **27TH: THE US AUTHORITIES** approve the drug Viagra, saying it helped two-thirds of impotent men.

## APRIL

- **1ST: A US FEDERAL JUDGE** dismisses the sexual harassment lawsuit brought by Paula Jones against President Clinton.
- **3RD: RECORD PRODUCER** Frank Farian finds 32-year-old Rob Pilatus – half of disgraced pop duo Milli Vanilli – dead from a drink/drugs overdose in a hotel room in Frankfurt, Germany.
- **4TH: THE LONGEST SUSPENSION BRIDGE** in the world, the Akashi Kaikyo Bridge in Japan, opens linking Shikoku and Honshu. The 3,910-meter (4,277 yard) bridge cost about $3.8 billion to build.
- **5TH: COZY (COLIN) POWELL**, a top UK rock drummer, dies in a car crash, age 50.

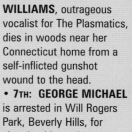

**And He Loved Her**

- **APRIL 17TH: LINDA McCARTNEY**, wife of ex-Beatle Paul, dies of breast cancer in Tucson, Arizona, at the age of 56.

- **6TH: WENDY O. WILLIAMS**, outrageous vocalist for The Plasmatics, dies in woods near her Connecticut home from a self-inflicted gunshot wound to the head.
- **7TH: GEORGE MICHAEL** is arrested in Will Rogers Park, Beverly Hills, for showing his penis to an undercover police officer in the restroom.
- **10TH: THE NORTHERN IRELAND** Good Friday Accord is reached. It creates three interconnected bodies of government: one within Northern Ireland, one between the north and rest of Ireland, and a third between the Irish Republic and United Kingdom.
- **11TH: THE TRIBUTE TO BURT BACHARACH** concert takes place at Hammerstein Ballroom,

- **APRIL 18TH: *LIFE THRU A LENS*** by Robbie Williams reaches Number One on the UK albums chart. It's the biggest solo hit so far for the former boy-band star, who's struck up a winning writing partnership with classically-trained muso Guy Chambers.

New York, featuring Dionne Warwick, Elvis Costello, All Saints, The Pretenders, Sheryl Crow, Wynona Judd, and others.
- **13TH: DOLLY**, the world's first cloned sheep, gives natural birth to a healthy baby lamb.
- **15TH: POL POT**, once-feared leader of the Khmer Rouge, dies at the age of 73, avoiding prosecution for the deaths of two million Cambodians.
- **29TH: SOUTH CAROLINA'S** Irmo High School cancels an Indigo Girls concert scheduled for May 7, following parental complaints about "the sexuality issue." The fact that singers Amy Ray and Emily Saliers are lesbians... Meanwhile, Brazil announces a plan to protect an area of Amazon forest the size of Colorado.

## Hill Top

- **AUGUST 25TH: LAURYN HILL** of The Fugees releases her first solo album, *The Miseducation Of Lauryn Hill*. It will debut at US Number One.

# Nu-metal Jackets

**J**UNE 8TH: *THE FAMILY VALUES TOUR* tour sets off from the War Memorial, Rochester, New York State. As well as the likes of Ice Cube, the tour includes some of the leading lights of the bougeoning nu-metal scene: Korn, Limp Bizkit, Rammstein, and Orgy. Taking a lead from rock innovators like Faith No More and Helmet, nu-metal burns brightly, if briefly, with acts like Limp Bizkit, Korn, Papa Roach, Linkin Park, Godsmack, POD, Staind, and The Deftones adding rap vocals, DJs, and samples to the guitar, bass & drum combo. In the process, they introduce the world to some very baggy shorts. Predictably, the initial impetus soon fragments, as anomalies like Slipknot, the indefinable Queens Of The Stone Age, and acts like Marilyn Manson (the antithesis of the jock-rock nu-metallers) begin to surface, all jostling together for slots on Ozzfest, the tour organised by Ozzy Osbourne, the granddaddy of metal.

**MAY**

**JUNE**

---

ribs and chest. The Stones have to reschedule several shows in the European leg of their Bridges To Babylon tour.
- **23RD:** *THE LIMITED SERIES* by Garth Brooks debuts on the US album chart at Number One... Meanwhile Protestants and Catholics in Northern Ireland vote to approve the new peace accord.
- **24TH: PHILADELPHIA MAYOR** Ed Rendell declares that May 24th will be Van Halen Day in Philadelphia.
- **31ST: 'GINGER SPICE'** Geri Halliwell announces she has split from the Spice Girls to pursue a solo career.

- **MAY 4TH: THE CORRS** achieve their first UK Top Ten singles chart hit with 'Dreams'.

- **5TH: MICHIGAN** introduces a bill that limits concert attendance by anyone under the age of 18.
- **7TH: STEVE PERRY**, vocalist with Journey, announces that he is quitting the band for health reasons.
- **11TH: INDIA UNDERTAKES** its first underground test of an atomic device, in direct violation of a global ban on nuclear testing... Meanwhile in Europe, a French mint produces the first of Europe's single-currency coins, known as the Euro.
- **14TH: GEORGE MICHAEL** pleads no contest to committing a lewd act in a toilet, is fined $810, given 80 hours of community service, and ordered to undergo counseling.
- **16TH: ROLLING STONES**, guitarist Keith Richards falls from a ladder in his library, injuring his

## All The Way

- **MAY 14TH: FRANK SINATRA** – the greatest popular singer of the 20th century – dies of a heart attack in Los Angeles, at the age of 82.

- **JUNE 5TH: REPORTS OF BOB HOPE'S DEMISE** on the Associated Press website prove to be greatly exaggerated. Bob in fact lives a further five years (until 27th July 2003), finally achieving the ripe old age of 100.

- **1ST: STONE TEMPLE PILOTS** singer Scott Weiland is arrested before a solo concert at Irving Plaza, New York City, for possession of heroin.
- **2ND: ROYAL CARIBBEAN CRUISES** pays $9 million to settle charges of dumping waste at sea.
- **8TH: THE MEMORIAL** service held for Linda McCartney at London's St Martin-in-the-Fields church brings together publicly the

- **JUNE 19TH: INDUCTEES TO** the Hollywood Walk Of Fame for 1999 are John Fogerty, Patsy Cline, Charley Pride, Frankie Valli & The Four Seasons, and country superstar Reba McEntire (right).

three surviving Beatles, Paul, George, and Ringo, for the first time in 30 years. Other mourners include Elton John, Sting, Peter Gabriel, George Martin, Billy Joel, David Gilmour, and Neil Tennant... Meanwhile, in the US, Charlton Heston is elected president of The National Rifle Association.
- **10TH: PAUL SIMON,** Motown founder Berry Gordy, and the writing team Fats Domino and Dave Bartholomew are inducted into the Songwriters' Hall of Fame at a ceremony at the Sheraton New York hotel in New York City.
- **11TH: THE UNITED NATIONS** declares an official famine in Sudan when it becomes clear that more than a million people are likely to starve. It estimates that up to 1.2 million people could die in the south of the country.
- **30TH: SYSTEM OF A DOWN** release their self-titled debut album.

• **AUGUST 18TH: KORN RELEASE** the album *Follow The Leader*, which will go straight to Number in the US and Canada.

**JULY**

**AUGUST**

• **5TH: BASKETBALL STAR** Dennis Rodman, shirtless, shoeless, and drunk, staggers on-stage with Pearl Jam in Dallas, plays the fool for 45 minutes, then stumbles off... Meanwhile Japan joins the space race, launching the Planet-B probe to Mars in another attempt to find out whether the 'red planet' ever supported life.

• **7TH: CANADIAN HARMONY-ROCKERS** Barenaked Ladies release their sixth album, *Stunt*... And Michael Jackson and cable television magnate Don Barden announce they intend to build an entertainment complex in Detroit, to be called the Majestic Kingdom. It will feature a theme park and a casino hotel on the city's waterfront.

• **8TH: THE ROY ORBISON** estate files a $12 million suit for unpaid royalties against Sony.

• **12TH: FRED DURST**, vocalist with Limp Bizkit, is arrested in St Paul, Minnesota, and charged with kicking a security man in the head at the band's Roy Wilkins Auditorium show.

• **14TH: LOS ANGELES** sues 15 tobacco companies for $2.5 billion over the dangers of passive smoking.

• **17TH: PAMELA KEARY**, a 17-year-old girl serving 12 years for murder, absconds from a correctional institute in Shakopee, Minnesota, and goes to see Smashing Pumpkins play a free show in Minneapolis. She is re-arrested at the show... Meanwhile, what are believed to be the remains of Russian royal family, the Romanovs, are reburied in St Petersburg, exactly 80 years after they were brutally murdered by Bolshevik revolutionaries.

• **23RD: MORE THAN 50** 'carbon-copy' mice are cloned by scientists at the University of Hawaii.

• **25TH: PRESIDENT CLINTON** avoids a subpoena to appear before a federal grand jury regarding the Monica Lewinsky case, by agreeing to give videotaped testimony.

• **27TH: TWO FORMER MEMBERS** of Blondie, Frank Infante and Nigel Harrison, are reported to be suing their bandmates for $1m on grounds of "financial misconduct."

• **28TH: WHEN OL' DIRTY BASTARD** of the Wu-Tang Clan fails to make a scheduled court appearance in Virginia on a charge of shoplifting Nike trainers, the judge issues a warrant for his arrest.

• **31ST: THE SPACECRAFT** Lunar Prospector, which has been orbiting the moon, is deliberately crashed into the polar ice cap in an effort to find water under the lunar surface. None is discovered.

• **4TH: IT'S REPORTED** that Patricia Glassop, mother of deceased INXS singer Michael Hutchence, has begun legal action to recover property, stocks, cash, and publishing royalties worth an estimated Australian $30 million (US $20 million) from his manager, Andrew Paul.

• **5TH: IRAQI PRESIDENT** Saddam Hussein starts being obstructive with UN weapons inspectors.

• **7TH: US EMBASSIES** in Nairobi, Kenya, and Dar es Salaam, Tanzania, are the targets of bombs, killing 190 people. A man called Osama bin Laden will later prove to have been behind the attacks.

• **10TH: CHER'S ALBUM** *Heart Of Stone* is certified by the RIAA as having sold three million copies in the US.

• **12TH: SWISS BANKS** agree to pay $1.25 billion to the victims of the World War II Holocaust. The money represents funds placed in Swiss banks by German Jews during the war and not repaid to relatives.

• **15TH: IN OMAGH**, Northern Ireland, 29 people die and over 200 are injured when a massive car bomb explodes the town centre. A breakaway republican grouping, the 'Real IRA,' has planned and executed the attack.

• **20TH: US CRUISE MISSILES** hit suspected terrorist bases in Afghanistan and the Sudan.

• **21ST: AFTER BEING MISSING** in action for most of the 1990s, Terence Trent D'Arby reveals via a website that, "I am a holographic representation in the third dimension of what was requested by your souls that one of your favourite artists be. I sent a portion of my soul to embody as an artist called TTD to favour that request."

• **28TH: THE PRIME MINISTER** of Pakistan imposes an Islamic legal system based on the Koran.

• **AUGUST 21ST: POSH SPICE**, Victoria Adams, is reported to be three months pregnant. She's engaged to UK soccer star David Beckham of Manchester United. The pair are set to be one of the world's golden couples in the years to come.

• **AUGUST 17TH: PRESIDENT CLINTON** finally admits, on national television, that he had an "inappropriate" relationship with Monica Lewinsky.

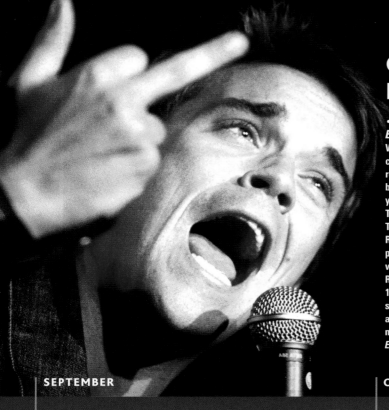

## Great Expectations

• **November 7th:** *I'VE BEEN EXPECTING YOU* by Robbie Williams enters the UK album chart at Number One. It seals his reputation as one of the UK's biggest stars. By the end of this year, he'll have had seven UK Top Ten hits since going solo in 1996. The US still remains immune to Robbie's cheeky, self-referential pop-rock charms – though it won't be for lack of trying on Robbie's part. In early 1999 he'll prepare a special compilation and tour for the US market, entitled *The Ego Has Landed*.

## Lonely Bells

**N**OVEMBER 22ND: *TUBULAR BELLS* composer Mike Oldfield places an ad in the personal column of the London *Sunday Times*: "Very successful, good looking musician/composer, 43, fun-loving with occasional artistic moods, seeks lovely affectionate lady 25-35 to share extraordinary life of romance, travel and mutual shared interests." Despite underestimating his age – he's really 45 – he's not exaggerating about the success. Having had another handful of hit albums since his 1973 blockbuster *Tubular Bells*, he is by now a multi-millionaire. He will have several relationships from such ads, though eventually opts to live with a woman he met on a wild spree in Ibiza.

**SEPTEMBER**

**OCTOBER**

• **September 25th:** **IT IS REPORTED THAT** The Backstreet Boys are beginning a lawsuit against their manager, Louis J. Pearlman, who also discovered the band and produced their first two albums. The band feels Pearlman is keeping more than his fair share of their earnings. Still more popular in Europe than they are at home, they'll soon be the US's top-selling act, and also have a British Number One in 1999.

• **1st:** **DAVID BOWIE** launches his Internet service provider business, Bowienet, offering a basic Internet services and exclusive David Bowie news and online content.

• **3rd:** **'I DON'T WANT TO MISS A THING'** by Aerosmith reaches Number One in the US Top 40 singles chart...

• **3rd:** **A SWISSAIR PLANE** flying from New York to Geneva crashes in the sea off the coast of Nova Scotia, just over an hour after taking off. All 229 people on board the McDonnell Douglas MD-11 aircraft are killed.

• **6th:** **THIRTY YEARS** after its original release, The Pretty Things use the Internet to broadcast the first full performance of their influential rock opera, *S.F. Sorrow*, live from the Abbey Road studio in which it was recorded.

• **9th:** **JOHNNY ROTTEN** (John Lydon) appears as a defendant on television court program *Judge Judy*. The action is brought by a former drummer, who sues Rotten for allegedly head-butting him.

• **10th:** **GARY GLITTER** appears in court on child pornography charges... Tonight, Madonna does well at MTV's 15th Annual Video Music Awards, winning Best Video and Best Female Video for her *Ray Of Light*. Rapper-actor Will Smith collects two trophies, Best Male Video and Best Rap Video.

• **13th:** **THE NEW YORK TIMES** has to close its website after hackers known as HFG (Hacking for Girlies) continually add offensive material.

• **22nd:** **THOUSANDS OF CIVILIANS** are forced to flee their homes in Kosovo after Serbian police, soldiers and armed civilians flood into the north of the province.

• **23rd:** **GARTH BROOKS** wins entertainer of the year at the 32nd Annual Country Music Association Awards, for a record fourth consecutive time.

• **23rd:** **IT IS ANNOUNCED** that a recent series of 17 fund-raising concerts by the Smashing Pumpkins has raised $2,686,973.59 for such charities as the Make A Wish Foundation, Street Outreach Services, and various AIDS organisations

• **29th:** **JAY-Z RELEASES** the album *Vol 2: Hard Knock Life*.

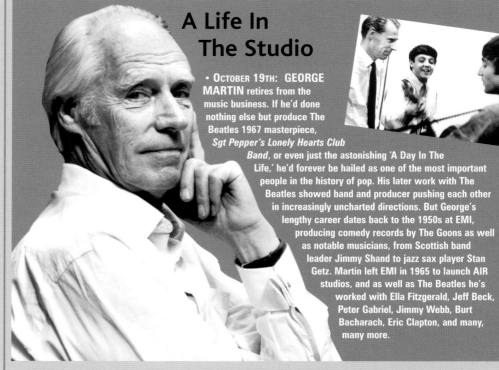

## A Life In The Studio

• **October 19th:** **GEORGE MARTIN** retires from the music business. If he'd done nothing else but produce The Beatles 1967 masterpiece, *Sgt Pepper's Lonely Hearts Club Band*, or even just the astonishing 'A Day In The Life,' he'd forever be hailed as one of the most important people in the history of pop. His later work with The Beatles showed band and producer pushing each other in increasingly uncharted directions. But George's lengthy career dates back to the 1950s at EMI, producing comedy records by The Goons as well as notable musicians, from Scottish band leader Jimmy Shand to jazz sax player Stan Getz. Martin left EMI in 1965 to launch AIR studios, and as well as The Beatles he's worked with Ella Fitzgerald, Jeff Beck, Peter Gabriel, Jimmy Webb, Burt Bacharach, Eric Clapton, and many, many more.

• **9th:** **BRUCE SPRINGSTEEN** testifies in the High Court, London, as part of an ongoing battle against bootleggers.

• **13th:** **THE CROSSROADS CENTRE** (a drug rehabilitation centre paid for by Eric Clapton) opens in Antigua.

• **14th:** **THE ALBUM** *Backstreet Boys* by The Backstreet Boys is certified as seven times platinum in the US by the RIAA.

• **15th:** **'ONE WEEK'** by Barenaked Ladies reaches Number One on the US Top 40 singles chart.

• **16th:** **UK POLICE** place Chile's former dictator General Pinochet under house arrest during his treatment for a medical condition in Britain.

• **19th:** **A WARRANT IS ISSUED** for the arrest of Bobby Brown for parole violation, following his recent release after spending five days in jail on a drunk driving charge.

• **20th:** **FORMER SPICE GIRL** Geri Halliwell is appointed a goodwill ambassador by the UN.

• **22nd:** **THE UN** reveals that two million children have been killed in wars in the last decade.

• **26th:** **AMONG THOSE** to whom President Clinton awards the 1998 Medal of the Arts are 1950s New Orleans rocker Antoine 'Fats' Domino, and folk singer Ramblin' Jack Elliott.

• **November 9th:** **MICHAEL JACKSON** agrees a settlement with the UK's *Daily Mirror* over pictures that claimed to show his face disfigured by cosmetic surgery. The *Mirror* will later acknowledge that the photographs do not accurately represent Jackson's true appearance. And no, that's not one of them above – it's a model of Jacko made entirely from Lego bricks.

• NOVEMBER 17TH: 'N SYNC begin their first headlining tour in Orlando, Florida, with

## NOVEMBER

• **3RD: BATMAN CREATOR** Bob Kane dies at the age of 83.
• **5TH: THE WU-TANG KLAN'S** ODB is arrested while climbing over a security gate, apparently attempting to attack his ex-girlfriend.
• **9TH: RICK JAMES** is hospitalized, after suffering a stroke in Denver.
• **11TH: A NEW RECORD** for the longest blindfolded skywalk is set by Jay Cochrane, after he walks 600ft between the towers of the Flamingo Hilton in Las Vegas.
• **13TH: PRESIDENT CLINTON** agrees to pay Paula Jones $850,000 to drop her sexual harassment lawsuit.
• **14TH:** *UP*, the new album by R.E.M., enters the US chart at No3, its highest position.

• **NOVEMBER 4TH: *COME ON OVER*** by Canadian singer-songwriter Shania Twain is certified as a six times platinum album in the US. It contains no fewer than nine US and/or UK hit singles, including 'You're Still The One' and 'That Don't Impress Me Much.' In 1994 Shania married producer Robert John 'Mutt' Lange (who'd worked with the likes of Def Leppard, Bryan Adams, and AC/DC), and the pair started collaborating on Twain's second album, *The Woman In Me*. Its assured combination of catchy, country-intoned tunes and glossy production sold over 20 million copies around the world. Follow-up *Come On Over* sells even more – making Shania (born Eileen Edwards) one of the world's top stars.

## DECEMBER

### Cher Amour

• **NOVEMBER 10TH: CHER RELEASES** her career-reviving new album *Believe*, on the back of the transatlantic chart-topping single of the same name. That has been her biggest US hit for more than 20 years.

• **5TH: IT IS ANNOUNCED** that the Garth Brooks album *Double Live* has sold 1,085,373 copies in its first week of release in the US, giving it the highest one-week sales of any album to date.
• **6TH: A POLL OF LISTENERS** to BBC Radio 2 in the UK results in The Eagles' single 'Hotel California' being chosen as their all-time easy-listening favorite.
• **8TH: THE FBI OPENS** its files on Frank Sinatra to the public, revealing more than 1,300 pages of material. They contain unproven accusations of Communist party and Mafia links.
• **10TH: ASTRONAUTS** open the doors to the new international space station positioned 250 miles above the Earth's surface.
• **11TH: CANADIAN LIQUOR GIANT** Seagram buys out record giant Polygram and its associated companies Island and Mercury. Meanwhile it's announced that the entire genetic blueprint of a worm has been successfully mapped by scientists.

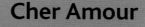

• **14TH: A CHART-FIXING ROW** erupts in the UK, after Sir Andrew Lloyd Webber and his lyricist Tim Rice (seen together right) write a letter to *The Times* of London, suggesting that the UK Top 40 is "little more than a guide to the most successful record company marketing departments."
• **16TH: THE US AND UK** fire missiles at Iraq in response to Saddam Hussein's refusal to comply with UN weapons inspectors.
• **19TH: UK MUSIC TRADE** weekly *Music Week* reports that, having topped nine official European airplay charts, Cher's single 'Believe' is about to become the biggest airplay hit of 1998 across Europe.
• **20TH: A 27-YEAR-OLD** Houston woman gives birth to the only known living octuplets.
• **21ST: TWO DISSIDENTS** are sentenced by a Chinese court to long prison terms for attempting to organize an opposition party.
• **25TH: POSH SPICE** Victoria Beckham gives soccer-player boyfriend David Beckham a £220,000 silver Ferrari 550 Maranello for Christmas, to add to his other four cars.
• **29TH: KHMER ROUGE** leaders apologise for the genocide they were responsible for in Cambodia.

# 1999
## January–April

## Slim's Chance

FEBRUARY 23RD 1999: EMINEM releases *The Slim Shady LP,* his debut album on a major label. A month later it will be certified as double platinum, having climbed to Number Two in the US. He also has his first hit single, 'My Name Is,' which peaks at Number Two in the UK (but only reaches 36 in the US at this stage). Hi-jacking black music like Elvis did back in the 1950s, Detroit-based Marshall Mathers has made his way up largely via open-mike nights (as recreated in the later movie *8 Mile*). But he has avoided comparisons with the likes of Vanilla Ice by demonstrating a genuinely deep affinity with rap music. A hugely gifted lyricist, he has convinced Dr Dre, who is not easily convinced. Dre has not only championed the skinny white boy, but produced this remarkable debut.

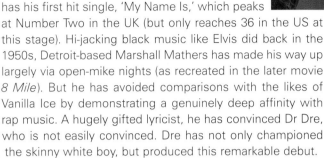

### JANUARY

- **1ST: ELEVEN MEMBER** states of the European Union (but not the UK, yet) change their national currencies to the Euro. But coins and notes will not be available until January 2002.
- **7TH: THE IMPEACHMENT** trial of President William Jefferson Clinton begins before the US Senate. It's the first time in US history that an elected president has been impeached and stood trial. (Andrew Johnson, in the 19th century, was impeached, but he wasn't elected, having succeeded the assassinated Abe Lincoln. Richard Nixon was also impeached, but resigned rather than stand trial.) On February 12th, the Senate will vote to acquit President Clinton of perjury and obstruction of justice, after Clinton tells the country he is "profoundly sorry" for what he has said and done in the Monica Lewinsky affair.
- **9TH: GANG STARR'S** Guru is relieved of $10,000 in jewelry outside a recording studio in Queens, New York.
- **11TH: THE 26TH** Annual American Music Awards are held at Shrine Auditorium, Los Angeles. Celine Dion is Favorite Pop/Rock Female Artist and Favorite Adult/Contemporary Artist. Pearl Jam is Favorite Alternative Music Artist. Rapper/actor Will Smith collects three trophies for his album Big Willie Style.

- **13TH: JAMIROQUAI SINGER** Jay Kay is arrested in Madrid Airport, after throwing a temper tantrum on his way home from a holiday in Tenerife with television presenter girlfriend Denise Van Outen.
- **14TH: METALLICA SUE** the famous lingerie maker Victoria's Secret, claiming that by manufacturing Metallica lip pencils the company has infringed the group's trademark.
- **15TH: WU-TANG CLAN** rapper Ol' Dirty Bastard is arrested in Brooklyn on charges of attempted murder following a shootout. The charge will be dismissed in February because no gun is found. The same month, he is arrested in Hollywood for wearing a bullet-proof vest, after being pulled over for driving erratically. He is sentenced to a year's drug rehabilitation and three years' probation.
- **19TH: HUNDREDS OF LEADING** European recording artists, led by Jean-Michel Jarre, ask the European Parliament for protection against Internet music piracy.
- **20TH: *TALK ON CORNERS*** by The Corrs is certified as a UK six-times platinum disc by the BPI.
- **21ST: OVER 9,000 POUNDS** of cocaine headed for Houston is intercepted by the US Coast Guard. It is one of the largest drug busts in US history.

### Fatboy Skank

- **JANUARY 10TH: 'PRAISE YOU'** by Fatboy Slim reaches Number One on the UK singles chart – just as the UK DJ is becoming one of the most talked-about new music-makers in the hipper regions of the US at the moment. It's especially impressive bearing in mind the Fatboy Slim alias started as a fun side-project for 35-year-old semi-retired pop star Norman Cook. Having had 1980s success with The Housemartins and Beats International, Cook then took experimental funk-pop outfit Freakpower on the road for a last fling at fame – until suddenly finding he's become the world's most in-demand DJ/producer/remixer.

### FEBRUARY

- **FEBRUARY 7TH: 'MARIA,'** the comeback single by Blondie, reaches Number One on the UK singles chart – still who are still more popular in the UK than in the US.

- **4TH: AMADOU DIALLO**, an unarmed West African immigrant, dies after being shot 41 times in front of his Bronx home by four plain-clothes New York City police officers, who explain he was "acting defensively."
- **8TH: THE NOVELIST** Iris Murdoch dies after succumbing to Alzheimer's disease, a mental decline poignantly described by her husband, John Bayley, in his memoir *Iris*, published in the year before her death and later made into a successful movie.
- **13TH: MONICA** has her third US Number One with 'Angel Of Mine.' Her first, back in June last year, was her duet with Brandy, 'This Boy Is Mine,' since when Brandy has also

had a solo Number One, with 'Have You Ever.'
- **15TH: ROLLING STONES DAY** is declared by the governor of Minnesota, who also controversially declines to endorse National Prayer Day… And tonight turns out to be Robbie Williams Night in the UK: after arriving at the London Docklands Arena by helicopter, Williams pulls off a hat-trick at the BRIT Awards, winning the categories for Best British Male Solo Artist, Best British Single ('Angels'), and Best Video (for 'Millennium').
- **17TH: IT'S ANNOUNCED** that Eric Clapton hopes to raise $750,000 from an auction of 100 of his 150 guitars, as a benefit for the Crossroads

• **JANUARY 30TH:** **THE OFFSPRING** hit the top of the UK charts with the single 'Pretty Fly (For A White Guy),' taken from their transatlantic Top Ten album *Americana*. Though this is their first breakthrough into the mainstream charts on either side of the Atlantic, the California 'new-punk' group have been a feature on the alternative rock scene since the mid 1980s, finding increased success in the mid Nineties guitar-band explosion ignited by Nirvana, when their ska-core-punk album *Smash* hit Number Four on the US album chart (and 21 in the UK).

## Not Yet A Woman

• **JANUARY 12TH:** '...BABY ONE MORE TIME' is released by 17-year-old Britney Spears. By the end of the month it will be Number One in the US, and shortly afterwards in the UK. Her seemingly instant stardom is propelled not just by the slick dance-pop cultivated by Swedish producer Max Martin, but by the video for '...Baby One More Time,' in which she dresses as a rather mature school girl – in its way almost as provocative as Madonna's video for 'Like A Prayer,' thus attracting unbuyable publicity and no little controversy. Britney – who started her showbiz career on *The New Mickey Mouse Club* on the Disney Channel in 1992 – then turns her sexy image on its head by espousing a virtuous 'no-sex before marriage' message, ensuring, deliberately ot not, that she is almost never out of the media for the next few years. She will become the world's biggest-selling teenage act.

Center, his alcohol and drug rehabilitation facility on Antigua.
• **18TH:** **THE CLINTON** administration warns Serbian president Slobodan Milosevic to choose peace with ethnic Albanians in Kosovo, or face a devastating military strike.

• **19TH:** **MEL B,** 'Scary' of the Spice Girls (above), has a baby girl, Phoenix Chi. "Oh, you are lovely," she declares. "Now, where's the champagne?"
• **24TH:** **THE 41ST ANNUAL GRAMMY AWARDS** are held in New York. Celine Dion does quite well. Her 'My Heart Will Go On' gets Best Female Pop Vocal Performance, Song Of The Year, Record Of The Year, and Best Song Written Specifically For A Motion Picture Or Television.
• **28TH:** **MARTI PELLOW** of Wet Wet Wet is rushed to hospital after collapsing on the floor of his London hotel.room.

• **2ND:** **DUSTY SPRINGFIELD** dies from cancer at home in Henley-on-Thames, UK.
• **2ND:** **JAY-Z** releases a new single, 'Hard Knock Life.'
• **4TH:** **MONICA LEWINSKY'S** book about her affair with President Clinton is rushed into the bookstores.
• **6TH:** **STANLEY KUBRICK** – who made only three movies, *The Shining* (1980), *Full Metal Jacket* (1987), and *Eyes Wide Shut* (1999) in the last 20 years of his life – dies at the age of 70.
• **8TH:** **NEW YORK YANKEES** baseball star Joe DiMaggio, once married to Marilyn Monroe, dies in Hollywood at age 84. His last words, apparently, were "I finally get to see Marilyn."
• **11TH:** **'BELIEVE' BY CHER** repeats its European success when it reaches No1 in the US Top 40 singles chart.

• **MARCH 7TH:** 'WHEN THE GOING GETS TOUGH' by Boyzone (below) reaches Number One on the UK singles chart. This is the Irish boy-band's last year together, but in their five-year career they'll have clocked up a remarkable 16 consecutive Top Five hits in the UK, six of them Number Ones. In the US they fail to chart at all. Six weeks from now, Westlife – a new Irish boy-band ready to succeed to the Boyzone throne – score their first UK Number One single with 'Swear It Again.' In fact, Westlife (inset) will be even more successful than their predecessors, topping the UK charts no fewer than 11 times in their first three years, usually with predictable slushy ballads.

• **13TH:** **TODAY IS DECLARED** 'N Sync Day in New Haven, Connecticut, and the group is honoured in a ceremony before their show this evening... Meanwhile Evander Holyfield, the WBA/IBF champion, and Lennox Lewis, the WBC champion, keep their respective boxing titles after fighting to a controversial draw in New York.
• **16TH:** **THE RIAA** launches Diamond Awards, for sales of ten million copies or more of an audio recording. No Doubt's Tragic Kingdom becomes one of the first albums to receive the Diamond award, and other winners include Alanis Morissette, Pearl Jam, Green Day, No Doubt, and the Backstreet Boys.
• **24TH:** **THIRTY-NINE PEOPLE** are killed when fire erupts in the Mont Blanc tunnel in France. The enclosed fire burns fiercely for two whole days.

• **5TH:** **THE UNITED NATIONS** suspends sanctions against Libya after General Gaddafi surrenders two suspected Libyan intelligence agents for trial in the 1988 Pan Am bombing over Lockerbie.
• **8TH:** **'NO SCRUBS'** by TLC reaches Number One on the US Top 40 singles chart. It's their third US Number One – though their first chart entry since 1995 – and their biggest UK hit (it reaches Number Three).
• **9TH:** **LAURYN HILL** is in court in Newark, New Jersey because four musicians, known as New-Ark Entertainment, are seeking performer/co-writer and co-producer royalties for work they claim to have done on her hit album *The Miseducation Of Lauryn Hill*.
• **15TH:** **PUFF DADDY** barges into the office of Steve Stoute, president of Interscope Records' Urban Music Division, and attacks him with a champagne bottle, a chair, and a phone. Stoute ends up with a broken arm and injuries to his ribs.
• **16TH:** **SINEAD O'CONNOR** gives up a long custody battle for her daughter Roisin, and hands the child over to John Waters, her father,

who is a columnist on the *Irish Times* newspaper in Dublin.
• **20TH:** **ON THE 110TH** anniversary of Hitler's birthday, staff and students are massacred at the Columbine High School in Denver, Colorado, by two students, Eric Harris and Dylan Theobald. The final death toll of 15 includes the two attackers. The families of most of the victims will later be awarded $2.5m after suing the gunmen's parents, and the people who sold the boys the weapons.
• **21ST:** **THE FORMER LEADER** of Dexy's Midnight Runners, Kevin Rowland (below), writes to Alan McGee, head of his new label Creation Records, explaining that he has taken to wearing women's dresses, stockings, and suspenders, but he is not transvestite nor homosexual. "It's me as a man expressing my soft, sexy side," he says.

# 1999

May–August

• JUNE 2ND: **SLIPKNOT** release their first legitimate album, entitled *Slipknot* – though the scary-mask-wearing nine-piece did release an obscure own-label CD in 1996 called *Mate, Feed, Kill, Repeat*.

## Peer-To-Peer Fear

**J**UNE 16TH: **THE US COURT OF APPEAL** finds that a 1992 federal music piracy law does not prohibit a palm-sized device that can download high-quality digital music files from the Internet and play them at home. MP3 files have arrived. They are a means of compressing music files, previously unmanageably large, to ten per cent of their normal size, without a fatal loss of quality. Almost simultaneously, a Boston college student called Shawn Fanning, with two friends, launches a new computer program that will change the way many people use the Internet. He calls it Napster (a name he uses in web chatrooms). The software lets music fans share songs stored as MP3 files on their computers – it becomes known as peer-to-peer (P2P) file sharing – and helps them find each other through a central directory at the Napster site. They can, and do, swap anything: bootlegs, rare tracks, and current releases by major artists. It all seems so easy and

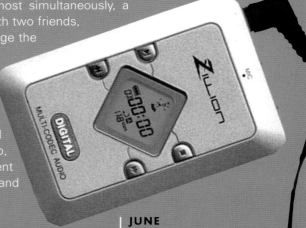

**MAY**

**JUNE**

• MAY 8TH: 'LIVIN' LA VIDA LOCA' by Ricky Martin reaches Number One on the US Top 40 singles chart.

• **1ST: A GROUP** of US mountain climbers discovers the body of George Mallory on Mount Everest. Mallory died in June of 1924 in an attempt to become the first person to reach the summit.

• **4TH: SEVERAL SEVERE TORNADOES** hit the Midwest U.S. overnight, killing at least 45 people

• **6TH: RANDY CASTILLO** is named as the replacement drummer for Tommy Lee of Mötley Crüe, who left last month.

• **7TH: A JURY RULES** that *The Jenny Jones Show* and Warner Bros are liable in the shooting to death of Scott Amedure, who was killed by Jonathan Schmitz, another guest on the show, after revealing he had a secret, same-sex crush on Schmitz. Three days later, Schmitz went to Amedure's home with a shotgun and fired two fatal blasts. He is later sentenced to 25-50 years in prison.

• **10TH: CEZANNE'S PAINTING** *Still Life With Curtain, Pitcher, & Bowl Of Fruit* sells for $60.5 million.

• **17TH: TABLOID PHOTOGRAPHER** Eric Ford is sentenced to six months at a halfway house, three years probation and 150 hours of community service for eavesdropping on a call between Tom Cruise and Nicole Kidman and then selling a recording of the conversation.

• **18TH: REGGAE STAR** Augustus Pablo, born Horace Swaby, dies in Kingston, Jamaica, following a life-long struggle against the nervous disorder myasthenia gravis.

• **18TH: BACKSTREET BOYS** release the album *Millennium*, which sells 1.1 million in its first week, breaking the sales record held by Garth Brooks.

• **27TH: THE 44TH ANNUAL IVOR NOVELLO AWARDS** ceremony takes place at the Grosvenor House Hotel, London. The team of Robbie Williams & Guy Chambers is named in the Songwriter Of The Year category, while Williams' hit single 'Angels' is Most Performed Work.

• **1ST: BLINK 182** release a new album, *Enema Of The State*, in the US. It will reach Number Nine on the US album chart.

• **8TH: THE RED HOT CHILI PEPPERS** release a new album, Californication... Meanwhile, in the UK, Coldplay sign a publishing deal with BMG Records... Also in Britain, disgraced former Tory government minister Jonathan Aitken is jailed for 18 months after he admits lying during a failed libel action against *The Guardian* newspaper and Granada TV.

• **9TH: NATO AND YUGOSLAVIA** sign a peace agreement over Kosovo.

• **18TH: MORE THAN 4,000 PEOPLE** take to the streets of London in protest at the debt owed by the world's poorest countries – but the peaceful gathering becomes violent after a small crowd of demonstrators begins attacking buildings and smashing windows.

• **19TH: HORROR WRITER** Stephen King is struck from behind by a mini-van while walking along a road in Maine.

• **25TH: R.E.M. PLAY** at the Glastonbury Festival, UK. Other acts at the event include Hole,

painless, what can be the harm? Inevitably the Recording Industry Association of America (RIAA), which represents most record labels, is concerned, to put it mildly. "We love the idea of using technology to build artist communities," it states, "but Napster is about facilitating piracy." In December, the RIAA sues Napster for copyright infringement. The publicity attracts even more Napster users – at one point estimated at 60 million – and inspires copy-cat sites, like Gnutella, and a dozen more over the next five years. But Napster bears the brunt of the industry's hysteria and vitriol. Rock band Metallica are one of its most vociferous opponents, and launch their own law suit against Fanning's company. Other artists, like Chuck D of Public Enemy, speak out in defense of Napster, arguing that major labels already have too much control over the music we hear, and the income it generates. Some are even inspired to offer free file downloads of their own music. By 2001, various court judgements will have crippled Napster, until it's effectively shut down – though there will be talk of a (strictly legal) Napster 2 in 2003. The technology will of course survive, and if ways can be found of generating income for the artists involved – most music file sharers are also music buyers, after all, so wouldn't object to paying a fair price – no one will lose out, apart from the traditional record companies. Which is why they are so worried.

## Travis Travel

**M**AY 24TH: **TRAVIS RELEASE** their second album, *The Man Who*, in the UK. It will reach Number One there, a full 13 weeks later, and provide them with four hit singles. Though they haven't had any chart success in the US as yet, they will be invited to support Oasis on their next US tour, and win quite a few new friends that way with songs that are well-crafted and easy on the ear, dogged determination, and a wee bit of charm.

---

**JULY**

**AUGUST**

## Hello J.Lo

• **JUNE 12TH:** **'IF YOU HAD MY LOVE'** by Jennifer Lopez reaches Number One on the US Top 40 singles chart. It's the first hit for the New York Bronx-born Puerto Rican actress turned singer, and the start of a hectic double career. Her next two albums, *J.Lo* and *This Is Me … Then*, will be chart-toppers as well.

Beautiful South, Bush, Blondie, Barenaked Ladies, Wilco, Pavement, and Kula Shaker.
• **28TH:** **IT'S REVEALED** that Hollywood spiritualist Father Gilberto has performed a 20-minute exorcism on former Mötley Crüe drummer Tommy Lee to release the demons that his ex-wife Pamela Anderson's psychic says have made him bad.
• **29TH:** **LEIF GARRETT** is arrested at an apartment in Los Angeles, then freed on $10,000 bail. He later pleads guilty to possession of heroin and cocaine. The singer, actor, and former teen heart-throb had three US Top 40 hits in the 1970s.

• **JUNE 18TH:** *THE MATRIX*, starring Keanu Reeves and Laurence Fishburne, is launched in the UK, after much anticipation. In the two months since it opened in the US, it's already managed the rare feat of becoming a box office smash and a cult movie at the same time.

• **1ST:** **AT HIS 37-ACRE** London estate, Sir Elton John holds his Summer Ball, a £1,000 ($1500)-a-ticket "white tie and tiara" function raising cash for Elton's Aids Foundation charity. It's attended by two Spice Girls (Mel C and Emma Bunton), Rolling Stones' singer Mick Jagger, Jerry Hall, Catherine Zeta Jones & Michael Douglas, Sir David Frost, designer Jasper Conran, and DJ Paul Gambaccini. Elton performs two songs, 'Crocodile Rock' and 'Your Song.'
• **7TH:** **PLEADING GUILTY** to a charge of illegal gun possession, Coolio is sentenced to ten days in jail, 40 hours of community service, and two years' probation.
• **9TH:** **THE STATE OF INDIANA** renames a 25-mile stretch of Interstate Route 65 as Kenneth Babyface Edmonds Highway. The musician has donated $50,000 to establish VH1's Save The Music campaign in the state, which is where he was born.
• **13TH:** **LIMP BIZKIT** release the album *Significant Other*, which gives them a US Number One.
• **16TH:** **THE SEARCH BEGINS** for the missing plane that was carrying John F. Kennedy Jr, his wife Carolyn, and her sister Lauren Bessette, on a flight from New Jersey to Massachusetts. It will later transpire that the plane crashed near Martha's Vineyard the night before, killing all three aboard. Kennedy's body is found five days later.
• **17TH:** **'BILLS, BILLS, BILLS'** by Destiny's Child reaches No1 in the US Top 40 singles chart. Ten days later they release their second album, *The Writing's On the Wall*, in the US.
• **18TH:** **OFFSPRING'S** Dexter Holland beats up life-size inflatable figures of the Backstreet Boys with a bat at a gig in Berkeley, California.
• **26TH:** **SHANIA TWAIN'S** album *Come On Over* is certified by the RIAA as 12-times platinum in the US. Meanwhile Marilyn Monroe's personal items (1,500 pieces in all) are put on display at Christie's in New York City, prior to going on sale.

• **JUNE 22ND:** **CHRISTINA AGUILERA** releases 'Genie In A Bottle.' By July it will be her first US Number One single, and by October it'll be Number One in the UK as well. She follows this up with three more chart toppers in the next few years, each more 'Dirrty' than the last.

• **1ST:** **JUST 15 MINUTES** before showtime, Whitney Houston claims she has bronchitis and decides to cancel an appearance at Concord Pavilion, Concord, California. The city officials sue her for $100,000.
• **2ND:** **AT LEAST 278 PEOPLE** are killed in eastern India, when two trains collided at a station.
• **4TH:** **CHRISTINA AGUILERA** releases her self-titled debut album.
• **5TH:** **MUSIC WRITTEN** by Johann Sebastian Bach, part of the musical estate of one of Bach's sons that was lost during World War II after being moved out of Germany, is found in a museum in Kiev, Ukraine... Meanwhile Blink 182 begin shooting the video for their new single 'All the Small Things.'
• **9TH:** **RUSSIAN PRESIDENT** Boris Yeltsin fires Prime Minister Sergei Stepashin and his entire cabinet for the fourth time in 17 months. A week later, former KGB man Vladimir Putin is confirmed as new Russian prime minister.
• **10TH:** **PAUL 'BONEHEAD' ARTHURS** leaves Oasis.
• **14TH:** **WHEN TICKETS** for the Backstreet Boys' upcoming US tour go on sale, all 39 cities sell out in just over one hour.
• **17TH:** **MORE THAN 15,000** people die in an earthquake in western Turkey.
• **25TH:** **'N SYNC** host a charity basketball game in Atlanta, Georgia, to raise money for children's hospitals.
• **27TH:** **THE LAST CREW** to inhabit Russian space station Mir return to Earth. They have been forced to abandon the space station for financial reasons.
• **30TH:** **RED HOT CHILI PEPPERS**, Offspring, Terrorvision, Silverchair, Feeder, Pitchshifter, Mansun, Flaming Lips, Sparklehorse, Fountains Of Wayne, Ice-T and more play on the third and last day of the Carling Weekend festival at Temple Newsam Park, Leeds, UK.

## Oye Santana

**O**CTOBER 23RD: 'SMOOTH' by Santana becomes the last Number One of the 20th century on the US Top 40 singles chart. It's also the first hit single for the Latin-rock veteran and his group since 1982, and comes from the star-studded chart-topping comeback album, *Supernatural*. 'Smooth' itself has vocals from Rob Thomas of rock band matchbox twenty, and the album's guest contributors include Dave Matthews, Wyclef Jean, Eric Clapton, and Everlast. An early exponent of what is later termed 'world music,' virtuoso guitarist Carlos Santana pioneered the polyrythmic fusion of Cuban, South American and African music with soul, blues, jazz, funk, and rock, creatin a sound that was, in the late 1960s at least, unique. Throughout his varied career he has worked with leading musicians of all genres, from John Lee Hooker and Herbie Hancock to Bob Dylan and Bob Marley.

## SEPTEMBER

- **2ND: BOB DYLAN AND PAUL SIMON** begin a joint US tour at the Coral Sky Amphitheater, West Palm Beach, Florida.
- **7TH: VIACOM**, owner of MTV, announces it plans to buy CBS (and it will do so, for $50 billion).
- **8TH: LOUIS 'MOONDOG' HARDIN**, the enigmatic New York City street performer, who dressed in elaborate garb and garnered great acclaim as a composer and conductor, dies of heart failure, at the age of 83.
- **12TH: GRAHAM NASH**, veteran of Crosby, Stills etc, breaks both legs when a huge wave throws him across his boat on the seas near his home on the Hawaiian island of Kauai.
- **13TH: BEVERLY HILLS** police officer Marcelo Rodriguez, who arrested George Michael on charges of lewd behaviour in a public park last year, files a $10 million slander lawsuit against the singer, alleging he slandered him in subsequent media interviews, by claiming he was entrapped. He also objects to the song and video for 'Outside.' It includes a camp dancer dressed as a policeman. The case will be dismissed in California in 2000, but then permitted to proceed by the court of appeal.
- **14TH: RCA/BMG** begins a $150m legal action against 'N Sync, who have recently quit the label to move to Zomba Records.
- **17TH: EMINEM** has a $10 million lawsuit filed against him by his mother, who claims he's made defamatory remarks in several interviews.
- **20TH: A MULTINATIONAL** peacekeeping force lands in East Timor in an attempt to end the violence that has beset the region since its people voted overwhelmingly for independence from Indonesia.
- **23RD: BONO OF U2** has an audience with Pope John Paul II in the papal summer house, near Rome, Italy.
- **27TH: STING RELEASES** *Brand New Day*, his first album in three years. It will win two Grammys.
- **30TH: IN TOKAIMURA**, Japan, radiation leaks from a nuclear facility after workers accidentally set off an uncontrolled chain reaction, which continues intermittently for 20 hours. Around 120 workers receive dangerously high doses of radiation. Two of them later die from the effects.

## Solo Spice

. **NOVEMBER 7TH:** 'LIFT ME UP' by former Spice Girl Geri Halliwell reaches Number One on the UK singles chart. The former Ginger Spice has a new image, which will soon include blonde-ish hair, a carb-free anorexic look, and a sound she herself describes as "Julie Andrews meets Johnny Rotten." She enjoys four solo Number Ones in the UK over the next couple of years, and growing US fame.

## Dreamcasting

• **SEPTEMBER 9TH:** **THE SEGA DREAMCAST** games system goes on sale, on the back of a hype-driven promotional campaign. By 1pm today, all Toys 'R' Us locations in the US have run out of stocks.

**OCTOBER**

**NOVEMBER**

**DECEMBER**

• **5TH:** **THE CORRS** record their MTV *Unplugged* album at Ardmore Studios, outside Dublin, Ireland.
• **6TH:** **AT THE MOBO** (Music Of Black Origin) Awards in London, Lauryn Hill gets the Best International Act award, while Jamaican DJ Mr Vegas takes home the Best Reggae Act award.
• **12TH:** **PERVEZ MUSHARRAF** seizes power in Pakistan in a bloodless coup that topples Prime Minister Nawaz Sharif... Meanwhile, when Bruce Springsteen plays at the America West Arena, Arizona, he is joined by Sam Moore of Sam & Dave for a version of 'Soul Man.'
• **18TH:** **JOE HIGGS,** known as the godfather of roots reggae, dies of cancer in the United States, at age 59.
• **22ND:** **CHINA ENDS** its first-ever human rights conference by defying Western definitions of civil liberties.
• **25TH:** **RAGE AGAINST THE MACHINE** release the album *The Battle Of Los Angeles*.

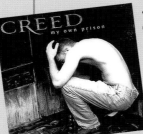

## Oye Enrique

• **SEPTEMBER 4TH:** 'BAILAMOS' by Enrique Iglesias reaches Number One on the US Top 40 singles chart. Enrique is the son of former heart-throb crooner Julio Iglesias, who was the most successful Spanish singer ever.

• **3RD:** *MY OWN PRISON* by grungey rockers Creed is certified as a quadruple platinum album in the US by the RIAA. At the same time, *Human Clay*, their new Number One album, is declared double platinum.
• **4TH:** **UNITED NATIONS** economic sanctions are imposed against the Taliban in Afghanistan, for refusing to turn over Osama bin Laden, charged with masterminding the 1998 bombings of the US embassies in Kenya and Tanzania.
• **6TH:** **AUSTRALIANS** overwhelmingly reject a proposal to break their remaining ties with the British monarchy and become a republic by replacing Queen Elizabeth with a president.
• **9TH:** **THE CO-FOUNDER** of Atlantic Records, Herb Abramson, dies in Las Vegas, Nevada.
• **15TH:** **REPRESENTATIVES** from China and the United States sign a major trade agreement that will allow China to join the World Trade Organization (WTO).
• **19TH:** **SINEAD O'CONNOR** visits ex-Pogues singer Shane MacGowan in his apartment in Kentish Town, London. Finding him openly using heroin, she reports him to the local police, and MacGowan is arrested.
• **28TH:** **A NAKED MAN** wielding a samurai sword enters a church in Surrey, UK, and injures 11 churchgoers, four severely. Eden Strang will later be detained indefinitely in a psychiatric hospital.
• **29TH:** **US SOUL SINGER** Curtis Knight dies at the age of 54.
• **29TH:** **SIR ELTON JOHN** upsets the Scout movement by performing at a Stonewall gay rights concert in London with a troupe of male strippers dressed as Boy Scouts.
• **30TH:** **THE BEEF-ON-THE-BONE BAN,** imposed at the height of the 'mad cow' BSE scare, is finally lifted by the UK government – putting T-bone steaks back on British menus.

• **2ND:** **AT A LISTENING PARTY** for Q-Tip's solo album *Amplified* at the Kit Kat Club, New York City, producer Lance 'Un' Rivera is stabbed in abdomen and shoulder during an argument about bootlegging. Police name rapper Jay-Z as one of the men they want to question. He denies the assault, but later pleads guilty and gets three years' probation.
• **4TH:** **FOLLOWING REPORTS** that Microsoft is bidding buy the Grateful Dead's musical archive, the group issues an announcement that, "The vault is not for sale. Not to Microsoft. Not to anyone."
• **8TH:** **A JURY IN MEMPHIS** finds that Rev Martin Luther King Jr was the victim of a murder conspiracy, not the convicted 'lone assassin' James Earl Ray. Ray died in April 1998 without ever receiving a new hearing, despite protests from many, including some in King's family.
• **12TH:** **BACKSTREET BOYS** end the 20th century with the ten-times platinum *Millennium* being declared the best-selling album of the year.
• **14TH:** **PAUL MCCARTNEY** plays at the Cavern Club in Liverpool for the first time since 1963. The show is webcast live and more than three million people attempt to gain Internet access to the concert. Even though only one million succeed, it's still the highest audience for a webcast to date.
• **17TH:** **GROVER WASHINGTON** dies in New York, at age 56, just after taping a performance for CBS's *The Saturday Early Show*. The show is aired the next day.
• **18TH:** **ANTI-LOGGING** environmental activist Julia 'Butterfly' Hill descends from ancient redwood tree in California, ending her two-year long protest.
• **26TH:** **AFTER A DECADE** of illness and paralysis, soul star Curtis Mayfield dies in a hospital at Roswell, Georgia, at 57.
• **27TH:** **PUFF DADDY** and girlfriend Jennifer Lopez are arrested in New York following a shooting incident in Times Square
• **30TH:** **GUITARIST GEORGE HARRISON** is stabbed in the chest at his home, Friar Park, Oxfordshire, while fending off intruder Michael Abram. Police claim it was a deliberate attempt to harm the ex-Beatle rather than a bungled robbery, but they don't know the motive. Abram is later treated for schizophrenia. George quips from his hospital bed, "He wasn't a burglar, but he certainly wasn't auditioning for the Traveling Wilburys." Humour aside, Harrison and his wife Olivia, who was slightly injured, are traumatised by the incident.
• **31ST:** **MISSING THE OPPORTUNITY** to have lived in three separate centuries by just hours, Sarah Knauss dies in Allentown, Pennsylvania, at the age of 119 years. The world's oldest person (born September 24th, 1880), she was older than both the Brooklyn Bridge and the Statue Of Liberty.

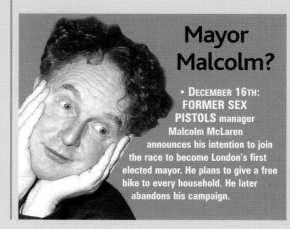

## Mayor Malcolm?

• **DECEMBER 16TH:** FORMER SEX PISTOLS manager Malcolm McLaren announces his intention to join the race to become London's first elected mayor. He plans to give a free bike to every household. He later abandons his campaign.

# 21st Century

# 2000

## January–April

- **1ST: DESPITE WIDESPREAD PANIC** by religious sects, computer bug theorists, and worrywarts generally, the world fails to come to an end as the new millennium dawns.
- **6TH: OKLAHOMA STATE** Prison carries out the first US execution of the 21st century.
- **10TH: DAVID BOWIE** opens his own online banking business, Bowiebanc.com, backed by the online banking firm USABancShares.com.
- **10TH: IT'S ANNOUNCED** that America Online (AOL) will buy Time Warner for $162bn, in the largest-ever corporate merger, .
- **11TH: WHITNEY HOUSTON** is caught with 15.2 grams of marijuana at Keahole-Kona International airport, Kailua-Kona, Hawaii, but she boards a plane before she can be arrested.
- **11TH: SMASHING PUMPKINS** manager Sharon Osbourne resigns from her job, declaring that frontman Billy Corgan is impossible to work with.
- **16TH: CALIFORNIA'S** state Capitol building in Sacramento is attacked by a man driving a truck loaded with evaporated milk. The driver dies in the incident and the world remains none the wiser as to what he hoped to achieve.
- **24TH: TIME WARNER** and UK music company EMI unveil plans for a merger intended to create the world's biggest record company, with a combined annual turnover of $7.4 billion (£4.9 billion). It all sounds cut and dried – but the plan will be abandoned in October (at least for a while), under pressure from the European Commission which is worried it would concentrate too much music market power in the hands of too few companies. It is said to be still investigating the AOL Time Warner merger...
- **25TH: D'ARCY WRETZKY,** former bassist of Smashing Pumpkins, is arrested in Chicago, Illinois, on charges of possessing crack cocaine.
- **30TH: BRITNEY SPEARS** is the latest musical guest to appear on animated TV series *The Simpsons* as a cartoon version of herself.
- **31ST: DR HAROLD SHIPMAN,** a middle-aged doctor with a practice near Manchester, UK, is found guilty of murdering 15 patients, mostly for no reason. Police believe the total number of victims may be 365.

- **JANUARY 7TH: US TOY MANUFACTURER McFarlane Toys** announces the start of production of a line of Kid Rock action figures. Soon to be better known as Pamela Anderson's latest beau, Kid 'Bob Ritchie' Rock is the white rapper beloved of the US 'jock rock' market. As such, he is the polar opposite of Emimen, though both revel in a bit of controversy and the bad-boy image. Still, Kid Rock makes Eminem seem tasteful.

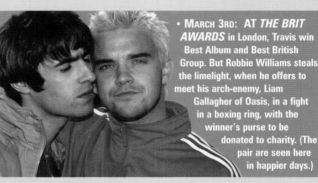

- **MARCH 3RD: AT *THE BRIT AWARDS*** in London, Travis win Best Album and Best British Group. But Robbie Williams steals the limelight, when he offers to meet his arch-enemy, Liam Gallagher of Oasis, in a fight in a boxing ring, with the winner's purse to be donated to charity. (The pair are seen here in happier days.)

- **3RD: IT'S REPORTED THAT ABBA** have turned down an offer of $1 billion to reform for a series of concerts. Co-founder Benny Andersson has been quoted as saying, "Fans had better make the most of [tribute band] Björn Again, because that's the closest they are going to get to seeing Abba. Abba will never reform."
- **7TH: ROBERT PICKETT** fires several shots at the White House, Washington, DC, near the South Lawn, before being subdued by a shot in the knee... Meanwhile US rapper The Big Punisher (born Christopher Rios) dies of a heart attack – he's 28 years old and weighs 700 pounds (315kgs).
- **8TH: MARVEL COMICS** announce that Stan Lee will create a Backstreet Boys comic... And The Spice Girls appear in the High Court, London, where they are being sued by Italian motor scooter manufacturers Aprilia. The company signed a $750,000 marketing deal with the band, to make scooters bearing their five-girl silhouette logo. Then Geri Halliwell left, rendering the logos obsolete, and damaging sales prospects.
- **12TH: PEANUTS CREATOR** Charles M. Schulz dies at age 77. His final comic strip appears in newspapers the following day.
- **17TH: COLUMBIA RECORDS** announces that two new members, Farrah Franklin and Michelle Williams, have joined Destiny's Child, alongside Beyoncé Knowles and Kelly Rowland.
- **19TH: 'THANK GOD I FOUND YOU'** by Whitney Houston reaches Number One in the US Top 40 singles chart.
- **22ND: THE CITY OF AUTLAN DE NAVARRO** in Mexico announces plans to build a public monument to Carlos Santana.
- **23RD:** Sean 'Puff Daddy' Combs is indicted for bribing his driver with money and jewelry to claim ownership of a gun that police recovered from Comb's car following a shooting at a New York nightclub in December last year... And tonight at the 42nd Annual Grammy Awards, Eminem wins two Grammies, for 'My Name Is' (Best Rap Solo Performance) and *Slim Shady* (Best Rap Album).
- **25TH: IT'S ANNOUNCED** that Britney Spears will be releasing her CD *Bubble Gum* in March.

- **1ST: FORMER CHILEAN DICTATOR** General Augusto Pinochet is told by UK Home Secretary Jack Straw that he will not be extradited on torture charges, and so can return to Chile tomorrow.
- **2ND: RAPPER DMX** is arrested while driving in New York without a license and found to be in possession of marijuana.... Coincidentally, a few days later female rapper Foxy Brown is charged with aggravated unlicensed operation of a vehicle after she crashes her car into a fence down the road in Brooklyn, requiring medical attention.
- **9TH: CHRISSIE HYNDE** of The Pretenders is arrested outside a New York City branch of The Gap while protesting with members of animal rights organisation PETA
- **18TH: 'SAY MY NAME'** by Destiny's Child (below) reaches Number One on the US Top 40

## Craig Says Bo

**A**PRIL 9TH: 'FILL ME IN' by Craig David reaches Number One on the UK singles chart. Initially finding favour as the face of the UK 'garage' scene, providing vocals for the Artful Dodger's 'Rewind (The Crowd Say Bo Selecta),' it's this chart-topping solo debut that makes Craig David, at 17, the youngest ever British male to hit the UK top slot. The album *Born To Do It* follows, blending pop, garage, and R&B to fine effect, selling over seven million copies, and earning a Grammy nomination for 'Seven Days.' He draws acclaim from big names like Elton John, J-Lo, and Sting, who'll work on his 'Rise And Fall' single.

• **M**ARCH 28TH: **ONE WEEK** after 'N Sync's album *No Strings Attached* is released, it's become the fastest-selling album ever – with 2.4 million copies bought in just seven days.

### APRIL

singles chart... And the historic Ryman Auditorium in Nashville, the home of the Grand Ole Opry for more than 30 years, is celebrated by the US Postal Service when it issues a 20-cent stamped postcard that features the venue.

• **20**TH: **FORMER BLACK PANTHER** Jamil Abdullah Al-Amin, once known as H. Rap Brown, is captured following a shootout that leaves a sheriff's deputy dead.

• **21**ST: **ALANIS MORISSETTE** opens as the star of feminist play *The Vagina Monologues* at Westside Theater, New York City. It is set to run for two weeks.

• **22**ND: **THE LONDON SUNDAY TIMES'S** annual Rich List reveals former Beatle Paul McCartney to be the UK's richest rock star, with a fortune estimated at some £500m ($750m).

• **3**RD: **THE US FEDERAL COURT** rule that Microsoft has violated antitrust laws by keeping "an oppressive thumb" on its competitors.

• **7**TH: **AN EYE WITNESS** reports that Neil Young appears close to an on-stage heart attack when he sees kids dancing happily to his song 'Ohio' – about four students killed by US National Guardsmen at Kent State University in 1970 – at the otherwise triumphant CSNY gig in Madison Square Garden, New York City.

• **10**TH: **SONY MUSIC** announce plans to make commercial digital downloads available to US consumers, offering songs from Lauryn Hill, Pearl Jam, Michael Jackson, and others.

• **11**TH: **NO DOUBT** release the album *The Return Of Saturn*.

• **13**TH: **METALLICA** file a $100,000 compensation lawsuit against Internet file-sharing software pioneers Napster Inc, alleging that it encourages music piracy... Meanwhile Paul McCartney's girlfriend Heather Mills wins $316,700 in damages for a 1993 accident involving a British motorcycle police officer. The out-of-court-settlement was for the loss of her left leg.

• **14**TH: **RUSSIA FINALLY APPROVES** the START II treaty which calls for the scrapping of US and Russian nuclear warheads.

• **17**TH: **IT'S REPORTED** that glam rock star Gary Glitter, disgraced in a child porn scandal, has left the UK to live in Cuba.

• **21**ST: **RESEARCHERS** in North Carolina discover that the heart of a 66 million-year-old dinosaur was more like that of a mammal or bird than that of a reptile.

• **A**PRIL 4TH: **PINK RELEASES** her debut album, *Can't Take Me Home*. Hopping nimbly between R&B and rock, Alecia 'Pink' Moore, with her ever-changing hair color, began her musical career as a back-up singer in the short-lived Basic Instinct, then as part of the equally brief Choice, before landing a solo contract with LeFace Records. A string of big-selling records soon follows.

## Tragic Pop Princess (1)

**J**UNE 17TH: 'TRY AGAIN' BY AALIYAH, from the soundtrack of the movie *Romeo Must Die*, reaches Number One on the US Top 40 singles chart, purely on the basis of airplay. It is the first song in history to reach the top slot without a commercial release. Aaliyah's talent first came to public attention as a child when she appeared on the TV show *StarSearch*. But she stayed on at school (a performing arts school in Detroit) until she met R. Kelly, who helped produce her debut album, *Age Ain't Nothing But A Number*. Unfortunately for Mr Kelly, age meant more than a number in legal terms. He married Aaliyah when she was only 15, but the marriage had to be annulled shortly afterwards. Aaliyah's talent and looks have ensured she's had several hit singles since, and also developed a successful acting career, including roles in *Romeo Must Die* and later *Queen Of The Damned*. But just when the future seems bright, tragedy looms – on August 20th, 2001, Aaliyah will die when her plane crashes in the Caribbean while she's making a video. She is still just 21.

**MAY**  **JUNE**

• **1ST: VARIOUS EVENTS** protesting against global capitalism are held throughout the US and Europe – but in London a peaceful protest descends into widespread rioting... Perhaps inspired by the day's events, fans storm Brixton Academy in London to gain free access to tonight's Eminem concert. Bum rushing the show, as it were.

• **7TH: 'OOOPS! – I DID IT AGAIN'** by Britney Spears reaches Number One on the UK singles chart. It is also Number One in Canada.

• **9TH: THE US FEDERAL APPEALS COURT** upholds a decision (worth $5.4 million) that Michael Bolton plagiarised parts of the song 'Love Is A Wonderful Thing' by the Isley Brothers.

• **10TH: "EXHAUSTION** caused by an ear infection combined with severe flu" is the reason given when teen pop star Christina Aguilera cancels her upcoming UK visit.

• **15TH: EURYTHMICS STAR** and film director Dave Stewart reveals that he had to drop a Jimi Hendrix song from an acid trip scene in soon-to-be-released All Saints movie *Honest*, because the Hendrix estate doesn't want Jimi's music associated with sex or drugs.

• **18TH: THE ARTIST** formerly known as The Artist Formerly Known As Prince, or that squiggly symbol, announces he is reclaiming the name Prince, because his contract with Warner-Chappell expired at the end of 1999. Tonight, he may well party.

• **27TH: LISA 'LEFT EYE' LOPES** unveils a new line of pyjamas from her clothing collection

• **31ST: JANET JACKSON** reveals she is getting a divorce from dancer Rene Elizondo. The announcement comes as something of a surprise, as the marriage has been kept secret for nine years. Last year the pair said they were ending their 13-year relationship, but denied they were married.

• **JUNE 18TH: TIGER WOODS** wins the US Open Golf championship by 15 shots. A month later he wins the British Open, the youngest ever winner of the Grand Slam, and soon establishes himself as one of the greatest golfers of all time.

• **8TH: SINEAD O'CONNOR** decides that she is a lesbian in an interview with *Curve* magazine in its July-August 2000 issue. But she will apparently have a relapse when she opts to marry for a second time (to British journalist Nick Sommerlad) in 2001.

• **11TH: NEW YORK CITY** police lodge a protest against a new Bruce Springsteen song, inspired by the 1999 police slaying of unarmed West African immigrant Amadou Diallo.

• **20TH: THE DEFTONES** release a new album, *White Pony*, in the US.

• **21ST: TLC ARE AWARDED** a six-times platinum disc for the album *Fanmail*.

• **25TH: US AND BRITISH** researchers announce they have completed a rough draft of the genetic makeup of human beings. The work to date has taken ten years.

• **27TH: A SAN FRANCISCO** appeals court decides The Rolling Stones improperly borrowed 'Love in Vain' and 'Stop Breakin' Down' from the back-catalog of blues legend Robert Johnson, having wrongly assumed the songs were out of copyright and therefore in the public domain.

• **29TH: THE GRAVES** of Ronnie Van Zant and Steve Gaines of Lynyrd Skynyrd are vandalized.

• **30TH: ROLLING STONE** Ronnie Wood checks into a clinic in London for alcohol abuse.

• **30TH: NINE FANS** are killed at the Roskilde Festival in Denmark, headlined by Pearl Jam and The Cure.

## Little Big Voice

• **JUNE 13TH: ANASTACIA** releases her debut album, *Not That Kind*, in the US. Small of stature but huge of voice, the extrovert singer-songwriter's achieves a US Number One in July with her first single, 'I'm Outta Love,' and a UK Number Six later in the year.

## Tragic Pop Princess (2)

• JUNE 20TH: **THE EVA CASSIDY ALBUM** *Time After Time* is released, building on the phenomenon begun by her previous hit albums, *Songbird,* and *Live At Blues Alley.* Cassidy's story is a perfect reminder of the power of recorded music – and also of the lack of foresight of most record companies, who like to think they know what people want. Eva died of cancer in 1996, at the age of 33, having been rejected by established labels because she only sang other people's songs and didn't stick to one style. But what they missed was a voice that instantly captivates, and makes people want

to hear more – whatever she happens to sing. It took an unlikely champion, a middle-aged UK DJ with a BBC radio show, to incite the public demand that made record execs hastily cobble together archive material into best-selling albums. Eva's music will inevitably run out, but unknown to her, her voice will touch many lives for years to come.

## Napster Update

**MAY 5TH: INTERNET** file-sharing pioneers Napster Inc lose the first round of a copyright suit brought by the RIAA, which alleges they encourage music piracy. Later this month, Public Enemy's Chuck D will testify about the benefits of Napster, and online music distribution in general, to the US Congress. Then, on July 11th, Lars Ulrich of Metallica, Roger McGuinn, formerly of The Byrds, Napster CEO Hank Barry, and others appear before a Senate judiciary committee investigating the copyright implications of downloading music from the Internet. On June 26th, an injunction is passed ordering Napster to remove all copyright material from its directories.

### JULY

• JULY 25TH: **AN AIR FRANCE CONCORDE** supersonic passenger jet crashes just after take-off from Charles De Gaulle Airport, Paris, killing 114. Subsequent investigation reveals the plane suffered a burst tyre, having apparently struck some metal debris on the runway that caused an explosion in the fuel tanks.

• 5TH: **EUAN BLAIR,** teenage son of UK prime minister Tony Blair, is arrested after police find him laying on the ground drunk in London's West End.
• 7TH: **EMERGENCY SERVICES** are called to Eminem's home at Sterling Heights, Michigan, where his wife, Kimberly, has attempted suicide... Meanwhile *Harry Potter & The Goblet Of Fire* by J.K Rowling becomes the biggest selling book in the history of online retailing, when Amazon.com announces it has sold almost 400,000 copies.
• 9TH: **POSH SPICE** Victoria Beckham has her live solo debut in London, but it's learned later that she actually mimed to backing tracks.
• 10TH: **KID ROCK'S** ex-manager Stephen Hutton files a lawsuit against his former client in New York City for breach of contract and "unjust enrichment." Hutton wants $4 million damages from Mr Rock and his company, Top Dog Records Inc... And a jewelry store in Beverly Hills, LA, files a $1.45 million lawsuit against Michael Jackson over an allegedly damaged diamond-encrusted wristwatch.
• 12TH: **YUSUF ISLAM,** formerly Cat Stevens, is detained on arrival in Israel, then deported because the intelligence service believes he has contributed funds to Hamas, the Islamic terrorist group.
• 26TH: **OASIS STORMS OFF-STAGE** after being hailed with bottles, cans, and coins at a Swiss music festival. Two weeks later they walk off again, this time in Portugal, when drummer Alan White is hit by a rock.

### AUGUST

• 4TH: **CELEBRATIONS** take place all over the UK to mark the 100th birthday of Queen Elizabeth, the Queen Mother.
• 7TH: **THE FAMILY** of Jimi Hendrix wins a case to evict the unrelated holder of the www.jimihendrix.com Internet address.
• 12TH: **THE RUSSIAN** Northern Fleet command loses contact with a nuclear submarine (the Kursk) which sank eight days ago in the Barents Sea. Despite belated attempts to rescue the crew, all 118 men aboard will be pronounced dead on August 22nd.
• 16TH: **EMINEM** files papers to begin divorce proceedings against his wife

Kimberley Mathers at Macomb County Court, Michigan.
• 18TH: **IT'S ANNOUNCED** that Courtney Love is being sued by film-company Background Productions, makers of the upcoming film *Beat,* for breach of contract, fraud, defamation, and infliction of emotional stress on crew-members.
• 22ND: **THE SECOND ANNUAL** Source Hip-Hop Awards Show in Pasadena, California, is cut short when a brutal fight erupts in the audience, resulting in injuries to Havoc of Mobb Depp and Krayzie Bone of Bone-Thugs-N-Harmony. The incident overshadows the real purpose of the event, which is the presentation of lifetime achievement awards to former NWA members Dr Dre and Ice Cube.
• 23RD: **KENNY LOGGINS** is awarded a star on the Hollywood Walk Of Fame. The singer-songwriter has recently branched out into a line of relationship advice books and tapes.
• 25TH: **JACK NITZSCHE,** legendary songwriter, arranger, and producer – co-creator of the famous Wall Of Sound with Phil Spector – dies at the age of 63 at Queen Of Angels Hospital, Los Angeles. The cause of his death is cardiac arrest, caused by a recurring bronchial infection.
• 26TH: **'DOESN'T REALLY MATTER'** by Janet Jackson reaches Number One on the US Top 40 singles chart.

• JULY 22ND: **'BENT' BY Matchbox Twenty** reaches Number One on the US Top 40 singles chart. Led by Rob Thomas (left) Matchbox Twenty first stormed the US charts with 1997's *Yourself Or Someone Like You.* While the group's brand of guitar rock at first resembles a hybrid of Tom Petty & The Heartbreakers and Pearl Jam, Thomas emerges as a perspicacious songwriter, able to adapt his style at will.

# One Step Closer

**O**CTOBER 24TH: LINKIN PARK (right) release the album *Hybrid Theory*. Purveyors of hip-hop influenced hardcore rock, Linkin Park – vocalists Chester Bennington and Mike Shinoda, guitarist Brad Delson, turntablist Joseph Hahn, drummer Rob Bourdon, and bassist Phoenix – began life at high school in southern California during the mid 1990s, and landed a publishing deal after just one show at legendary LA venue the Whiskey A Go Go. Signing on the dotted line with Warner Brothers, they promptly delivered *Hybrid Theory*, which goes on to become the best-selling album of 2001 (and will sell over 14 million copies in the next three years). They make a connection with tens of thousands of like-minded youths all over the US (and score a few Top 40 singles in the UK as well). They grab a Grammy for Best Hard Rock Performance, as well as nominations for Best Rock Album and Best New Artist. Expectations will be high for their follow-up album, but the band won't let the pressure affect them, despite their youth, and their fans are obviously more than happy with the results: when *Meteora* is released in 2003, more than 800,000 copies fly off the shelves in the US in just one week.

## SEPTEMBER

## OCTOBER

• **OCTOBER 1ST: BOY GEORGE** is made an honorary citizen of Philadelphia, Pennsylvania, on the city's Boy George Tribute Day, acknowledging his services to the gay community.

• **1ST: RADIOHEAD** begin a UK tour in their own circus big top tent, with the first of two nights at Tredegar House, Newport, South Wales.
• **6TH: US DISTRICT** Judge Jed Rakoff rules that MP3.com has violated copyrights, and awards Universal Music $250 million in damages.
• **7TH: WHEN TIM C** of Rage Against The Machine climbs a stage prop at the MTV Awards in New York, he is taken away in handcuffs and held by police.
• **15TH: THE INQUIRY** into the deaths of nine rock fans at Roskilde Festival clears headline band Pearl Jam of any blame... Meanwhile, the 27th Olympic Games begin in Sydney.
• **16TH: 'MUSIC' BY MADONNA** reaches Number One in the US Top 40 chart.
• **19TH: A 'PSYCHEDELIC' JACKET** worn by Jimi Hendrix is sold to the Hard Rock Café for $53,000 when it comes up at auction at Sotheby's in London.

• **2ND: DEPUTY JUDGE** Nicholas Strauss, in the High Court, London, rules that Robbie Williams breached copyright when he used lines from the Woody Guthrie song 'I Am the Way' in his composition 'Jesus In A Camper Van.' ... And John Lennon's murderer Mark David Chapman is denied parole by the New York State Board of Parole.
• **3RD: BENJAMIN ORR**, co-founder of The Cars, dies of pancreatic cancer, at 53.

• **4TH: PRESIDENT SLOBIDAN MILOSEVIC** leaves office after widespread demonstrations throughout Serbia and the withdrawal of Russian support
• **12TH: WHILE REFUELLING** in Yemen, the USS Cole, a US Navy destroyer, is attacked by a small boat packed with explosives: 17 crew-members are killed and at least 39 injured.
• **14TH: 'COME ON OVER BABY'** by Christina Aguilera reaches No1 in the US Top 40

• **OCTOBER 1ST: KYLIE MINOGUE**, former Aussie soap actress turned pop goddess, performs a star turn at the spectacular closing ceremony of the Olympic Games in Sydney, Australia.

NOVEMBER

DECEMBER

• **DECEMBER 22ND: MADONNA MARRIES 32-YEAR-OLD** movie director/producer Guy Ritchie in Skibo Castle, Scotland.

singles chart.. And a lawsuit is filed against Don Henley in Arkansas by a fan who was hit by a maraca during a concert.
• **19TH: ZACK DE LA ROCHA**, vocalist with Rage Against The Machine, quits the band.

• **NOVEMBER 7TH: ANDREA CORR** of The Corrs is voted the 'most beautiful woman in the world' in a survey in the UK.

• **5TH: WESTLIFE** notch up their seventh consecutive UK singles chart topper with 'My Love' – equalling the record set by

The Beatles in 1966.
• **7TH: IT BECOMES CLEAR** that it's going to be one of the closest presidential elections in

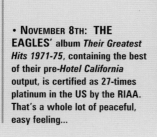

• **NOVEMBER 8TH: THE EAGLES'** album *Their Greatest Hits 1971-75*, containing the best of their pre-*Hotel California* output, is certified as 27-times platinum in the US by the RIAA. That's a whole lot of peaceful, easy feeling...

the history of the US when the counting and recounting of Florida's ballots last for more than a month. The final (but still disputed) official count gives George W. Bush victory by only 537 votes.
• **11TH: 'WITH ARMS WIDE OPEN'** by Creed reaches No1 in the US Top 40 chart.
• **17TH: A SENTENCE** of life-plus-22 years with no prospect of parole is pronounced on 40-year-old Gabriel Gomez, killer of Sandra

Rosas, wife of Los Lobos frontman Cesar Rojas.
• **19TH: IT'S REVEALED** in the UK press that The Spice Girls have no plans to release any more records.
• **28TH: NINE MILLION PEOPLE** watch a Madonna concert over the Internet. The 29-minute, six-song event, from London's Brixton Academy is, according to MSN.com, a record for such events, with nine million logging on to the site.

## One & Only

• **DECEMBER 19TH: UK SINGER-SONGWRITER** Kirsty MacColl is hit and killed by a speedboat while scuba-diving with her two sons off the coast of Mexico. She was 41. Her biggest hit was her 1987 duet with The Pogues on 'Fairytale Of New York,' but she made some excellent, witty solo albums, including *Electric Landlady*, and recently *Tropical Brainstorm*.

• **2ND: THE SMASHING PUMPKINS** play their final show together, in Chicago, Illinois.
• **4TH: O.J. SIMPSON** is involved in an incident in Miami, accused of scratching another motorist's face while pulling off the man's glasses.
• **10TH: THE SMASH HITS** Poll Winners' Party 2000 takes place at the London Arena, with a line-up including Britney Spears, Billie Piper, a1, Samantha Mumba, Westlife, Sonique, Ronan Keating, Steps, Savage Garden, Texas, and Five.
• **14TH: AMERICAN BUSINESSMAN** Edmond Pope is released from a Russian prison for humanitarian reasons, after being held for 20 years on espionage charges.
• **16TH: NASA'S GALILEO** spacecraft discovers that Ganymede, a moon of Jupiter, appears to have a liquid saltwater ocean beneath a surface of solid ice.
• **18TH: THE ALBUM** Baby, One More Time by Britney Spears is certified as a US 13-times platinum disc by the RIAA.
• **19TH: ROBUCK 'POPS' STAPLES**, patriarch of revered R&B band The Staple Singers, dies after suffering concussion in a fall near his home in Dalton, Illinois.
• **31ST: JAMES BROWN** astounds his audience at the Blue Note jazz club, Las Vegas, Nevada, when he becomes involved in an altercation with two women in front of the stage. He confiscates their video camera, knocks drinks off their table and kicks over their chairs.

# 2001
## January–April

• **MARCH 18TH: JOHN PHILLIPS**, leader of The Mamas & The Papas (above, and on the left in the inset photo, in his 1960s heyday), dies of heart failure, after a month in a Los Angeles hospital following a shoulder injury.

**JANUARY**

**FEBRUARY**

## Wannabe Famous?

• **FEBRUARY 28TH: AT *THE BRIT AWARDS*** in London, Hear'say (above), the band created by the TV show *Popstars*, make their live performance debut... Meanwhile, the first US series of *Popstars* has just launched on the WB channel, and after hundreds of excruciating auditions in front of a panel of industry judges (admittedly not as scathingly unkind as the UK panelists), the 'best' singers will eventually be put together to form the anodynely glamorous Eden's Crush (below). A second series will later create Scene 23, while a Canadian *Popstars* series introduces Sugar Jones. None will set the world alight. But thousands of wannabe starlets still continue to turn up for similar TV shows over the next couple of years. Is this simply a more honest approach to the business of pop entertainment? After all, you could claim Berry Gordy 'manufactured' acts on Motown, and certainly The Monkees were carefully put together for the TV audience in the mid 1960s. But how many people auditioned for The Monkees, compared with the number of entrants for *Popstars*? Nowadays everyone who stands up to sing in a karaoke bar thinks they can become a star. When even the hundreds of audition failures are screened endlessly on TV, Andy Warhol's quip that everyone will be famous for 15 minutes seems to be literally coming true.

• **1ST: GUNS N' ROSES** begin their comeback tour with a show at the House Of Blues, Las Vegas, Nevada, their first in seven years.
• **4TH: A POLL HELD** by Madame Tussaud's Waxworks in London reveals that Liam Gallagher of Oasis has come third in the 'Most Hated Characters' category – just below Adolf Hitler and Slobodan Milosevic.
• **13TH: WHILE IN RIO DE JANIERO**, Brazil, for the Rock In Rio III Festival, Britney Spears and Justin Timberlake spend the weekend holed up in the Intercontinental Hotel but later say they have not had sex.
• **17TH: IT IS ANNOUNCED** by Metallica that Jason Newstead has chosen to leave the band.
• **20TH: REPUBLICAN GEORGE W. BUSH** is inaugurated as the 43rd President of the US, succeeding Democrat Bill Clinton.
• **24TH: SLIPKNOT** launch their latest evil tactic to control the minds of impressionable young fans – the Slipknot lunchbox... The last of the seven convicts (dubbed the Texas seven by the media) who escaped from prison in San Antonio in December, then robbed a sports store, killing a police officer and escaping with $70,000, are finally apprehended in Colorado Springs.
• **26TH: A 7.9 RICHTER SCALE EARTHQUAKE** hits Gujarat, India, killing 20,000 and destroying much of the historic city.
• **27TH: A NEWLY DISCOVERED** species of dinosaur is named Masiakasaurus Knopfleri because the music of Dire Straits (led by Mark Knopfler) was being played when it was dug up.

## Rock Of Ages

• **FEBRUARY 12TH: AT A PRESS CONFERENCE** in London's Savoy Hotel, original Roxy Music members Bryan Ferry (left), Phil Manzanera, and Andy Mackay announce they will reform to tour together this summer for the first time in 18 years, taking in the UK, Europe, Canada, and the US. They're not the only ones jumping (or perhaps easing themselves gently) onto the reunion bandwagon: Donald Fagen and Walter Becker have resurrected Steely Dan (below); Blondie are back on the road, and in the charts; The Who have dragged themselves on-stage for the umpteenth time; and Crosby, Stills, Nash, & recently Young are back. Meanwhile, The Eagles did it a few years ago, The Osmonds are threatening to do it, Genesis may reconvene and even all four Monkees have toured and recorded together recently, albeit briefly, for the first time in three decades. And of course, The Rolling Stones are planning a 40th anniversary reunion tour for 2002, although that's less of a surprise to anyone, as they've barely stopped in 40 years. We're now seeing punk and new romantic tours on the 'nostalgia' circuit, once reserved for ageing 1960s popsters (who are still performing there too). But these high-profile, highly-paid superstar reunions divide audiences and critics between sentimental middle-aged frenzy and cynical contempt. Brian Eno, who's spurned the chance to re-join Roxy Music for a lucrative tour, is in the latter camp, telling *Rolling Stone* magazine: "I'm not interested any more. It's obvious why it's being done. Why does anyone have a reunion?" Apart from a boost to the pension fund, the one thing it does provide is proof, if it were needed, that rock is no longer just for the young and rebellious, as it may have been for previous generations. Parents now drag their kids to rock concerts, rather than the other way around – and most bizarre of all, they sometimes even like the same music.

• **9TH: DON FELDER** of The Eagles files a lawsuit in Los Angeles Superior Court against his former bandmates, Don Henley and Glenn Frey, claiming to have been wrongfully dismissed from the group in early 2001.
• **11TH: ELLEN MACARTHUR** completes the Vendee Globe yacht race, becoming the fastest woman ever to sail single-handedly around the world.
• **12TH: SONY MUSIC** announces that Lauryn Hill has settled out of court with the four musicians known as New-Ark Entertainment who had been seeking co-writing and co-production credits and a third of the profits from Hill's album The

*Miseducation Of Lauryn Hill*.
• **17TH: 'MS JACKSON'** by Outkast reaches Number One on the US Top 40 singles chart.
• **20TH: FBI AGENT** Robert Phillip Hanssen is arrested as a Russian spy.
• **21ST: THE FIRST OUTBREAK** of foot & mouth disease in the UK for over 20 years is confirmed, beginning at an abattoir in Essex and spreading throughout the UK. At its worst, 25 new cases are identified a day, and the final number will reach over 2,000 by the end of the year.
• **24TH: AT THE GRAMMY AWARDS** in Los Angeles, Elton John performs a duet with Eminem.

MARCH

APRIL

## Cuba Back On the Map

• **FEBRUARY 17TH: UK BAND MANIC STREET PREACHERS** become the first high-profile 'Western' act to perform an official concert in Cuba for 20 years (since Billy Joel in 1979), and the first British band in 40 years. Fidel Castro is among the audience of 5000 (paying only 25 cents for a ticket) at the Karl Marx Theatre in Havana. Bass player Nicky Wire insists the group's desire to play on the island is "not like a student Che Guevara sort of thing – it's just that for me Cuba is the last great symbol that really fights against the Americanisation of the world." Interest in Cuba in general has been revived since the 1997 album *Buena Vista Social Club*, the result of a year Ry Cooder spent on the island, recording with veteran Cuban musicians, such as pianist Ruben Gonzalez and guitarist Eliades Ochoa, and singers Ibrahim Ferrer, Omara Portuondo (seen together left), and Company Segundo. Although the Buena Vista Social Club has a retro feel about it, it points to the next generation too, with younger musicians such as Juan De Marcos's Afro-Cuban All-Stars participating. Indeed movie director Wim Wenders is so impressed that he makes a *Buena Vista Social Club* documentary about the musicians and their lives, and that also becomes a massive hit.

---

• **1ST: THE SOUL TRAIN AWARDS** are held in Los Angeles. Destiny's Child win Best Entertainer Award, Jagged Edge win Best Group, and R. Kelly wins both Best Male Solo Single and Best Album.

• **4TH: GLENN HUGHES**, the original biker in Village People, dies of cancer at his Manhattan home, at age 51. He has requested that he be buried in his leather biking costume.

• **7TH: IN A MOVE** to outflank bootleggers, no less than seven 'official bootleg' CDs, recorded by Pearl

Jam during a recent tour, debut on the Billboard Hot 200 album chart.

• **8TH: DIVERS** raise the wreck of Donald Campbell's boat, Bluebird, from the bottom of Coniston Water in Cumbria, UK, where it has remained since it crashed in 1967. Campbell – the only person to have held both land and water speed records at the same time – died as he attempted to take back the world water speed record.

• **16TH: PUFF DADDY** is cleared of gun-related charges relating to a December 1999 incident outside a

club in Times Square, New York.

• **19TH: CALIFORNIA** officials order the first of two days of rolling blackouts.

• **22ND: THE BODY** of James Hanratty, hanged as a murderer in 1962, is exhumed from his grave at Carpenters Park cemetery, Hertfordshire, UK, for DNA samples to be taken to uphold the original verdict.

• **23RD: AFTER 15 YEARS** in space, the Russians space lab Mir returns to Earth, disintegrating as it re-enters the atmosphere somewhere above the South Pacific.

• **1ST: FORMER YUGOSLAVIAN** president Slobodan Milosevic is arrested and taken to prison after an armed stand-off at his Belgrade villa.

• **3RD: A DOLL BASED** on Eminem is banned from sale in Woolworths stores in the UK.

• **4TH: ROB ZOMBIE'S** goresplattered horror movie *House Of 1,000 Corpses* is refused distribution in US cinemas.

• **5TH: DUTCH LORRY DRIVER** Perry Wacker is sentenced to 14 years in prison for his part in the deaths of 58 illegal Chinese immigrants who were found suffocated in the back of his lorry when it was searched at the ferry port in Dover, UK, last June.

• **11TH: CHINA RELEASE** the 24 crew-members of a US surveillance plane they had been holding since April 1st.

• **15TH: JOEY RAMONE**, founder member of The Ramones dies of lymphatic cancer.

• **21ST: PETER BUCK** of R.E.M. is arrested at the UK's Heathrow Airport as a result of an alleged 'air rage' incident, involving charges of causing criminal damage to the plane, being drunk on an aircraft, and two counts of assaulting cabin crew.

• **28TH: A BILLIONAIRE BUSINESSMAN**, Dennis Tito (60) from California, becomes the first paying passenger to go into outer space, setting off from Kazakhstan for an eight-day holiday aboard the International Space Station.

• **30TH: DESTINY'S CHILD** hold an album release party for their new album, *Survivor*, at the Park restaurant in New York City.

• **APRIL 14TH: 'ALL FOR YOU'** by Janet Jackson reaches Number One on the US Top 40 singles chart.

## Farming Today

• **FEBRUARY 3RD: PAPA ROACH** (left) announce they have signed Alien Ant Farm (right) to their New Noize record label. AAA will go on to have their biggest international hit with their metallized cover of Michael Jackson's 'Smooth Criminal.'

# 2001

May–August

## Different Strokes

**A**UGUST 26TH: **THE STROKES** receive a rousing reception at the UK's *Reading Festival*. The five friends – Julian Casablancas (vocals), Fabrizio Moretti (drums), Albert Hammond Jr (guitar), Nick Valensi (guitar), and Nikolai Fraiture (bass) – first met at the Music Building in New York. They have gone from "just having some fun" with their updated take on the Velvet Underground and Television, to creating a buzz at downtown Manhattan clubs, to being *the* new band on both sides of the Atlantic, and all seemingly overnight. Their career is not harmed by their good looks, on-stage showmanship, or acclaimed debut album *Is This It?*, which proves something of a catalyst for a whole 'new' rock movement, and helps to rekindle interest in post-dance guitar bands everywhere.

## The Blues Will Never Die...

• JUNE 21ST: **BLUES GIANT** John Lee Hooker dies in his sleep, age 83, at home in the San Francisco Bay Area, California.

## Queen Bs

**J**UNE 2ND: 'Lady Marmalade' by Lil' Kim (below), Christina Aguilera, Mya, & Pink reaches Number One on the US Top 40 .

## Up-dated

• AUGUST 7TH: **USHER RELEASES** his fourth US album. Called *8701* – which, you'll notice, is today's date – its slickly-produced melodic R&B provides another huge seller for the 22-year-old singer.

---

| MAY | JUNE | JULY | AUGUST |

### MAY

• 6TH: **PRINCE RELEASES** a new single, 'The Work – Pt 1,' as an officially sanctioned Napster download.

• 8TH: **LOU REED** issues an official statement denying numerous Internet rumours of his death, and pointing out that he is currently working on his latest project in Amsterdam, Holland... Meanwhile Ronnie Biggs, 71-year-old ex-train robber, is returned to prison for the first time since he escaped 35 years ago. He has become seriously ill and has flown back from exile in Brazil to the UK for medical treatment.

• 9TH: **TOM PETTY & THE HEARTBREAKERS** begin their US tour at Gill Coliseum, Corvallis, Oregon.

• 15TH: **A NEW RECORD** label, Flawless, is launched by Fred Durst of Limp Bizkit.

• 16TH: **BRITISH DEPUTY PRIME MINISTER** John Prescott assaults Craig Evans at an election rally in Wales after Evans throw an egg at him.

• 17TH: **IT'S REPORTED** that Madonna has broken existing box office records at Earl's Court, London. Her upcoming UK shows there were the fastest sellers the venue had ever experienced - with the first show in July selling out in 15 minutes.

• 27TH: **STEVEN TYLER** of Aerosmith upsets the crowd at the Indianapolis 500 car race in Indiana when he sings the US National Anthem, changing the line "The land of the free and the home of the brave" to "The land of the free and the home of the Indianapolis 500."

### JUNE

• 5TH: **ALICIA KEYS** releases her debut album, *Songs in A Minor*. In its first week, it sells more than 235,000 copies.

• 8TH: **MARC CHAGALL'S** painting *Study For 'Over Vitebsk'* is stolen from the Jewish Museum in New York City. A group called the International Committee for Art & Peace announces it will return the painting, worth about $1 million, when there is peace in the Middle East.

• 9TH: **UK PRIME MINISTER** Tony Blair celebrates his first day back in office. Yesterday he achieved a landslide majority, prompting his opposite number, William Hague, to resign as leader of the Conservative Party. The turnout for the election was the lowest since 1918.

• 11TH: **TIMOTHY MCVEIGH** is executed

• JUNE 12TH: **BLINK-182** release their latest party-punk album, *Take Off Your Pants And Jacket.*

• AUGUST 24TH: **MICK JAGGER** of The Rolling Stones is reported to be furious when his picture appears on the front cover of *Saga*, a UK magazine for senior citizens.

in Terre Haute Federal Penitentiary, Indiana, by lethal injection, after he admitted responsibility for the deaths of 168 people in the Oklahoma City bombing of 1995. He was the first federal prisoner to be executed in 38 years.

• 21ST: **IT'S ANNOUNCED** that the Beastie Boys' label, Grand Royal, has negotiated a deal with Napster Inc to release and feature a number of songs from its artists.

• 29TH: **EMINEM** is sentenced to one year of probation on charges of carrying a concealed weapon and brandishing a weapon. The charges relate back to a confrontation with Insane Clown Posse in a parking lot in Michigan last year.

### JULY

• 2ND: **CONSTRUCTION** of the Stax Museum begins on a site in Memphis, Tennessee.

• 7TH: **'U REMIND ME'** by Usher reaches Number One on the US Top 40 singles chart.

• 9TH: **GEORGE HARRISON**, formerly of The Beatles, is in hospital in Zurich, Switzerland, being treated for a cancerous brain tumour... Meanwhile The Backstreet Boys temporarily halt their Black & Blue World Tour because A.J. McLean needs to enter a treatment centre for depression and alcohol abuse. The tour resumes on August 24th.

• 10TH: **KURT COBAIN'S** former wife Courtney Love sues his former bandmates Dave Grohl and Krist Novoselic in the latest battle over his estate.

• 10TH: **IT'S ANNOUNCED** that Jennifer Lopez has insured her hair, currently appearing in a Loreal ad, for $50m... And 96 years after British soccer player Alf Common became the world's first £1,000 ($1,600) footballer, Spanish club Real Madrid pays the highest transfer fee yet, coughing up more than £45m ($70m) to Italy's Juventus for French star Zinedine Zidane.

• 11TH: **SHOCK-ROCKERS** Slipknot are seen for the first time without their masks in an unofficial book published today.

• 13TH: **THE LEGAL BATTLE** between Metallica and Napster is reported to have been settled with Napster agreeing to block access to files that artists don't want users to share. In return, Metallica agrees to make some tracks available for download via Napster, but not for free.

### AUGUST

• 16TH: **AFTER BITTER DISPUTES** with her record label, Lisa 'Left Eye' Lopes of TLC fame releases her solo album, *Supernova*, by streaming it from her own website.

• 17TH: **RED HOT CHILI PEPPERS** cancel their upcoming concert in Tel Aviv due to the current political unrest in Israel.

• 16TH: **PAUL BURRELL**, former butler to Diana, Princess Of Wales, is charged with theft from her estate of items reportedly worth £5m ($7.5m). In October 2002, his trial will collapse after the

Queen reveals Burrell told her he was storing some of Princess Diana's belongings.

• 24TH: **NASA** announces that the Upper Atmosphere Research Satellite project – best known for monitoring a hole in the ozone layer over Antarctica – will end by September 30th this year due to budget restrictions.

• 27TH: **WORK BEGINS** on a World War II memorial in the U.S. capital's historic national Mall, between the Washington Monument and the Lincoln Memorial.

• AUGUST 18TH: **'FALLIN'' BY ALICIA KEYS** reaches Number One on the US Top 40 singles chart.

# 2001

## September–December

# Nine Eleven

**S**EPTEMBER 11TH 2001: THE TWIN TOWERS of the World Trade Center in New York are destroyed, and the Pentagon in Washington DC attacked, when four passenger airliners are hi-jacked by suicidal terrorists, who will rapidly be linked to Osama bin Laden's al-Quaeda, an Islamic fundamentalist network. More than 3,000 lives are lost. In the traumatized aftermath, pop and rock music plays its own role in uniting a devastated city and the watching world. Not all music is seen as helpful, though: the Clear Channel radio network issues a 'don't-play' list of 150 songs, including John Lennon's 'Imagine,' and Buddy Holly's 'That'll Be The Day.' Three days later, Rage Against The Machine's website is

## SEPTEMBER

- **SEPTEMBER 8TH: THE ALBUM** *Toxicity* by radical rockers System Of A Down enters the US chart at Number One.

- **1ST: AT THE DRAGONCON,** Atlanta, Georgia, The International Horror Guild presents Alice Cooper with its Living Legend Award, for influencing the horror field.
- **5TH:** *JUNICHIRO KOIZUMI PRESENTS: My Favorite Elvis Songs* is released exclusively in Japan. All the songs in the collection were picked by Japan's prime minister.
- **6TH: EBAY INC** is found not liable for copyright infringement after bootleg copies of a Charles Manson documentary are auctioned via its site.
- **14TH: NINTENDO RELEASES** its GameCube console in Japan.
- **15TH: METALLICA** action figures go on sale.
- **22ND: A JURY** dismisses claims against Cher brought by an accountant who insists he lost his job after uncovering labour violations during the building of her Malibu mansion.
- **29TH: JENNIFER LOPEZ** marries dancer/choreographer Cris Judd in Los Angeles. They will divorce within nine months.

## OCTOBER

- **4TH: NATO** offers the United States open access to its airfields and seaports in its declared war on terrorism. Three days later, the US and Great Britain begin air-strikes in Afghanistan in response to its support for terrorism and Osama bin Laden. President George W. Bush then presents a list of the world's 22 most wanted terrorists.
- **5TH: IT IS CONFIRMED,** following rumors, that internationally successful Australian duo Savage Garden have split.
- **6TH: MARILYN MANSON** appears in court in Clarkston, Michigan, facing charges of alleged indecent assault.
- **9TH: BOB DYLAN** is refused entry to his own show at Central Point, Oregon, because he doesn't have a backstage pass.

- **14TH: AN ISRAELI** plane bound for Russia is destroyed over the Black Sea by a Ukrainian military missile, set off during a training exercise: 76 passengers lose their lives.
- **18TH: SLIPKNOT** are among the US acts who decide to postpone all foreign tour dates, citing the World Trade Center terrorist attacks as a reason for not flying.
- **24TH: IT IS REPORTED** that Britney Spears has incurred the displeasure of her sponsors Pepsi, with whom she has signed a deal worth some $97 million. She has been seen in public drinking a rival firm's soft drinks. A Pepsi spokesman says it will "be made clear to her she should drink only Pepsi." ... Meanwhile, the Mars Odyssey spacecraft successfully enters orbit around Mars.

- **OCTOBER 2ND: GARBAGE RELEASE** the much-anticipated new album *beautifulgarbage* – the band's first since 1998's eulogized *Version 2.0*, and only their third since forming in 1995. Many know Butch Vig as the master-producer behind some of the most groundbreaking albums of the grunge/alternative guitar movement, including Nirvana's *Nevermind*, Sonic Youth's *Dirty*, and the Smashing Pumpkins' *Gish* and *Siamese Dream*. So his own band, Garbage – formed with vocalist Shirley Manson (left) and guitarists Steve Marker and Duke Erikson, plus Vig on drums – may well have come as something of a shock. Because while there is undeniably an aggressive and noisy aspect to the Garbage sound, there's an equally unapologetic pop element. The combination of crunching riffs, thunderous drums, and plenty of pop hooks ensures over four million sales and several Grammys for their debut. The 1998 follow-up pushed the punishing but melodic Garbage imprint even further. The new album, *Beautifulgarbage*, challenges yet again, being replete with string-driven ballads, bubblegum pop, and heavy nods towards Phil Spector.

## NOVEMBER

- **NOVEMBER 13TH: SHAKIRA** releases the album *Laundry Service*. Former child prodigy Shakira, a half-Lebanese Colombian, has been a star on the Latin market for some years, writing and performing her own material – she was named Latin Female Artist Of The Year at the 1998 *World Music Awards* – but her crossover breakthrough has been helped by working with Gloria and Emilio Estefan on some English language recordings. The first international hit single from the new album will be 'Whatever Whenever,' co-written with Gloria Estefan.

- **3RD: 'FAMILY AFFAIR'** by Mary J. Blige reaches Number One on the US Top 40 chart.
- **4TH: THE UNITED STATES** sends humanitarian aid to Cuba – the first commercial food shipment from the US to the island in nearly 40 years – after Hurricane Michelle hits the country, destroying crops and thousands of homes.
- **6TH: THE DESTINY'S CHILD** album *The Writing's On the Wall* is certified as eight-times platinum by the RIAA.
- **7TH: THE NEW .BIZ WEBSITE** domain extension is officially launched.
- **12TH: THE NORTHERN**

closed, allegedly by the US secret service, angered that the group has voiced opinions not in line with the US government's view of the terrorist attack. On September 20th, a telethon is broadcast to raise money for the victims' families. *America: A Tribute To Heroes* features Stevie Wonder, Sting, Tom Petty, Mariah Carey, Bruce Springsteen, Celine Dion, Dixie Chicks, Wyclef Jean, Billy Joel, Neil Young with members of Pearl Jam, Limp Bizkit, and Goo Goo Dolls. On October 20th, a huge *Concert For New York City* is held at Madison Square Garden. Paul McCartney (above left) hosts the event, raising more money for victims' families, with Bon Jovi, Destiny's Child, Janet Jackson, Elton John, Mick Jagger, David Bowie, The Who, Bono & The Edge of U2, and others.

**• NOVEMBER 29TH: GEORGE HARRISON,** the former Beatle – a man who inspired a generation to take up the electric guitar, with his monumental pop riffs and chiming chords – dies of cancer in Los Angeles, at the age of 58.

## DECEMBER

**ALLIANCE** take Kabul, capital of Afghanistan, from the ruling Taliban. They insist they also have control over most of the northern areas of the county.

**• 15TH: A MICROSCOPIC** speck of DNA ensures a 65-year-old farm labourer from the English midlands is jailed for life for the murder of schoolboy Roy Tutill, 33 years ago. It's thought to be the longest known gap between a crime being committed and the perpetrator being brought to justice.

**• 21ST: MICROSOFT** proposes giving $1 billion in computers, software, training, and cash to more than 12,500 of the poorest schools in the US, as part of a deal to settle the company's antitrust lawsuits.

**• 23RD: UK POP IMPRESARIO** and former pop star Jonathan King is sentenced to seven years in jail for sex assaults on boys as young as 14.

**• 28TH: SONGS IN A MINOR**, the album by Alicia Keys, is certified as a quadruple platinum disc by the RIAA.

**• NOVEMBER 20TH: PINK** releases the album *M!SSUNAZTOOD*.

**• DECEMBER 22ND: 'HOW YOU REMIND ME'** by Canadian rockers Nickelback reaches Number One on the US Top 40 singles chart. The song will climb to Number Four in the UK, although not until next spring.

**• 3RD: THE VH1 MUSIC AWARDS** 2001 ceremony is held at the Shrine Auditorium, Los Angeles. Favorite Group is the Dave Matthews Band, Favorite Male Artist is Lenny Kravitz, and Favorite Female Artist is Gwen Stefani of No Doubt.

**• 5TH: AFGHAN LEADERS** sign a pact to create a temporary administration for post-Taliban Afghanistan, which includes two women in the cabinet structure.

**• 7TH: JAY-Z** gets three years' probation after admitting to having stabbed a producer during an argument about bootlegging.

**• 11TH: THE UNITED NATIONS** gives Alanis Morissette its Global Tolerance Award for her work in promoting open-mindedness through the arts

**• 12TH: ACTRESS WINONA RYDER** is arrested at Saks Fifth Avenue in Beverly Hills, LA, for shoplifting and possessing pharmaceutical drugs without a prescription.

**• 15TH: SIENA HEIGHTS UNIVERSITY**, Michigan, begins offering a class called Animated Philosophy & Religion, covering the spiritual and metaphysical side of popular culture, taking particular note of the TV series *The Simpsons*.

**• 16TH: THE OBSERVER** newspaper in the UK reports that a notebook has been found at an al-Quaeda training camp in southern Afghanistan, containing a blueprint for a bomb attack on London's financial district.

**• 17TH: ILLINOIS STATE** opens a child sex abuse investigation into R. Kelly, based on an alleged videotape that is said to show him engaging in various sex acts with a girl of 14. The police are also investigating the girl's parents.

**• 18TH: THE ALBUM *CORE*** by Stone Temple Pilots is certified as eight times platinum in the US... Meanwhile Mötley Crüe's Tommy Lee wins a court battle with ex-wife Pamela Anderson to get unsupervised visits to their two children.

**• DECEMBER 13TH: DAVE GROHL & KRIST NOVOSELIC** file a countersuit against Courtney Love, charging her with manipulating the memory and work of her dead husband, Kurt Cobain, for the benefit of her own career. Since the demise of Cobain and Nirvana, bassist Novoselic's career has been low-key (though he's just got a new band called Eyes Adrift), but former drummer Grohl has emerged as the true keeper of the Nirvana flame. In 1995 he resolutely stepped from behind his drum stool and unleashed the Foo Fighters, featuring Pat Smear (guitar), Nate Mendel (bass), William Goldsmith (drums), and Grohl himself (below) on guitar and lead vocals. Their debut surprised critics and fans alike with the quality of its material. They were even stronger on the follow-up, *The Colour & The Shape*. But the group's shifting line-up (and Grohl's brief moonlighting with Queens Of The Stone Age) has had fans fearing The Foo Fighters are finished. Not so. Grohl and co will release the triumphant *One By One* album in 2002, and confirm the band's status as the standard-bearers of new guitar rock.

# 2002
## January–April

### Euro Dollar?

• **JANUARY 1ST: THE EURO REPLACES** the national currencies of 12 EEC countries: only Denmark, Sweden, and the UK retain their old notes and coins. Allowing for fluctuating exchange rates, one Euro is worth roughly $1.1.

---

## JANUARY

• **JANUARY 14TH: JON BON JOVI** begins a nine-episode acting stint on popular TV show *Ally McBeal.*

• **3RD: SOUNDSCAN REPORTS** that, with 4.8 million sales, Linkin Park's *Hybrid Theory* was the best-selling US album of the past 12 months.

• **7TH: JON LEE**, drummer with Feeder, is found dead at his home in Miami, Florida, having committed suicide by hanging himself. He was 33.

• **8TH: THE BLACK CROWES** announce that, "For the time being, Chris Robinson is pursuing a solo career, and Steve Gorman has left the band for personal reasons."

• **9TH: AT THE AMERICAN MUSIC AWARDS** in the Shrine Auditorium, Los Angeles, Alicia Keys wins Favourite New Artist (Pop/Rock), and Favourite New Artist (Soul/R&B).

• **10TH: WOMEN** can now get the morning-after contraception pill free in pharmacies in France.

• **13TH: US PRESIDENT** George W. Bush faints after choking on a pretzel while watching a football game on television.

• **21ST: AROUND 50 PEOPLE** are killed when a lava flow from Mount Nyiragongo in the Congo ignites a gas station while they are there trying to steal fuel.

• **23RD: EMI ANNOUNCES** it will pay Mariah Carey $28 million to leave the label. Her contract was planned to last for several albums, and was estimated to be worth $100 million.

• **25TH: *LES MISERABLES*** becomes the second-longest running show in Broadway history, after its 6,138th performance. *Cats*, which closed in 2000, still holds the record for longevity, at 7,485 shows.

• **30TH: GEORGE W. BUSH**, recovered from his choking incident, uses his State of the Union address to the US Congress to drop some very heavy hints about upcoming aggression, using the phrase "axis of evil" to describe America's enemies. He specifically mentions North Korea, Iran, and Iraq.

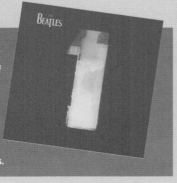

• **JANUARY 8TH: WHEN CREED** begin their seventh week at the top of the US album chart with *Weathered*, they equal the record for longest-running Number One of the 21st century. The record was set by The Beatles with their 2001 compilation *1*, which, amazingly, was the first time a Beatles album had ever topped the US end-of-year best-selling lists.

---

## FEBRUARY

• **2ND: GEORGE HARRISON'S** re-released 'My Sweet Lord' comes to the end of a week at Number One in the UK in the wake of the former Beatle's death. It's replaced at the top by Enrique Iglesias' 'Hero' ... Meanwhile, in the US, *Drive* by Alan Jackson reaches Number One on the US album chart, finally displacing Creed's record-breaking chart-topper *Weathered*.

• **12TH: THE TRIAL** of former Yugoslavian President Slobodan Milosevic begins at the UN tribunal in The Hague.

• **13TH: RUDOLPH GIULIANI**, the former mayor of New York City, receives an honorary knighthood from Queen Elizabeth II... Meanwhile Zal Yanovsky, lead guitarist of the Lovin' Spoonful, dies of a heart attack in Kingston, Ontario, Canada.

• **17TH: GEORGE MICHAEL'S HOME** in Hampstead, London, is burgled, and $140,000 in paintings, jewelry and clothing are stolen – as is his $114,000 Aston Martin sports car.

• **FEBRUARY 9TH: ALMOST 14 MILLION** British TV viewers watch the final of *Pop Idol*, a televised talent contest and sequel to the *Popstars* group hunt, this time designed to create a new solo pop star. The winner is Will Young, though the close runner-up, Gareth Gates, will also get a record contract and have some chart success. The series will soon be exported to the States as *American Idol*, with one of the same judges, big-trousered, big-mouthed A&R man Simon Cowell (right). He will quickly become better-known than any of the would-be 'idols,' getting bookings as a guest on TV chat shows, and even *The Simpsons*. Ironically, Cowell will end up being voted one of America's "Top Five Entertainers."

## Roots Music

**F**EBRUARY 20TH: At the BRIT Awards ceremony in London, the Best British Male Artist award goes to Robbie Williams (again), Best British Female Artist is Dido (left), and Best British Group is Travis. A week later, across the pond at the 44th Annual Grammy Awards in Los Angeles, Record Of The Year is U2's 'Walk On,' Song Of The Year is 'Fallin'' by Alicia Keys. But the surprising Album Of The Year is the soundtrack of the movie *O Brother Where Art Thou*. Directed by Joel and Ethan Coen, and starring George Clooney as a singing convict, this film seemed solid art-house fare, but in fact it kick-started an extraordinary new enthusiasm among mainstream audiences for traditional American roots music. The album ended up topping the pop charts.

## Wild Frontier

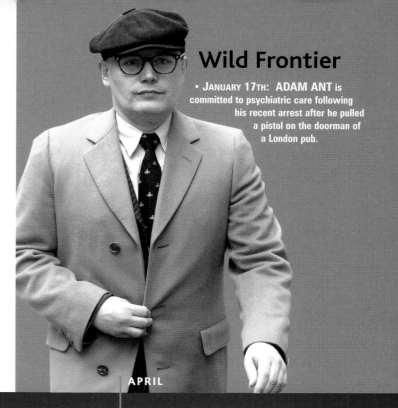

• JANUARY 17TH: ADAM ANT is committed to psychiatric care following his recent arrest after he pulled a pistol on the doorman of a London pub.

**MARCH**

**APRIL**

• FEBRUARY 7TH: **FOURTEEN YEARS** after her last US hit, Kylie Minogue – or SexKylie as she's now termed in the press – reaches Number 20 on the US singles chart with 'Can't Get You Out Of My Head.' After early Stock/Aitken/Waterman production-line confections like 'I Should Be So Lucky,' Kylie gradually started exerting more control over her career and choice of material, dating INXS frontman Michael Hutchence, who encouraged her new sexy image, and working with the likes of Nick Cave . She becomes a more respected (and much desired) dance-pop diva, finally breaking in the US this year with *Fever*.

• FEBRUARY 27TH: **SPIKE MILLIGAN** dies of kidney failure at the age of 83. Milligan was founder member and script-writer of *The Goons*, as well as being a poet, novelist and musician – and probably the most influential comedian in post-war Britain. The Monty Python team would acknowledge their debt to his anarchic and surreally inventive style. He's seen above (on the left) working with Goons colleague Peter Sellers.

• 4TH: *SONGS IN A MINOR* by Alicia Keys is certified as five-times platinum in the US.
• 9TH: **'AIN'T IT FUNNY'** by Jennifer Lopez reaches Number One on the US Top 40 singles chart.
• 12TH: **LEAKED DOCUMENTS** reveal that although deceased rock star Michael Hutchence, singer with INXS, earned $45m in his career, and was estimated to be worth over $21m when he died, he has left just $33,000. It's believed most of this will go to Amnesty International and Greenpeace. The rest of INXS, meanwhile, have re-grouped and relaunched their career, with a new frontman, New Zealand singer Jon Stevens, and are preparing for a North American tour this summer.
• 13TH: **ACTOR TODD BRIDGES**, former star of television's *Diff'rent Strokes* and *Roots*, defeats rapper Vanilla Ice on Fox Television's *Celebrity Boxing*.
• 15TH: **BURGER KING** in the US begin selling veggie burgers – the first non-meat burgers to be sold nationally by a fast food chain.
• 16TH: *UNDER RUG SWEPT* by Alanis Morrisette reaches Number One on the US album chart.
• 19TH: **THE LARGEST** US-led ground offensive since the Gulf War (Operation Anaconda) ends in eastern Afghanistan.
• 21ST: **THE EARLIEST RECORDED** photographic image, an 1825 print of a man leading a horse, by French inventor Joseph Nicephore Niepce, is sold in Paris for $443,220.
• 23RD: **SLIPKNOT** end a world tour at the NK Hall, Tokyo, Japan.
• 28TH: **BILLY WILDER**, German-born director of such classic Hollywood movies as *Some Like It Hot*, *Double Indemnity*, and *Sunset Boulevard*, dies at the grand age of 95.
• 30TH: **THE QUEEN MOTHER** dies in her sleep in Windsor, UK, at 101 years old.

• MARCH 5TH: **THE OSBOURNES**, a fly-on-the-wall documentary series about life with Ozzy Osbourne, is shown for the first time, on MTV in the US.

• 4TH: **MEGADETH** break up, due to an injury that leaves Dave Mustaine unable to play guitar. He even puts his gear up for sale.
• 5TH: **AT ISLEWORTH CROWN COURT**, London, Peter Buck of R.E.M. is cleared of charges arising from an "air rage" incident a year ago.
• 9TH: **EMINEM AGREES** to pay $100,000 to John Guerra for allegedly hitting him in the head and face with a handgun, after he had kissed Kim Mathers, Eminem's wife.
• 12TH: **THE SOUTH AFRICAN** version of *Sesame Street* announces it will be introducing a character who is HIV-positive.
• 19TH: **LAYNE STALEY**, vocalist with Alice In Chains, is found dead at home in Seattle, Washington. Heroin equipment is found nearby.
• 20TH: **'FOOLISH'** by Ashanti tops the US Top 40 singles chart, on the same day as her album, *Ashanti*, enters the album chart at Number One.
• 21ST: **IN THE FIRST ROUND** of the French presidential elections, socialist Prime Minister Lionel Jospin is defeated by the neo-fascist Jean-Marie Le Pen. Jacques Chirac, a conservative, will win the second round on May 5th.
• 24TH: **IN THE ONGOING** battle for control of the legacy of Kurt Cobain, Judge Robert Alsdorf turns down a request from former Nirvana members Dave Grohl and Krist Novoselic to have Courtney Love tested by a psychiatrist.
• 25TH: **LISA 'LEFT-EYE' LOPES** of TLC dies, at age 30, in a car wreck in Honduras, where she's been on holiday.
• 25TH: **SOUTH AFRICAN** Mark Shuttleworth blasts off from Baikonur in Kazakhstan to become the first African citizen in orbit. A place on the mission cost him over $22million.
• 29TH: **PAUL McCARTNEY** gets an order preventing Christie's auction house from selling the hand-written lyrics to his song 'Hey Jude.'

# 2002

- **JANUARY 4TH: THE HIGHEST NEW** entry in the US album chart this week is *C'Mon, C'Mon* by Sheryl Crow, straight in at Number Two.

## Hyper-Bjork

**A**UGUST 30TH: BJORK'S west London flat is robbed while she sleeps... The Icelandic vocalist, whose biggest chart success to date came with her mid-1990s albums *Post* and *Homogenic*, is about to release two major collections of her work. There's a *Greatest Hits* volume, compiled from fans' voting, and a box set of her own selections called *Family Tree*, spread over five mini and one full-size CD, which traces her intriguing musical development from teenage years to date, much of it previously unreleased. The box includes solo work, and a variety of collaborations, with acts ranging from her cult Icelandic band The Sugarcubes to 808 State's Graham Massey and the classical Brodsky quartet. To call Bjork Gudmundsdottir – born in Reykjavik in 1965 – a little eccentric is an understatement. But to call her a little talented is equally short of the mark.

## MAY

- **2ND: IN THE WORST RIOTING** in London for a decade, more than 100 police are injured after an important soccer match between local team Millwall and Birmingham City.
- **6TH: LEGENDARY** songwriter/producer Otis Blackwell, composer of 'Don't Be Cruel,' 'All Shook Up,' and many others, dies in Nashville, Tennessee. He was 70.
- **6TH: DUTCH FAR-RIGHT LEADER** Pim Fortuyn is shot to death outside a radio station in Hilversum. In the subsequent general election his party make significant gains.
- **9TH: HAVING ALLEGEDLY** been paid a vast sum to leave her previous label, Virgin/EMI, Mariah Carey signs a new record deal, which will include the formation of her own record label, with Island/Def Jam.
- **16TH: ALEC CAMPBELL**, the last survivor of the ill-fated Gallipoli campaign of 1915, dies in Tasmania at age 103. Soldier, builder, carpenter, and economist, he will be given a state funeral at St David's Cathedral, and the whole of Australia observes a minute's silence.
- **17TH: JAY-Z DECIDES** against buying a $6.5m penthouse after his criminal record was pinned up in the building.
- **22ND: A JURY IN ALABAMA** convicts former Ku Klux Klansman Bobby Frank Cherry of murder in a 1963 church bombing that killed four girls.
- **24TH: DRYDEN MITCHELL** of Alien Ant Farm is airlifted from Spain to London for treatment following a tour bus crash.

## JUNE

- **JUNE 11TH: KORN STARTS** its first tour for two years, and singer Jonathan Davis shows off his new microphone stand, specially commissioned by the band from 'Alien' creator H.R. Giger. The 60-year-old Swiss-born artist and designer, who says he has become a fan of the band's music, was given complete design freedom by Davis, other than stipulating that the stand be "very erotic, biomechanical and, most importantly, as moveable as possible."

- **5TH: R. KELLY IS ARRESTED** in Polk County, Florida, on child pornography charges.
- **8TH: *THE EMINEM SHOW*** by Eminem enters the US album chart at Number One.
- **11TH: A REPORT** by The International Federation of the Phonographic Industry (IFPI) shows that illegal sales of recordable CDs (in other words bootlegs) tripled during the year 2001 to 450 million units.
- **20TH: FORBES MAGAZINE** in the US lists Britney Spears as the world's "most powerful celebrity." The ranking is not based on physical strength, you'll be relieved to hear, but on such criteria as financial clout, media coverage, and general influence on the world at the moment. Other rock stars further down the list include Madonna, U2, 'N Sync, and Mariah Carey.
- **24TH: A PAINTING** from Claude Monet's *Water Lilies* series sells for $20.2 million.
- **26TH: LOTS OF DRYING** out this month in the entertainment world: soul legend Diana Ross is in a Malibu drink and drugs rehabilitation centre, in order to "resolve some personal issues;" Columbia Records have announced that Billy Joel has signed himself into a substance abuse and psychiatric hospital in New Canaan, Connecticut; and today David Hasselhoff, star of Baywatch (and apparently the most popular singer in Germany in the 1980s), checks into The Betty Ford Clinic.

- **JUNE 3RD: A ROCK FESTIVAL** is staged around Buckingham Palace, London, as part of Queen Elizabeth II's Golden Jubilee celebrations. Artists performing include Brian May of Queen (who opens the proceedings by playing the 'National Anthem' standing on the roof of the palace, left), Paul McCartney, Brian Wilson, Robbie Williams, Ricky Martin, Annie Lennox, Bryan Adams, Eric Clapton, Tom Jones, 'Baby Spice' Emma Bunton, Cliff Richard, Tony Bennett, and, perhaps the biggest surprise in a fairly 'safe' line-up, Ozzy Osbourne.

- **JUNE 27TH: JOHN ENTWISTLE**, bass player with The Who for 38 years, dies from a heart attack in a Las Vegas hotel room, at the age of 57.

Releasing her first album (a collection of Icelandic folk songs) at just 11, she joined the Icelandic punk scene with groups like Spit & Snot, Cork That Bitch's Arse, and then KUKL, before The Sugarcubes. But while she found the band fun, she felt restricted too. Her 1993 solo *Debut* blended intriguing dance beats with her astonishing voice. Becoming a club favorite, Bjork shot to unexpected fame and fortune. Yet her taste for experimentation still remains strong.

**JULY**

**AUGUST**

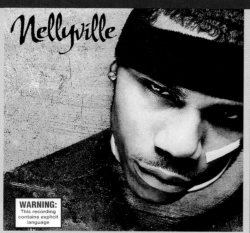

• **JULY 13TH:** *NELLYVILLE* by Nelly enters *Billboard*'s US album chart at Number One. He'll also have hits with 'N Sync and Kelly Rowland from Destiny's Child.

• **3RD: IT'S REPORTED** that Michael Jackson and Sony Music are to buy country music publisher Acuff-Rose for $157m), securing rights to 55,000 songs, including the works of Hank Williams, The Everly Brothers, and Roy Orbison.
• **10TH: THE RUBENS** painting Massacre Of The Innocents sells for $76.2 million at Sotheby's auction house.
• **15TH: A BOAT CAPTAINED** by Bob Segar wins its division in the 78th annual Port Huron-to-Mackinac Island Race... Meanwhile cable channel VH1 confirms it is working on a reality TV show, in the same vein as *The Osbournes*, that will feature Liza Minnelli.
• **23RD: TWO EXAMPLES** of fan-abuse today: Britney Spears angers Mexican fans when she appears to flip the bird towards them on arrival at Mexico City airport; and Rod Stewart, performing at Cardiff Castle, in Wales, kicks a football into the crowd, as he often does. Unfortunately, this time he breaks the finger of audience member Steve Tudor.
• **25TH: PRODUCER GARY BINKOW** sues Ozzy Osbourne, claiming that Ozzy and wife Sharon stole the idea for the popular MTV rockumentary, *The Osbournes*, from him.

• **3RD: IT'S REPORTED** that Latin pop sensation Shakira is unhurt after her helicopter was forced to make an emergency landing in bad weather on a baseball field in the Dominican Republic... Meanwhile, *Busted Stuff* by the Dave Matthews Band goes straight into Billboard's US album chart at Number One.
• **13TH: AEROSMITH**, Kid Rock, and a re-formed Run-DMC begin a US tour at the PNC Bank Amphitheater, Holmdel, New Jersey.
• **14TH: DURING THE OZZFEST TOUR**, Dave Williams, vocalist with Drowning Pool, is found dead on the band's tour bus in Manassas, Virginia. He is 30 years old.
• **21ST: IN PAKISTAN**, President General Pervez Musharraf unilaterally amends the Pakistani constitution, extends his term in office, and grants himself powers that included the right to dissolve parliament.
• **29TH: PEPSI DUMPS** rapper Ludacris after he is criticized by influential US radio commentator Bill O'Reilly as a "subversive influence on children."
• **29TH: PUDDLE OF MUDD** (right) releases a new single, called 'She Hates Me.'

## A Man & His Tape Recorder

• **JULY 19TH: CELEBRATED MUSICOLOGIST** Alan Lomax (right) dies in Mease Countryside Hospital, Florida, at age 87. From the 1930s onward, working initially with his father John, Lomax preserved and documented America's musical heritage by making thousands of location and studio recordings of folk, blues, and jazz musicians – many of them not recorded before, or since. His best known 'discoveries' include Leadbelly (left), Son House (below), Memphis Slim, and Muddy Waters, but he also assembled a priceless archive of field recordings of ordinary people making music at work and play. Lomax has been called "the most important folklorist of the 20th century." His work has been described as "capturing the human spirit in song" -- and he's been acclaimed and respected by everyone from Pete Seeger and The Rolling Stones to David Byrne and Brian Eno. Indeed, without his priceless recordings, much of the heritage of American music we take for granted now may have been lost to posterity.

# 2002

## September–December

SEPTEMBER | OCTOBER | NOVEMBER

- **SEPTEMBER 4TH:** **AVRIL LAVIGNE'S** debut album *Let Go* is certified as having sold two million copies. The first single, 'Complicated,' is also a best-seller, and at 17 it looks like Avril may well have lots more to come. After a frustrating false start with an earlier album, the Canadian skater-punk tomboy with a big voice, a grungey guitar, a head full of energetic teen angst, and some great pop-rock tunes has found the right formula with successful but sympathetic AOR producer Clif Magness.

## SEPTEMBER

- **10TH:** **CHRIS COWIE**, producer of *Top Of The Pops*, the UK's most powerful music show, attacks the pop chart system, claiming that most new Top Ten entries "are there because of clever marketing practises employed by record companies, not because they are popular."
- **11TH:** **THE EXHIBIT** 'September 11: Bearing Witness to History' has opened at the Smithsonian's National Museum of American History in Washington, DC.
- **12TH:** **ROD STEWART** is in court in Malibu, California, to support his son Sean, who's been charged with kicking 19-year old Jason Rogland unconscious outside a restaurant nine months ago. Sean will be sentenced to 90 days in jail, and required to have treatment for drug problems. Meanwhile, the house in which Nirvana's Kurt Cobain lived as a child (from 11-15 years), is sold on eBay for $210,000. (It was valued recently at under $60,000.)
- **16TH:** **PINK'S** new single is 'Just Like A Pill.'
- **19TH:** **AROUND 750** rebel soldiers attempt to overthrow the government of Ivory Coast, west Africa, prompting US troops to land six days later to help move foreigners, including Americans, to safer areas.
- **23RD:** **THE LARGEST EARTHQUAKE** in the UK for more than ten years occurs in the West Midlands: it measures 4.8 on the Richter scale.
- **27TH:** **THE RED HOT CHILLI PEPPERS** begin a South American tour at the Plaza de Toros, Guadalajara, Mexico.

- **SEPTEMBER 14TH:** *HOME* **BY THE DIXIE CHICKS** enters the US album chart at Number One.

## OCTOBER

- **OCTOBER 1ST:** **THE WHITE STRIPES**, a manic, minimalist, guitar & drums, husband & wife (or is it brother & sister?) duo, stage a free open-air afternoon gig to 9,000 fans in Union Square, New York City. But power is cut by local authorities when the duo play longer than their allotted 60 minutes.

- **2ND:** **ROBBIE WILLIAMS** signs the biggest album deal in British history, with EMI. It is said to guarantee him $80m.
- **11TH:** **EMINEM** plays an unannounced show at Michigan State University, East Lansing, Michigan, after an advance screening of *8 Mile*, his forthcoming movie.
- **12TH:** **A MASSIVE BOMB** destroys a crowded nightspot, the Sari Club, in the resort of Kuta in Bali, Indonesia. It claims 190 victims – mostly tourists, including many Australians.
- **16TH:** **IT'S REPORTED** that North Korea has told the US it has a secret nuclear weapons program, in violation of an 1994 agreement... Meanwhile, Corey Taylor of Slipknot drops strong hints that the band's next album may be their last.
- **25TH:** **AN $800,000 HOUSE** owned by Aretha Franklin in Bloomfield, Michigan, burns down, although Franklin has not lived in the house for two years.

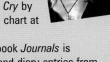

- **OCTOBER 5TH:** *BELIEVE* **BY DISTURBED** enters the US album chart at Number One.

- **26TH:** **RUSSIAN** authorities pump poison gas into a Moscow theater where Chechen separatist rebels are holding over 800 hostages, killing 116 hostages and all 50 terrorists.
- **30TH:** **OAKWOOD POSTAL** station in LA is renamed the Nat King Cole Post Office.
- **31ST:** **THERE'S TALK** of a new bio-pic movie on the life of Ozzy Osbourne. Ozzy's wife Sharon is quoted as saying she would like Johnny Depp to play Ozzy.

## NOVEMBER

- **2ND:** **NINE CONSPIRATORS** are arrested in London in connection with an alleged plot to kidnap Victoria Beckham (aka Posh Spice of the Spice Girls) and hold her for £5m ($7.5m) ransom... Meanwhile *Cry* by Faith Hill enters the US album chart at Number One.
- **4TH:** **THE KURT COBAIN** book *Journals* is published: it contains letters and diary entries from the 1980s up to 1994, the last year of his life.
- **7TH:** **A CROWD OF 9,000** riot when they learn that Guns N' Roses have unexpectedly pulled out of tonight's show at the GM Place, Vancouver, Canada.
- **11TH:** **MICROSOFT** chairman Bill Gates pledges $100 million to fight AIDS in India.
- **12TH:** **STAN LEE**, the creator of Spider-Man, the Incredible Hulk, and Daredevil, files a lawsuit against Marvel Entertainment, claiming the company has cheated him out of millions of dollars in movie profits.
- **13TH:** **BILL WYMAN**, a music journalist based in Atlanta, Georgia, receives a 'cease-and-desist' letter from attorneys representing Rolling Stones ex-bassist Bill Wyman. The bassist wants the writer to stop using his name, even though the writer was born with it – unlike the bass player, who was born William Perks.
- **15TH:** **MYRA HINDLEY**, vilified co-murderer of several children in the UK's 'Moors Murders' case of the 1960s, dies at the age of 60 from respiratory failure a West Suffolk hospital, having served 36 years of a life sentence.
- **19TH:** **THE OIL TANKER PRESTIGE**, en route from Latvia to Gibraltar, breaks in two and sinks off the north-west coast of Spain and Portugal with 70,000 tons of heavy fuel oil aboard – it causes a marine and environmental disaster.
- **20TH:** **THE US GOVERNMENT** completes its takeover of security at 424 airports nationwide.
- **21ST:** **NATO** invites Latvia, Estonia, Lithuania, Bulgaria, Romania, Slovakia, and Slovenia to become members.
- **26TH:** The Backstreet Boys start legal action in New York against Zomba Records, seeking $75m for violation of trademark, $5m for a lost advance, and at least $20m in punitive damages.

# War Is In The Air

**O**CTOBER 13TH: **PRESIDENT BUSH** tells the United Nations General Assembly that Iraq presents a "grave and gathering danger" and that the US, "will not allow any terrorist or tyrant to threaten civilisation with weapons of mass murder." Bush says Washington wants to work through the UN Security Council, but warns that military action will be unavoidable if Iraq fails to comply with UN resolutions.

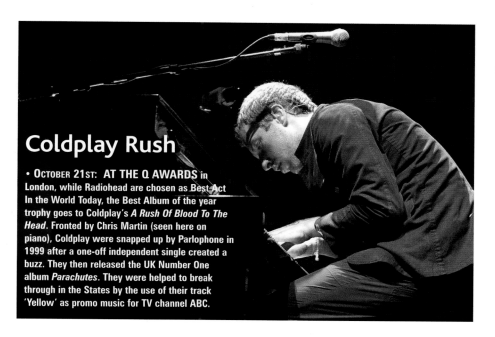

## Coldplay Rush

• **O**CTOBER 21ST: **AT THE Q AWARDS** in London, while Radiohead are chosen as Best Act In the World Today, the Best Album of the year trophy goes to Coldplay's *A Rush Of Blood To The Head*. Fronted by Chris Martin (seen here on piano), Coldplay were snapped up by Parlophone in 1999 after a one-off independent single created a buzz. They then released the UK Number One album *Parachutes*. They were helped to break through in the States by the use of their track 'Yellow' as promo music for TV channel ABC.

## DECEMBER

• **1ST: A SPECIAL** live World AIDS Day concert is held, featuring Alicia Keys playing in Cape Town, South Africa, while the Dave Matthews Band and Missy Elliott play in Seattle, Washington. The event is broadcast on MTV.

• **3RD: PETER GARRETT** quits Australian stars Midnight Oil after 25 years as vocalist.

• **4TH: IT'S ANNOUNCED** that Korn have been forced to cancel the five remaining US dates on the Pop Sux! Tour because lead singer Jonathan Davis has strained vocal chords.

• **7TH:** *UP!* **BY SHANIA TWAIN** enters *Billboard*'s US album chart at Number One. ... Meanwhile two Van Gogh paintings are stolen from the Van Gogh Museum in Amsterdam, Netherlands.

• **9TH: BRITNEY SPEARS** files for a restraining order against a 41-year-old Japanese man she claims has been stalking her... While tonight at the Billboard Awards in the MGM Grand, Las Vegas, Nevada, Nelly wins in the categories of Best Artist and Best Male Artist, while Ashanti walks off with the Female Artist and Top New Pop Artist awards.

• **12TH: LES PAUL**, 87-year-old guitar-playing legend who gave his name to a revered electric guitar model, offers memorabilia from his music career to Waukesha County's historical society for an exhibit.

• **16TH: LIZA MINNELLI** and her new husband, David Gest, file a $23 million dollar lawsuit against VH1, MTV Networks, Viacom and Remote Productions, Inc. for breach of contract, after plans for a reality show based on their lives are dropped.

• **18TH: NINE COMPETING** designs are unveiled for renovating the site of the destroyed World Trade Center. A decision is expected early next year.

• **19TH: BEYONCÉ KNOWLES** of Destiny's Child is reported to have been signed as the new face of Pepsi, with effect from the end of this year.

• **30TH: EMINEM'S** album *The Eminem Show* is declared the biggest seller of the year in the US, with more than 7.4 million copies sold.

• **31ST: RAPPER 50 CENT** and four other men are arrested and charged with criminal possession of a weapon.

• **O**CTOBER 30TH: **DJ JAM MASTER JAY** of Run-DMC (real name Jason Mizell, below left) is shot dead in his New York City recording studio, at the age of just 37. He was the musical innovator behind the Run-DMC sound from the early 1980s – perhaps the first time a DJ and his turntable techniques took centre-stage in a gigging group – and as such was recognised as one of the pioneers of 'old-skool' hip-hop. He was also much admired and respected for his interest and involvement in the hip-hop community at large. To add a twist to the tragedy, as is often the way of these things, the group has just been enjoying its most successful period since its heyday more than 15 years ago.

# 2003

## January–April

**M**ARCH 12TH: US RADIO STATIONS begin dropping Dixie Chicks tracks from their playlists because of vocalist Natalie Maines' recent statement – faced with the imminent US invasion of Iraq – that the group is ashamed of coming from the same state as President George Bush... On March 16th, President Bush, UK Prime Minister Blair, and Spanish Premier Aznar will set a deadline of the next night for the UN Security Council to back their call for immediate Iraqi disarmament... The following day Bush delivers a live television address, insisting "Saddam Hussein and his sons must leave Iraq within 48 hours ... their refusal to do so will result in military conflict." On March 20th, 90 minutes after President Bush's deadline expires,

## JANUARY

- **5TH: NORTH KOREA** withdraws from the global nuclear arms control treaty.
- **7TH: POLLSTAR**, the music business information service, reveals that Paul McCartney, touring for the first time in nine years, was the top live concert attraction in the US during 2002, grossing $103.3m.
- **10TH: IT'S ANNOUNCED** that Eminem has signed a $3m deal with US sportswear manufacturers Nesi Apparel. He is to launch his own line of clothing, under the brandname Shady.
- **14TH: PETE TOWNSHEND** of The Who is arrested in connection with allegations that he has been downloading child pornography onto his home computer.

Townshend explains that his use of an Internet website, advertising child porn, was for the purposes of research for an autobiography. But he is pilloried in the press.
- **20TH: AT THE ANNUAL** MIDEM music business conference in Cannes, France, Robbie Williams reveals that he thinks Internet music piracy is acceptable, saying, "I think it's great, really I do. There is nothing anyone can do about it."
- **22ND: SCIENTISTS IN CHINA** find the fossilized remains of a dinosaur with four feathered wings in Liaoning Province. They suggest it is an early ancestor of birds, though birds only have two wings.
- **26TH: BILLY JOEL** is hospitalized after crashing his car into a tree.
- **27TH: UN WEAPONS** inspectors Hans Blix and Mohammed El Baradei present a report to the Security Council saying they have not been able to find proof that Iraq has any weapons of mass destruction, or the facilities to produce them... A day later, President Bush, in his State Of The Union address, will promise to present fresh evidence about Iraq's weapons programs, and vows to lead a military campaign if the Iraqis do not disarm.

- **JANUARY 25TH: *COME AWAY WITH ME*** by Norah Jones reaches Number One on the album chart in the US and almost everywhere else. Legendary jazz label Blue Note chooses to describe its new signing as "jazz-informed" – she studied jazz at college – but while jazz purists are sceptical, the mainstream music buyer laps it up. Jones is the daughter of revered sitar player Ravi Shankar, but was raised by her mother in Texas, before moving to Greenwich Village, New York, where she was spotted playing piano and singing in local bars. Perhaps viewed initially as a "new Diana Krall," her massive success (winning eight Grammys, for instance – see story on the right) means she's now just Norah Jones, way out on her own.

## FEBRUARY

- **FEBRUARY 24TH: AT TONIGHT'S *Grammy Awards*** ceremony, Norah Jones picks up an armful of trophies: Album Of The Year for *Come Away With Me*, plus Record Of The Year, Song Of The Year, Best New Artist, and Best Pop Vocal Album, and Best Female Pop Vocal Performance, for the hit single 'Don't Know Why.' Her album also wins awards for sound engineering & production. Also at the event: Eminem receives Best Rap Album award, and performs 'Lose Yourself,' backed by The Roots (the rap group, not the reggae band of the same name); Dixie Chicks pick up three awards; and 'N Sync – fronted by Justin Timberlake (right), who's just had his first solo hit – perform a tribute to The Bee Gees.

- **1ST: THE US SPACE SHUTTLE** Columbia explodes while re-entering Earth's atmosphere, killing all seven astronauts aboard instantly. It's believed that protective tiles were damaged at launch and over-heated on re-entry.
- **4TH: AS SHE LANDS** at the UK's Heathrow Airport on a Virgin Airlines transatlantic flight, Courtney Love is arrested for having been abusive to cabin staff... Meanwhile US Secretary of State Colin Powell presents evidence to the UN concerning Iraq's material breach of UN Resolution 1441.
- **7TH: SANDRA BOHN** is fined $74 under the federal Fisheries Act for petting a killer whale in Nootka Sound in Canada.
- **15TH: OFFICIALS CONFIRM** 150,000 US military personnel are now in and around the Gulf as part of the build-up for a possible war with Iraq, despite massive

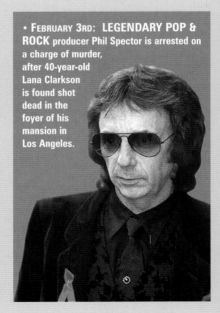

- **FEBRUARY 3RD: LEGENDARY POP & ROCK** producer Phil Spector is arrested on a charge of murder, after 40-year-old Lana Clarkson is found shot dead in the foyer of his mansion in Los Angeles.

explosions are heard in Iraq's capital, Baghdad. An official statement reads: "The opening stages of the disarmament of the Iraqi regime have begun." The band R.E.M. are among the musicians making clear their opposition to the invasion. They make available an anti-war song, 'The Final Straw,' online at their official website. On April 9th, US tanks drive unhindered into public squares in Baghdad for the first time. In a symbolic moment, an American armored vehicle helps a crowd of cheering Iraqis pull down a huge statue of Saddam Hussein (left).

• JANUARY 12TH: **MAURICE GIBB** of the Bee Gees (above right, and inset) – keyboard player, vocalist, and one-third of this creative, and obviously still close, partnership since the late 1950s – dies in the Mount Sinai Medical Center, Miami, Florida, following a heart attack, at the age of 53.

## MARCH

## APRIL

• FEBRUARY 1ST: **B2K AND P. DIDDY** (the artist formerly known as Puff Daddy, above) reach Number One on the US Top 40 singles chart with 'Bump, Bump, Bump.'

anti-war protests taking place across the world.
• 17TH: **THE MAYOR OF LONDON**, Ken Livingstone, introduces 'congestion charging', a fee for driving into Central London. It's the first time such a traffic-cutting experiment has been tried in a major city.
• 20TH: **A FIRE** caused by pyrotechnics used by the band Great White at the Station nightclub in Rhode Island, causes the deaths of more than 90 members of the audience. The band's guitarist, Ty Longley, is also killed.
• 20TH: **JOHNNY PAYCHECK** dies, at the age of 64.
• 26TH: **IT'S ANNOUNCED** that The Cure have signed a three album recording contract with I AM Recordings – making them labelmates with Korn, Limp Bizkit, and Slipknot.

• 1ST: **IRAQ BEGINS** destroying its al-Samoud medium-range missiles, which are in breach of UN resolutions. Hans Blix, the weapons inspector, describes the move as "very significant."
• 6TH: **SMOKEY ROBINSON** is awarded The National Medal of the Arts by US President George W. Bush, at the White House, Washington, DC.
• 8TH: **'IN DA CLUB'** by 50 Cent reaches Number One on the US Top 40 singles chart... meanwhile, while Bryan Adams plays at Donau Arena, Regensburg, Germany, 24-year-old audience member Christiane Kittel emerges from a coma she has been in for seven years.
• 12TH: **THE CHINESE GOVERNMENT** insist the Rolling Stones remove 'Brown Sugar,' 'Honky Tonk Women,' 'Beast Of Burden,' and 'Let's Spend The Night Together' from their upcoming performances in Shanghai and Beijing.
• 18TH: **ALAN KEITH**, believed to be the world's oldest broadcasting DJ, dies at the age of 94. Originally an actor and stand-up comedian, he's been a familiar voice on the BBC since 1933 (yes, 70 years), and has presented the same popular 'easy-listening' music show, *Your 100 Best Tunes*, on the radio since 1959.
• 24TH: **MADONNA MAKES** her new single 'American Life' available as an officially sanctioned digital download, at a cost of $1.49, though only to US listeners. A CD version of the track will go into shops a few weeks later.

• APRIL 3RD: **LINKIN PARK** enter the US album chart at Number One with their second album, *Meteora*.

• 6TH: **AT CANADA'S** annual Juno Awards ceremony, Avril Lavigne wins Best Single for 'Complicated,' plus Best Album and Best Pop Album for *Let Go*.

She also scoops the Best New Artist prize.
• 8TH: **IT'S REPORTED** that 32-year-old sanitation engineer DeAngelo Bailey is beginning a legal action against Eminem, because he feels the song 'Brain Damage,' on the rapper's *Slim Shady* album, portrays him incorrectly as a bully.
• 10TH: **THREE GUNMEN** open fire on a five-car convoy containing rapper Snoop Dogg (who's now dropped the "Doggy," though it's clearly not changed his luck) as it passes through the mid-city area of Los Angeles. One bodyguard is injured, but Snoop Dogg is unharmed.
• 11TH: **IT'S ANNOUNCED** that Sheryl Crow will be one of 49 celebrities designing their own brassieres for auction by Sothebys.com to raise money for breast cancer research.
• 15TH: **FLEETWOOD MAC** release the album *Say You Will*. It's their first since 1987 to feature new contributions from the reunited Stevie Nicks and Lyndsey Buckingham – though it's without Christine McVeigh, who's decided to quit, after 30 years, and move back to England.
• 21ST: **NINA SIMONE** dies at home in the South Of France, at the age of 70.
• 21ST: **EVEL KNIEVEL**, famed stunt motorbiker, signs over exclusive rights to allow the production of *Evel Knievel: The Rock Opera*. Whatever next...?

## The Future Is Here...

• APRIL 29TH: **APPLE COMPUTER** – which is currently rumored to be attempting to buy Universal Music from Vivendi (as indeed is Microsoft, which is all very interesting) – announces the launch of a new online record-buying operation, the iTunes Music Store, which it claims will revolutionize the way music is bought and distributed. It's a shrewd concept, though fraught with potential difficulties. The user can choose from (so far) 200,000 songs on the website – mostly by well-known artists – having previewed them first, and then can buy individual songs for 99 cents each. So if you only want one or two songs from an artist, or from an album, you can just buy those songs. Or you can purchase the whole album if you prefer. The songs can also, crucially, be burned onto CD, downloaded to an iPod player, or transferred to up to three other (Mac) computers. All of which makes it the most liberal and, crucially, legal music file-sharing service yet created. It catches on quickly: within a week, Apple's chief executive Steve Jobs will be claiming it has sold over one million songs – so far just in the US, and just to Mac owners – making Apple "the largest online music company in the world." The future of music-buying seems to have arrived, ostensibly with the blessing of the RIAA, record labels, and artists, all of whom appear happy with the deal. It's potentially bad news for conventional record stores, of course. But as Apple informs us on its website: "Rock and roll will never die. It is, however, being reborn."

# Index

## PICTURE CREDITS

Photographs and illustrations in this book are reproduced with permission from the following copyright holders, and we are grateful for their help. Most were supplied by Redfern's (indicated in the key below by initials RF) and Rex Features (RX). Many of the other images are from the Balafon Image Bank, managed by Backbeat UK; and also Image.net; NASA; Cartoon Network: www.wattstax.com; Tias.com; Angel's Vintage Attic, PO Box 464, Florida 34673. We would also like to thank the various record companies who gave permission for reproduction of record artwork etc. In the key below, the page number(s) is/are followed by an identifier and then the initial key or name of the supplier.

### 1950s
8-9 Elvis RX. Haley RF. 11 Guys & Dolls RX; Woman/Beast/Earth RX. 12 Sinatra RX; Doris & Rock RX. 13 card RX; hoop RX; Ball & Hope RX. 14 RF. 15 tranny RX; Dean RX. 16 Ella RF; Miles RF. 17 Jungle RX; Chuck RF; Jerry RF.

### 1960s
18-19 Jimi RX. 20 Cash RF. 21 Freed RF; Cochran RF. 22 Gordy RX; Eichmann RX; Shadows RX. 23 Berry RF; Elvis RX. 24 King/Goffin RX; Cline RF. 24-25 Douglas RX. 26 Castro RX; Flintstones, Cartoon Network. 27 Wilson RX; Lewis RX; Gagarin RX. 28 Cavern RX; Cooper RX. 29 wall RX; Sinatra RX. 30 beatnik RX; Dylan RF. 31 Burke RF; Dion RF. 32 PPPM RF; Richard RX; Hepburn RX. 33 Korner RF. 34 Best RF; soup RX; Pitney RX; Isleys RF; Charles RF. 35 Monroe RX; Jones RX. 36 Spector RF; Richard RF; Moore RX; Hillbillies RX. 37 Meek RF; L&S RF; Lawrence RX; Martha RX; Brown RF. 38-39 fans RX. 40 Rats RF; Miracles RF; Lancaster RX. 41 Getz RF; Boys RX. 42 J&D RF; Ness RX; King RX. 43 beach RX; T&B RX; Bennett RF; Wonder RF. 44 Dusty RX. 44-45 funeral RX. 45 Washington RF 46 Sellers RX; Clay RX; Beatles RX. 47 Millie RF; Mustang RX. 48 Jagger RX; Yardbirds RX; Sutch RX. 48-49 Poppins, Disney Channel. 49 Bacharach RX; Warwick RX; Seasons RF. 50 Kuryakin RX; Marx RX. 51 Manfreds RX. Orbison RX; Cooke RF; Clark RX. Supremes RX. 52-53 Supremes RF. 54 X RX; Cole RF. 55 Vietnam RX; L&H RX; Beck RX. 56 knees RX; Twiggy RX. 56-57. 57 S&C RX; survival RX. Airplane RF. 60 Fairport RX; Batman RX. 60-61 Sinatra RF. 61 Reverie RF; march RX. 62 M&Ps RF; Sellers RX; Turners RF. 63 Dead RF; Clift RX; Bruce RX; Spoonful RX. 64 Trek RX; Donovan RX; Tops RX. 65 Panther RX; Donald, Disney Channel; Thunderbirds RX. 66-67 Morrison RF. 68 BGs RX; Young RF; Aretha RX; Shaw RF; Gaye RX. 70 Jimi RF; Beatles RX; roller RX; King RX; De Gaulle RX. 71 Floyd RX; Gentry RF; Epstein RX. 72 T&J, Cartoon Network; Hair RX; Poitier RX. 73 Guthrie RF; Redding RF; Nillson RF; Queen RX. 74 Elvis RF; 2001 RX; Kitt RX. 75 funeral RX; Branson RX; bridge RX. 76 Alpert RF; Hopkin RX; Graduate RX. 77 Bowie RF; Beck RX; Parsons RF. 78 Who RX; Brown RX. 79 Circus RX. Elvis RX; Barbarella RX. 80-81 moon RX. 82 Sly RF. 82-83 Mac RX. 83 Campbell RF; Dekker RX; Karloff RX. 84 J&Y RX; Leary RX; Oz RX. 84-85 Jimi RX. 85 Jones RX; Manson RX; Bowie RX. 86 Cliff RX; Minh RX; Crimson RX. 87 Rider RX; Harris RX; Jacksons RF.

### 1970s
88-89 Bowie RX. 90 Greenbaum RX. 91 Zep RX; Pablo RX; Lowe RF. 92 Sabbath RX. 92-93 Carpenters RX. 93 MASH RX; Jerry RX. 94 Elvis RX; Mayfield RF; Bolan RX. 95 Joplin RF; Jimi RF; Piggy RX; Patridges RX. 96 Harrison RF; Chanel RX; Temps RF. 97 Taylor RX; Osmonds RF. 98 Fairport RF; Morrison RX; Mitchell RX. 99 Armstrong RF; concert RF. 100 Stewart RF; Lennon RX; Orange RX. 100-101 Shaft RX. 101 Hayes RX; Vincent RF. 102 Flack RX; Stevens RX; Nilsson RF; Badfinger RF; Floyd RF; Jackson RF. 103 girl RX; soldiers RX; Byrd RF; M&N RX. 104 Slade RX. 105 Roxy RX; Staples, www.wattstax.com; Tull RF. 106 Ross RX; O'Sullivan RX. 107 Simon RF. 108-109 John RX. 110 Coward RX. 111 Wailers (4) RD; Godfather RX; Dawn RF; R&M RX. 114 Sydney RX; Rings (2) RX; Knight RX. 114-115 oilmen RX. 115 Darin RF; Exorcist RX. 118 Parton RX; Wakeman RX. 119 Springsteen RF; Nixon RX; Heimlich RX; Ellington RF; Dan RF. 120 Selassie RX; Lennon RF; Lydon 120-121 boxers RX. 121 AWB RX; Douglas RX. 122-123 Wonder RX. 124 Skynyrd RX; Quo RX; Baxter RX; Labelle RX. 125 Kraftwerk RF; Ripperton RX; Mercury RX. 10cc RX; Denver RF; Evel RX; Jaws RX. 127

### 1980s
160 Floyd RF; Scott RX. 161 Hitchcock RX; Springsteen RX. 162 Curtis RF; Abba RF; Pryor RX. 163 Fame RX; Summer RX. 164 Bonham RX; newspaper RX; Ross RX. 165 Marley RX; Streisand RX; McQueen RX; monkey RX. 166 Adam RX; Ultravox RF; Murdoch RX. 167 Spandau RX; Strange RX; Hite RX; Hinckley RX; Depeche RX. 168 Easton RF; Smokey RX. 169 Go-Go's RF; Anderson RX; Diana RX. 170 Flash RX; S&G RF. 171 Yazoo RF; Paisley RX; Olivia RX. 172 Carnes RX; Ozzy RX. 173 Clinton RX; Elvis RF; motor RX; Bowie RX. 174 Bambaataa RF; Cell RX; ET RX. 175 Waters RX; League RX; Vaughan RX. 176 Jett RX; Mellencamp RX; Jam RF. 177 Devo RX; Basil RX; Jackson RX. 180 Gaye RX; John RX. 180-181 Duran RF. 181 Swanson RX; Dexy's RX; Jackson RX. 182 Bowie RX; Jamerson RX; Niven RX. 183 R.E.M. RX; Madness RF. 184 Smiths RF; Tyler RF; Eurythmics RF. 185 Morrissey RF; Richie RF; Greenham RX; Thriller RX. 186 Madonna RX; Tarzan RX; Frankie RF. 187 Collins RX; Basie RF. 188 Ghostbusters RX; Prince RF. 189 Sade RF; Turner RX. 190 Brighton RX; Cosby RX. 190-191 Wham! RF. 191 Def RX; Nightmare RX; Geldof RX. 194 Tears RX. 195 Speedwagon RF; miners RX. 196 Aid RF; Bowie RF; Minds RX. 197 Dire RX; boat RX; Becker RX. 198 Gates RX; Bush RX; Brynner RX. 199 Gorby RX; Housemartins RF; Sinclair RX. 200 Cabaret RX; Vandross RF; Jackson RX. 201 Boys RF; Turner RX; Chernobyl RX; Clint RX. 202 DMC RF; Brown RX; Cameo RX. 203 Geldof RX; Gun RX; country (3) RX. 204 Chuck RF. 204-205 Metallica RF. 205 Bangles RX; Banana RX; Lauper RX; Jovi RX. 208 Warhol RX; Houston RX. 209 Beasties RF; Bakker RX; House RX. 210 Astaire RX; Wilde RX; Enemy RF. 211 U2 RF; Cool RF; Hammond RF. 212 trees RX; Tiffany RF. 213 Order RF; Douglas RX; Michael RF. 214 Estefan RF; Astley RX; Harrison RX. 215 INXS RF; Dion RX; Dynasty RX. 216 Chapman RF; Salt RX; Hynde RX. 217 Buchanan RF; Def RX. 218 UB40 RX; Slash RX. 219 rave RX; Poison RF; crash RX. 220-221. 222 Abdul RX; Soul RF; Rushdie RX. 223 oil RX; Milli RX; Roxette RX; Cats RX. 224 Pixies RX; China RX; Gameboy RX; Cannibals RX. 225 Nails RX; Wyman RX; Joker RX. 226 Cure RX; wall RX; quake RX; Warren RX. 227 Crue RF; Brooks RF.

### 1990s
228-229 Nirvana RX. 230 Tribe RX; Collins RF; Mandela RX; B52s RX; O'Connor RF. 231 Saddam RX; Soul RF; Macca RX. 232 Hammer RX. 233 Carey RF; Waits RF; Madonna RF; Wall RX. 234 Blur RX; Bernstein RF; Smith RX. 235 tunnel RX; Zevon RX; Deee RF. 236 King RX; Scott RF. 237 Thunders RF; Buckley RX. 238 R.E.M. RF; Ice-T RX; NWA RX; Cube RX. 239 Adams RX; Megadeth RF; Metallica RF. 240 Peppers RF. 240-241 Nirvana RX. 241 Dawn RX; Freddie RX; U2 RX. 242 Kurt & Courtney RX; Groening RX; Wayne RX. 242-243 Fred RX. 243 George & Elt RX. 244 Boyz RF; Bowie RX; Kross RX. 245 Quayle RX; Sting RX; palace RX; Jackal RX. 246 Radiohead RF; Shamen RX; Lang RX; Dyke RF. 247 Rage RF; Young RF. 248-249 TLC RX. 250 2PAC RX; Clapton RX; Clinton RX. 251 Doctors RX; Depeche RX; Ronson RX; Stevens RX; Merchant RX; Lovett RX; Berners-Lee RX; Park RX. 253 That RX. 254 Jam RF; Crows RF; Pumpkins RX. 255 Snoop RX; Zappa RF. 256 Amos RF; Osmond RX. 257 Cobain RX; Base RX; Beck RF; Nails RX. 258 Prodigy RX; Oasis RX. 259 Crow RX; Blige RX; Woodstock RX; Zep RF. 260 Korn RX; Cranberries RX. 261 Castle RX; Topac RX; Crosby RF; Sonny RX. 262-263 RX. 264 Lee RX; 265 That RF; Kobe RX; Edwards RF; Oklahoma RX; Tokyo RX. 266 Love RX; Alanis RX. 267 Grant RX; Hendrix RX; Garcia RX; 268 Beatles RF; Coolio RX; Stones RX. 269 Dean RX; Doubt RX. 270 Blige RF; Zoo RX. 271 Pistols RX; Cocker RX; Manics RF. 272 slayer RF; Spice RX; Matthews RX. 273 Ali RX. 274 Shakur RX. 275 Mozza RX;

Braxton RX; Criminals RX. 276 Phish RX; sheep RX; Notorious RX. 277 Liam RX; Prodigy RX. 278 Cardigans RF; Perry RX; Puff RX. 279 Kuti RF; Harris RF; Orbital RX. 280 Cruise RX; Elt RX. 281 Wang-Tu RF; Aqua RF; Hutchence RF. 282-283 Child RF. 284 Titanic RX; Garden RX. 285 Verve RX; Linda RX. 286 Hill RF; Corrs RX; Hope RX; Sinatra RF; McEntire RX. 288 Williams RF; Oldfield RX; Martin RF; Beatles RX; Jackson RX. 289 Sync RF; Twain RF. 290 Eminem RF; Blondie RF; Slim RF. 291 Spears RF; Offspring RF; Mel RX; Boyzone RF; Westlife RF; Rowland RF. 292 Martin RX. 293 Lopez RF; Matrix RX; Aguilera RX. 294 Santana RX; Enrique RF; Julio RF. 295 Halliwell RF; McLaren RX.

### 21st Century
298 David RF; Robbie & Liam RF; Kid RF. 299 Child RF; Pink RF. 399 Aaliyah RF; Anastacia RF; Woods RX. 301 Concorde RX; Matchbox RF. 302 George RX; Kylie RX. 303 Linkin RF; Madonna RX; MacColl RF; Corr! RX. 304 Phillips RX; M&Ps RF; Roxy RX; Hear'say RX; Dan RX; Crush RX. 305 Buena RX; Jackson RF; Alien RF; Roach RF. 306 Hooker RF. 307 Kim RF; Usher RF; Jagger RF; Keys RF. 308 Towers RX; Zero RX; Garbage RF. 309 McCartney RX; Harrison RF; Nickelback RF; Foo RX. 310 Hepburn RX. 312 Korn RF; Entwistle x2 RF; May RX. 313 Bjork RF; Mudd RF; House RF; Leadbelly RF; Lomax RF. 314 Lavigne RF; Stripes RX; Chicks RX. 315 Coldplay RX; Run-DMC RF. 316 Timberlake RF; Jones RF; Spector RX. 317 statue RX; Gibb RX; BGs RX; Diddy RF.

## CONTRIBUTORS

This book is based on Johnny Black's unique rock timeline database. Other contributors: Andy Basire; Paul Quinn; Hugh Gregory; Daniel Duffell; Sean McManus.

Project editor: Paul Quinn
Text editor: John Morrish
Designer: Denise Wright

With thanks to: Tony Bacon, Nigel Osborne, Paul Cooper, Phil Richardson; Mark Brend; John Ryall.

The editorial team and publishers would also like to acknowledge the following sources, which have proved invaluable in the research and compilation of this book.

**Books, periodicals & websites**
The AllMusicGuide; Billboard; Rolling Stone; NME; Mojo; washingtonpost.com; Our American Century (Time-Life Books); The Great Rock Discography, Martin C. Strong; Guinness Book Of British Hit Singles/Albums (Ed David Roberts); Billboard Book Of Top 40 Hits, Joel Whitburn; The NME Rock and Roll Years; The Q Encyclopedia of Rock Stars; The Penguin Encyclopedia of Popular Music; The Virgin Encyclopaedia of Popular Music; Rock Day by Day (Guinness); Reggae Explosion The Story of Jamaican Music – Chris Salewicz & Adrian Boot (Virgin); The A to Z of Record Labels – Brian Southall (Sanctuary); The 20th Century Year by Year (Marshall); The Chronicle of the 20th Century (Dorling Kindersley); Chronology Of World History (Hutchinson); When The Music's Over – Robin Denslow (Faber & Faber); deadoraliveinfo.com; news.bbc.co.uk; www.who2.com; David Wimble, indiebible.com; sean.co.uk; Cornflakes & Classics; 5years.com; and countless other fan sites, whose obsessive collection of seemingly insignificant detail is a boon to any book such as this. Apart from the ones who just make it up, of course.

*"Work five years, and 20 years hanging around." Charlie Watts, asked in 1988 if he still enjoyed The Rolling Stones after 25 years.*